Saab 900

Service and Repair Manual

A K Legg LAE MIMI and Spencer Drayton

Models covered (3512 - 256)

Saab 900 3 and 5 door Hatchback and Coupe models, including special/limited editions
October 1993 to 1998

Petrol models: 2.0 litre (1985cc) and 2.3 litre (2290cc) normally-aspirated, 2.0 litre (1985cc) Turbo

Does not cover 2.5 litre (2498cc) V6 petrol engine or 'Sensonic' semi-automatic transmission.
Covers most mechanical features of Convertible models.

ABCDE
FGHIJ
KLMNO
PQR

A book in the **Haynes Service and Repair Manual Series**

ISBN **1 85960 512 5**

British Library Cataloguing in Publication Data
A catalogue record for this book is available from the British Library.

Printed in the USA

Haynes Publishing
Sparkford, Nr Yeovil, Somerset BA22 7JJ, England

Haynes North America, Inc
861 Lawrence Drive, Newbury Park, California 91320, USA

Editions Haynes S.A.
Tour Aurore - La Défense 2, 18 Place des Reflets,
92975 PARIS LA DEFENSE Cedex France

Haynes Publishing Nordiska AB
Box 1504, 751 45 UPPSALA, Sverige

Contents

LIVING WITH YOUR SAAB 900

Contents

REPAIRS AND OVERHAUL

The new Saab 900 was introduced in the UK in October 1993 as a replacement for the existing 900 series. It was originally available in 3 and 5 door Hatchback versions with 2.0 and 2.3 litre normally aspirated petrol engines, and a turbocharged 2.0 litre petrol engine. A 3-door Coupe model was launched in March 1994.

Models may be fitted with a five-speed manual transmission or four-speed automatic transmission mounted on the left-hand side of the engine. The 2.5 litre V6 engine and the 'Sensonic' automatic clutch system fitted to Turbo models as an option, are not covered in this Manual.

All models have front-wheel-drive with fully-independent front suspension and torsion beam rear suspension. Power steering (PAS), an Anti-lock Braking System (ABS) and a driver's air bag are fitted as standard to all models.

For the home mechanic, the Saab 900 is a relatively straightforward vehicle to maintain and repair, since design features have been incorporated to reduce the actual cost of ownership to a minimum, and most of the items requiring frequent attention are easily accessible.

Saab 900 S i Hatchback

Saab 900SE 2.0 Turbo Coupé

The Saab 900 Team

Haynes manuals are produced by dedicated and enthusiastic people working in close co-operation. The team responsible for the creation of this book included:

Authors	**A. K. Legg** (LAE MIMI) **Spencer Drayton**
Sub-editor	**Sophie Yar**
Editor & Page Make-up	**Steve Churchill**
Workshop manager	**Paul Buckland**
Photo Scans	**John Martin**
Cover illustration & Line Art	**Roger Healing**
Wiring diagrams	**Matthew Marke**

We hope the book will help you to get the maximum enjoyment from your car. By carrying out routine maintenance as described you will ensure your car's reliability and preserve its resale value.

Your Saab 900 manual

The aim of this manual is to help you get the best value from your vehicle. It can do so in several ways. It can help you decide what work must be done (even should you choose to get it done by a garage), provide information on routine maintenance and servicing, and give a logical course of action and diagnosis when random faults occur. However, it is hoped that you will use the manual by tackling the work yourself. On simpler jobs, it may even be quicker than booking the car into a garage and going there twice, to leave and collect it. Perhaps most important, a lot of money can be saved by avoiding the costs a garage must charge to cover its labour and overheads.

The manual has drawings and descriptions to show the function of the various components, so that their layout can be understood. Then the tasks are described and photographed in a clear step-by-step sequence.

References to the 'left' or 'right' are in the sense of a person in the driver's seat, facing forward.

Acknowledgements

Thanks are due to the Champion Spark Plug Company who supplied the illustrations of various spark plug conditions and to Duckhams Oils, who provided lubrication data. Thanks are also due to Draper Tools Limited, who provided some of the workshop tools, and to all those people at Sparkford who helped in the production of this manual.

We take great pride in the accuracy of information given in this manual, but vehicle manufacturers make alterations and design changes during the production run of a particular vehicle of which they do not inform us. No liability can be accepted by the authors or publishers for loss, damage or injury caused by any errors in, or omissions from, the information given.

Project vehicle

The main vehicle used in the preparation of this manual, and which appears in many of the photographic sequences, was a 1996 Saab 900 S 2.0 litre 5-door Hatchback with manual transmission.

Working on your car can be dangerous. This page shows just some of the potential risks and hazards, with the aim of creating a safety-conscious attitude.

General hazards

Scalding

• Don't remove the radiator or expansion tank cap while the engine is hot.

• Engine oil, automatic transmission fluid or power steering fluid may also be dangerously hot if the engine has recently been running.

Burning

• Beware of burns from the exhaust system and from any part of the engine. Brake discs and drums can also be extremely hot immediately after use.

Crushing

• When working under or near a raised vehicle, always supplement the jack with axle stands, or use drive-on ramps. ***Never venture under a car which is only supported by a jack.***

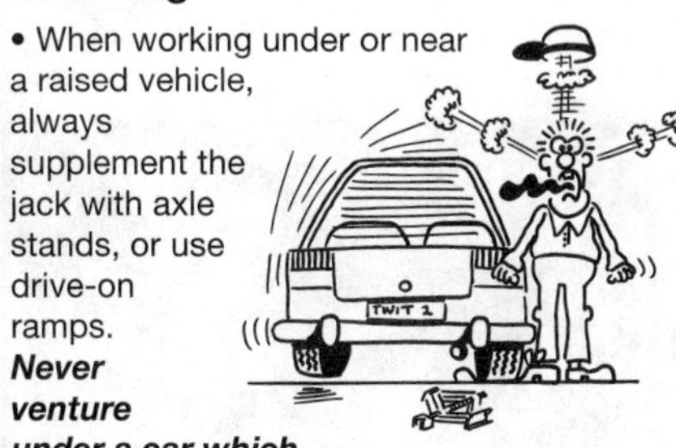

• Take care if loosening or tightening high-torque nuts when the vehicle is on stands. Initial loosening and final tightening should be done with the wheels on the ground.

Fire

• Fuel is highly flammable; fuel vapour is explosive.

• Don't let fuel spill onto a hot engine.

• Do not smoke or allow naked lights (including pilot lights) anywhere near a vehicle being worked on. Also beware of creating sparks (electrically or by use of tools).

• Fuel vapour is heavier than air, so don't work on the fuel system with the vehicle over an inspection pit.

• Another cause of fire is an electrical overload or short-circuit. Take care when repairing or modifying the vehicle wiring.

• Keep a fire extinguisher handy, of a type suitable for use on fuel and electrical fires.

Electric shock

• Ignition HT voltage can be dangerous, especially to people with heart problems or a pacemaker. Don't work on or near the ignition system with the engine running or the ignition switched on.

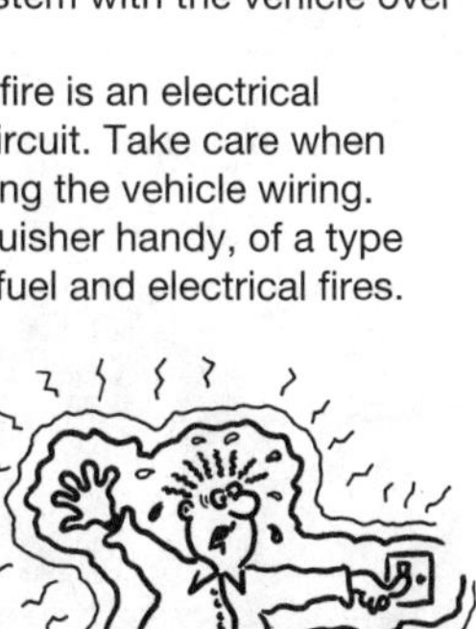

• Mains voltage is also dangerous. Make sure that any mains-operated equipment is correctly earthed. Mains power points should be protected by a residual current device (RCD) circuit breaker.

Fume or gas intoxication

• Exhaust fumes are poisonous; they often contain carbon monoxide, which is rapidly fatal if inhaled. Never run the engine in a confined space such as a garage with the doors shut.

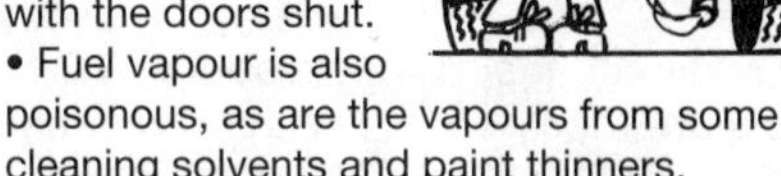

• Fuel vapour is also poisonous, as are the vapours from some cleaning solvents and paint thinners.

Poisonous or irritant substances

• Avoid skin contact with battery acid and with any fuel, fluid or lubricant, especially antifreeze, brake hydraulic fluid and Diesel fuel. Don't syphon them by mouth. If such a substance is swallowed or gets into the eyes, seek medical advice.

• Prolonged contact with used engine oil can cause skin cancer. Wear gloves or use a barrier cream if necessary. Change out of oil-soaked clothes and do not keep oily rags in your pocket.

• Air conditioning refrigerant forms a poisonous gas if exposed to a naked flame (including a cigarette). It can also cause skin burns on contact.

Asbestos

• Asbestos dust can cause cancer if inhaled or swallowed. Asbestos may be found in gaskets and in brake and clutch linings. When dealing with such components it is safest to assume that they contain asbestos.

Special hazards

Hydrofluoric acid

• This extremely corrosive acid is formed when certain types of synthetic rubber, found in some O-rings, oil seals, fuel hoses etc, are exposed to temperatures above 400ºC. The rubber changes into a charred or sticky substance containing the acid. *Once formed, the acid remains dangerous for years. If it gets onto the skin, it may be necessary to amputate the limb concerned.*

• When dealing with a vehicle which has suffered a fire, or with components salvaged from such a vehicle, wear protective gloves and discard them after use.

The battery

• Batteries contain sulphuric acid, which attacks clothing, eyes and skin. Take care when topping-up or carrying the battery.

• The hydrogen gas given off by the battery is highly explosive. Never cause a spark or allow a naked light nearby. Be careful when connecting and disconnecting battery chargers or jump leads.

Air bags

• Air bags can cause injury if they go off accidentally. Take care when removing the steering wheel and/or facia. Special storage instructions may apply.

Diesel injection equipment

• Diesel injection pumps supply fuel at very high pressure. Take care when working on the fuel injectors and fuel pipes.

Warning: Never expose the hands, face or any other part of the body to injector spray; the fuel can penetrate the skin with potentially fatal results.

Remember...

DO

• Do use eye protection when using power tools, and when working under the vehicle.

• Do wear gloves or use barrier cream to protect your hands when necessary.

• Do get someone to check periodically that all is well when working alone on the vehicle.

• Do keep loose clothing and long hair well out of the way of moving mechanical parts.

• Do remove rings, wristwatch etc, before working on the vehicle – especially the electrical system.

• Do ensure that any lifting or jacking equipment has a safe working load rating adequate for the job.

DON'T

• Don't attempt to lift a heavy component which may be beyond your capability – get assistance.

• Don't rush to finish a job, or take unverified short cuts.

• Don't use ill-fitting tools which may slip and cause injury.

• Don't leave tools or parts lying around where someone can trip over them. Mop up oil and fuel spills at once.

• Don't allow children or pets to play in or near a vehicle being worked on.

The following pages are intended to help in dealing with common roadside emergencies and breakdowns. You will find more detailed fault finding information at the back of the manual, and repair information in the main chapters.

If your car won't start and the starter motor doesn't turn

- ☐ If it's a model with automatic transmission, make sure the selector is in 'P' or 'N'.
- ☐ Open the bonnet and make sure that the battery terminals are clean and tight.
- ☐ Switch on the headlights and try to start the engine. If the headlights go very dim when you're trying to start, the battery is probably flat. Get out of trouble by jump starting (see next page) using a friend's car.

If your car won't start even though the starter motor turns as normal

- ☐ Is there fuel in the tank?
- ☐ Is there moisture on electrical components under the bonnet? Switch off the ignition, then wipe off any obvious dampness with a dry cloth. Spray a water-repellent aerosol product (WD-40 or equivalent) on ignition and fuel system electrical connectors like those shown in the photos. Pay special attention to the ignition coil wiring connector and HT leads.

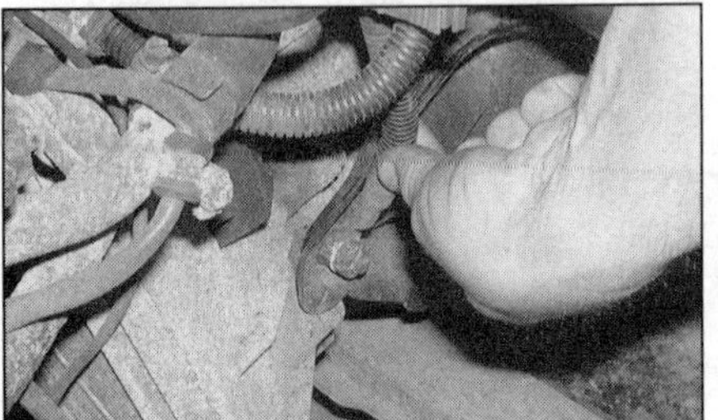

A Check the condition and security of all earth cables.

B Check the ignition system LT wiring connectors.

C Check the security of the HT leads on the distributor.

Check that electrical connections are secure (with the ignition switched off) and spray them with a water dispersant spray like WD40 if you suspect a problem due to damp

D Check that the battery cables are securely connected.

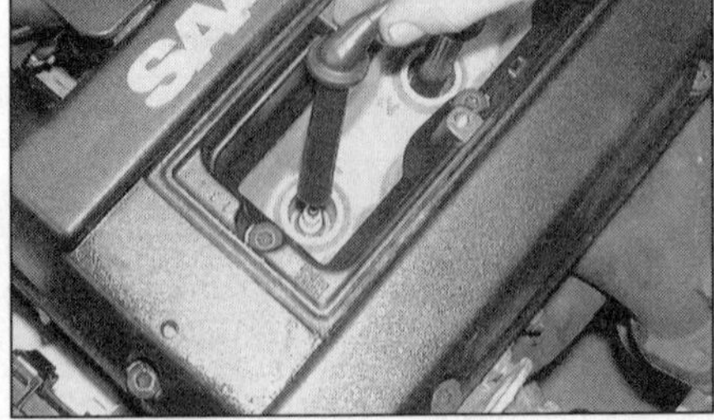

E Check the security of the HT leads on the spark plugs.

Jump starting

HAYNES HiNT ***Jump starting will get you out of trouble, but you must correct whatever made the battery go flat in the first place. There are three possibilities:***

1 The battery has been drained by repeated attempts to start, or by leaving the lights on.

2 The charging system is not working properly (alternator drivebelt slack or broken, alternator wiring fault or alternator itself faulty).

3 The battery itself is at fault (electrolyte low, or battery worn out).

When jump-starting a car using a booster battery, observe the following precautions:

- ✔ Before connecting the booster battery, make sure that the ignition is switched off.
- ✔ Ensure that all electrical equipment (lights, heater, wipers, etc) is switched off.
- ✔ Take note of any special precautions printed on the battery case.
- ✔ Make sure that the booster battery is the same voltage as the discharged one in the vehicle.
- ✔ If the battery is being jump-started from the battery in another vehicle, the two vehicles MUST NOT TOUCH each other.
- ✔ Make sure that the transmission is in neutral (or PARK, in the case of automatic transmission).

1 Connect one end of the red jump lead to the positive (+) terminal of the flat battery

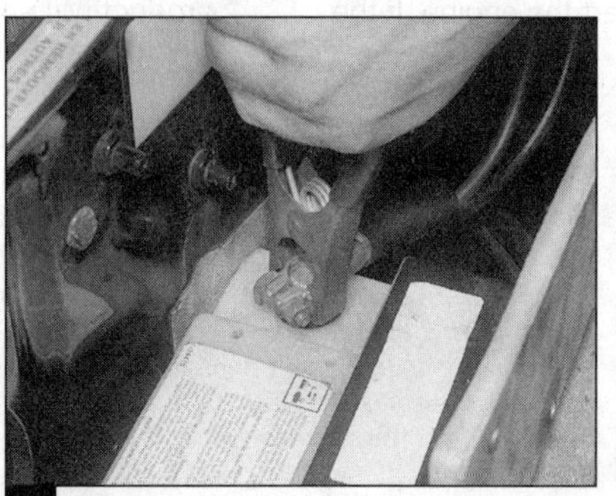

2 Connect the other end of the red lead to the positive (+) terminal of the booster battery.

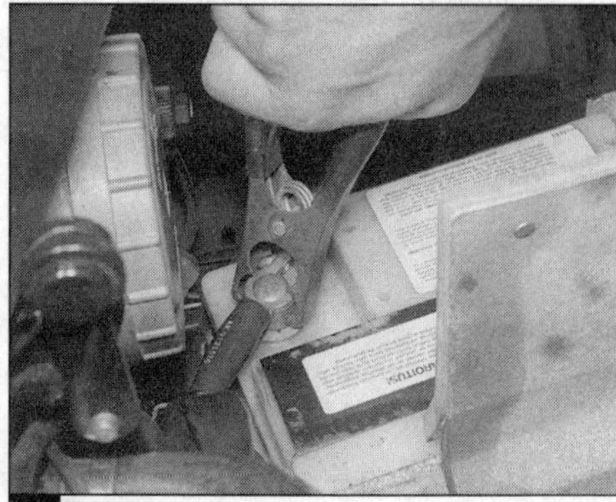

3 Connect one end of the black jump lead to the negative (-) terminal of the booster battery

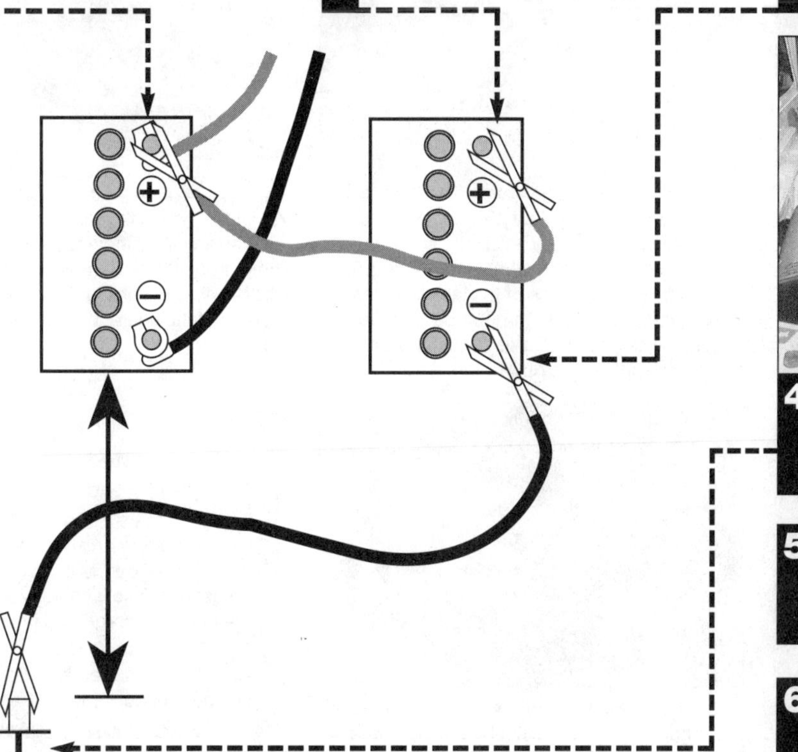

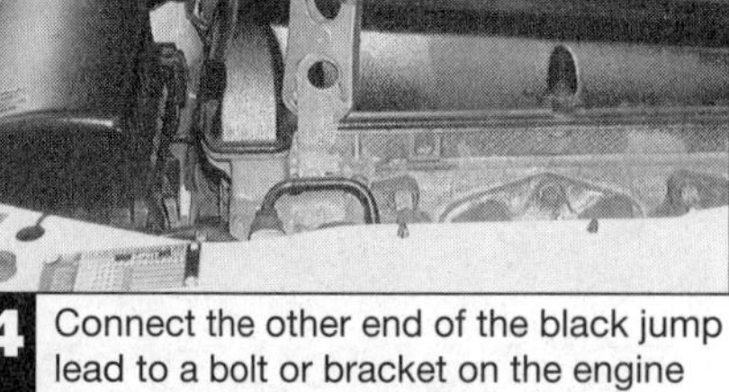

4 Connect the other end of the black jump lead to a bolt or bracket on the engine block, well away from the battery, on the vehicle to be started.

5 Make sure that the jump leads will not come into contact with the fan, drive-belts or other moving parts of the engine.

6 Start the engine using the booster battery and run it at idle speed. Switch on the lights, rear window demister and heater blower motor, then disconnect the jump leads in the reverse order of connection. Turn off the lights etc.

Wheel changing

Warning: Do not change a wheel in a situation where you risk being hit by another vehicle. On busy roads, try to stop in a lay-by or a gateway. Be wary of passing traffic while changing the wheel - it is easy to become distracted by the job in hand.

Preparation

- ☐ When a puncture occurs, stop as soon as it is safe to do so.
- ☐ Park on firm level ground, if possible, and well out of the way of other traffic.
- ☐ Use hazard warning lights if necessary.
- ☐ If you have one, use a warning triangle to alert other drivers of your presence.
- ☐ Apply the handbrake and engage first or reverse gear (or Park on models with automatic transmission.
- ☐ Chock the wheel diagonally opposite the one being removed – a couple of large stones will do for this.
- ☐ If the ground is soft, use a flat piece of wood to spread the load under the jack.

Changing the wheel

1 The spare wheel, jack and wheel removal tools are stored beneath a cover in the luggage compartment.

2 Unscrew the retaining nut and lift out the spare wheel. Place it beneath the sill as a precaution against the jack failing. Note that on all models, the spare wheel is of the 'space saver' type.

3 On models with steel wheels, use the special tool to pull the wheel trim from the wheel. On models with alloy wheels, use the tool provided to prise off the centre cap.

4 Before you raise the jack, loosen each wheel bolt by half a turn only.

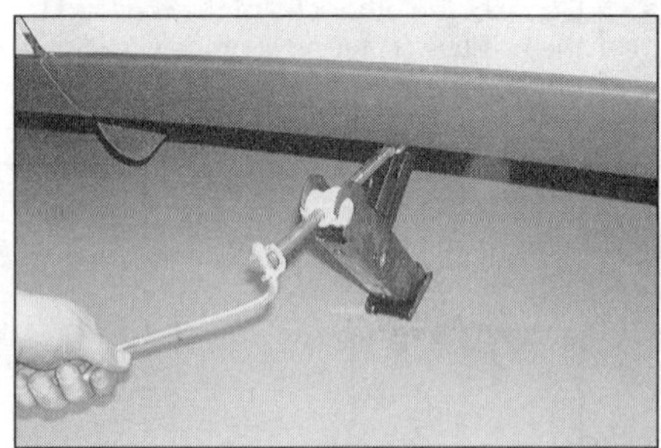

5 Locate the jack head below the reinforced jacking points (indicated by the cut-outs in the sill), nearest the wheel to be changed. Turn the handle until the base of the jack touches the ground then make sure that the base is located directly below the sill. Raise the vehicle until the wheel is clear of the ground.

6 If the tyre is flat make sure that the vehicle is raised sufficiently to allow the spare wheel to be fitted. Remove the bolts and lift the wheel from the vehicle. Place it beneath the sill in place of the spare as a precaution against the jack failing.

7 Fit the spare wheel, then insert each of the wheel bolts and tighten them moderately using the wheel brace.

8 Lower the vehicle to the ground, then finally tighten the wheel bolts in a diagonal sequence. Refit the wheel trim. Note that the wheel bolts should be tightened to the specified torque at the earliest opportunity.

Finally...

- ☐ Remove the wheel chocks.
- ☐ Stow the jack and tools in the correct locations in the car.
- ☐ Check the tyre pressure on the wheel just fitted. If it is low, or if you don't have a pressure gauge with you, drive slowly to the nearest garage and inflate the tyre to the right pressure.
- ☐ Have the damaged tyre or wheel repaired as soon as possible.

Warning: You should not exceed 50 mph when driving the vehicle with a 'Space Saver' spare wheel fitted - consult your vehicle handbook for further information.

Identifying leaks

Puddles on the garage floor or drive, or obvious wetness under the bonnet or underneath the car, suggest a leak that needs investigating. It can sometimes be difficult to decide where the leak is coming from, especially if the engine bay is very dirty already. Leaking oil or fluid can also be blown rearwards by the passage of air under the car, giving a false impression of where the problem lies.

Warning: Most automotive oils and fluids are poisonous. Wash them off skin, and change out of contaminated clothing, without delay.

The smell of a fluid leaking from the car may provide a clue to what's leaking. Some fluids are distictively coloured. It may help to clean the car carefully and to park it over some clean paper overnight as an aid to locating the source of the leak. Remember that some leaks may only occur while the engine is running.

Sump oil

Engine oil may leak from the drain plug...

Oil from filter

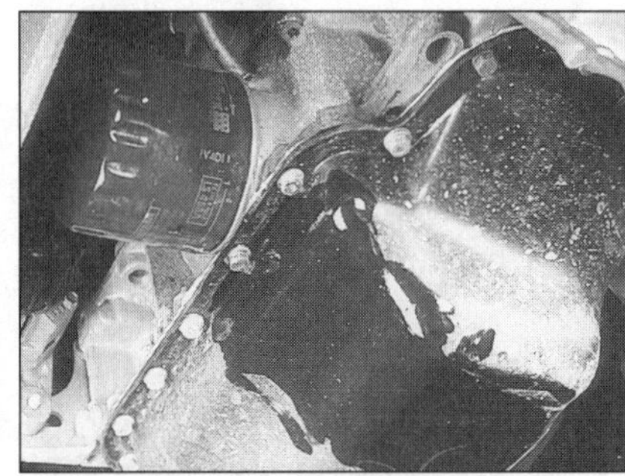

...or from the base of the oil filter.

Gearbox oil

Gearbox oil can leak from the seals at the inboard ends of the driveshafts.

Antifreeze

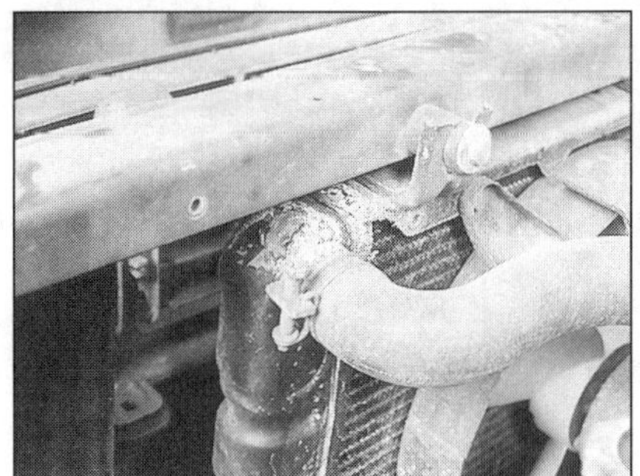

Leaking antifreeze often leaves a crystalline deposit like this.

Brake fluid

A leak occurring at a wheel is almost certainly brake fluid.

Power steering fluid

Power steering fluid may leak from the pipe connectors on the steering rack.

Towing

When all else fails, you may find yourself having to get a tow home – or of course you may be helping somebody else. Long-distance recovery should only be done by a garage or breakdown service. For shorter distances, DIY towing using another car is easy enough, but observe the following points:

☐ Use a proper tow-rope – they are not expensive. The vehicle being towed must display an 'ON TOW' sign in its rear window.

☐ Always turn the ignition key to the 'on' position when the vehicle is being towed, so that the steering lock is released, and that the direction indicator and brake lights will work.

☐ Only attach the tow-rope to the towing eyes provided.

☐ Before being towed, release the handbrake and select neutral on the transmission.

☐ Note that greater-than-usual pedal pressure will be required to operate the brakes, since the vacuum servo unit is only operational with the engine running.

☐ On models with power steering, greater-than-usual steering effort will also be required.

☐ The driver of the car being towed must keep the tow-rope taut at all times to avoid snatching.

☐ Make sure that both drivers know the route before setting off.

☐ Only drive at moderate speeds and keep the distance towed to a minimum. Drive smoothly and allow plenty of time for slowing down at junctions.

☐ The driver of the towing vehicle must accelerate very gently from a standstill and must bear in mind the extra length of the vehicle being towed, when pulling out at junctions, roundabouts etc.

☐ A front towing eye is provided behind a cover panel in the spoiler beneath the front bumper. A rear towing eye is provided beneath the rear of the vehicle.

☐ On models with automatic transmission, special precautions apply as follows (if in doubt, do not tow, or transmission damage may result):

a) The car may only be towed in the forward direction

b) The gear selector lever must be in the 'N' position

c) An additional 2 litres of fluid must be added to the transmission (see Chapter 1)

d) Do not exceed 30 mph when towing.

e) After towing, the excess transmission fluid must be drained out and the fluid level restored to its normal level.

Introduction

There are some very simple checks which need only take a few minutes to carry out, but which could save you a lot of inconvenience and expense.

These "Weekly checks" require no great skill or special tools, and the small amount of time they take to perform could prove to be very well spent, for example;

☐ Keeping an eye on tyre condition and pressures, will not only help to stop them wearing out prematurely, but could also save your life.

☐ Many breakdowns are caused by electrical problems. Battery-related faults are particularly common, and a quick check on a regular basis will often prevent the majority of these.

☐ If your car develops a brake fluid leak, the first time you might know about it is when your brakes don't work properly. Checking the level regularly will give advance warning of this kind of problem.

☐ If the oil or coolant levels run low, the cost of repairing any engine damage will be far greater than fixing the leak, for example.

Underbonnet check points

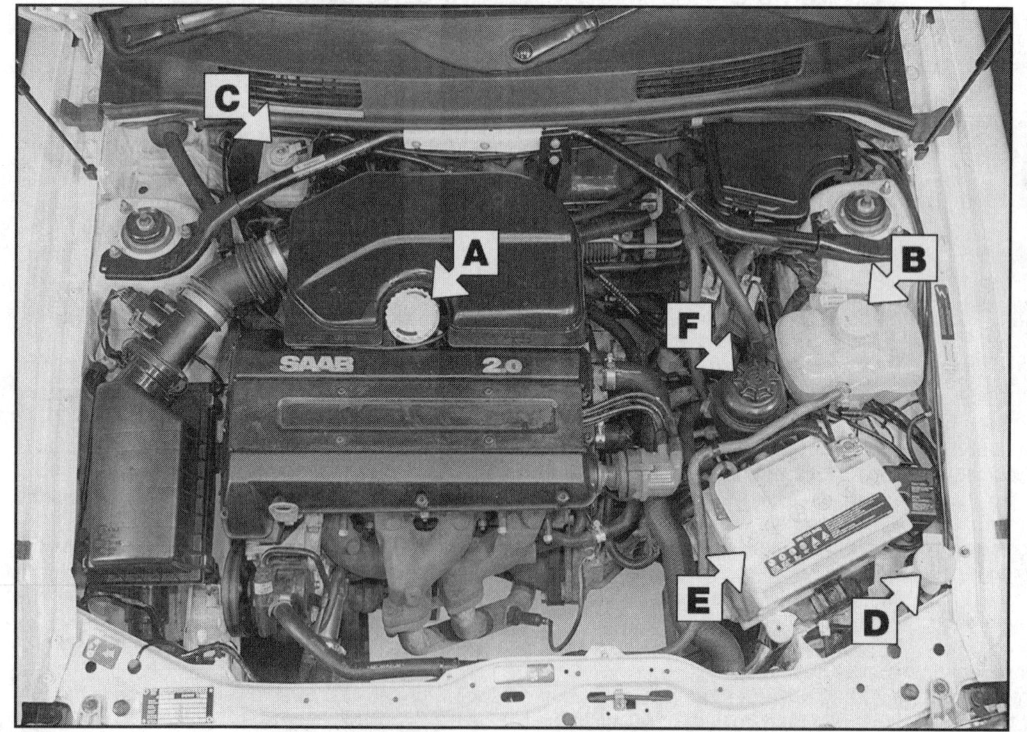

◀ 2.0 litre engine

A *Engine oil level filler cap and dipstick*

B *Coolant reservoir (expansion tank)*

C *Brake fluid reservoir*

D *Washer fluid reservoir*

E *Battery*

F *Power steering fluid reservoir*

Engine oil level

Before you start

✔ Make sure that your car is on level ground.
✔ Check the oil level before the car is driven, or at least 5 minutes after the engine has been switched off.

If the oil is checked immediately after driving the vehicle, some of the oil will remain in the upper engine components, resulting in an inaccurate reading on the dipstick!

The correct oil

Modern engines place great demands on their oil. It is very important that the correct oil for your car is used (See "Lubricants, fluids and tyre pressures").

Car Care

- If you have to add oil frequently, you should check whether you have any oil leaks. Place some clean paper under the car overnight, and check for stains in the morning. If there are no leaks, the engine may be burning oil *(see "Fault Finding").*
- Always maintain the level between the upper and lower dipstick marks (see photo 3). If the level is too low severe engine damage may occur. Oil seal failure may result if the engine is overfilled by adding too much oil.

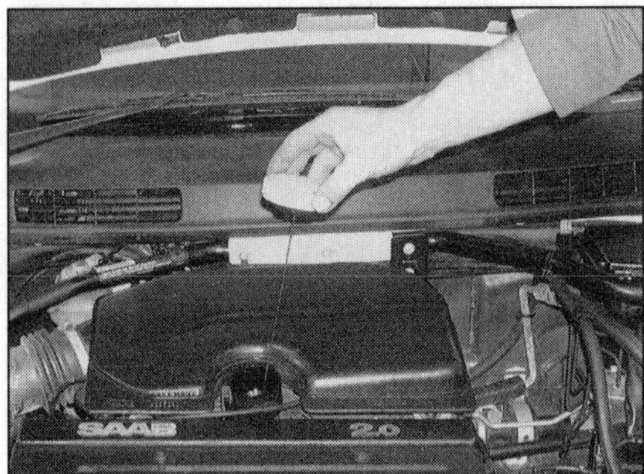

1 The dipstick is located at the centre of the engine (see *"Underbonnet Check Points"* on page 0•10 for exact location). Unscrew the cap and withdraw the integral dipstick.

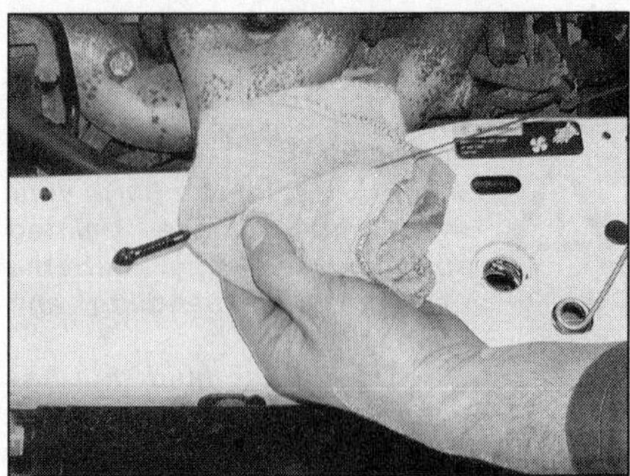

2 Using a clean rag or paper towel remove all oil from the dipstick. Insert the clean dipstick into the tube as far as it will go, then withdraw it again.

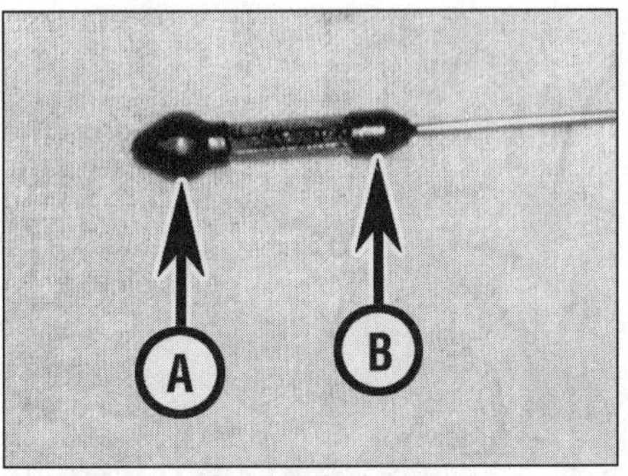

3 Note the oil level on the end of the dipstick, which should be between the upper mark (B) and lower mark (A). Approximately 1.0 litre of oil will raise the level from the lower mark to the upper mark.

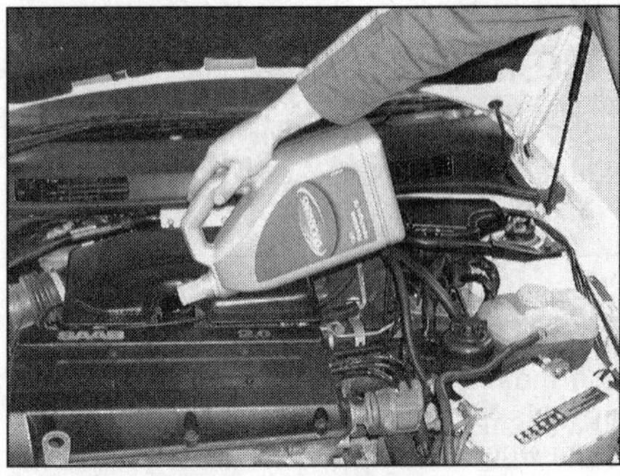

4 Oil is added through the filler cap. Rotate the cap through a quarter-turn anti-clockwise and withdraw it. Top-up the level. A funnel may help to reduce spillage. Add the oil slowly, checking the level on the dipstick often. Do not overfill.

Coolant level

Warning: DO NOT attempt to remove the expansion tank pressure cap when the engine is hot, as there is a very great risk of scalding. Do not leave open containers of coolant about, as it is poisonous.

Car Care

- With a sealed-type cooling system, adding coolant should not be necessary on a regular basis. If frequent topping-up is required, it is likely there is a leak. Check the radiator, all hoses and joint faces for signs of staining or wetness, and rectify as necessary.
- It is important that antifreeze is used in the cooling system all year round, not just during the winter months. Don't top-up with water alone, as the antifreeze will become too diluted.

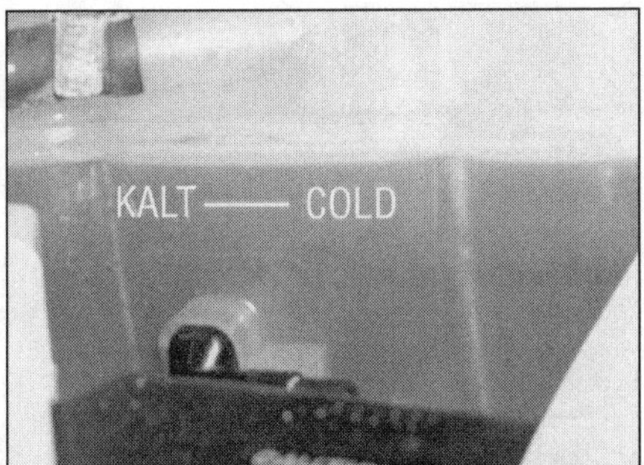

1 The coolant level varies with the temperature of the engine. When the engine is cold, the coolant level should be slightly above the KALT/COLD mark on the side of the tank. When the engine is hot, the level will rise.

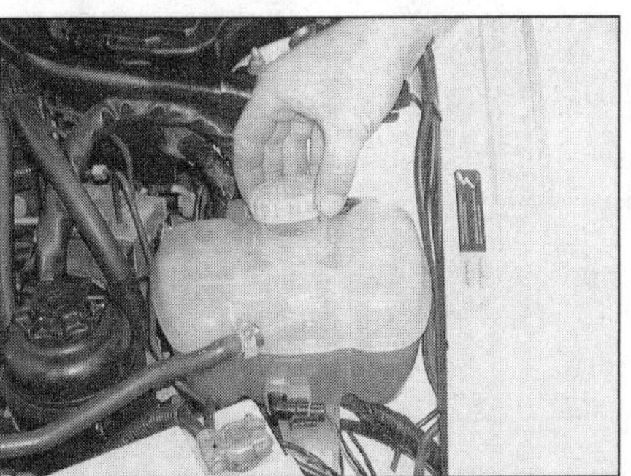

2 If topping up is necessary, **wait until the engine is cold**. Slowly unscrew the expansion tank cap, to release any pressure present in the cooling system, and remove it.

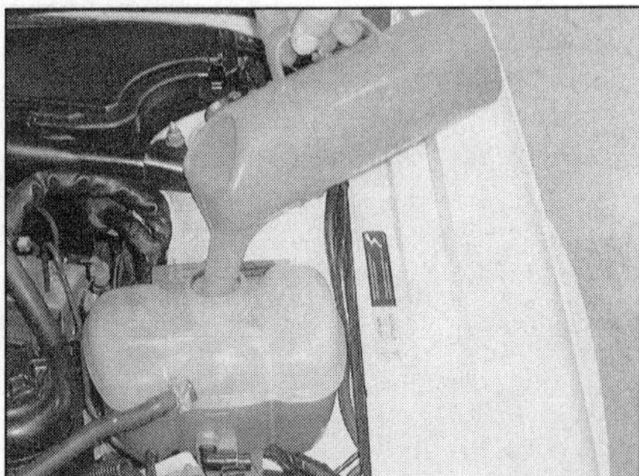

3 Top up the level by adding a mixture of water and antifreeze to the expansion tank. A funnel may help to reduce spillage. Refit the cap and tighten it securely.

Brake fluid level

Warning:
- ***Brake fluid can harm your eyes and damage painted surfaces, so use extreme caution when handling and pouring it.***
- ***Do not use fluid that has been standing open for some time, as it absorbs moisture from the air, which can cause a dangerous loss of braking effectiveness.***

- ***Make sure that your car is on level ground.***
- ***The fluid level in the reservoir will drop slightly as the brake pads wear down, but the fluid level must never be allowed to drop below the "MIN" mark.***

Safety First!

- If the reservoir requires repeated topping-up this is an indication of a fluid leak somewhere in the system, which should be investigated immediately.
- If a leak is suspected, the car should not be driven until the braking system has been checked. Never take any risks where brakes are concerned.

1 The "MAX" and "MIN" marks are indicated on the front of the reservoir. The fluid level must be kept between the marks at all times.

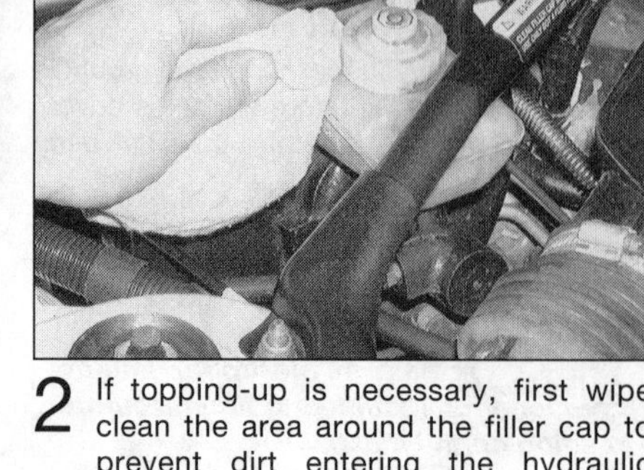

2 If topping-up is necessary, first wipe clean the area around the filler cap to prevent dirt entering the hydraulic system.

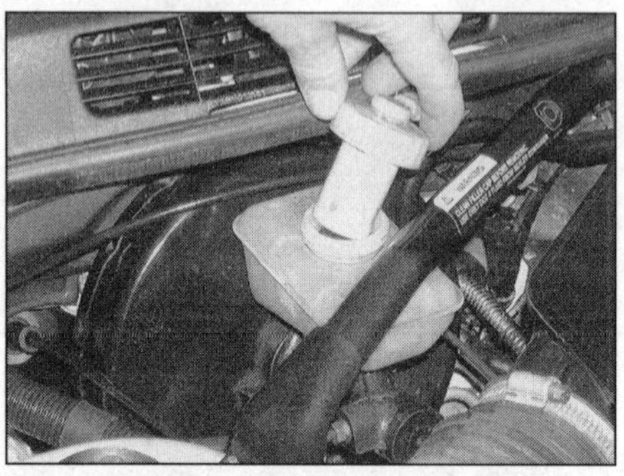

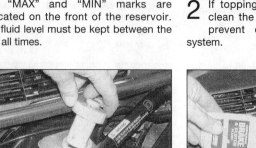

3 Unscrew the cap and place it on an absorbent rag, with the wiring still attached.

4 Carefully add fluid, taking care not to spill it onto the surrounding components. Use only the specified fluid; mixing different types can cause damage to the system. After topping-up to the correct level, securely refit the cap and wipe off any spilt fluid.

Screen washer fluid level

Screenwash additives not only keep the winscreen clean during foul weather, they also prevent the washer system freezing in cold weather - which is when you are likely to need it most. Don't top up using plain water as the screenwash will become too diluted, and will freeze during cold weather. ***On no account use coolant antifreeze in the washer system - this could discolour or damage paintwork.***

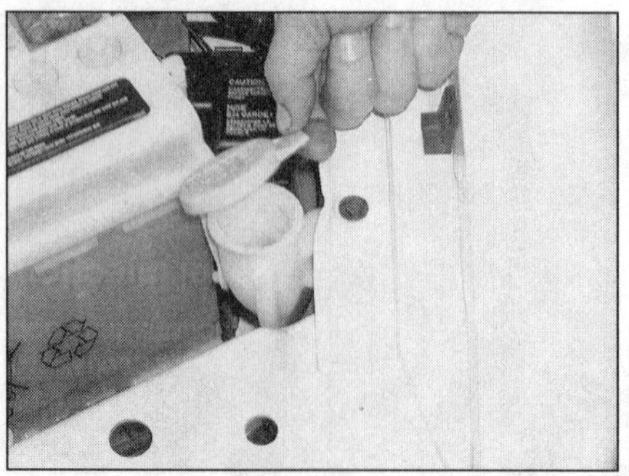

1 The reservoir for the windscreen and rear window (where applicable) washer systems is located on the front left-hand side of the engine compartment. If topping-up is necessary, open the cap.

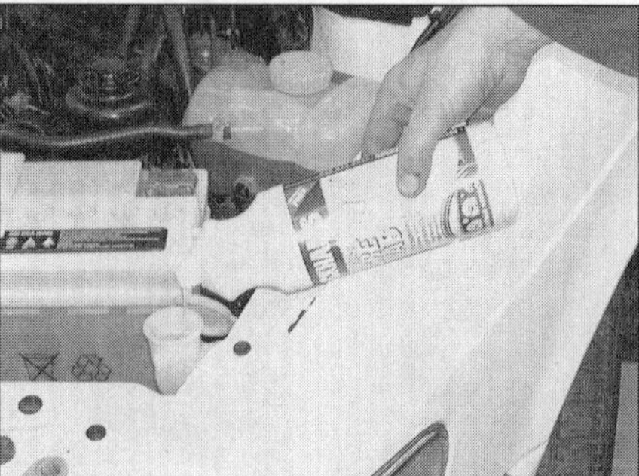

2 When topping-up the reservoir a screenwash additive should be added in the quantities recommended on the bottle.

Power steering fluid level

Before you start:

✔ Park the vehicle on level ground.

✔ With the engine idling, turn the steering wheel slowly from lock to lock 2 or 3 times and set the front wheels at the straight-ahead position, then stop the engine.

✔ The engine should be turned off.

For the check to be accurate, the steering must not be turned once the engine has been stopped.

Safety First!

● The need for frequent topping-up indicates a leak, which should be investigated immediately.

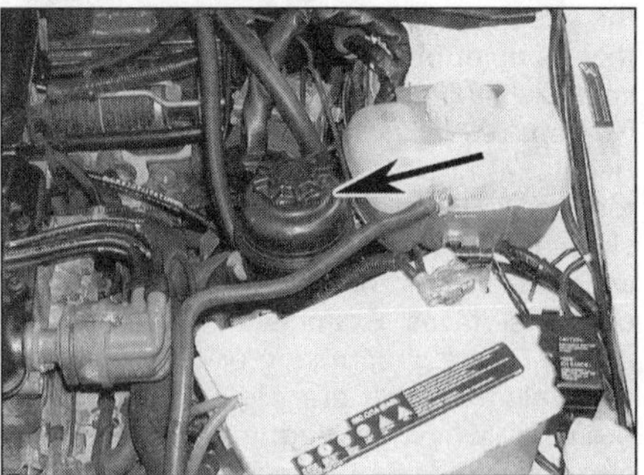

1 The power steering fluid reservoir is located on the left-hand side of the engine compartment behind the battery. The fluid level should be checked with the engine stopped.

2 Unscrew the filler cap from the top of the reservoir, and wipe all fluid from the cap dipstick with a clean rag. Refit the filler cap, then remove it again. Note the fluid level on the dipstick.

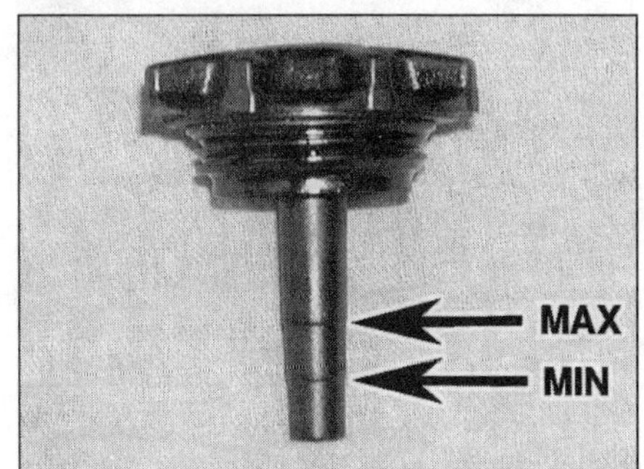

3 When the engine is cold, the fluid level should be between the upper ("MAX") and lower marks ("MIN") on the dipstick. Where only one mark is provided, the level should be between the bottom of the dipstick and the mark.

4 Top up the fluid level using the specified type of fluid (do not overfill the reservoir), then refit and tighten the filler cap.

Wiper blades

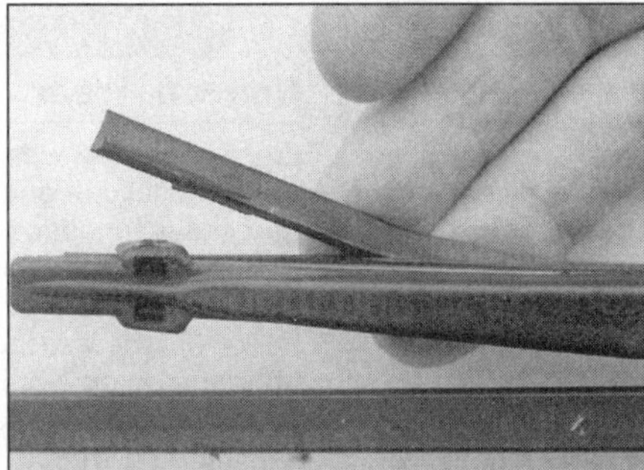

1 Check the condition of the wiper blades; if they are cracked or show any signs of deterioration, or if the glass swept area is smeared, renew them. Wiper blades should be renewed annually.

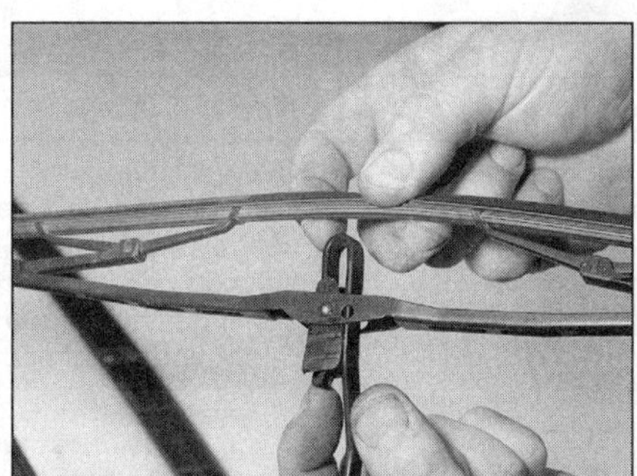

2 To remove a windscreen wiper blade, pull the arm fully away from the screen until it locks. Swivel the blade through 90°, press the locking tab with your fingers and slide the blade out of the arm's hooked end.

Tyre condition and pressure

It is very important that tyres are in good condition, and at the correct pressure - having a tyre failure at any speed is highly dangerous. Tyre wear is influenced by driving style - harsh braking and acceleration, or fast cornering, will all produce more rapid tyre wear. As a general rule, the front tyres wear out faster than the rears. Interchanging the tyres from front to rear ("rotating" the tyres) may result in more even wear. However, if this is completely effective, you may have the expense of replacing all four tyres at once!

Remove any nails or stones embedded in the tread before they penetrate the tyre to cause deflation. If removal of a nail does reveal that the tyre has been punctured, refit the nail so that its point of penetration is marked. Then immediately change the wheel, and have the tyre repaired by a tyre dealer.

Regularly check the tyres for damage in the form of cuts or bulges, especially in the sidewalls. Periodically remove the wheels, and clean any dirt or mud from the inside and outside surfaces. Examine the wheel rims for signs of rusting, corrosion or other damage. Light alloy wheels are easily damaged by "kerbing" whilst parking; steel wheels may also become dented or buckled. A new wheel is very often the only way to overcome severe damage.

New tyres should be balanced when they are fitted, but it may become necessary to re-balance them as they wear, or if the balance weights fitted to the wheel rim should fall off. Unbalanced tyres will wear more quickly, as will the steering and suspension components. Wheel imbalance is normally signified by vibration, particularly at a certain speed (typically around 50 mph). If this vibration is felt only through the steering, then it is likely that just the front wheels need balancing. If, however, the vibration is felt through the whole car, the rear wheels could be out of balance. Wheel balancing should be carried out by a tyre dealer or garage.

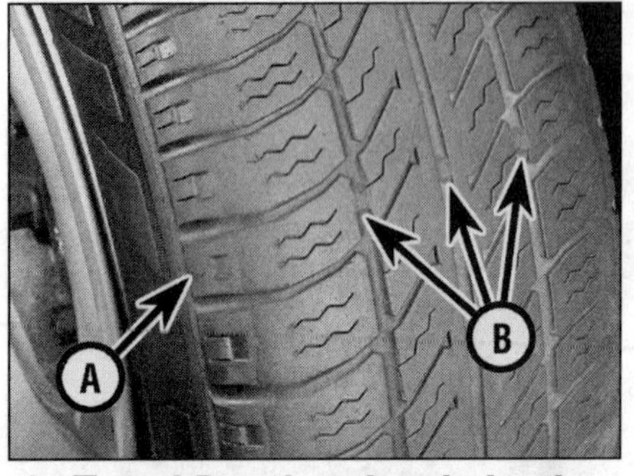

1 ***Tread Depth - visual check***
The original tyres have tread wear safety bands (B), which will appear when the tread depth reaches approximately 1.6 mm. The band positions are indicated by a triangular mark on the tyre sidewall (A).

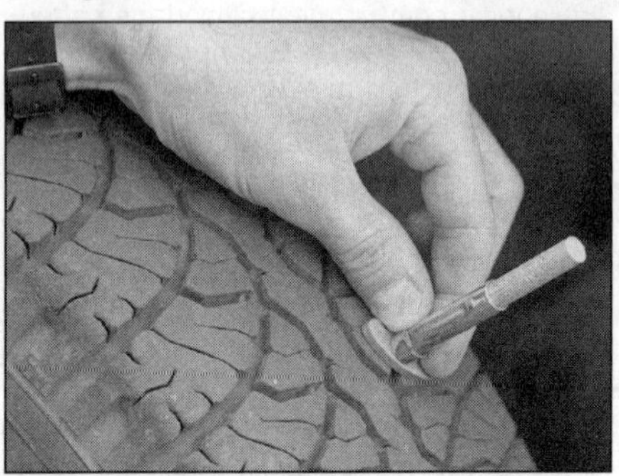

2 ***Tread Depth - manual check***
Alternatively, tread wear can be monitored with a simple, inexpensive device known as a tread depth indicator gauge.

3 ***Tyre Pressure Check***
Check the tyre pressures regularly with the tyres cold. Do not adjust the tyre pressures immediately after the vehicle has been used, or an inaccurate setting will result.

Tyre tread wear patterns

Shoulder Wear

Underinflation (wear on both sides)
Under-inflation will cause overheating of the tyre, because the tyre will flex too much, and the tread will not sit correctly on the road surface. This will cause a loss of grip and excessive wear, not to mention the danger of sudden tyre failure due to heat build-up.
Check and adjust pressures
Incorrect wheel camber (wear on one side)
Repair or renew suspension parts
Hard cornering
Reduce speed!

Centre Wear

Overinflation
Over-inflation will cause rapid wear of the centre part of the tyre tread, coupled with reduced grip, harsher ride, and the danger of shock damage occurring in the tyre casing.
Check and adjust pressures

If you sometimes have to inflate your car's tyres to the higher pressures specified for maximum load or sustained high speed, don't forget to reduce the pressures to normal afterwards.

Uneven Wear

Front tyres may wear unevenly as a result of wheel misalignment. Most tyre dealers and garages can check and adjust the wheel alignment (or "tracking") for a modest charge.
Incorrect camber or castor
Repair or renew suspension parts
Malfunctioning suspension
Repair or renew suspension parts
Unbalanced wheel
Balance tyres
Incorrect toe setting
Adjust front wheel alignment
Note: *The feathered edge of the tread which typifies toe wear is best checked by feel.*

Battery

***Caution:** Before carrying out any work on the vehicle battery, read the precautions given in "Safety first" at the start of this manual.*

✔ Make sure that the battery tray is in good condition, and that the clamp is tight. Corrosion on the tray, retaining clamp and the battery itself can be removed with a solution of water and baking soda. Thoroughly rinse all cleaned areas with water. Any metal parts damaged by corrosion should be covered with a zinc-based primer, then painted.

✔ Periodically (approximately every three months), check the charge condition of the battery as described in Chapter 5A.

✔ If the battery is flat, and you need to jump start your vehicle, see ***Roadside Repairs***.

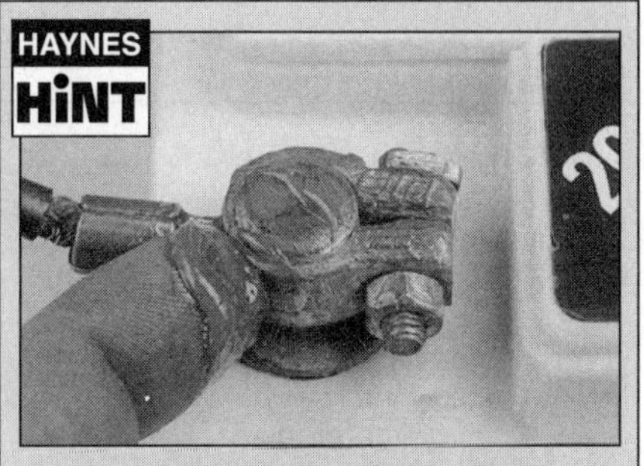

Battery corrosion can be kept to a minimum by applying a layer of petroleum jelly to the clamps and terminals after they are reconnected.

1 The battery is located at the front, left-hand side of the engine compartment. The exterior of the battery should be inspected periodically for damage such as a cracked case or cover.

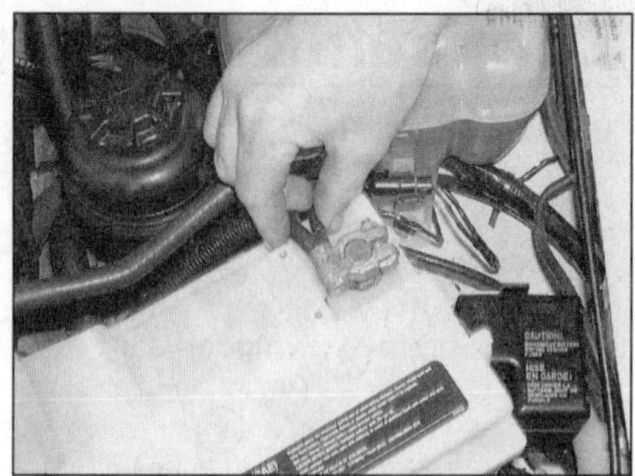

2 Check the tightness of battery clamps to ensure good electrical connections. You should not be able to move them. Also check each cable for cracks and frayed conductors.

3 If corrosion (white, fluffy deposits) is evident, remove the cables from the battery terminals, clean them with a small wire brush, then refit them. Automotive stores sell a tool for cleaning the battery post . . .

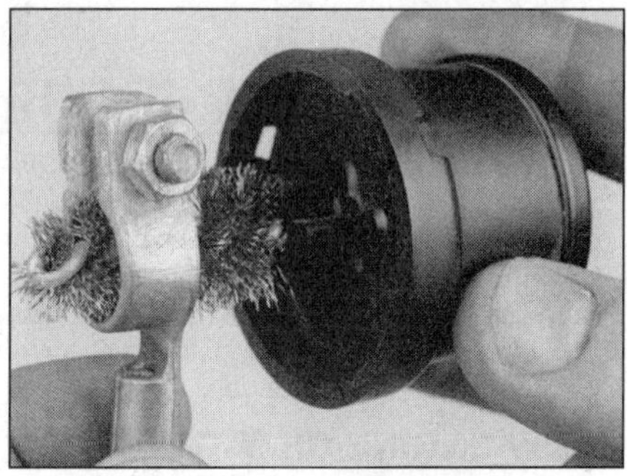

4 . . . as well as the battery cable clamps

Electrical systems

✔ Check all external lights and the horn. Refer to the appropriate Sections of Chapter 12 for details if any of the circuits are found to be inoperative.

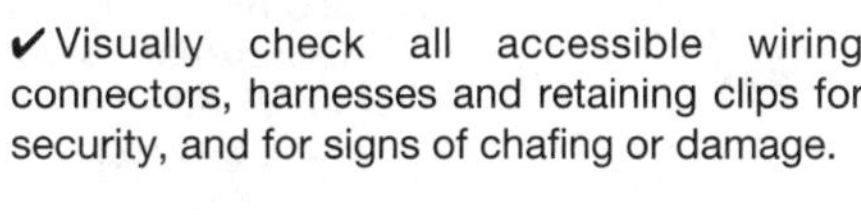

✔ Visually check all accessible wiring connectors, harnesses and retaining clips for security, and for signs of chafing or damage.

If you need to check your brake lights and indicators unaided, back up to a wall or garage door and operate the lights. The reflected light should show if they are working properly.

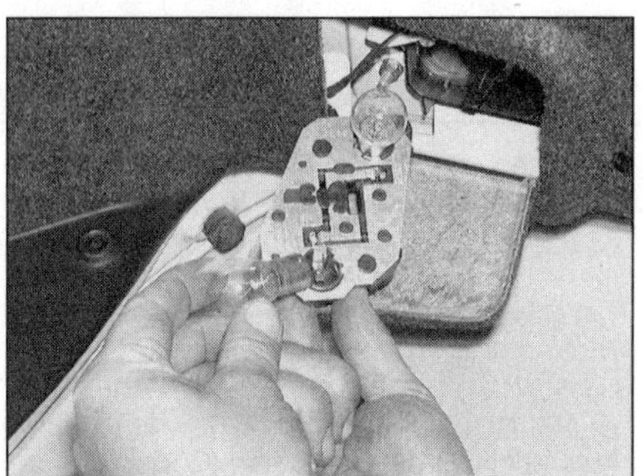

1 If a single indicator light, stop-light or headlight has failed, it is likely that a bulb has blown and will need to be replaced. Refer to Chapter 12 for details. If both stop-lights have failed, it is possible that the switch has failed (see Chapter 9).

2 If more than one indicator light or headlight has failed, it is likely that either a fuse has blown or that there is a fault in the circuit (see Chapter 12). The main fuses are located beneath a cover on the driver's side of the facia. Pull up and remove the cover, then pull out the bottom of the fusebox. Additional fuses and relays are located in the left-hand side of the engine compartment.

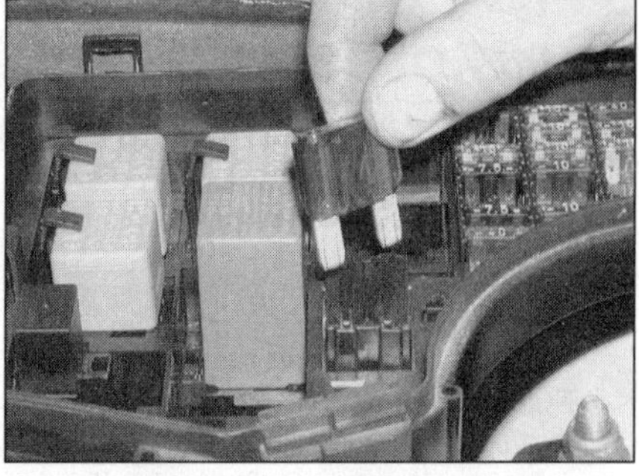

3 To replace a blown fuse, remove it - where applicable using the plastic tool provided. Fit a new fuse of the same rating, available from car accessory shops. It is important that you find the reason that the fuse blew (see *"Electrical fault finding"* in Chapter 12).

Lubricants and fluids

Engine	Saab Turbo Engine Oil or equivalent, to specification API SG/SH or CCMC G4/G5, viscosity of 10W30, 10W40, 5W30 or 5W40 *(Duckhams QXR Premium Petrol Engine Oil)*
Cooling system	Saab antifreeze only
Manual gearbox:	
Models up to 1997 model year	Mineral motor oil to specification API SF/CC, SF/CD, viscosity 10W30 or 10W40 *(Duckhams QXR Premium Petrol Engine Oil)*
Models from 1997 model year	Saab synthetic manual transmission oil only
Automatic transmission	Dexron II type ATF *(Duckhams ATF Autotrans III)*
Power steering reservoir	Saab Power Steering Fluid only
Brake fluid reservoir	Hydraulic fluid to SAE J1703, DOT 3 or DOT 4 *(Duckhams Universal Brake and Clutch Fluid)*

Choosing your engine oil

Engines need oil, not only to lubricate moving parts and minimise wear, but also to maximise power output and to improve fuel economy. By introducing a simplified and improved range of engine oils, Duckhams has taken away the confusion and made it easier for you to choose the right oil for your engine.

HOW ENGINE OIL WORKS

• *Beating friction*

Without oil, the moving surfaces inside your engine will rub together, heat up and melt, quickly causing the engine to seize. Engine oil creates a film which separates these moving parts, preventing wear and heat build-up.

• *Cooling hot-spots*

Temperatures inside the engine can exceed 1000° C. The engine oil circulates and acts as a coolant, transferring heat from the hot-spots to the sump.

• *Cleaning the engine internally*

Good quality engine oils clean the inside of your engine, collecting and dispersing combustion deposits and controlling them until they are trapped by the oil filter or flushed out at oil change.

OIL CARE - FOLLOW THE CODE

To handle and dispose of used engine oil safely, always:

- ***Avoid skin contact with used engine oil. Repeated or prolonged contact can be harmful.***
- ***Dispose of used oil and empty packs in a responsible manner in an authorised disposal site. Call 0800 663366 to find the one nearest to you. Never tip oil down drains or onto the ground.***

Tyre pressures (cold)

Note: *Pressures apply to original-equipment tyres, and may vary if any other make or type of tyre is fitted; check with the tyre manufacturer or supplier for correct pressures if necessary. A full load means a total of five occupants and their luggage. For fewer occupants, subtract 0.1 bar per person from the pressures given below.*

Tyre size	Front	Rear
185/65 R15 88H:		
Up to 3 persons, up to 160 km/h	30 psi (2.1 bar)	30 psi (2.1 bar)
Full load, up to 160 km/h	32 psi (2.2 bar)	32 psi (2.2 bar)
Full load, sustained speeds over 160 km/h	35 psi (2.4 bar)	35 psi (2.4 bar)
195/60 R15 88V:		
Up to 3 persons, up to 160 km/h	32 psi (2.2 bar)	32 psi (2.2 bar)
Full load, up to 160 km/h	35 psi (2.4 bar)	35 psi (2.4 bar)
Full load, sustained speeds over 160 km/h	38 psi (2.6 bar)	38 psi (2.6 bar)
205/50 ZR16:		
Up to 3 persons, up to 160 km/h	33 psi (2.3 bar)	33 psi (2.3 bar)
Full load, up to 160 km/h	36 psi (2.5 bar)	36 psi (2.5 bar)
Full load, sustained speeds over 160 km/h	39 psi (2.7 bar)	39 psi (2.7 bar)

Chapter 1
Routine maintenance and servicing

Contents

Degrees of difficulty

Easy, suitable for novice with little experience 	**Fairly easy,** suitable for beginner with some experience 	**Fairly difficult,** suitable for competent DIY mechanic	**Difficult,** suitable for experienced DIY mechanic	**Very difficult,** suitable for expert DIY or professional 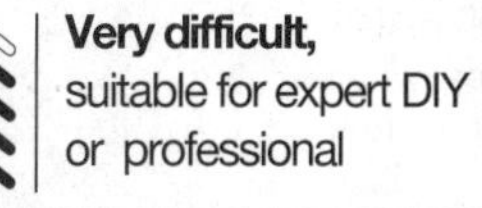

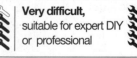

Servicing specifications

Lubricants and fluids
See end of "*Weekly checks*"

Capacities

Engine oil	
All engines (with filter change)	4.0 litres
Between dipstick 'MAX' and 'MIN' markings	1.0 litres
Cooling system	8.5 litres
Transmission	
Manual (drain and refill)	1.8 litres
Automatic (drain and refill)	3.25 litres
Braking system	
System capacity	0.58 litres
Fluid reservoir capacity	0.24 litres
Fuel tank	68.0 litres
Screen wash	4.7 litres
Power assisted steering	
Saloon models:	
Up to chassis No. V2022749	0.75 litres
From chassis No. V2022750	1.0 litres
Cabriolet models:	
Up to chassis No. T7003150	0.75 litres
From chassis No. T7003151	1.0 litres

Engine

Oil filter	Champion C104

Cooling system

Antifreeze mixture:*	
50% antifreeze	Protection down to -37°C
55% antifreeze	Protection down to -45°C

***Note:** *Refer to antifreeze manufacturer for latest recommendations.*

Fuel system

Air filter element	Champion recommendation not available
Fuel filter	Champion L204

Windscreen wipers

Windscreen	Champion VX53
Rear screen	Champion X51

Ignition system

Firing order	1 - 3 - 4 - 2	
Spark plugs:	**Type**	**Electrode gap***
2.0 engine	Champion RC6YCC	0.8 mm
2.3 litre engine	Champion RC9YCC	0.8 mm

**The spark plug gap quoted is that recommended by Champion for their specified plug listed above. If spark plugs of any other type are to be fitted, refer to their manufacturer's recommendations.*

Brakes

Front brake pad friction material minimum thickness	5.0 mm
Rear brake pad friction material minimum thickness	5.0 mm

Tyre pressures
Refer to the end of "*Weekly checks*"

Torque wrench settings

	Nm	lbf ft
Engine oil sump drain plug	25	19
Spark plugs	27	20
Manual transmission drain, level and filler plugs	50	37
Automatic transmission drain plug	35	26
Wheel bolts:		
Steel wheels	100	74
Alloy wheels	117	86

The maintenance intervals in this manual are provided with the assumption that you will be carrying out the work yourself. These are the minimum maintenance intervals recommended by the manufacturer for vehicles driven daily. If you wish to keep your vehicle in peak condition at all times, you may wish to perform some of these procedures more often. We encourage frequent maintenance, because it enhances the efficiency, performance and resale value of your vehicle.

If the vehicle is driven in dusty areas, used to tow a trailer, or driven frequently at slow speeds (idling in traffic) or on short journeys, more frequent maintenance intervals are recommended.

When the vehicle is new, it should be serviced by a factory-authorised dealer service department, in order to preserve the factory warranty.

Every 250 miles (400 km) or weekly

☐ Refer to "*Weekly checks*"

At 6000 miles (10 000 km) and every 12 000 miles (20 000 km) thereafter

☐ Reset the service indicator (Section 3)
☐ Engine oil and filter - renewal (Section 4)
☐ Underbonnet/underbody hose condition and fluid leak - check (Section 5)
☐ Headlight beam alignment - check (Section 6)
☐ Front brake pad wear - check (Section 7)
☐ Rear brake pad wear - check (Section 8)
☐ Braking system operation - check (Section 9)
☐ Handbrake operation - check (Section 10)
☐ Driveshaft gaiter condition - check (Section 11)
☐ Exhaust system - check (Section 12)
☐ Suspension and steering condition and operation - check (Section 13)
☐ Coolant antifreeze concentration - check (Section 14)
☐ Automatic transmission fluid level - check (Section 15)
☐ Auxiliary drivebelt condition - check (Section 16)
☐ Ventilation air filter element - renewal (Section 17)
☐ Hinges and locks - lubrication (Section 18)
☐ Seat belt condition - check (Section 19)
☐ Road test (Section 20)
☐ Air bag system - check (Section 21)

Every 24 000 miles (40 000 km)

☐ Manual transmission oil level - check (Section 22)
☐ Wheel alignment - check (Section 23)
☐ Brake fluid - renewal (Section 24) *

**The interval for this service item is based on time *and* mileage. It must be carried out every 2 years, or every 24 000 miles (40Ê000 km), whichever comes sooner.*

Every 36 000 miles (60 000 km)

☐ Spark plugs - renewal (Section 25)
☐ Air filter element - renewal (Section 26)

Every 48 000 miles (80 000 km)

☐ Coolant - renewal (Section 27) *

**The interval for this service item is based on time *and* mileage. It must be carried out every 3 years or every 48 000 miles (80 000 km), whichever comes sooner.*

1

Every 60 000 miles (100 000 km)

☐ Automatic transmission fluid - renewal (Section 28)

Every 102 000 miles (170 000 km)

☐ Fuel filter - renewal (Section 29)

Underbonnet view of a 1996 Saab 900S 2.0 litre model

1 Brake fluid reservoir
2 Engine oil filler cap and dipstick
3 Fusebox
4 Suspension strut top mounting
5 Power steering fluid reservoir
6 Coolant expansion tank
7 Battery
8 Windscreen washer fluid reservoir filler cap
9 Ignition distributor
10 Spark plugs (hidden)
11 Power steering pump
12 Auxiliary drivebelt
13 Air cleaner housing
14 Air mass flow meter
15 Ignition HT leads

Front underbody view of a 1996 Saab 900S 2.0 litre model

1 Engine oil filter
2 Engine oil sump drain plug
3 Driveshaft
4 Front suspension subframe
5 Front suspension radius arm
6 Front suspension lower control arm
7 Transmission
8 Lambda sensor
9 Brake caliper
10 Radiator electric cooling fan
11 Exhaust system front pipe

Rear underbody view of a 1996 Saab 900S 2.0 litre model

1 Rear brake caliper
2 Exhaust system tail box
3 Rear suspension anti-roll bar
4 Rear suspension beam axle
5 Rear suspension coil spring
6 Rear suspension shock absorber lower mounting
7 Handbrake cable
8 Fuel tank
9 Fuel filter

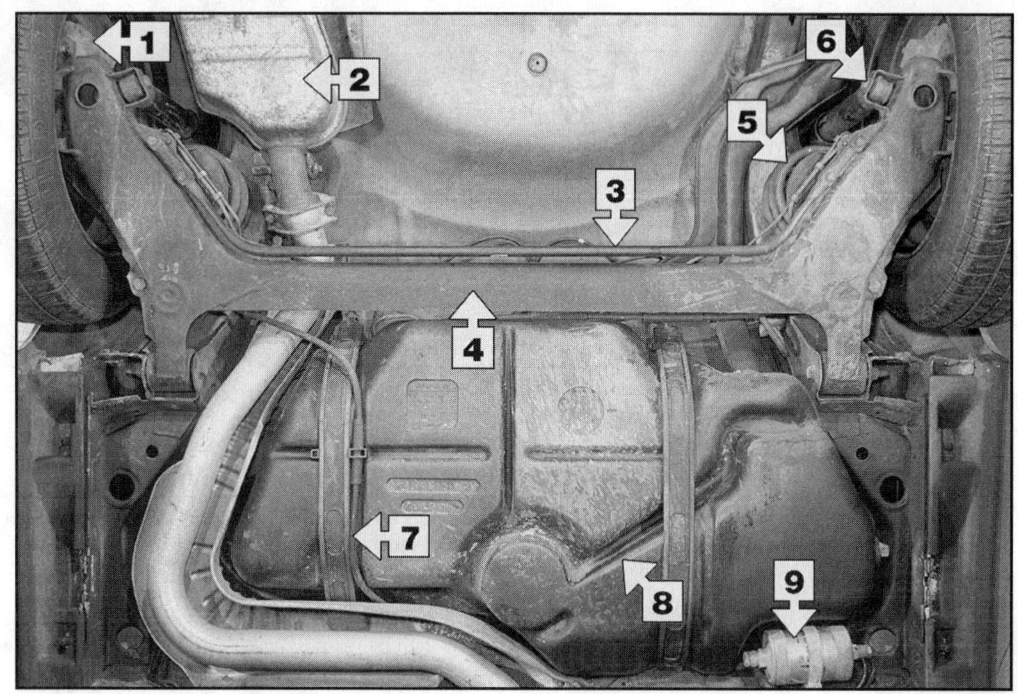

1 General information

1 This Chapter is designed to help the home mechanic maintain his/her vehicle for safety, economy, long life and peak performance.

2 The Chapter contains a master maintenance schedule, followed by Sections dealing specifically with each task in the schedule. Visual checks, adjustments, component renewal and other helpful items are included. Refer to the accompanying illustrations of the engine compartment and the underside of the vehicle for the locations of the various components.

3 Servicing your vehicle in accordance with the mileage/time maintenance schedule and the following Sections will provide a planned maintenance programme, which should result in a long and reliable service life. This is a comprehensive plan, so maintaining some items but not others at the specified service intervals, will not produce the same results.

4 As you service your vehicle, you will discover that many of the procedures can - and should - be grouped together, because of the particular procedure being performed, or because of the close proximity of two otherwise-unrelated components to one another. For example, if the vehicle is raised for any reason, the exhaust system could be inspected at the same time as the suspension and steering components.

5 The first step in this maintenance programme is to prepare yourself before the actual work begins. Read through all the Sections relevant to the work to be carried out, then make a list and gather together all the parts and tools required. If a problem is encountered, seek advice from a parts specialist, or a dealer service department.

2 Intensive maintenance

1 If, from the time the vehicle is new, the routine maintenance schedule is followed closely, and frequent checks are made of fluid levels and high-wear items, as suggested throughout this manual, the engine will be kept in relatively good running condition, and the need for additional work will be minimised.

2 It is possible that there will be times when the engine is running poorly due to the lack of regular maintenance. This is even more likely if a used vehicle, which has not received regular and frequent maintenance checks, is purchased. In such cases, additional work may need to be carried out, outside of the regular maintenance intervals.

3 If engine wear is suspected, a compression test (refer to Chapter 2A) will provide valuable information regarding the overall performance of the main internal components. Such a test can be used as a basis to decide on the extent of the work to be carried out. If, for example, a compression test indicates serious internal engine wear, conventional maintenance as described in this Chapter will not greatly improve the performance of the engine, and may prove a waste of time and money, unless extensive overhaul work (Chapter 2B) is carried out first.

4 The following series of operations are those most often required to improve the performance of a generally poor-running engine:

Primary operations

a) Clean, inspect and test the battery ("Weekly checks", Chapter 5A)
b) Check all the engine-related fluids ("Weekly checks").
c) Check the condition and tension of the auxiliary drivebelt (Section 16).
d) Renew the spark plugs (Section 25).
e) Inspect the distributor cap, rotor arm and HT leads - as applicable (Chapter 5B).
f) Check the condition of the air cleaner filter element, and renew if necessary (Section 26).
g) Renew the fuel filter (Section 29).
h) Check the condition of all hoses, and check for fluid leaks (Section 5).

5 If the above operations do not prove fully effective, carry out the following secondary operations:

Secondary operations

a) Check the charging system (Chapter 5A).
b) Check the ignition system (Chapter 5B).
c) Check the fuel system (Chapter 4A).
d) Renew the distributor cap and rotor arm - as applicable (Chapter 5B).
e) Renew the ignition HT leads - as applicable (Chapter 5B).

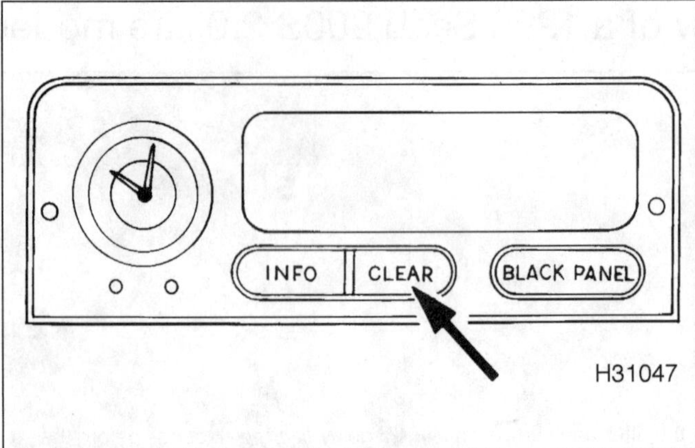

3.2 On the SID panel, press and hold the 'CLEAR' button for 8 seconds, then release it

4.3 Slacken and remove the sump oil drain plug

Every 12 000 miles (20 000 km)

3 Reset the service indicator

1 On some models, the facia-mounted SID (Saab Information Display) system incorporates a service interval indicator. When the distance covered between services approaches 12,000 miles, a visual warning is displayed. The service indicator is then manually reset to zero, after the vehicle has been serviced.

2 On the SID panel, press and hold the 'CLEAR' button for 8 seconds, then release it **(see illustration)**. During this period, the display should read 'CLEAR' for the first four seconds, followed by 'SERVICE' for the remaining 4 seconds. An audible signal will also be sounded during this time. The service indicator will then be reset.

4.4a Allow some time for the old oil to drain . . .

4.4b . . . noting that it may be necessary to reposition the container as the oil flow slows to a trickle

4 Engine oil and filter - renewal

HAYNES HiNT ***Frequent oil and filter changes are the most important preventative maintenance procedures that can be undertaken by the DIY owner. As engine oil ages, it becomes diluted and contaminated. The oil filter gradually becomes clogged with contaminants and debris, lessening its flow capacity and causing reduced oil pressure. These effects can combine to cause premature engine wear, if left unchecked. High-mileage vehicles, and those which are subjected to a lot of short distance or stop-start driving will have a higher-than-average rate of oil contamination. In these circumstances, owners may prefer to carry out engine oil and filter renewal at 6000 mile/10 000 km intervals instead of at the normal 12000 mile/20 000 km interval.***

1 Before starting this procedure, gather together all the necessary tools and materials. Also make sure that you have plenty of clean rags and newspapers handy, to mop up any spills. Ideally, the engine oil should be warm, as it will drain better, and more built-up sludge will be removed with it. Take care, however, not to touch the exhaust or any other hot parts of the engine when working under the vehicle.

2 To avoid any possibility of scalding, and to protect yourself from possible skin irritants and other harmful contaminants in used engine oils, it is advisable to wear gloves when carrying out this work. Access to the underside of the vehicle will be greatly improved if it can be raised on a lift, driven onto ramps, or jacked up and supported on axle stands (see *"Jacking and vehicle support"*). Whichever method is chosen, make sure that the vehicle remains level, or if it is at an angle, that the drain plug is at the lowest point.

3 Slacken the drain plug about half a turn **(see illustration)**. Position the draining container under the drain plug, then remove the plug completely. If possible, try to keep the plug pressed into the sump while unscrewing it by hand the last couple of turns. As the plug releases from the threads, move it away sharply so the stream of oil issuing from the sump runs into the container, not up your sleeve! Recover the sealing washer from the drain plug.

4 Allow some time for the old oil to drain, noting that it may be necessary to reposition the container as the oil flow slows to a trickle **(see illustrations)**.

5 After all the oil has drained, wipe off the drain plug with a clean rag. Check the sealing washer for condition, and renew it if necessary **(see illustration)**. Clean the area around the drain plug opening, and refit the plug. Tighten the plug to the specified torque.

4.5 Renew the sump oil drain plug washer if necessary

4.7a Slacken the oil filter using a removal tool . . .

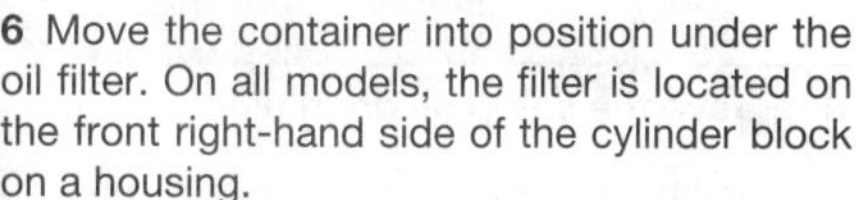

6 Move the container into position under the oil filter. On all models, the filter is located on the front right-hand side of the cylinder block on a housing.

7 Using an oil filter removal tool if necessary, slacken the filter initially, then unscrew it by hand the rest of the way **(see illustrations)**. Note that on the B204 and B234 engines, the oil filter is located very close to the sump. Use of a strap-type removal tool is possible on these engines. Empty the oil from the old filter into the container, and discard the filter.

8 Use a clean rag to remove all oil, dirt and sludge from the filter sealing area on the engine. Check the old filter to make sure that the rubber sealing ring hasn't stuck to the engine. If it has, carefully remove it.

9 Apply a light coating of clean engine oil to the sealing ring on the new filter, then screw it into position on the engine **(see illustrations)**. Tighten the filter firmly by hand only - **do not** use any tools. Wipe clean the filter and sump drain plug.

10 Remove the old oil and all tools from under the car, then lower the car to the ground (if applicable).

11 Remove the oil filler cap and withdraw the dipstick from the top of the filler tube. Fill the engine, using the correct grade and type of oil (see "*Lubricants and fluids*"). An oil can spout or funnel may help to reduce spillage. Pour in half the specified quantity of oil first, then wait a few minutes for the oil to fall to the sump. Continue adding oil a small quantity at a time until the level is up to the lower mark on the dipstick. Adding a further 1.0 litre will bring the level up to the upper mark on the dipstick. Insert the dipstick, and refit the filler cap **(see illustrations)**.

12 Start the engine and run it for a few minutes; check for leaks around the oil filter seal and the sump drain plug. Note that there may be a delay of a few seconds before the oil pressure warning light goes out when the engine is first started, as the oil circulates through the engine oil galleries and the new oil filter, before the pressure builds up.

13 Switch off the engine, and wait a few minutes for the oil to settle in the sump once more. With the new oil circulated and the filter completely full, recheck the level on the dipstick, and add more oil as necessary.

14 Dispose of the used engine oil safely, in accordance with the guidance given in the Reference Section.

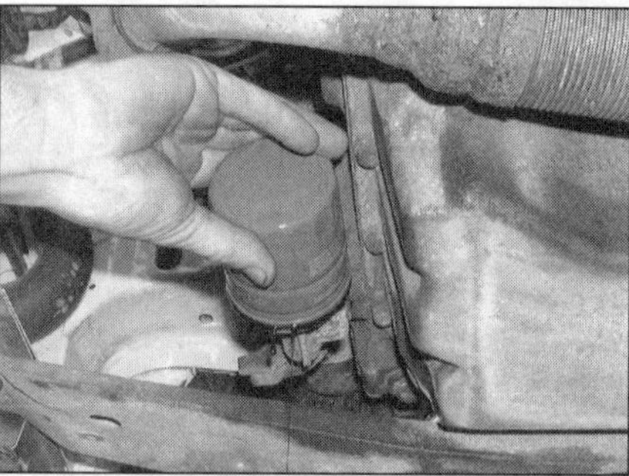

4.7b . . . and remove it from the engine

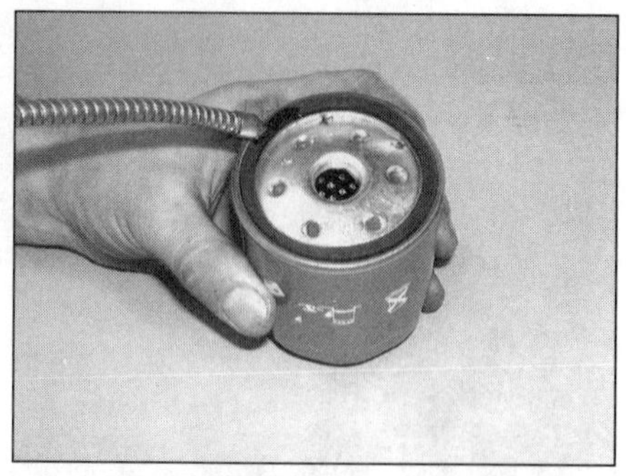

4.9a Apply a light coating of clean engine oil to the sealing ring on the new filter . . .

4.9b . . . then screw it into position on the engine

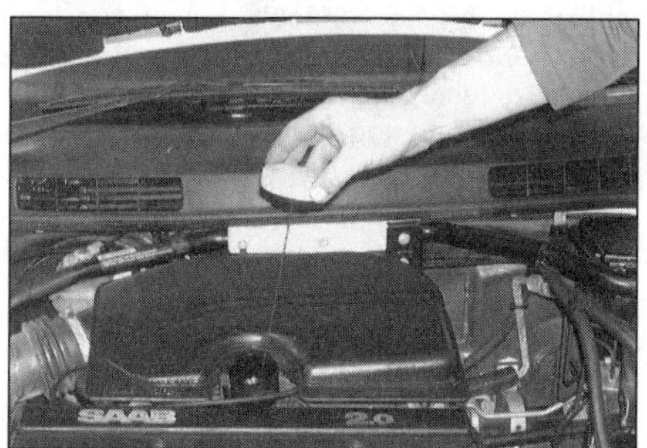

4.11a Remove the oil filler cap and withdraw the dipstick from the top of the filler tube

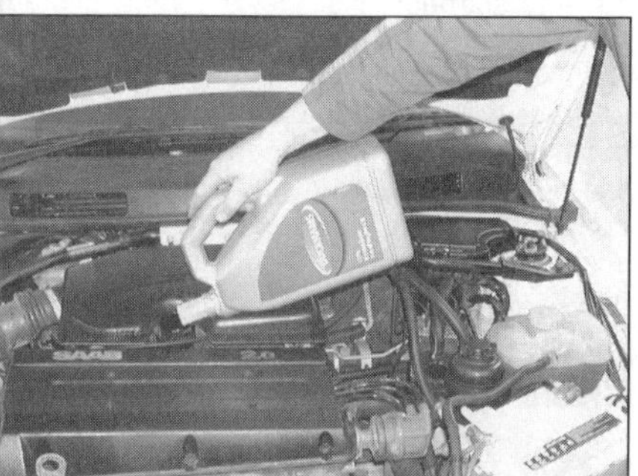

4.11b Fill the engine, using the correct grade and type of oil

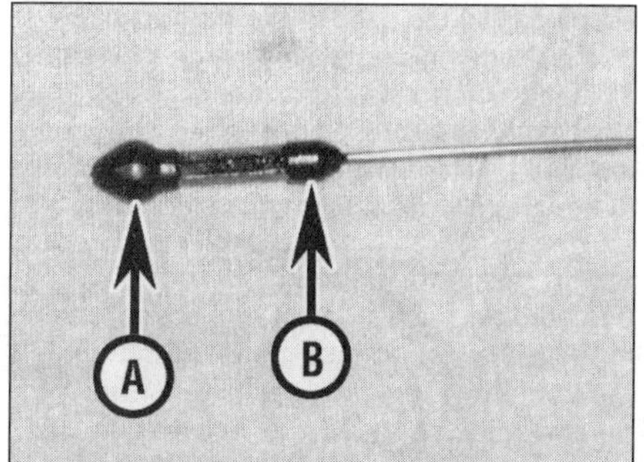

4.11c Lower mark(A) and upper mark(B) on the engine oil dipstick

5 Underbonnet/underbody hose condition and fluid leak - check

1

Cooling system

Warning: Refer to the safety information given in "Safety First" and Chapter 3 before disturbing any of the cooling system components.

1 Carefully check the radiator and heater coolant hoses along their entire length. Renew any hose which is cracked, swollen or which shows signs of deterioration. Cracks will show up better if the hose is squeezed. Pay close attention to the clips that secure the hoses to the cooling system components. Hose clips that have been over-tightened can pinch and puncture hoses, resulting in cooling system leaks **(see illustration)**.

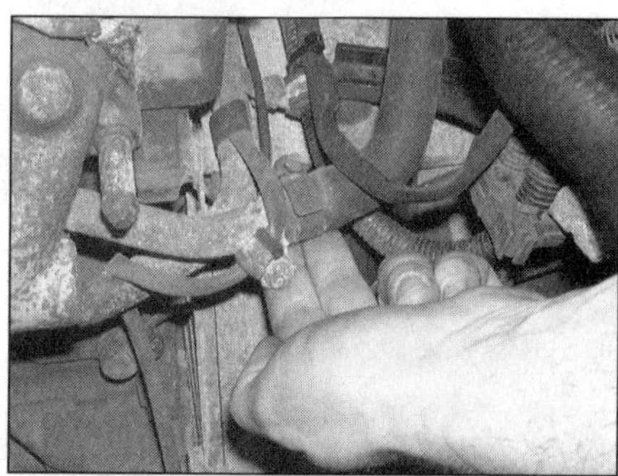

5.1 Check all cooling system hoses for signs of leakage

A leak in the cooling system will usually show up as white- or rust-coloured, crusty deposits around the area of the leak

2 Inspect all the cooling system components (hoses, joint faces etc.) for leaks. Where any problems of this nature are found on system components, renew the component or gasket with reference to Chapter 3 **(see Haynes Hint)**.

Fuel system

Warning: Refer to the safety information given in "Safety First" and Chapter 4A before disturbing any of the fuel system components.

3 Petrol leaks can be difficult to pinpoint, unless the leakage is significant and hence easily visible. Fuel tends to evaporate quickly once it comes into contact with air, especially in a hot engine bay. Small drips can disappear before you get a chance to identify the point of leakage. If you suspect that there is a fuel leak from the area of the engine bay, leave the vehicle overnight then start the engine from cold, with the bonnet open. Metal components tend to shrink when they are cold, and rubber seals and hoses tend to harden, so any leaks will be more apparent whilst the engine is warming up from a cold start.

4 Check all fuel lines at their connections to the fuel rail, fuel pressure regulator and fuel filter. Examine each rubber fuel hose along its length for splits or cracks. Check for leakage from the crimped joints between rubber and metal fuel lines. Examine the unions between the metal fuel lines and the fuel filter housing. Also check the area around the fuel injectors for signs of O-ring leakage.

5.9 Examine the power steering fluid supply and return hoses and pipes for signs of leakage

5.7a Inspect the area around the camshaft cover joint face for signs of engine oil leakage

5 To identify fuel leaks between the fuel tank and the engine bay, the vehicle should be raised and securely supported on axle stands (see "*Jacking and vehicle support*"). Inspect the petrol tank and filler neck for punctures, cracks and other damage. The connection between the filler neck and tank is especially critical. Sometimes a rubber filler neck or connecting hose will leak due to loose retaining clamps or deteriorated rubber.

6 Carefully check all rubber hoses and metal fuel lines leading away from the petrol tank. Check for loose connections, deteriorated hoses, kinked lines, and other damage. Pay particular attention to the vent pipes and hoses, which often loop up around the filler neck and can become blocked or kinked, making tank filling difficult. Follow the fuel supply and return lines to the front of the vehicle, carefully inspecting them all the way for signs of damage or corrosion. Renew damaged sections as necessary.

Engine oil

7 Inspect the area around the camshaft cover, cylinder head, oil filter and sump joint faces. Where applicable, check the area around the ignition distributor mounting flange **(see illustrations)**. Bear in mind that, over a period of time, some very slight seepage from these areas is to be expected - what you are really looking for is any indication of a serious leak caused by gasket failure. Engine oil seeping from the base of the timing belt cover or the transmission bellhousing may be an indication of crankshaft or transmission input shaft oil seal failure. Should a leak be found, renew the failed gasket or oil seal by referring to the appropriate Chapters in this manual.

Automatic transmission fluid

8 Where applicable, check the hoses leading to the transmission fluid cooler at the front of the engine bay for leakage. Look for deterioration caused by corrosion and damage from grounding, or debris thrown up from the road surface. Automatic transmission fluid is a thin oil and is usually red in colour.

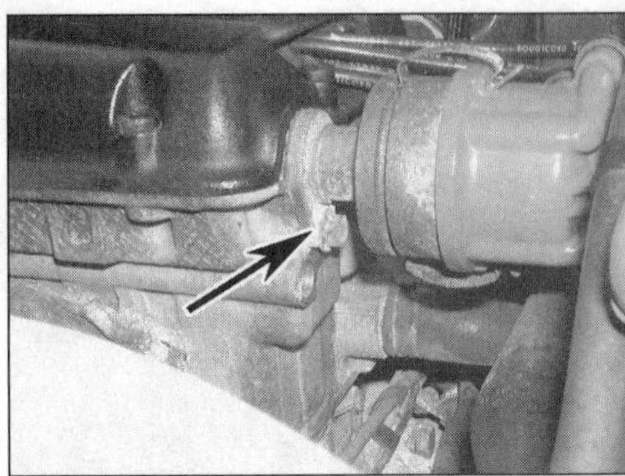

5.7b Where applicable, check the area around the ignition distributor mounting flange

Power assisted steering (PAS) fluid

9 Examine the hose running between the fluid reservoir and the power steering pump, and the return hose running from the steering rack to the fluid reservoir. Also examine the high pressure supply hose between the pump and the steering rack **(see illustration)**.

10 Check the condition of each hose carefully. Look for deterioration caused by corrosion and damage from grounding, or debris thrown up from the road surface.

11 Pay particular attention to crimped unions, and the area surrounding the hoses that are secured with adjustable worm drive clips. Like automatic transmission fluid, PAS fluid is a thin oil, and is usually red in colour.

Air conditioning refrigerant

Warning: Refer to the safety information given in "Safety First" and Chapter 3, regarding the dangers of disturbing any of the air conditioning system components.

12 The air conditioning system is filled with a liquid refrigerant, which is retained under high pressure. If the air conditioning system is opened and depressurised without the aid of specialised equipment, the refrigerant will immediately turn into gas and escape into the atmosphere. If the liquid comes into contact with your skin, it can cause severe frostbite. In addition, the refrigerant contains substances which are environmentally damaging; for this reason, it should not be allowed to escape into the atmosphere in an uncontrolled fashion.

13 Any suspected air conditioning system leaks should be immediately referred to a Saab dealer or air conditioning specialist. Leakage will be shown up as a steady drop in the level of refrigerant in the system.

14 Note that water may drip from the condenser drain pipe, underneath the car, immediately after the air conditioning system has been in use. This is normal, and should not be cause for concern.

Brake fluid

Warning: Refer to the safety information given in "Safety First" and Chapter 9, regarding the dangers of handling brake fluid.

5.15 Check the area around the base of brake fluid reservoir, for signs of leakage

15 With reference to Chapter 9, examine the area surrounding the brake pipe unions at the master cylinder for signs of leakage. Check the area around the base of fluid reservoir, for signs of leakage caused by seal failure **(see illustration)**. Also examine the brake pipe unions at the ABS hydraulic unit.

16 If fluid loss is evident, but the leak cannot be pinpointed in the engine bay, the brake calipers and underbody brake lines should be carefully checked with the vehicle raised and supported on axle stands (see *"Jacking and vehicle support"*). Leakage of fluid from the braking system is a serious fault that must be rectified immediately.

17 Brake/clutch hydraulic fluid is a toxic substance with a watery consistency. New fluid is almost colourless, but it becomes darker with age and use.

Unidentified fluid leaks

18 If there are signs that a fluid of some description is leaking from the vehicle, but you cannot identify the type of fluid or its exact origin, park the vehicle overnight and slide a large piece of card underneath it. Providing that the card is positioned in roughly the right location, even the smallest leak will show up on the card. Not only will this help you to pinpoint the exact location of the leak, it should be easier to identify the fluid from its colour. Bear in mind, though, that the leak may only be occurring when the engine is running!

Vacuum hoses

19 Although the braking system is hydraulically-operated, the brake servo unit amplifies the effort applied at the brake pedal, by making use of the vacuum in the inlet manifold, generated by the engine. Vacuum is ported to the servo by means of a large-bore hose. Any leaks that develop in this hose will reduce the effectiveness of the braking system, and may affect the running of the engine.

20 In addition, a number of the underbonnet components, particularly the emission control components, are driven by vacuum supplied from the inlet manifold via narrow-bore hoses. A leak in a vacuum hose means that air is being drawn into the hose (rather than escaping from it) and this makes leakage very difficult to detect. One method is to use an old length of vacuum hose as a kind of stethoscope - hold one end close to (but not in!) your ear and use the other end to probe the area around the suspected leak. When the end of the hose is directly over a vacuum leak, a hissing sound will be heard clearly through the hose. Care must be taken to avoid contacting hot or moving components, as the engine must be running, when testing in this manner. Renew any vacuum hoses that are found to be defective.

6 Headlight beam alignment - check

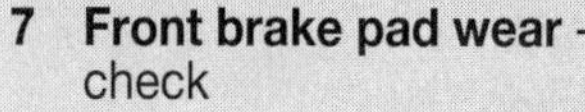

Refer to Chapter 12 for details

7 Front brake pad wear - check

1 Firmly apply the handbrake, then jack up the front of the vehicle and support it securely on axle stands (see *"Jacking and Vehicle Support"*). Remove the front roadwheels.

2 For a quick check, the pad thickness can be checked via the inspection hole on the front of the caliper **(see illustration)**. Using a steel rule, measure the thickness of the pad lining including the backing plate. This must not be less than that indicated in the Specifications.

3 The view through the caliper inspection hole gives a rough indication of the state of the brake pads. For a comprehensive check, the brake pads should be removed and cleaned. The operation of the caliper can then also be checked, and the condition of the brake disc itself can be fully examined on both sides.

4 If any pad's friction material is worn to the specified thickness or less, *all four pads must be renewed as a set.* Refer to Chapter 9 for details.

5 On completion, refit the roadwheels and lower the vehicle to the ground.

7.2 The brake pad wear can be measured through the aperture in the front brake caliper

8 Rear brake pad wear - check

1 Firmly apply the handbrake, then jack up the rear of the vehicle and support it securely on axle stands (see *"Jacking and Vehicle Support"*). Remove the rear roadwheels.

2 For a quick check, the pad thickness can be carried out via the inspection hole on the rear of the caliper. Using a steel rule, measure the thickness of the pad lining including the backing plate. This must not be less than that indicated in the Specifications.

3 The view through the caliper inspection hole gives a rough indication of the state of the brake pads. For a comprehensive check, the brake pads should be removed and cleaned. The operation of the caliper can then also be checked, and the condition of the brake disc itself can be fully examined on both sides.

4 If any pad's friction material is worn to the specified thickness or less, *all four pads must be renewed as a set.* Refer to Chapter 9 for details.

5 On completion, refit the roadwheels and lower the vehicle to the ground.

9 Braking system operation - check

1 Depress the footbrake pedal and check that it feels firm without excessive travel. If it feels 'spongy', air is present in the hydraulic system, and it will be necessary to bleed the system as described in Chapter 9.

2 Check that the brakes operate evenly on both sides of the vehicle, and that there is no tendency to pull to one side.

3 Check the vacuum servo unit as described in Chapter 9.

10 Handbrake operation - check

1 Chock the front wheels, then jack up the rear of the vehicle and support on axle stands (see *"Jacking and Vehicle Support"*).

2 Fully release the handbrake lever.

3 Apply the lever to the 6th notch position, and check that both rear wheels are locked when attempting to turn them by hand.

4 If adjustment is necessary, refer to Chapter 9.

5 Lower the vehicle to the ground.

11 Driveshaft gaiter condition - check

1 With the front of the vehicle raised and securely supported on stands, turn the steering onto full lock then slowly rotate the

11.1 Checking the condition of the driveshaft gaiters

roadwheel. Inspect the condition of the outer constant velocity (CV) joint rubber gaiters while squeezing the gaiters to open out the folds **(see illustration)**. Check for signs of cracking, splits or deterioration of the rubber which may allow the grease to escape and lead to water and grit entry into the joint. Also check the security and condition of the retaining clips. Repeat these checks on the inner CV joints. If any damage or deterioration is found, the gaiters should be renewed as described in Chapter 8.

2 At the same time check the general condition of the CV joints themselves by first holding the driveshaft and attempting to rotate the wheel. Repeat this check by holding the inner joint and attempting to rotate the driveshaft. Any appreciable movement indicates wear in the joints, wear in the driveshaft splines or loose driveshaft retaining nut.

12 Exhaust system - check

Warning: *If the engine has been running take care not to touch the exhaust system, especially the front section, as it may still be hot.*

1 Position the car over an inspection pit, or on car ramps. Alternatively, raise the front or rear of the car and support on axle stands (see "*Jacking and vehicle support*").

2 Examine the exhaust system over its entire length, checking for any damaged, broken or missing mountings, security of the pipe retaining clamps, and condition of the system with regard to rust and corrosion.

3 Look for signs of leakage - a leak normally shows up as a black sooty stain. With the engine running, have an assistant place a wad of rag over the exhaust tailpipe, while you listen for the rhythmic "fluffing" sound characteristic of an exhaust leak.

4 It may be possible to repair a minor leak yourself, using one of the proprietary exhaust sealing products available, but more serious damage will require the replacement of one or more sections of the exhaust system - refer to Chapter 4A.

5 Lower the vehicle to the ground on completion.

13.4 Check for wear in the hub bearings by grasping the wheel and trying to rock it

13 Suspension and steering condition and operation - check

Front suspension and steering check

1 Raise the front of the vehicle, and securely support it on axle stands (see "*Jacking and Vehicle Support*").

2 Visually inspect the balljoint dust covers and the steering rack-and-pinion gaiters for splits, chafing or deterioration. Any wear of these components will cause loss of lubricant, together with dirt and water entry, resulting in rapid deterioration of the balljoints or steering gear.

3 On vehicles with power steering, check the fluid hoses for chafing or deterioration, and the pipe and hose unions for fluid leaks. Also check for signs of fluid leakage under pressure from the steering gear rubber gaiters, which would indicate failed fluid seals within the steering gear.

4 Grasp the roadwheel at the 12 o'clock and 6 o'clock positions, and try to rock it **(see illustration)**. Very slight free play may be felt, but if the movement is appreciable, further investigation is necessary to determine the source. Continue rocking the wheel while an assistant depresses the footbrake. If the movement is now eliminated or significantly reduced, it is likely that the hub bearings are at fault. If the free play is still evident with the footbrake depressed, then there is wear in the suspension joints or mountings.

5 Now grasp the wheel at the 9 o'clock and 3 o'clock positions, and try to rock it as before. Any movement felt now may again be caused by wear in the hub bearings or the steering track-rod balljoints. If the outer balljoint is worn, the visual movement will be obvious. If the inner joint is suspect, it can be felt by placing a hand over the rack-and-pinion rubber gaiter and gripping the track-rod. If the wheel is now rocked, movement will be felt at the inner joint if wear has taken place.

6 Using a large screwdriver or flat bar, check for wear in the suspension mounting bushes by levering between the relevant suspension component and its attachment point. Some movement is to be expected, as the mountings are made of rubber, but excessive wear should be obvious. Also check the condition of any visible rubber bushes, looking for splits, cracks or contamination of the rubber.

7 With the car standing on its wheels, have an assistant turn the steering wheel back and forth, about an eighth of a turn each way. There should be very little, if any, lost movement between the steering wheel and roadwheels. If this is not the case, closely observe the joints and mountings previously described. In addition, check the steering column universal joints for wear, and also check the rack-and-pinion steering gear itself.

8 The front suspension mountings should be checked for tightness at the first 6000 mile (10 000 km) service.

Rear suspension check

9 Chock the front wheels, then jack up the rear of the vehicle and support securely on axle stands (see "*Jacking and Vehicle Support*").

10 Working as described previously for the front suspension, check the rear hub bearings, the suspension bushes and the strut or shock absorber mountings (as applicable) for wear.

11 The rear suspension mountings should be checked for tightness at the first 6000 mile (10 000 km) service.

Shock absorber check

12 Check for any signs of fluid leakage around the shock absorber body, or from the rubber gaiter around the piston rod. Should any fluid be noticed, the shock absorber is defective internally, and should be renewed. **Note:** *Shock absorbers should always be renewed in pairs on the same axle.*

13 The efficiency of the shock absorber may be checked by bouncing the vehicle at each corner. Generally speaking, the body will return to its normal position and stop after being depressed. If it rises and returns on a rebound, the shock absorber is probably suspect. Also examine the shock absorber upper and lower mountings for any signs of wear.

14 Coolant antifreeze concentration - check

1 With the engine cold, unscrew and remove the filler cap from the expansion tank located on the left-hand side of the engine compartment.

2 Using a proprietary tester, draw out some of the coolant and check the concentration of the antifreeze. The testers are available from car accessory shops **(see illustration)**.

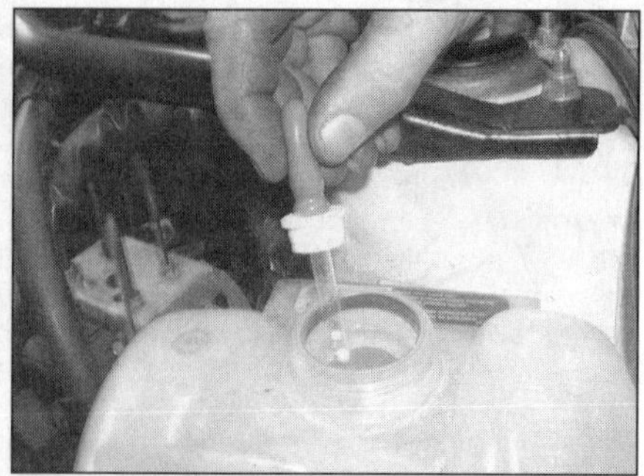

14.2 Using a proprietary tester, draw out some of the coolant and check the concentration of the antifreeze

3 If it is necessary to increase the strength of the antifreeze, determine the amount of antifreeze to add to the system with reference to the "*Specifications*". Where it is necessary to add a large proportion of antifreeze, consider draining the complete system and refilling it with reference to Section 27. If only a small amount of antifreeze needs to be added, drain off some of the coolant, then add the antifreeze and finally top-up the system with reference to *"Weekly Checks"*.

4 On completion, refit and tighten the expansion tank filler cap.

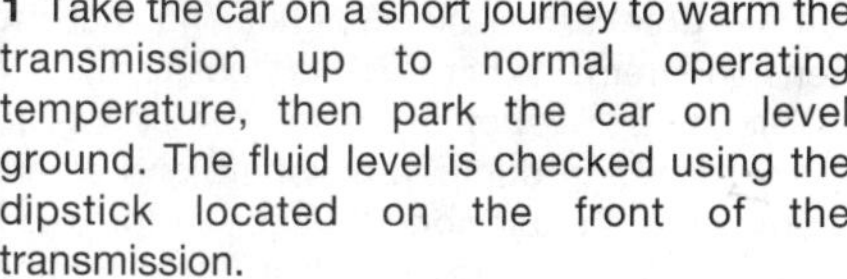

15 Automatic transmission fluid level - check

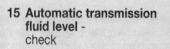

1 Take the car on a short journey to warm the transmission up to normal operating temperature, then park the car on level ground. The fluid level is checked using the dipstick located on the front of the transmission.

2 With the engine idling, select "D" for approximately 15 seconds, then engage "R" and wait a further 15 seconds. Do this again in position "P", and leave the engine idling.

3 Release the locking catch and withdraw the dipstick from the tube. Wipe all the fluid from its end with a clean rag or paper towel. Insert the clean dipstick back into the tube as far as it will go, then withdraw it once more. Note the fluid level on the end of the dipstick - there are two sets of level marks, the lower ones are for a fluid temperature of 20°C, and the upper ones are for a temperature of 80°C **(see illustrations)**. If the engine is at normal operating temperature, use the upper level marks.

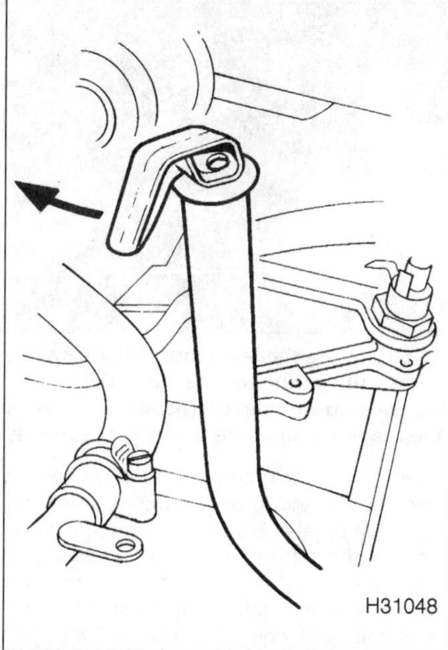

15.3a Release the locking catch and withdraw the dipstick from the tube

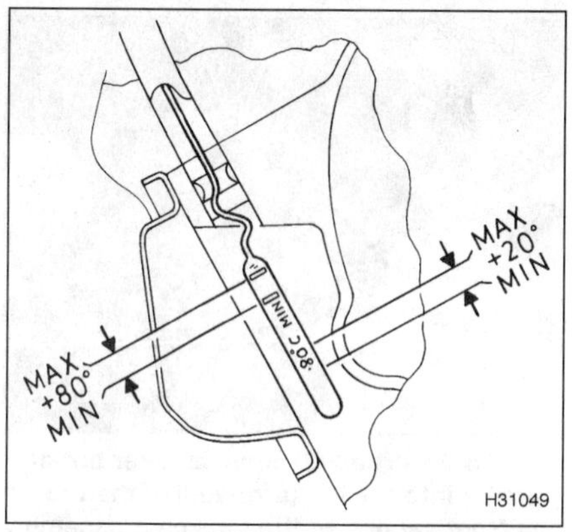

15.3b Note the two sets of level marks on the end of the dipstick (see text for details)

4 If topping-up is necessary, add fluid as necessary via the dipstick tube until the level is on the upper mark on the dipstick. **Note:** *Never overfill the transmission so that the fluid level is above the upper mark. Use a funnel with a fine mesh gauze, to avoid spillage and to ensure that no foreign matter enters the transmission.*

5 After topping-up, take the car on a short run to distribute the fresh fluid, then recheck the level again, topping-up if necessary.

6 Always maintain the level between the two dipstick marks. If the level is allowed to fall below the lower mark, fluid starvation may result, which could lead to severe transmission damage.

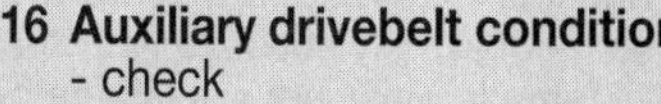

16 Auxiliary drivebelt condition - check

1 On all engines, a single, multi-grooved auxiliary drivebelt is used to transmit drive from the crankshaft pulley to the coolant pump, alternator, power steering pump and on models equipped with air conditioning, the refrigerant compressor. The drivebelt is guided by two idler pulleys and is tensioned automatically by a spring loaded tensioner pulley.

Auxiliary drivebelt - condition check

2 For better access to the drivebelt, apply the handbrake then jack up the front of the car and support it on axle stands (see "*Jacking and vehicle support*"). Remove the right-hand front roadwheel, then remove the lower section of the plastic liner from under the right-hand wheel arch, to expose the crankshaft pulley. Remove the air cleaner and its associated intake air ducting with reference to Chapter 4A **(see illustrations)**.

3 Using a suitable socket and extension bar fitted to the crankshaft pulley bolt, rotate the crankshaft so that the entire length of the drive-belt(s) can be examined. Examine the drivebelt for cracks, splitting, fraying, or other damage **(see illustration)**. Check also for signs of glazing (shiny patches) and for separation of the belt plies. Renew the belt if worn or damaged.

16.2a Remove the lower section of the plastic liner from under the right-hand wheel arch, to expose the crankshaft pulley

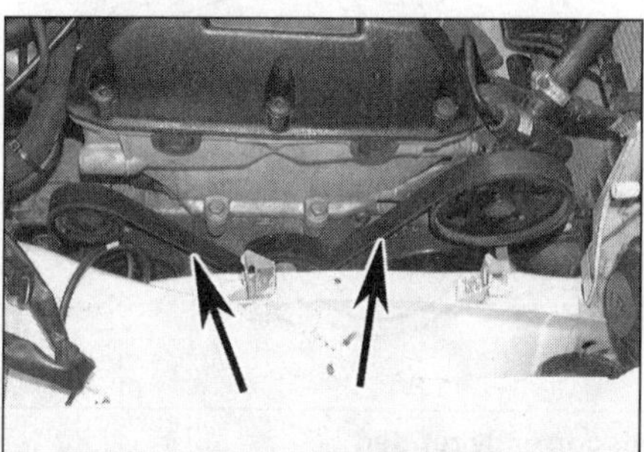

16.2b Remove the air cleaner and its ducting to expose the auxiliary drivebelt (arrowed)

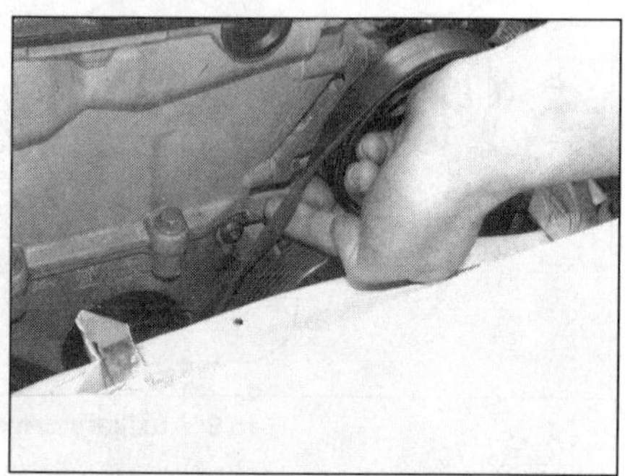

16.3 Examining the auxiliary drivebelt for signs of wear or damage

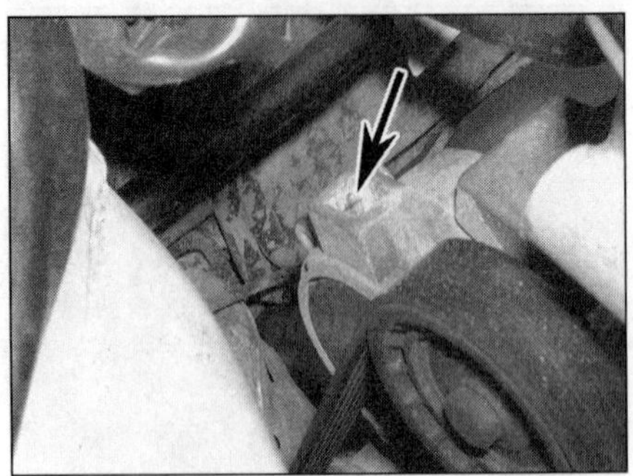
16.6a Insert a 1/2" drive breaker bar or similar into the lug (arrowed) at the top of the front section of the tensioner assembly

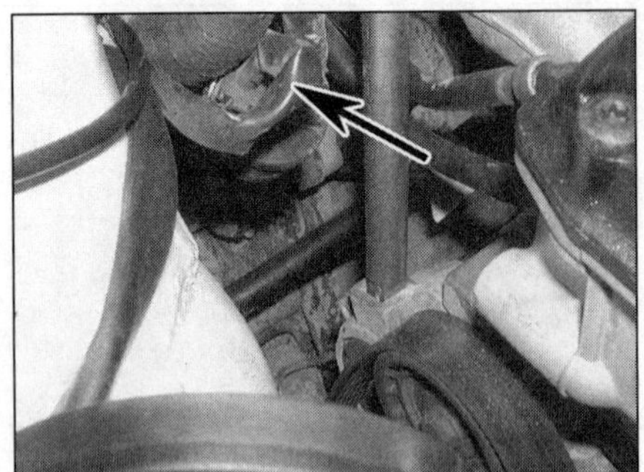
16.6b Rotate the tensioner anticlockwise, against the spring tension, until the locking lug lines up with the corresponding hole in the rear section of the tensioner assembly

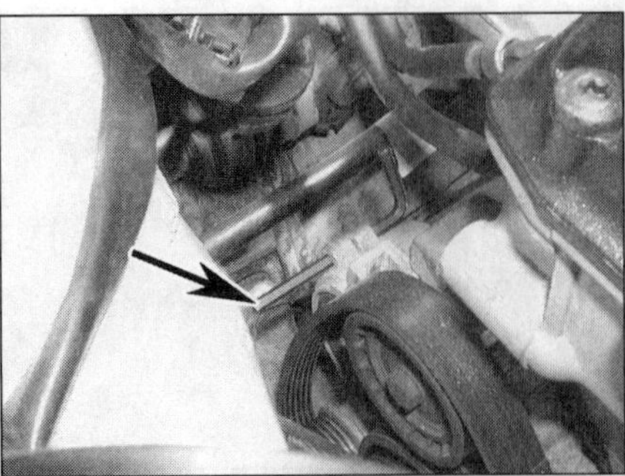
16.7 Use a 6mm drill bit or similar tool (arrowed) to lock the tensioner assembly in position

4 Grasp the belt mid-way between two of the pulleys and pull it directly away from the pulleys, so it deflects by about 25mm. Check that the automatic tensioner causes the belt to return to its normal position smoothly and without resistance.

Auxiliary drivebelt - removal and refitting

Removal

5 If not already done, carry out the operations described in paragraph 3.

6 The tensioner pulley spring must now be compressed and locked in position. Insert a 1/2" drive breaker bar or similar into the lug at the top of the front section of the tensioner assembly. Rotate the tensioner anticlockwise, against the spring tension, until the locking lug lines up with the corresponding hole in the rear section of the tensioner assembly. Note that the tensioner spring is very strong, and considerable pressure is required to compress it, but **do not** try to force it beyond the limit of its travel **(see illustrations)**.

16.8 Removing the auxiliary drivebelt from the crankshaft pulley

7 Hold the tensioner in position, then slide a 6mm drill bit (or similar tool) through the tensioner locking lug and engage it with the hole in the rear section of the tensioner assembly **(see illustration)**. Release the effort on the breaker bar slowly, checking that the tensioner remains in the locked position.

8 Slip the drivebelt from the water pump, power steering pump, crankshaft (and where applicable, the air conditioning compressor) pulleys, then remove it from the engine compartment, via the right-hand wheel arch **(see illustration)**.

Refitting

9 Locate the drivebelt over all the pulleys, making sure that the multi-grooved side is correctly engaged with the grooves on the pulleys. The accompanying illustration shows the correct belt **(see illustration)**.

10 Compress the tensioner spring using a breaker bar as described for the removal procedure. Remove the locking tool and then slowly release the tensioner, allowing it to apply pressure to the rear surface of drivebelt.

11 Ensure that the belt is correctly seated on all the pulleys, then start the engine and allow it to idle for a few minutes. This will allow the tensioner to settle in position and distribute the tension evenly throughout the belt. Stop the engine and check once again that the belt is correctly seated on all the pulleys.

12 On completion, refit the plastic wheel arch liner and roadwheel, and then lower the car to the ground.

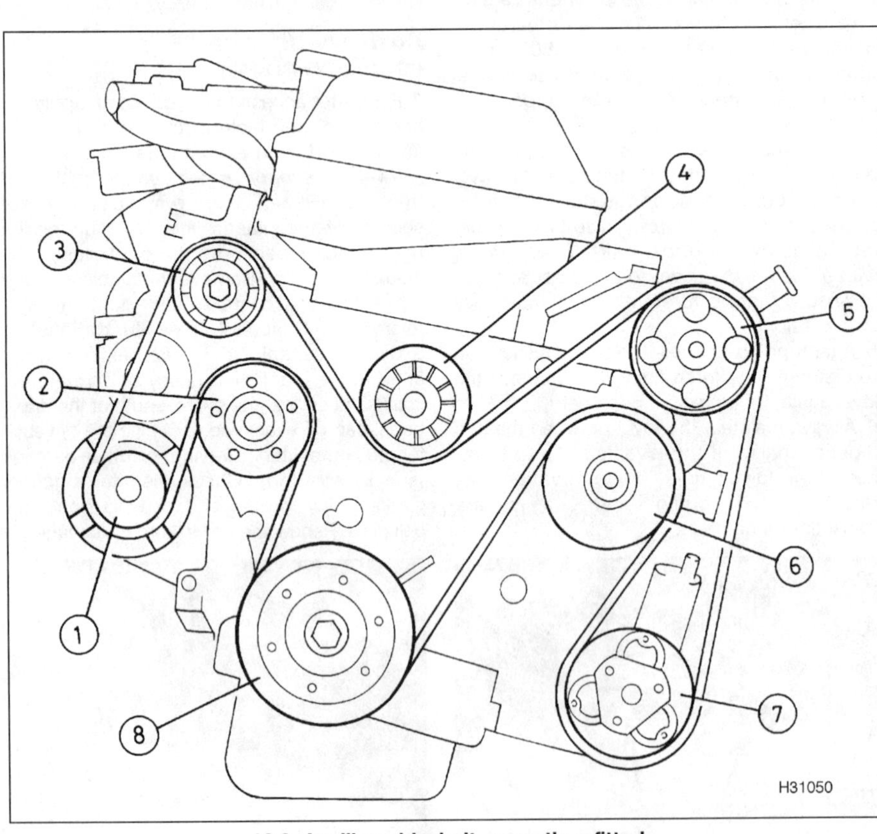

16.9 Auxiliary drivebelt correctly refitted

1 Alternator
2 Tensioner
3 Idler pulley
4 Idler pulley
5 Power steering pump
6 Coolant pump
7 Air conditioning refrigerant compressor (where fitted)
8 Crankshaft pulley

17 Ventilation air filter element - renewal

1 Remove the windscreen wiper arms as described in Chapter 12.
2 Pull the weatherstrip from the bulkhead.
3 Lift up the bulkhead cover and disconnect the washer tube from the adapter.
4 Unclip and remove the ventilation air filter element **(see illustration)**.
5 Fit the new element using a reversal of the removal procedure.

17.4 Unclip and remove the ventilation air filter element

18 Hinges and locks - lubrication

1 Work around the vehicle and lubricate the hinges of the bonnet, doors and tailgate with a light machine oil.
2 Lightly lubricate the bonnet release mechanism with a smear of grease.
3 Check carefully the security and operation of all hinges, latches and locks. Check that the central locking system operates correctly.
4 Check the condition and operation of the bonnet and tailgate struts, renewing them if either is leaking or no longer able to support the bonnet/tailgate.

19 Seat belt condition - check

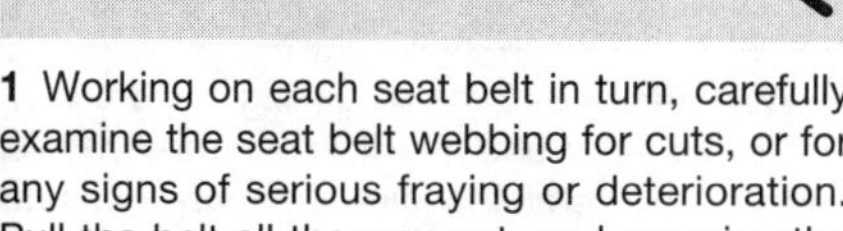

1 Working on each seat belt in turn, carefully examine the seat belt webbing for cuts, or for any signs of serious fraying or deterioration. Pull the belt all the way out, and examine the full extent of the webbing.
2 Fasten and unfasten the belt, ensuring that the locking mechanism holds securely, and releases properly when intended. Check also that the retracting mechanism operates correctly when the belt is released.
3 Check the security of all seat belt mountings and attachments which are accessible, without removing any trim or other components, from inside the vehicle.

20 Road test

Instruments and electrical equipment

1 Check the operation of all instruments and electrical equipment.
2 Make sure that all instruments read correctly, and switch on all electrical equipment in turn to check that it functions properly. Check the function of the heating, air conditioning and automatic climate control systems.

Steering and suspension

3 Check for any abnormalities in the steering, suspension, handling or road "feel".
4 Drive the vehicle, and check that there are no unusual vibrations or noises.
5 Check that the steering feels positive, with no excessive "sloppiness", or roughness, and check for any suspension noises when cornering, or when driving over bumps. Check that the power steering system operates correctly. Check that the cruise control system (where fitted) operates correctly.

Drivetrain

6 Check the performance of the engine, clutch (manual transmission), transmission and driveshafts. On Turbo models, check that the boost pressure needle moves up to the upper limit of the orange zone during sharp acceleration. The needle may occasionally enter the red zone for an instant, but if this happens frequently, or for extended periods, a problem may exist within the turbo boost control mechanism (see Chapter 4A).
7 Listen for any unusual noises from the engine, clutch (manual transmission) and transmission.
8 Make sure that the engine runs smoothly when idling, and that there is no hesitation when accelerating.
9 On manual transmission models, check that the clutch action is smooth and progressive, that the drive is taken up smoothly, and that the pedal travel is correct. Also listen for any noises when the clutch pedal is depressed. Check that all gears can be engaged smoothly, without noise, and that the gear lever action is not abnormally vague or "notchy".
10 On automatic transmission models, make sure that all gearchanges occur smoothly without snatching, and without an increase in engine speed between changes. Check that all the gear positions can be selected with the vehicle at rest. If any problems are found, they should be referred to a Saab dealer.
11 Listen for a metallic clicking sound from the front of the vehicle, as the vehicle is driven slowly in a circle with the steering on full lock. Carry out this check in both directions. If a clicking noise is heard, this indicates wear in a driveshaft joint, in which case, refer to Chapter 8.

Check the operation and performance of the braking system

12 Make sure that the vehicle does not pull to one side when braking, and that the wheels do not lock prematurely when braking hard.
13 Check that there is no vibration through the steering when braking.
14 Check that the handbrake operates correctly, without excessive movement of the lever, and that it holds the vehicle stationary on a slope.
15 Test the operation of the brake servo unit (where applicable) as follows. With the engine off, depress the footbrake four or five times to exhaust the vacuum. Start the engine, holding the brake pedal depressed. As the engine starts, there should be a noticeable "give" in the brake pedal as vacuum builds up. Allow the engine to run for at least two minutes, and then switch it off. If the brake pedal is depressed now, it should be possible to detect a slight 'hiss' from the servo as the pedal is depressed. After about four or five applications, no further sound should be heard.

21 Air bag system - check

1 The following work can be carried out by the home mechanic, however if an electronic fault is apparent, it will be necessary to take the car to a Saab dealer, who will have the necessary diagnostic equipment to extract fault codes from the system.
2 Turn the ignition switch to the drive position (ignition warning lights on), and check that the SRS (Supplementary Restraint System) warning light is illuminated for 3 to 4 seconds. After this period the light should go out, indicating that the system has been checked and is functioning correctly.
3 If the warning light remains on or refuses to light, have the system checked by a Saab dealer.
4 Visually examine the steering wheel centre pad and the passenger airbag module for external damage. If damage is evident, consult a Saab dealer.
5 In the interests of safety, make sure that there are no loose items inside the car which could be thrown onto the airbag modules in the event of an accident.

22.2 Unscrew the transmission oil level plug, using a suitable Allen key (arrowed)

22.3a The transmission oil filler plug (arrowed) is located at the top of the transmission casing

Every 24 000 miles (40 000 km)

22 Manual transmission oil level - check

***Note:** A suitable Allen key will be required to unscrew the manual transmission filler and level plugs (as applicable). This can be obtained from most motor factors, or from your Saab dealer.*

1 Make sure that the car is parked on a level surface. Wipe clean the area around the level plug, which is located on the left hand side of the differential casing at the rear of the transmission, behind the left-hand driveshaft. Access to the plug can be gained from the engine compartment.

2 Unscrew the plug, using a suitable Allen key or hex bit and wipe it clean **(see illustration)**. The oil level should reach the lower edge of the level hole. A certain amount of oil will have gathered behind the level plug, and will trickle out when it is removed; this does **not** necessarily indicate that the level is correct. To ensure that a true level is established, wait until the initial trickle has stopped, then use a length of clean wire, bent into a right angle, as a dipstick.

3 If the oil level requires topping-up, wipe clean the area around the filler plug, which is located on top of the transmission. Unscrew the plug, and wipe it clean **(see illustrations)**.

22.3b Unscrew the plug using a suitable Allen key

4 Add oil as necessary until a steady trickle of oil can be seen emerging from the level hole **(see illustration)**. Use **only** good-quality oil of the specified grade. A funnel will be helpful when adding oil to the transmission through the filler plug aperture.

Caution: On some later models, the transmission is filled with synthetic oil, and must be topped up with oil of the same type and grade - do not top up with mineral transmission oil. Where synthetic oil is used, the transmission filler plug will be labelled 'USE ONLY SAAB OIL NO. 87 48 733'. Refer to "Lubricants and fluids" at the end of "Weekly checks" for details.

5 When the level is correct, refit and tighten the filler plug (and where necessary, the level plug) to the specified torque wrench setting. Wipe off any spilt oil.

23 Wheel alignment - check

Refer to Chapter 10.

24 Brake fluid - renewal

Note: *The interval for this service item is based on time and mileage. It must be carried out every 2 years,* ***or*** *every 24 000 miles (40 000 km), whichever comes sooner.*

Warning: Brake hydraulic fluid can harm your eyes and damage painted surfaces, so use extreme caution when handling and pouring it. Do not use fluid that has been standing open for some time, as it absorbs moisture from the air. Excess moisture can cause a dangerous loss of braking effectiveness.

1 The procedure is similar to that for the bleeding of the hydraulic system as described in Chapter 9.

2 Working as described in Chapter 9, open the first bleed screw in the sequence, and pump the brake pedal gently until nearly all the old fluid has been emptied from the master cylinder reservoir. Top-up to the "MAX" level with new fluid, and continue pumping until only the new fluid remains in the reservoir, and new fluid can be seen emerging from the bleed screw. Tighten the screw, and top the reservoir level up to the "MAX" level line.

Old hydraulic fluid is invariably much darker in colour than the new, making it easy to distinguish the two.

3 Work through all the remaining bleed screws in the sequence until new fluid can be seen at all of them. Be careful to keep the master cylinder reservoir topped-up to above the "MIN" level at all times, or air may enter the system and greatly increase the length of the task.

4 When the operation is complete, check that all bleed screws are securely tightened, and that their dust caps are refitted. Wash off all traces of spilt fluid, and recheck the master cylinder reservoir fluid level.

5 Check the operation of the brakes before taking the car on the road.

22.4 Topping up the transmission

25.2a Remove the screws . . .

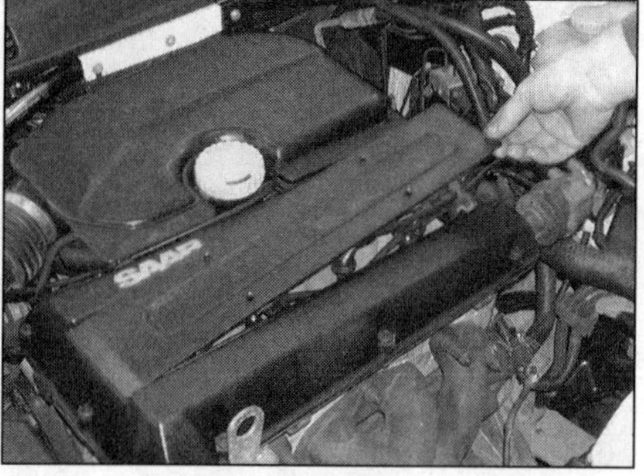

25.2b . . . and lift the inspection cover from the centre of the camshaft cover

25.3 Cylinder number markings cast into the cylinder head

Every 36 000 miles (60 000 km)

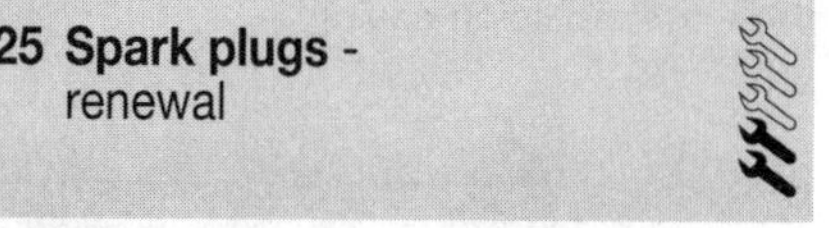

25 Spark plugs - renewal

1 The correct functioning of the spark plugs is vital for the correct running and efficiency of the engine. It is essential that the plugs fitted are appropriate for the engine. If this type is used and the engine is in good condition, the spark plugs should not need attention between scheduled replacement intervals. Spark plug cleaning is rarely necessary, and should not be attempted unless specialised equipment is available, as damage can easily be caused to the firing ends.

Models without Direct Ignition

2 Remove the screws, and lift the inspection cover from the centre of the camshaft cover **(see illustrations)**.

3 If the marks on the spark plug (HT) leads cannot be seen, mark the leads "1" to "4", to correspond to the cylinder the lead serves (No 1 cylinder is at the timing chain end of the engine) **(see illustration)**.

4 Pull the leads from the plugs by gripping the end fitting, not the lead, otherwise the lead connection may be fractured **(see illustration)**. With all the leads disconnected, lift the rubber grommet from the distributor end of the cylinder head, and position the leads to one side.

Models with Direct Ignition

5 Carry out the following operations with reference to Chapter 5B:

a) Disconnect the wiring multi-plug from the flywheel end of the ignition cartridge.

b) Unscrew the four screws securing the ignition cartridge to the top of the cylinder head. An Allen key or hex bit will be required for this.

c) Where applicable, unscrew the bolt and release the cartridge wiring support clip.

d) Where applicable, unscrew the bolt and disconnect the earth lead.

e) Carefully lift the ignition cartridge, at the same time releasing it from the tops of the spark plugs.

All models

6 It is advisable to remove the dirt from the spark plug recesses using a clean brush, vacuum cleaner or compressed air before removing the plugs, to prevent dirt dropping into the cylinders.

7 Unscrew the plugs using a spark plug spanner, suitable box spanner or a deep socket and extension bar. Keep the socket aligned with the spark plug - if it is forcibly moved to one side, the ceramic insulator may be broken off. As each plug is removed, examine it as follows.

8 Examination of the spark plugs will give a good indication of the condition of the engine. If the insulator nose of the spark plug is clean and white, with no deposits, this is indicative of a weak mixture or too hot a plug (a hot plug transfers heat away from the electrode slowly, a cold plug transfers heat away quickly).

9 If the tip and insulator nose are covered with hard black-looking deposits, then this is indicative that the mixture is too rich. Should the plug be black and oily, then it is likely that the engine is fairly worn, as well as the mixture being too rich.

10 If the insulator nose is covered with light tan to greyish-brown deposits, then the mixture is correct, and it is likely that the engine is in good condition.

11 The electrode gap is of considerable importance as, if it is too large or too small, the size of the spark and its efficiency will be seriously impaired. The gap should be set to the value given in the Specifications.

25.4 Pull the HT leads from the spark plugs by gripping the end fitting, not the lead itself

12 To set the gap, measure it with a feeler blade or wire gauge and then bend open, or closed, the outer plug electrode until the correct gap is achieved. The centre electrode should never be bent, as this will crack the insulator and cause plug failure, if nothing worse. If using feeler blades, the gap is correct when the appropriate-size blade is a firm sliding fit. Note that some models may be fitted with multi-electrode spark plugs - no attempt to adjust the electrode gap should be made on this type of spark plug.

13 Special spark plug electrode gap adjusting tools are available from most motor accessory shops, or from some spark plug manufacturers.

14 Before fitting the spark plugs, check that the threaded connector sleeves are tight, and that the plug exterior surfaces and threads are clean. It is very often difficult to insert spark plugs into their holes without cross-threading them. To avoid this possibility, fit a short length of hose over the end of the spark plug **(see Haynes Hint)**.

It is very often difficult to insert spark plugs into their holes without cross-threading them. To avoid this possibility, fit a short length of 5/16 inch internal diameter rubber hose over the end of the spark plug. The flexible hose acts as a universal joint to help align the plug with the plug hole. Should the plug begin to cross-thread, the hose will slip on the spark plug, preventing thread damage to the aluminium cylinder head. Remove the rubber hose, and tighten the plug to the specified torque using the spark plug socket and a torque wrench.

1

25.15 Refit the spark plugs and tighten them to the specified torque

25.18 Press the HT lead guides (arrowed) into their respective slots in the cylinder head

26.1 The air cleaner is located on the front right-hand corner of the engine compartment

26.2 Release the clips and remove the cover from the air cleaner housing

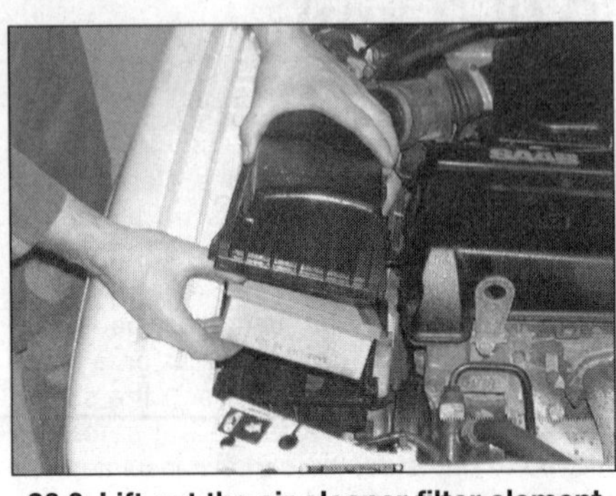
26.3 Lift out the air cleaner filter element

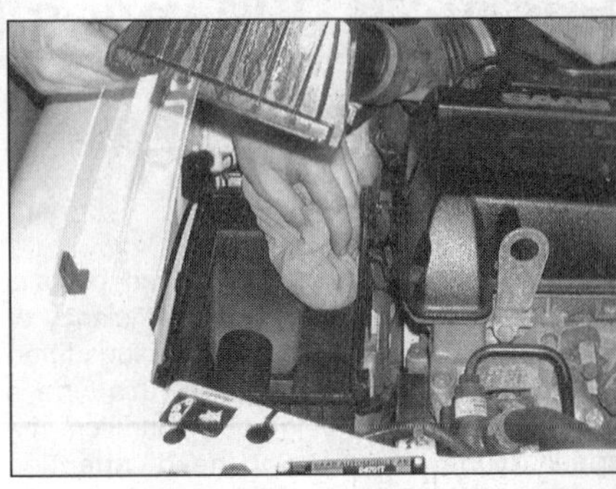
26.4 Wipe out the inner surfaces of the cover and main housing

15 Remove the rubber hose (if used), and tighten the plug to the specified torque (see Specifications) using the spark plug socket and a torque wrench. Refit the remaining plugs in the same way **(see illustration)**.

16 Where applicable, reconnect the HT leads in the correct firing order (see Specifications)

Models with Direct Ignition

17 Refit the ignition cartridge using a reversal of the removal procedure. Tighten the four screws to the specified torque (see Chapter 5B Specifications).

Models without Direct Ignition

18 Connect the HT leads in their correct order, and refit the rubber grommet. Press the HT lead guides into their respective slots in the cylinder head **(see illustration)**.

19 Refit the inspection cover, and tighten the retaining screws.

26 Air filter element - renewal

1 The air cleaner is located on the front right-hand corner of the engine compartment, and the air inlet is taken from the front of the car behind the radiator grille area **(see illustration)**.

2 Release the toggle clips, and remove the top cover from the air cleaner filter housing **(see illustration)**.

3 Lift out the air cleaner filter element, noting which way round it is fitted **(see Illustration)**.

4 Wipe clean the inner surfaces of the cover and main housing **(see illustration)**, then locate the new element in the housing, making sure that the sealing lip is correctly engaged with the edge of the housing.

5 Refit the cover, and secure with the toggle clips.

6 Reconnect the air ducting and secure it by tightening the hose clip.

Every 48 000 miles (80 000 km)

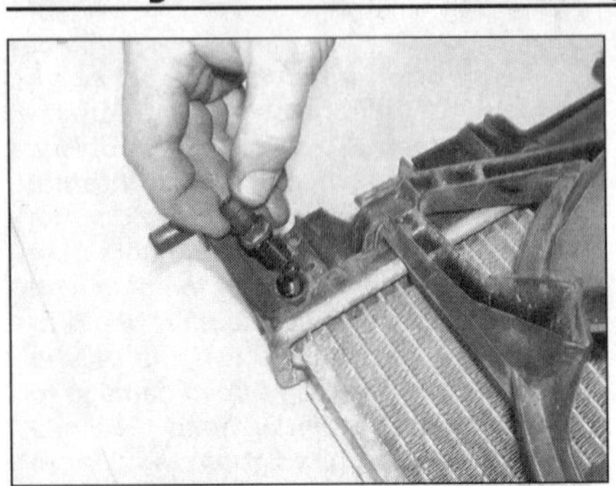
27.3 The drain plug is located on the left-hand side of the radiator

27 Coolant - renewal

Note: *The interval for this service item is based on time and mileage. It must be carried out every 3 years* ***or*** *every 48 000 miles (80 000 km), whichever comes sooner.*

Cooling system draining

Warning: Wait until the engine is cold before starting this procedure. Do not allow antifreeze to come into contact with your skin, or with the painted surfaces of the vehicle. Rinse off spills immediately with plenty of water.

1 With the engine completely cold, remove the expansion tank filler cap. Turn the cap anti-clockwise, wait until any pressure remaining in the system is released, then unscrew it and lift it off.

2 Where applicable, remove the engine undershield, then position a suitable container beneath the left-hand side of the radiator.

3 Loosen the drain plug, and allow the coolant to drain into the container **(see illustration)**. If necessary, attach a hose to the drain plug to direct the coolant into the container.

4 When the flow of coolant stops, tighten the drain plug and where necessary refit the undershield.
5 If the coolant has been drained for a reason other than renewal, then provided it is clean and less than two years old, it can be re-used, though this is not recommended.

Cooling system flushing

6 If coolant renewal has been neglected, or if the antifreeze mixture has become diluted, then in time, the cooling system may gradually lose efficiency, as the coolant passages become restricted due to rust, scale deposits and other sediment. The cooling system efficiency can be restored by flushing the system clean.
7 The radiator should be flushed independently of the engine, to avoid unnecessary contamination.

Radiator flushing

8 Disconnect the top and bottom hoses and any other relevant hoses from the radiator, with reference to Chapter 3.
9 Insert a garden hose into the radiator top inlet. Direct a flow of clean water through the radiator, and continue flushing until clean water emerges from the radiator bottom outlet.
10 If after a reasonable period, the water still does not run clear, the radiator can be flushed with a good proprietary cleaning agent. It is important that the manufacturer's instructions are followed carefully. If the contamination is particularly bad, remove the radiator and insert the hose in the bottom outlet, and reverse-flush the radiator, then refit it.

Engine flushing

11 Remove the thermostat as described in Chapter 3, then temporarily refit the thermostat cover. If the radiator top hose has been disconnected, temporarily reconnect the hose.
12 With the top and bottom hoses disconnected from the radiator, insert a garden hose into the radiator top hose. Direct a clean flow of water through the engine, and continue flushing until clean water emerges from the radiator bottom hose.
13 On completion of flushing, refit the thermostat and reconnect the hoses with reference to Chapter 3.

Cooling system filling

14 Before attempting to fill the cooling system, make sure that all hoses and clips are in good condition, and that the clips are tight. Note that an antifreeze mixture must be used all year round, to prevent corrosion of the engine components.
15 Remove the expansion tank filler cap and slowly fill the system until the coolant level reaches the MAX mark on the side of the expansion tank.
16 Refit and tighten the expansion tank filler cap.
17 Start the engine, and allow it to run until it reaches normal operating temperature (until the cooling fan cuts in and out).
18 Stop the engine, and allow it to cool, then re-check the coolant level with reference to "*Weekly checks*". Top-up the level if necessary and refit the expansion tank filler cap. Where applicable, refit the engine undershield.

Antifreeze mixture

19 The antifreeze should always be renewed at the specified intervals. This is necessary not only to maintain the antifreeze properties, but also to prevent corrosion which would otherwise occur as the corrosion inhibitors become progressively less effective.
20 Always use an ethylene-glycol based antifreeze which is suitable for use in mixed-metal cooling systems. The quantity of antifreeze and levels of protection are given in the Specifications.
21 Before adding antifreeze, the cooling system should be completely drained, preferably flushed, and all hoses checked for condition and security.
22 After filling with antifreeze, a label should be attached to the expansion tank, stating the type and concentration of antifreeze used, and the date installed. Any subsequent topping-up should be made with the same type and concentration of antifreeze.
23 Do not use engine antifreeze in the windscreen/tailgate washer system, as it will cause damage to the vehicle paintwork. A screenwash additive should be added to the washer system in the quantities stated on the bottle.

Every 60 000 miles (100 000 km)

28 Automatic transmission fluid - renewal

1 Take the car on a short journey to warm the transmission up to normal operating temperature. Position the car over an inspection pit, or alternatively jack up the front and rear of the car and support on axle stands (see "*Jacking and vehicle support*"). Whichever method is used, make sure that the car is level for checking the fluid level later.
2 Position a suitable container beneath the transmission, then unscrew the drain plug and allow the fluid to drain **(see illustration)**. Note that a special adapter key will be required to unscrew the plug.

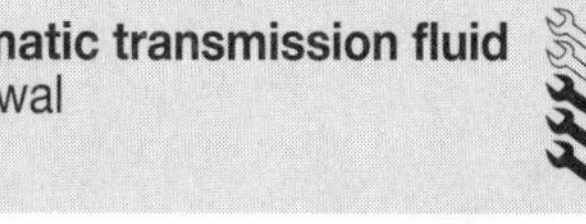

Warning: The fluid will be very hot, so take necessary precautions to prevent scalding. The use of thick waterproof gloves is recommended.

3 With all the fluid drained, wipe clean the plug and refit it to the automatic transmission housing. Where applicable fit a new sealing washer. Tighten the plug to the specified torque.
4 Fill the automatic transmission with the specified grade and quantity of fluid. Referring to Section 15, top it up to the correct level. Use the low temperature set of dipstick markings first, then take the car for a run. With the fluid at operating temperature, re-check the fluid level using the high temperature set of dipstick markings.

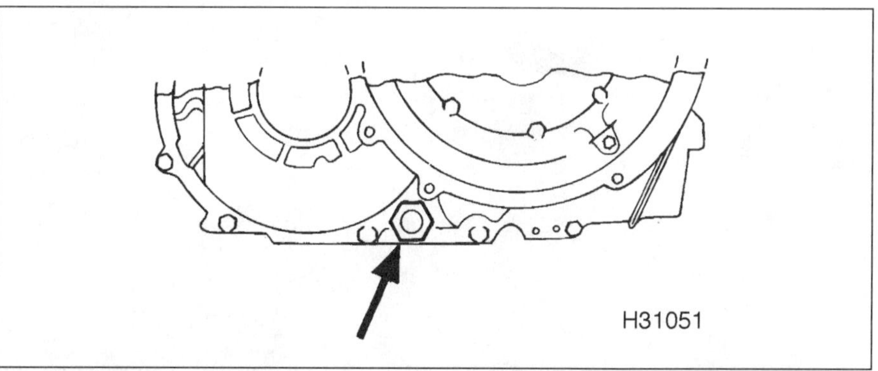

28.2 Location of the automatic transmission fluid drain plug (arrowed)

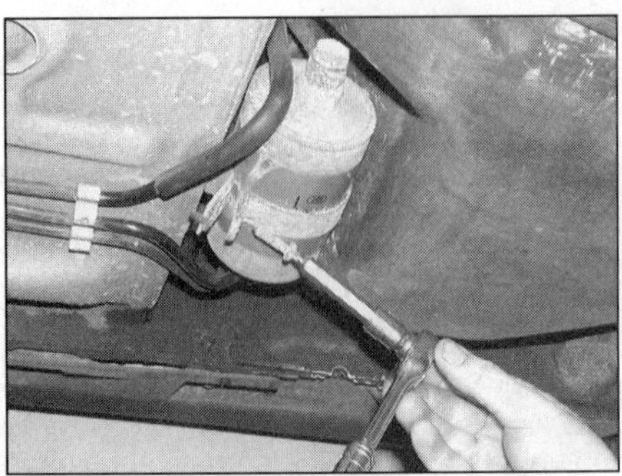

29.6 Loosen the fuel filter mounting bracket securing screw

29.7 Unscrew the banjo coupling bolts from each end of the filter

29.9 Make sure that the direction of flow arrow on the filter body is pointing towards the outlet which leads to the engine compartment

Every 102 000 miles (170 000 km)

29 Fuel filter - renewal

Warning: Before carrying out the following operation, refer to the precautions given in "Safety first!" at the beginning of this manual, and follow them implicitly. Petrol is a highly-dangerous and volatile liquid, and the precautions necessary when handling it cannot be overstressed.

1 On all models, the fuel filter is mounted adjacent to the fuel tank underneath the rear of the car.

2 Depressurise the fuel system with reference to Chapter 4A.

3 Chock the front wheels, then jack up the rear of the car and support on axle stands (see *"Jacking and vehicle support"*).

4 Pull off the plastic guard where fitted, then clean the areas around the fuel filter inlet and outlet unions.

5 Position a small container or cloth rags beneath the filter to catch spilt fuel.

6 Loosen the mounting bracket securing screw **(see illustration)**.

7 Unscrew the banjo coupling bolts from each end of the filter, while holding the coupling with a further spanner **(see illustration)**. Recover the sealing washers.

8 Remove the filter from its mounting bracket, noting the direction of the arrow marked on the filter body, loosen the retaining clip and withdraw the filter from under the car.

9 Locate the new filter in the retaining clip, then fit and tighten the securing screw. Make sure that the direction of flow arrow on the filter body is pointing towards the outlet which leads to the engine compartment **(see illustration)**.

10 Check the condition of the sealing washers, and renew them if necessary.

11 Refit the banjo couplings and hoses to each end of the filter, together with the sealing washers. Tighten the bolts securely, while holding the couplings with a second spanner.

12 Wipe away any excess fuel, refit the plastic cover where fitted, then lower the car to the ground.

13 Start the engine, and check the filter hose connections for leaks.

14 The old filter should be disposed of safely, bearing in mind that it will be highly inflammable.

Chapter 2 Part A:
Engine in-car repair procedures

Contents

Degrees of difficulty

Easy, suitable for novice with little experience 	**Fairly easy,** suitable for beginner with some experience 	**Fairly difficult,** suitable for competent DIY mechanic 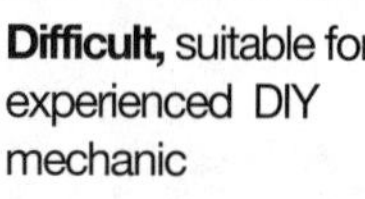	**Difficult,** suitable for experienced DIY mechanic	**Very difficult,** suitable for expert DIY or professional

Specifications

Engine (general)

Designation:	
1985 cc engine (without balance shafts)	B206i
1985 cc engine (with balance shafts)	B204i
1985 cc turbo engine	B204L
2290 cc engine	B234i
Bore	90.00 mm
Stroke:	
1985 cc engine	78.00 mm
2290 cc engine	90.00 mm
Direction of crankshaft rotation	Clockwise (viewed from right-hand side of vehicle)
No 1 cylinder location	At timing chain end of engine
Maximum power/torque:	
B206i	98 kW @ 6100 rpm/180 Nm @ 4300 rpm
B204i	96 kW @ 6100 rpm/177 Nm @ 4300 rpm
B204 Turbo:	
Manual	136 kW @ 5500 rpm/263 Nm @ 2100 rpm
Automatic	136 kW @ 5750 rpm/230 Nm @ 2000 rpm
B234i	110 kW @ 5700 rpm/210 Nm @ 4300 rpm

Camshafts

Drive	Simplex chain from crankshaft
Number of bearings	5 per camshaft
Camshaft bearing journal diameter (outside diameter)	28.922 to 28.935 mm
Endfloat:	
Up to 1993	0.14 to 0.35 mm
1994 on	0.08 to 0.35 mm

Lubrication system

Oil pump type	Bi-rotor type, driven off the crankshaft
Minimum oil pressure at 80°C	2.7 bars at 2000 rpm, using 10W30 engine oil.
Oil pressure warning switch operating pressure	0.3 to 0.5 bar
Clearance between pump outer rotor and timing cover housing	0.03 to 0.08 mm
Pressure release valve opens at	3.8 bar
Oil cooler thermostat opens at	80°C

Engine codes

The engine code is situated on the left-hand front of the cylinder block and is stamped directly onto the cylinder block.

Torque wrench settings

Torque wrench settings	Nm	lbf ft
Automatic transmission driveplate	95	70
Balance shaft chain idler sprocket	25	18
Balance shaft sprocket	42	31
Big-end bearing cap nuts	48	35
Camshaft bearing cap	15	11
Camshaft sprocket	63	47
Crankshaft pulley bolt	175	129
Cylinder head bolts:		
Stage 1	60	44
Stage 2	80	59
Stage 3	Angle-tighten through 90°	
Cylinder head cover	15	11
Engine oil drain plug	25	18
Engine-to-transmission bolts	70	52
Right hand engine mounting:		
Mounting to bracket	39	29
Mounting to body	73	54
Left hand engine mounting:		
Mounting to bracket	39	29
Mounting to body	73	54
Bracket to transmission	45	33
Rear engine mounting:		
Bracket to transmission	39	29
Mounting to subframe	39	29
Subframe front mounting bolts	115	85
Subframe centre mounting bolts	190	140
Subframe rear mounting bolts:		
Stage 1	110	81
Stage 2	Angle tighten through 75°	
Flywheel	80	59
Main bearing cap bolts	110	81
Oil cooler hose unions	18	13
Piston cooling jet	18	13
Plug for camshaft chain tensioner	22	16
Plug for oil cooler thermostat	60	44
Plug for oil pressure reducing valve	30	22
Sump bolts	22	16
Timing chain tensioner body	63	47
Timing cover bolts	22	16

1 General information

How to use this Chapter

This Part of Chapter 2 describes those repair procedures that can reasonably be carried out on the engine while it remains in the car. If the engine has been removed from the car, and is being dismantled as described in Part B, any preliminary dismantling procedures can be ignored.

Note that, while it may be possible to overhaul items such as the piston/connecting rod assemblies while the engine is in the car, such tasks are not normally carried out as separate operations. Usually, several additional procedures (including the cleaning of components and of oilways) have to be carried out, and these are more easily carried out with the engine removed from the vehicle. For this reason, all such tasks are classed as major overhaul procedures, and are described in Part B of this Chapter.

Part B describes the removal of the engine/transmission from the vehicle, and the full overhaul procedures that can then be carried out.

Engine description

The engine is of in-line four-cylinder, double-overhead camshaft (DOHC), 16-valve type, mounted transversely at the front of the car. The transmission is attached to its left-hand end. The Saab 900 is fitted with 1985 cc or 2290 cc versions of the engine; later versions of the 1985 cc engine and all 2290 cc engines are fitted with balance shafts in the cylinder block, to reduce vibrations. All engines are controlled by full engine management systems; a variant of the Bosch Motronic system is fitted to normally aspirated models, and the Saab-manufactured "Trionic" engine management system is fitted to 1985 cc Turbo models; see Chapter 4A for further details.

The crankshaft runs in five main bearings. Thrustwashers are fitted to the centre main bearing to control crankshaft endfloat.

The connecting rods rotate on horizontally-split bearing shells at their big-ends. The pistons are attached to the connecting rods by fully-floating gudgeon pins, which are retained in the pistons by circlips. The aluminium-alloy pistons are fitted with three piston rings - two compression rings and an oil control ring.

The cylinder block is of cast-iron, and the cylinder bores are an integral part of the cylinder block. The inlet and exhaust valves are closed by coil springs, and operate in guides pressed into the cylinder head; the valve seat inserts are also pressed into the cylinder head, and can be renewed separately if worn. There are four valves per cylinder.

The camshafts are driven by a single-row timing chain, and they operate the 16 valves via hydraulic cam followers. The hydraulic cam followers maintain a predetermined clearance between the low point of the cam lobe and the end of the valve stem, using hydraulic chambers and a tension spring. The followers are fed with oil from the main engine lubrication circuit.

The balance shafts (fitted to all 2290 and later 1985 cc engines) are driven in counter-rotation by a small single-row chain from a sprocket on the front of the crankshaft. The balance shaft chain run is controlled by two fixed guide rails and an idler sprocket. The chain is located on the outside of the main camshaft timing chain, with its tension being controlled by a dedicated oil pressure-driven tensioner.

The engine mountings are hydraulic, and provide a dual damping action which helps to control engine vibrations over a wide range of frequencies.

Lubrication is by means of a bi-rotor oil pump, driven from the front of the crankshaft and located in the timing cover. A relief valve in the timing cover limits the oil pressure at high engine speeds by returning excess oil to the sump. Oil is drawn from the sump through a strainer and, after passing through the oil pump, is forced through an externally-mounted filter and oil cooler into galleries in the cylinder block/crankcase. From there, the oil is distributed to the crankshaft (main bearings), balance shafts (where applicable) camshaft bearings and hydraulic cam followers. On Turbo models, it also lubricates the water-cooled turbocharger and the crankcase-mounted piston cooling jets. The big-end bearings are supplied with oil via internal drillings in the crankshaft, while the camshaft lobes and valves are lubricated by splash, as are all other engine components.

Repair operations possible with the engine in the car

The following work can be carried out with the engine in the car:

a) Compression pressure - testing.
b) Cylinder head cover - removal and refitting.
c) Timing cover - removal and refitting.
d) Timing chain, balance shaft chain (later models), guides and tensioner - removal and refitting.
e) Camshaft oil seals - renewal.
f) Camshafts - removal, inspection and refitting.
g) Cylinder head - removal and refitting.
h) Cylinder head and pistons - decarbonising (refer to Part B of this Chapter).
i) Sump - removal and refitting.
j) Oil pump - removal, overhaul and refitting.
k) Crankshaft oil seals - renewal.
l) Flywheel/driveplate - removal, inspection and refitting.
m) Engine/transmission mountings - inspection and renewal.

2 Compression test - description and interpretation

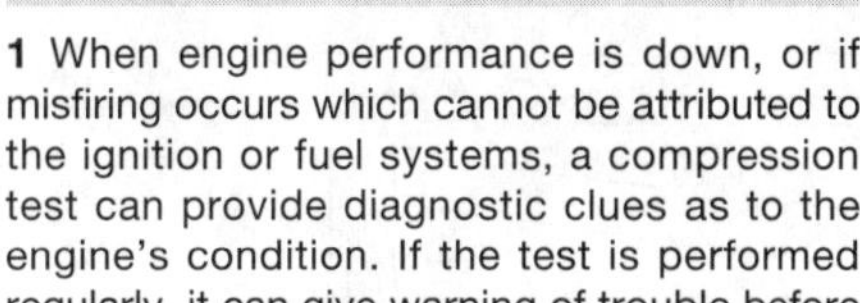

1 When engine performance is down, or if misfiring occurs which cannot be attributed to the ignition or fuel systems, a compression test can provide diagnostic clues as to the engine's condition. If the test is performed regularly, it can give warning of trouble before any other symptoms become apparent.
2 The engine must be fully warmed-up to normal operating temperature, the battery must be fully charged, and all the spark plugs must be removed (Chapter 1). The aid of an assistant will also be required.
3 On normally aspirated models with Bosch Motronic engine management, disable the ignition system by disconnecting the LT lead from the ignition coil. See Chapter 5B for further details.
4 On Turbo models with Trionic engine management, disable the ignition system by disconnecting the wiring plug from the Direct Ignition cartridge, referring to Chapter 5B for further information.
5 To prevent unburnt fuel from being supplied to the catalytic converter, the fuel pump must also be disabled by removing the relevant fuse and/or relay; see Chapter 4A as applicable for further details.
6 Fit a compression tester to the No 1 cylinder spark plug hole - the type of tester which screws into the plug thread must be used to obtain accurate readings.
7 Have the assistant depress the accelerator pedal fully, and crank the engine on the starter motor; after one or two revolutions, the compression pressure should build up to a maximum figure, and then stabilise. Record the highest reading obtained.
8 Repeat the test on the remaining cylinders, recording the pressure in each.
9 All cylinders should produce very similar pressures; a difference of more than 2 bars between any two cylinders indicates a fault. Note that the compression should build up quickly in a healthy engine; low compression on the first stroke, followed by gradually-increasing pressure on successive strokes, indicates worn piston rings. A low compression reading on the first stroke, which does not build up during successive strokes, indicates leaking valves or a blown head gasket (a cracked cylinder head could also be the cause). Deposits on the undersides of the valve heads can also cause low compression.
10 The manufacturer does not state specific compression pressures, but as a guide, any cylinder pressure of below 10 bars can be considered as less than healthy. Refer to a Saab dealer or other specialist if in doubt as to whether a particular pressure reading is acceptable.
11 If the pressure in any cylinder is low, carry out the following test to isolate the cause. Introduce a teaspoonful of clean oil into that cylinder through its spark plug hole, and repeat the test.
12 If the addition of oil temporarily improves the compression pressure, this indicates that bore or piston wear is responsible for the pressure loss. No improvement suggests that leaking or burnt valves, or a blown head gasket, may be to blame.
13 A low reading only from two adjacent cylinders is almost certainly due to the head gasket having blown between them; the presence of coolant in the engine oil will confirm this.
14 If one cylinder is about 20 percent lower than the others and the engine has a slightly rough idle, a worn camshaft lobe could be the cause.
15 On completion of the test, refit the spark plugs and reconnect the ignition system and fuel pump as necessary.

3 Top dead centre (TDC) for No 1 piston - locating

1 TDC timing marks are provided in the form of a slot machined into the crankshaft pulley and a corresponding bar cast into the timing chain cover. In addition, TDC marks are provided on the flywheel and rear oil seal housing - these are useful if the engine is being dismantled on the bench **(see illustration)**. **Note:** *With the timing marks correctly aligned, piston Nos 1 (at the timing chain end of the engine) and 4 (at the flywheel end of the engine) will be at top dead centre (TDC), with piston No 1 on its compression stroke.*
2 For access to the crankshaft pulley bolt, jack up the front of the car and support on axle stands (see *"Jacking and vehicle support"*). Remove the right-hand front wheel, then remove the screws and detach the inspection cover from the right-hand wheelarch liner.
3 Using a socket on the crankshaft pulley, turn the engine until the TDC slot in the crankshaft pulley is aligned with the bar on the timing cover **(see illustration)**. No 1 piston (at the timing chain end of the engine) will be at the top of its compression stroke.

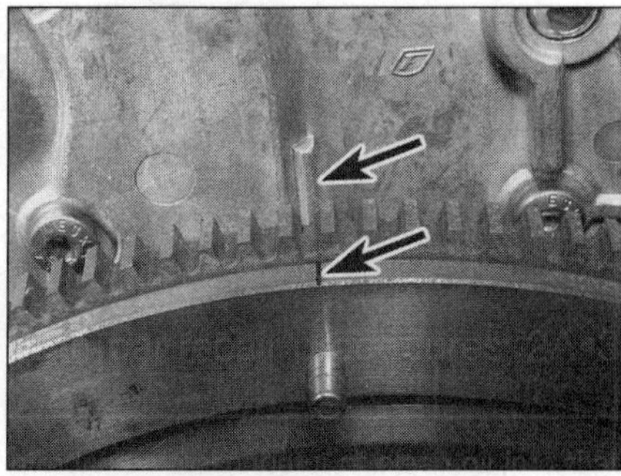

3.1 TDC timing marks (arrowed) on the flywheel and engine backplate

2A

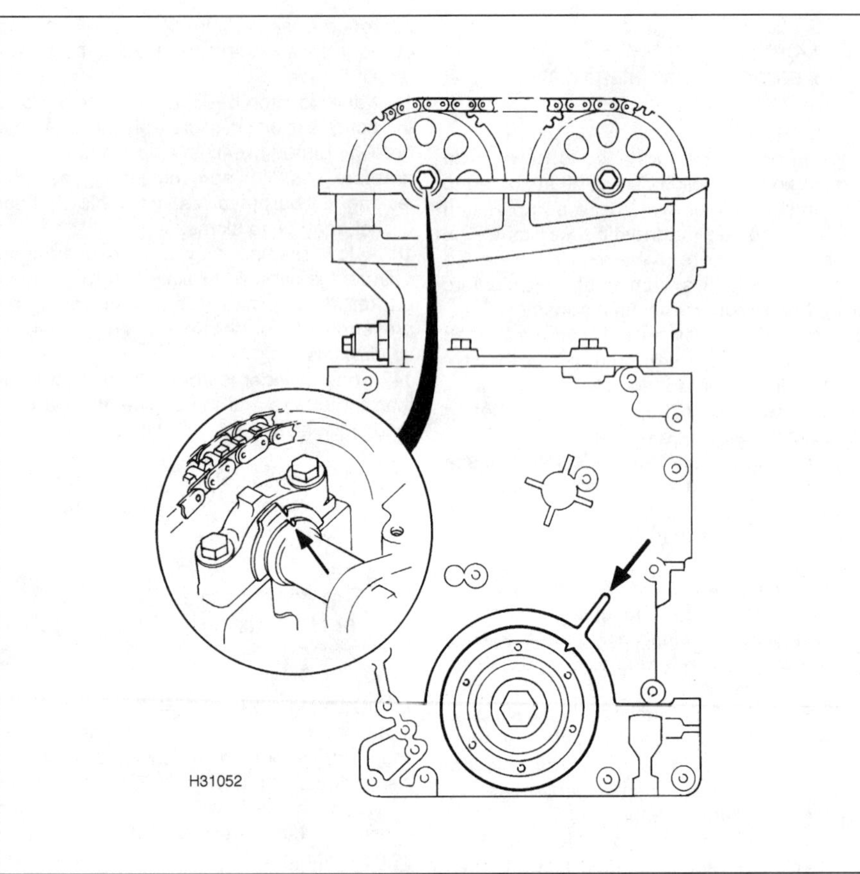

3.3 TDC timing marks on the crankshaft pulley, timing cover, camshafts and camshaft bearing caps

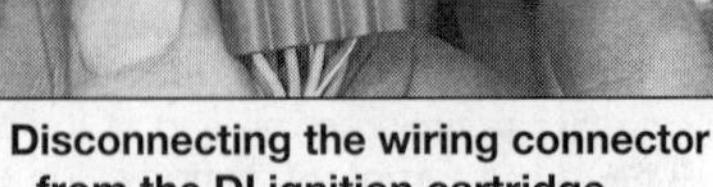

4.1 Disconnecting the wiring connector from the DI ignition cartridge

The compression stroke can be confirmed by removing the No 1 spark plug, and checking for compression with a finger over the plug hole as the piston approaches the top of its stroke. No compression indicates that the cylinder is on its exhaust stroke and is therefore one crankshaft revolution out of alignment.

4 Remove the cylinder head cover with reference to Section 4.

5 Check that the TDC marks at the sprocket ends of the camshafts are aligned with the corresponding TDC marks on the camshaft bearing caps **(refer to illustration 3.3)**. If necessary, turn the crankshaft to bring the marks into alignment.

4 Cylinder head cover - removal and refitting

Removal

1 Unscrew the screws and remove the inspection cover or ignition cartridge (as applicable) from the centre of the cylinder head cover; refer to Chapter 5B if necessary **(see illustration)**.

2 On models not fitted with DI ignition, disconnect the HT leads from the spark plugs.

3 Unbolt and remove the cylinder head cover, and remove the gasket **(see illustrations)**. If the cover is stuck, tap it gently with the palm of your hand to free it.

Refitting

4 Clean the contact surfaces of the cylinder head cover and cylinder head. Locate the gasket securely in the groove in the cylinder head cover.

5 Refit the cylinder head cover, and insert the securing bolts. Tighten the bolts progressively, starting with the bolts at the transmission end of the engine, and then the central bolt at the timing end. Work around the cover in a spiral fashion until all the bolts are tightened to the specified torque.

6 Where applicable, reconnect the HT leads to the spark plugs.

7 Refit the inspection cover or direct ignition cartridge (as applicable) to the centre of the cylinder head cover, and tighten the screws.

5 Timing cover - removal and refitting

Note 1: *Removal of the timing cover can be accomplished with the engine in situ, however note that if the cover is being removed to permit removal of the balance shaft chain and sprockets, this can only be achieved after the engine has been removed from the vehicle, due to the lack of clearance between the engine and the side of the engine compartment.*

Note 2: *This procedure describes removal of the timing cover, leaving the cylinder head in*

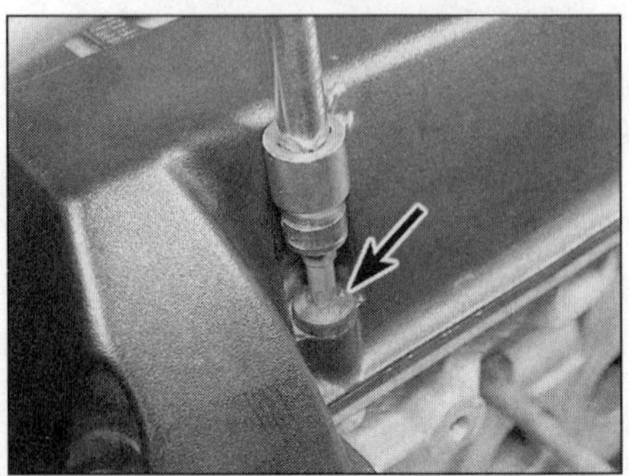

4.3a Removing the cylinder head cover retaining screws

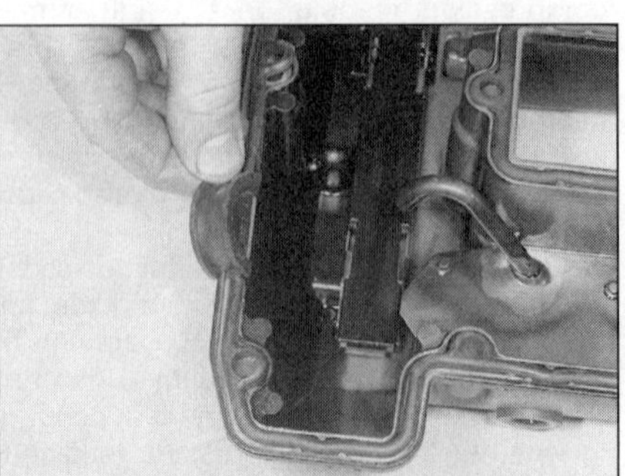

4.3b The split rubber plugs are incorporated into the outer gasket

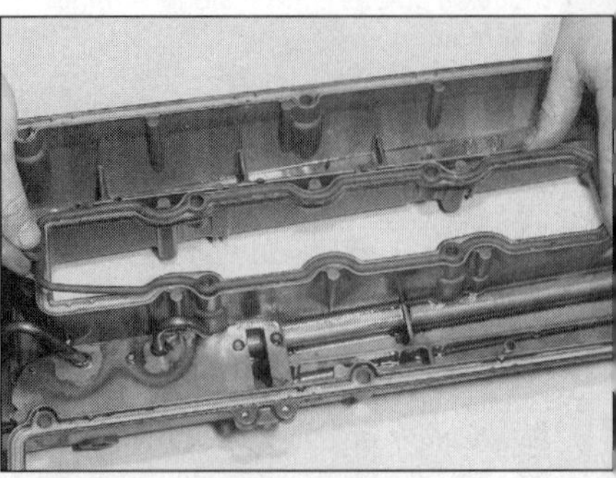

4.3c Removing the cylinder head cover inner gasket

5.10 Loosening the crankshaft pulley bolt

5.11a Remove the crankshaft pulley bolt . . .

5.11b . . . and slide the pulley off the crankshaft

position. The alternative method (which is less likely to damage the cylinder head gasket) is to remove the cylinder head first.

Removal

1 Disconnect the battery negative lead and position it away from the terminal.

2 Remove the air cleaner assembly, air mass meter and intake ducting, as described in Chapter 4A.

3 Unscrew the bolt securing the coolant pipe to the engine, above the knock sensor.

4 Apply the handbrake, then jack up the front of the car and support on axle stands (see *"Jacking and vehicle support"*). Remove the right-hand front wheel.

5 Drain the engine oil and coolant, with reference to Chapter 1.

6 Unscrew the retaining screws, and remove the right-hand front wing moulding and front wheelarch liner.

5.19a View of the bolts securing the timing cover to the cylinder block

7 Remove the auxiliary drivebelt with reference to Chapter 1.

8 Unbolt and remove the auxiliary drivebelt tensioner unit (and where applicable, the mounting bracket).

9 Have an assistant hold the crankshaft stationary, by engaging 4th gear and applying the handbrake (manual transmission models only). Alternatively, remove the flywheel protection plate from the underside of the transmission bellhousing.

10 Loosen the crankshaft pulley bolt using a long socket bar. Note that the bolt is tightened to a very high torque **(see illustration)**.

11 Fully unscrew the crankshaft pulley bolt, and slide the pulley off the end of the crankshaft **(see illustrations)**.

12 Unscrew the coolant pipe and oil cooler pipe supports (as applicable) from the timing cover.

13 Withdraw the coolant pipe from the rear of the water pump (where applicable) then remove the water pump with reference to Chapter 3.

14 Unscrew the bolt securing the power steering pump steady bar to the timing cover. Recover the nut from the rear of the timing cover.

15 Unscrew the upper bolt for the alternator, and the two securing bolts for the power steering pump, then withdraw the bracket and the steady bar.

16 Loosen the alternator lower mounting bolt, and swivel the alternator to one side.

17 Unscrew the mounting bolts, and remove the alternator and power steering pump mounting bracket from the timing cover.

18 Unbolt and remove the sump with reference to Section 10.

19 Unscrew and remove the bolts securing the timing cover to the cylinder block, sump and cylinder head. Note that the bolts are of different lengths. Note the two upper bolts on the cylinder head and the two lower bolts in the sump **(see illustrations)**.

20 Taking care not to damage the cylinder head gasket, carefully withdraw the timing cover complete with the oil pump from the nose of the crankshaft. Where fitted, remove the gaskets from the cylinder block.

21 Thoroughly clean all traces of sealant from the contact faces of the timing cover, sump, cylinder head and block. Make sure that the groove in the sump is free of all sealant.

22 If required, remove the oil pump from the timing cover, with reference to Section 11.

Refitting

23 Apply a bead of suitable sealant to the sump. Locate new gaskets on the cylinder block - if necessary, hold the gaskets in position using a little grease. Where there are no gaskets fitted, apply a bead of suitable sealant to the timing cover flanges **(see illustration)**.

24 Carefully locate the timing cover on the cylinder block, at the same time engaging the oil supply pipe from the block with the hole near the bottom of the timing cover, where applicable.

25 Insert and tighten the timing cover retaining bolts to the specified torque. Insert loosely the upper and lower bolts securing the timing cover to the cylinder head and sump.

5.19b Removing one of the bolts securing the timing cover to the sump

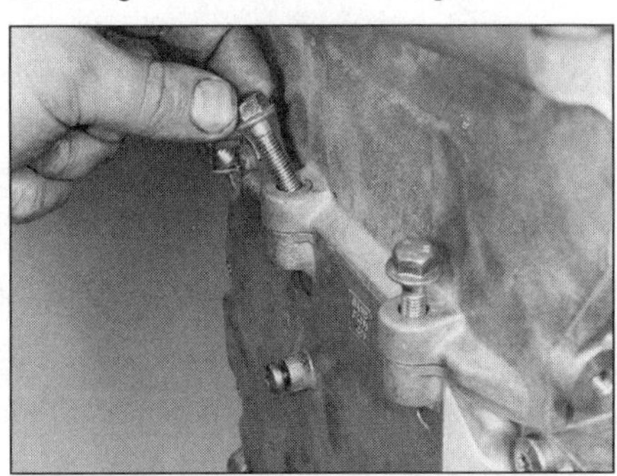

5.19c Removing the upper bolts securing the timing cover to the cylinder head

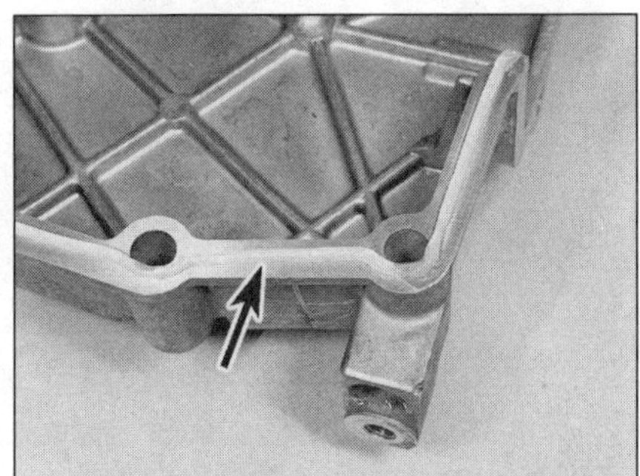

5.23 Sealant on the timing cover flanges

6.2 Removing the oil pump drive dog from the crankshaft

6.3a "INL" mark on the inlet balance shaft front bearing

6.3b "EXH" mark on the exhaust balance shaft front bearing

6.4a Unscrew the bolts . . .

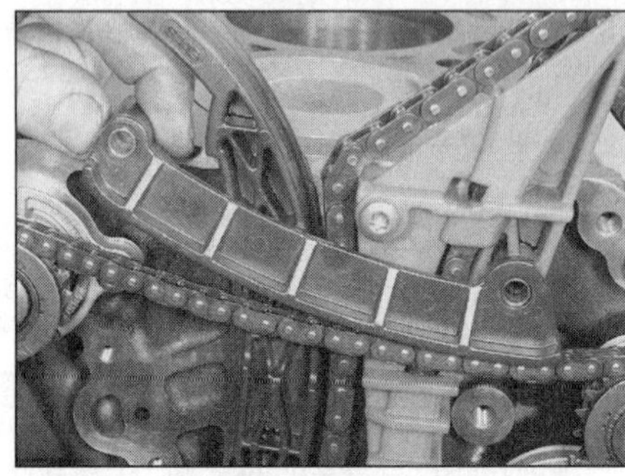

6.4b . . . and remove the balance shaft chain upper guide

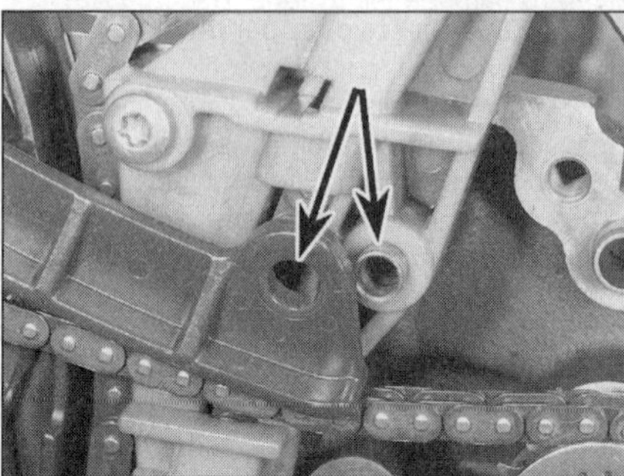

6.4c Note how the upper guide locates on the dowel

6.4d Removing the balance shaft chain tensioner . . .

6.4e . . . and side guide

6.5a Loosen . . .

6.5b . . . and remove the idler retaining bolt (note alignment marks between idler and chain) . . .

6.5c . . . then withdraw the idler and remove the balance shaft chain

6.5d The idler is in two parts

6.6 Removing the balance shaft chain sprocket from the front of the crankshaft

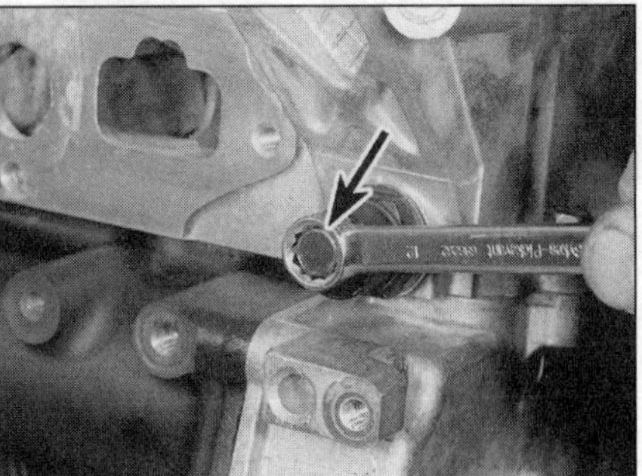

6.9a Unscrew the centre bolt . . .

6.9b . . . and remove the spring . . .

26 Where applicable, refit the oil pump with reference to Section 11.

27 Tighten the two upper and two lower timing cover bolts to the specified torque.

28 Refit the alternator and power steering pump mounting bracket, and tighten the bolts.

29 Swivel the alternator towards the engine, then refit the alternator/power steering pump bracket and the steady bar, and tighten all bolts to the specified torque.

30 Slide the crankshaft pulley onto the crankshaft, then insert the pulley bolt. Tighten the bolt to the specified torque, while an assistant holds the crankshaft stationary using a wide-bladed screwdriver inserted in the starter ring gear.

31 Refit the drivebelt tensioner assembly, and tighten the bolts. Before locating the assembly on the stub, apply a little grease to the bearing surfaces

32 Refit the water pump, with reference to Chapter 3.

33 Refit the auxiliary drivebelt with reference to Chapter 1.

34 Refit the moulding and front wheelarch liner under the right-hand front wing, and tighten the retaining screws.

35 Check that the sump drain plug and the coolant drain plug are tight, and that the splash guard is fitted under the radiator. Refit the right-hand front wheel, and lower the car to the ground.

36 Where applicable, refit and tighten the bolt securing the coolant pipe above the knock sensor.

37 Where applicable, refit the starter motor.

38 Reconnect the battery negative lead.

39 Fill the engine with the correct grade and quantity of oil.

40 Refill the cooling system, with reference to Chapter 1.

41 Start the engine, and run it to normal operating temperature. Check for oil and coolant leaks.

6 Timing chain and sprockets - removal, inspection and refitting

Removal

1 Position the crankshaft at TDC compression for No 1 piston (timing chain end of the engine) as described in Section 3.

2 Remove the timing cover as described in Section 5. Also remove the oil pump drive dog from the crankshaft **(see illustration)**.

3 The balance shafts are "timed" at TDC, but since they rotate at twice the speed of the crankshaft, they may also be correctly "timed" at BDC. Check that the timing marks on the shafts are correctly aligned with the marks on the front of the cylinder block/bearing housing.

Apply alignment markings (small dabs of paint are ideal) to the chain and sprockets, to ensure correct refitting.

Note that the balance shaft sprockets are marked "inlet" and "exhaust" for their positions, but both front bearings are marked identically. However, as the bearings are located with single bolts, the "inlet" and "exhaust" marks will always be correctly located at the top of the bearings **(see illustrations)**.

4 Unbolt the balance shaft chain upper guide, then remove the tensioner and side guide **(see illustrations)**.

5 Unbolt the idler from the block, then release the chain from the balance shaft sprockets and crankshaft sprocket. Note that the idler is in two parts **(see illustrations)**.

6 Slide the balance shaft chain sprocket from the front of the crankshaft **(see illustration)**. Note that the word "Saab" is facing outwards.

7 Unscrew the retaining bolts, and remove the sprockets from the ends of the balance shafts. To do this, hold the sprockets stationary with a chain-type oil filter removal tool or similar. Keep the sprockets identified for position.

8 Remove the cylinder head cover as described in Section 4.

9 Unscrew and remove the timing chain tensioner from the rear of the cylinder head. To do this, first unscrew the centre bolt and remove the spring, then unscrew and remove the tensioner from the cylinder head **(see illustrations)**.

10 While holding each camshaft stationary with a spanner on the flats at the flywheel/driveplate end of the camshaft, loosen (but do not remove) the camshaft sprocket securing bolts.

2A

6.9c . . . then unscrew the tensioner . . .

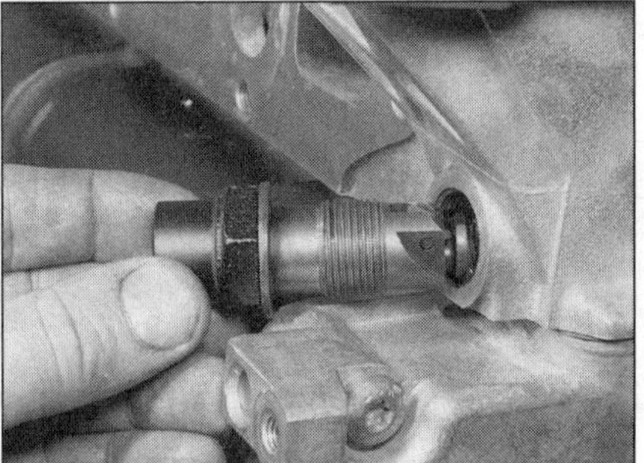

6.9d . . . and remove it from the cylinder head

6.9e The timing chain tensioner components

6.11 Removing the sprocket from the end of the inlet camshaft

6.13a Remove the retaining bolt . . .

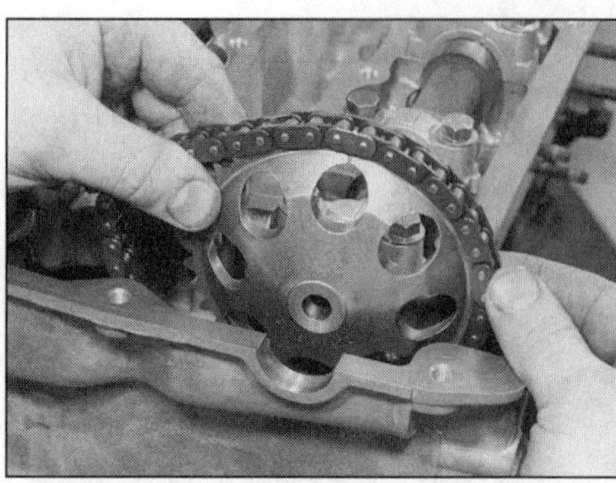
6.13b . . . then disengage the sprocket from the chain

11 Unscrew and remove the bolt, and withdraw the sprocket from the end of the inlet camshaft **(see illustration)**. Hold the timing chain with one hand, and release the sprocket from it with the other hand.

12 Identify each sprocket for position. Note that each sprocket has a projection which engages with a cut-out in the end of the camshaft.

13 Unscrew the bolt and withdraw the sprocket from the end of the exhaust camshaft, then disengage it from the chain **(see illustrations)**.

14 Unscrew the bolts, and remove the timing chain fixed guide from the cylinder block **(see illustrations)**.

15 Unbolt the chain retainer from the cylinder block, then disengage the timing chain and remove the sprocket from the end of the crankshaft **(see illustrations)**. If necessary, remove the Woodruff key from the groove in the crankshaft using a screwdriver.

Inspection

16 The timing chain **(see illustration)** (and where applicable, the balance shaft chain) should be renewed if the sprockets are worn, or if the chain is loose and noisy in operation. It's a good idea to renew the chain as a matter of course if the engine is stripped down for overhaul. The rollers on a very badly worn chain may be slightly grooved. To avoid future problems, if there's any doubt at all about the chain's condition, renew it. The chain tensioner and guides should be examined and if necessary renewed at the same time (refer to Section 7).

6.14a Unscrew the bolts . . .

6.14b . . . and remove the timing chain fixed guide

6.15a Removing the timing chain retainer (arrowed) from the cylinder block

6.15b Removing the crankshaft sprocket from the end of the crankshaft

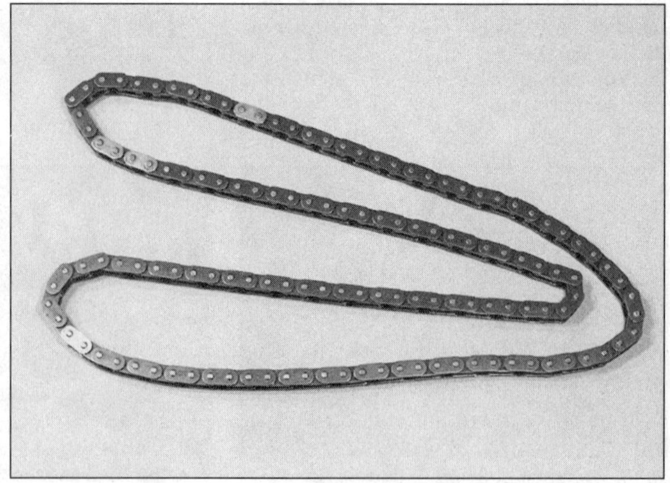
6.16 Timing chain removed from the engine

6.19a Where timing chain has bright links, these must be aligned with the slot in the sprocket (arrowed)

6.19b Tightening the timing chain retainer bolts

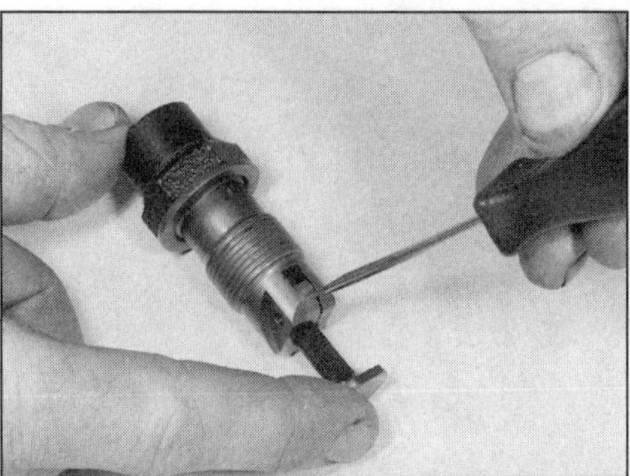

6.25 Setting the timing chain tensioner

17 Examine the teeth on the crankshaft sprocket, camshaft sprockets (and where applicable, the balance shaft sprockets) for wear. Each tooth forms an inverted "V". If worn, the side of each tooth under tension will be slightly concave ("hooked") in shape, when compared with the other side of the tooth (ie one side of the inverted "V" will be concave when compared with the other). If the teeth appear to be worn, the sprockets must be renewed.

Refitting

18 Locate the Woodruff key in the groove in the crankshaft. Tap it fully into the groove, making sure that its plane surface is parallel to the crankshaft.

19 Engage the timing chain with the crankshaft sprocket, then locate the crankshaft sprocket on the end of the crankshaft, making sure that it locates correctly on the Woodruff key. Where the timing chain has bright links, locate the single bright link at the bottom of the sprocket, aligned with the slot in the sprocket. Refit the chain retainer and tighten the bolts **(see illustrations)**.

20 Locate the timing chain in the fixed guide, then refit the guide and tighten the bolts.

21 Refit the sprocket to the end of the exhaust camshaft, insert the bolt and finger-tighten it at this stage. **Do not** apply thread-locking fluid to the threads of the bolt.

22 Check that the crankshaft and camshafts are still aligned at their TDC positions.

23 Feed the timing chain up through the cylinder head aperture, and locate it on the exhaust camshaft sprocket, making sure that it is taut between the two sprockets. Check that it is correctly located on the guides. Where the chain has a bright link, make sure that it is aligned with the timing mark.

24 Engage the inlet sprocket with the timing chain so that the engagement cut-out and projection are in alignment, then locate the sprocket on the inlet camshaft, and insert the bolt. Finger-tighten the bolt at this stage. **Do not** apply thread-locking fluid to the threads of the bolt. Where the chain has a bright link, make sure that it is aligned with the timing mark.

25 Set the timing chain tensioner by pressing down on the ratchet with a screwdriver, then push the plunger fully into the tensioner, and release the ratchet **(see illustration)**. Check the tensioner washer for condition and renew it if necessary.

26 Insert the tensioner body in the cylinder head, and tighten to the specified torque.

27 Insert the spring and plastic guide pin in the tensioner, then fit the plug together with a new O-ring, and tighten it to the specified torque. **Note:** *New tensioners are supplied with the tensioner spring held pre-tensioned with a pin.* ***Do not*** *remove this pin until after the tensioner has been tightened into the cylinder head.* When the engine is started, hydraulic pressure will take up any remaining slack.

28 Temporarily refit the crankshaft pulley bolt, and rotate the engine two complete turns clockwise. Check that the timing marks still align correctly. Remove the pulley bolt. Where the chain has bright links, note that these will not now be aligned with the timing marks.

29 Fully tighten the camshaft sprocket bolts to the specified torque, while holding the camshafts with a spanner on the flats.

30 Refit the cylinder head cover with reference to Section 4.

31 Refit the sprockets to the ends of the balance shafts, and tighten the retaining bolts.

32 Locate the balance shaft chain sprocket on the front of the crankshaft, with the word "Saab" facing outwards.

33 Fit the chain to the sprockets, making sure that the timing marks are aligned correctly **(see illustration)**.

34 Refit the idler to the front of the block, and tighten the retaining bolt.

35 Refit the side guide, tensioner and upper guide to the balance shaft chain **(see illustration and Tool Tip)**.

36 Rotate the crankshaft one turn, and check that the balance shaft timing marks are still correctly aligned.

37 Refit the timing cover with reference to Section 5.

6.33 The balance shaft timing marks must be correctly aligned before refitting the chain

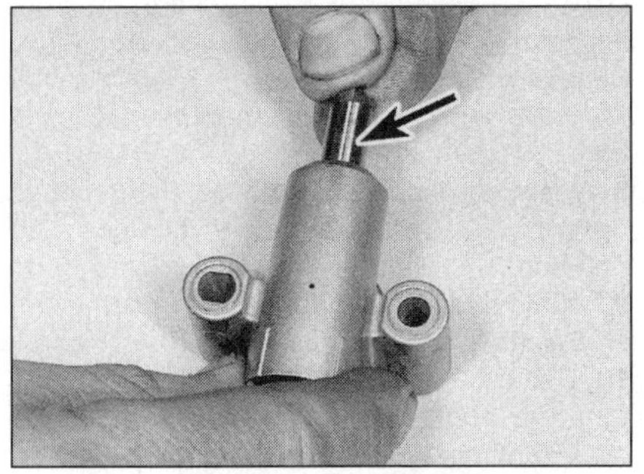

6.35 Depress the balance shaft chain tensioner plunger (arrowed) and retain with a plastic cable-tie

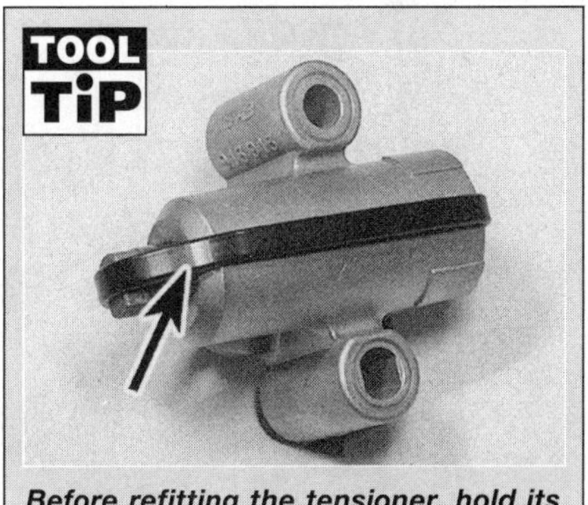

Before refitting the tensioner, hold its plunger depressed by fitting a plastic cable-tie around it. Cut the tie after refitting.

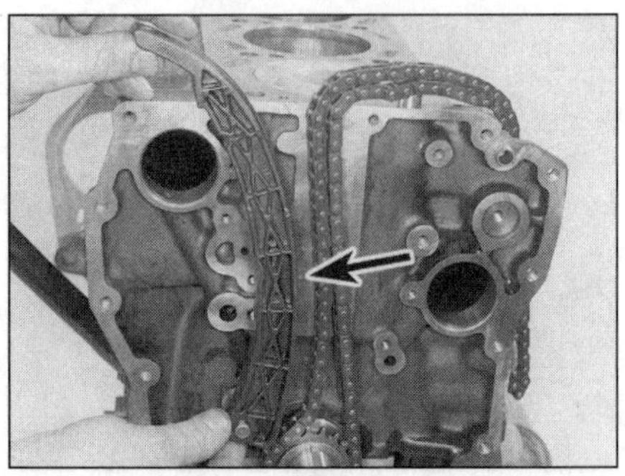

7.2 Removing the pivoting guide from the pin on the cylinder block

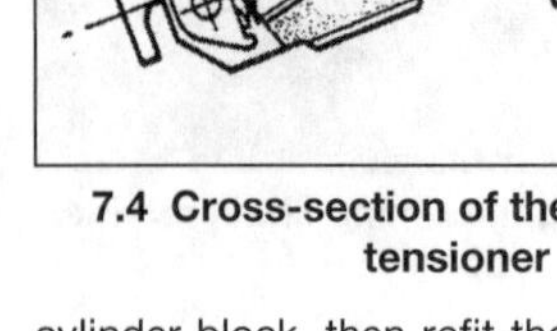

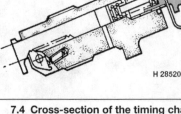

7.4 Cross-section of the timing chain tensioner

8.13 The camshaft bearing caps are marked for position here (arrowed)

7 Timing chain guides and tensioner - removal, inspection and refitting

Removal

1 Remove the timing chain as described in Section 6; note that this procedure includes removal of the fixed guide and balance shaft chain guides. The timing chain need not be removed from the crankshaft sprocket.

2 Unbolt and remove the fixed timing chain guide and release the pivoting guide from the pin on the cylinder block **(see illustration)**.

Inspection

3 Inspect the chain guides for damage and excessive wear, and renew them if necessary.

4 Clean the tensioner plunger and body, and examine them for damage and wear **(see illustration)**. On models manufactured after 1988, the plunger may be removed by depressing the ratchet against the spring. If the plunger or body is excessively scored, the complete tensioner should be renewed.

Refitting

5 Locate the pivoting guide on the pin on the cylinder block, then refit the fixed guide and tighten the retaining bolts.

6 Refit the timing chain with reference to Section 6.

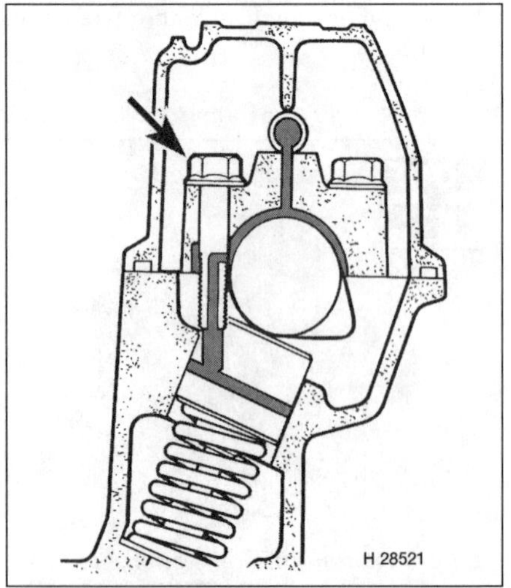

8.14a The camshaft bearing cap inner bolts (arrowed) are hollow for the oil supply to the hydraulic cam followers

8 Camshaft(s) and hydraulic cam followers - removal, inspection and refitting

Note: *The following procedure describes removal and refitting of the camshafts and hydraulic cam followers with the cylinder head in position in the car. If necessary, the work can be carried out on the bench, with the cylinder head removed from the engine. In this case, start the procedure at paragraph 12, after removing the cylinder head.*

Removal

1 Open the bonnet, and clean the engine around the cylinder head.

2 Apply the handbrake, then jack up the front of the car and support on axle stands (see *"Jacking and vehicle support"*). Remove the right-hand front wheel.

3 Remove the screws, and withdraw the front wing moulding and wheelarch liner from under the right-hand front wing.

4 Disconnect the battery negative lead, and position the lead away from the battery terminal.

5 Disconnect the crankcase breather hose (and where applicable, the vacuum control unit hose), and position them to one side.

6 Unscrew the screws, and remove the inspection cover or DI ignition cartridge from the centre of the cylinder head cover (refer to Chapter 5B if necessary).

7 Where applicable, disconnect the HT leads from the spark plugs.

8 Where applicable, remove the distributor as described in Chapter 5B, and position it to one side.

9 Unbolt and remove the cylinder head cover as described in Section 4.

10 Using a socket on the crankshaft pulley, turn the engine until the TDC slot in the crankshaft pulley is aligned with the timing bar on the timing cover. If necessary, refer to Section 3 for more information. Check also that the TDC marks on the sprocket ends of the camshafts are aligned with the corresponding TDC marks on the camshaft bearing caps.

11 Unscrew and remove the timing chain tensioner from the rear of the cylinder head.

12 While holding each camshaft stationary with a spanner on the special flats at the transmission end of the camshaft, unscrew the bolts, then withdraw the sprockets and allow them to rest on the timing chain guides. Note that the sprockets have projections which engage with cut-outs in the ends of the camshafts. The timing chain cannot come off the crankshaft sprocket, since there is a guide located below the sprocket.

13 Check that the camshaft bearing caps and the camshafts are identified for position. The bearing caps are stamped "1" to "5" on the inlet side, and "6" to "10" on the exhaust side - do not confuse these marks with the moulded markings on each cap **(see illustration)**.

14 Progressively unscrew the bearing cap bolts, so that the caps are not stressed unduly by the valve springs. Ensure that the bearing caps closest to the open valves are removed last, to avoid stressing the camshaft unduly. Fully remove the bolts and lift off the caps, then lift the camshafts from the cylinder head. Note that the bearing cap inner bolts (except at the timing chain end) have black heads, and incorporate drillings for the oil supply to the hydraulic cam followers; always make sure that the correct bolts are fitted **(see illustrations)**. Keep the camshafts carefully identified for location.

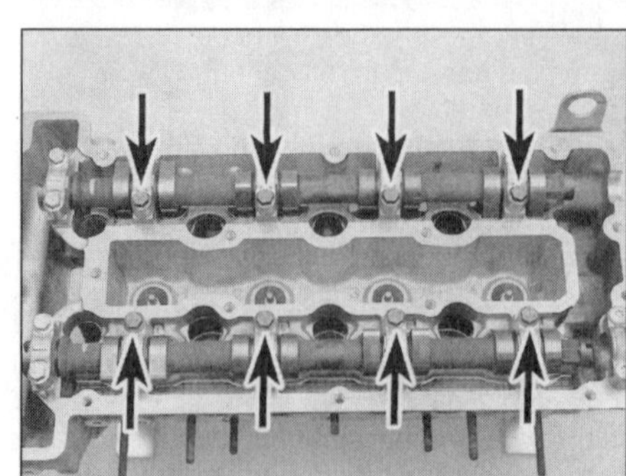

8.14b Locations (arrowed) of the black-headed inner bearing cap bolts incorporating oil drillings

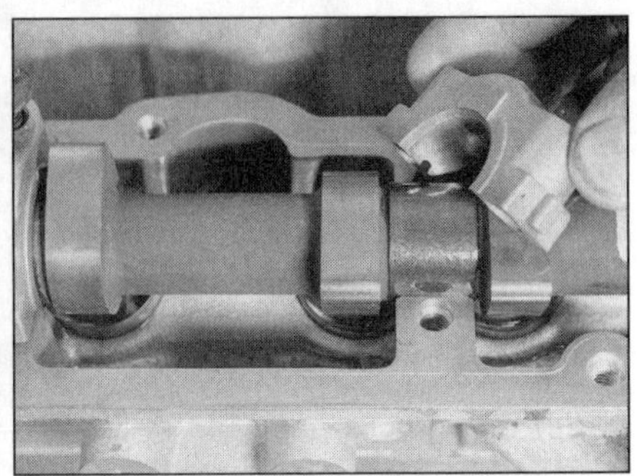

8.14c Removing a camshaft bearing cap

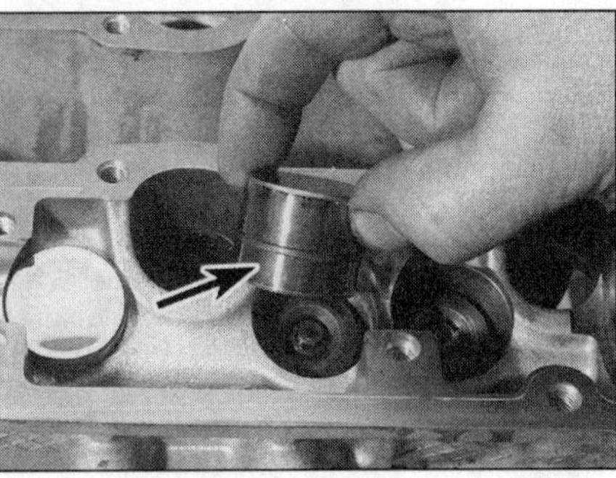

8.15a Removing a hydraulic cam follower

8.15b Hydraulic cam follower removed from the cylinder head. Cam followers should be stored in an oil bath while removed

15 Obtain sixteen small, clean plastic containers, and number them "1i" to "8i" (inlet) and "1e" to "8e" (exhaust). Alternatively, divide a larger container into sixteen compartments, similarly marked for the inlet and exhaust camshafts. Using a rubber sucker or a magnet, withdraw each hydraulic cam follower in turn, and place it in its respective container **(see illustrations)**. **Do not** interchange the cam followers. To prevent the oil draining from the hydraulic cam followers, pour fresh oil into the containers until it covers them.

Caution: Take great care to avoid scratching the cylinder head bores as the followers are withdrawn.

Inspection

16 Examine the camshaft bearing surfaces and cam lobes for signs of wear ridges and scoring. Renew the camshaft if any of these conditions are apparent. Examine the condition of the bearing surfaces on the camshaft journals, in the camshaft bearing caps, and in the cylinder head. If the head or cap bearing surfaces are worn excessively, the cylinder head will need to be renewed. If the necessary measuring equipment is available, camshaft bearing journal wear can be checked by direct measurement and comparison with the specifications given.

17 Camshaft endfloat can be measured by locating each camshaft in the cylinder head, refitting the sprockets, and using feeler blades between the shoulder on the front of the camshaft and the front bearing surface on the cylinder head.

18 Check the hydraulic cam followers where they contact the bores in the cylinder head for wear, scoring and pitting. Occasionally, a hydraulic cam follower may be noisy and require renewal, and this will have been noticed when the engine was running. It is not easy to check a cam follower for internal damage or wear once it has been removed; if there is any doubt, the complete set of cam followers should be renewed.

19 Clean the internal drillings of the hollow camshaft bearing cap bolts, to ensure oil supply to the hydraulic cam followers.

Refitting

20 Lubricate the bores for the hydraulic cam followers in the cylinder head, and the followers themselves, then insert them in their original positions **(see illustration)**.

21 Lubricate the bearing surfaces of the camshafts in the cylinder head.

22 Locate the camshafts in their correct positions in the cylinder head, so that the valves of No 1 cylinder (timing chain end) are closed, and the valves of No 4 cylinder are "rocking".

23 The timing marks on the sprocket ends of the camshafts should be pointing upwards.

24 Lubricate the bearing surfaces in the bearing caps, then locate them in their correct positions and insert the retaining bolts. Progressively tighten the bolts to the specified torque.

Note: *Ensure that the black-coloured oil supply bolts are in their correct positions **(see illustration 8.14b)**.*

25 Check that each camshaft is at its TDC position - the timing marks are located on the front of the camshafts, and must be aligned with the mark on the bearing caps.

26 Check that the TDC "0" mark on the flywheel/driveplate is still aligned with the timing mark on the transmission. On later models, check that the TDC slot in the crankshaft pulley is aligned with the timing bar on the timing cover.

27 Locate the sprockets on the camshafts, fitting the exhaust one first, followed by the inlet one. Do not fully tighten the bolts at this stage. Check that the timing chain is correctly located on the guides and sprockets.

28 Refit the timing chain tensioner, with reference to Section 6.

29 Using a socket on the crankshaft pulley, rotate the engine two complete turns clockwise, then check that the TDC timing marks are still correctly aligned.

30 Fully tighten the camshaft sprocket retaining bolts to the specified torque, while holding them stationary with a spanner on the special flats provided **(see illustration)**.

31 Clean the contact surfaces of the cylinder head cover and cylinder head. Refit the cylinder head cover with reference to Section 4.

32 Where applicable, check that the distributor rotor is aligned with the timing mark, then refit the distributor and cap with reference to Chapter 5B.

33 Where applicable, reconnect the HT leads to the spark plugs.

34 Refit the inspection cover or DI ignition cartridge to the centre of the cylinder head cover, and tighten the securing screws.

35 Reconnect the crankcase breather hose.

36 Refit the front wing moulding and wheelarch liner under the right-hand front wing, and tighten the screws.

37 Refit the right-hand front wheel, and lower the car to the ground.

38 Reconnect the battery negative lead.

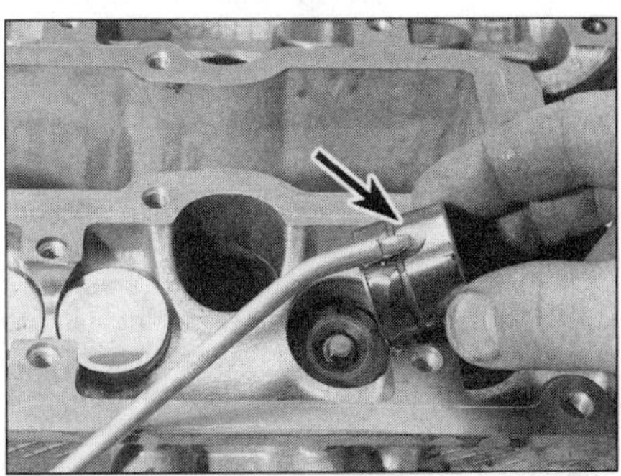

8.20 Oiling a hydraulic cam follower prior to fitting

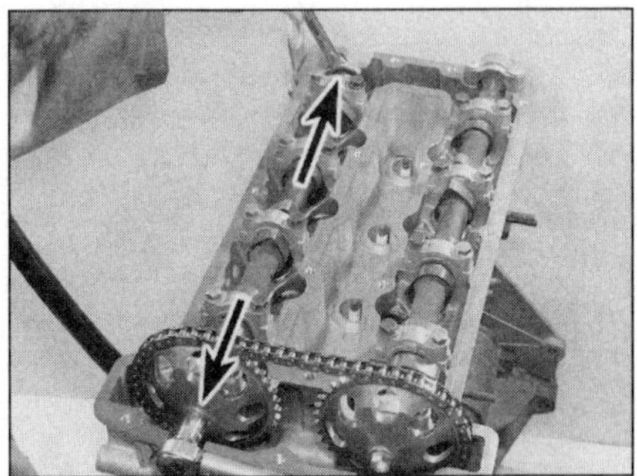

8.30 Tightening the camshaft sprocket retaining bolts, using a spanner on the camshaft flats to hold it stationary

9.25 Removing a cylinder head bolt

9 Cylinder head - removal and refitting

Removal

1 Open the bonnet, and clean the engine around the cylinder head.
2 Apply the handbrake, then jack up the front of the car and support on axle stands (see *"Jacking and vehicle support"*). Remove the right-hand front wheel.
3 Disconnect the battery negative lead, and position the lead away from the battery terminal.
4 Remove the screws, and withdraw the front wing moulding and wheelarch liner from under the right-hand front wing.
5 Drain the cooling system, with reference to Chapter 1.
6 With reference to Chapter 4A, remove the air cleaner assembly from the engine compartment. On normally aspirated models, unplug the wiring from the mass air flow meter, then remove the intake air ducting. On Turbo models, release the hose clips and remove the turbocharger-to-intercooler and intercooler-to-throttle body intake air ducts. Cover the turbocharger port with a cloth to prevent the ingress of debris.
7 Remove the securing screws and lift the intake resonator (normally-aspirated models) or the cover panel (Turbo models) away from the inlet manifold.
8 Refer to Chapter 1 and remove the auxiliary drivebelt.

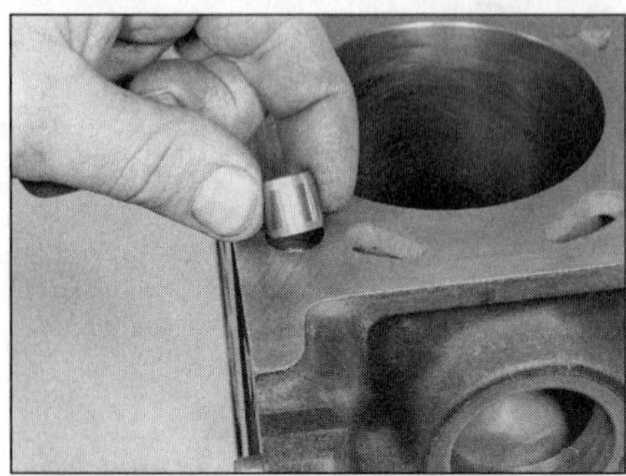

9.27 Removing a cylinder head locating dowel

9 Unbolt the power steering pump from its mountings, with reference to Chapter 10 and secure to one side using nylon cable ties or similar. Note that there is no need to disconnect the hydraulic fluid hoses from the pump.
10 Remove the securing screws and disconnect the air cleaner-to-turbocharger intake elbow (together with its associated crankcase breather hose) from the turbocharger.
11 On Turbo models, unbolt and remove the turbocharger bracing bracket. Refer to Chapter 4A and unbolt the exhaust system front pipe from the turbocharger (or exhaust manifold on normally-aspirated models).
12 Slacken the hose clips and disconnect the cabin heater and throttle body pre-heater coolant hoses from the cylinder head. On Turbo models, unscrew the union bolts and disconnect the coolant supply and return pipes from the turbocharger.
13 On Turbo models, unscrew the union bolts and disconnect the oil supply and return pipes from the turbocharger.
14 On models with direct ignition, refer to Chapter 5B and unplug the wiring connector from the DI cartridge.
15 Unbolt the support bracket and release the engine oil dipstick tube from the cylinder head.
16 Release the hose clips (where applicable) and disconnect the vacuum and crankcase breather hoses from the cylinder head cover.
17 Unbolt and remove the engine lifting eyes from the inlet manifold and move the wiring harness bracket to one side. Refer to Chapter 4A and remove the inlet manifold from the cylinder head.
18 Remove the securing bolts and disconnect the radiator top hose at the thermostat housing.
19 Remove all four spark plugs, as described in Chapter 1.
20 Unbolt and remove the cylinder head cover, as described in Section 4.
21 Using a socket on the crankshaft pulley, turn the engine until the TDC mark on the crankshaft pulley is aligned with the timing mark on the timing cover, and No 1 piston (at the timing chain end of the engine) is at the top of its compression stroke. If necessary, refer to Section 3 for more information. Check also that the TDC marks on the sprocket ends of the camshafts are aligned with the corresponding TDC marks on the camshaft bearing caps.
22 Unscrew and remove the timing chain tensioner from the rear of the cylinder head.
23 While holding each camshaft stationary with a spanner on the special flats at the flywheel/driveplate end of the camshaft, unscrew the bolts, then disengage the sprockets from the chain and remove from the engine.
24 Unscrew and remove the two bolts securing the timing cover to the cylinder head. The bolts screw into the bottom of the head.
25 Working in the reverse of the sequence shown in illustration 9.40a, progressively slacken the ten cylinder head bolts by half a turn at a time, until all bolts can be unscrewed by hand **(see illustration)**. The bolts require the use of a Torx socket to unscrew them, as they have six external splines.
26 With all the cylinder head bolts removed, check that the timing chain is positioned so that the pivoting chain guide will not obstruct removal of the head. Lift the cylinder head directly from the top of the cylinder block, and place it on the workbench. If necessary, enlist the help of an assistant, since the cylinder head is quite heavy. If the cylinder head is stuck, try rocking it slightly to free it from the gasket - **do not** insert a screwdriver or similar tool between the gasket joint, otherwise the gasket mating faces will be damaged. The head is located on dowels, so do not try to free it by tapping it sideways.
27 Remove the gasket from the top of the block, noting the two locating dowels. If the locating dowels are a loose fit, remove them and store them with the head for safe-keeping **(see illustration)**. Do not discard the gasket - it may be needed for identification purposes.
28 If the cylinder head is to be dismantled for overhaul, remove the camshafts as described in Section 8.

Preparation for refitting

29 The mating faces of the cylinder head and cylinder block must be perfectly clean before refitting the head. Use a hard plastic or wood scraper to remove all traces of gasket and carbon; also clean the piston crowns. Take particular care during the cleaning operations, as the soft aluminium alloy is damaged easily. Also, make sure that the carbon is not allowed to enter the oil and water passages - this is particularly important for the lubrication system, as carbon could block the oil supply to the engine's components. Using adhesive tape and paper, seal the water, oil and bolt holes in the cylinder block.

To prevent carbon entering the gap between the pistons and bores, smear a little grease in the gap. After cleaning each piston, use a small brush to remove all traces of grease and carbon from the gap, then wipe away the remainder with a clean rag.

Clean all the pistons in the same way.
30 Check the mating surfaces of the cylinder block and the cylinder head for nicks, deep scratches and other damage. If slight, they may be removed carefully with a file, but if excessive, machining may be the only alternative to renewal.
31 If warpage of the cylinder head gasket surface is suspected, use a straight-edge to check it for distortion. Refer to Part B of this Chapter if necessary.

9.35 Position a new cylinder head gasket on the cylinder block

32 Check the condition of the cylinder head bolts, and particularly their threads, whenever they are removed. Wash the bolts in suitable solvent, and wipe them dry. Check each for any sign of visible wear or damage, renewing any bolt if necessary. Measure the length of each bolt, and compare with the length of a new bolt. Although Saab do not actually specify that the bolts must be renewed, it is strongly recommended that the bolts are renewed as a complete set if the engine has completed a high mileage.

Refitting

33 Where removed, refit the camshafts with reference to Section 8.

34 Wipe clean the mating surfaces of the cylinder head and cylinder block/crankcase. Check that the two locating dowels are in position on the cylinder block.

35 Position a new gasket on the cylinder block surface, making sure that it is fitted the correct way round **(see illustration)**.

36 Check that each camshaft is at its TDC position - the timing marks are located on the front of the camshaft, and must be aligned with the marks on the bearing caps.

37 Rotate the crankshaft one quarter of a turn away from TDC; this will position all four pistons part-way along their bores, keeping them out of way during cylinder head refitting.

38 Check that the timing chain is located correctly on the chain guides, then carefully lower the cylinder head onto the block, aligning it with the locating dowels.

39 Apply a smear of grease to the threads, and to the underside of the heads, of the cylinder head bolts. Insert the bolts, and screw them in finger-tight.

40 Working progressively and in the sequence shown, tighten the cylinder head bolts to their Stage 1 torque setting, using a torque wrench **(see illustrations)**.

41 Using the same sequence, tighten the cylinder head bolts to their Stage 2 torque setting.

42 With all the cylinder head bolts tightened to their Stage 2 setting, working again in the given sequence, angle-tighten the bolts further through the specified Stage 3 angle, using a socket and extension bar. It is recommended that an angle-measuring

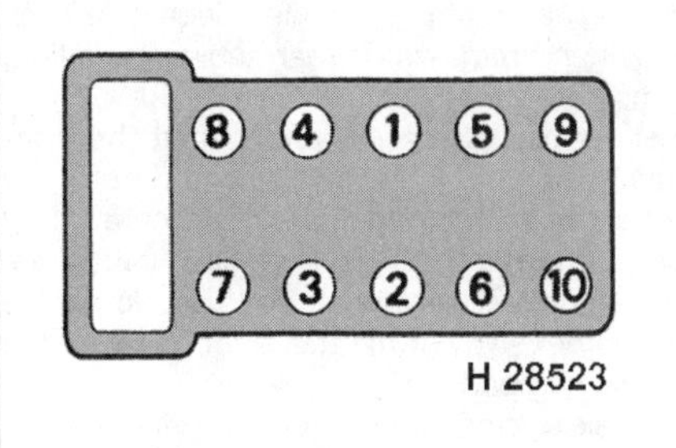

9.40a Cylinder head bolt tightening sequence

gauge is used during this stage of the tightening, to ensure accuracy **(see illustration)**.

If a gauge is not available, use white paint to make alignment marks between the bolt head and cylinder head prior to tightening; the marks can then be used to check that the bolt has been rotated through the correct angle during tightening.

43 Rotate the crankshaft through one quarter of a turn back to its TDC position (see Section 3).

44 Insert and tighten the two bolts securing the timing cover to the cylinder head.

45 With reference to Chapter 3, check that the camshafts are both aligned at their respective TDC positions. Engage the camshaft sprockets with the timing chain (with reference to Section 6 if necessary) and then locate the sprockets on the camshafts, fitting the inlet one first, followed by the exhaust one. Do not fully tighten the bolts at this stage. Check that the timing chain is correctly located on the guides and sprockets.

46 Refit the timing chain tensioner with reference to Section 6.

47 Using a socket on the crankshaft pulley, rotate the engine two complete turns clockwise, then check that the TDC timing marks are still correctly aligned.

48 Fully tighten the camshaft sprocket retaining bolts to the specified torque, while holding each camshaft stationary, using a spanner on the special flats machined into the transmission end of each shaft.

49 Refit the cylinder head cover as described in Section 4, then refit the spark plugs with reference to Chapter 1.

50 Fit the DI cartridge (Turbo models) or the inspection cover (all other models) to the cylinder head cover. Where applicable, refit the ignition distributor with reference to Chapter 5B.

51 Refit the inlet manifold with reference to Chapter 4A. Bolt the engine lifting eyelets and the wiring harness support bracket in position.

52 Reconnect the coolant hoses for the throttle body pre-heater, thermostat housing and cabin heater to their respective ports on

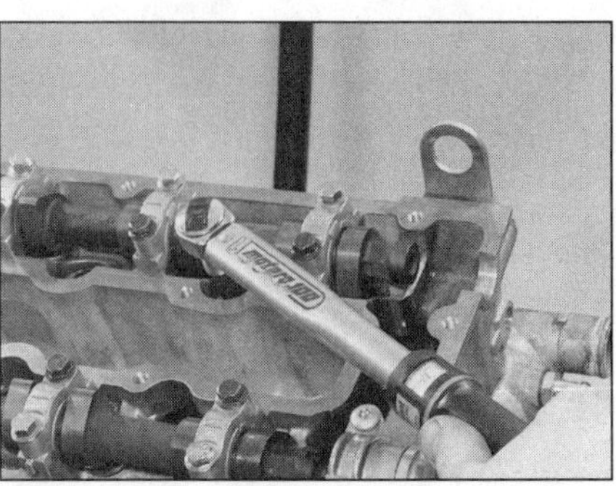

9.40b Tightening the cylinder head bolts with a torque wrench

the cylinder head, tightening the hose clips securely.

53 Position the engine oil dipstick tube against the cylinder head and secure it with the retaining screw.

54 Reconnect the vacuum and crankcase breather hoses to the cylinder head cover.

55 On Turbo models, reconnect the coolant and oil supply and return pipes to the turbocharger, tightening the union bolts to the specified torque.

56 With reference to Chapter 4A refit the exhaust system front pipe to the turbocharger (Turbo models) or exhaust manifold (normally aspirated models) and tighten the bolts to the specified torque.

57 On Turbo models, refit the turbocharger bracing bracket; insert and tighten the bolt to the cylinder block first.

58 Refit the power steering pump with reference to Chapter 10, then refit the auxiliary drivebelt with reference to Chapter 1.

59 On normally aspirated models, refit the intake air ducting, mass air flow meter and air cleaner housing with reference to Chapter 4A.

60 On Turbo models, refit the turbocharger inlet elbow and crankcase breather pipe, securing them in position with the retaining screws. Remove the cover from the turbocharger port, then refit the turbocharger-to-intercooler and intercooler-to-throttle body intake air ducts.

61 Refit the resonator (normally aspirated models) or cover panel (Turbo models) to the top of the inlet manifold.

62 Reconnect the battery negative lead.

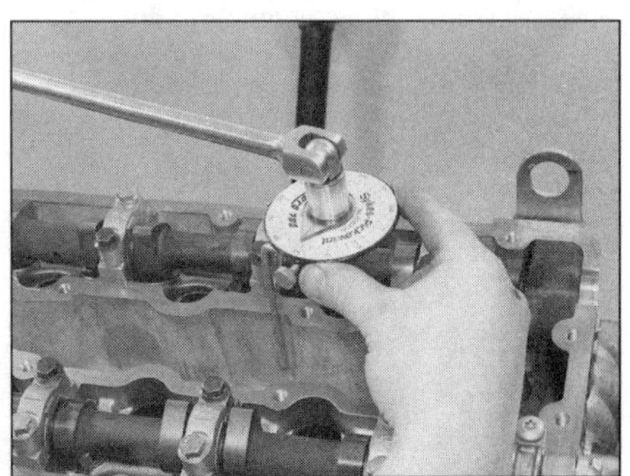

9.42 Using an angle-measuring gauge to tighten the cylinder head bolts through their Stage 3 angle

63 Refit the central panel under the radiator, followed by the right-hand front wing wheelarch liner and moulding.
64 Refit the right-hand front wheel, and lower the car to the ground.
65 Refill the cooling system (see Chapter 1).
66 Start the engine, observing the precautions given in Chapter 2B, Section 20.

10 Sump - removal and refitting

Removal

1 Firmly apply the handbrake, then jack up the front of the car and support it on axle stands (see *"Jacking and vehicle support"*). Disconnect the battery negative lead.
2 Drain the engine oil, then clean and refit the engine oil drain plug, tightening it to the specified torque. Remove the dipstick from its tube and place clean rag over the engine oil filler neck to prevent the ingress of debris. If the engine is nearing its service interval when the oil and filter are due for renewal, it is recommended that the filter is also removed, and a new one fitted. After reassembly, the engine can then be refilled with fresh oil. Refer to Chapter 1 for further information.
3 Mount a lifting beam across the engine compartment, in-line with the front suspension turrets. Attach the jib to the engine lifting eyelet at the left hand end of the cylinder head. Raise the jib until the beam just starts to take the weight of the engine.
4 Unplug the lambda sensor wiring at the connector, located on a bracket at the left hand end of the cylinder head.
5 Raise the front of the vehicle and support it securely on axle stands (see *"Jacking and vehicle support"*). Remove both front roadwheels.
6 Remove the securing screws and lower the undertray away from the front spoiler.
7 With reference to Chapter 4A, unbolt the exhaust system intermediate pipe from the front pipe, then unbolt the front pipe from the turbocharger or exhaust manifold, as applicable. Unbolt the front pipe from its support bracket and withdraw it from the underside of the engine compartment.

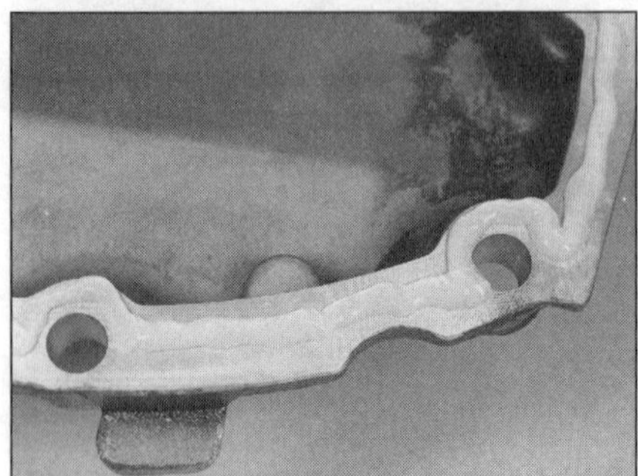

10.16 Apply a bead of sealant to the sump flange

8 Ensure that the lifting beam is supporting the engine and transmission adequately, then unbolt and remove the rear engine mounting, with reference to Section 17.
9 Refer to Chapter 10 and unbolt the front suspension lower arm balljoints from the bottom of both hub carriers. Position a trolley jack underneath the suspension subframe, then remove the securing bolts and lower the subframe away from the underside of the engine compartment.
10 Release the oil level sensor wiring from its retaining clips, then unplug the wiring from the sensor at the connector.
11 Where applicable, unscrew the bolts, and remove the bracket and oil return pipe for the turbo unit from the sump.
12 Unbolt and remove the sump exhaust heat shield, then progressively unscrew and remove the bolts securing the sump to the cylinder block, leaving one or two bolts in position to prevent the sump falling.
13 Remove the remaining bolts, and lower the sump to the ground. If necessary, break the joint between the sump and crankcase by striking the sump with the palm of your hand.
14 While the sump is removed, take the opportunity to check the oil pump pick-up/strainer for signs of clogging or damage.

Refitting

15 Clean all traces of sealant from the mating surfaces of the cylinder block/crankcase and sump, then use a clean rag to wipe out the sump and the engine's interior.
16 Ensure that the sump and cylinder block/crankcase mating surfaces are clean and dry, then apply a bead of suitable sealant to the sump flange **(see illustration)**.
17 Offer up the sump and refit its retaining bolts, tightening them progressively to the specified torque.
18 Refit the heat shield, then reconnect the oil level sensor wiring.
19 Refit the suspension subframe with reference to Chapter 10. Reconnect the suspension lower arms to the hub carriers and tighten the balljoint securing nuts to the specified torque.
20 Refit the rear engine mounting with reference to Section 17.
21 Refer to Chapter 4A and refit the exhaust system front pipe. Apply a suitable anti-seize agent to the front pipe-to-turbocharger securing nut studs, and tighten the nuts to the specified torque. Fit the front pipe-to-support bracket securing bolt and tighten it securely.
22 Refit the undertray to the front spoiler and tighten the securing screws.
23 Refit both front roadwheels and lower the vehicle to the ground. Remove the lifting beam and reconnect the lambda sensor wiring.
24 Refill the engine with the correct quantity and grade of oil as described in Chapter 1, then clean and refit the dipstick/filler cap.
25 Start the engine and allow it to warm up. Check around the sump mating surface for signs of leakage.

11 Oil pump - removal, inspection and refitting

Removal

1 Apply the handbrake, then jack up the front of the car and support on axle stands (see *"Jacking and vehicle support"*). Remove the right-hand front wheel.
2 Remove the screws, and remove the front wing moulding followed by the front wheelarch liner.
3 Remove the auxiliary drivebelt with reference to Chapter 1.
4 Unscrew and remove the centre bolt from the crankshaft pulley. To do this, the crankshaft must be held stationary using one of the following methods. On manual transmission models, have an assistant depress the brake pedal and engage 4th gear. Alternatively, remove the starter motor as described in Chapter 5A, then insert a stout flat-bladed screwdriver through the transmission bellhousing and engage it with the starter ring gear to prevent the crankshaft turning. On automatic transmission models, use the latter method only.
5 Pull the crankshaft pulley and hub from the end of the crankshaft. If it is tight, careful use of two levers may be required.
6 Extract the large circlip, then withdraw the oil pump cover from the timing cover. Note that the circlip has a high tension, and a large pair of circlip pliers will be required to compress it. Also note the alignment arrows on the cover and timing cover **(see illustrations)**.
7 Remove the O-ring seal from the groove in the cover **(see illustration)**.
8 Note the position of the crankshaft oil seal in the oil pump cover, then prise it out with a screwdriver **(see illustration)**.

Inspection

9 Wipe clean the inner faces of the pump rotors, and identify them for position with a marker pen. It is important that the rotors remain in their correct original positions on reassembly. Note that the outer rotor position is identified by the punch hole facing outwards.
10 Remove the rotors from the timing cover

11.6a Using circlip pliers to remove the oil pump cover circlip

11.6b Withdrawing the oil pump cover from the timing cover

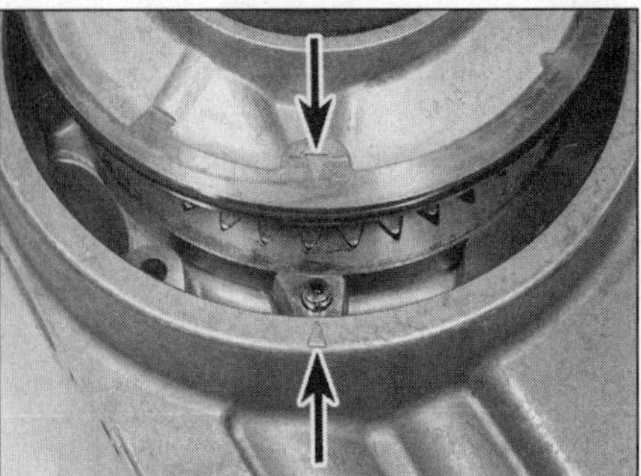

11.6c Alignment arrows on the oil pump cover

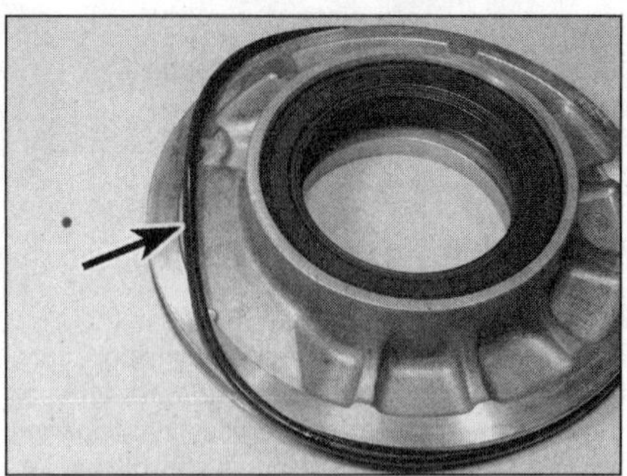

11.7 Removing the O-ring seal from the groove in the oil pump cover

(oil pump body), keeping them identified for position **(see illustrations)**.

11 Unscrew the plug, and remove the relief valve spring and plunger, noting which way round they are fitted **(see illustrations)**. Recover the plug washer.

12 Clean all components, and examine them for wear and damage. Examine the pump rotors and body for signs of wear ridges and scoring. Using a feeler blade check the clearance between the outer rotor and the timing cover, with reference to the Specifications **(see illustration)**. If worn excessively, the complete pump assembly must be renewed.

13 Examine the relief valve plunger for signs of wear or damage, and renew if necessary. The condition of the relief valve spring can only be measured by comparing it with a new one; if there is any doubt about its condition, it should also be renewed.

14 If there are any signs of dirt or sediment in the oil pump, it will be necessary to remove the sump (see Section 10), and clean the pick-up/strainer.

15 Insert the relief valve plunger and spring, then refit the plug together with a new washer, and tighten the plug.

16 Lubricate the rotors with fresh engine oil, then insert them in the oil pump body in their original positions. The outer rotor must be positioned with the identification mark facing outwards.

Refitting

17 Wipe clean the oil seal seating in the oil pump casing, then drive a new oil seal into the casing, making sure that it enters squarely and is fitted in the previously-noted position.

18 Fit a new O-ring seal, then insert the oil pump in the timing cover, making sure that the alignment arrows point to each other. Refit the large circlip in the groove with its chamfer facing outwards, and the opening facing downwards.

19 Locate the crankshaft pulley and hub on the end of the crankshaft. Insert the centre bolt and tighten it to the specified torque, holding the crankshaft stationary using one of the methods described in paragraph 5.

20 Refit the auxiliary drivebelt with reference to Chapter 1.

21 Refit the wing liner and moulding, and tighten the screws.

22 Refit the right-hand front wheel, and lower the car to the ground.

23 Before running the engine, disconnect the ignition wiring harness to the distributor or DI ignition cartridge to disable the ignition system (see Chapter 5B), then remove the fuel pump fuse (see Chapter 12). Crank the engine on the starter motor until oil pressure is restored and the oil pressure warning light is extinguished. Restore the ignition and fuel systems, and run the engine to check for oil leaks.

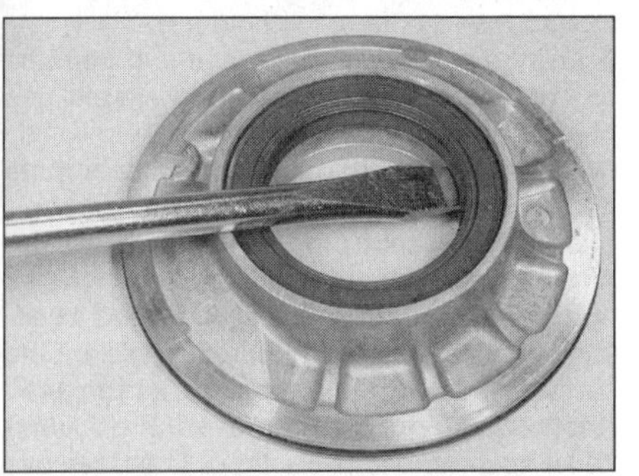

11.8 Prising out the crankshaft oil seal from the oil pump cover

11.10a Removing the inner rotor . . .

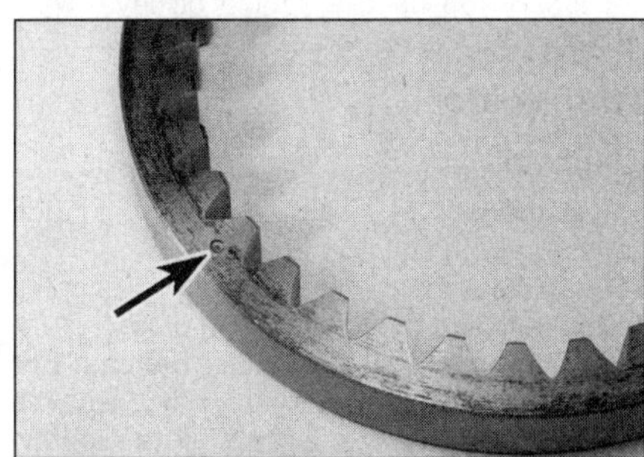

11.10b . . . and outer rotor from the timing cover. Note that the position mark (arrowed) is facing outwards

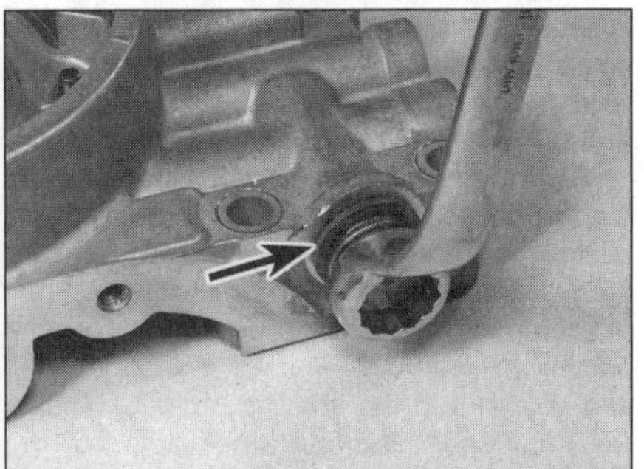

11.11a Unscrew the plug (arrowed) . . .

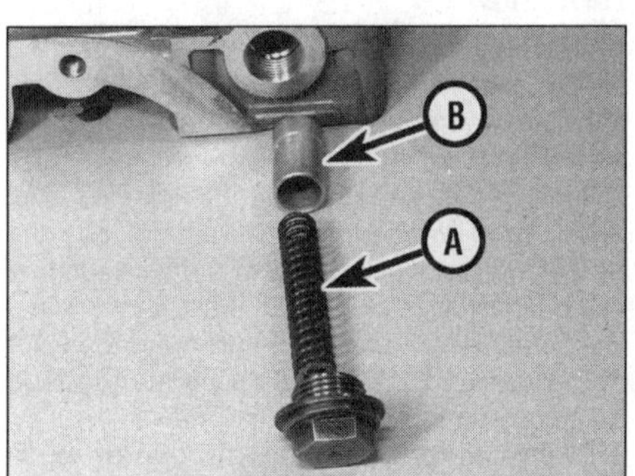

11.11b . . . and remove the relief valve spring (A) and plunger (B)

11.12 Checking the clearance between the oil pump outer rotor and the timing cover

12 Oil cooler and thermostat - removal and refitting

Oil cooler

Removal

1 An oil cooler is fitted to Turbo models only. It is connected to ports on an adapter fitted to the oil filter, and the adapter also incorporates an oil thermostat. To remove the oil cooler, first drain the engine oil as described in Chapter 1, then refit and tighten the drain plug.

2 Jack up the front of the car and support it securely on axle stands (see "*Jacking and vehicle support*"). Slacken and withdraw the securing screws, and remove the front lower spoiler.

3 Position a suitable container beneath the oil cooler on the right-hand side of the engine compartment. Unscrew the unions from the top and bottom of the oil cooler, and disconnect the oil supply and return hoses. Allow any oil to drain into the container.

4 Unscrew the mounting bolts and remove the oil cooler from the engine compartment.

Refitting

5 Refitting is a reversal of removal, but tighten the unions to the specified torque. Fill the engine with oil with reference to Chapter 1. On completion, start the engine and run it at a fast idle speed for several minutes, to allow the oil to fill the oil cooler. Check and if necessary top-up the engine oil level with reference to "*Weekly checks*".

Thermostat

Removal

6 The thermostat is mounted on the right hand side of the oil filter adapter.

7 Drain the engine oil as described in Chapter 1, then refit and tighten the drain plug.

8 Position a suitable container beneath the thermostat, then unscrew the plug, recover the seal and allow the surplus oil to run into the container.

9 Withdraw the thermostat and spring from the filter adapter.

13.2 Disconnecting the wiring from the oil pressure switch

Refitting

10 Fit the new thermostat into the filter adapter, ensuring that the flange rests on the machined recess in the housing.

11 Slide the spring into position, then fit the seal to the plug and screw the plug into the filter housing, tightening it to the correct torque.

12 Fill the engine with oil with reference to Chapter 1. On completion, start the engine and run it at a fast idle speed for several minutes, then check around the thermostat plug for signs of leakage. Check the engine oil level and top-up if necessary (see "*Weekly checks*").

13 Oil pressure warning light switch - removal and refitting

Removal

1 The oil pressure switch is screwed into the rear of the cylinder block, beneath the inlet manifold. First jack up the front of the car, and support on axle stands (see "*Jacking and vehicle support*").

2 Disconnect the wiring from the switch terminal **(see illustration)**.

3 Unscrew the switch from the cylinder block. Be prepared for slight loss of oil. If the switch is to be left removed for any length of time, plug the hole, to prevent the entry of debris.

Refitting

4 Wipe clean the threads of the switch and the location aperture. Do not insert tools or wire into the hole at the tip of the switch, in an attempt to clean it out; as this may damage the internal components.

5 Insert the switch into the cylinder block and tighten it securely.

6 Reconnect the wiring to the switch terminal.

7 Start the engine and check for leakage, then lower the car to the ground.

14 Oil level sensor - removal and refitting

Removal

1 The oil level sensor (where fitted) is located on the rear of the sump, and consists of a float and transducer. A warning light on the instrument panel is illuminated when the ignition is switched on and the engine oil level is low. After illuminating the warning light, the sensor will not operate again until the ignition has been switched off for at least 5 minutes.

2 Apply the handbrake, then jack up the front of the car and support on axle stands (see "*Jacking and vehicle support*").

3 Drain the engine oil with reference to Chapter 1.

4 Disconnect the wiring from the oil level sensor on the rear of the sump.

5 Wipe clean the area around the sensor, then unscrew the mounting screws and withdraw the sensor from the sump. Remove the gasket.

Refitting

6 Refitting is a reversal of the removal procedure, but clean the contact surfaces and fit a new gasket. Tighten the mounting screws progressively.

15 Crankshaft oil seals - renewal

Right-hand oil seal

1 Apply the handbrake, then jack up the front of the car and support on axle stands (see "*Jacking and vehicle support*"). Remove the right-hand front wheel.

2 Remove the front wing plastic moulding, followed by the front wheelarch liner.

3 Remove the auxiliary drivebelt with reference to Chapter 1.

4 Unscrew and remove the centre bolt from the crankshaft pulley. To do this, the crankshaft must be held stationary using one of the following methods. On manual transmission models, have an assistant depress the brake pedal and engage 4th gear. Alternatively, remove the starter motor as described in Chapter 5A, then insert a flat-bladed screwdriver through the bellhousing and jam the starter ring gear to prevent the crankshaft turning. On automatic transmission models, use the latter method only.

5 Pull the crankshaft pulley and hub from the end of the crankshaft. If it is tight, careful use of two levers may be required.

6 Note the fitted depth of the oil seal in its housing, then using a screwdriver, carefully prise the oil seal from the oil pump casing. Alternatively, punch or drill two small holes opposite each other in the seal. Thread a self-tapping screw into each hole, and pull on the screw heads with pliers to extract the seal. Another method is to remove the oil pump cover as described in Section 11, and remove the oil seal on the bench.

7 Clean the seating in the oil pump casing, then lubricate the lips of the new oil seal with clean engine oil, and locate it squarely on the oil pump casing. Make sure that the closed side is facing outwards. Using a suitable tubular drift (such as a socket) which bears only on the hard outer edge of the seal, tap the seal into position, to the same depth in the casing as the original was prior to removal **(see illustration)**.

8 Locate the crankshaft pulley and hub on the end of the crankshaft. Insert the centre bolt and tighten it to the specified torque, holding the crankshaft stationary using one of the methods described in paragraph 5.

9 Refit the auxiliary drivebelt with reference to Chapter 1.

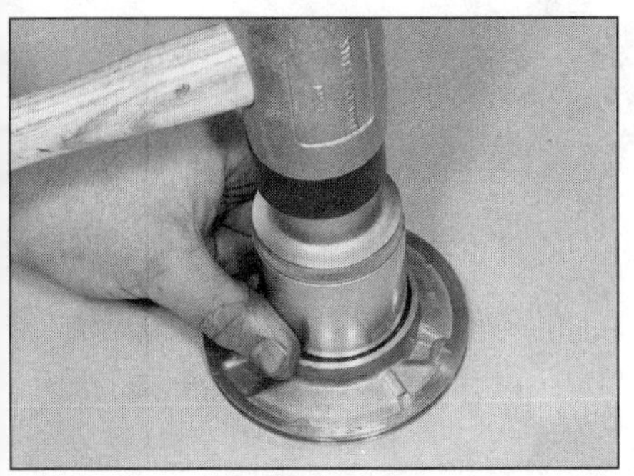

15.7 Fitting a new oil seal to the oil pump cover

10 Refit the wheelarch liner front section and moulding, and tighten the screws.

11 Refit the right-hand front wheel, and lower the car to the ground.

Left-hand oil seal

12 Remove the flywheel/driveplate as described in Section 16.

13 Make a note of the fitted depth of the seal in its housing. Punch or drill two small holes opposite each other in the seal. Thread a self-tapping screw into each hole, and pull on the screw heads with pliers to extract the seal. Alternatively, use a screwdriver to prise out the oil seal.

14 Clean the seal housing, then lubricate the lips of the new seal with clean engine oil, and carefully locate the seal on the end of the crankshaft.

15 Using a suitable tubular drift, which bears only on the hard outer edge of the seal, drive the seal into position, to the same depth in the housing as the original was prior to removal.

16 Wipe clean the oil seal, then refit the flywheel/driveplate as described in Section 16.

16 Flywheel/driveplate - removal, inspection and refitting

Removal

1 Remove the transmission as described in Chapter 7A or 7B.

2 On manual transmission models, remove the clutch assembly as described in Chapter 6.

3 Prevent the flywheel/driveplate from turning by jamming the ring gear teeth with a wide-bladed screwdriver or similar tool. Alternatively, bolt a metal link between the flywheel/driveplate (using the clutch or torque converter bolt holes) and the cylinder block/crankcase.

4 Unscrew and remove the retaining bolts, remove the locking tool, then remove the flywheel/driveplate from the crankshaft flange. Note that the unit is located by a single dowel pin, and cannot be fitted incorrectly.

Inspection

5 On manual transmission models, if the flywheel's clutch mating surface is deeply scored, cracked or otherwise damaged, the flywheel must be renewed. However, it may be possible to have it surface-ground; seek the advice of a Saab dealer or engine reconditioning specialist.

6 Similarly check the condition of the driveplate on automatic transmission models.

7 If the ring gear is badly worn or has missing teeth, it may be possible to renew it. This job is best left to a Saab dealer or engine reconditioning specialist. The temperature to which the new ring gear must be heated for installation is critical and, if not done accurately, the hardness of the teeth will be destroyed.

Refitting

8 Clean the mating surfaces of the flywheel/driveplate and crankshaft. Clean the threads of the retaining bolts and the crankshaft holes.

If a suitable tap is not available, cut two slots into the threads of an old flywheel bolt, and use the bolt to clean the threads.

9 Ensure that the locating dowel is in position, then offer up the flywheel and locate it on the dowel.

10 Apply locking fluid to the threads of the retaining bolts. Insert and tighten them to the specified torque, holding the flywheel/driveplate stationary using one of the methods described in paragraph 3 **(see illustration)**.

11 On manual transmission models, refit the clutch assembly as described in Chapter 6.

12 Refit the transmission with reference to Chapter 7A or 7B.

17 Engine/transmission mountings - inspection and renewal

Inspection

1 For improved access, raise the front of the car and support it securely on axle stands (see *"Jacking and vehicle support"*).

2 The engine mountings are located at the front right-hand side, beneath the left-hand side of the transmission, and at the rear of the engine. With the exception of the upper right-hand mounting, all mountings are of hydraulic type, incorporating an inner chamber filled with oil. Vibration damping is progressive depending on the load applied, and works for both horizontal and vertical movement.

3 Check the mounting rubbers to see if they are cracked, hardened or separated from the metal at any point; renew the mounting if any such damage or deterioration is evident.

4 Check that all the mounting's fasteners are securely tightened.

5 Using a large screwdriver or a crowbar, check for wear in the mounting by carefully levering against it to check for freeplay. Where this is not possible, enlist the aid of an assistant to move the engine/transmission back and forth, or from side to side, while you watch the mounting. While some freeplay is to be expected even from new components, excessive wear should be obvious. If excessive freeplay is found, check first that the fasteners are securely tightened, then if necessary renew any worn components as described below.

16.10 Apply locking fluid to the bolt threads, and tighten to the specified torque

Renewal

Right-hand engine mounting

6 Apply the handbrake, then jack up the front of the car and support on axle stands (see *"Jacking and vehicle support"*). Remove the right-hand front wheel.

7 Remove the screws, and withdraw the right-hand front wing plastic moulding and front wheelarch liner.

8 Remove the securing screws and detach the plastic undertray from the front spoiler.

9 Position a trolley jack underneath the engine and raise the jack head until it is just taking the weight of the engine. Ensure that the jack head does not bear on the underside of the sump. Alternatively, position a lifting beam across the engine bay and support the engine by the lifting eyelet located at the rear right hand side of the cylinder head.

10 Unscrew the bolts securing the engine mounting bracket to the bodywork **(see illustration)**. Lower the jack slightly, until the engine mounting bracket is clear of the bodywork. Take care to avoid straining the rear and left-hand engine mountings as you do this.

17.10 Unscrew the bolts securing the right-hand engine mounting bracket to the bodywork

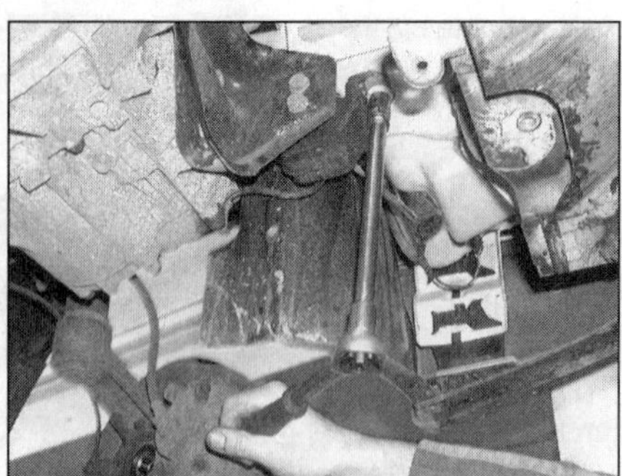
17.17 Unscrew the bolts securing the left-hand engine/transmission mounting bracket to the bodywork

17.18 Remove the engine/transmission mounting with its mounting bracket from the transmission casing

11 Slacken and withdraw the centre bolt and remove the engine mounting from its bracket.

12 Fit the new mountings using a reversal of the removal procedure, making sure that the nuts are tightened to the correct torque.

Left-hand engine/transmission mounting

13 Apply the handbrake, then jack up the front of the car and support on axle stands (see "*Jacking and vehicle support*"). Remove the left-hand front wheel.

14 Remove the screws, and withdraw the left-hand front wing plastic moulding and front wheelarch liner.

15 Remove the securing screws and detach the plastic undertray from the front spoiler.

16 Position a trolley jack underneath the transmission and raise the jack head until it is just taking the combined weight of the engine and transmission. On models with automatic transmission, ensure that the jack head does not bear on the underside of the transmission sump. Alternatively, position a lifting beam across the engine bay and support the engine by the lifting eyelet located at the rear left hand side of the cylinder head.

17 Unscrew the bolts securing the engine/transmission mounting bracket to the bodywork **(see illustration)**. Lower the jack slightly, until the engine mounting bracket is clear of the bodywork. Take care to avoid straining the rear and right-hand engine mountings as you do this.

18 Slacken and withdraw the bolts and remove the engine/transmission mounting, together with its mounting bracket, from the transmission casing **(see illustration)**.

19 Fit the new mounting using a reversal of the removal procedure, making sure that the nuts are tightened to the correct torque.

Rear engine mounting

20 Mount a lifting beam across the engine compartment, in-line with the front suspension turrets. Attach the jib to the engine lifting eyelet at the left hand end of the cylinder head. Raise the jib until the beam just starts to take the weight of the engine.

21 Unplug the lambda sensor wiring at the connector, located on a bracket at the left hand end of the cylinder head.

22 Raise the front of the vehicle and support it securely on axle stands (see "*Jacking and vehicle support*"). Remove both front roadwheels.

23 With reference to Chapter 4A, unbolt the exhaust system intermediate pipe from the front pipe, then unbolt the front pipe from the turbocharger or exhaust manifold, as applicable. Unbolt the front pipe from its support bracket and withdraw it from the underside of the engine compartment.

24 Ensure that the lifting beam is supporting the engine and transmission adequately, then slacken and withdraw the rear engine mounting centre bolts **(see illustration)**.

25 Unbolt the engine mounting from the rear of the transmission casing and remove it from the engine compartment **(see illustration)**.

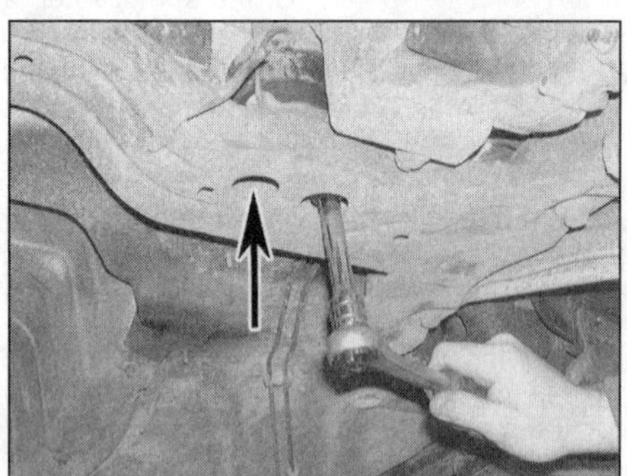
17.24 Slacken and withdraw the rear engine mounting centre bolts

17.25 Rear engine mounting bracket-to-transmission casing bolts (arrowed) (transmission removed for clarity)

Chapter 2 Part B:
Engine removal and overhaul procedures

Contents

Degrees of difficulty

Easy, suitable for novice with little experience 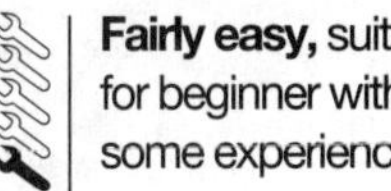

Fairly easy, suitable for beginner with some experience 

Fairly difficult, suitable for competent DIY mechanic 

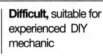

Difficult, suitable for experienced DIY mechanic

Very difficult, suitable for expert DIY or professional

2B

Specifications

Cylinder head

Height:	
New	139.4 to 139.6 mm
Minimum	139.0 mm
Valve guide to valve stem clearance (max)	0.50 mm (measured on valve head raised 3 mm above seat)

Valves

Valve head diameter:	
Inlet	33.0 mm
Exhaust	29.0 mm
Valve seat cutting angle	45°
Valve stem diameter:	
Inlet	6.960 to 6.975 mm
Exhaust	6.965 to 6.980 mm
Valve spring free length	44.0 to 47.0 mm

Balance shafts

Outer bearing diameter	20.000 - 20.021 mm
Outer journal diameter	19.947 - 19.960 mm
Inner bearing diameter	39.988 - 40.043 mm
Inner journal diameter	39.892 - 39.908 mm
Outer bearing clearance	0.040 - 0.074 mm
Maximum inner bearing clearance	0.18 mm
Endfloat	0.050 - 0.450 mm

Cylinder block

Cylinder bore diameter:	
Standard (A)	90.000 to 90.012 mm
Standard (B)	90.003 to 90.020 mm
Standard (B+)	90.011 to 90.030 mm
First oversize	90.500 to 90.512 mm
Second oversize	91.000 to 91.012 mm

Balance shafts

Endfloat	0.050 to 0.450 mm
Diameter of journal:	
Larger, inner	39.900 ± 0.008 mm
Smaller, outer	19.947 to 19.960 mm
Diameter of bearing:	
Larger, inner	39.988 to 40.043 mm
Smaller, outer	20.000 to 20.021 mm
Bearing running clearance (maximum)	0.080 to 0.151 mm

Pistons

Note: *Piston diameter is measured at right-angles to the gudgeon pin hole, at the specified distance from the bottom of the skirt.*

Distance from bottom of skirt:	
B204L	9.3 mm
B206i, B204i and B234i	11.0 mm
Piston diameter:	
Standard A	89.971 to 89.980 mm
Standard AB	89.980 to 89.989 mm
Standard B	89.989 to 90.000 mm
Standard C	90.000 to 90.013 mm
First oversize (0.5 mm)	90.472 to 90.488 mm
Second oversize (1.0 mm)	90.972 to 90.988 mm
Piston/cylinder classification (clearance):	
A/A	0.020 to 0.041 mm
AB/A	0.011 to 0.032 mm
AB/B	0.014 to 0.040 mm
B/B	0.006 to 0.031 mm
B/B+	0.011 to 0.041 mm

Connecting rods

Maximum weight difference between any two connecting rods	6.0 g

Crankshaft

Endfloat	0.06 to 0.31 mm
Main bearing journal diameter:	
Standard	57.981 to 58.000 mm
First undersize	57.731 to 57.750 mm
Second undersize	57.481 to 57.500 mm
Third undersize	57.237 to 57.250 mm
Fourth undersize	56.987 to 57.000 mm
Main bearing running clearance	0.014 to 0.062 mm
Big-end bearing journal diameter:	
Standard	51.981 to 52.000 mm
First undersize	51.731 to 51.750 mm
Second undersize	51.481 to 51.500 mm
Third undersize	51.237 to 51.250 mm
Fourth undersize	50.987 to 51.000 mm
Big-end bearing running clearance	0.020 to 0.068 mm
Maximum bearing journal out-of-round	0.005 mm
Maximum journal taper	0.005 mm

Piston rings

End gaps:	
Top compression ring	0.30 to 0.50 mm
Second compression ring	0.15 to 0.65 mm
Oil control ring	0.38 to 1.40 mm
Side clearance in groove:	
Top compression ring	0.050 to 0.082 mm
Second compression ring	0.040 to 0.072 mm
Oil control ring	(Not applicable)

Torque wrench settings

Refer to Chapter 2A Specifications.

1 General information

Included in this Part of Chapter 2 are details of removing the engine from the vehicle, and general overhaul procedures for the cylinder head, cylinder block/crankcase, and all engine internal components.

The information given ranges from advice concerning preparation for an overhaul and the purchase of replacement parts, to detailed step-by-step procedures covering removal, inspection, renovation and refitting of engine internal components.

After Section 8, all instructions are based on the assumption that the engine has been removed from the vehicle. For information concerning in-car engine repair, as well as the removal and refitting of those external components necessary for full overhaul, refer to Part A of this Chapter. Ignore any preliminary dismantling operations described in Part A that are no longer relevant once the engine has been removed from the vehicle.

2 Engine overhaul - general information

It is not always easy to determine when, or if, an engine should be completely overhauled, as a number of factors must be considered.

High mileage is not necessarily an indication that an overhaul is needed, while low mileage does not preclude the need for an overhaul. Frequency of servicing is probably the most important consideration. An engine which has had regular and frequent oil and filter changes, as well as other required maintenance, should give many thousands of miles of reliable service. Conversely, a neglected engine may require an overhaul very early in its life.

Excessive oil consumption is an indication that piston rings, valve seats and/or valve guides are in need of attention. Make sure that oil leaks are not responsible before deciding that the rings and/or guides are worn. Perform a compression test, as described in Part A of this Chapter, to determine the likely cause of the problem.

Check the oil pressure with a gauge fitted in place of the oil pressure switch, and compare it with that specified (see Chapter 2A Specifications). If it is extremely low, the main and big-end bearings, and/or the oil pump, are probably worn out.

Loss of power, rough running, knocking or metallic engine noises, excessive valve gear noise, and high fuel consumption may also point to the need for an overhaul, especially if they are all present at the same time. If a complete service does not remedy the situation, major mechanical work is the only solution.

An engine overhaul involves restoring all internal parts to the specification of a new engine. During an overhaul, the cylinders are rebored (where necessary) and the pistons and the piston rings are renewed. New main and big-end bearings are generally fitted; if necessary, the crankshaft may be renewed or reground, to restore the journals. The valves are also serviced as well, since they are usually in less-than-perfect condition at this point. While the engine is being overhauled, other components, such as the distributor (where applicable), starter and alternator, can be overhauled as well. The end result should be an as-new engine that will give many trouble-free miles.

Note: *Critical cooling system components such as the hoses, thermostat and water pump should be renewed when an engine is overhauled. The radiator should be checked carefully, to ensure that it is not clogged or leaking. Also, it is a good idea to renew the oil pump whenever the engine is overhauled.*

Before beginning the engine overhaul, read through the entire procedure, to familiarise yourself with the scope and requirements of the job. Overhauling an engine is not difficult if you follow carefully all of the instructions, have the necessary tools and equipment, and pay close attention to all specifications. It can, however, be time-consuming. Plan on the car being off the road for a minimum of two weeks, especially if parts must be taken to an engineering works for repair or reconditioning. Check on the availability of parts, and make sure that any necessary special tools and equipment are obtained in advance. Most work can be done with typical hand tools, although a number of precision measuring tools are required for inspecting parts to determine if they must be renewed. Often the engineering works will handle the inspection of parts, and will offer advice concerning reconditioning and renewal.

Note: *Always wait until the engine has been completely dismantled, and until all components (especially the cylinder block/crankcase and the crankshaft) have been inspected, before deciding what service and repair operations must be performed by an engineering works. The condition of these components will be the major factor to consider when determining whether to overhaul the original engine, or to buy a reconditioned unit. Do not, therefore, purchase parts or have overhaul work done on other components until they have been thoroughly inspected.*

As a general rule, time is the primary cost of an overhaul, so it does not pay to fit worn or sub-standard parts.

As a final note, to ensure maximum life and minimum trouble from a reconditioned engine, everything must be assembled with care, in a spotlessly-clean environment.

3 Engine removal - methods and precautions

If you have decided that the engine must be removed for overhaul or major repair work, several preliminary steps should be taken.

Locating a suitable place to work is extremely important. Adequate workspace, along with storage space for the vehicle, will be needed. If a workshop or garage is not available, at the very least, a flat, level, clean work surface is required.

Cleaning the engine compartment and engine/transmission before beginning the removal procedure will help keep tools clean and organised.

An engine hoist or A-frame will also be necessary. Make sure the equipment is rated in excess of the combined weight of the engine and transmission. Safety is of primary importance, considering the potential hazards involved in lifting the engine/transmission out of the vehicle.

If this is the first time you have removed an engine, an assistant should ideally be available. Advice and aid from someone more experienced would also be helpful. There are many instances when one person cannot simultaneously perform all of the operations required when lifting the engine out of the vehicle.

Plan the operation ahead of time. Before starting work, arrange for the hire of, or obtain, all of the tools and equipment you will need. Some of the equipment necessary to perform engine/transmission removal and installation safely and with relative ease (in addition to an engine hoist) is as follows: a heavy-duty trolley jack, complete sets of spanners and sockets, wooden blocks, and plenty of rags and cleaning solvent for mopping up spilled oil, coolant and fuel. If the hoist must be hired, make sure that you arrange for it in advance, and perform all of the operations possible without it beforehand. This will save you money and time.

Plan for the vehicle to be out of use for quite a while. An engineering works will be required to perform some of the work which the average owner cannot accomplish without special equipment. These places often have a busy schedule, so it would be a good idea to consult them before removing the engine, in order to accurately estimate the amount of time required to rebuild or repair components that may need work.

Always be extremely careful when removing and refitting the engine/transmission. Serious injury can result from careless actions. Plan ahead and take your time, and a job of this nature, although major, can be accomplished successfully.

The engine and transmission is removed by lowering it from the underside of the engine compartment.

4 Engine and transmission - removal, separation and refitting

Removal

Note: *The engine can be removed from the car only as a complete unit with the transmission; the two are then separated for overhaul. The engine/transmission is lowered from the underside of the engine compartment. Note that is possible to remove the transmission, leaving the engine in situ - refer to Chapter 7A or 7B (as applicable) for details.*

1 Park the vehicle on firm, level ground. Chock the rear wheels, then firmly apply the handbrake. Jack up the front of the vehicle, and securely support it on axle stands (see *"Jacking and vehicle support"*).

2 Remove both front wheels, then unbolt both wing mouldings and front wheelarch liners, for access to either side of the engine.

3 Unbolt and remove the centre splash guard panel from under the radiator.

4 Drain the coolant with reference to Chapter 1. Save the coolant if it is fit for re-use.

Warning: The engine should be cold before draining the coolant.

5 With the coolant drained, refit and tighten the drain plugs.

6 Remove the bonnet as described in Chapter 11. Alternatively, disconnect the support struts from the bonnet, and support it in the fully-open position.

7 Remove the battery with reference to Chapter 5A.

8 Refer to Chapter 4A and remove the air cleaner, intake ducting, air flow meter (where applicable). Unbolt the resonator assembly or cover panel, as applicable from above the throttle body.

9 Detach the throttle cable from the throttle body, with reference to Chapter 4A.

10 On models with cruise control, disconnect the cruise control actuator cable from the throttle body, then unplug the wiring harness and remove the cruise control unit from the engine compartment together with the actuator cable.

4.36 Mark around the periphery of the subframe to act as a guide to correct alignment on refitting

11 Disconnect the fuel supply and return hoses at the quick release unions as described in Chapter 4A, Section 14. Plug both sides of the open fuel lines to minimise leakage and to prevent the ingress of foreign material.

12 Disconnect the evaporative loss system vapour hose from the side of the throttle body.

13 Unscrew the union and disconnect the braking system vacuum hose from the inlet manifold; see Chapter 9 for details.

14 On Turbo models, with reference to Chapter 4A, unbolt the manifold pressure sensor from the engine compartment cross brace, and the boost pressure control valve from the front right hand side of the engine compartment, and allow them to rest on top of the engine, with their respective hoses and wiring still connected.

15 Remove the auxiliary drivebelt as described in Chapter 1.

16 With reference to Chapter 10, unbolt the power steering fluid pump from its mounting bracket and secure it, with the hoses still attached, to the front of the engine compartment using nylon cable ties or similar.

17 On Turbo models, slacken the clips and remove the air cleaner-to-intercooler and intercooler-to-throttle body intake ducts from the engine compartment.

18 With reference to Chapter 3, slacken the hose clips and disconnect the radiator top and bottom coolant hoses from the radiator stubs. Similarly, disconnect the coolant expansion tank hose from the radiator.

19 On models with air conditioning, unplug the wiring harness and then unbolt the refrigerant compressor from its mounting bracket. Secure the compressor to a suitable point at the front of the engine compartment (but not the suspension subframe) using nylon cable ties or similar. Take great care to avoid straining the refrigerant hoses or pipework.

20 Remove the cover from the secondary fusebox, then unscrew the nut and detach the battery supply cable from the side of the fusebox.

21 Unscrew the nut(s) and disconnect the earth cable from the front and top of the transmission casing.

22 Unplug the wiring from the reversing lamp switch at the connector on the top of the transmission casing.

23 With reference to Chapter 5B, disconnect the ignition system LT wiring from the DI cartridge, or distributor, as applicable. On models with Bosch Motronic engine management, disconnect the HT king lead from the distributor.

24 Disconnect the crankshaft sensor, lambda sensor and cooling fan switch wiring at the connectors, located on the mounting bracket at the left hand end of the cylinder head. The connectors are released by pulling out their sliding locking bars.

25 On models with automatic transmission, unplug the breather hose from the front of the transmission casing; plug the open port to prevent the ingress of foreign material.

26 Disconnect the gear selector cable (automatic models) or shaft (manual models) at the rear of the transmission casing; refer to Chapter 7A or 7B for details. On automatic models, also unplug the transmission control system wiring harness, at the two multiway connectors located underneath the engine compartment secondary fusebox.

27 On models with manual transmission, refer to Chapter 6 and disconnect the clutch cable from the top of the transmission. On later models with a hydraulic clutch, disconnect the hydraulic fluid supply pipe from the slave cylinder.

28 On models with central locking, remove the cover panel from the underside of the facia (see Chapter 11) and disconnect the wiring from the central locking control unit. Locate the engine wiring harness connectors mounted nearby and disconnect them. Pull the engine wiring harness carefully through the bulkhead grommet into the engine compartment. Coil up the harness and place it on top of the engine; cover the connectors with a plastic bag to prevent damage and contamination.

29 Remove the right- and left-hand driveshafts, as described in Chapter 8. The intermediate driveshaft together with its bearing and mounting bracket can be left in position.

30 Unbolt the exhaust system front pipe and catalytic converter from the exhaust manifold or turbocharger (as applicable) and intermediate pipe. Unbolt the catalytic converter from its support bracket, then remove the front pipe and catalytic converter from the vehicle.

31 On models with automatic transmission, disconnect the transmission fluid cooler hoses from the transmission and position them to one side; be prepared for some transmission fluid loss as you do this. Plug the open ports to prevent contamination.

32 On Turbo models, undo the unions and disconnect the supply and return hoses from the engine oil cooler. Plug the hoses to prevent contamination.

33 Position an engine lifting hoist over the engine compartment. Attach the lifting jib to the eyelets at either end of the cylinder head. Raise the hoist until it is just taking the weight of the engine.

34 With reference to Chapter 2A, Section 17 detach the rear engine mounting from the front suspension subframe by slackening the centre bolt and withdrawing it through the access hole in the underside of the subframe.

35 Refer to Chapter 10 and unbolt both suspension lower arm balljoints from the underside of the hub carriers. If required, unbolt the ends of the anti-roll bar from the lower arms to increase available clearance.

36 Position a pair of trolley jacks underneath the suspension subframe and raise them until the jack heads rest against the underside of the subframe. Mark around the periphery of the subframe to act as a guide to correct alignment on refitting **(see illustration)**.

37 Progressively slacken and withdraw each of the six subframe securing bolts. Note that the bolts are of different lengths and diameters - make a note of their fitted positions to aid refitting. Ensure that the engine hoist is taking the weight of the engine/transmission as the unit will tend to pivot towards the rear of the engine compartment as the subframe is removed.

38 Slowly lower the subframe away from the underside of the engine compartment using the trolley jacks. Recover the spacer washers fitted to the two rearmost bolts **(see illustrations)**.

39 Unbolt and remove the right- and left-hand engine/transmission mountings, with reference to Chapter 2A, Section 17.

40 Make a final check that any components which would prevent the removal of the engine/transmission from the car have been removed or disconnected. Ensure that components such as the gearchange selector rod, clutch cable and accelerator cable are secured so that they cannot be damaged on removal.

41 Slowly lower the engine/transmission assembly from the engine compartment, making sure that it clears the components on the surrounding panels **(see illustration)**. In particular, make sure that it clears the ABS unit and the radiator. Enlist the help of an assistant during this procedure, as it may be necessary to tilt and twist the assembly slightly to clear the body panels. Lower the assembly to the ground and remove it from the underside of the engine compartment.

Separation of transmission from engine

42 If the engine is to be dismantled, working as described in Chapter 1, drain the oil and if required remove the oil filter. Clean and refit the drain plug, tightening it securely.

43 Support the engine/transmission assembly on suitable blocks of wood, on a workbench (or failing that, on a clean area of the workshop floor).

44 Remove the starter motor with reference to Chapter 5A.

45 If the alternator has not yet been removed, unscrew the nut and disconnect the lead from the rear of the alternator. Also disconnect the charge warning light lead from the alternator. Unscrew the alternator mounting bolts and withdraw the alternator from the engine, with reference to Chapter 5A.

Manual transmission models

46 On Turbo models, unscrew the bolt securing the turbo oil pipe bracket to the transmission.

47 Unbolt and remove the flywheel protection plate from the underside of the transmission bellhousing.

48 Ensure that both engine and transmission are adequately supported, then with reference to Chapter 7A, unscrew the bolts securing the transmission housing to the engine. Note the correct fitted positions of each bolt as they are removed, to use as a reference on refitting. Withdraw the transmission directly from the engine **(see illustration)**. Take care not to allow the weight of the transmission to bear on the input shaft and clutch friction plate.

4.38a Slowly lower the subframe away from the underside of the engine compartment using the trolley jacks

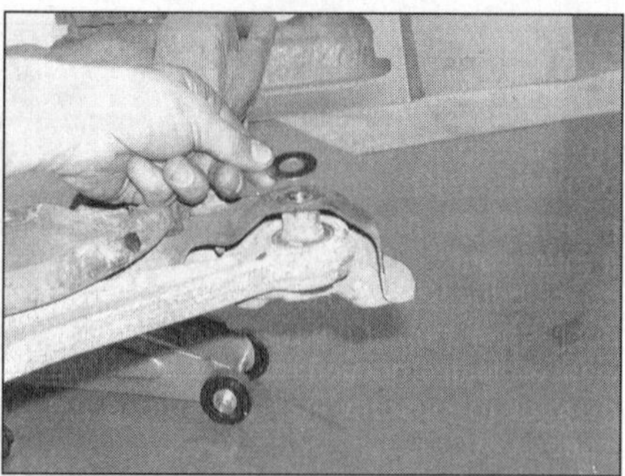

4.38b Recover the spacer washers fitted to the two rearmost bolts

Automatic transmission models

49 Remove the breather valve from the top of the transmission.

50 Working through the aperture exposed by the removal of the bellhousing lower cover plate, unscrew the bolts securing the flywheel to the torque converter. To bring each bolt into view, turn the engine using a socket on the crankshaft pulley bolt.

51 Saab technicians use a special tool to hold the torque converter inside the transmission while the transmission is separated from the engine. The tool is quite basic, and consists of a plate which engages the torque converter through the timing hole in the top of the transmission.

52 Support the weight of the transmission, preferably using a hoist.

53 Ensure that both engine and transmission are adequately supported, then unscrew the bolts securing the transmission housing to the engine. Note the correct fitted positions of each bolt as they are removed, to use as a reference on refitting. Withdraw the transmission directly from the engine (see Chapter 7B for details). Make sure that the torque converter stays inside the transmission bellhousing, otherwise it may fall out and be damaged.

Reconnection of transmission to engine

Automatic transmission models

54 Carefully offer the transmission to the engine. Make sure that the torque converter is held fully engaged with the transmission, using the special tool described earlier in this procedure.

55 Insert and tighten to the specified torque the bolts securing the transmission to the engine.

56 Remove the special tool, then insert and tighten to the specified torque the three bolts securing the flywheel to the torque converter. Turn the engine by means of a socket on the crankshaft pulley.

57 Refit the breather valve to the top of the transmission.

Manual transmission models

Caution: If a new clutch slave cylinder has been fitted, or if any hydraulic fluid has been allowed to drain from the existing slave cylinder, the cylinder must be primed and bled BEFORE the transmission is refitted; see Chapter 6 for details.

58 Apply a smear of high-melting-point grease to the splines of the transmission input shaft. Do not apply too much, otherwise there is a possibility of the grease contaminating the clutch friction plate.

59 Carefully offer the transmission to the engine. Ensure that the weight of the transmission is not allowed to hang on the input shaft as it is engaged with the clutch

4.41 Slowly lower the engine/transmission assembly from the engine compartment

4.48 Separating the transmission from the engine (manual transmission shown)

4.63 Guide the engine/transmission assembly into the engine compartment carefully, to ensure that it clears all surrounding components

friction disc. Insert and tighten to the specified torque the bolts securing the transmission to the engine.

60 Refit the lower cover plate to the transmission bellhousing, and tighten the bolts.

61 On Turbo models, insert and tighten the bolts securing the turbo oil pipe bracket to the transmission.

All models

62 Refit the starter motor and alternator with reference to Chapter 5A.

Refitting

63 Refit the engine and transmission by following the removal procedure in reverse, noting the following points **(see illustration)**:

a) Hoist the engine and transmission into position in the engine compartment, then refit the right- and left-hand engine mountings as described in Chapter 2A. Refit the suspension subframe ensuring that the spacer washers are fitted to the two rearmost bolts, observing the alignment markings made during removal. Delay tighten the subframe securing bolts to their final torque until the rear engine mounting has been refitted.

b) Tighten all nuts and bolts to the specified torque.

c) Renew all copper sealing washers on unions, as applicable.

d) Reconnect the accelerator cable with reference to Chapter 4A as applicable.

e) With reference to Chapter 6, reconnect the clutch cable. On later models with a hydraulic clutch, reconnect the fluid supply pipe to the slave cylinder, then bleed the clutch hydraulic system.

f) Ensure that all wiring has been securely reconnected, and all nuts and bolts have been tightened.

g) Refill the engine and transmission with the correct quantity and grade of oil/fluid, with reference to Chapter 1.

h) Refill the cooling system with reference to Chapter 1.

i) Check and if necessary top-up the power steering fluid, with reference to "Weekly checks".

5 Engine overhaul - dismantling sequence

1 It is much easier to dismantle and work on the engine if it is mounted on a portable engine stand. These stands can often be hired from a tool hire shop. Before the engine is mounted on a stand, the flywheel/driveplate should be removed, so that the stand bolts can be tightened into the end of the cylinder block/crankcase.

2 If a stand is not available, it is possible to dismantle the engine with it blocked up on a sturdy workbench, or on the floor. Be extra careful not to tip or drop the engine when working without a stand.

3 If you are going to obtain a reconditioned engine, all the external components must be removed first, to be transferred to the replacement engine (just as they will if you are doing a complete engine overhaul yourself). These components normally include the following, but check with your engine supplier first:

a) Alternator mounting bracket (Chapter 5A).

b) The distributor (where applicable), HT leads or Direct Ignition cartridge and spark plugs, as applicable (Chapter 1 and Chapter 5B).

c) Thermostat and housing (Chapter 3).

d) The dipstick tube, where applicable.

e) Air conditioning compressor mounting bracket (Chapter 3).

f) The fuel injection system and emission control components (Chapter 4A and 4B).

g) All electrical switches and sensors, and the engine wiring harness.

h) Inlet and exhaust manifolds (Chapter 4A).

i) Oil filter (Chapter 1).

j) Engine mounting brackets (Part A of this Chapter).

k) Flywheel/driveplate (Part A of this Chapter).

When removing the external components from the engine, pay close attention to details that may be helpful or important during refitting. Note the fitted position of gaskets, seals, spacers, pins, washers, bolts, and other small items.

4 If you are obtaining a "short" engine (which consists of the engine cylinder block/crankcase, crankshaft, pistons and connecting rods all assembled), then the cylinder head and sump will have to be removed also.

5 If you are planning a complete overhaul, the engine can be dismantled, and the internal components removed, in the order given below, referring to Part A of this Chapter unless otherwise stated:

a) Inlet and exhaust manifolds (Chapter 4A).

b) Cylinder head (Chapter 2A).

c) Timing chain and balance shaft chain, sprockets and tensioners (Chapter 2A).

d) Flywheel/driveplate (Chapter 2A).

e) Balance shafts (where applicable) (Section 9).

f) Sump (Chapter 2A).

g) Piston/connecting rod assemblies (Section 10).

h) Crankshaft (Section 11).

6 Before beginning the dismantling and overhaul procedures, make sure that you have all of the correct tools necessary. Refer to "*Tools and working facilities*" for further information.

6 Cylinder head - dismantling

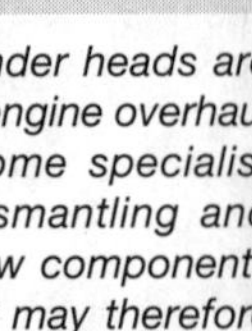

Note: *New/reconditioned cylinder heads are obtainable from Saab, or from engine overhaul specialists. Be aware that some specialist tools are required for the dismantling and inspection procedures, and new components may not be readily available. It may therefore be more practical and economical for the home mechanic to purchase a reconditioned head, rather than dismantle, inspect and recondition the original head.*

1 Remove the cylinder head as described in Part A, then unbolt the external components including manifolds, engine lifting eyes and the distributor blanking plug, according to model **(see illustrations)**.

2 Remove the camshafts and hydraulic cam

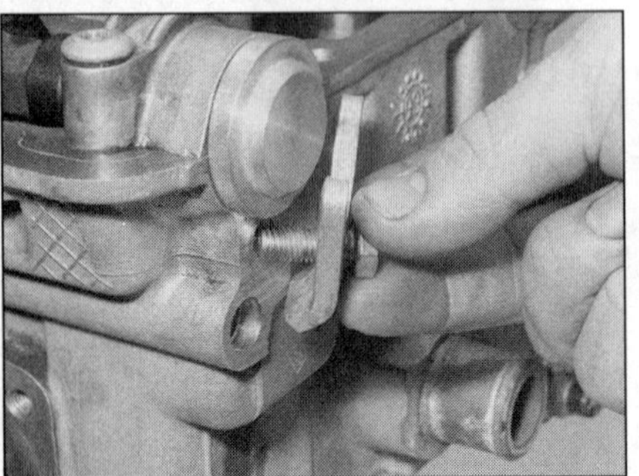

6.1a Unbolt the clamp . . .

6.1b . . . and remove the distributor blanking plug

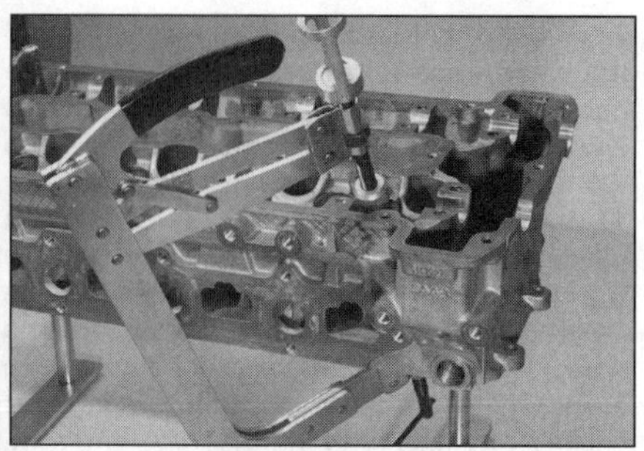

6.4a Using a compressor to compress the valve springs in order to remove the split collets

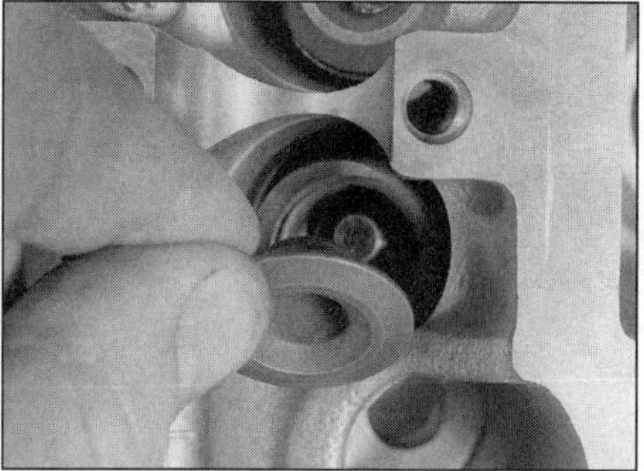

6.4b Removing the spring retainer . . .

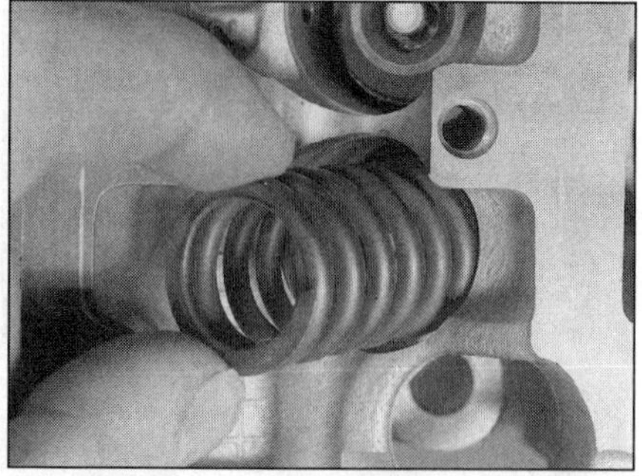

6.4c . . . valve spring . . .

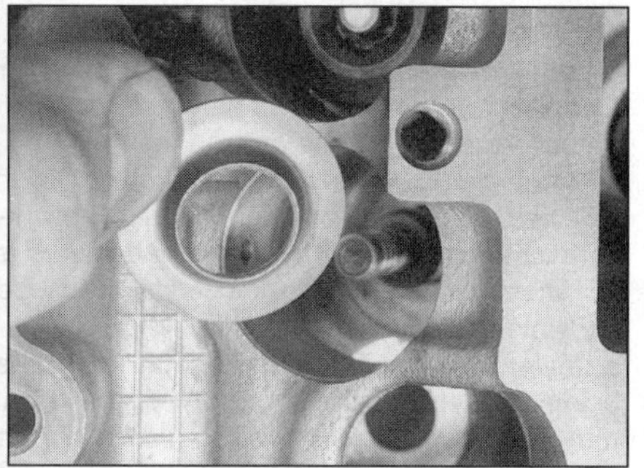

6.4d . . . and seat

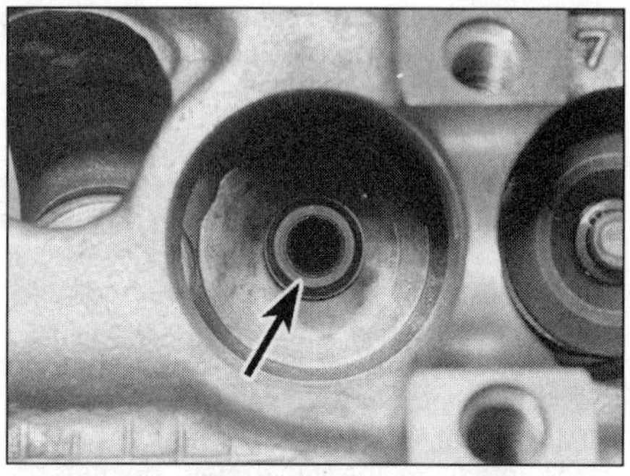

6.4e Valve stem seal location

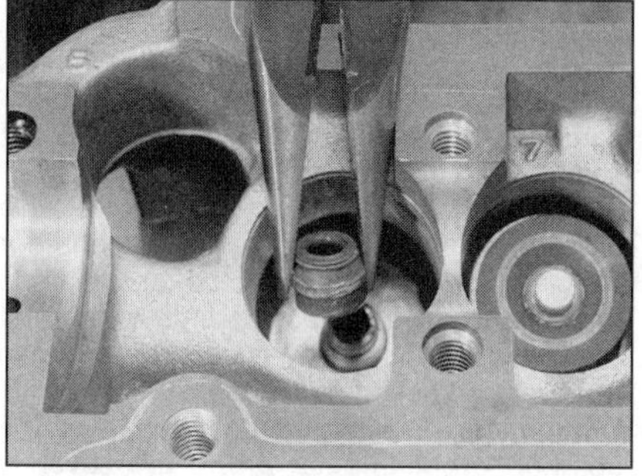

6.4f Removing a valve stem seal

followers, with reference to Chapter 2A.

3 Before removing the valves, consider obtaining plastic protectors for the hydraulic cam follower bores. When using certain valve spring compressors, the bores can easily be damaged, should the compressor slip off the end of the valve. The bores form a sealing surface around the hydraulic cam followers and will cause leakage if damaged.

The cam follower bore protectors can be obtained from a Saab dealer; alternatively, a protector may be made out of plastic cut from a washing-up liquid container or similar.

4 Position the protector in the cam follower bore, then using a valve spring compressor, compress the valve spring until the split collets can be removed. Release the compressor, and lift off the spring retainer, spring and seat. Using a pair of pliers, carefully extract the valve stem seal from the top of the guide **(see illustrations)**.

5 If, when the valve spring compressor is screwed down the spring retainer sticks, gently tap the top of the tool, directly over the retainer, with a light hammer. This will free the retainer.

6 Withdraw the valve through the combustion chamber.

7 It is essential that each valve is stored together with its collets, retainer, spring, and spring seat. The valves should also be kept in their correct sequence, unless they are so badly worn that they are to be renewed. If they are going to be kept and used again, place each valve assembly in a labelled polythene bag or similar small container **(see illustrations)**. Note that No 1 cylinder is nearest to the timing chain end of the engine.

8 With all the valves removed, use a pair of pliers to pull the valve seals from the tops of the guides.

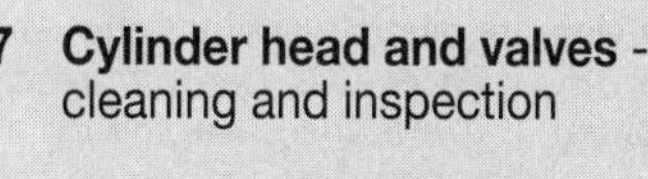

7 Cylinder head and valves - cleaning and inspection

1 Thorough cleaning of the cylinder head and valve components, followed by a detailed inspection, will enable you to decide how much valve service work must be carried out during the engine overhaul. **Note:** *If the engine has been severely overheated, it is best to assume that the cylinder head is warped - check carefully for signs of this.*

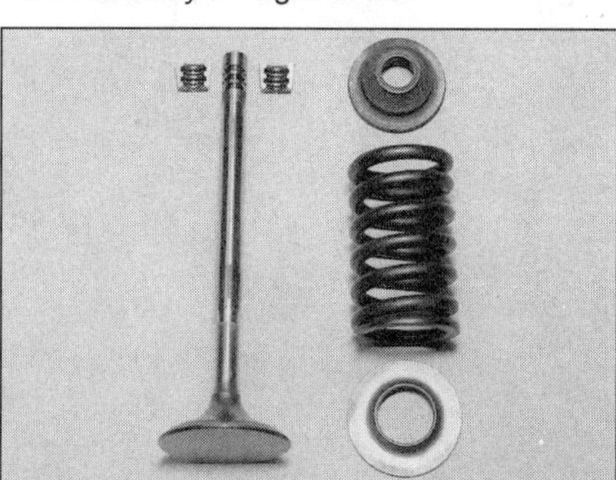

6.7a The valve spring components

Cleaning

2 Scrape away all traces of old gasket material from the cylinder head.

3 Scrape away the carbon from the combustion chambers and ports, then wash the cylinder head thoroughly with paraffin or a suitable solvent.

4 Scrape off any heavy carbon deposits that may have formed on the valves, then use a power-operated wire brush to remove deposits from the valve heads and stems. Take great care to avoid eroding metal from the sealing surface of the valve head or the valve stems.

Inspection

Note: *Be sure to perform all the following inspection procedures before concluding that the services of a machine shop or engine overhaul specialist are required. Make a list of all items that require attention.*

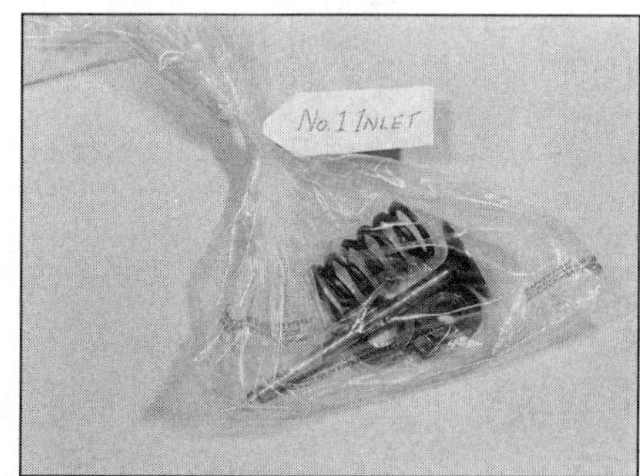

6.7b Place each valve and its associated components in a labelled polythene bag

7.6 Checking the cylinder head gasket face for distortion

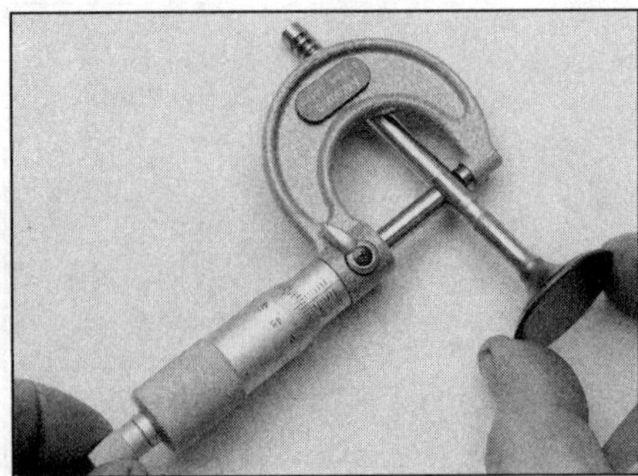

7.10 Measuring a valve stem diameter

Cylinder head

5 Inspect the head very carefully for cracks, evidence of coolant leakage, and other damage. If cracks are found, a new cylinder head should be obtained.

6 Use a straight-edge and feeler blade to check that the cylinder head surface is not distorted **(see illustration)**. If it is, it may be possible to have it machined, provided that the cylinder head is not reduced to less than the specified height.

7 Examine the valve seats in each of the combustion chambers. If they are severely pitted, cracked, or burned, they will need to be renewed or re-cut by an engine overhaul specialist. If they are only slightly pitted, this can be removed by grinding-in the valve heads and seats with fine valve-grinding compound, as described below. Note that the exhaust valves have a hardened coating and, although they may be ground-in with paste, they must not be machined.

8 Check the valve guides for wear by inserting the relevant valve, and checking for side-to-side motion of the valve. A very small amount of movement is acceptable. If the movement seems excessive, remove the valve. Measure the valve stem diameter (see below), and renew the valve if it is worn. If the valve stem is not worn, the wear must be in the valve guide, and the guide must be renewed. The renewal of valve guides is best carried out by a Saab dealer or engine overhaul specialist, who will have the necessary tools available.

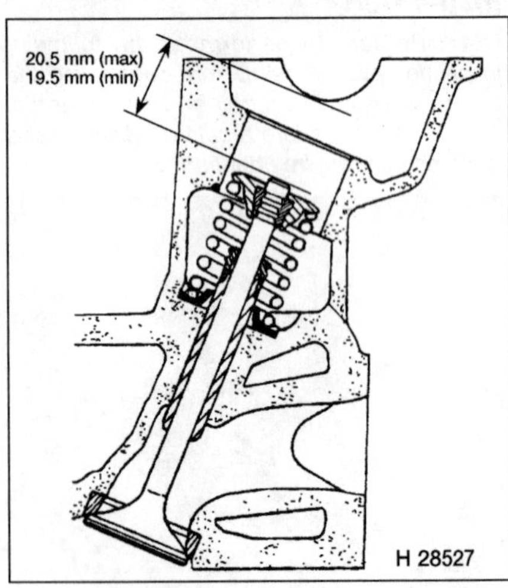

7.16 Check the depth of the valve stems below the camshaft bearing surface

Valves

9 Examine the head of each valve for pitting, burning, cracks, and general wear. Check the valve stem for scoring and wear ridges. Rotate the valve, and check for any obvious indication that it is bent. Look for pits and excessive wear on the tip of each valve stem. Renew any valve that shows any such signs of wear or damage.

10 If the valve appears satisfactory at this stage, measure the valve stem diameter at several points using a micrometer **(see illustration)**. Any significant difference in the readings obtained indicates wear of the valve stem. Should any of these conditions be apparent, the valve(s) must be renewed.

11 If the valves are in satisfactory condition, they should be ground (lapped) into their respective seats, to ensure a smooth, gas-tight seal. If the seat is only lightly pitted, or if it has been re-cut, fine grinding compound should be used to produce the required finish. Coarse valve-grinding compound should *not* be used, unless a seat is badly burned or deeply pitted. If this is the case, the cylinder head and valves should be inspected by an expert, to decide whether seat re-cutting, or even the renewal of the valve or seat insert (where possible) is required.

12 Valve grinding is carried out as follows. Place the cylinder head upside-down on a bench.

13 Smear a trace of (the appropriate grade of) valve-grinding compound on the seat face, and press a suction grinding tool onto the valve head. With a semi-rotary action, grind the valve head to its seat, lifting the valve occasionally to redistribute the grinding compound. A light spring placed under the valve head will greatly ease this operation.

7.18 Checking the valve spring free length

14 If coarse grinding compound is being used, work only until a dull, matt even surface is produced on both the valve seat and the valve, then wipe off the used compound, and repeat the process with fine compound. When a smooth unbroken ring of light grey matt finish is produced on both the valve and seat, the grinding operation is complete. *Do not* grind-in the valves any further than absolutely necessary, or the seat will be prematurely sunk into the cylinder head.

15 When all the valves have been ground-in, carefully wash off *all* traces of grinding compound using paraffin or a suitable solvent, before reassembling the cylinder head.

16 To ensure that the hydraulic cam followers operate correctly, the depth of the valve stems below the camshaft bearing surface must be within certain limits. It may be possible to obtain a Saab checking tool from a dealer, but if not, the check may be made using a steel rule and straight-edge. Check that the dimension is within the limits given in the Specifications by inserting each valve in its guide in turn, and measuring the dimension between the end of the valve stem and the camshaft bearing surface **(see illustration)**.

17 If the dimension is not within the specified limits, adjustment must be made either to the end of the valve stem or to the valve seat height. If lower than the minimum amount, the length of the valve stem must be reduced, and if more than the maximum amount, the valve seat must be milled. Seek the advice of a Saab dealer or engine reconditioning specialist.

Valve components

18 Examine the valve springs for signs of damage and discoloration, and measure their free length **(see illustration)**.

19 Stand each spring on a flat surface, and check it for squareness **(see illustration)**. If any of the springs are less than the minimum free length, or are damaged, distorted or have lost their tension, obtain a complete new set of springs.

20 Obtain new valve stem oil seals, regardless of their apparent condition.

7.19 Checking the valve springs for squareness

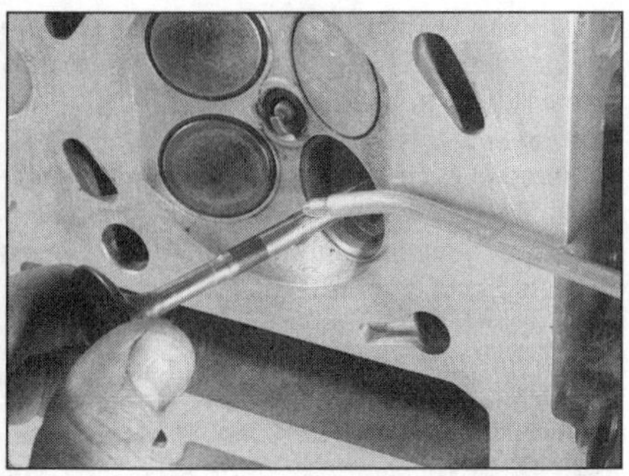
8.1 Inserting a valve in the cylinder head

8.2 Using a socket to fit the valve stem seals

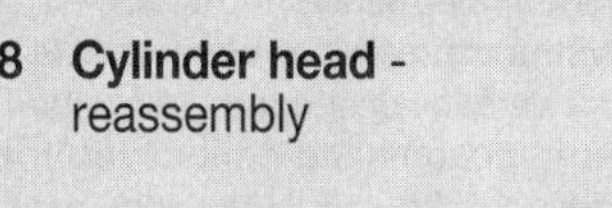

8 Cylinder head - reassembly

1 Lubricate the stems of the valves, and insert the valves into their original locations **(see illustration)**. If new valves are being fitted, insert them into the locations to which they have been ground.

2 Working on the first valve, dip the new valve stem seal in clean engine oil. Carefully locate it over the valve and onto the guide. Take care not to damage the seal as it is passed over the valve stem. Use a suitable socket or metal tube to press the seal firmly onto the guide **(see illustration)**.

3 Refit the valve spring followed by the spring retainer, then locate the plastic protector in the hydraulic cam follower bore.

4 Compress the valve spring, and locate the split collets in the recess in the valve stem **(see Haynes Hint)**. Release the compressor and remove the protector, then repeat the procedure on the remaining valves.

5 With all the valves installed, place the cylinder head flat on the bench and, using a hammer and interposed block of wood, tap the end of each valve stem to settle the components.

6 Refit the hydraulic cam followers and camshafts with reference to Part A, Section 8.

7 Refit the external components removed in Section 6. When refitting the distributor blanking plug, check and if necessary renew the O-ring seal.

8 The cylinder head may now be refitted as described in Part A of this Chapter.

Use a little dab of grease to locate the collets on the valve stems, and to hold them in place while the spring compressor is released

9 Balance shafts - removal, inspection and refitting

Removal

1 Position the crankshaft at TDC on the compression for No 1 piston (timing chain end of the engine) as described in Chapter 2A.

2 Remove the timing cover as described in Chapter 2A.

3 The balance shafts are "timed" at TDC, but since they rotate at twice the speed of the crankshaft, they may also be correctly "timed" at BDC. Check that the timing marks on the shafts are correctly aligned with the marks on the bearing brackets. As an extra precaution, apply dabs of paint to the chain and sprockets, to ensure correct refitting. Note that the balance shaft sprockets are marked "inlet" and "exhaust" for position, but the front bearings are marked identically. However, as the bearings are located with single bolts, the "inlet" and "exhaust" marks will always be correctly located at the top of the bearings.

4 Unbolt the balance shaft chain upper guide, then remove the tensioner and side guide.

5 Unscrew the retaining bolt and remove the idler from the block.

6 Release the chain from the balance shaft sprockets and crankshaft sprocket.

7 Unscrew the bearing retaining bolts, and withdraw the balance shafts from the cylinder block **(see illustrations)**. Keep the shafts identified for position.

Caution: Take great care to avoid scoring the inside of the bearing with the lobes of the balance shaft as it is withdrawn.

8 Unscrew the retaining bolts, and remove the sprockets from the ends of the balance shafts, while holding each shaft in a soft-jawed vice.

Inspection

9 Clean the balance shafts and examine the bearing journals for wear and damage. The bearings inside the cylinder block should also be examined. If these are excessively worn or damaged, get advice from a Saab dealer or engine reconditioning specialist. Although the bearings can be renewed, the renewal procedure requires access to specialised workshop equipment.

9.7a Unscrew the bearing retaining bolts . . .

9.7b . . . and withdraw the exhaust balance shaft from the cylinder block

9.7c Removing the inlet balance shaft from the cylinder block

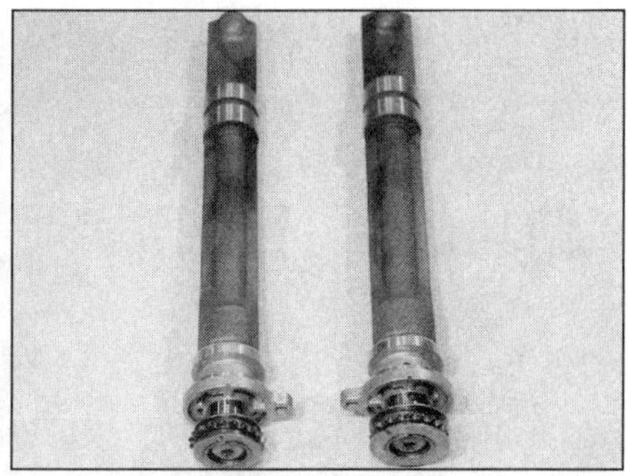
9.7d The two balance shafts removed from the engine

10.5a Removing a big-end bearing cap

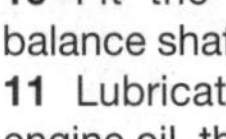

Refitting

10 Fit the sprockets to the ends of the balance shafts, and tighten the retaining bolts.

11 Lubricate the bearing journals with clean engine oil, then insert the balance shafts in the cylinder block in their correct positions.

12 Locate the balance shaft chain sprocket on the front of the crankshaft, with the word "Saab" facing outwards.

13 Fit the chain to the sprockets, and refit the idler to the front of the block, making sure that the timing marks remain aligned correctly.

14 Refit the side guide, tensioner and upper guide to the balance shaft chain.

15 Rotate the crankshaft one turn, and check that the balance shaft sprockets are still correctly aligned.

16 Refit the timing cover with reference to Chapter 2A.

11.5 The main bearing caps are numbered from the timing chain end of the engine

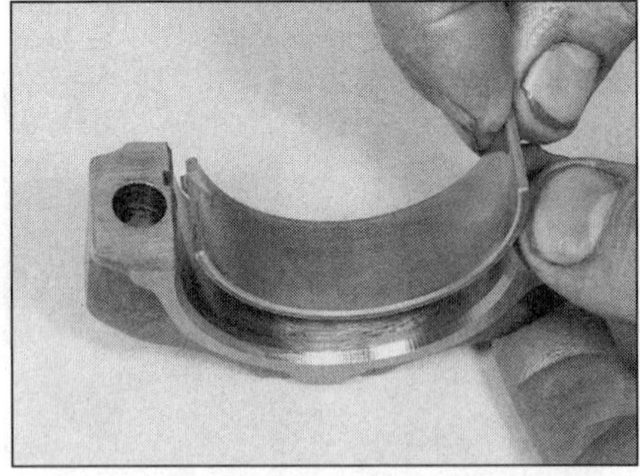

10.5b Removing a bearing shell from a big-end bearing cap

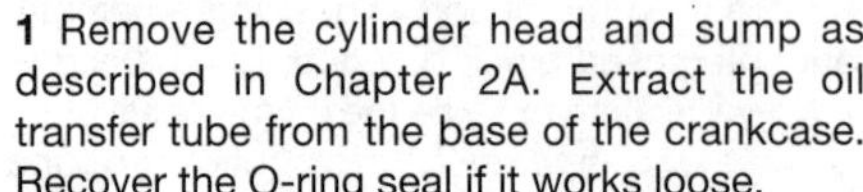

10 Piston/connecting rod assembly - removal

1 Remove the cylinder head and sump as described in Chapter 2A. Extract the oil transfer tube from the base of the crankcase. Recover the O-ring seal if it works loose.

2 If there is a pronounced wear ridge at the top of any bore, it may be necessary to remove it with a scraper or ridge reamer, to avoid piston damage during removal. Such a ridge indicates excessive wear of the cylinder bore.

3 Using a hammer and centre-punch, paint or similar, mark each connecting rod big-end bearing cap with its respective cylinder number on the flat machined surface provided; if the engine has been dismantled before, note carefully any identifying marks made previously.

4 Turn the crankshaft to bring pistons 1 and 4 to BDC (bottom dead centre).

5 Unscrew the nuts from No 1 piston big-end bearing cap. Take off the cap, and recover the bottom half bearing shell. If the bearing shells are to be re-used, tape the cap and the shell together **(see illustrations)**.

6 To prevent the possibility of damage to the crankshaft bearing journals, tape over the connecting rod stud threads.

7 Using a hammer handle, push the piston up through the bore, and remove it from the top of the cylinder block. Recover the bearing shell, and tape it to the connecting rod for safe-keeping.

8 Loosely refit the big-end cap to the connecting rod, and secure with the nuts - this will help to keep the components in their correct order.

9 Remove No 4 piston assembly in the same way.

10 Turn the crankshaft through 180° to bring pistons 2 and 3 to BDC (bottom dead centre), and remove them in the same way.

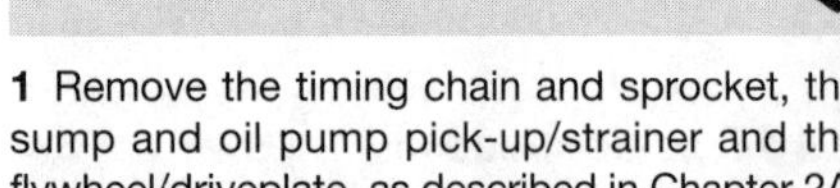

11 Crankshaft - removal

1 Remove the timing chain and sprocket, the sump and oil pump pick-up/strainer and the flywheel/driveplate, as described in Chapter 2A.

2 Remove the pistons and connecting rods, as described in Section 10. **Note:** *If no work is to be done on the pistons and connecting rods, there is no need to remove the cylinder head, or to push the pistons out of the cylinder bores. The pistons should just be pushed far enough up the bores so that they are positioned clear of the crankshaft journals.*

3 Check the crankshaft endfloat with reference to Section 14, then proceed as follows.

4 Unbolt and remove the crankshaft rear oil seal housing from the end of the cylinder block, noting the correct fitted locations of the locating dowels. If the locating dowels are a loose fit, remove them and store them with the housing for safe-keeping. Remove the gasket.

5 Cylinder identification numbers should already be cast onto the base of each main bearing cap **(see illustration)**. If not, number the cap and crankcase using a centre-punch as was done for the connecting rods and caps.

6 Unscrew and remove the main bearing cap retaining bolts, and withdraw the caps complete with bearing shells **(see illustrations)**. Tap the caps with a wooden or plastic-faced mallet if they are stuck.

7 Remove the bearing shells from the caps, but keep them with their relevant caps and identified for position to ensure correct refitting **(see illustration)**.

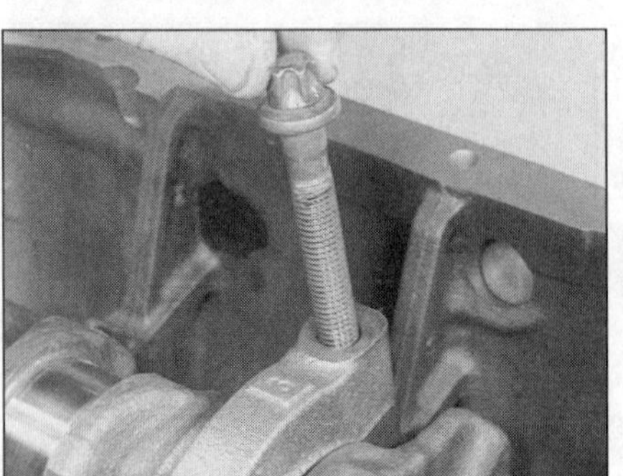

11.6a Unscrew and remove the main bearing cap bolts . . .

11.6b . . . and remove the main bearing caps

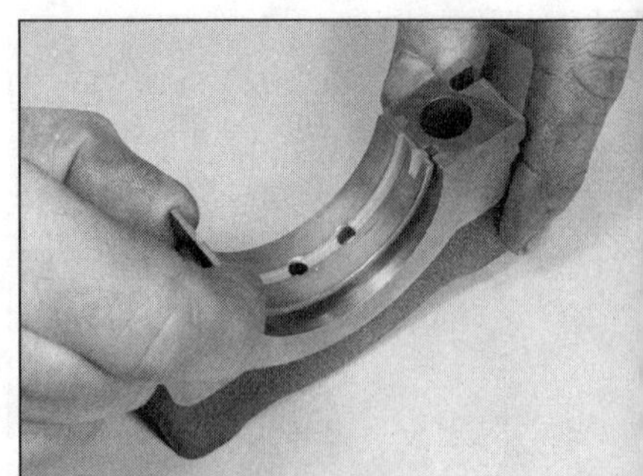

11.7 Removing a main bearing shell from its cap

11.8 Lifting the crankshaft from the crankcase

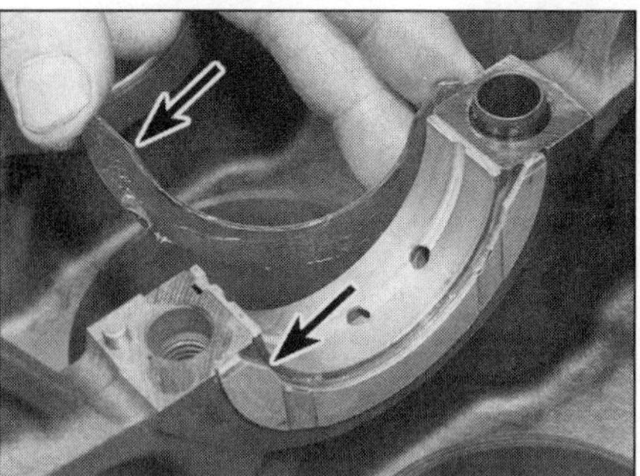

11.9a Removing the thrustwashers (arrowed) . . .

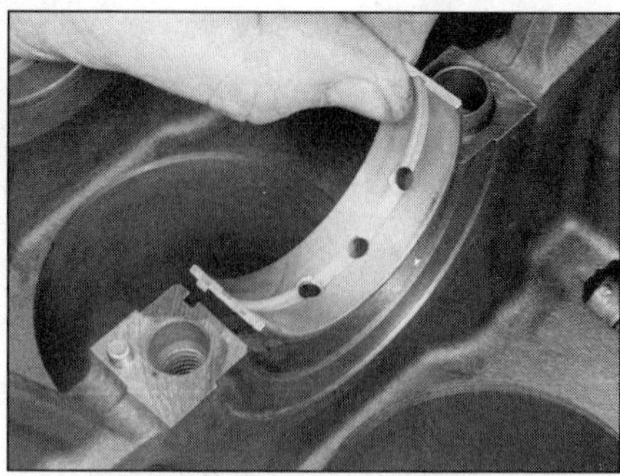

11.9b . . . and main bearing shells

8 Carefully lift the crankshaft from the crankcase **(see illustration)**. Take great care to avoid damaging the reluctor ring.

9 Remove the upper bearing shells from the crankcase, keeping them identified for position. Also remove the thrustwashers at each side of the centre main bearing, and store them with the bearing cap **(see illustrations)**.

10 With the crankshaft removed, the crankshaft position sensor reluctor may be removed if necessary, by unscrewing the screws and withdrawing the reluctor over the end of the crankshaft **(see illustration)**. Note that the screws are arranged so that it is only possible to refit the reluctor in one position.

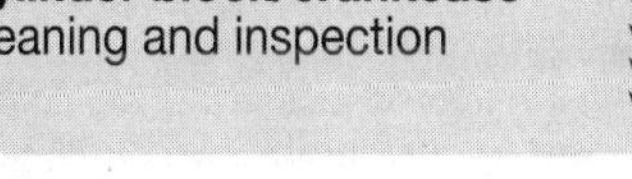

12 Cylinder block/crankcase - cleaning and inspection

Cleaning

1 Remove all external components and electrical switches/sensors from the block. For complete cleaning, the core plugs should ideally be removed, as follows. Drill a small hole in the plugs, then insert a self-tapping screw into the hole. Pull out the plugs by pulling on the screw with a pair of grips, or by using a slide hammer. Also unbolt the four piston oil jets from the crankcase on Turbo engines **(see illustration)**.

2 Scrape all traces of sealant from the cylinder block/crankcase, taking care not to damage the gasket/sealing surfaces.

3 Remove all oil gallery plugs (where fitted). The plugs are usually very tight - they may have to be drilled out, and the holes re-tapped. Use new plugs when the engine is reassembled.

4 If the cylinder block/crankcase is extremely dirty, it should be steam-cleaned.

5 Clean all oil holes and oil galleries, and flush all internal passages with warm water until the water runs clear. Dry thoroughly, and apply a light film of oil to all mating surfaces, to prevent rusting. Also oil the cylinder bores. If you have access to compressed air, use it to speed up the drying process, and to blow out all the oil holes and galleries.

Warning: Wear eye protection when using compressed air!

6 If the cylinder block is not very dirty, you can do an adequate cleaning job with very hot, soapy water and a stiff brush. Take plenty of time, and do a thorough job. Regardless of the cleaning method used, be sure to clean all oil holes and galleries very thoroughly, and to dry all components well. On completion, protect the cylinder bores as described above, to prevent rusting.

7 All threaded holes must be clean, to ensure accurate torque readings during reassembly. To clean the threads, run the correct-size tap into each of the holes to remove rust, corrosion, thread sealant or sludge, and to restore damaged threads **(see illustration)**. If possible, use compressed air to clear the holes of debris produced by this operation.

Warning: Wear eye protection when cleaning out these holes in this way!

8 Apply suitable sealant to the new oil gallery plugs, and insert them into the holes in the block. Tighten them securely. Refit and tighten the piston oil jets to the bottom of the crankcase on Turbo engines.

9 If the engine is not going to be reassembled right away, cover it with a large plastic bag to keep it clean; protect all mating surfaces and the cylinder bores as described above, to prevent rusting.

Inspection

10 Visually check the cylinder block for cracks and corrosion. Look for stripped threads in the threaded holes. If there has been any history of internal water leakage, it may be worthwhile having an engine overhaul specialist check the cylinder block/crankcase with special equipment. If defects are found, have them repaired if possible; otherwise, a new block will be needed.

11 Check each cylinder bore for scuffing and scoring. Check for signs of a wear ridge at the top of the cylinder, indicating that the bore is excessively worn.

12 The cylinder bores and pistons are matched and classified according to five codes (see *"Specifications"*). The code is stamped on the piston crowns, and on the front of the cylinder block **(see illustrations)**. Note that any combination of classifications may occur on a cylinder block.

13 Wear of the cylinder bores and pistons can be measured by inserting the relevant piston (without piston rings) in its bore and using a feeler blade. Alternatively, hire or borrow a proprietary bore gauge. Make the

2B

11.10 Location of the screws securing the crankshaft position sensor reluctor

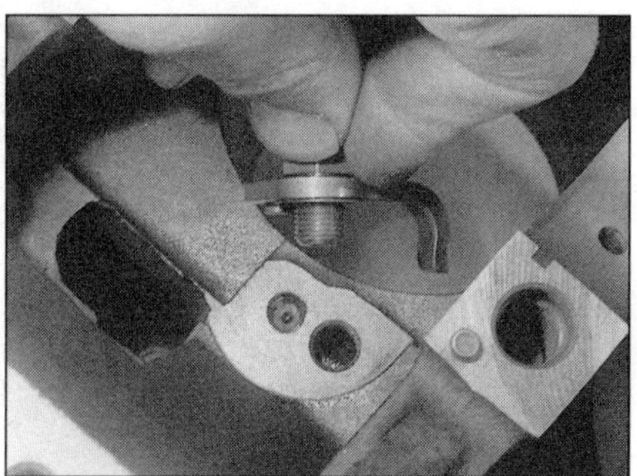

12.1 Removing an oil jet from the crankcase

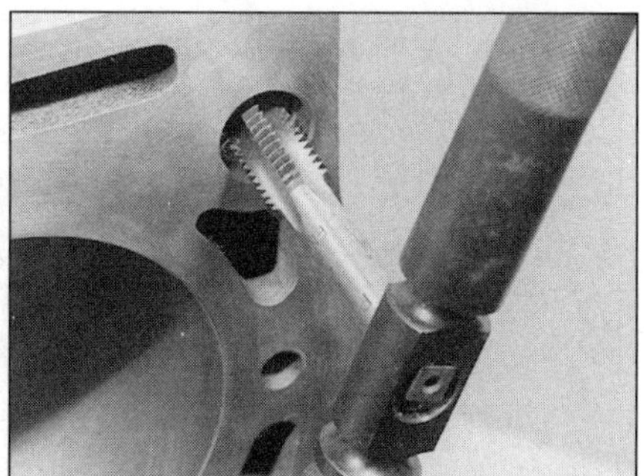

12.7 Cleaning a cylinder head bolt hole in the cylinder block using a tap

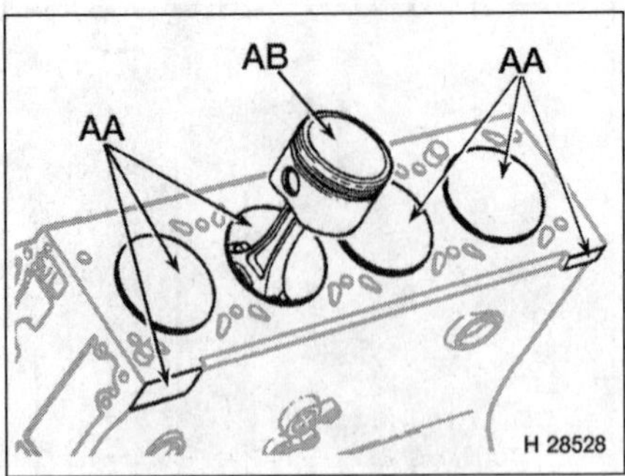

12.12a Piston and cylinder bore classification code locations

12.12b Cylinder bore classification on the front of the block

12.12c Piston classification on the piston crown

checks with the piston near the top of its bore, and also at the bottom of its bore, where the most wear occurs. If the clearance is more than the amount given in the Specifications, a reborn should be considered, and the opinion of an engine reconditioner sought. Note that individual pistons made by different manufacturers must not be used in the same engine.

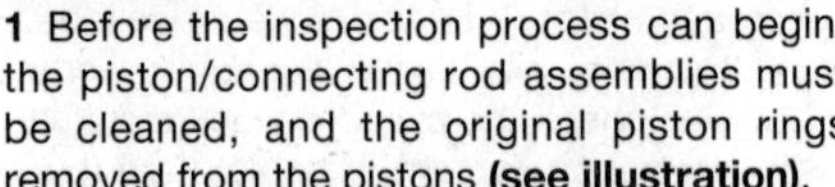

13 Piston/connecting rod assembly - inspection

1 Before the inspection process can begin, the piston/connecting rod assemblies must be cleaned, and the original piston rings removed from the pistons **(see illustration)**.

2 Carefully expand the old rings over the top of the pistons. The use of two or three old feeler blades will be helpful in preventing the rings dropping into empty grooves as they are withdrawn **(see illustrations)**. Be careful not to scratch the piston with the ends of the ring. The rings are brittle, and will snap if they are spread too far. They're also very sharp - protect your hands and fingers. Note that the third ring incorporates an expander. Always remove the rings from the top of the piston. Keep each set of rings with its piston, if the old rings are to be re-used.

3 Scrape away all traces of carbon from the top of the piston. A hand-held wire brush (or a piece of fine emery cloth) can be used, once the majority of the deposits have been scraped away.

4 Remove the carbon from the ring grooves in the piston, using an old ring. Break the ring in half to do this (be careful not to cut your fingers - piston rings are sharp). Be careful to remove only the carbon deposits - do not remove any metal, and do not nick or scratch the sides of the ring grooves.

5 Once the deposits have been removed, clean the piston/connecting rod assembly with paraffin or a suitable solvent, and dry thoroughly. Make sure that the oil return holes in the ring grooves are clear.

6 If the pistons and cylinder bores are not damaged or worn excessively, and if the cylinder block does not need to be rebored, the original pistons can be refitted. Normal piston wear shows up as even vertical wear on the piston thrust surfaces, and slight looseness of the top ring in its groove.

7 Carefully inspect each piston for cracks around the skirt, around the gudgeon pin holes, and at the piston ring "lands" (between the ring grooves).

8 Look for scoring and scuffing on the piston skirt, holes in the piston crown, and burned areas at the edge of the crown. If the skirt is scored or scuffed, the engine may have been suffering from overheating, and/or abnormal combustion which caused excessively high operating temperatures. The cooling and lubrication systems should be checked thoroughly. Scorch marks on the sides of the pistons show that blow-by has occurred. A hole in the piston crown, or burned areas at the edge of the piston crown, indicates that abnormal combustion (pre-ignition, knocking, or detonation) has been occurring. If any of the above problems exist, the causes must be investigated and corrected, or the damage will occur again. The causes may include incorrect ignition timing and/or fuel/air mixture.

9 Corrosion of the piston, in the form of pitting, indicates that coolant has been leaking into the combustion chamber and/or the crankcase. Again, the cause must be corrected, or the problem may persist in the rebuilt engine.

10 Where needed, pistons can be purchased from a Saab dealer.

11 Examine each connecting rod carefully for signs of damage, such as cracks around the big-end and small-end bearings. Check that the rod is not bent or distorted. Damage is highly unlikely, unless the engine has been seized or badly overheated. Detailed checking of the connecting rod assembly can only be carried out by a Saab dealer or engine repair specialist with the necessary equipment.

12 The gudgeon pins are of the floating type, secured in position by two circlips, and the pistons and connecting rods can be separated and reassembled as follows.

13 Using a small flat-bladed screwdriver, prise out the circlips, and push out the gudgeon pin **(see illustrations)**. Hand pressure should be sufficient to remove the pin. Identify the piston, gudgeon pin and rod to ensure correct reassembly.

14 Examine the gudgeon pin and connecting rod small-end bearing for signs of wear or damage. Wear can be cured by renewing both the pin and bush. Bush renewal, however, is a specialist job - hydraulic press facilities are required, and the new bush must be reamed accurately.

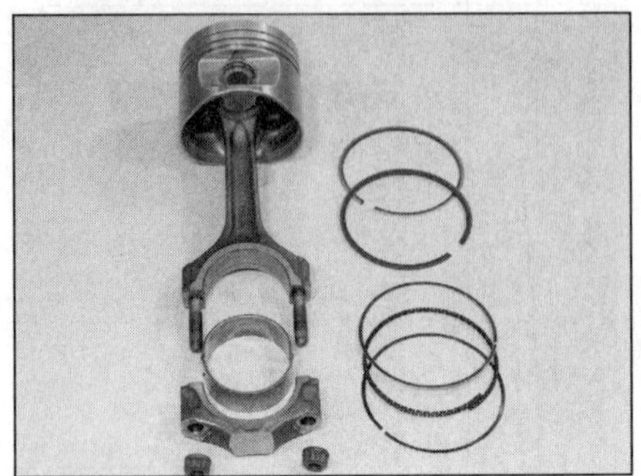

13.1 Piston/connecting rod assembly components

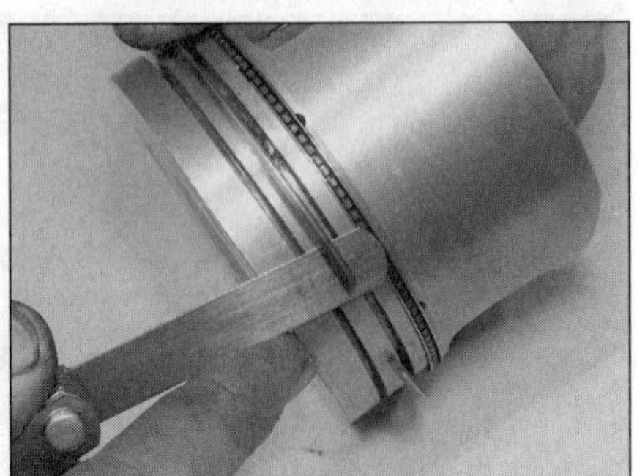

13.2a Removing a piston compression ring with the aid of a feeler blade

13.2b Removing the oil control ring

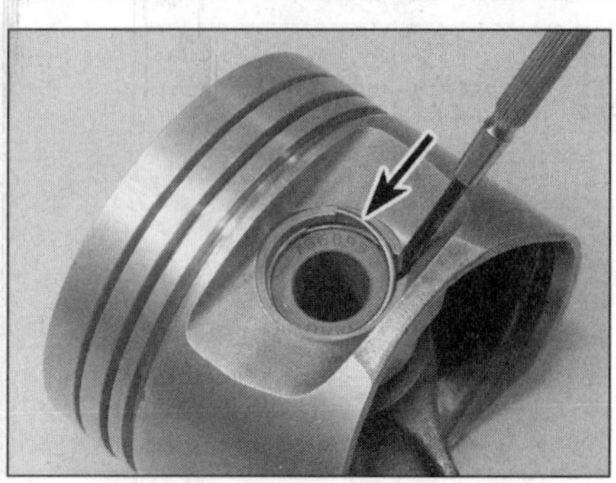

13.13a Prise out the gudgeon pin circlip . . .

13.13b . . . then withdraw the gudgeon pin and separate the piston from the connecting rod

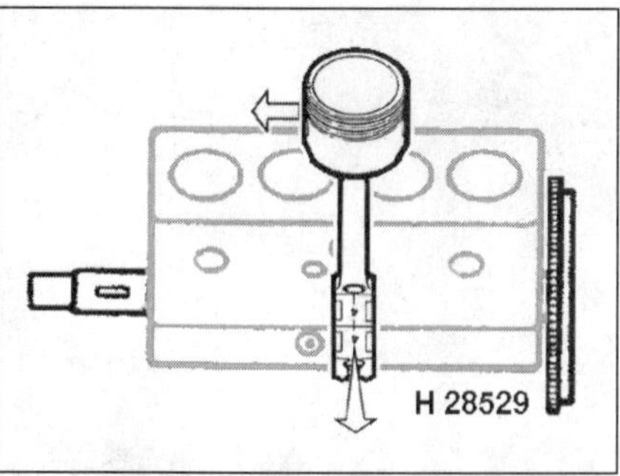

13.17 Relationship of the piston and connecting rod

15 The connecting rods themselves should not be in need of renewal, unless seizure or some other major mechanical failure has occurred. Check the alignment of the connecting rods visually, and if the rods are not straight, take them to an engine overhaul specialist for a more detailed check.

16 Examine all components, and obtain any new parts from your Saab dealer. If new pistons are purchased, they will be supplied complete with gudgeon pins and circlips. Circlips can also be purchased individually.

17 Position the piston so that the arrow stamped onto the crown faces the timing chain end of the engine, and the numbers on the connecting rod and big-end cap face the exhaust side of the cylinder block. With the piston held in your hand and the arrow on the crown facing the left, the connecting rod numbering should face towards you **(see illustration)**. Apply a smear of clean engine oil to the gudgeon pin. Slide it into the piston and through the connecting rod small-end. Check that the piston pivots freely on the rod, then secure the gudgeon pin in position with the circlips. Ensure that each circlip is correctly located in its groove in the piston.

Note: *The circlip end gap must face upwards, ie towards the piston crown.*

18 Measure the piston diameters, and check that they are within limits for the corresponding bore diameters. If the piston-to-bore clearance is excessive, the block will have to be rebored, and new pistons and rings fitted.

14 Crankshaft - inspection

Checking crankshaft endfloat

1 If the crankshaft endfloat is to be checked, this must be done when the crankshaft is still installed in the cylinder block/crankcase, but is free to move (see Section 11).

2 Check the endfloat using a dial gauge in contact with the end of the crankshaft. Push the crankshaft fully one way, and then zero the gauge. Push the crankshaft fully the other way, and check the endfloat **(see illustration)**. The result can be compared with the specified amount, and will give an indication as to whether new thrustwashers are required.

3 If a dial gauge is not available, feeler blades can be used. First push the crankshaft fully towards the flywheel end of the engine, then use feeler blades to measure the gap between the No 3 crankpin web and the centre main bearing thrustwasher **(see illustration)**.

Inspection

4 Clean the crankshaft using paraffin or a suitable solvent, and dry it, preferably with compressed air if available. Be sure to clean the oil holes with a pipe cleaner or similar probe, to ensure that they are not obstructed.

Warning: Wear eye protection when using compressed air!

5 Check the main and big-end bearing journals for uneven wear, scoring, pitting and cracking.

6 Big-end bearing wear is accompanied by distinct metallic knocking when the engine is running (particularly noticeable when the engine is pulling from low speed), and some loss of oil pressure.

7 Main bearing wear is accompanied by severe engine vibration and rumble - getting progressively worse as engine speed increases - and again by loss of oil pressure.

8 Check the bearing journal for roughness by running a finger lightly over the bearing surface. Any roughness (which will be accompanied by obvious bearing wear) indicates that the crankshaft requires regrinding (where possible) or renewal.

9 If the crankshaft has been reground, check for burrs around the crankshaft oil holes (the holes are usually chamfered, so burrs should not be a problem, unless regrinding has been carried out carelessly). Remove any burrs with a fine file or scraper, and thoroughly clean the oil holes as described previously.

10 Using a micrometer, measure the diameter of the main and big-end bearing journals, and compare the results with the Specifications **(see illustration)**. By measuring the diameter at a number of points around each journal's circumference, you will be able to determine whether or not the journal is out-of-round. Take the measurement at each end of the journal, near the webs, to determine if the journal is tapered. Compare the results obtained with those given in the Specifications.

14.2 Using a dial gauge to check the crankshaft endfloat

14.3 Using feeler blades to check the crankshaft endfloat

14.10 Measuring a crankshaft big-end bearing journal diameter

15.1 **"STD" marking on the backing of a big-end bearing shell**

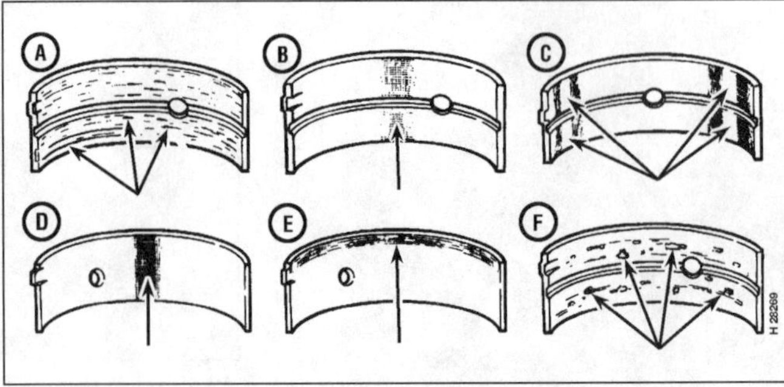

15.2 Typical bearing failures

A Scratched by dirt; dirt embedded into bearing material
B Lack of oil; overlay wiped out
C Improper seating; bright (polished) sections
D Tapered journal; overlay gone from entire surface
E Radius ride
F Fatigue failure; craters or pockets

11 Check the oil seal contact surfaces at each end of the crankshaft for wear and damage. If the seal has worn a deep groove in the surface of the crankshaft, consult an engine overhaul specialist; repair may be possible, but otherwise a new crankshaft will be required.

15 Main and big-end bearings - inspection

1 Even though the main and big-end bearings are renewed during the engine overhaul, the old bearings should be retained for close examination, as they may reveal valuable information about the condition of the engine. The bearing shells are graded by thickness, the grade of each shell being indicated by the colour code marked on it - they may also have markings on their backing faces **(see illustration)**. Standard shells are colour-coded yellow-yellow, or red-blue. The only shells available as spares are colour-coded yellow. No specific dimensions are quoted by Saab.

2 Bearing failure can occur due to lack of lubrication, the presence of dirt or other foreign particles, overloading the engine, or corrosion **(see illustration)**. Regardless of the cause of bearing failure, the cause must be corrected (where applicable) before the engine is reassembled, to prevent it from happening again.

3 When examining the bearing shells, remove them from the cylinder block/crankcase, the main bearing caps, the connecting rods and the connecting rod big-end bearing caps. Lay them out on a clean surface in the same general position as their location in the engine. This will enable you to match any bearing problems with the corresponding crankshaft journal. *Do not* touch any shell's bearing surface with your fingers while checking it, or the delicate surface may be scratched.

4 Dirt and other foreign matter gets into the engine in a variety of ways. It may be left in the engine during assembly, or it may pass through filters or the crankcase ventilation system. It may get into the oil, and from there into the bearings. Metal chips from machining operations and normal engine wear are often present. Abrasives are sometimes left in engine components after reconditioning, especially when parts are not thoroughly cleaned using the proper cleaning methods. Whatever the source, these foreign objects often end up embedded in the soft bearing material, and are easily recognised. Large particles will not embed in the bearing, and will score or gouge the bearing and journal. The best prevention for this cause of bearing failure is to clean all parts thoroughly, and keep everything spotlessly-clean during engine assembly. Frequent and regular engine oil and filter changes are also recommended.

5 Lack of lubrication (or lubrication breakdown) has a number of interrelated causes. Excessive heat (which thins the oil), overloading (which squeezes the oil from the bearing face) and oil leakage (from excessive bearing clearances, worn oil pump or high engine speeds) all contribute to lubrication breakdown. Blocked oil passages, which usually are the result of misaligned oil holes in a bearing shell, will also oil-starve a bearing, and destroy it. When lack of lubrication is the cause of bearing failure, the bearing material is wiped or extruded from the steel backing of the bearing. Temperatures may increase to the point where the steel backing turns blue from overheating.

6 Driving habits can have a definite effect on bearing life. Full-throttle, low-speed operation (labouring the engine) puts very high loads on bearings, tending to squeeze out the oil film. These loads cause the bearings to flex, which produces fine cracks in the bearing face (fatigue failure). Eventually, the bearing material will loosen in pieces, and tear away from the steel backing.

7 Short-distance driving leads to corrosion of bearings, because insufficient engine heat is produced to drive off the condensed water and corrosive gases. These products collect in the engine oil, forming acid and sludge. As the oil is carried to the engine bearings, the acid attacks and corrodes the bearing material.

8 Incorrect bearing installation during engine assembly will lead to bearing failure as well. Tight-fitting bearings leave insufficient bearing running clearance, and will result in oil starvation. Dirt or foreign particles trapped behind a bearing shell result in high spots on the bearing, which lead to failure.

9 *Do not* touch any shell's bearing surface with your fingers during reassembly; there is a risk of scratching the delicate surface, or of depositing particles of dirt on it.

Bearing shells should be renewed as a matter of course during engine overhaul; to do otherwise is false economy. Refer to Section 18 for details of bearing shell selection.

16 Engine overhaul - reassembly sequence

1 Before reassembly begins, ensure that all new parts have been obtained, and that all necessary tools are available. Read through the entire procedure, to familiarise yourself with the work involved, and to ensure that all items necessary for reassembly of the engine are at hand. In addition to all normal tools and materials, thread-locking compound will be needed. A suitable tube of sealant will also be required for the joint faces that are fitted without gaskets.

2 In order to save time and avoid problems, engine reassembly can be carried out in the following order:

a) Crankshaft (Section 18).
b) Piston/connecting rod assemblies (Section 19).

c) Sump (Chapter 2A).
d) Balance shafts (Section 9).
e) Flywheel/driveplate (Chapter 2A).
f) Timing chain and balance shaft chain, sprockets and tensioners (Chapter 2A).
g) Cylinder head (Chapter 2A).
h) Inlet and exhaust manifolds (Chapter 4A).
i) Engine external components.

3 At this stage, all engine components should be absolutely clean and dry, with all faults repaired. The components should be laid out (or in individual containers) on a completely clean work surface.

17 Piston rings - refitting

1 Before fitting new piston rings, the ring end gaps must be checked as follows.

2 Lay out the piston/connecting rod assemblies and the new piston ring sets, so that the ring sets will be matched with the same piston and cylinder during the end gap measurement and subsequent engine reassembly.

3 Insert the top ring into the first cylinder, and push it down the bore using the top of the piston **(see illustration)**. This will ensure that the ring remains square with the cylinder walls. Position the ring near the bottom of the cylinder bore, at the lower limit of ring travel; this is especially important if the cylinder bores display signs of wear. Note that the top and second compression rings are different.

4 Measure the end gap using feeler blades, and compare the measurements with the figures given in the Specifications **(see illustration)**.

5 If the gap is too small (unlikely if genuine Saab parts are used), it must be enlarged, or the ring ends may contact each other during engine operation, causing serious damage. Ideally, new piston rings providing the correct end gap should be fitted. As a last resort, the end gap can be increased by filing the ring ends very carefully with a fine file. Mount the file in a vice with soft jaws, slip the ring over the file with the ends contacting the file face, and slowly move the ring to remove material from the ends. Take care, as piston rings are sharp, and are easily broken.

6 With new piston rings, it is unlikely that the end gap will be too large. If the gaps are too large, check that you have the correct rings for your particular engine and recheck the cylinder bore measurements.

7 Repeat the checking procedure for each ring in the first cylinder, and then for the rings in the remaining cylinders. Remember to keep rings, pistons and cylinders matched up.

8 Once the ring end gaps have been checked and if necessary corrected, the rings can be fitted to the pistons.

9 Fit the piston rings using the same technique as for removal. Fit the bottom (oil control) ring first, and work up. When fitting the oil control ring, first insert the expander, then fit the lower and upper rings with the ring gaps both on the non-thrust side of the piston, with approximately 60° between them. Ensure that the second compression ring is fitted the correct way up, with the word "TOP" uppermost. Arrange the gaps of the top and second compression rings on opposite sides of the piston, above the ends of the gudgeon pin **(see illustration)**. **Note:** *Always follow any instructions supplied with the new piston ring sets - different manufacturers may specify different procedures. Do not mix up the top and second compression rings, as they have different cross-sections.*

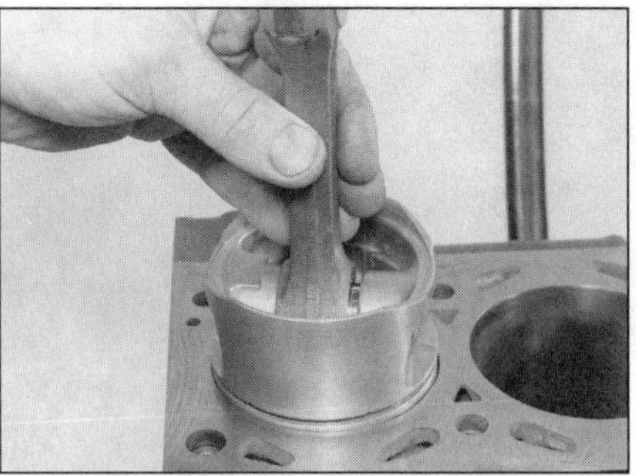

17.3 Using the top of a piston to push a piston ring into the bore

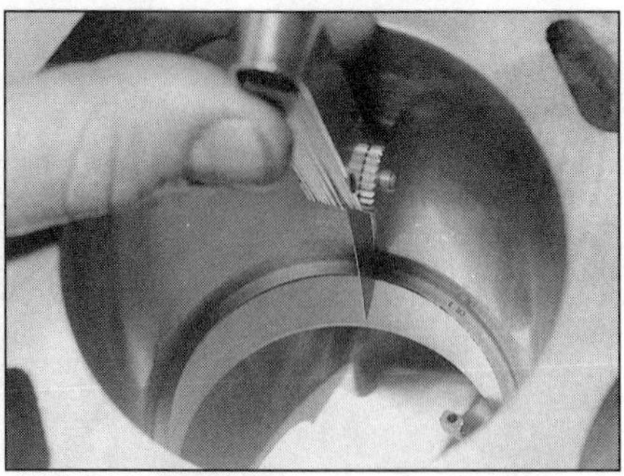

17.4 Measuring a piston ring end gap

18 Crankshaft - refitting and main bearing running clearance check

Selection of new bearing shells

1 The main bearing shells are classified for thickness as described in the following table (Specific dimensions are not quoted by Saab):

Shell	Colour
Thinnest	Red
+0.005 mm	Yellow
+0.010 mm	Blue

Note that up to the second undersize, it is possible to mix different thicknesses of shell in order to obtain the correct running clearance. Commence the procedure with the two thinnest shells, then if the clearance is too great, fit one thick shell with one thin shell, and make the check again. If the clearance is still too great, fit two thick shells.

Main bearing running clearance check

2 Clean the backs of the bearing shells, and the bearing locations in both the cylinder block and the main bearing caps.

3 Press the bearing shells into their locations, ensuring that the tab on each shell engages in the notch in the cylinder block or main bearing cap location. Take care not to touch any shell's bearing surface with your fingers.

4 The running clearance may be checked using one of two methods.

5 One method (which will be difficult to achieve without a range of internal micrometers or internal/external expanding calipers) is to refit the main bearing caps to the cylinder block/crankcase, with the bearing shells in place. With the cap retaining bolts correctly tightened, measure the internal diameter of each assembled pair of bearing shells. If the diameter of each corresponding crankshaft journal is measured and then subtracted from the bearing internal diameter, the result will be the main bearing running clearance.

6 The second (and more accurate) method is to use a product known as "Plastigauge". This consists of a fine thread of perfectly-round plastic, which is compressed between the bearing shell and the journal. When the cap and shell are removed, the plastic is deformed, and can be measured with a special card gauge supplied with the kit. The running clearance is determined from this gauge. Plastigauge may be available from your Saab dealer; otherwise, enquiries at one of the larger specialist motor factors should produce the name of a stockist in your area. The procedure for using Plastigauge is as follows.

7 With the main bearing upper shells in place, carefully lay the crankshaft in position. Do not use any lubricant at this stage; the crankshaft journals and bearing shells must be perfectly clean and dry.

8 Cut several lengths of the appropriate-size Plastigauge (they should be slightly shorter than the width of the main bearings), and

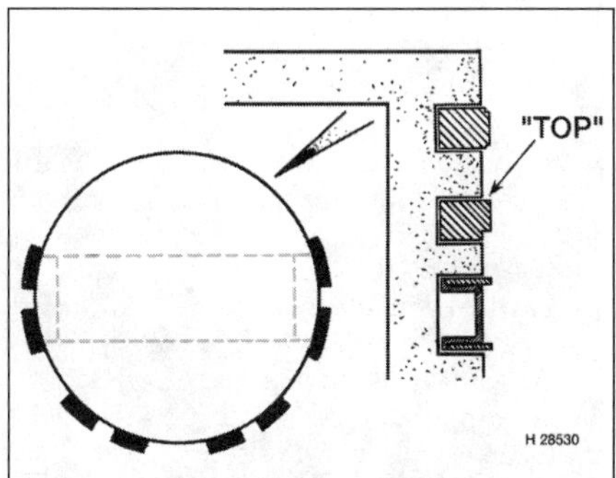

17.9 Piston ring cross-section and gap positioning

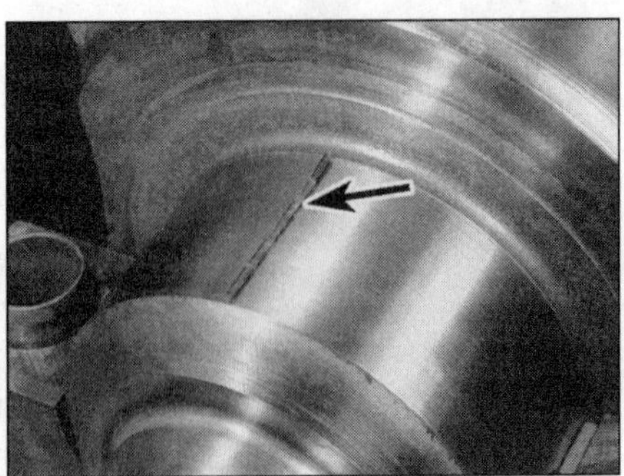

18.8 Plastigauge in place on the crankshaft main bearing journal

18.9 Tightening a main bearing cap bolt

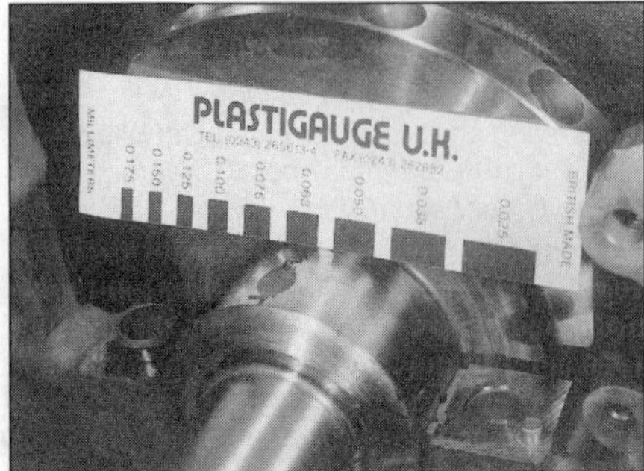

18.11 Measuring the width of the deformed Plastigauge using the card gauge

place one length on each crankshaft journal axis **(see illustration)**. The length of Plastigauge should be placed approximately 6.0 mm to one side of the centre-line of the journal. Avoid placing the Plastigauge close to an oil drilling.

9 With the main bearing lower shells in position, refit the main bearing caps, then insert the bolts and tighten them progressively to the specified torque **(see illustration)**. Take care not to disturb the Plastigauge, and *do not* rotate the crankshaft at any time during this operation.

10 Unscrew the bolts and remove the main bearing caps, again taking great care not to disturb the Plastigauge or rotate the crankshaft.

11 Compare the width of the crushed Plastigauge on each journal to the scale printed on the Plastigauge envelope, to obtain the main bearing running clearance **(see illustration)**. Compare the clearance measured with that given in the Specifications at the start of this Chapter.

12 If the clearance is significantly different from that expected, the bearing shells may be the wrong size (or excessively worn, if the original shells are being re-used). Before deciding that different-size shells are required, make sure that no dirt or oil was trapped between the bearing shells and the main bearing caps or block when the clearance was measured. If the Plastigauge was wider at one end than at the other, the crankshaft journal may be tapered.

13 If the clearance is not as specified, use the reading obtained, along with the shell thicknesses quoted above, to calculate the necessary grade of bearing shells required. When calculating the bearing clearance required, bear in mind that it is always better to have the running clearance towards the lower end of the specified range, to allow for wear in use.

14 Where necessary, obtain the required grades of bearing shell, and repeat the running clearance checking procedure as described above.

15 On completion, carefully scrape away all traces of the Plastigauge material from the crankshaft and bearing shells. Use your fingernail, or a wooden or plastic scraper which is unlikely to score the bearing surfaces.

Final crankshaft refitting

16 Carefully lift the crankshaft out of the cylinder block once more. Where applicable, refit the crankshaft position sensor reluctor if removed, and tighten the screws.

17 Using a little grease, stick the upper thrustwashers to each side of the centre main bearing upper location; ensure that the oilway grooves on each thrustwasher face outwards (away from the cylinder block).

18 Place the bearing shells in their locations in the caps as described earlier. If new shells are being fitted, ensure that all traces of protective grease are cleaned off, using paraffin. Wipe dry the shells and connecting rods with a lint-free cloth. Liberally lubricate each bearing shell in the cylinder block/crankcase with clean engine oil **(see illustration)**.

19 Lower the crankshaft into position so that Nos 2 and 3 cylinder crankpins are at TDC. In this position, Nos 1 and 4 cylinder crankpins will be at BDC, ready for fitting No 1 piston. Check the crankshaft endfloat as described in Section 14.

20 Lubricate the lower bearing shells in the main bearing caps with clean engine oil. Make sure that the locating lugs on the shells engage with the corresponding recesses in the caps.

21 Fit the main bearing caps to their correct locations, ensuring that they are fitted the correct way round (the bearing shell lug recesses in the block and caps must be on the same side). Insert the bolts loosely.

22 Progressively tighten the main bearing cap bolts to the specified torque wrench setting.

23 Check that the crankshaft rotates freely.

24 Refit the piston/connecting rod assemblies to the crankshaft, as described in Section 19.

25 Before refitting the crankshaft rear oil seal housing, fit a new rear oil seal in the housing, with reference to Chapter 2A. Use a mallet and block of wood to drive it into the housing, or alternatively, use the block of wood in a vice **(see illustrations)**.

26 Apply suitable sealant to the contact faces of the rear oil seal housing, then smear a little oil on the oil seal lips, and refit the

18.18 Lubricating the main bearing shells

18.25a Driving the crankshaft rear oil seal into the housing

18.25b Fitting the crankshaft rear oil seal using a block of wood in a vice

18.26a Adhesive tape over the end of the crankshaft will prevent damage to the oil seal when refitting

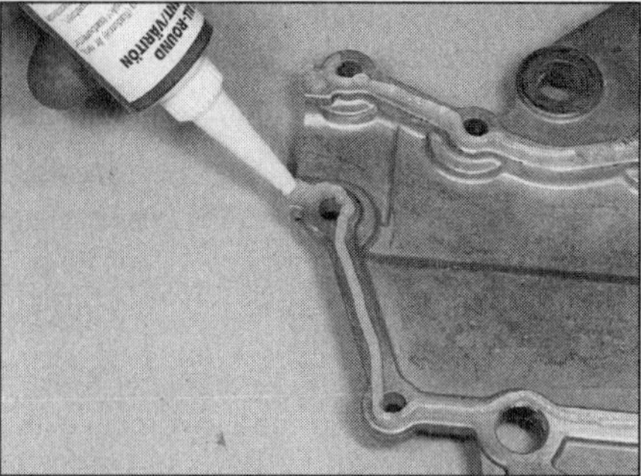
18.26b Applying sealant to the rear oil seal housing

18.26c Refitting the rear oil seal housing (engine backplate)

locating dowels where necessary. Locate the housing on the rear of the cylinder block. To prevent damage to the oil seal as it locates over the crankshaft, make up a guide out of a plastic container, or alternatively use adhesive tape. Once the housing is in position, remove the guide or tape, then insert the bolts and tighten them to the specified torque **(see illustrations)**.

27 Refit the flywheel/driveplate, oil pick-up/strainer and sump, with reference to Part A of this Chapter.

28 Where removed, refit the cylinder head as described in Chapter 2A.

29 Refit the timing chain and sprocket as described in Chapter 2A.

19 Piston/connecting rod assembly - refitting and big-end bearing running clearance check

Selection of bearing shells

1 The big-end bearing shells are classified for thickness in the same manner as the main bearing shells, as described in Section 18. Note that up to the second undersize, it is possible to mix different thicknesses of shell, in order to obtain the correct running clearance. Commence the procedure with the two thinnest shells, then if the clearance is too great, fit one thick shell with one thin shell, and make the check again. If the clearance is still too great, fit two thick shells.

Big-end bearing running clearance check

2 The clearance can be checked in either of two ways.

3 One method is to refit the big-end bearing cap to the connecting rod before refitting the pistons to the cylinder block, ensuring that they are fitted the correct way round, with the bearing shells in place. With the cap retaining nuts correctly tightened, use an internal micrometer or vernier caliper to measure the internal diameter of each assembled pair of bearing shells. If the diameter of each corresponding crankshaft journal is measured and then subtracted from the bearing internal diameter, the result will be the big-end bearing running clearance.

4 The second, and more accurate, method is to use Plastigauge (see Section 18) after refitting the pistons to the cylinder block. The following paragraphs describe the latter method, together with the refitting of the pistons to the cylinder block.

5 Position the cylinder block either on its side or on the flywheel/driveplate end.

6 Lay out the assembled pistons and rods in order, with the bearing shells, connecting rod caps and nuts.

7 Clean the backs of the bearing shells, and the bearing locations in both the connecting rod and bearing cap. If new shells are being fitted, ensure that all traces of protective grease are cleaned off, using paraffin.

8 Press the bearing shells into their locations, ensuring that the tab on each shell engages in the notch in the connecting rod and cap. Take care not to touch any shell's bearing surface with your fingers. If the original bearing shells are being used for the check, ensure that they are refitted in their original locations.

9 Lubricate the cylinder bores, pistons and piston rings with clean engine oil, then lay out each piston/connecting rod assembly in its respective position. Do not lubricate the bearing shells at this stage.

10 Start with assembly No 1. Make sure that the piston rings are still spaced as described in Section 17, then clamp them in position with a piston ring compressor **(see illustration)**.

11 Insert the piston/connecting rod assembly into the top of cylinder No 1. Ensure that the notch or arrow on the piston crown is pointing towards the timing chain end of the engine. Using a block of wood or hammer handle against the piston crown, tap the assembly into the cylinder bore until the piston crown is flush with the top of the cylinder **(see illustrations)**. Make sure that the ends of the big-end bearing cap bolts do not scratch the bore walls.

12 With the No 1 crankpin at the bottom of its stroke, guide the connecting rod onto it while tapping the top of the piston with the hammer handle.

13 Place a strand of Plastigauge on the crankpin journal.

14 Refit the big-end bearing cap, using the marks made or noted on removal to ensure that they are fitted the correct way round.

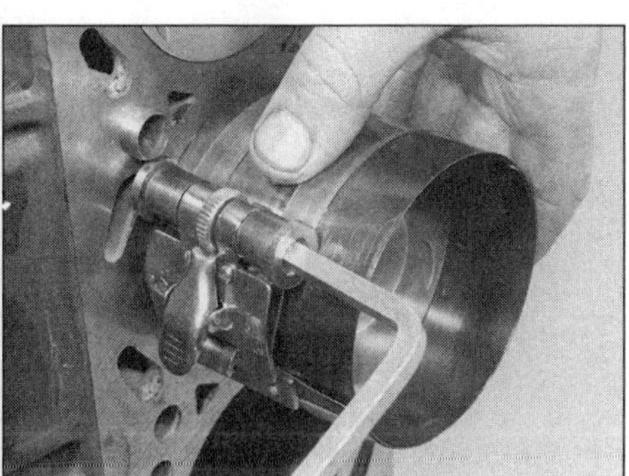
19.10 Piston ring compressor fitted over the piston rings

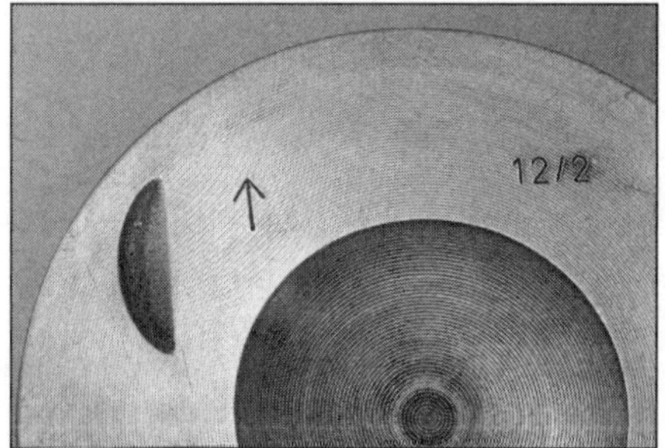

19.11a The arrow on the piston crown must point towards the timing chain end of the engine

19.11b Using a hammer handle to tap the piston down the cylinder bore

19.14 Tightening the big-end bearing cap nuts

Tighten the bearing cap nuts to the specified torque **(see illustration)**. Take care not to disturb the Plastigauge or rotate the crankshaft during the tightening sequence.

15 Dismantle the assembly, then use the scale printed on the Plastigauge envelope to obtain the big-end bearing running clearance.

16 If the clearance is significantly different from that specified, the bearing shells may be the wrong size (or excessively worn, if the original shells are being re-used). If necessary, select different shells as described in paragraph 1. Make sure that no dirt or oil was trapped between the bearing shells and the cap or connecting rod when the clearance was measured. If the Plastigauge was wider at one end than at the other, the crankpins may be tapered.

17 Push the No 1 piston/connecting rod assembly to the top of the cylinder, then refit the No 4 piston/connecting rod assembly and repeat the bearing running clearance check. With Nos 1 and 4 pistons at the top of their bores, refit Nos 2 and 3 pistons and repeat the bearing running clearance check on these.

18 On completion, carefully scrape away all traces of the Plastigauge material from the crankshaft and bearing shells. Use your fingernail, or some other object which is unlikely to score the bearing surfaces.

Final piston/connecting rod refitting

19 Position No 1 crankpin at the bottom of its stroke. Liberally lubricate the crankpin and both bearing shells. Taking care not to mark the cylinder bores, tap the piston/connecting rod assembly down the bore and onto the crankpin. Refit the big-end bearing cap, tightening its retaining nuts finger-tight at first. Note that the faces with the identification marks must match (which means that the bearing shell locating tabs abut each other).

20 Tighten the bearing cap retaining nuts evenly and progressively to the specified torque setting.

21 Rotate the crankshaft. Check that it turns freely; some stiffness is to be expected if new components have been fitted, but there should be no signs of binding or tight spots.

22 Refit the remaining three piston/connecting rod assemblies to their crankpins in the same way.

23 Refit the oil transfer tube to the base of the crankcase, using a new O-ring seal. Refit the sump and cylinder head with reference to Chapter 2A.

20 Engine - initial start-up after overhaul

1 With the engine refitted in the vehicle, double-check the engine oil and coolant levels (see "*Weekly checks*"). Make a final check that everything has been reconnected, and that there are no tools or rags left in the engine compartment.

2 Remove the spark plugs. On models with a distributor, disable the ignition system by disconnecting the LT wiring from the ignition coil. On models with Direct Ignition, disconnect the wiring plug from the ignition cartridge (refer to Chapter 5B if necessary). Remove the fuel pump fuse, to prevent unburned fuel from contaminating the catalytic converter.

3 Turn the engine on the starter until the oil pressure warning light goes out. Refit the spark plugs, and reconnect the coil lead to the distributor cap or DI cartridge wiring (as applicable) and refit the fuel pump fuse.

4 Start the engine, noting that this may take a little longer than usual, due to the fuel system components having been disturbed.

5 While the engine is idling, check for fuel, water and oil leaks. Don't be alarmed if there are some odd smells and smoke from parts getting hot and burning off oil deposits.

6 Assuming all is well, keep the engine idling until hot water is felt circulating through the top hose then switch off the engine.

7 After a few minutes, recheck the oil and coolant levels as described in "*Weekly checks*", and top-up as necessary.

8 If new pistons, rings or crankshaft bearings have been fitted, the engine must be treated as new, and run-in for the first 500 miles (800 km). *Do not* operate the engine at full-throttle, or allow it to labour at low engine speeds in any gear. It is recommended that the oil and filter are changed at the end of this period (see Chapter 1).

Chapter 3
Cooling, heating and ventilation systems

Contents

Degrees of difficulty

Easy, suitable for novice with little experience 

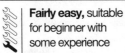

Fairly easy, suitable for beginner with some experience 

Fairly difficult, suitable for competent DIY mechanic 

Difficult, suitable for experienced DIY mechanic 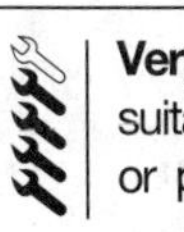

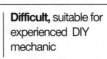

Very difficult, suitable for expert DIY or professional

Specifications

General

Expansion tank cap opening pressure	1.4 to 1.5 bars

Thermostat

Opening temperature	89°C ± 2°C

Electric cooling fan

Cut-in temperature (ignition on):	
Stage 1	100° ± 2°C
Stage 2	113° ± 2°C
Cut-out temperature (ignition off):	
Turbo engines	103° ± 2°C
Non-turbo engines	110° ± 2°C
Cut-out temperature (ignition on):	
Turbo engines	99° ± 2°C
Non-turbo engines	106° ± 2°C
Air conditioning system switch-off temperature (engine temp. rising)	126° ± 2°C
Air conditioning system switch-on temperature (engine temp. cooling)	125° ± 0.5°C

Engine temperature sensor

Resistance:	
At 0°C	5.7 kohms
At 20°C	2.4 kohms
At 30°C	1.6 kohms
At 50°C	800 ohms
At 85°C	300 ohms
At 110°C	140 ohms
At 130°C	100 ohms

Torque wrench settings	Nm	lbf ft
Automatic transmission oil cooler hoses to radiator	25	19
Thermostat housing	22	16

1 General information and precautions

General information

1 The cooling system is of pressurised type, comprising a water pump driven by the auxiliary drivebelt, a crossflow radiator, electric cooling fan, a thermostat, heater matrix and all associated hoses. The expansion tank is located on the left-hand side of the engine compartment.

2 The system functions as follows. Cold coolant in the bottom of the radiator passes through the bottom hose to the water pump, where it is pumped around the cylinder block and head passages. After cooling the cylinder bores, combustion surfaces and valve seats, the coolant reaches the underside of the thermostat, which is initially closed. The coolant passes through the heater, and is returned via the cylinder block to the water pump.

3 When the engine is cold, the coolant circulates only through the cylinder block, cylinder head, throttle housing and heater. On turbo models it also passes through the turbocharger. When the coolant reaches a predetermined temperature, the thermostat opens, and the coolant passes through the top hose to the radiator. As the coolant circulates through the radiator, it is cooled by the inrush of air when the car is in forward motion, and also by the action of the electric cooling fan when necessary. Upon reaching the bottom of the radiator, the coolant has now cooled, and the cycle is repeated.

4 When the engine is at normal operating temperature, the coolant expands, and some of it is displaced into the expansion tank. Coolant collects in the tank, and is returned to the radiator when the system cools.

5 The electric cooling fan mounted on the rear of the radiator is controlled by a thermostatic switch. At a predetermined coolant temperature, the switch/sensor actuates the fan.

Precautions

Warning: Do not attempt to remove the expansion tank filler cap, or to disturb any part of the cooling system, while the engine is hot, as there is a high risk of scalding. If the expansion tank filler cap must be removed before the engine and radiator have fully cooled (even though this is not recommended), the pressure in the cooling system must first be relieved. Cover the cap with a thick layer of cloth, to avoid scalding, and slowly unscrew the filler cap until a hissing sound is heard. When the hissing has stopped, indicating that the pressure has reduced, slowly unscrew the filler cap until it can be removed; if more hissing sounds are heard, wait until they have stopped before unscrewing the cap completely. At all times, keep well away from the filler cap opening, and protect your hands.

Warning: Do not allow antifreeze to come into contact with your skin, or with the painted surfaces of the vehicle. Rinse off spills immediately, with plenty of water. Never leave antifreeze lying around in an open container, or in a puddle in the driveway or on the garage floor. Children and pets are attracted by its sweet smell, but antifreeze can be fatal if ingested.

Warning: If the engine is hot, the electric cooling fan may start rotating even if the engine is not running. Be careful to keep your hands, hair and any loose clothing well clear when working in the engine compartment.

Warning: Refer to Section 10 for precautions to be observed when working on models with air conditioning.

2 Cooling system hoses - disconnection and renewal

1 The number, routing and pattern of hoses will vary according to model, but the same basic procedure applies. Before commencing work, make sure that the new hoses are to hand, along with new hose clips if needed. It is good practice to renew the hose clips at the same time as the hoses.

2 Drain the cooling system, as described in Chapter 1, saving the coolant if it is fit for re-use. Squirt a little penetrating oil onto the hose clips if they are corroded.

3 Loosen and release the hose clips from the hose concerned.

4 Unclip any wires, cables or other hoses which may be attached to the hose being removed. Make notes for reference when reassembling if necessary. The hoses can be removed with relative ease when new, however on an older vehicle they may be stuck to the outlet.

5 If a hose proves stubborn, try to release it by rotating it before attempting to work it off. Take care not to damage the pipe stubs or hoses. Note in particular that the radiator hose stubs are fragile; do not use excessive force when attempting to remove the hoses.

If all else fails, cut hoses with a sharp knife, then slit them so that they can be peeled off in two pieces. While expensive, this is preferable to buying a new radiator.

6 Before fitting the new hose, smear the stubs with washing-up liquid or a suitable rubber lubricant to aid fitting. Do not use oil or grease, which may attack the rubber.

7 Fit the hose clips over the ends of the hose, then fit the hose over its stubs. Work the hose into position. When satisfied, locate and tighten the hose clips.

8 Refill the cooling system as described in Chapter 1. Run the engine, and check that there are no leaks.

9 Recheck the tightness of the hose clips on any new hoses after a few hundred miles.

10 Top-up the coolant level if necessary (see "*Weekly checks*").

3 Radiator - removal, inspection and refitting

Note: *If the reason for removing the radiator is to cure a leak, it is worth trying the effect of a radiator sealing compound first - this is added to the coolant, and will often cure minor leaks with the radiator in situ.*

Removal

1 On turbo models, remove the intercooler as described in Chapter 4A.

2 Depress the upper clips and remove the grille for access to the radiator.

3 Where fitted, remove the engine oil cooler and suspend it to one side with string or wire.

4 On models with air conditioning, unbolt the condenser and position it to one side without disconnecting the hoses.

5 Remove the battery as described in Chapter 5A.

6 Drain the cooling system as described in Chapter 1.

7 On turbo models, disconnect and remove the intercooler bypass hose and the inlet hose from the throttle housing.

8 Loosen the clip and disconnect the expansion tank purge hose from the top right-hand side of the radiator **(see illustration)**.

3.8 Disconnecting the expansion tank purge hose from the top of the radiator

9 Loosen the clip and disconnect the top hose from the top left-hand side of the radiator **(see illustration)**.

10 Disconnect the electric cooling fan wiring.

11 Unscrew the bolt and release the power steering pump fluid supply hose from its location above the radiator. Unbolt the cable bracket from the battery mounting platform,

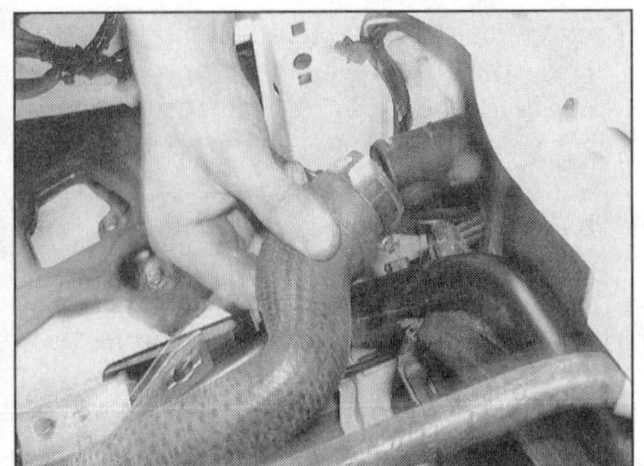
3.9 Disconnecting the top hose from the radiator

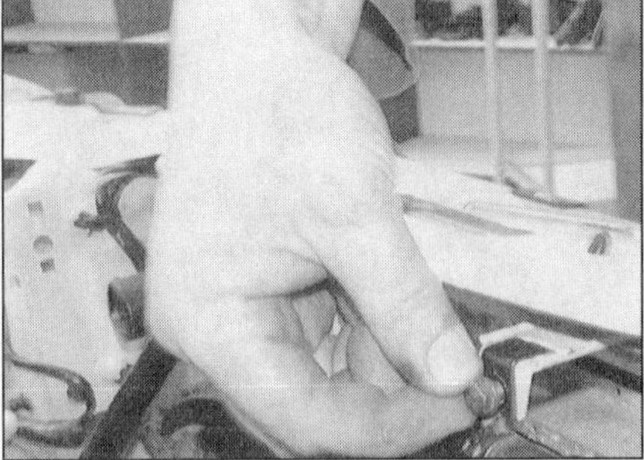
3.11a Unscrew the bolt securing the PAS fluid supply hose to the crossmember . . .

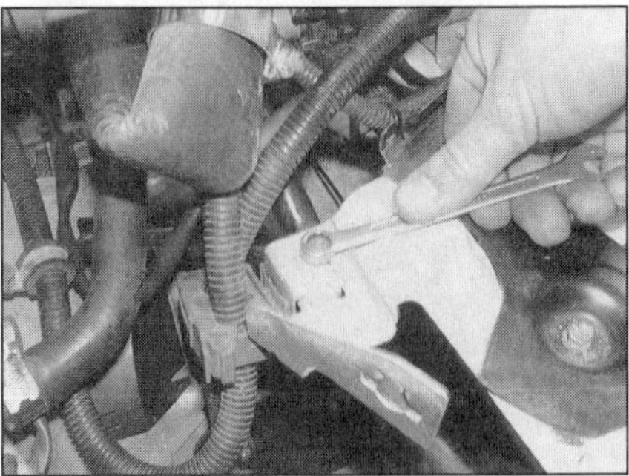
3.11b . . . then unbolt the cable bracket from the battery mounting platform . . .

then tie the fluid supply hose away from the radiator **(see illustrations)**.

12 Where fitted, undo the screws and remove the cover from over the electric cooling fan.

13 On automatic transmission models, disconnect the oil cooler hoses from the radiator and plug them to prevent entry of dust and dirt. Also release the hose bracket from the radiator.

14 Loosen the clip and disconnect the bottom hose from the radiator **(see illustration)**.

15 Release the upper clamps by squeezing them together, then move the radiator rearwards and lift it from the rubber grommets in the front valance and withdraw from the engine compartment **(see illustrations)**. Take care not to damage the radiator cooling fins. On models with air conditioning, unclip the cable for the compressor as the radiator is lifted.

Inspection

16 If the radiator has been removed due to suspected blockage, reverse-flush it as described in Chapter 1. Clean dirt and debris from the radiator fins, using an air line or a soft brush.

Caution: Be careful, as the fins are sharp, and easily damaged.

17 If necessary, a radiator specialist can perform a "flow test" on the radiator, to establish whether an internal blockage exists.

18 A leaking radiator must be referred to a specialist for permanent repair. Do not attempt to weld or solder a leaking radiator.

19 If the radiator is to be sent for repair, or is to be renewed, remove the cooling fan thermostatic switch.

20 Inspect the condition of the upper and lower radiator mounting rubbers, and renew them if necessary.

Refitting

21 Apply a little washing up liquid to the rubber grommets located in the front valance; this will assist the radiator location pins to enter the grommets.

22 Carefully lower the radiator into position and locate it in the lower rubber grommets. Press the radiator firmly downwards and push it forwards into the upper mountings, then refit the upper clamps to secure.

23 On models with air conditioning, refit the cable for the compressor.

24 On automatic transmission models, reconnect the oil cooler hoses. Also attach the hose support bracket to the radiator.

25 Reconnect the bottom hose and tighten the clip.

26 Where fitted, refit the cover over the electric cooling fan and tighten the screws.

27 Refit the power steering pump fluid supply hose to the crossmember and tighten the bolt. Refit the cable bracket to the battery mounting platform.

28 Reconnect the electric cooling fan wiring.

29 Reconnect the top hose and tighten the clip.

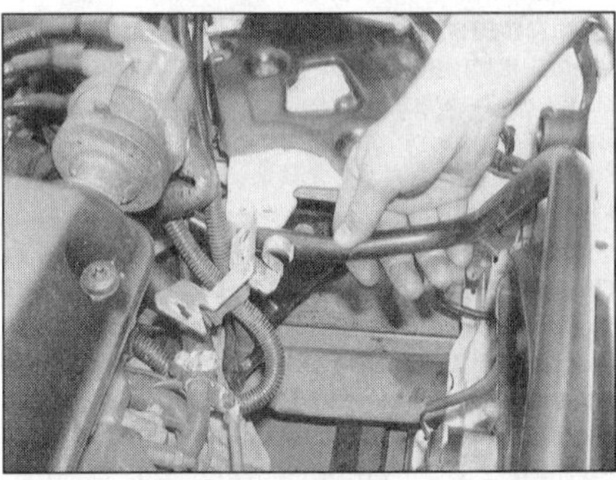
3.11c . . . and move the hose away from the radiator

30 Reconnect the expansion tank purge hose to the top right-hand side of the radiator, and tighten the clip. Secure the hose with the clips to the crossmember.

31 On turbo models, reconnect the intercooler bypass hose and the throttle housing inlet hose.

32 Refit the battery with reference to Chapter 5A.

33 On models with air conditioning, refit the condenser and grille.

34 On turbo models, refit the intercooler with reference to Chapter 4A.

35 Check that the radiator drain plug is tight, then refill and bleed the cooling system as described in Chapter 1.

36 Start the engine and check the cooling system for leaks.

3.14 Disconnecting the bottom hose from the radiator

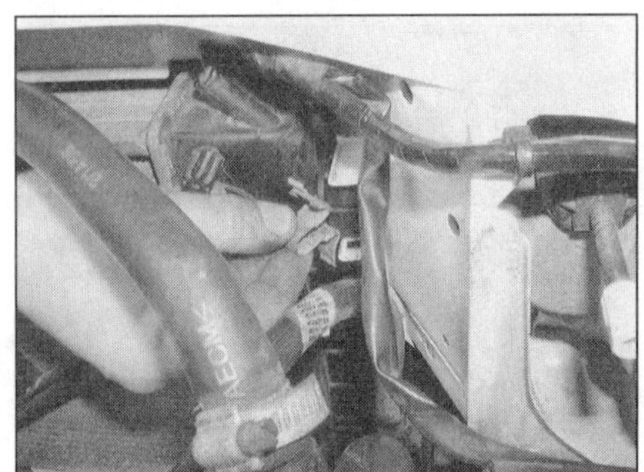
3.15a Remove the upper clamps . . .

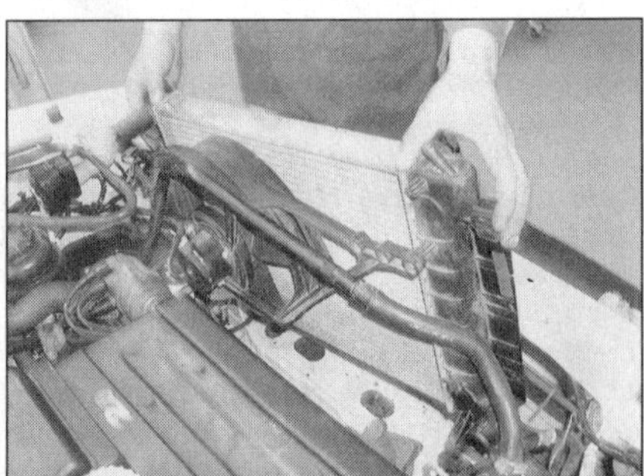
3.15b . . . then lift the radiator from the engine compartment

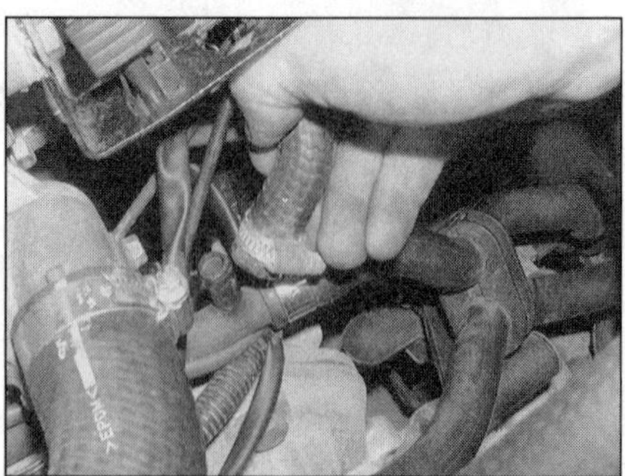

4.4a Disconnect the pre-heating coolant hose from the rigid pipe . . .

4.4b . . . then unbolt the rigid pipe from the thermostat cover

4.5 Remove the thermostat cover . . .

4 Thermostat - removal, testing and refitting

Removal

1 Drain the cooling system as described in Chapter 1.

2 On turbo models remove the cover, then disconnect and remove the intercooler bypass hose and the inlet hose from the throttle body.

3 Unscrew the bolt and disconnect the rigid coolant pipe from the water pump, then unscrew the bolt which secures the pipe to the front left-hand corner of the engine. Remove the O-ring from the water pump.

4 Loosen the clip and disconnect the pre-heating coolant hose from the throttle body or from the rigid pipe, then unbolt the pipe from the thermostat cover **(see illustrations)**.

5 Unscrew the bolts and remove the thermostat cover **(see illustration)**. There is no need to disconnect the top hose from the cover.

6 Remove the thermostat from the cylinder head or thermostat cover **(see illustration)**.

Testing

7 A rough test of the thermostat may be made by suspending it with a piece of string in a container full of water. Heat the water to bring it to the boil - the thermostat must open by the time the water boils. If not, renew it.

8 If a thermometer is available, the precise opening temperature of the thermostat may be determined and compared with the figures given in the Specifications. The opening temperature is normally marked on the thermostat.

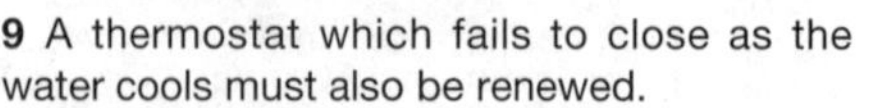

9 A thermostat which fails to close as the water cools must also be renewed.

10 If necessary renew the rubber ring on the outer periphery of the thermostat.

Refitting

11 Locate the thermostat in the cover, making sure that the air bleed hole is uppermost.

12 Refit the cover to the cylinder head and tighten the bolts securely.

13 Using a new O-ring, refit the rigid coolant pipe to the water pump and tighten the bolt.

14 Reconnect the hose to the throttle body and secure the pipe to the thermostat cover.

15 On turbo models, reconnect the intercooler bypass hose and the inlet hose to the throttle body, then refit the cover.

16 Refill and bleed the cooling system as described in Chapter 1.

5 Electric cooling fan - testing, removal and refitting

Testing

1 Current supply to the cooling fan is controlled by a relay which is earthed by the Integrated Central Electronics Control Module (see Chapter 12). The module is supplied with the engine cooling system temperature by a sensor. On models with air conditioning, the cooling fan is also controlled by the air conditioning control unit. Note that some models are equipped with two cooling fans.

2 If the fan does not appear to work, first check that the wiring plug located near the cooling fan is intact. Note that Saab technicians use an electronic tester to check the Control Module for fault codes, and if necessary a Saab dealer should carry out a diagnostic check to locate the fault.

3 If a multimeter is available, a check can be made of the relay which controls the fan. Remove the relay and connect a voltmeter between terminal 30 and earth. With the ignition switched on, terminal 30 should have a reading of 12 volts.

4 Now connect a bridging wire between terminals 30 and 87. If the cooling fan now works, the relay is proved faulty and should be renewed.

5 If the relay and the wiring are in good condition, the fault must lie in the motor itself. The motor can be checked by disconnecting it from the wiring loom, and connecting a 12-volt supply directly to it.

Removal

6 Disconnect and remove the battery (see Chapter 5A).

7 Disconnect the wiring from the electric cooling fan.

8 Unscrew the bolt securing the power steering fluid supply hose to the radiator crossmember. If necessary, unbolt the hose support from the battery bracket, then move the hose to one side.

9 Unclip the cooling system purge hose from the radiator crossmember.

10 Unscrew the mounting bolt(s) and slide the cooling fan assembly sideways to disengage it from the location slots **(see illustrations)**. Lift the assembly from the engine compartment.

4.6 . . . and remove the thermostat from the cylinder head

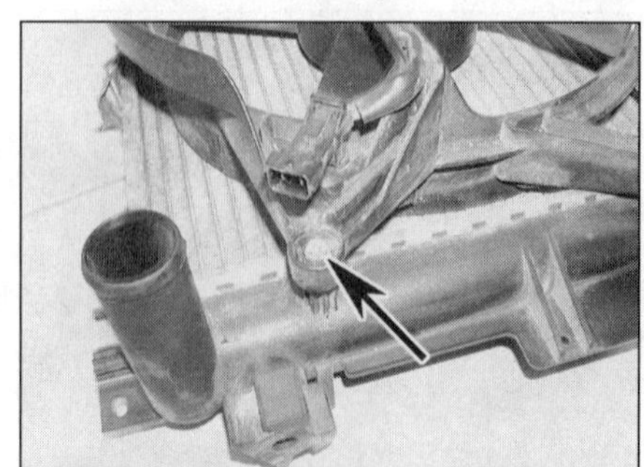

5.10a Unscrew the mounting bolt . . .

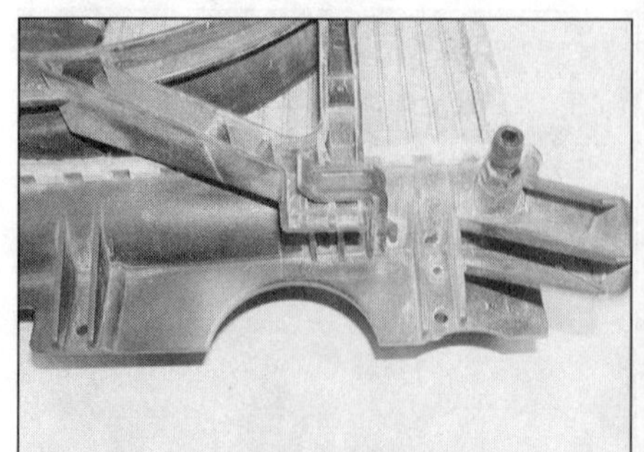

5.10b . . . and slide the cooling fan assembly from the location slots

5.11 Cooling fan motor mounting nuts

11 Unscrew the nuts and remove the fan motor from the housing **(see illustration)**. Where two fans are fitted, also remove the resistor.

Refitting

12 Refitting is a reversal of removal.

6 Coolant temperature sensor - testing, removal and refitting

Testing

1 The engine coolant temperature sensor is located in the left-hand end of the cylinder head. The resistance of the sensor varies according to the temperature of the coolant.

2 To test the sensor, disconnect the wiring at the plug then connect an ohmmeter to the sensor.

3 Determine the temperature of the coolant, then compare the resistance with the information given in the Specifications. If the reading is incorrect, the sender must be renewed.

Removal

4 Drain the cooling system as described in Chapter 1.

5 With the wiring disconnected, unscrew the sensor and remove it from the cylinder head.

Refitting

6 Insert the sensor and tighten securely.

7 Reconnect the wiring.

8 Refill the cooling system as described in Chapter 1.

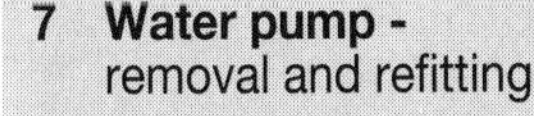

7 Water pump - removal and refitting

Removal

1 Drain the cooling system as described in Chapter 1.

2 Remove the air cleaner as described in Chapter 4A.

3 On turbo models, disconnect the intercooler inlet hose and the bypass hose from the throttle body.

4 Remove the auxiliary drivebelt with reference to Chapter 1.

5 Remove the power steering pump with reference to Chapter 10, but do not disconnect the fluid hoses. Tie the pump to the radiator crossmember with string or wire.

6 Unbolt the power steering pump mounting bracket from the cylinder head **(see illustration)**.

7.6 Removing the power steering pump mounting bracket from the cylinder head

7 Loosen the clip and disconnect the bottom hose from the water pump **(see illustration)**.

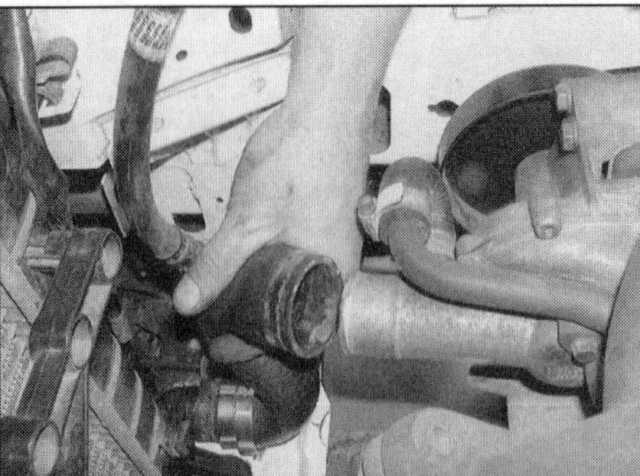

7.7 Disconnecting the bottom hose from the water pump

8 Unscrew the bolt and disconnect the rigid coolant pipe from the water pump, then unscrew the bolt which secures the pipe to the front left-hand corner of the engine **(see illustration)**. Remove the O-ring from the water pump.

7.8 Remove the bolt securing the rigid coolant pipe to the front left-hand side of the cylinder head

9 Loosen the clip and disconnect the pre-heating coolant hose from the throttle body or from the rigid pipe **(see illustration)**, then unbolt the pipe from the thermostat cover. Move the rigid pipe away from the water pump.

7.9 Disconnecting the pre-heating hose from the rigid coolant pipe

10 On turbo models, remove the boost pressure control valve with reference to Chapter 4A and position it to one side.

11 Loosen the clip and disconnect the heater return hose from the water pump.

12 Unscrew the mounting bolts and withdraw the water pump from the front of the cylinder block **(see illustrations**.

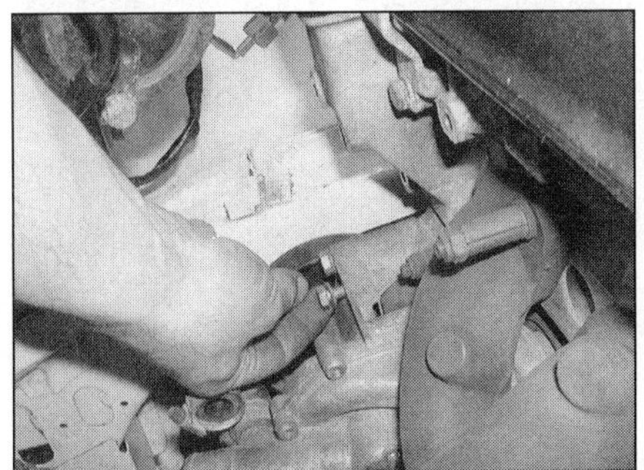

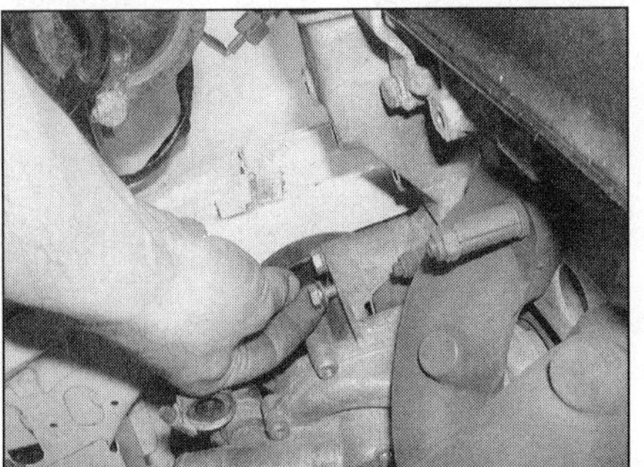

7.12a Unscrew the mounting bolts . . .

7.12b . . . and withdraw the water pump from the front of the cylinder block

13 Remove the adapter sleeve and O-rings from the aperture in the cylinder block **(see illustration)**.

14 The water pump may be obtained as a complete unit, or alternatively just the impeller/pulley section may be obtained. To separate the two sections, first mark them in relation to each other. Unscrew the bolts and separate the two halves **(see illustration)**.

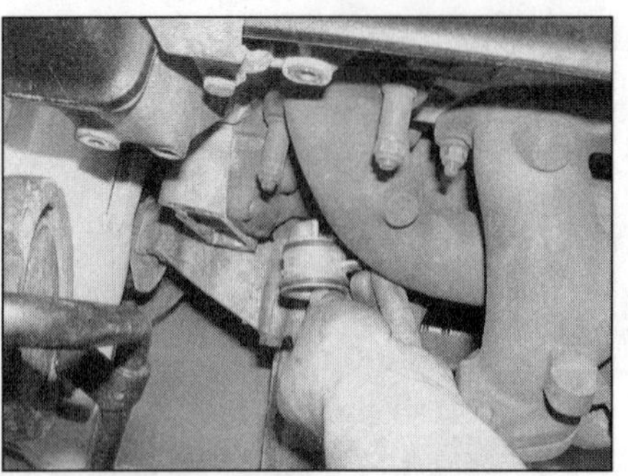
7.13 Removing the adapter sleeve and O-rings from the cylinder block

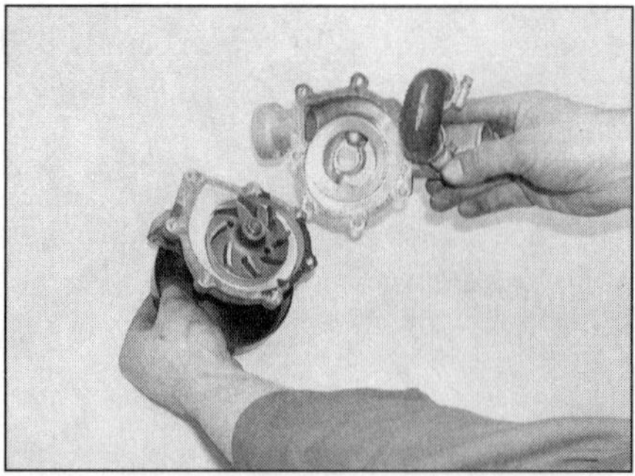
7.14 Separating the two halves of the water pump

Refitting

15 If separated, clean the mating faces and assemble the two halves together with a new gasket. Insert the bolts and tighten securely.

16 Refit the adapter sleeve to the cylinder block together with new O-rings. Apply a little vaseline to the O-rings to help them enter the cylinder block.

17 Locate the water pump on the cylinder block then insert the bolts and tighten securely.

18 Reconnect the heater return hose and tighten the clip.

19 On turbo models, refit the boost pressure control valve with reference to Chapter 4A.

20 Refit the rigid coolant pipe to the water pump together with a new O-ring and tighten the bolts.

21 Reconnect the pre-heating coolant hose to the throttle body and tighten the clip.

22 Locate the rigid pipe on the thermostat cover and tighten the bolt. Refit and tighten the bolt securing the coolant pipe to the front left-hand corner of the engine.

23 Reconnect the bottom hose to the water pump and tighten the clip.

24 Refit the power steering pump mounting bracket to the cylinder head and tighten the bolts.

25 Refit the power steering pump with reference to Chapter 10.

26 Refit the auxiliary drivebelt with reference to Chapter 1.

27 On turbo models, refit the intercooler inlet hose and the bypass hose to the throttle body.

28 Refit the air cleaner as described in Chapter 4A.

29 Refill and bleed the cooling system as described in Chapter 1.

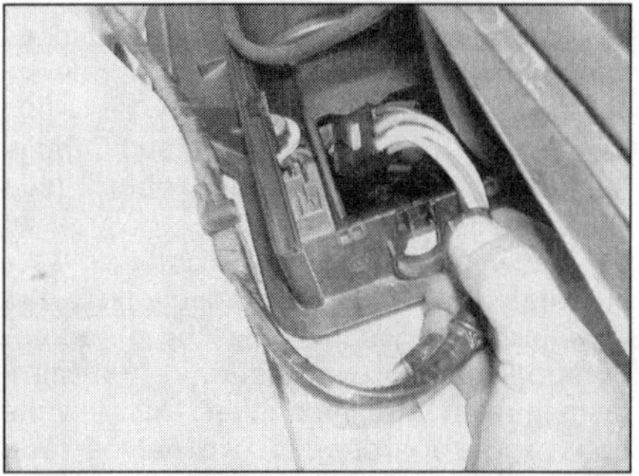
9.3 Disconnecting the heater motor wiring

8 Heating and ventilation system - general information

1 Three types of heating/ventilation system are fitted - the Standard system controlled manually, the Standard system with air conditioning also controlled manually, and the Automatic Climate Control (ACC) system which maintains the temperature inside the car at a selected temperature, regardless of the temperature outside the car. The basic heating/ventilation unit is common to all versions, and consists of air ducting from the centrally-located heater assembly to a central vent and two side vents, with an extension leading from the bottom of the heater through the centre console to the rear passenger footwell areas. A four-speed heater blower motor is fitted.

2 The heating and ventilation controls are mounted in the centre of the facia. Cable-controlled flap valves are contained in the air distribution housing, to divert the air to the various ducts and vents.

3 Cold air enters the system through the grille at the bottom of the windscreen. If required, the airflow is boosted by the blower, and then flows through the various ducts, according to the settings of the controls. Stale air is expelled through ducts at the rear of the vehicle. If warm air is required, the cold air is passed over the heater matrix, which is heated by the engine coolant.

4 On models fitted with air conditioning, a recirculation switch enables the outside air supply to be closed off, while the air inside the vehicle is recirculated. This can be useful to prevent unpleasant odours entering from outside the vehicle, but should only be used briefly, as the recirculated air inside the vehicle will soon become stale.

5 A solar sensor located on top of the facia panel, detects increased solar radiation, and increases the speed of the blower motor. This is necessary in order to increase the throughput of air in the vehicle.

9 Heating and ventilation system components - removal and refitting

Heater blower motor

Removal

1 Remove the wiper motor and linkage as described in Chapter 12.

2 Unclip the pollen filter from over the heater motor.

3 Disconnect the wiring from the heater motor **(see illustration)**.

4 Unscrew the bolts and remove the pollen filter frame **(see illustrations)**.

5 Unclip and remove the cover **(see illustrations)**.

6 Undo the screw securing the wiring socket to the bulkhead **(see illustration)**.

7 Undo the remaining screws and lift the heater motor from the bulkhead.

9.4a Unscrew the bolts . . .

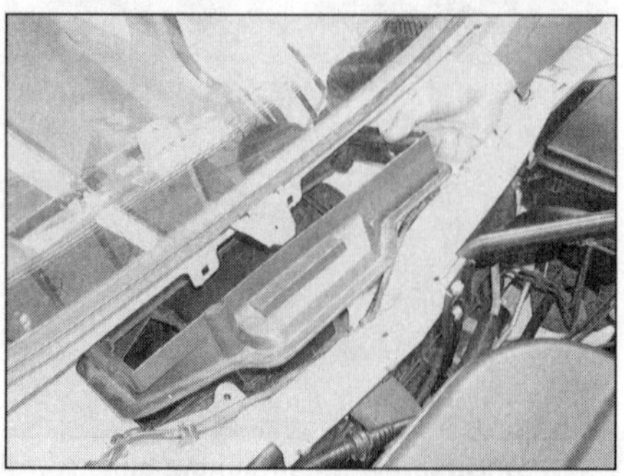
9.4b . . . and remove the pollen filter frame

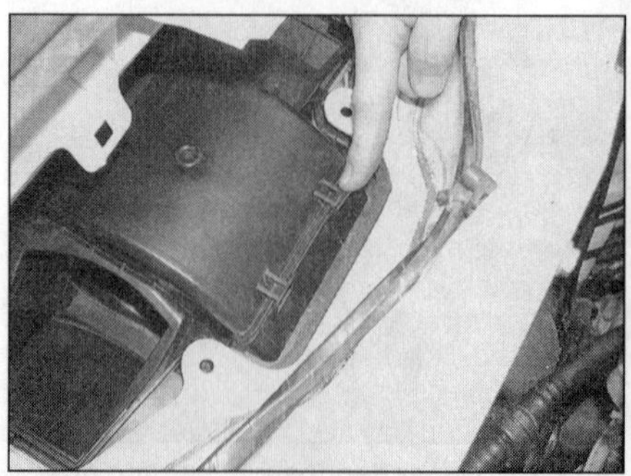
9.5a Release the clips . . .

9.5b . . . and remove the cover from over the heater blower motor

9.6 Heater blower motor wiring socket

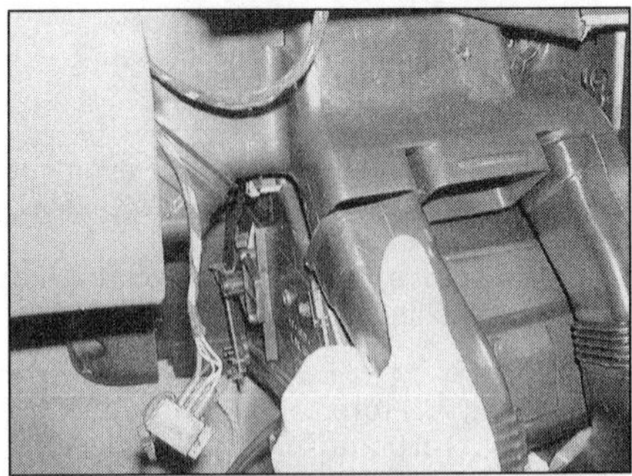
9.13 Removing the air ducts from the rear of the heater housing

Refitting

8 Refitting is a reversal of removal.

Heater matrix

Removal

9 Where fitted, remove the air duct from the rear of the engine compartment.

10 Fit hose clamps to the heater hoses at the bulkhead.

11 Identify the hoses for position, then loosen the clips and disconnect them from the heater matrix. Plug the stubs to prevent coolant spilling onto the floor when the matrix is removed from inside the car.

12 Remove the centre console as described in Chapter 11.

13 Release the cable ties and remove the air ducts from the rear of the heater housing **(see illustration)**.

14 Unclip the rear cover from the heater housing **(see illustration)**.

15 Using a screwdriver, release the clips securing the two hoses to the heater matrix **(see illustration)**.

16 Place cloth rags beneath the matrix, then release the clips on each side of the heater housing and pull the hoses down from the matrix. Expect some loss of coolant.

17 Carefully slide the heater matrix from the housing.

Refitting

18 Refitting is a reversal of removal.

Heater housing

Removal

19 On models with air conditioning, the refrigerant must be evacuated by a qualified engineer.

Warning: Do not attempt to carry out this work yourself, as it is potentially dangerous.

20 Remove the facia panel (see Chapter 11).

21 On models with air conditioning, unscrew the bolt and disconnect the refrigerant hoses at the bulkhead.

22 Fit hose clamps on the heater hoses at the bulkhead, then loosen the clips and disconnect them.

23 Working inside the car, remove the lower trim panel from the facia with reference to Chapter 11.

24 Release the cable ties, then disconnect and remove the air ducts from the rear of the heater housing.

25 Disconnect the air ducts from the sides of the heater housing.

26 Remove the windscreen wiper motor and linkage with reference to Chapter 12.

27 Inside the car, unscrew the dashboard crossmember mounting nuts and bolts.

28 Unbolt the support bracket from the heater housing.

29 Where a passenger airbag is fitted, remove the knee guard from the bulkhead.

30 Remove the steering column as described in Chapter 10.

31 Unscrew the nuts and fold out the support brackets from the top of the pedal assembly.

32 Unscrew the bolts securing the fusebox to the dashboard crossmember.

33 Note how the wiring cables are located, then remove the dashboard crossmember.

34 Disconnect the wiring from the heater housing.

35 In the engine compartment, remove the heater blower motor as described in paragraphs 1 to 7.

36 Unscrew the bolts and remove the motor mounting frame from the top of the bulkhead.

37 Inside the engine compartment, unscrew the bolts securing the heater housing to the lower floor.

38 Place polythene sheeting or cloth rags in the passenger compartment, then withdraw the heater housing.

Refitting

39 Refitting is a reversal of removal.

Heater control panel

Removal

40 Unscrew the bolt and remove the centre console side panel for access to the rear of the heater control panel.

41 Carefully press out the panel from the rear, and disconnect the control shaft.

42 Disconnect the wiring. Note the location of the plugs to ensure correct refitting.

43 Release the clip and disconnect the control cable.

44 Withdraw the heater control panel.

45 If necessary, the switch panel can be removed by pulling off the knobs and removing the screws. Also if necessary disconnect the control cables from the heater housing **(see illustration)**.

Refitting

46 Refitting is a reversal of removal.

9.14 Unclip the rear cover from the heater housing

9.15 Releasing the heater hose clips from the matrix

9.45 Control cable on the side of the heater housing

Automatic Climate Control (ACC) Module

Removal

47 Using a screwdriver, carefully prise out the two switches each side of the ACC panel, and disconnect the wiring.

48 Press out the ACC Module from behind and disconnect the wiring.

Refitting

49 Refitting is a reversal of removal, but on completion calibrate the ACC system by pressing the 'AUTO' and 'OFF' buttons simultaneously.

Solar sensor

Removal

50 At the centre top of the facia panel, slide the solar sensor cover rearwards.

51 Disconnect the wiring.

52 With the cover on the bench, depress and twist the sensor anticlockwise to remove it from the cover.

Refitting

53 Refitting is a reversal of removal, but on completion calibrate the ACC system by pressing the 'AUTO' and 'OFF' buttons simultaneously.

Interior temperature sensor

Removal

54 Remove the control module as described earlier.

55 Depress the covers each side of the temperature sensor, then pull the cover from the sensor.

56 Using a screwdriver, release the catches and press the sensor inwards.

57 Withdraw the sensor and disconnect the wiring.

Refitting

58 Refitting is a reversal of removal, but on completion calibrate the ACC system by pressing the 'AUTO' and 'OFF' buttons simultaneously.

Mixed air sensor

Removal

59 Remove the glovebox as described in Chapter 11.

60 Undo the screw and remove the panel from the side of the centre console.

61 Remove the air duct for the floor ventilation, then unhook the mixed air sensor and disconnect the wiring. Press out the sensor leads from the connector.

Refitting

62 Refitting is a reversal of removal, but on completion calibrate the ACC system by pressing the 'AUTO' and 'OFF' buttons simultaneously.

Air distribution stepping motor

Removal

63 Remove the control module as described earlier.

64 Undo the screws and remove the stepping motor.

65 Disconnect the wiring.

Refitting

66 Refitting is a reversal of removal, but on completion calibrate the ACC system by pressing the 'AUTO' and 'OFF' buttons simultaneously.

Air blending stepping motor

Removal

67 Remove the glovebox, then undo the screws and remove the panel from the side of the centre console.

68 Remove the air duct from the floor.

69 Disconnect the wiring.

70 Undo the screws and withdraw the air blending stepping motor.

Refitting

71 Refitting is a reversal of removal, but on completion calibrate the ACC system by pressing the 'AUTO' and 'OFF' buttons simultaneously.

Fan control unit

Removal

72 Remove the glovebox as described in Chapter 11.

73 Undo the screw and remove the panel from the side of the centre console.

74 Remove the floor air duct.

75 Undo the screw and remove the protective cover.

76 Undo the screws and remove the fan control unit, then disconnect the wiring.

Refitting

77 Before refitting the control unit, smear some silicon paste on the surface which contacts the evaporator. Tighten the screws.

78 Reconnect the wiring and start the ventilation fan. Check that no condensate leaks from the control unit.

79 Refit the protective cover and the floor air duct.

80 Refit the panel to the side of the centre console, then refit the glovebox.

81 On completion, calibrate the ACC system by pressing the 'AUTO' and 'OFF' buttons simultaneously.

10 Air conditioning system - general information and precautions

General information

1 Air conditioning is available as an option on all models. It enables the temperature of air inside the car to be lowered, and also dehumidifies the air, which makes for rapid demisting and increased comfort.

2 The cooling side of the system works in the same way as a domestic refrigerator. Refrigerant gas is drawn into a belt-driven compressor, and passes into a condenser mounted in front of the radiator, where it loses heat and becomes liquid. The liquid passes through a receiver and expansion valve to an evaporator, where it changes from liquid under high pressure to gas under low pressure. This change is accompanied by a drop in temperature, which cools the evaporator. The refrigerant returns to the compressor, and the cycle begins again.

3 Air drawn through the evaporator passes to the air distribution unit. The air conditioning system is switched on with the switch located on the heater panel.

4 The heating side of the system works in the same way as on models without air conditioning.

5 The compressor operation is controlled by an electromagnetic clutch on the drive pulley. Any problems with the system should be referred to a Saab dealer.

Precautions

6 When working on the air conditioning system, it is necessary to observe special precautions. If for any reason the system must be disconnected, entrust this task to your Saab dealer or a refrigeration engineer.

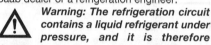

Warning: The refrigeration circuit contains a liquid refrigerant under pressure, and it is therefore dangerous to disconnect any part of the system without specialised knowledge and equipment. The refrigerant is potentially dangerous, and should only be handled by qualified persons. If it is splashed onto the skin, it can cause frostbite. It is not itself poisonous, but in the presence of a naked flame (including a cigarette) it forms a poisonous gas. Uncontrolled discharging of the refrigerant is dangerous, and potentially damaging to the environment. Do not operate the air conditioning system if it is known to be short of refrigerant, as this may damage the compressor.

11 Air conditioning system components - removal and refitting

Warning: Do not attempt to open the refrigerant circuit. Refer to the precautions given in Section 10.

1 The only operation which can be carried out easily without discharging the refrigerant is renewal of the compressor drivebelt. This is described in Chapter 1, Section 16. All other operations must be referred to a Saab dealer or an air conditioning specialist.

2 If necessary for access to other components, the compressor can be unbolted and moved aside, **without** disconnecting its flexible hoses, after removing the drivebelt.

3 Access to the condenser is gained by removing the grille.

Chapter 4 Part A:
Fuel and exhaust systems

Contents

Degrees of difficulty

Easy, suitable for novice with little experience 

Fairly easy, suitable for beginner with some experience 

Fairly difficult, suitable for competent DIY mechanic

Difficult, suitable for experienced DIY mechanic 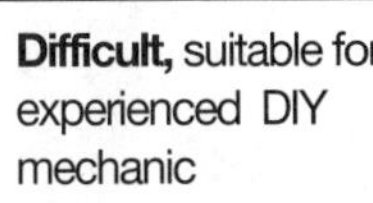

Very difficult, suitable for expert DIY or professional

Specifications

System type

1985 cc models with B206i or B204i engines	Bosch Motronic 2.10.2 engine management system
1985 cc Turbo models with B204L engine	Saab Trionic engine management system
2290 cc models with B234I engine	Bosch Motronic 2.10.2 engine management system

Fuel system data (Bosch Motronic 2.10.2 engine management system)

Air mass flow meter	
Operating temperature	165°C
Output:	
No flow	0.2 V
4 grammes/sec	1.0 V
33 grammes/sec	2.6 V
133 grammes/sec	4.6 V
Electronic Control Unit (ECU)	
Quiescent power consumption	<2.5 mA
Throttle Position Sensor	
Resistance:	
At idle	2.4 to 3.4 V
At full throttle	0.7 to 1.0 V
Idle Air Control Valve (IAC)	
No. of coils	2
Coil winding resistance	9 to 15 Ω
Operating frequency	100Hz
Coolant temperature sensor	
Resistance:	
20°C	2.3 to 2.7 kΩ
60°C	565 to 670 Ω
90°C	200 to 240 Ω
Fuel injectors	
Resistance	14.5 ± 0.35 Ω
Flow capacity	107 ml per 30 secs

Fuel system data (Bosch Motronic 2.10.2 engine management system) (continued)

Crankshaft position sensor

Resistance	540 Ω
Sensor to reluctor disc clearance	0.4 to 1.3 mm

Lambda sensor

Preheater rating	12 W
Sensor resistance	4.0 Ω
Output signal range	0 to 1.0 V

Fuel pressure regulator

Opening fuel pressure	3.0 bar

Fuel pump/gauge sender unit

Fuel pump capacity	700ml per 30 secs at 3.0 bar
Fuel gauge sender resistance:	
Full tank	350 Ω
Empty tank	35 Ω

Idle speed

All models	900 rpm, controlled by ECU (not adjustable)

Exhaust gas CO content

All models	Controlled by ECM (not adjustable)

Fuel system data (Saab Trionic engine management system)

Manifold absolute pressure sensor (expressed in absolute pressure)

Pressure	Voltage (approx)
-0.75 bar	0.48
-0.50 bar	0.95
0 bar	1.9
0.25 bar	2.4
0.50 bar	2.8
0.75 bar	3.3

Inlet air temperature sensor

Temperature (°C)	Voltage (V)
-30	4.5
-10	3.9
20	2.4
40	1.5
60	0.9
80	0.54
90	0.41

Throttle position switch	Resistance (Ω)	Voltage (V)
Pins 1 and 2	1.6 to 2.4	5 ± 0.1
Pins 2 and 3 - idling	0.8 to 1.2	0.5 ± 0.4
Pins 2 and 3 - wide open	2.0 to 3.0	4.5 ± 0.4

Crankshaft position sensor

Resistance (pins 1 and 2)	540 ± 55 Ω

Fuel pressure regulator

Opening fuel pressure	3.0 ± 0.1 bar

Injectors

Resistance at 20°C	12.0 ± 0.35 Ω
Flow capacity	176 ± 14 ml/30 seconds
Maximum flow difference between injectors	18 ml

Idle air control valve

Resistance at 20°C	7.7 ± 1 Ω

Fuel pump

Type	Electric immersed in fuel tank
Capacity at 3.0 bars	700 ml/30 seconds (minimum)
Fuel gauge sender unit winding resistance	33 to 370 Ω

Idle speed

All models	Controlled by ECM 900 ± 50 rpm (not adjustable)

Fuel system data (Saab Trionic engine management system) (continued)

Exhaust gas CO content		
All models	Controlled by ECM (not adjustable)	
Boost control valve		
Winding resistance	3 ± 1 Ω	
Turbocharger		
Basic boost pressure	0.40 ± 0.03 bar	
Maximum boost pressure	0.8 bar	
Pressure switch opens at	1.05 bar	
Recommended fuel	95 RON unleaded	
Torque wrench settings	**Nm**	**lbf ft**
Coolant temperature sensor	13	9
Crankshaft position sensor screw	8	6
Exhaust front pipe to exhaust manifold	40	30
Exhaust front pipe to turbocharger	25	18
Exhaust manifold to cylinder head	25	18
Exhaust system joint nuts and bolts	20	15
Fuel filter unions	21	15
Fuel pump securing ring	75	55
Inlet manifold to cylinder head	22	16
Lambda sensor	45	33
Throttle body to inlet manifold	8	6
Turbocharger to exhaust manifold	22	16

1 General information and precautions

The fuel supply system consists of a fuel tank mounted under the rear of the car (with an electric fuel pump immersed in it), a fuel filter, and the fuel feed and return lines. The fuel pump supplies fuel to the fuel rail, which acts as a reservoir for the four fuel injectors which inject fuel into the inlet tracts. A fuel filter is incorporated in the feed line from the pump to the fuel rail, to ensure that the fuel supplied to the injectors is clean. The filter is mounted adjacent to the fuel tank.

The engine management system is of Bosch Motronic type (normally-aspirated models) or Saab Trionic type (Turbo models). Refer to the relevant Sections for further information on the operation of each of the relevant fuel injection systems.

A cruise control system is fitted as standard equipment on 'SE' models, and is available as an option on 'S' models.

Turbo models are fitted with a water-cooled turbocharger (see Sections 16 and 17 for more information). Boost pressure is controlled by the Saab Motronic engine management, as detailed in Sections 7 and 15.

Precautions

Warning: Many of the procedures in this Chapter require the disconnection of fuel lines, which may result in some fuel spillage. Before carrying out any operation on the fuel system, refer to the precautions given in "Safety first!" and follow them implicitly. Petrol is a highly-dangerous and volatile liquid, and the precautions necessary when handling it cannot be overstressed.

2 Air cleaner assembly - removal and refitting

Removal

1 Ensure that the ignition is switched off, then unplug the wiring from the air mass flow meter.

2 Release the spring clips and separate the air mass flow meter from the rear of the air cleaner housing (where applicable, see Section 14). Rest the meter carefully on the inner wing - do not allow to hang unsupported as this risks damage to the delicate internal components. On Turbo models, release the hose clips and disconnect the air ducting from the air cleaner housing.

3 Release the spring clips and remove the cover from the air cleaner housing. Lift out the air filter element, noting which way up it is fitted, see Chapter 1 for details.

4 Undo the securing nuts and lift the air cleaner housing out of the engine compartment **(see illustration)**. If required, the intake duct can be removed by depressing the locking button and withdrawing the duct from the front of the housing.

Warning: Do not run the engine with the air cleaner housing and/or ducting removed, particularly on Turbo models - the depression at the turbocharger intake may increase very suddenly if the engine speed is raised above idle.

Refitting

5 Refitting is a reversal of removal. Where applicable, ensure that the air mass flow meter wiring is securely reconnected.

2.4 Lift the air cleaner housing out of the engine compartment (non-turbo model shown)

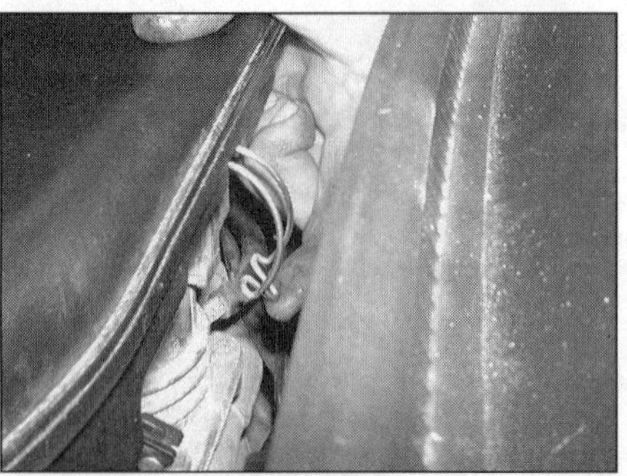

3.1a Release the clips . . .

3 Accelerator cable - removal, refitting and adjustment

Removal

1 Working in the engine compartment, undo the screws/release the clips and lift off the cover panel (Turbo models) or resonator assembly (normally aspirated models) from the top of the throttle body **(see illustrations)**.
2 Open the throttle by hand slightly, unhook the accelerator cable from the throttle disc arm and then release the throttle. Extract the spring clip and withdraw the accelerator cable outer from its mounting bracket **(see illustrations)**.
3 Release the accelerator cable from any securing clips in the engine compartment.
4 Working in the drivers footwell, disconnect

3.2a Unhook the accelerator cable from the throttle disc arm . . .

3.2b . . . then extract the spring clip and withdraw the accelerator cable outer from its mounting bracket

3.1b . . . and lift the resonator assembly (non-turbo model shown) from the top of the throttle body

the accelerator cable from the top of the accelerator pedal with reference to Section 4 **(see illustration)**.
5 Pull the accelerator cable through the bulkhead into the engine compartment and remove it from the vehicle.

Refitting

6 Pass the accelerator cable through the bulkhead aperture and into the space behind the facia, above the drivers footwell .
7 Lay the cable in position through the engine compartment securing it with the retaining clips, where applicable. Ensure that the cable is not kinked or twisted at any point.
8 Insert the end of the cable outer into its mounting bracket at the throttle body and secure it in position with the metal spring clip.
9 Open the throttle by hand slightly, then hook the end of the cable inner into the recess in the throttle disc arm. Release the throttle and allow it to return to its idle stop.

Adjustment

10 Have an assistant depress the accelerator pedal to the wide-open throttle position. On models with manual transmission, the pedal should be touching its stop. On models with automatic transmission, the pedal should be just touching, but **not** operating, the kick-down switch. Hold the pedal stationary in this position.

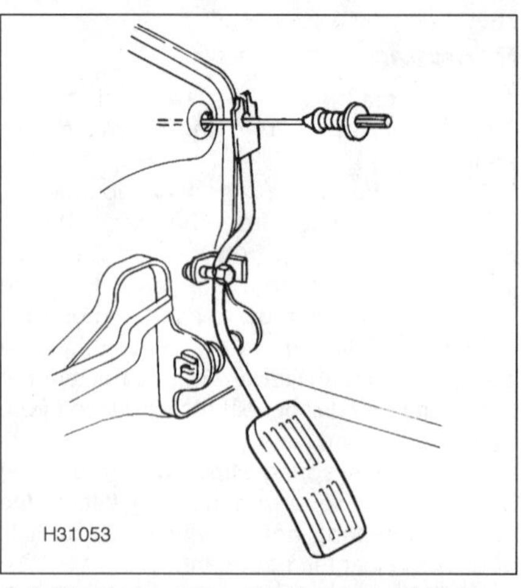

3.4 Disconnect the accelerator cable from the top of the accelerator pedal

11 Working in the engine compartment, turn the knurled knob at the end of the accelerator cable outer until the throttle disc arm reaches its full-throttle stop.
12 Release the accelerator pedal and allow it to return to its rest position.
13 Woking in the drivers footwell, turn the pedal adjustment screw, located on the accelerator pedal arm just above the pivot shaft, so that any slack in the cable inner is eliminated.
14 At the throttle body, verify that the throttle arm still rests against its idle stop.
15 Refit the cover panel/resonator assembly over the inlet manifold and throttle body.
16 Refit the lower cover panel to the underside of the facia.

4 Accelerator pedal - removal and refitting

Removal

1 Disconnect the accelerator cable from the throttle body, with reference to Section 3.
2 Working in the driver's footwell, release the fasteners and detach the lower cover panel from the underside of the facia. On certain models, it may be necessary to first undo the screws and release the diagnostic connector from the underside of the facia.
3 Reach up behind the facia and unhook the accelerator cable from the top of the accelerator pedal.
4 Compress the pedal return spring and release it from the pedal arm.
5 Using a pair of pliers, pull the locking clip from the end of the pedal pivot shaft and recover the bush.
6 Withdraw the pedal from its mounting bracket and remove it from the vehicle **(see illustration)**.

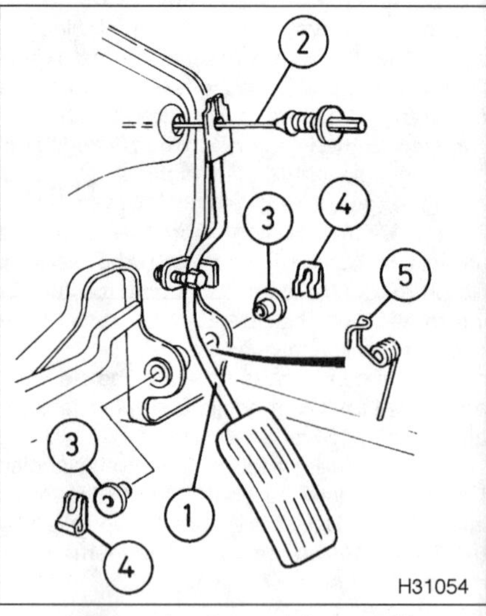

4.6 Accelerator pedal assembly

1 Pedal
2 Accelerator cable
3 Bush
4 Locking clip
5 Return spring

Refitting

7 Refitting is a reversal of removal. On completion, adjust the throttle cable with reference to Section 3.

5 Cruise control system - description and component renewal

Description

1 The cruise control system allows the driver to preselect the speed of the car and then release the accelerator pedal. The cruise control system then adjusts the throttle automatically to maintain a constant road speed. The system is deactivated when either the clutch or brake pedals are depressed, when neutral gear is selected (models with automatic transmission) or when the main cruise control switch is switched off. The system has a memory function which allows a pre-selected cruising speed to be resumed, if the operation of the cruise control has been interrupted by depressing the brake or clutch pedals.

2 When the cruise control system is active, the pre-selected road speed may be increased or decreased in small increments, by means of the multi-function cruise control system switch.

3 In the event of a fault in the cruise control system, first check all relevant wiring for security. Further testing is best left to a Saab dealer, who will have the necessary diagnostic equipment to find the fault quickly.

4 The main components of the system fitted to later models are as follows:

a) ***Control module**: the control module incorporates an electric stepper motor, which operates the control cable attached to the throttle butterfly lever on the throttle housing. The module is supplied with the speed of the car by signals sent from the speedometer in the instrument panel. The system is not operative at speeds below 20 mph, nor above 137 mph. When the cruise control system is active on Turbo models, the engine management system ECU is informed of this fact by a signal, to ensure smoother control of the car's speed. The ECU determines the vehicle's road speed from a signal supplied by the Anti-lock Braking System (ABS) ECU.*

b) ***Switches**: the main multi-function control switch for the cruise control system is integral with the steering column left-hand stalk switch. Switches mounted behind the facia and operated by the brake and clutch pedals deactivate the system when either pedal is depressed. As a fail-safe, the brake pedal cruise control switch is earthed through the brake stop-light bulbs, via the main stop light switch - if this circuit develops a fault, the cruise control system will not operate.*

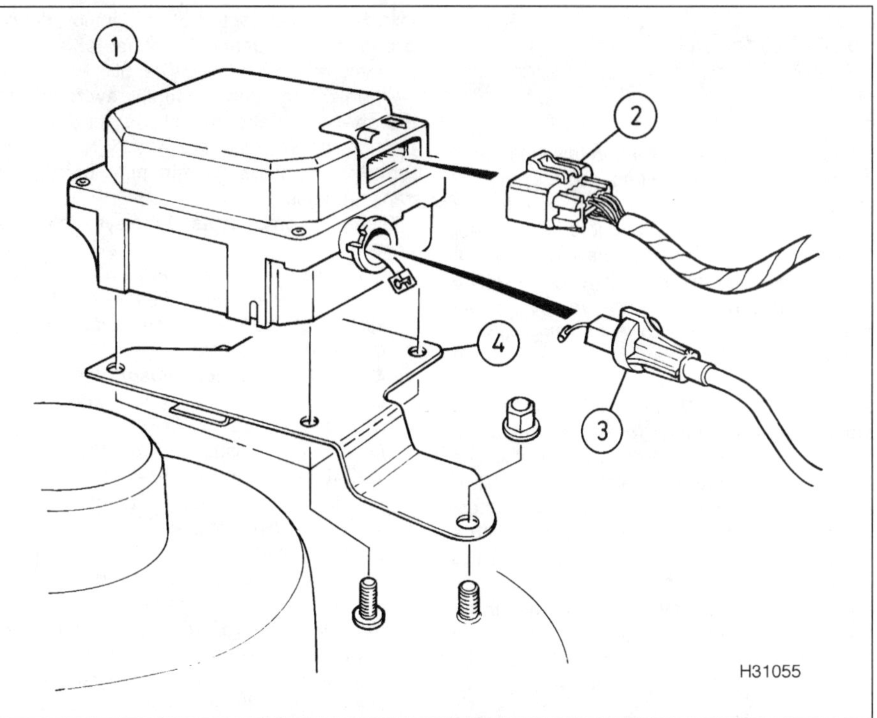

5.7 Cruise control system components

1 Electronic control unit
2 Wiring harness multi-way connector
3 Control cable
4 Mounting bracket

c) ***Indicator light**: the 'CRUISE' indicator light on the instrument panel is illuminated whenever the cruise control system is operating.*

Component renewal

Electronic Control Unit

5 The cruise control system ECU is located in the engine compartment, behind the right hand front suspension turret. Ensure that the ignition is switched before proceeding.

6 Turn the control cable union to disengage the bayonet fixing. Withdraw the cable outer from the control unit slightly, then unhook the cable inner from the internal control chain. Unplug the wiring from the control unit at the multi-way connector.

7 Slacken and withdraw the bolt that secures the control unit mounting bracket to the bodywork. Turn the bracket over, then undo the retaining screws and detach the control unit from the mounting bracket **(see illustration)**.

8 Refitting is a reversal of removal.

Control cable

9 Disconnect the control cable from the control unit as described in the previous sub-Section.

10 Undo the securing screws and remove the cover panel/resonator assembly from above the inlet manifold.

11 Disconnect the accelerator cable from the throttle disc arm, as described in Section 3, then unhook the control cable inner from the throttle disc arm.

12 Depress the locking tabs and release the control cable outer from the accelerator cable mounting bracket,

13 Release the control cable from its securing clips, then remove the control cable from the engine compartment.

14 Refitting is a reversal of removal.

Multi-function control switch

15 Refer to the information given in Chapter 12, Section 4 for the removal of the direction indicator/dip beam/main beam steering column stalk switch.

Pedal switches

16 Remove the fasteners and detach the lower cover panel from the drivers side of the facia. On certain models, it may be necessary to first undo the screws and release the diagnostic connector from the underside of the facia.

17 Reach behind the facia and unplug the wiring from the relevant switch.

18 Carefully prise the switch from its mounting bracket.

19 To refit the switch, carefully pull the switch plunger out, then depress the brake/clutch pedal (as applicable). Insert the switch into its mounting bracket, and slowly release the pedal until it contacts the switch plunger. Reconnect the wiring securely.

Stop-light switch

20 Refer to the information given in Chapter 9.

6 Unleaded petrol - general information and usage

Note: *The information given in this Chapter is correct at the time of writing, and applies only to fuels currently available in the UK. If updated information is thought to be required, check with a Saab dealer. If travelling abroad, consult one of the motoring organisations (or a similar authority) for advice on the petrols available, and their suitability for your vehicle.*

1 The fuel recommended by Saab is given in the Specifications at the start of this Chapter.

2 RON and MON are different testing standards; RON stands for Research Octane Number (also written as RM), while MON stands for Motor Octane Number (also written as MM).

3 All Saab 900 models covered in this manual are designed to run on unleaded fuel with a minimum octane rating of 91 RON; 95 RON unleaded fuel is recommended. All models are equipped with a catalytic converter, and **must** be run on unleaded fuel only. Under no circumstances should leaded fuel be used, as this will damage the catalytic converter.

7 Engine management system - general information

Trionic engine management system

The Saab Trionic engine management system controls three functions of the engine from a single electronic control unit (ECU). The three functions comprise the fuel injection system, ignition system, and on Turbo models, the turbocharger boost control system. Details of the components related to the ignition function are given in Chapter 5B.

The system is microprocessor-controlled, and the fuel system provides the correct amount of fuel necessary for complete combustion under all engine conditions. Data from various sensors is processed in the ECU, in order to determine the opening period of the fuel injectors for the exact amount of fuel to be injected into the inlet manifold.

The system is of sequential type, where fuel is injected in sequence with the engine's firing order. Conventional sequential fuel injection systems requires a camshaft sensor, which works in conjunction with the crankshaft position sensor to indicate which cylinder at TDC is on its compression stroke and which is on its exhaust stroke. The Trionic system has no camshaft sensor, it determines each cylinder's stroke by applying a small, direct current voltage across each spark plug. When a cylinder on its combustion stroke approaches TDC, this voltage causes an ionisation current to flow across the terminals of the spark plug, thus indicating which cylinder requires fuel injection and ignition next. Sequential control of the ignition timing to control combustion knock is achieved in the same manner (see Chapter 5B).

When the ignition is initially switched on and after the fuel pump is operating, all the injectors operate simultaneously for a short period; this helps to minimise cold start cranking times.

The main components of the system are as follows:

a) ***ECU**: the electronic control unit controls the entire operation of the fuel injection system, ignition system and turbocharger boost control system.*
b) ***Crankshaft position sensor**: the crankshaft position sensor provides a datum for the ECU to calculate the position of the crankshaft in relation to TDC. The sensor is triggered by a reluctor disc that rotates inside the crankcase.*
c) ***Manifold absolute pressure (MAP) sensor**: the MAP sensor provides a voltage to the ECU, proportional to the pressure in the inlet manifold.*
d) ***Inlet air temperature sensor**: the inlet air temperature sensor provides the ECU with signals which enable it to calculate the density of the air entering the engine.*
e) ***Engine coolant temperature sensor**: the engine coolant temperature sensor informs the ECU of the engine temperature.*
f) ***Throttle position sensor**: the throttle position sensor informs the ECU of the throttle valve position.*
g) ***Lambda sensor**: the lambda sensor provides the ECU with constant feedback on the oxygen content of the exhaust gases.*
h) ***Ignition discharge module and spark plugs** : the ignition discharge module (or cartridge) contains four HT coils connected directly to the spark plugs (see Chapter 5B).*
i) ***Injectors**: each fuel injector consists of a solenoid-operated needle valve, which opens under the commands from the ECU. Fuel from the fuel rail is then delivered through the injector nozzle into the inlet manifold.*
j) ***Boost pressure control (solenoid) valve**: the boost pressure control valve (also referred to as the solenoid valve) controls the operation of the turbocharger. Under certain conditions (ie in 1st gear), boost pressure is reduced.*
k) ***Idle air control valve**: the idle air control valve controls the volume of air bypassing the throttle butterfly. The system maintains the engine idle speed under all conditions of load imposed by the alternator, air conditioning compressor, or when a gear other than P or N is selected on automatic transmission models. If there is a break in the idle air control valve circuit, the valve opening is set by an internal spring, to control the engine speed at approximately 1000 rpm. The idle air control valve is also used as an exhaust emission control device; when the engine is on overrun, insufficient air intake can cause poor combustion leading to high emissions of hydrocarbons. During these conditions, the ECU opens the IAC to increase air intake flow and control hydrocarbon emissions.*
l) ***EVAP canister-purge valve**: the EVAP canister-purge valve is operated when the engine is started, to purge fuel accumulated in the canister. In order to allow the lambda sensor to compensate for the additional fuel, the system is operated in short phases.*
m) ***Fuel pump**: the fuel pump is housed in the fuel tank. The pump housing incorporates a separate feed pump which supplies the main fuel pump with pressurised fuel, free of air bubbles.*

Bosch Motronic engine management system

The operation of the Bosch Motronic engine management system is very similar to the Saab Trionic system described in the previous sub-Section. Principal differences are detailed below.

a) ***Ignition system:** a conventional ignition system is employed, using a separate HT ignition coil and rotary distributor. Combustion knock detection is provided by means of a cylinder block-mounted knock sensor (see Chapter 5B for details).*
b) ***Air mass flow meter:** engine load is measured by means of a hot-film type air mass flow meter, rather than by measuring inlet manifold depression. The meter houses a heated metal filament which is mounted in the flow of the air intake. The temperature reduction in the wire caused by the flow of air over it causes a change in electrical resistance, which is converted to a variable voltage output signal. Measuring air mass flow, rather than volume flow compensates for the changes in air density encountered when driving on roads at different altitudes above sea level. Note that this method of measurement also precludes the need for a measurement of inlet air temperature.*
c) ***Camshaft position sensor:** The ignition distributor houses the camshaft position sensor. It informs the ECU when cylinder No 1 is on its combustion stroke, allowing sequential fuel injection and ignition timing (for combustion knock control) to be employed.*

'Check Engine' indicator

With either type of engine management system, if the 'Check Engine' warning light comes on, the car should be taken to a Saab dealer at the earliest opportunity. A complete test of the engine management system can then be carried out, using dedicated Saab electronic diagnostic test equipment. The engine management system can be set into a 'self-test' mode, which will cause it to display any stored fault code information by flashing the 'Check Engine' light in a coded sequence. This sequence can then be interpreted to determine what faults have been detected by the engine management system; refer to Section 13 for greater detail.

8 Fuel supply system - precautions and depressurisation

Note: *Refer to the warning at the end of Section 1 before proceeding.*

Warning: The following procedure will merely relieve the pressure in the fuel system - remember that fuel will still be present in the system components, and to take precautions accordingly before disconnecting any of them.

1 The fuel system referred to in this Section is defined as the tank-mounted fuel pump, the fuel filter, the fuel injectors, the fuel rail and the pressure regulator, and the metal pipes and flexible hoses connected between these components. All these contain fuel, which will be under pressure while the engine is running and/or while the ignition is switched on.

Warning: Residual fuel pressure may remain for some time after the ignition has been switched off, and must be relieved before any of these components are disturbed for servicing work.

2 Open the fusebox, beneath a cover panel adjacent to the instrument panel (see "*Weekly checks*") and remove the fuel pump fuse (fuse number 32).

3 Turn the ignition key and crank the engine. If it starts and runs, allow it to idle until it stops through fuel starvation; this should not take more than a few seconds. Try to start it two more times, to ensure that all pressure has been relieved.

4 Disconnect the battery negative terminal, then refit the fuel pump fuse.

5 Place a suitable container beneath the relevant connection/union to be disconnected, and have a large rag ready to soak up any escaping fuel not being caught by the container.

6 Slowly loosen the connection or union nut (as applicable) to avoid a sudden release of pressure, and position the rag around the connection to catch any fuel spray which may be expelled. Once the pressure is released, disconnect the fuel line.

Cut the fingers from an old pair of rubber gloves and secure them over the open fuel lines or ports with elastic bands, to minimise fuel loss and to prevent the entry of dirt into the fuel system.

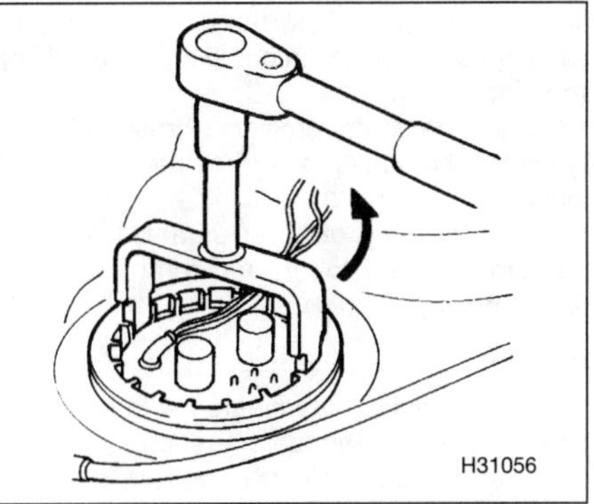

9.3 Unscrew and remove the locking ring from the top of the fuel pump

9 Fuel pump - removal and refitting

Warning: Refer to the precautions given in Section 1 and the information detailed in the "Safety First!" Section of this manual, before disturbing any component in the fuel supply system.

Note: *On all models, the fuel pump also incorporates the fuel gauge sender unit.*

Removal

1 Disconnect the battery negative cable and position it away from the terminal.

2 Remove the fuel tank as described in Section 12.

3 The unit is secured by a screwed ring. Saab technicians use a special tool to unscrew the ring, but a large pair of grips (water pump pliers) inserted between the serrations on the inside edge of the ring will achieve the same result. Unscrew and remove the ring **(see illustration)**. Note the location arrows on the top of the pump and tank.

4 Carefully lift the pump flange away from the surface of the fuel tank. Allow the excess fuel to drain back into the tank, then rotate the pump clockwise through about one quarter of a turn and withdraw it from the fuel tank **(see illustration)**. Recover the O-ring seal from the tank aperture.

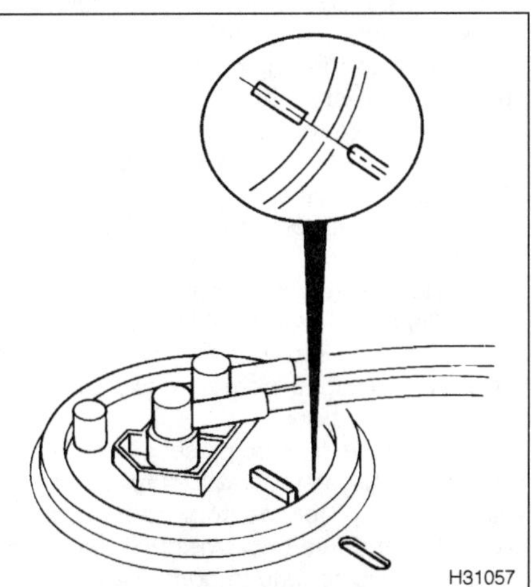

9.6 When refitting the fuel pump, ensure that the markings on the fuel pump and tank are aligned

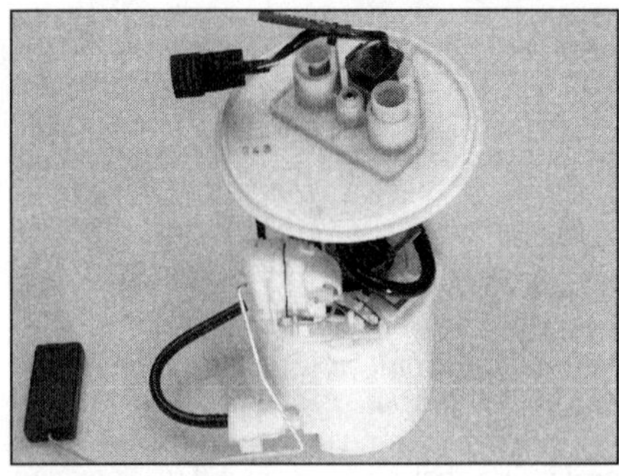

9.4 Fuel pump removed from the fuel tank

Refitting

5 Fit a new O-ring seal to the fuel tank aperture, pressing it firmly into its recess.

6 Lower the fuel pump into the fuel tank, rotating it to ensure that the alignment markings on the fuel pump and tank line up **(see illustration)**.

7 Screw the large plastic locking ring into position and tighten it using the method described for its removal.

8 Refit the fuel tank as described in Section 12.

9 Reconnect the battery negative cable.

10 Fuel pump relay - removal and refitting

Removal

1 The fuel pump relay is located on the main relay board, behind the facia (see Chapter 12 for exact location).

2 Disconnect the battery negative cable and position it away from the terminal.

3 Release the fasteners and detach the lower cover panel from the driver's side of the facia.

4 Remove the securing screws and lower the fuseboard away from the facia.

5 The fuel pump relay is the one labelled 'F'; 2nd column from the left, 2nd row from the top.

6 Grasp the relay and pull it squarely from the relay board.

Refitting

7 Refitting is a reversal of removal. Ensure that the relay is pushed firmly into its base.

11 Fuel gauge sender unit - removal and refitting

On all models, the fuel gauge sender unit is integral with the fuel pump; refer to Section 9 for details.

12 Fuel tank - removal, repair and refitting

Warning: Refer to the precautions given in Section 1, and the information detailed in the "Safety First!" Section of this manual, before disturbing any component in the fuel supply system.

1 Before removing the fuel tank, it is preferable that all the fuel is first removed from the tank. Since a fuel tank drain plug is not provided, carry out the removal operation when the tank is almost empty.

Removal

2 Disconnect the battery negative cable and position it away from the terminal.

3 Select first gear (manual transmission) or 'Park' (automatic transmission) and chock the front wheels securely. Raise the rear of the car and support it securely on axle stands (see "*Jacking and vehicle support*").

4 Loosen the clips and disconnect the filler neck hose from the tank. Also disconnect the breather hose.

5 Slacken and withdraw the fuel filter securing screw. Detach the fuel filter from the side of the fuel tank.

6 Position a trolley jack centrally underneath the fuel tank, with a plank of wood placed on the jack head. Raise the jack until it just starts to take the weight of the fuel tank.

7 Progressively undo the nuts securing the fuel tank support straps to their respective mounting brackets **(see illustration)**. Unhook the ends of each support strap from their brackets, as they become slack.

8 Lower the jack slightly, to gain access to the top of the fuel tank - do not fully lower it at this point.

9 Carefully release all fuel lines from their retaining clips on top and sides of the fuel tank.

10 Unplug the two wiring connectors from the top of the fuel pump.

11 Label the fuel return and supply hoses to aid refitting later, then disconnect them from the top of the fuel pump. Do this by depressing the locking tabs at the sides of each quick-release union. Be prepared for some fuel leakage.

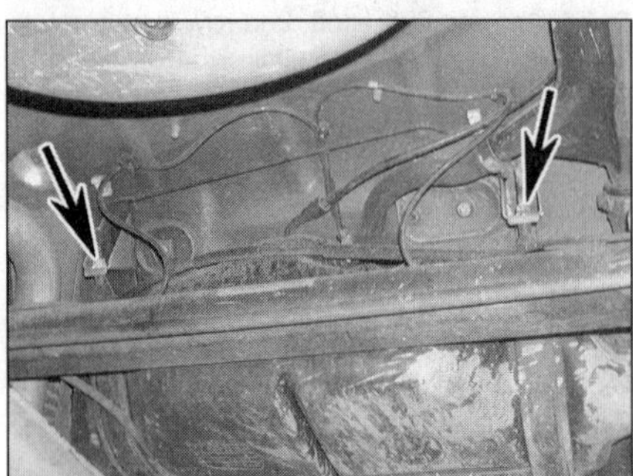

12.7 Progressively undo the nuts (arrowed) securing the fuel tank support straps to their respective mounting brackets

12 Disconnect any remaining breather hoses or cables that may prevent the removal of the tank.

13 With the help of an assistant, lower the fuel tank to the ground and remove it from under the car.

Repair

14 If the tank is contaminated with sediment or water, remove the fuel pump and wash the tank out with clean fuel. In certain cases, it may be possible to have small leaks or minor damage repaired. Seek the advice of a suitable specialist before attempting to repair the fuel tank.

Refitting

15 Refitting is a reversal of removal, noting the following points:

a) *Inspect the O-rings at the fuel supply and return quick release unions, on the top of the fuel pump.*
b) *Ensure that all fuel lines and breather hoses are correctly routed and are not kinked or twisted.*
c) *Tighten the fuel tank support straps securely.*

13 Engine management system - testing, checking and adjustment

General information

1 On models with either Bosch Motronic or Saab Trionic engine management systems, the engine idle speed and air-to-fuel mixture (and hence the exhaust gas CO content) are automatically controlled by the ECU. The *checking* of idle speed and mixture is possible on all models by using a tachometer and exhaust gas analyser, but some difficulty may be experienced connecting a conventional tachometer to the engine on Turbo models fitted with Direct Ignition. In addition, as all models are fitted with catalytic converters, the levels of CO, HC and NOx produced may be difficult to measure accurately, with anything other than professional test equipment, if the system is operating normally. However, it may be possible to at least confirm the existence of a fuelling or ignition fault, by detecting high levels of one or more of these exhaust gas pollutants, using a commercially available exhaust gas analyser.

2 If a fault appears to be present in the engine management system, first ensure that all the system wiring connectors are securely connected and free of corrosion. Then ensure that the fault is not due to poor maintenance - ie, check that the air cleaner filter element is clean, that the fuel filter has been renewed at the specified interval, and that the spark plugs and associated HT components (including the distributor and ignition coil, where applicable) are in good condition. Also check that the engine breather hoses are clear and undamaged. Finally, check that the cylinder compression pressures are correct, referring to Chapters 1, 2A and 5B for further information.

3 If these checks fail to reveal the cause of the problem, the car should be taken to a Saab dealer for testing. A diagnostic connector is incorporated in the engine management system wiring harness, into which a special Saab electronic diagnostic tester can be plugged. The tester will identify any faults detected by the engine management system ECU by interpreting fault codes stored in the ECU's memory. It also allows system sensors and actuators to be tested remotely without disconnecting them or removing them from the vehicle. This alleviates the need to test all the system components individually, using conventional test equipment. The diagnostic connector is located on the underside of the facia, on the driver's side of the vehicle.

'Check Engine' indicator

4 With either type of engine management system, if the 'Check Engine' warning light comes on, the car should be taken to a Saab dealer at the earliest opportunity. A complete test of the engine management system can then be carried out, using dedicated Saab electronic diagnostic test equipment. The engine management system can be set into a 'self-test' mode, which will cause it to display any stored fault code information by flashing the 'Check Engine' light in a coded sequence. This sequence can then be interpreted to determine what faults have been detected by the engine management system. It should be noted that fault codes displayed by the flashing 'Check Engine' indicator are limited to those types of malfunction that would lead to increased exhaust emissions or evaporative loss emissions. For a comprehensive diagnosis of the entire engine management system, the vehicle must be taken to a Saab dealer or fuel injection system specialist.

5 To initiate the 'self-test' sequence, carry out the steps detailed in the following sub-Sections.

Turbo models with Saab Trionic engine management

6 Switch off the engine and turn the ignition switch to the 'OFF' position. Wait for a few seconds, then turn the ignition switch to the 'ON' position, without starting the engine.

7 The 'Check Engine' indicator will start to flash. A 3 second long flash, followed by a pause followed by another 3 second long flash indicates that the flash code is about to be displayed. After a short pause, count the number of short flashes that follow - this corresponds to the first fault code. After a pause of about 2 seconds, the next fault code will be displayed, if more than one malfunction has been detected. A long, 3 second flash indicates that all fault codes have been displayed.

8 The flash sequence then repeats itself, and continues to do so until the ignition is switched off, or the engine is started. The flash code diagnosis table is given below.

Flash Code	*Fault*
2	MAP sensor
3	Inlet air temperature sensor
4	Coolant temperature sensor
5	Throttle position sensor
6	Lambda sensor
7	Adaptation fault
8	Evaporative loss system purge valve
9	Electronic control unit (ECU) fault

Non-Turbo models with Bosch Motronic engine management

9 Locate the diagnostic connector, underneath the facia on the driver's side of the vehicle.

10 Obtain a length of thin, single-strand sheathed copper wire. Strip about 10 mm of the sheathing from either end of the wire.

11 Ensure that ignition is switched off, then carefully insert one end of the stripped wire into the position corresponding to pin 6 on the diagnostic connector.

12 Ensure that the free end of the wire is not touching any part of the vehicle, then turn the ignition switch to the 'ON' position, without starting the engine.

13 Touch the free end of the wire onto a good electrical earthing point (such as an exposed, unpainted part of the vehicle's bodywork) for a period of between 0.5 and 4.5 seconds.

14 The 'Check Engine' indicator will start to flash. A long flash indicates that the flash code is about to be displayed. Count the number of short flashes that follow - this corresponds to the first digit. After a short pause, count the number of short flashes that follow - this corresponds to the second digit. After a pause, the system displays the next stored fault, if more than one malfunction has been detected. The flash sequence then repeats itself, and continues to do so until the ignition is switched off, or the engine is started. The flash code diagnosis table is given below.

Flash Code	*Fault*
11	Secondary air injection relay
12	No fault
21	Air mass flow sensor
41	Coolant temperature sensor
51	Throttle position sensor
61	Lambda sensor
71	Long adaptation time
73	Short adaptation time
81	Evaporative loss system purge valve
91	Electronic control unit (ECU) Random Access Memory (RAM) fault
92	Electronic control unit (ECU) Read Only Memory (ROM) fault

14.9a Crankshaft position sensor securing screw (arrowed)

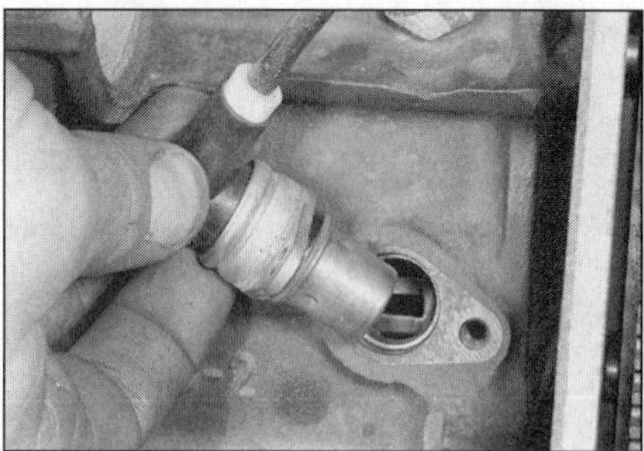

14.9b Removing the crankshaft position sensor from the cylinder block

14 Engine management system components (Bosch Motronic) - removal and refitting

Warning: Refer to the precautions given in Section 1, and the information detailed in the "Safety First" Section of this manual, before disturbing any component in the fuel supply system.

Electronic Control Unit (ECU)

Removal

1 Ensure that the ignition is switched off. Disconnect the battery negative cable and position it away from the terminal.

2 Working inside the vehicle, in the right hand footwell, remove the fixings and lower the cover panel away from the underside of the facia and steering column.

3 Peel back the carpet to expose the ECU mounted on the bodywork at the base of the A-pillar.

4 Release the locking lever and unplug the multiway wiring harness connector from the underside of the ECU.

5 Slacken and withdraw the securing screws and remove the ECU from the vehicle.

Refitting

6 Refitting is a reversal of removal. Ensure that the wiring harness multiway connector is secured with the locking lever. Note that if a new ECU has been fitted, it will gradually 'learn' the engines characteristics as the vehicle is driven. Drivability, performance and fuel economy may be slightly reduced during this period.

Crankshaft position sensor

Removal

7 The crankshaft position sensor is located on the front surface of the cylinder block, adjacent to the transmission bellhousing mating surface.

8 Note the routing of the wiring for the crankshaft position sensor. Disconnect the wiring at the connector located at the left hand end of the cylinder head. Release the wiring from the retaining clips along its length.

9 Remove the retaining screw and withdraw the sensor from its location on the front left-hand side of the cylinder block **(see illustrations)**. Recover the O-ring, noting how it is fitted. Clean the seating in the cylinder block.

Refitting

10 Refitting is a reversal of removal, ensuring that the O-ring is properly seated. Tighten the sensor securing screw to the specified torque. Ensure that the wiring is retained with the clips/cable ties, following its original routing, and that the multiway connector is securely reconnected.

Coolant temperature sensor

Removal

11 The sensor is threaded into the inlet manifold **(see illustration)**. Ensure that the engine is completely cold, then release the pressure in the cooling system by removing and then refitting the expansion tank filler cap (see "*Weekly checks*").

12 Release the clips and remove the intake air resonator assembly from the top of the throttle body.

13 Unplug the wiring connector from the sensor.

14 Unscrew the sensor from the lower inlet manifold. Be prepared for some coolant loss.

Refitting

15 Clean the threads, then insert the sensor into the inlet manifold, and tighten securely.

16 Refit the wiring connector, then refit the intake air resonator, ensuring that the two O-ring seals are properly seated.

17 Top up the cooling system with reference to "*Weekly checks*".

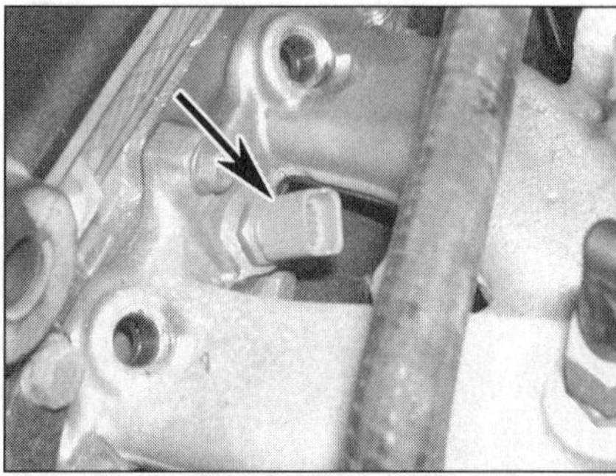

14.11 The coolant temperature sensor (arrowed) is threaded into the inlet manifold (fuel rail and injectors removed)

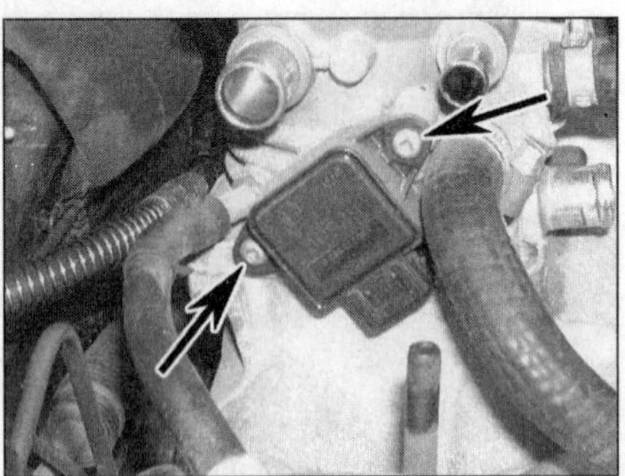
14.23 Throttle position sensor securing screws (arrowed)

14.26 Lambda sensor location in the exhaust system front pipe

Throttle position sensor

Removal

18 Ensure that the ignition switch is turned to the 'OFF' position.

19 Release the clips and remove the intake air resonator assembly from the top of the throttle body.

20 Release the clips and remove the crankcase breather hose from the cylinder head cover and throttle body.

21 Slide the idle air control valve from its mounting stud and move it to one side.

22 Unplug the wiring connector from the throttle position sensor.

23 Slacken and remove the securing screws, then withdraw the sensor from the end of the throttle spindle **(see illustration)**. Recover the O-ring seal.

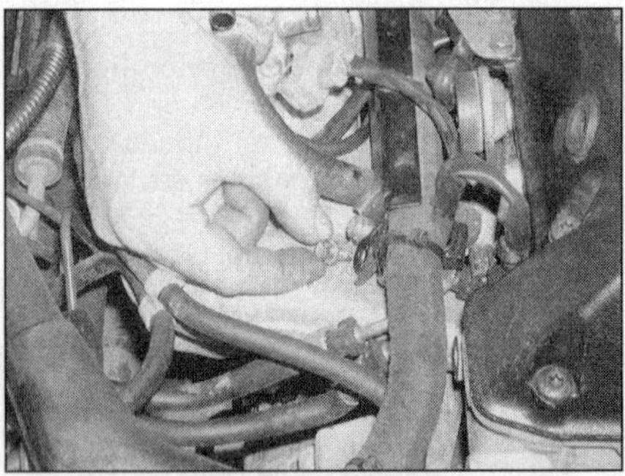
14.36a Slacken and withdraw the screws . . .

Refitting

24 Refitting is a reversal of removal. Ensure that the throttle position sensor O-ring seal is correctly seated. When refitting the intake air resonator to the throttle body, ensure that the two O-ring seals are properly seated.

Lambda sensor

Removal

25 Ensure that the ignition is switched to the 'OFF' position.

26 Unscrew the sensor from the exhaust system front pipe **(see illustration)**. A slotted socket will be required as the sensor incorporates a flying lead.

27 Release the sensor wiring from the retaining clips in the engine compartment, noting how it is routed.

28 Unplug the sensor wiring from the main harness at the connector situated at the left hand end of the cylinder head and remove it from the engine compartment.

Refitting

29 Refitting is a reversal of the removal procedure. Coat the threads of the sensor with a suitable high temperature anti-seize grease, then refit and tighten it to the specified torque.

Injectors, fuel rail and pressure regulator

Note: *Refer to the warning at the end of Section 1 before proceeding.*

Removal

30 Depressurise the fuel system as descried in Section 8. Ensure that the ignition switch is then turned to the 'OFF' position.

31 Release the clips and remove the intake air resonator assembly from the top of the throttle body.

32 Release the clips and remove the crankcase breather hose from the cylinder head cover and throttle body.

33 Slide the idle air control valve from its mounting stud and move it to one side.

34 Unbolt the dipstick tube from the rear of the cylinder head.

35 Refer to Section 3 and disconnect the accelerator cable from the throttle body. Where applicable, refer to Section 5 and disconnect the cruise control cable from the throttle body.

36 Slacken and withdraw the two screws securing the cable guide to the fuel rail. Release the cable ties and detach the wiring harness from the cable guide. Remove the cable guide from the engine compartment **(see illustrations)**.

37 Release the locking clips and then unplug the wiring from all four injectors **(see illustration)**. Mark each connector to avoid confusion on refitting.

38 Disconnect the fuel supply and return hoses from the right hand end of the fuel rail. The hoses incorporate quick release connectors, which ordinarily require access to a special separation tool. The tool consists of a plastic collar which slides between the fuel hose fitting and the fuel pipe leading to the fuel rail; when pushed into position, the tool splays out the four internal tabs inside the quick release fitting allowing the hose to be disconnected. The same effect can be achieved with a length of plastic tubing, cut along its length to allow it to be fitted over the fuel pipe. Note that the rubber grommets must be prised from the fittings, before the hoses can be disconnected **(see illustrations)**.

39 Remove the two screws securing the fuel rail to the cylinder head **(see illustration)**. Place a cloth beneath the fuel rail, to soak up fuel which will escape as the fuel rail is removed.

40 Lift the fuel rail from the inlet manifold complete with the fuel injectors. If required release the metal clamp and remove the fuel

14.36b . . . then remove the cable guide

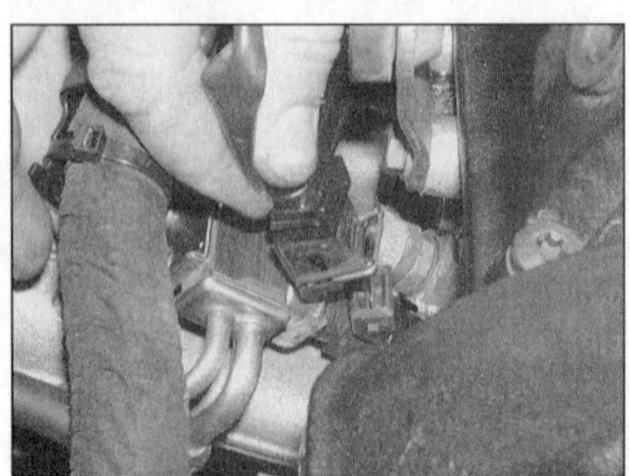
14.37 Unplug the wiring connectors from the fuel injectors

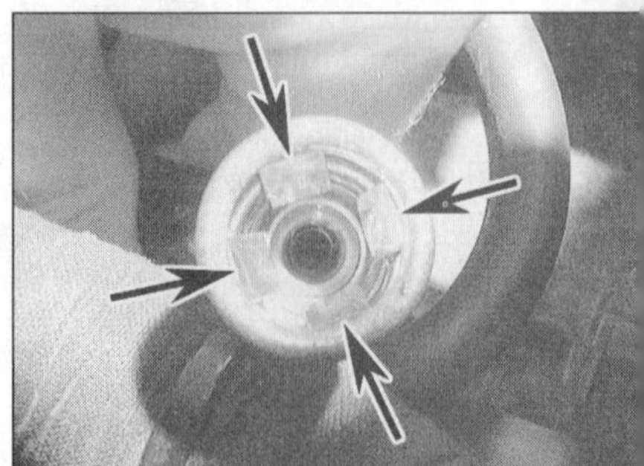
14.38a The quick release fitting contains four internal tabs (arrowed)

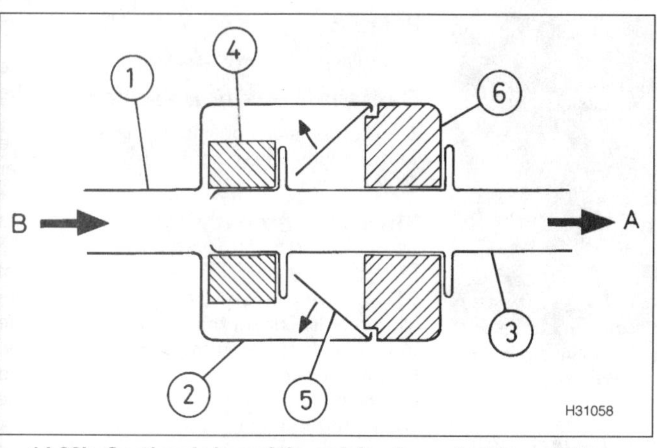

14.38b Sectional view of the quick release fuel hose fittings

A To fuel rail
B From fuel tank
1 Fuel hose
2 Quick release fitting
3 Fuel pipe
4 Seal
5 Spring tab
6 Grommet

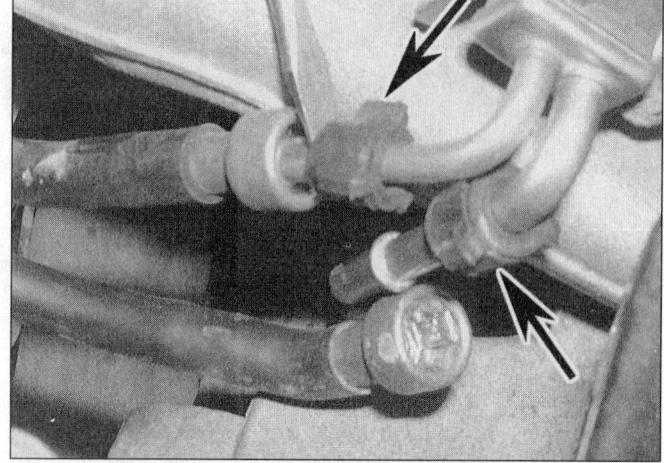

14.38c The rubber grommets must be prised from the fittings, before the hoses can be disconnected

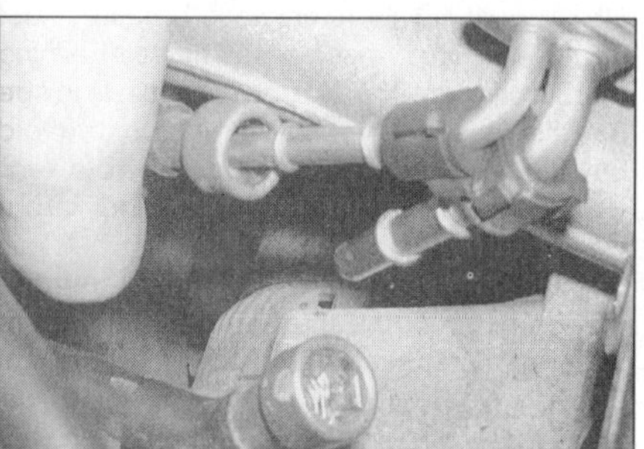

14.38d Disconnecting the fuel supply and return hoses from the fuel rail

pressure regulator from the left hand end of the fuel rail. Recover the O-ring seal **(see illustrations)**.

41 Prise out the retaining clips, and pull the injectors from the fuel rail **(see illustrations)**. Recover the rubber O-ring seals.

Refitting

42 Refitting is a reversal of the removal procedure. Fit the injectors to the fuel rail, then press the fuel rail and injectors into the inlet manifold as an assembly. Before locating the rubber O-rings in the inlet manifold, apply a little petroleum jelly to them, to facilitate entry of the injectors. Make sure that the correct wiring plugs are connected to the injectors. When refitting the intake air resonator to the throttle body, ensure that the two large O-ring seals are properly seated.

Idle air control valve

Removal

43 Ensure that the ignition switch is turned to the 'OFF' position.

44 Release the clips and remove the intake air resonator assembly from the top of the throttle body.

14.39 Remove the screws . . .

14.40a . . . and lift the fuel rail from the inlet manifold

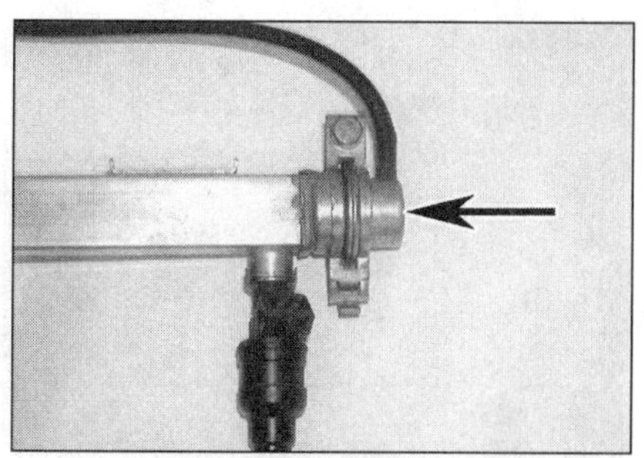

14.40b To remove the fuel pressure regulator (arrowed), undo the screw and release the metal clamp

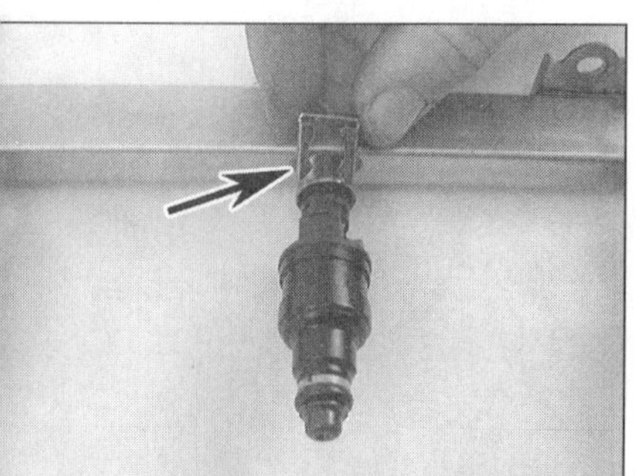

14.41a Prise out the retaining clips . . .

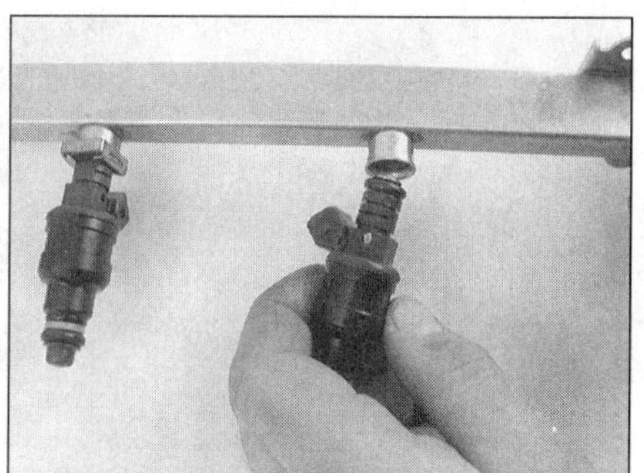

14.41b . . . and pull the injectors from the fuel rail

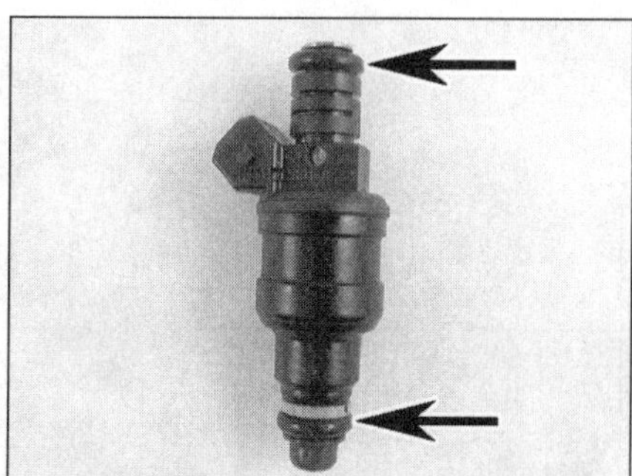

14.41c Renew the O-ring seals

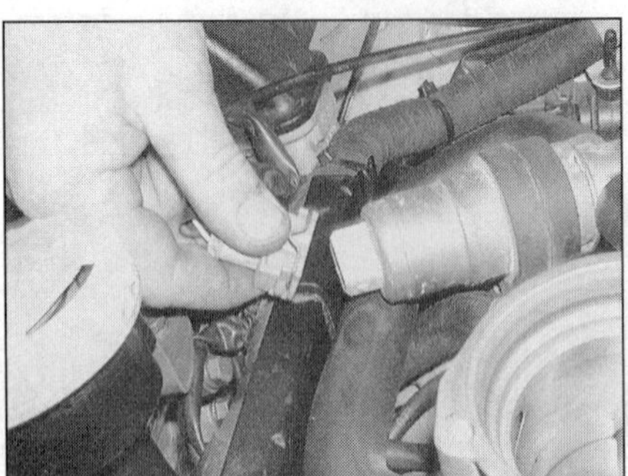

14.45a Unplug the wiring connector from the base of the valve . . .

45 Unplug the wiring connector from the base of the valve, then slide the valve from its mounting stud **(see illustrations)**.

46 Release the air hoses from the ports on the throttle body and then remove the valve from the engine compartment **(see illustrations)**.

Refitting

47 Refitting is a reversal of removal. When refitting the intake air resonator to the throttle body, ensure that the two O-ring seals are properly seated.

Evaporative loss system purge valve

Removal

48 Ensure that the ignition switch is turned to the 'OFF' position.

49 Remove the section of flexible intake air ducting that connects the air mass flow meter

14.45b . . . then slide the valve from its mounting stud (arrowed)

to the resonator assembly.

50 Unplug the wiring from the purge valve, then disconnect the vacuum hoses, noting their order of fitment to avoid confusion on refitting.

51 Release the valve from its mounting collar and remove it from the engine compartment.

Refitting

52 Refitting is a reversal of removal.

Air mass flow meter

Removal

53 Ensure that the ignition switch is turned to the 'OFF' position.

54 Unplug the wiring connector from the side of the air mass flow meter **(see illustration)**.

55 Slacken the hose clips, release the spring clips and detach the meter from the air cleaner and flexible intake air ducting **(see illustrations)**.

Refitting

56 Refitting is a reversal of removal.

Camshaft position sensor

57 The camshaft position sensor is integral with the ignition distributor; refer to Chapter 5B for details of its removal and refitting.

Throttle body

Removal

58 Remove the cover panel, then slacken the clip and disconnect the intake hose from the top of the throttle housing.

59 Disconnect the wiring plug from the throttle position sensor.

60 With the engine cold, unscrew the filler cap on the coolant expansion tank, then refit and tighten the cap.

61 Loosen the clips, then disconnect and plug the coolant hoses from the throttle housing.

62 Disconnect the crankcase breather hose from the throttle housing **(see illustration)**.

63 Disconnect the IAC valve hose from the throttle housing.

64 Disconnect the accelerator cable (and where necessary, the cruise control cable) with reference to Sections 3 and 5.

65 Slacken and remove the mounting screws, then lift the throttle housing from the inlet manifold **(see illustration)**. Recover the O-ring.

Refitting

66 Clean the contact surfaces of the throttle housing and inlet manifold, then refit the

14.46a Release the air hoses from the ports on the throttle body (arrowed) . . .

14.46b . . . and then remove the valve from the engine compartment

14.54 Unplug the wiring connector from the side of the air mass flow meter

14.55a Slacken the hose clips . . .

14.55b . . . release the clips and detach the meter from the air cleaner and flexible intake air ducting

14.62 Disconnect the crankcase breather hose from the throttle housing

14.65 Slacken and remove the throttle housing mounting screws

throttle housing together with a new O-ring. Tighten the mounting screws.

67 Reconnect and adjust the accelerator cable (and where necessary, the cruise control cable) with reference to Section 3.

68 Reconnect the IAC valve hose and the crankcase breather hose.

69 Reconnect the coolant hoses and tighten the clips.

70 Reconnect the wiring plug to the throttle position sensor.

71 Reconnect the rubber connecting hose to the throttle housing, and tighten the clip.

72 Top-up the cooling system with reference to "*Weekly checks*".

15 Engine management system components (Saab Trionic) - removal and refitting

Warning: Refer to the precautions given in Section 1, and the information detailed in the "Safety First!" Section of this manual, before disturbing any component in the fuel supply system.

Electronic Control Module (ECM)

Removal

1 Ensure that the ignition is switched off. Disconnect the battery negative cable and position it away from the terminal.

2 Working inside the vehicle, in the right hand footwell, remove the fixings and lower the cover panel away from the underside of the facia and steering column.

3 Peel back the carpet to expose the ECM mounted on the bodywork at the base of the A-pillar. Remove the central locking system relay from its mountings.

4 Release the locking lever and unplug the multiway wiring harness connector from the underside of the ECM.

5 Slacken and withdraw the securing screws and remove the ECM from the vehicle.

Refitting

6 Refitting is a reversal of removal. Ensure that the wiring harness multiway connector is secured with the locking lever. Note that if a new ECM has been fitted, it will gradually 'learn' the engines characteristics as the vehicle is driven. Drivability, performance and fuel economy may be slightly reduced during this period.

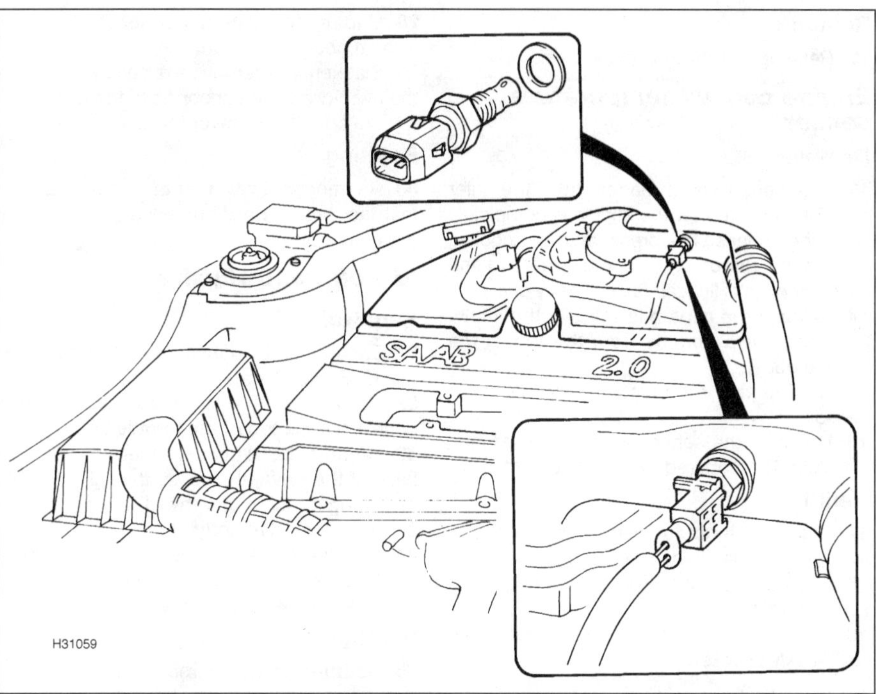

15.8 Inlet air temperature (IAT) sensor

Inlet air temperature sensor

Removal

7 Release the fixings and remove the cover panel from above the throttle body.

8 Disconnect the wiring from the sensor, which is located in the main air inlet duct to the throttle housing. Unscrew the sensor from the air inlet duct, and recover the sealing washer **(see illustration)**.

Refitting

9 Refitting is a reversal of removal, but check and if necessary renew the sealing washer.

Manifold absolute pressure (MAP) sensor

Removal

10 Release the fixings and remove the cover panel from above the throttle body **(see illustration)**.

11 Disconnect the wiring plug and vacuum hose, then remove the securing screw and detach the sensor from the underside of the engine compartment cross-bracing bar.

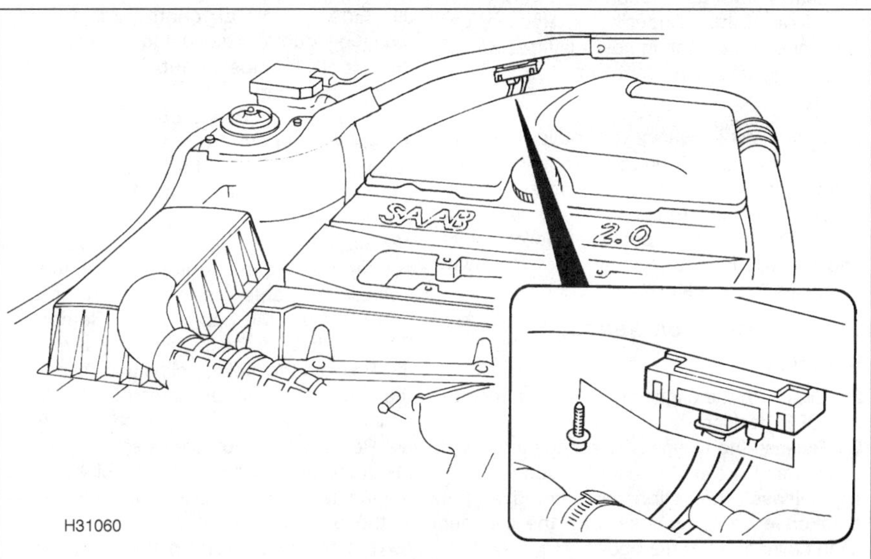

15.10 Manifold absolute pressure (MAP) sensor

Refitting

12 Refitting is a reversal of removal.

Engine coolant temperature sensor

Removal

13 The sensor is threaded into the inlet manifold. Ensure that the engine is completely cold, then release the pressure in the cooling system by removing and then refitting the expansion tank filler cap (see "*Weekly checks*").

14 Release the clips and remove the intake air resonator assembly from the top of the throttle body.

15 Unplug the wiring connector from the sensor.

16 Unscrew the sensor from the lower inlet manifold. Be prepared for some coolant loss.

Refitting

17 Clean the threads, then insert the sensor into the inlet manifold, and tighten securely.

18 Ensure that the wiring connector is securely refitted.

19 Top up the cooling system with reference to "*Weekly checks*".

Crankshaft position sensor

Removal

20 The crankshaft position sensor is located on the front surface of the cylinder block, adjacent to the transmission bellhousing mating surface.

21 Remove the cover from above the throttle body, then slacken the hose clips and remove the inlet air ducting, as necessary to gain access to the crankshaft position sensor. Note the routing of the wiring for the crankshaft position sensor. Disconnect the wiring at the connector located at the left hand end of the cylinder head. Release the wiring from the retaining clips along its length.

22 Remove the retaining screw and withdraw the sensor from its location on the front left-hand side of the cylinder block. Recover the collar and O-ring, noting how it is fitted. Clean the seating in the cylinder block.

Refitting

23 Refitting is a reversal of removal, ensuring that the collar and O-ring are properly seated. Tighten the sensor securing screw to the specified torque. Ensure that the wiring is retained with the clips/cable ties, following its original routing, and that the multiway connector is securely reconnected.

Throttle position sensor

Removal

24 Ensure that the ignition switch is turned to the 'OFF' position.

25 Release the fixings and remove the cover panel from the top of the throttle body.

26 Release the clips and remove the crankcase breather hose from the cylinder head cover and throttle body.

27 Slide the idle air control valve from its mounting stud and move it to one side.

28 Unplug the wiring connector from the throttle position sensor.

29 Slacken and remove the securing screws, then withdraw the sensor from the end of the throttle spindle. Recover the O-ring seal.

Refitting

30 Refitting is a reversal of removal. Ensure that the throttle position sensor O-ring seal is correctly seated.

Idle air control valve

Removal

31 Ensure that the ignition switch is turned to the 'OFF' position.

32 Release the fixings and remove the cover panel from the top of the throttle body.

33 Unplug the wiring connector from the base of the valve, then slide the valve from its mounting stud. Note the direction of flow arrow on the valve body.

34 Release the air hoses from the ports on the throttle body and then remove the valve from the engine compartment.

Refitting

35 Refitting is a reversal of removal. The direction of flow arrow on the valve body must face away from the throttle body.

Fuel supply rail, injectors and pressure regulator

Note: *Refer to the warning at the end of Section 1 before proceeding.*

Removal

36 Depressurise the fuel system as described in Section 8. Ensure that the ignition switch is then turned to the 'OFF' position.

37 Release the fixings and remove the cover panel from the top of the throttle body.

38 Release the clips and remove the crankcase breather hose from the cylinder head cover and throttle body.

39 Slide the idle air control valve from its mounting stud and move it to one side.

40 Unbolt the dipstick tube from the rear of the cylinder head.

41 Refer to Section 3 and disconnect the accelerator cable from the throttle body. Where applicable, refer to Section 5 and disconnect the cruise control cable from the throttle body.

42 Slacken and withdraw the two screws securing the cable guide to the fuel rail. Release the cable ties and detach the wiring harness from the cable guide. Remove the cable guide from the engine compartment.

43 Release the locking clips and then unplug the wiring from all four injectors. Mark each connector to avoid confusion on refitting.

44 Remove the two screws securing the fuel rail to the cylinder head. Place a cloth beneath the fuel rail, to soak up fuel which will escape as the fuel rail is removed.

45 Lift the fuel rail from the inlet manifold complete with the fuel injectors. If required, release the metal clamp and remove the fuel pressure regulator from the left hand end of the fuel rail. Recover the O-ring seal.

46 Prise out the retaining clips, and pull the injectors from the fuel rail. Recover the rubber O-ring seals.

Refitting

47 Refitting is a reversal of the removal procedure. Fit the injectors to the fuel rail, then press the fuel rail and injectors into the inlet manifold as an assembly. Before locating the rubber O-rings in the inlet manifold, apply a little petroleum jelly to them, to facilitate entry of the injectors. Make sure that the correct wiring plugs are connected to the injectors. When refitting the intake air resonator to the throttle body, ensure that the two O-ring seals are properly seated.

Throttle housing

Removal

48 Loosen the clip, and disconnect the rubber connecting hose from the throttle housing.

49 Disconnect the wiring plug from the throttle position sensor.

50 With the engine cold, unscrew the filler cap on the coolant expansion tank, then refit and tighten the cap.

51 Loosen the clips, then disconnect and plug the coolant hoses from the throttle housing.

52 Disconnect the crankcase breather hose from the throttle housing.

53 Disconnect the IAC valve hose from the throttle housing.

54 Disconnect the accelerator cable (and where necessary, the cruise control cable) with reference to Sections 3 and 5.

55 Unscrew the mounting nuts, and remove the throttle housing from the inlet manifold. Recover the O-ring.

Refitting

56 Clean the contact surfaces of the throttle housing and inlet manifold, then refit the throttle housing together with a new O-ring. Tighten the mounting bolts.

57 Reconnect and adjust the accelerator cable (and where necessary, the cruise control cable) with reference to Section 3.

58 Reconnect the IAC valve hose and the crankcase breather hose.

59 Reconnect the coolant hoses and tighten the clips.

60 Reconnect the wiring plug to the throttle position sensor.

61 Reconnect the rubber connecting hose to the throttle housing, and tighten the clip.

62 Top-up the cooling system with reference to "*Weekly checks*".

Boost control valve

Removal

63 The valve is located at the front right hand corner of the engine compartment.

64 Ensure that the ignition is switched off, then unplug the wiring connector from the valve.

65 Mark each of the hoses leading to the valve to identify their fitted positions, then release the clips and detach the hoses from the valve ports.

66 Undo the screws and remove the boost control valve from the engine compartment.

Refitting

67 Refitting is a reversal of removal. It is vitally important that the hoses are refitted to the correct ports on the boost control valve **(see illustration)**.

Boost pressure bypass valve

Removal

68 Unplug the vacuum hose from the top of the valve body.

69 Slacken the clips then disconnect the air intake ducts from the sides of the bypass valve **(see illustration)**.

Refitting

70 Refitting is a reversal of removal.

Lambda sensor

71 Refer to the information given in Section 14.

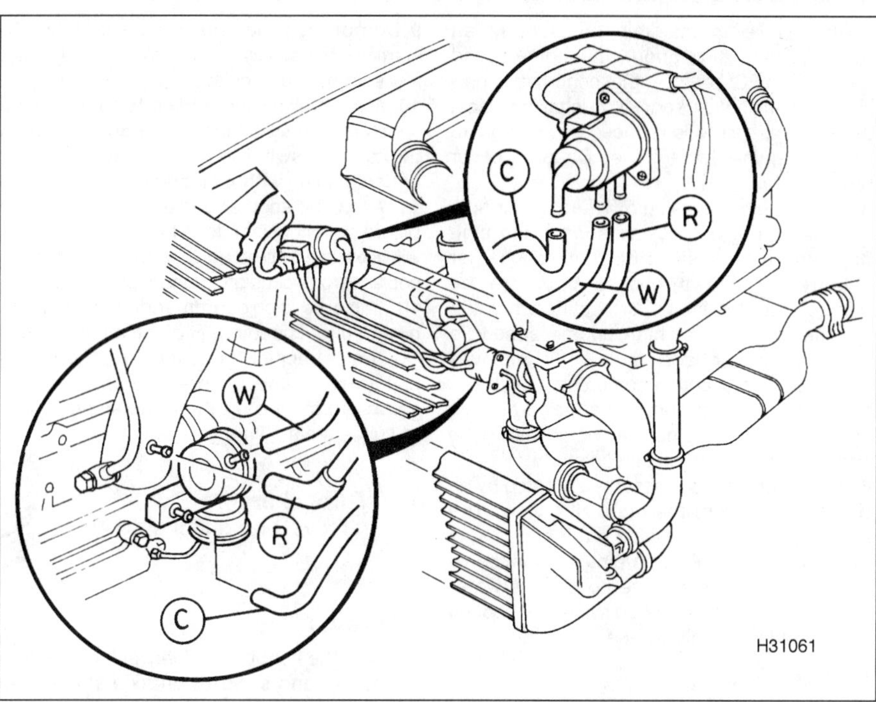

15.67 Boost pressure control valve location and hose connections

W Waste gate connection R Inlet air duct connection C Turbocharger connection

16 Turbocharger - description and precautions

Description

1 The turbocharger fitted to 2.0 litre Turbo models increases engine efficiency and performance by raising the pressure in the inlet manifold above atmospheric pressure. Instead of the inlet air being sucked into the combustion chambers, it is forced in under pressure. This leads to a greater charge pressure increase during combustion and improved fuel burning, which raises the thermal efficiency of the engine. Under these conditions, additional fuel is supplied by the fuel injection system, in proportion to the increased air flow.

2 Energy for the operation of the turbocharger comes from the exhaust gas. The gas flows through a specially-shaped housing (the turbine housing) and in so doing, spins the turbine wheel. The turbine wheel is attached to a shaft, at the end of which is another vaned wheel known as the compressor wheel. The compressor wheel spins in its own housing, and compresses the inlet air on the way to the inlet manifold.

3 Between the turbocharger and the inlet manifold, the compressed air passes through an intercooler. This is an air-to-air heat exchanger, mounted in front of the radiator and supplied with cooling air from the front grille and electric cooling fans. The temperature of the inlet air rises due to the compression action of the turbocharger - the purpose of the intercooler is to cool the inlet air again, before it enters the engine. Because cool air is denser than hot air, this allows a greater mass of air (occupying the same volume) to be forced into the combustion chambers, resulting in a further increase in the engine's thermal efficiency.

4 Boost pressure (the pressure in the inlet manifold) is limited by a wastegate, which diverts the exhaust gas away from the turbine wheel in response to a pressure-sensitive actuator. The wastegate valve is controlled by the engine management system ECU, via an electronic boost control valve. The ECU opens and closes (modulates) the boost valve several times a second, which results in manifold vacuum being applied to the wastegate valve in a series of rapid pulses - the duty ratio of the pulses depends primarily on engine speed and load. The ECU monitors boost pressure via the manifold pressure sensor, and uses the boost

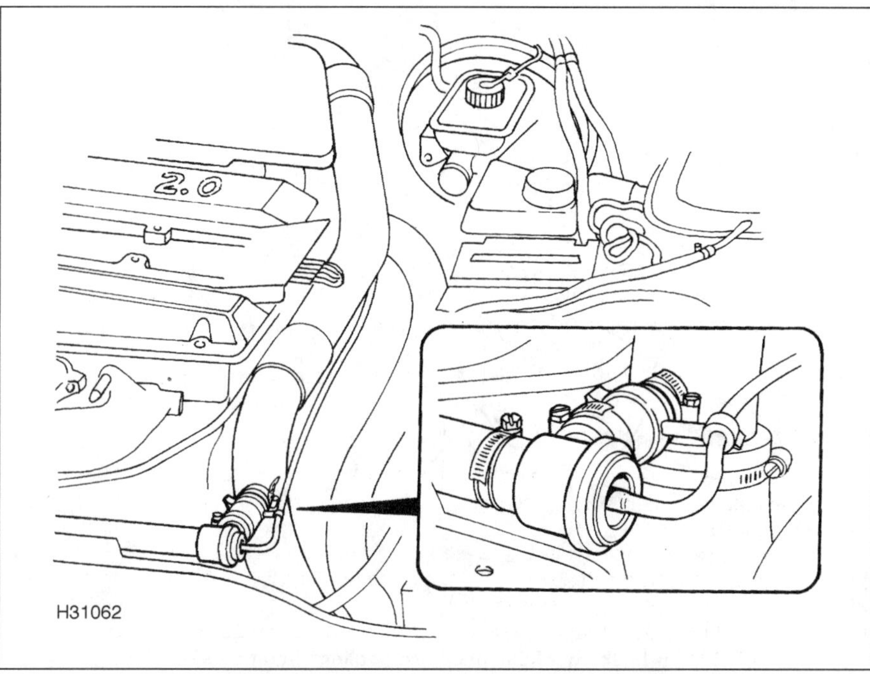

15.69 Boost pressure bypass valve location

control valve to maintain pressure at an optimum level throughout the engine speed range. If the ECU detects that combustion pre-ignition ('pinking' or 'knocking') is taking place, the boost pressure is reduced accordingly to prevent engine damage; see Chapter 5B for greater detail.

5 A boost bypass valve fitted in the air flow between the low pressure supply and high pressure delivery sides of the turbocharger compressor allows excess boost to be dumped into the intake air ducting when the throttle is closed at high engine speed (ie during overrun or deceleration). This improves drivabilty by preventing compressor stall (and therefore reducing turbo 'lag'), and also by eliminating the surging that would otherwise occur when the throttle is reopened.

6 The turbo shaft is pressure-lubricated by an oil feed pipe from the main oil gallery. The shaft "floats" on a cushion of oil and has no moving bearings. A drain pipe returns the oil to the sump. The turbine housing is water cooled and has a dedicated system of coolant supply and return pipes **(see illustration)**.

Precautions

7 The turbocharger operates at extremely high speeds and temperatures. Certain precautions must be observed during servicing activities, to avoid injury to the operator, or premature failure of the turbo.

8 Do not operate the turbo with any of its parts exposed, or with any of its hoses removed. Foreign objects falling onto the rotating vanes could cause excessive damage, and (if ejected) personal injury.

9 Do not race the engine immediately after start-up, especially if it is cold. Give the oil a few seconds to circulate.

10 Always allow the engine to return to idle speed before switching it off - do not blip the throttle and switch off, as this will leave the turbo spinning without lubrication.

11 Allow the engine to idle for a few minutes before switching off after a high-speed run. This will allow the turbine housing to cool before the coolant stops circulating under pressure.

12 Observe the recommended intervals for oil and filter changing, and use a reputable oil of the specified quality. Infrequent oil changes, or use of inferior oil, can cause carbon formation on the turbo shaft, leading to subsequent failure.

17 Turbocharger - removal and refitting

Removal

1 Apply the handbrake, then jack up the front of the car and support on axle stands (see *"Jacking and vehicle support"*).

2 Remove the shield from beneath the radiator, then drain the cooling system as described in Chapter 1.

3 Loosen the clips and disconnect the air hose between the turbocharger and intercooler. Similarly, remove the intake air hose that runs between the air cleaner and the turbocharger intake elbow, together with the boost pressure bypass valve.

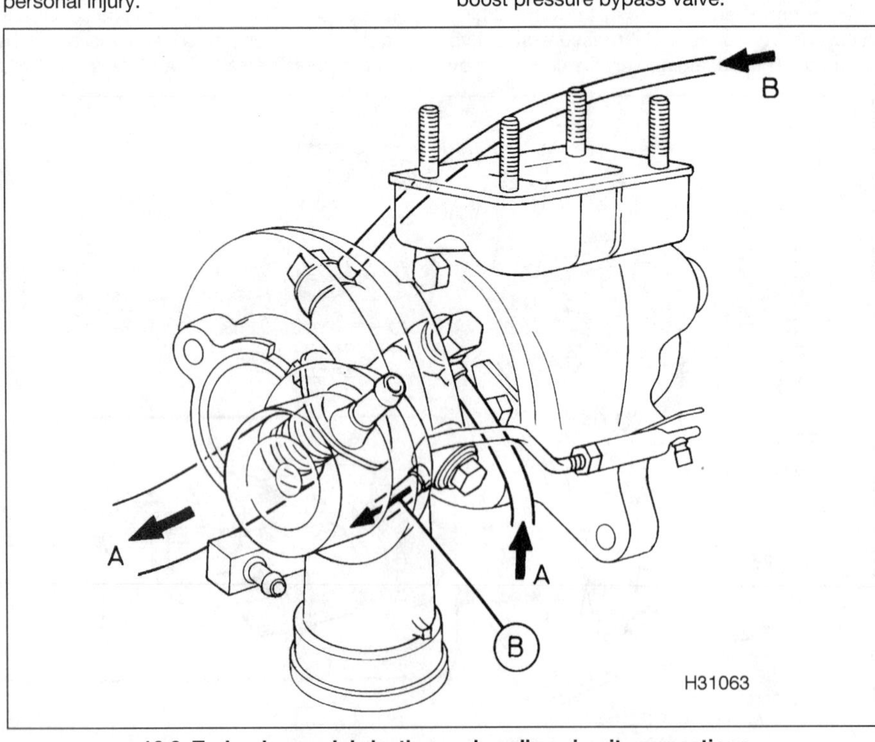

16.6 Turbocharger lubrication and cooling circuit connections

A Lubrication *B Cooling*

4 Unbolt and remove the exhaust system front pipe and catalytic converter.

5 Unbolt and remove the turbocharger bracing bracket. To improve access, remove the circlip and detach the diaphragm unit actuator arm from the waste gate shaft.

6 Slacken the unions and disconnect the oil supply and return pipes from the turbocharger. Plug the open ports to prevent contamination.

7 Mark the three hoses that run to the boost control valve, to identify their fitted positions. Release the clips and disconnect the hoses from the turbocharger, wastegate actuator and air hose.

8 Unbolt the intake elbow from the turbocharger inlet and remove it. Note that this entails unbolting and removing the crankcase ventilation pipe that is connected to the side of the intake elbow.

9 Undo the unions and detach the coolant supply and return unions from the turbine housing. Plug the open ports to prevent contamination.

10 Slacken and remove the turbocharger securing nuts then remove the turbocharger from the exhaust manifold studs.

Refitting

11 Refitting is a reversal of removal, noting the following points:

a) *Fill the turbocharger inter-chamber with clean engine oil, through the oil supply union on the turbocharger. This is important, as the turbocharger must have oil in it when the engine is started.*
b) *Thoroughly clean the exhaust manifold mating surface, before refitting the turbocharger.*
c) *Renew all copper union sealing washers, O-ring seals and gaskets where applicable.*
d) *Tighten all nuts, bolts and oil and coolant unions to the correct torque settings, where specified.*
e) *Apply a suitable high temperature, anti-seize compound to the threads of the exhaust system-to-turbocharger and exhaust manifold-to-turbocharger studs and nuts.*
f) *Ensure that the boost control valve hoses are refitted correctly to the turbocharger, wastegate actuator and air hose (refer to Section 15, illustration 15.67).*
g) *Refit the diaphragm unit actuator rod to the wastegate shaft and secure it with the circlip.*

12 On completion, check that the radiator drain plug is tight, then refit the shield panel.

13 Lower the car to the ground, then check and if necessary top-up the engine oil level (see *"Weekly checks"*). It is strongly recommended that the engine oil is changed before starting the engine if a new turbocharger has been fitted, as this will protect the turbo bearings during the "running-in" period.

14 Refill the cooling system (see Chapter 1).

15 It is recommended that the boost pressure is checked by a Saab dealer at the earliest opportunity.

18 Intercooler - removal and refitting

Removal

1 Remove the front grille as described in Chapter 11.
2 Refer to Chapter 12 and remove the horn, both headlights and both direction indicators.
3 Raise the front of the vehicle and support it securely on axle stands (see "*Jacking and vehicle support*"). Remove the front bumper, as described in Chapter 11.
4 Release the hose clips and disconnect the air hoses from the left hand end of the intercooler.
5 Slacken and withdraw the intercooler securing screws, together with the mounting pillars, washers and grommets.
6 Move the intercooler away from the front panel, lift it from its mountings, and withdraw it from the engine compartment.

Refitting

7 Refitting is a reversal of removal. Ensure that the air hose clips are securely tightened.

19 Inlet manifold - removal and refitting

Warning: Refer to the precautions given in Section 1, and the information detailed in the 'Safety First!' Section of this manual, before disturbing any component in the fuel supply system.

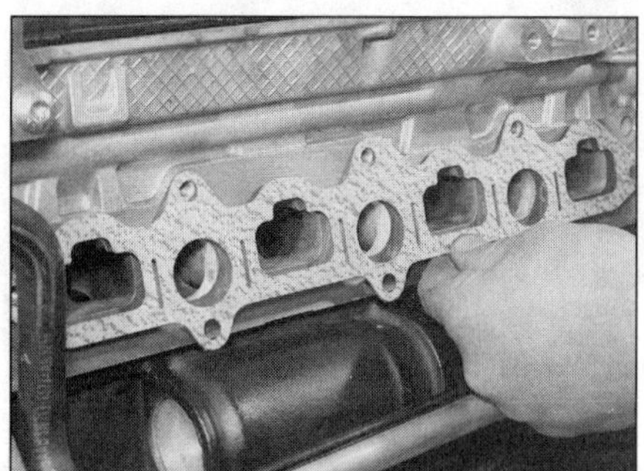

19.8a Fitting an inlet manifold gasket (non-turbo model shown)

Removal

1 Disconnect the battery negative lead.
2 Refer to Section 14 or 15 (as applicable) and remove the throttle housing from the inlet manifold.
3 Remove the fuel rail and fuel injectors from the inlet manifold as described in Section 14 or 15 (as applicable).
4 Disconnect the brake servo vacuum hose from the inlet manifold.
5 Unplug the wiring from the coolant temperature sensor as described in Section 14 or 15.
6 Unscrew the mounting bolts securing the inlet manifold to the cylinder head. Also unscrew the lower bolt from the steady bar.
7 Withdraw the inlet manifold from the cylinder head. Where applicable, carefully withdraw the intake air heating plate, unplugging the wiring at the multiway connector. Recover the gasket from the cylinder head.

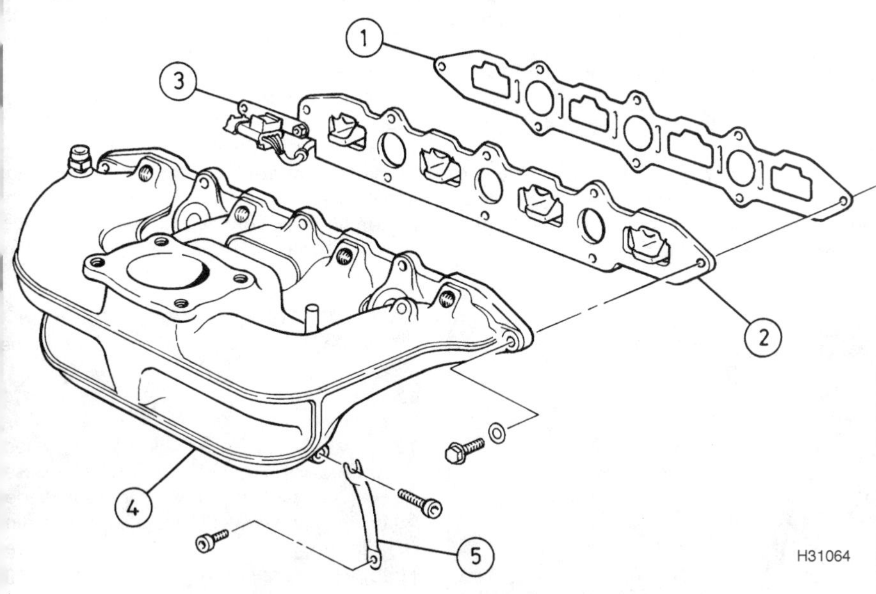

19.8b Inlet manifold and associated components - Turbo model shown

1 Gasket
2 Heating plate
3 Heating plate wiring connector
4 Inlet manifold
5 Support stay

Refitting

8 Refitting is a reversal of removal. Fit a new gasket and where applicable, reconnect the intake air heating plate wiring **(see illustrations)**. Ensure that the manifold retaining bolts are tightened to the specified torque.

20 Exhaust manifold - removal and refitting

Non-turbo models

Removal

1 Apply the handbrake, then jack up the front of the car and support on axle stands (see "*Jacking and vehicle support*").
2 Disconnect the lambda sensor wiring with reference to Section 14 or 15.
3 Remove the exhaust system front pipe and catalytic converter with reference to Section 21.
4 Remove the auxiliary drivebelt as described in Chapter 1. To gain access to the right-hand exhaust manifold nuts, the power steering fluid pump must be unbolted and moved aside; see Chapter 10 for details. Note that there is no need to disconnect the hydraulic fluid pipes.
5 Unscrew and remove the exhaust manifold mounting nuts, then lift the manifold from the cylinder head. Note that the manifold is in two sections; the centre section should be removed first, noting that on the remaining section, sleeves are fitted beneath all the mounting nuts **(see illustrations)**.

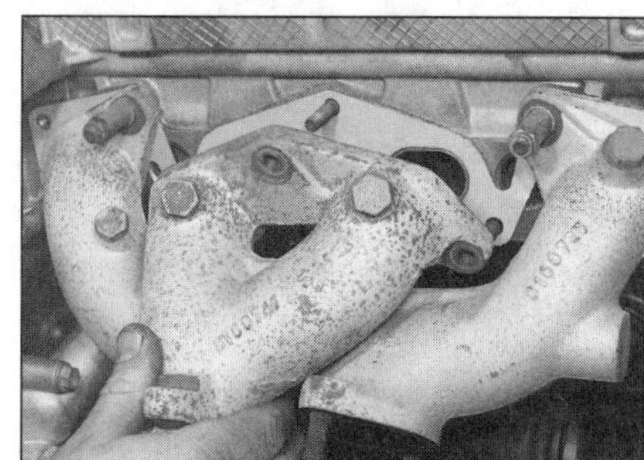

20.5a Removing the centre section of the exhaust manifold

20.5b Removing the sleeves from the outer section of the exhaust manifold

4A

20.5c Removing the outer section of the exhaust manifold

20.6 Removing the exhaust manifold gasket

20.8 Tighten the exhaust manifold nuts to the specified torque

6 Remove the gasket from the studs on the cylinder head **(see illustration)**.

Refitting

7 Clean the contact surfaces of the cylinder head and exhaust manifold.

8 Refit the exhaust manifold to the studs on the cylinder head together with a new gasket, then tighten the mounting nuts to the specified torque **(see illustration)**. Make sure that the sleeves are correctly located, as previously described. Refit the outer section of the manifold first, and tighten the mounting nuts to the specified torque, then refit the centre section and tighten the nuts.

9 Refit the power steering pump with reference to Chapter 10.

10 Refit the auxiliary drivebelt as described in Chapter 1.

11 Refit the exhaust front pipe with reference to Section 21.

12 Reconnect the lambda sensor wiring with reference to Section 14 or 15.

13 Lower the car to the ground.

Turbo models

Removal

14 Remove the turbocharger as described in Section 17.

15 The remainder of the removal procedure is as described for non-turbo models, noting that the manifold is a single-piece casting, and that sleeves are fitted beneath the outer mounting stud nuts only.

Refitting

16 Refitting is reversal of removal.

21 Exhaust system - general information and component removal

General information

1 The exhaust system consists of four sections:

a) The front pipe (incorporating a three-way catalytic converter on certain models).
b) The intermediate pipe (incorporating a three-way catalytic converter on certain models).
c) The intermediate silencer.
d) The rear silencer and tailpipe.

2 The exhaust system sections are joined by flanges with internal flared tube ends. The front pipe-to-manifold joint is gasketed, and is secured by studs and nuts. The front pipe and the connector pipes between the silencers are aluminium-plated. The silencers are made of chrome steel plate.

3 On all models, the lambda sensor is located in the front pipe. The catalytic converter is located either in the front pipe or in the front silencer and pipe.

4 On non-Turbo models, the front pipe is of twin-branch type. On Turbo models, the single front pipe incorporates an elbow at its front end which is connected to the turbocharger.

5 On all models, the system is suspended throughout its entire length by rubber mountings.

Removal

6 Each exhaust section can be removed individually. Alternatively, it is possible to remove the complete exhaust system in one piece.

7 To remove a section of the system, first jack up the front or rear of the car and support it on axle stands (see *"Jacking and vehicle support"*). Alternatively, position the car over an inspection pit, or on car ramps.

Front pipe (and catalytic converter where applicable)

Note: *Where a catalytic converter is fitted, do not drop the unit, as it contains a fragile ceramic element.*

8 On models with a catalytic converter, remove the lambda sensor as described in Section 14 or 15.

9 Unscrew the nuts and separate the flange joint between the front pipe and the intermediate pipe **(see illustration)**.

10 Unhook the mounting rubbers from the underbody **(see illustration)**. Where applicable, remove the bolt securing the catalytic converter to its support bracket.

11 Unscrew the nuts securing the front pipe to the turbocharger or exhaust manifold (as applicable), then lower the pipe between the engine and the front subframe crossmember **(see illustrations)**. Recover the gaskets.

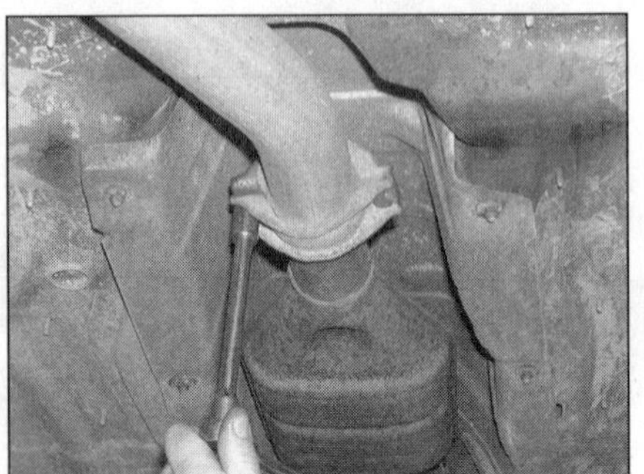

21.9 Unscrew the nuts and separate the flange joint between the front pipe and the intermediate pipe

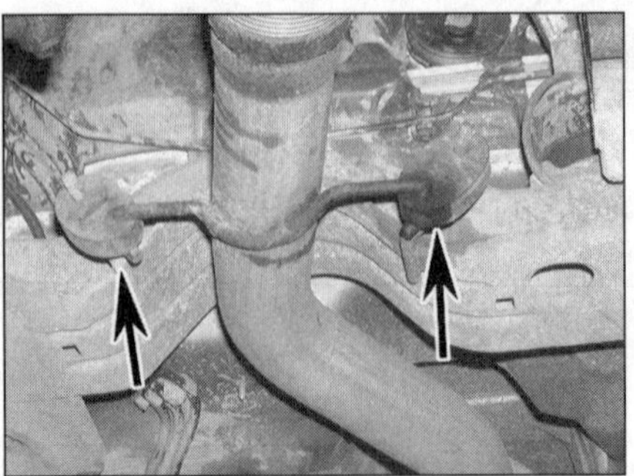

21.10 Unhook the mounting rubbers from the underbody

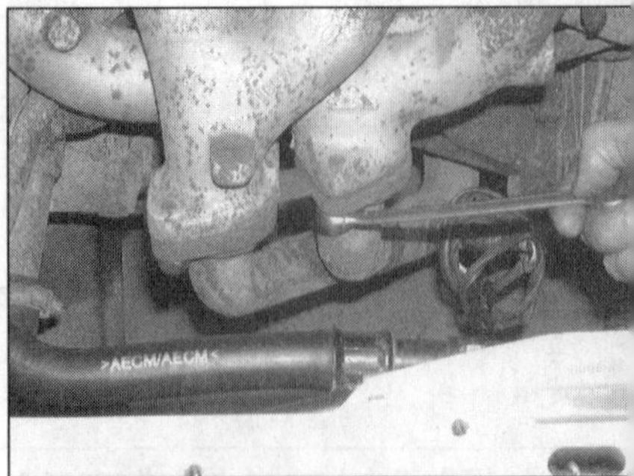

21.11a Unscrew the nuts securing the front pipe to the exhaust manifold (non-turbo model shown) . . .

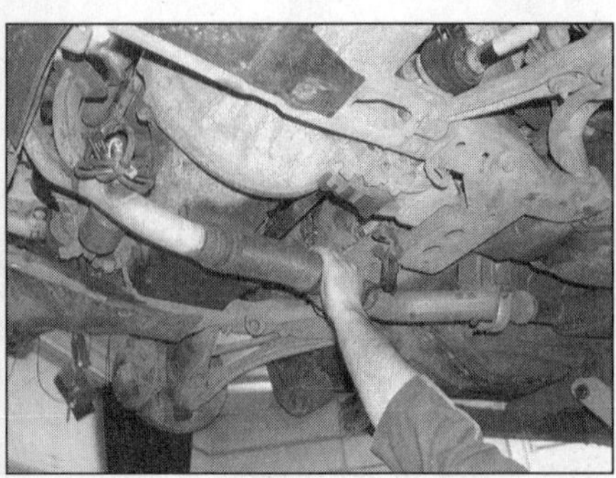

21.11b . . . then remove the front pipe

Intermediate pipe

Note: *Where a catalytic converter is fitted, do not drop the unit, as it contains a fragile ceramic element.*

12 Unscrew the nuts, and separate the flange joints connecting the intermediate pipe to the front pipe, and the intermediate silencer.

13 Unhook the mounting rubbers from the underbody, and lower the front silencer and pipe to the ground.

Intermediate silencer

14 Unscrew the nuts/bolts, and separate the flange joints connecting the intermediate silencer to the intermediate pipe, and to the rear silencer and tailpipe.

15 Unhook the mounting rubbers from the underbody, and lower the intermediate silencer and pipe to the ground.

Rear silencer and tailpipe

16 Unscrew the bolts, and separate the flange joint connecting the rear silencer and tailpipe to the intermediate silencer and pipe.

17 Unhook the mounting rubbers from the underbody, and lower the rear silencer and tailpipe to the ground.

Heat shields

18 The heat shields are secured to the underbody by bolts. Each shield can be removed once the relevant exhaust section has been removed.

Refitting

19 Each section is refitted by a reversal of the removal sequence, noting the following points:

a) *Ensure that all traces of corrosion have been removed from the flared tube ends in the flanges, and renew the front pipe-to-exhaust manifold/turbocharger gasket(s).*

b) *Inspect the rubber mountings for signs of damage or deterioration, and renew as necessary.*

c) *On models with a catalytic converter, refit the lambda sensor with reference to Section 14 or 15 as applicable.*

d) *Make sure that all rubber mountings are correctly located, and that there is adequate clearance between the exhaust system and underbody.*

Chapter 4 Part B: Emission control systems

Contents

Degrees of difficulty

Easy, suitable for novice with little experience 	**Fairly easy,** suitable for beginner with some experience 	**Fairly difficult,** suitable for competent DIY mechanic	**Difficult,** suitable for experienced DIY mechanic	**Very difficult,** suitable for expert DIY or professional

1 General information

1 All models use unleaded petrol and also have various other features built into the fuel system to help minimise harmful emissions. All models are equipped with a crankcase emission control system, a catalytic converter and an evaporative emission control system to keep fuel vapour emissions down to a minimum. In some markets, 2.3 litre models are also fitted with a secondary air injection system to further improve the exhaust gas emissions during engine warm-up. The emission control systems function as follows.

Crankcase emission control

2 To reduce the emission of unburned hydrocarbons from the crankcase into the atmosphere, the engine is sealed and the blow-by gases and oil vapour are drawn from inside the crankcase, through a wire mesh oil separator, into the inlet tract to be burned by the engine during normal combustion.

3 Under conditions of high manifold depression (idling, deceleration) the gases will be sucked positively out of the crankcase. Under conditions of low manifold depression (acceleration, full-throttle running) the gases are forced out of the crankcase by the (relatively) higher crankcase pressure; if the engine is worn, the raised crankcase pressure (due to increased blow-by) will cause some of the flow to return under all manifold conditions.

Exhaust emission control

4 To minimise the amount of pollutants which escape into the atmosphere, all models are fitted with a catalytic converter in the exhaust system. The system is of the closed-loop type, in which a lambda sensor in the exhaust system provides the fuel-injection/ignition system ECU with constant feedback, enabling the ECU to adjust the mixture to provide the best possible conditions for the converter to operate.

5 The lambda sensor's tip is sensitive to oxygen and sends the ECU a varying voltage depending on the amount of oxygen in the exhaust gases; if the intake air/fuel mixture is too rich, the exhaust gases are low in oxygen so the sensor sends a low-voltage signal, the voltage rising as the mixture weakens and the amount of oxygen rises in the exhaust gases. Peak conversion efficiency of all major pollutants occurs if the intake air/fuel mixture is maintained at the chemically-correct ratio for the complete combustion of petrol of 14.7 parts (by weight) of air to 1 part of fuel (the 'Stoichiometric ratio'). The sensor output voltage alters in a large step at this point, the ECU using the signal change as a reference point and correcting the intake air/fuel mixture accordingly by altering the fuel injector pulse width.

Evaporative emission control

6 To minimise the escape into the atmosphere of unburned hydrocarbons, an evaporative emissions control system is also fitted to all models. The fuel tank filler cap is sealed and a charcoal canister is mounted behind the right-hand front wing. The canister collects the petrol vapours generated in the tank when the car is parked and stores them until they can be cleared from the canister (under the control of the fuel-injection/ignition system ECU) via the purge valve into the inlet tract to be burned by the engine during normal combustion.

7 To ensure that the engine runs correctly when it is cold and/or idling and to protect the catalytic converter from the effects of an over-rich mixture, the purge control valve is not opened by the ECU until the engine has warmed up, and the engine is under load; the valve solenoid is then modulated on and off to allow the stored vapour to pass into the inlet tract.

Secondary air injection system

8 The purpose of the secondary air injection system is to decrease exhaust gas emissions when the engine is cold. The system achieves this by raising the temperature of the exhaust gases which has the effect of quickly warming the catalytic converter up to its normal operating temperature. Once the catalytic converter is up to temperature the air injection system is switched off.

9 The system consists of a pump, a non-return air valve and a solenoid valve and is controlled by the fuel-injection/ignition ECU. When the engine is cold, the solenoid valve switches the air valve to open and the pump injects a controlled amount of air into the cylinder head exhaust ports. The air then mixes with the exhaust gases, causing any unburned particles of the fuel in the mixture to be burnt in the exhaust port/manifold which effectively raises the temperature of the exhaust gases. Once the catalytic converter is up to temperature, the solenoid valve closes the air valve and the pump is switched off. A non-return valve prevents the exhaust gases passing through the air valve.

2 Emission control systems - testing and component renewal

Crankcase emission control

1 The components of this system require no attention other than to check that the hose(s) are clear and undamaged at regular intervals.

Evaporative emission control system

Testing

2 If the system is thought to be faulty, disconnect the hoses from the charcoal canister and purge control valve and check that they are clear by blowing through them. Full testing of the system can only be carried out using specialist electronic equipment which is connected to the engine management system diagnostic wiring connector (see Chapter 4A). If the purge control valve or charcoal canister are thought to be faulty, they must be renewed.

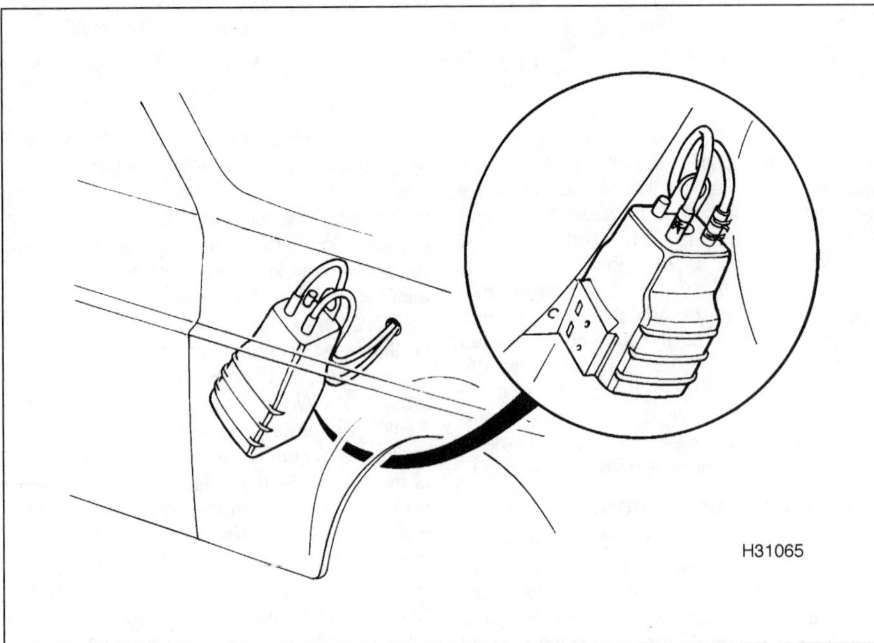

2.5 Disconnect the vapour hoses then slide the charcoal canister from its mounting bracket

Charcoal canister - renewal

3 The charcoal canister is located behind the right-hand front wing. To gain access to the canister, firmly apply the handbrake then jack up the front of the vehicle and support it on axle stands (see "*Jacking and vehicle support*").

4 Remove the retaining screws and fasteners and remove the wheelarch liner to gain access to the canister.

5 Mark the vapour hoses for identification purposes then disconnect. Slide the canister from its mounting bracket and remove it from the vehicle **(see illustration)**.

6 Refitting is a reverse of the removal procedure, ensuring the hoses are correctly and securely reconnected.

Purge valve - renewal

7 Refer to the information given in Chapter 4A, Section 14.

Exhaust emission control system

Testing

8 The performance of the catalytic converter can be checked only by measuring the exhaust gases using a good-quality, carefully-calibrated exhaust gas analyser, as described in Chapter 4A, Section 13.

9 If the CO level at the tailpipe is too high, the vehicle should be taken to a Saab dealer so that the complete fuel-injection and ignition systems, including the lambda sensor, can be thoroughly checked using the special diagnostic equipment. Once these have been checked and are known to be free from faults, the fault must be in the catalytic converter, which must be renewed.

Catalytic converter - renewal

10 Refer to Chapter 4A, Section 21.

Lambda sensor - renewal

11 Refer to the information given in Chapter 4A, Section 14.

3 Catalytic converter - general information and precautions

1 The catalytic converter is a reliable and simple device which needs no maintenance in itself, but there are some facts of which an owner should be aware if the converter is to function properly for its full service life.

Petrol models

a) DO NOT use leaded petrol in a car equipped with a catalytic converter - the lead will coat the precious metals, reducing their converting efficiency and will eventually destroy the converter.

b) Always keep the ignition and fuel systems well-maintained in accordance with the manufacturer's schedule.

c) *If the engine develops a misfire, do not drive the car at all (or at least as little as possible) until the fault is cured.*
d) *DO NOT push- or tow-start the car - this will soak the catalytic converter in unburned fuel, causing it to overheat when the engine does start.*
e) *DO NOT switch off the ignition at high engine speeds.*
f) *DO NOT use fuel or engine oil additives - these may contain substances harmful to the catalytic converter.*
g) *DO NOT continue to use the car if the engine burns oil to the extent of leaving a visible trail of blue smoke.*
h) *Remember that the catalytic converter operates at very high temperatures. DO NOT, therefore, park the car in dry undergrowth, over long grass or piles of dead leaves after a long run.*
i) *Remember that the catalytic converter is FRAGILE - do not strike it with tools during servicing work.*
j) *In some cases a sulphurous smell (like that of rotten eggs) may be noticed from the exhaust. This is common to many catalytic converter-equipped cars and once the car has covered a few thousand miles the problem should disappear.*
k) *The catalytic converter, used on a well-maintained and well-driven car, should last for between 50 000 and 100 000 miles - if the converter is no longer effective it must be renewed.*

4 Secondary air injection system - testing and component renewal

Note: *The secondary air injection system is only fitted to Swedish and U.S. specification 2.3 litre models.*

Testing

1 Comprehensive testing of the system can only be carried out using specialist electronic equipment which is connected to the engine management system diagnostic wiring connector (see Chapter 4A). If any component is thought to be faulty, it must be renewed.

Air injection pump and filter renewal

2 The pump is located in the engine compartment, behind the left hand headlight unit **(see illustration)**. To gain access to the pump, jack up the front of the car and rest it securely on axle stands (see "*Jacking and vehicle support*"). Remove the plastic spoilers from under the leading edge of the front bumper (see Chapter 11).

3 Disconnect the air hoses from the pump then undo the pump mounting bracket retaining nuts.

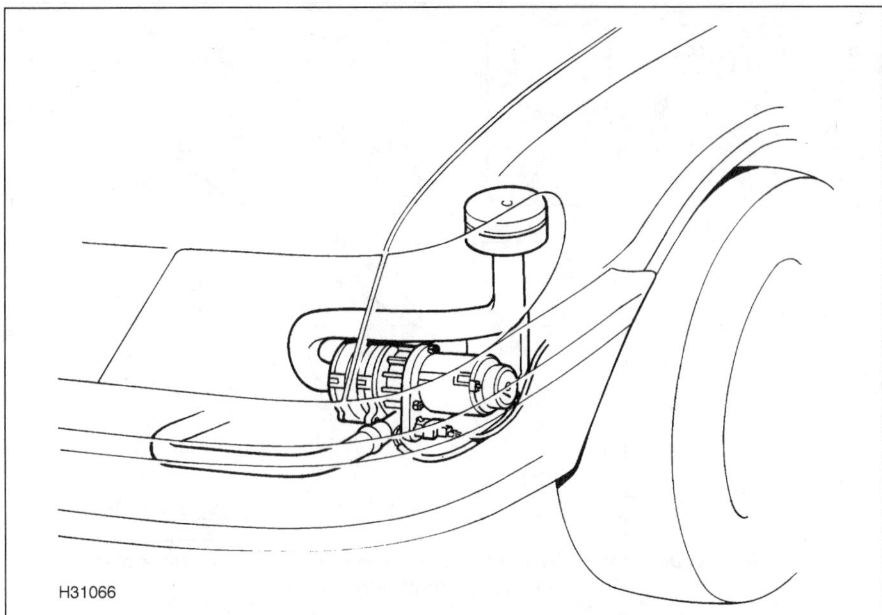

4.2 The air injection pump and filter is located in the engine compartment, behind the left hand headlight unit

4 Remove the pump assembly from the engine compartment, disconnecting the wiring connector as it becomes accessible. If necessary the pump and mounting bracket can then be separated.

5 Refitting is the reverse of removal, tightening the retaining nuts securely.

Solenoid valve renewal

6 The solenoid valve is mounted at the rear, left-hand side of the engine compartment, underneath the suspension cross-bracing bar **(see illustration)**. To locate the valve, trace the vacuum hose back from the air valve on the front of the engine.

7 Disconnect the wiring connector from the valve and detach the vacuum hoses, noting each one's correct fitted location.

8 Undo the retaining screws and remove the valve from the engine compartment.

9 Refitting is the reverse of removal, ensuring the vacuum hoses are correctly reconnected.

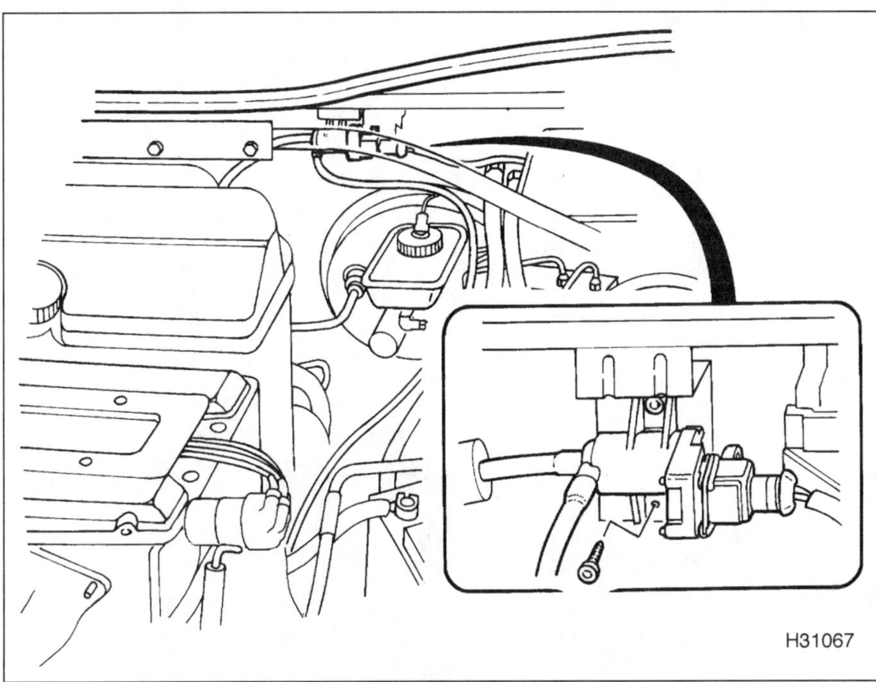

4.6 The solenoid valve is mounted at the rear, left-hand side of the engine compartment, underneath the suspension cross-bracing bar

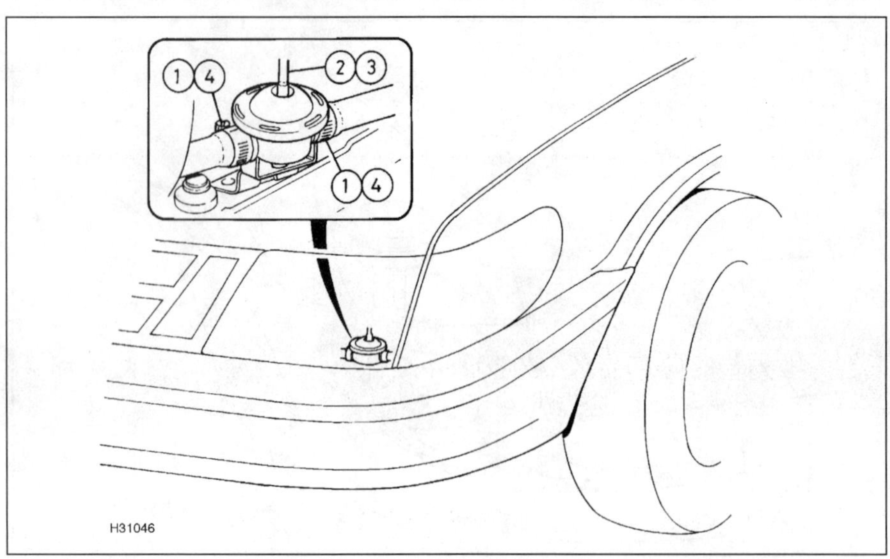

4.10 The vacuum control valve is located at the front left hand corner of the engine compartment

1-4 Hose clips *2-3 Vacuum hose*

Vacuum control valve renewal

10 The vacuum control valve is located at the front left hand corner of the engine compartment. To remove the valve, slacken the hose clips and detach the air hoses from either side of the valve. Unplug the vacuum hose from the top of the valve and remove it from the engine compartment **(see illustration)**.

11 Refitting is a reversal of removal.

Chapter 5 Part A:
Starting and charging systems

Contents

Degrees of difficulty

Easy, suitable for novice with little experience 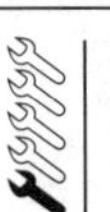

Fairly easy, suitable for beginner with some experience 

Fairly difficult, suitable for competent DIY mechanic 

Difficult, suitable for experienced DIY mechanic

Very difficult, suitable for expert DIY or professional 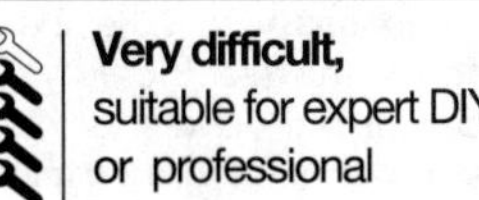

Specifications

System type	12-volt, negative earth
Battery	
Type	Lead-acid, "low-maintenance" or "maintenance-free" (sealed for life)
Battery capacity	60 Ampere-hours
Charge condition:	
Poor	12.5 Volts
Normal	12.6 Volts
Good	12.7 Volts
Electrolyte specific gravity:	
Charging (recommended)	1.21
Fully charged	1.28
Starting current:	
SAE	520 Amps
IEC	320 Amps
Alternator	
Type	Bosch KC 14V 40 - 70A, 45-90A or NC 14V 60-120A
Rated voltage	14 Volts
Output current:	
At 1800 rpm	40, 45 or 60 Amps
At 6000 rpm	70, 90 or 120 Amps
Minimum brush protrusion from holder	7.5 mm
Minimum slip ring diameter	14.8 mm
Starter motor	
Type	Bosch DW 12V
Output	1.4 kW

Torque wrench settings	**Nm**	**lbf ft**
Starter solenoid to starter	5	4
Starter through-bolts	3	2

5A

1 General information and precautions

General information

Because of their engine-related functions, the components of the starting and charging systems are covered separately from the body electrical devices such as the lights, instruments, etc (which are covered in Chapter 12). Refer to Part B of this Chapter for information on the ignition system.

The electrical system is of the 12-volt negative earth type.

The battery fitted as original equipment is of low-maintenance or "maintenance-free" (sealed for life) type. The battery is charged by the alternator, which is belt-driven from the crankshaft pulley. During the life of the car, the original battery may have been replaced by a standard type battery.

The starter motor is of the pre-engaged type, incorporating an integral solenoid. On starting, the solenoid moves the drive pinion into engagement with the flywheel/driveplate ring gear before the starter motor is energised. Once the engine has started, a one-way clutch prevents the motor armature being driven by the engine until the pinion disengages from the ring gear. Unlike some modern starter motors, it incorporates epicyclic reduction gears between the armature and the pinion.

Precautions

Further details of the various systems are given in the relevant Sections of this Chapter. While some repair procedures are given, the usual course of action is to renew the component concerned. The owner whose interest extends beyond mere component renewal should obtain a copy of the *"Automotive Electrical & Electronic Systems Manual"*, available from the publishers of this manual.

It is necessary to take extra care when working on the electrical system, to avoid damage to semi-conductor devices (diodes, transistors and integrated circuits), and to avoid the risk of personal injury. In addition to the precautions given in *"Safety first!"* observe the following when working on the system:

Always remove rings, watches, etc before working on the electrical system. Even with the battery disconnected, capacitive discharge could occur if a component's live terminal is earthed through a metal object. This could cause a shock or nasty burn.

Do not reverse the battery connections. Components such as the alternator, electronic control units, or any other components having semi-conductor circuitry, could be irreparably damaged.

If the engine is being started using jump leads and a slave battery, connect the batteries *positive-to-positive* and *negative-to-negative* (see *"Booster battery (jump) starting"*). This also applies when connecting a battery charger.

Caution: Never disconnect the battery terminals, the alternator, any electrical wiring, or any test instruments, when the engine is running.

Do not allow the engine to turn the alternator when the alternator is not connected.

Never "test" for alternator output by "flashing" the output lead to earth.

Never use an ohmmeter of the type incorporating a hand-cranked generator for circuit or continuity testing.

Always ensure that the battery negative lead is disconnected when working on the electrical system.

Before using electric-arc welding equipment on the car, disconnect the battery, alternator, and components such as the fuel injection/ignition electronic control unit, to protect them from the risk of damage.

The radio/cassette unit fitted as standard equipment on some models has a built-in security code, to deter thieves. If the power source to the unit is cut, the anti-theft system will activate. Even if the power source is immediately reconnected, the radio/cassette unit will not function until the correct security code has been entered. Therefore, if you do not know the correct security code for the radio/cassette unit, **do not** disconnect the battery negative terminal of the battery, nor remove the radio/cassette unit from the vehicle. Refer to *"Radio/cassette unit anti-theft system - precaution"* for further information.

2 Electrical fault-finding - general information

Refer to Chapter 12.

3 Battery - testing and charging

Standard and low-maintenance battery - testing

1 If the vehicle covers a small annual mileage, it is worthwhile checking the specific gravity of the electrolyte every three months, to determine the state of charge of the battery. Use a hydrometer to make the check, and compare the results with the following table. Note that the specific gravity readings assume an electrolyte temperature of 15°C (60°F); for every 10°C (18°F) below 15°C (60°F), subtract 0.007. For every 10°C (18°F) above 15°C (60°F), add 0.007. However, for convenience, the temperatures quoted in the following table are **ambient** (outdoor air) temperatures, above or below 25°C (77°F):

	Above 25°C (77°F)	**Below 25°C (77°F)**
Fully-charged	*1.210 to 1.230*	*1.270 to 1.290*
70% charged	*1.170 to 1.190*	*1.230 to 1.250*
discharged	*1.050 to 1.070*	*1.110 to 1.130*

2 If the battery condition is suspect, first check the specific gravity of electrolyte in each cell. A variation of 0.040 or more between any cells indicates loss of electrolyte or deterioration of the internal plates.

3 If the specific gravity variation is 0.040 or more, the battery should be renewed. If the cell variation is satisfactory but the battery is discharged, it should be charged as described later in this Section.

Maintenance-free battery - testing

4 In cases where a "sealed for life" maintenance-free battery is fitted, topping-up and testing of the electrolyte in each cell is not possible. The condition of the battery can therefore only be tested using a battery condition indicator or a voltmeter.

5 A battery with a built-in charge condition indicator may be fitted. The indicator is located in the top of the battery casing, and indicates the condition of the battery from its colour. If the indicator shows green, then the battery is in a good state of charge. If the indicator turns darker, eventually to black, then the battery requires charging, as described later in this Section. If the indicator shows clear/yellow, then the electrolyte level in the battery is too low to allow further use, and the battery should be renewed. **Do not** attempt to charge, load or jump-start a battery when the indicator shows clear/yellow.

6 If testing the battery using a voltmeter, connect the voltmeter across the battery, and compare the result with those given in the Specifications under "charge condition". The test is only accurate if the battery has not been subjected to any kind of charge for the previous six hours, including charging by the alternator. If this is not the case, switch on the headlights for 30 seconds, then wait four to five minutes after switching off the headlights before testing the battery. All other electrical circuits must be switched off, so check (for instance) that the doors and tailgate or bootlid are fully shut when making the test.

7 If the voltage reading is less than 12.2 volts, then the battery is discharged. A reading of 12.2 to 12.4 volts indicates a partially-discharged condition.

8 If the battery is to be charged, remove it from the vehicle (Section 4) and charge it as described in the following paragraphs.

Standard and low-maintenance battery - charging

Note: *The following is intended as a guide only. Always refer to the manufacturer's recommendations (often printed on a label attached to the battery) before charging a battery.*

9 Charge the battery at a rate of 3.5 to 4 amps, and continue to charge the battery at this rate until no further rise in specific gravity is noted over a four-hour period.

10 Alternatively, a trickle charger charging at the rate of 1.5 amps can safely be used overnight.

11 Specially rapid "boost" charges which are claimed to restore the power of the battery in 1 to 2 hours are not recommended, as they can cause serious damage to the battery plates through overheating.

12 While charging the battery, note that the temperature of the electrolyte should never exceed 37.8°C (100°F).

Maintenance-free battery - charging

Note: *The following is intended as a guide only. Always refer to the manufacturer's recommendations (often printed on a label attached to the battery) before charging a battery.*

13 This battery type requires a longer period to fully recharge than the standard type, the time taken being dependent on the extent of discharge, but it can take anything up to three days.

14 A constant-voltage type charger is required, to be set, where possible, to 13.9 to 14.9 volts with a charger current below 25 amps. Using this method, the battery should be usable within three hours, giving a voltage

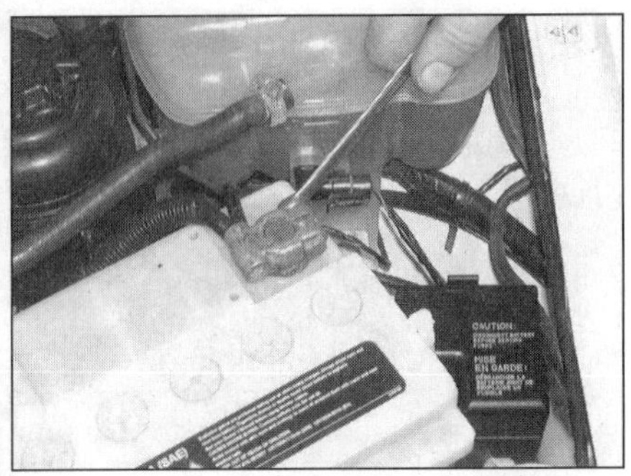

4.2a Loosen the clamp nut and disconnect the lead at the negative (earth) terminal

reading of 12.5 volts, but this is for a partially-discharged battery and, as mentioned, full charging can take considerably longer.

15 Use of a normal trickle charger should not be detrimental to the battery, provided excessive gassing is not allowed to occur, and the battery is not allowed to become hot.

4 Battery - removal and refitting

Removal

1 The battery is located on the left-hand side of the engine compartment.

2 Loosen the clamp nut and disconnect the lead at the negative (earth) terminal. Disconnect the lead at the positive terminal in the same way **(see illustrations)**.

3 Unscrew the bolt and remove the battery retaining clamp which secures the battery to the mounting bracket **(see illustration)**.

4 Lift the battery out of the engine compartment (take care not to tilt it excessively) **(see illustration)**.

Refitting

5 Refitting is a reversal of removal. Smear petroleum jelly on the terminals when reconnecting the leads, and always reconnect the positive lead first, and the negative lead last.

5 Charging system - testing

Note: *Refer to the warnings given in "Safety first!" and in Section 1 of this Chapter before starting work.*

1 If the ignition/no-charge warning light does not come on when the ignition is switched on, first check the alternator wiring connections for security. If satisfactory, check that the warning light bulb has not blown, and that the bulbholder is secure in its location in the instrument panel. If the light still fails to illuminate, check the continuity of the warning light feed wire from the alternator to the bulbholder. If all is satisfactory, the alternator is at fault, and should be taken to an auto-electrician for testing and repair, or else renewed.

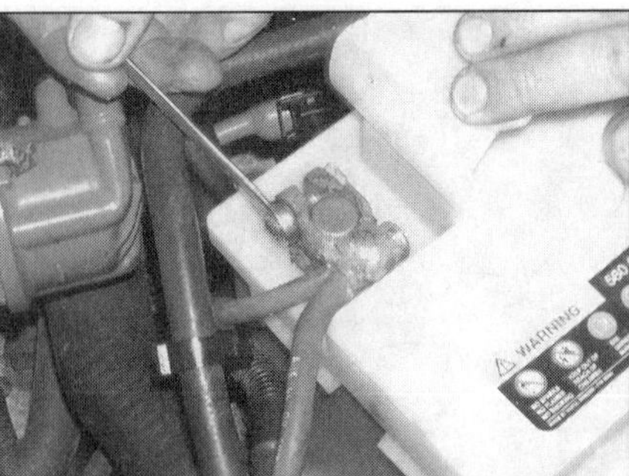

4.2b Loosen the clamp nut and disconnect the lead at the positive terminal

2 If the ignition warning light comes on when the engine is running, stop the engine. Check that the drivebelt is intact and correctly tensioned (see Chapter 1), and that the alternator connections are secure. If all is satisfactory, check the alternator brushes and slip rings as described in Section 8. If the fault persists, the alternator should be taken to an auto-electrician for testing and repair, or else renewed.

3 If the alternator output is suspect even though the warning light functions correctly, the regulated voltage may be checked as follows.

4 Connect a voltmeter across the battery terminals, and start the engine.

5 Increase the engine speed until the voltmeter reading remains steady; the reading should be approximately 12 to 13 volts, and no more than 14 volts.

6 Switch on as many electrical accessories (eg, the headlights, heated rear window and heater blower) as possible, and check that the alternator maintains the regulated voltage at around 13 to 14 volts.

7 If the regulated voltage is not as stated, the fault may be due to worn brushes, weak brush springs, a faulty voltage regulator, a faulty diode, a severed phase winding, or worn or damaged slip rings. The brushes and slip rings may be checked (see Section 8), but if the fault persists, the alternator should be taken to an auto-electrician for testing and repair, or else renewed.

4.4 Carefully lift the battery out of the engine compartment

4.3 Unscrew the bolt and remove the battery retaining clamp

6 Alternator drivebelt - removal, refitting and tensioning

Refer to the procedure given for the auxiliary drivebelt in Chapter 1.

7 Alternator - removal and refitting

Removal

1 Disconnect the battery negative lead.

2 Apply the handbrake, then jack up the front of the car and support on axle stands (see *"Jacking and vehicle support"*). Remove the right-hand front wheel.

3 Remove the right-hand front wing plastic moulding, followed by the front section of the wheelarch liner, for access to the engine.

4 Remove the auxiliary drivebelt as described in Chapter 1.

5 Note the position of the cables on the rear of the alternator, then unscrew the terminal nuts (where applicable) and disconnect the cables **(see illustration)**.

6 Unscrew the alternator upper and lower mounting bolts **(see illustration)**. Note that the lower bolt passes through the intermediate driveshaft bearing mounting bracket.

7 Withdraw the alternator via the right-hand wheel arch.

5A

7.5 Unscrew the terminal nuts (where applicable) and disconnect the cables from the rear of the alternator

7.6 Unscrew the alternator upper and lower mounting bolts (arrowed)

8.2a Unscrew the large terminal nut . . .

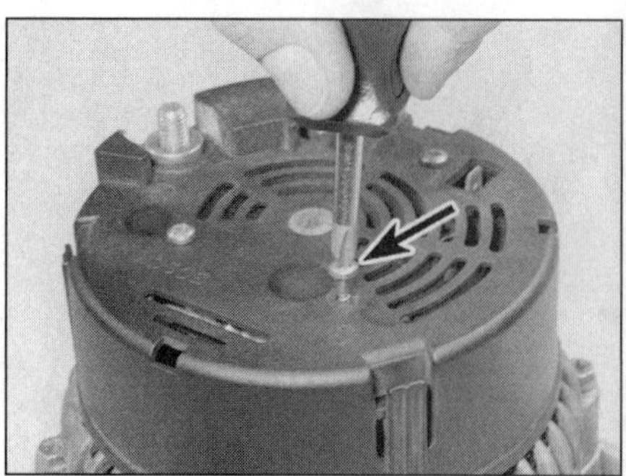
8.2b . . . and the screws securing the cover to the rear of the alternator

Refitting

8 Refitting is a reversal of removal. Ensure that the alternator mountings are securely tightened, and refit the auxiliary drivebelt as described in Chapter 1.

8 Alternator brushes and regulator - inspection and renewal

1 Remove the alternator (see Section 7).

2 Unscrew the large terminal nut and the screws securing the cover to the rear of the alternator **(see illustrations)**.

3 Using a screwdriver, lever off the cover, and remove it from the rear of the alternator **(see illustrations)**.

4 Unscrew and remove the two retaining screws, and remove the regulator/brush holder from the rear of the alternator **(see illustrations)**.

5 Measure the protrusion of each brush from its holder, using a steel rule or vernier calipers **(see illustration)**. If less than 5.0 mm, the brushes should be renewed, or a new assembly obtained. On early models, the brushes can be unsoldered and renewed, but on later models, this may not be the case.

6 Using a soldering iron, unsolder the brush wires from the terminals on top of the holder. **Note:** *Take care not to overheat the regulator.* Remove the brushes from the holder, complete with the tension springs.

7 Remove excess solder from the terminals, and clean the holders. It is important that the new brushes move freely in the holders.

8 Insert the new brushes in the holder, one at a time, and hold them against the spring tension with a pair of pliers while the wires are soldered onto the terminals. Do not release the brushes until the solder has cooled.

9 If the original brushes were in good condition, clean them and check that they move freely in their holders.

10 Clean the alternator slip-rings with a fuel-moistened cloth. Check for signs of scoring or burning on the surface of the slip-rings. It may be possible to have the slip rings renovated by an electrical specialist.

11 Refit the regulator/brush holder assembly, and securely tighten the retaining screws.

12 Refit the cover, then insert and tighten the retaining screws and refit the large terminal nut.

13 Refit the alternator with reference to Section 7.

9 Starting system - testing

Note: *Refer to the precautions given in "Safety first!" and in Section 1 of this Chapter before starting work.*

1 If the starter motor fails to operate when the ignition key is turned to the appropriate position, the following possible causes may apply:

a) The battery is faulty.

b) The electrical connections between the switch, solenoid, battery and starter motor are somewhere failing to pass the necessary current from the battery through the starter to earth.

c) The solenoid is faulty.

d) The starter motor is mechanically or electrically defective.

8.3a Lever off the cover . . .

8.3b . . . and remove it from the rear of the alternator

8.4a Unscrew and remove the two retaining screws . . .

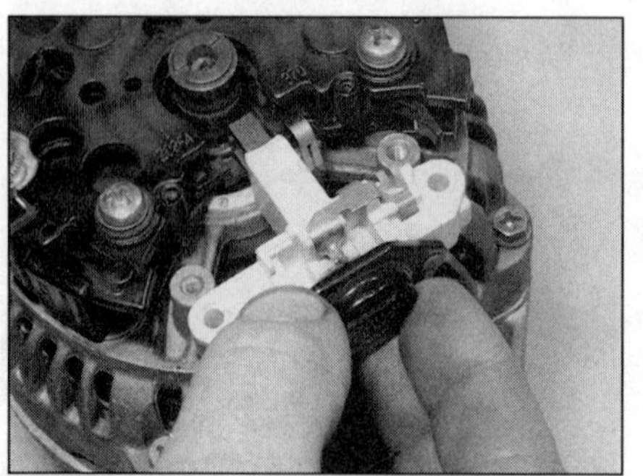
8.4b . . . and remove the regulator/brush holder from the rear of the alternator

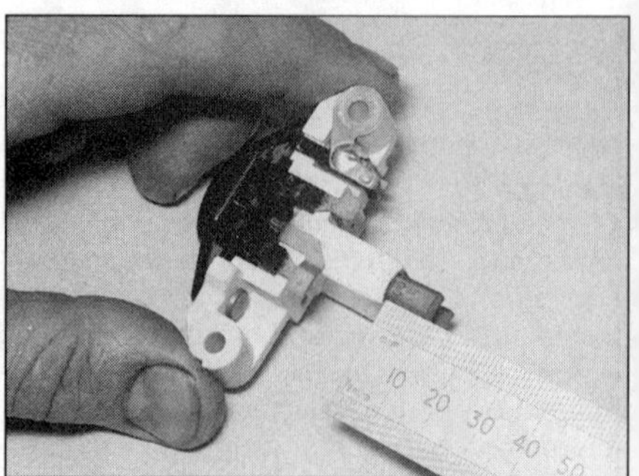

8.5 Measuring the protrusion of a brush from its holder, using a steel rule

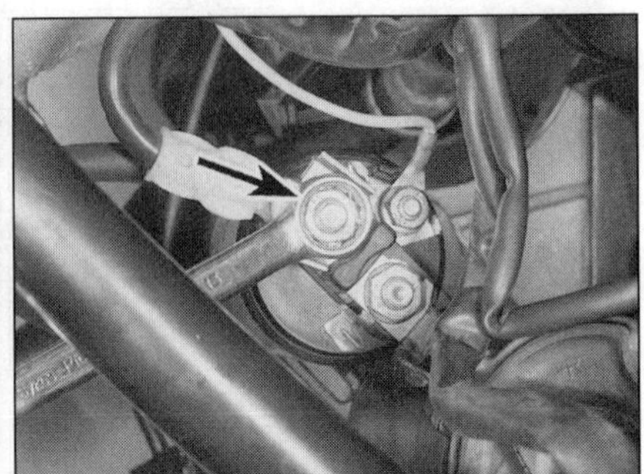

10.3 Unscrew the nut and disconnect the battery positive supply lead from the terminal on the solenoid

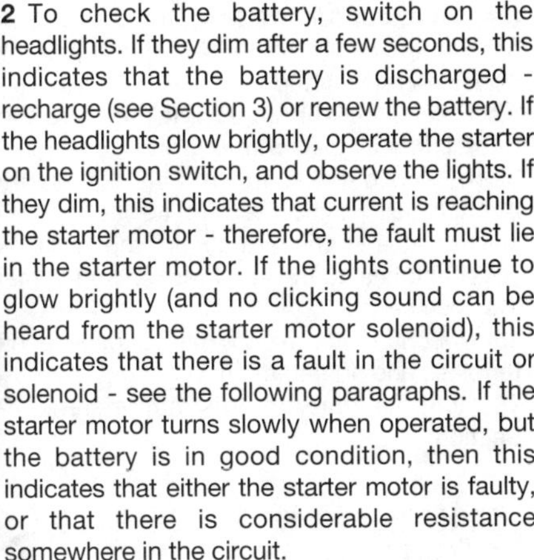

2 To check the battery, switch on the headlights. If they dim after a few seconds, this indicates that the battery is discharged - recharge (see Section 3) or renew the battery. If the headlights glow brightly, operate the starter on the ignition switch, and observe the lights. If they dim, this indicates that current is reaching the starter motor - therefore, the fault must lie in the starter motor. If the lights continue to glow brightly (and no clicking sound can be heard from the starter motor solenoid), this indicates that there is a fault in the circuit or solenoid - see the following paragraphs. If the starter motor turns slowly when operated, but the battery is in good condition, then this indicates that either the starter motor is faulty, or that there is considerable resistance somewhere in the circuit.

3 If a fault in the circuit is suspected, disconnect the battery leads, the starter/solenoid wiring and the engine/transmission earth strap. Thoroughly clean the connections, and reconnect the leads and wiring, then use a voltmeter or test light to check that full battery voltage is available at the battery positive lead connection on the solenoid, and that the earth is sound.

4 If the battery and all connections are in good condition, check the circuit by disconnecting the wire from the solenoid terminal. Connect a voltmeter or test light between the wire end and a good earth (such as the battery negative terminal), and check that the wire is live when the ignition switch is turned to the "start" position. If it is, then the circuit is sound - if not, the circuit wiring can be checked as described in Chapter 12.

10.5 Unscrew and remove the starter motor lower mounting nut (intermediate driveshaft removed)

5 The solenoid contacts can be checked by connecting a voltmeter or test light between the terminal on the starter side of the solenoid, and earth. When the ignition switch is turned to the "start" position, there should be a reading or lighted bulb, as applicable. If there is no reading or lighted bulb, the solenoid or contacts are faulty and the solenoid should be renewed.

6 If the circuit and solenoid are proved sound, the fault must lie in the starter motor. Begin checking the starter motor by removing it (see Section 10), and checking the brushes (see Section 11). If the fault does not lie in the brushes, the motor windings must be faulty. In this event, it may be possible to have the starter motor overhauled by a specialist, but check on the availability and cost of spares before proceeding, as it may prove more economical to obtain a new or exchange motor.

10 Starter motor - removal and refitting

Removal

1 The starter motor is located on the left-hand rear side of the engine, and is bolted to the engine backplate and transmission. First disconnect the battery negative lead.

2 Apply the handbrake, then jack up the front of the car and support on axle stands (see *"Jacking and vehicle support"*).

10.7 Withdraw the upper starter motor mounting bolt, from the transmission side of the bellhousing

3 Unscrew the nut and disconnect the battery positive supply lead from the terminal on the solenoid **(see illustration)**.

4 Where applicable, unbolt the positive cable support from the inlet manifold stay.

5 Unscrew and remove the starter motor lower mounting nut **(see illustration)**.

6 Remove the nut and disconnect the solenoid wire from the terminal blade.

7 Slacken and withdraw the upper starter motor mounting bolt, from the transmission side of the bellhousing **(see illustration)**.

8 Withdraw the starter motor from the bellhousing and remove it from the engine compartment **(see illustration)**.

Refitting

9 Refitting is a reversal of removal. Tighten all wire connections securely.

11 Starter motor - brush renewal

Note: *No minimum brush length is specified by the manufacturers, but it should be self-evident if the brushes are worn to the extent where renewal is required.*

1 Remove the starter motor as described in Section 10.

2 Unscrew the nut and disconnect the starter motor feed cable from the solenoid terminal **(see illustrations)**.

5A

10.8 Withdraw the starter motor from the bellhousing

11.2a Unscrew the nut . . .

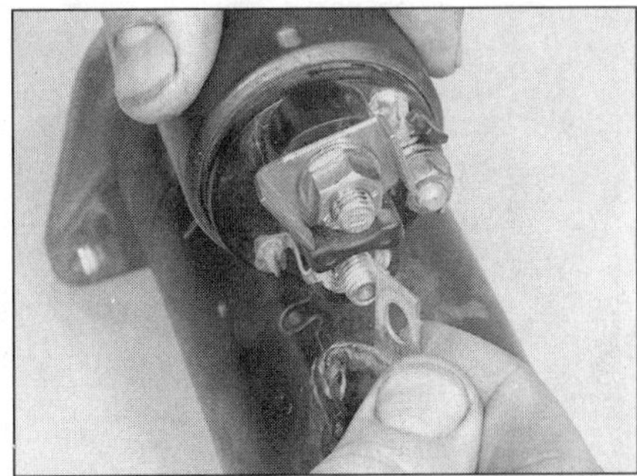

11.2b . . . and disconnect the starter motor feed cable from the solenoid terminal

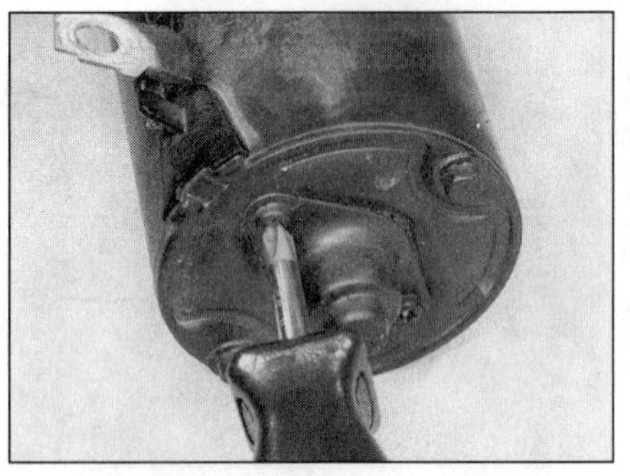

11.3a Unscrew and remove the two screws . . .

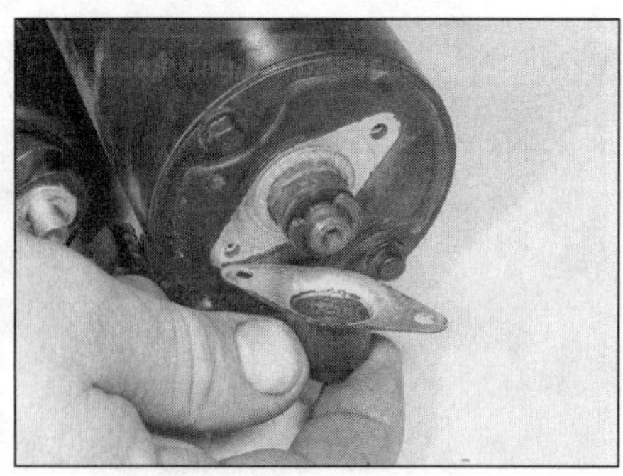

11.3b . . . lift off the cover . . .

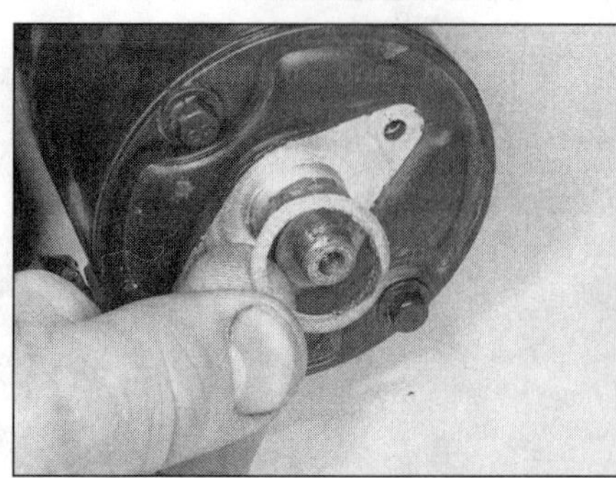

11.3c . . . and remove the seal

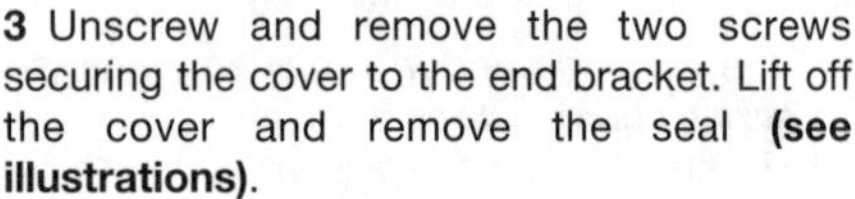

3 Unscrew and remove the two screws securing the cover to the end bracket. Lift off the cover and remove the seal **(see illustrations)**.

4 Extract the circlip, and remove the shim(s) and O-ring seal **(see illustration)**.

5 Unscrew the through-bolts securing the commutator end bracket and yoke to the pinion end bracket **(see illustration)**. Mark the end bracket in relation to the yoke.

6 Remove the commutator end bracket **(see illustration)**.

7 Withdraw the brush holder assembly, at the same time releasing the feed cable grommet from the yoke. If the commutator/armature requires attention or cleaning, withdraw it from the yoke at this stage, then remove the brush holder assembly **(see illustration)**. As the holder assembly is removed, the brushes will be pushed out of their holders by the springs, but will be retained by the leads.

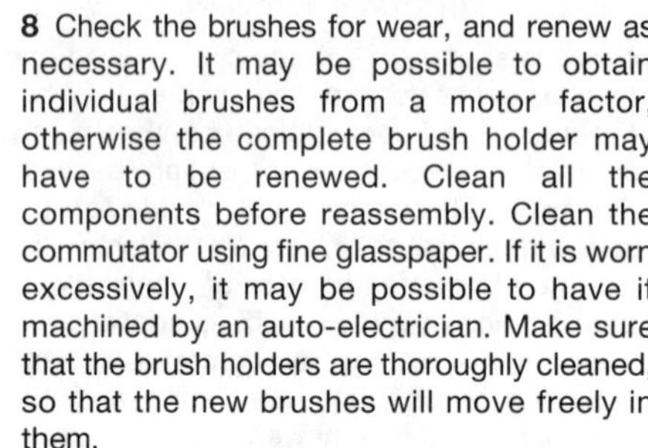

8 Check the brushes for wear, and renew as necessary. It may be possible to obtain individual brushes from a motor factor, otherwise the complete brush holder may have to be renewed. Clean all the components before reassembly. Clean the commutator using fine glasspaper. If it is worn excessively, it may be possible to have it machined by an auto-electrician. Make sure that the brush holders are thoroughly cleaned, so that the new brushes will move freely in them.

9 Locate the brush plate without the brush holders part-way onto the commutator, then centralise the brushes, and fit the holders and springs over the brushes **(see illustration)**.

10 If removed, refit the armature inside the yoke.

11 Slide the complete bush holder assembly onto the armature commutator, while guiding the feed cable grommet in the yoke slot.

12 Locate the commutator end bracket on the armature, followed by the O-ring seal, shim(s) and circlip. Make sure that the O-ring seal is correctly fitted.

13 Refit the end bracket, making sure that the mark is aligned with the previously-made mark on the yoke. Insert and tighten the through-bolts to the specified torque.

14 Refit the shims and circlip, then refit the cover and seal to the end bracket, and tighten the two screws.

15 Reconnect the feed cable to the solenoid terminal, and tighten the nut.

16 Refit the starter motor with reference to Section 10.

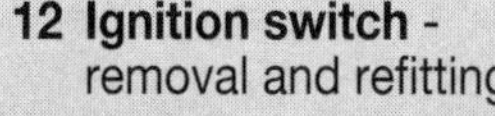

12 Ignition switch - removal and refitting

Removal

1 On models with manual transmission, refer to Chapter 7A and unbolt the gear change lever housing from the floorpan. Undo the screws and detach the locking plate holder and retaining spring from the underside of the gear lever housing. Prise out the locking plate pivot using a screwdriver, then remove the stop plate.

2 On models with automatic transmission, remove the selector lever assembly from the floorpan as described in Chapter 7B.

3 Unplug the wiring from the base of the ignition switch, then remove the switch retaining screws (5) and withdraw the

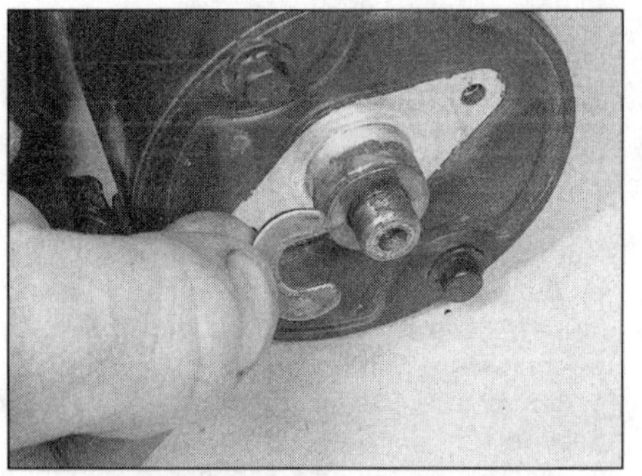

11.4 Extracting the circlip shim(s)

11.5 Unscrew the through-bolts . . .

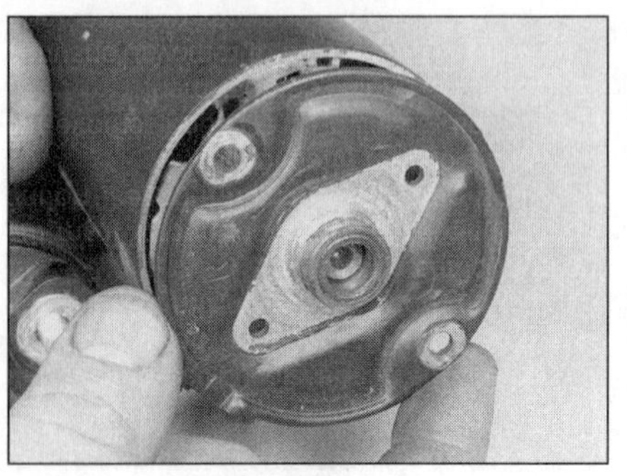

11.6 . . . and remove the commutator end bracket

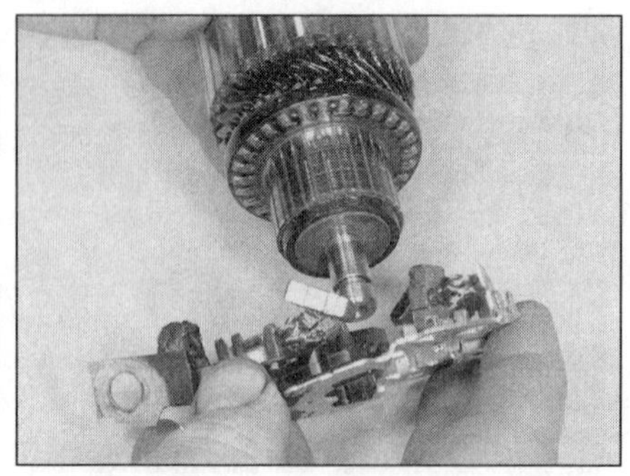

11.7 Removing the brush holder assembly

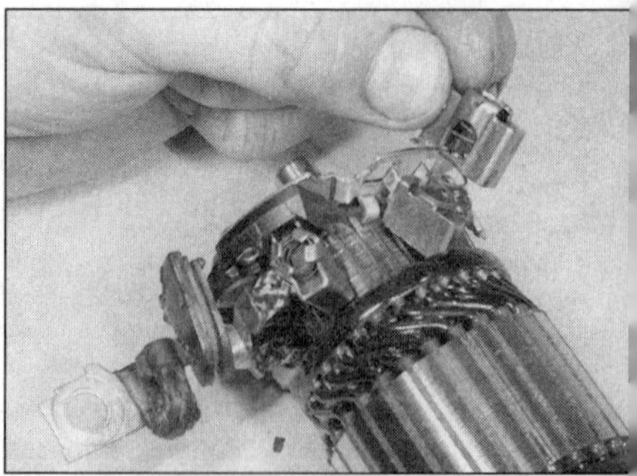

11.9 Fitting the brush holders

assembly from the base of the ignition lock **(see illustration)**. If required, remove the securing screw (4) and withdraw the lock from the lever housing.

Refitting

4 Locate the ignition lock in the housing, then fit and tighten the securing screw. Fit the ignition switch, then fit and tighten the ignition securing screws. Reconnect the wiring to the rear of the ignition switch.

5 On models with manual transmission, press the stop plate into position in the lever housing, then fit the locking plate into position, ensuring that the pivot pins snap into their respective recesses and that the bushings are correctly located. Fit the locking plate holder, then coat the threads of the securing screws with locking fluid and fit them. Fit the locking plate spring, then adjust the position of the locking plate by turning the locking plate holder securing screw, so that the edge of the locking plate is level with the heel in the lever housing. Ensure that the stop does not come into contact with the locking plate (see Chapter 7A).

6 On models with automatic transmission, check the adjustment of the parking lock mechanism, as described in Chapter 7B, Section 5.

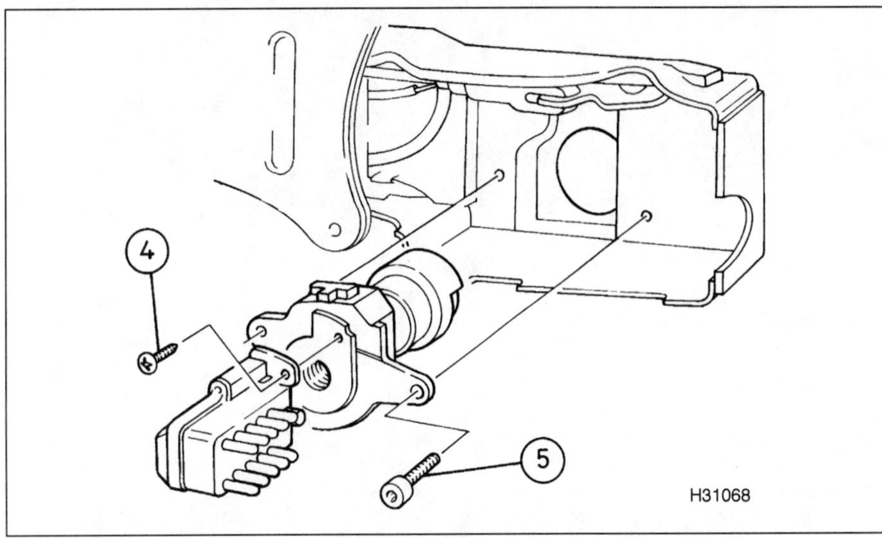

12.3 Remove the switch retaining screws and withdraw the assembly from the base of the ignition lock

7 Refer to Chapter 7A or 7B as applicable for details of refitting the gear change/selector lever assembly.

Notes

Chapter 5 Part B: Ignition system

Contents

Degrees of difficulty

Easy, suitable for novice with little experience 

Fairly easy, suitable for beginner with some experience 

Fairly difficult, suitable for competent DIY mechanic

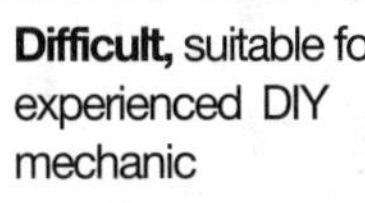

Difficult, suitable for experienced DIY mechanic

Very difficult, suitable for expert DIY or professional

Specifications

System type

2.0 litre non-turbo and 2.3 litre models	Hall-effect ignition, controlled by Bosch Motronic engine management system
2.0 litre Turbo models	Direct Ignition (DI), controlled by Saab Trionic engine management system

Hall-effect ignition system

Ignition HT coil winding resistances:	
Primary	0.52 to 0.76 ohms
Secondary	7200 to 8200 ohms
HT lead resistances:	
Coil-to-distributor	500 to 1500 ohms
Distributor-to-spark plug	2000 to 4000 ohms

Direct Ignition (DI) system

Ignition discharge cartridge:	
Capacitor voltage	400 volts
Ignition voltage (maximum)	40 000 volts
Ignition timing	Pre-programmed in ECU

Firing order

1-3-4-2 (No 1 cylinder at timing chain end)

Torque wrench settings

	Nm	lbf ft
Ignition cartridge (discharge module)	12	9
Knock detector	22	16
Spark plugs	27	20

5B

1 General information

Hall-effect ignition system

1 The system is a breakerless electronic ignition system, and comprises an impulse generator (Hall sensor in the distributor), the HT coil and spark plugs. The impulse generator uses the Hall-effect method to send signals to the Bosch Motronic engine management system electronic control unit (ECU), which then drives the low-tension circuit. The ECU monitors and regulates the ignition timing and dwell angle.

2 The distributor contains no centrifugal or vacuum advance mechanisms, as the speed and load related ignition advance is controlled solely by the engine management system.

Direct Ignition (DI) system

3 The Direct Ignition system uses a separate HT coil for each spark plug. The Saab Trionic engine management system electronic control module (ECM) monitors the engine by means of various sensors, in order to determine the most efficient ignition timing.

4 During starting at a crankshaft speed in excess of 150 rpm, HT sparks are triggered in the cylinder pair with the pistons at TDC. Under difficult conditions, multi-sparking occurs during this period, to aid starting. The ECU determines in which cylinder combustion is taking place by monitoring the flow of current across the spark plug electrodes, and then uses this information to determine the firing

5 When the ignition is switched off and the engine stops, the main relay remains operational for a further 6 seconds. During this period, the Trionic control module earths all the trigger leads 210 times a second for 5 seconds, in order to burn off impurities from the spark plug electrodes.

6 Because the system does not use any HT leads, radio suppression must be incorporated in the actual spark plugs, so resistor-type plugs must always be used.

7 The Direct Ignition system uses the

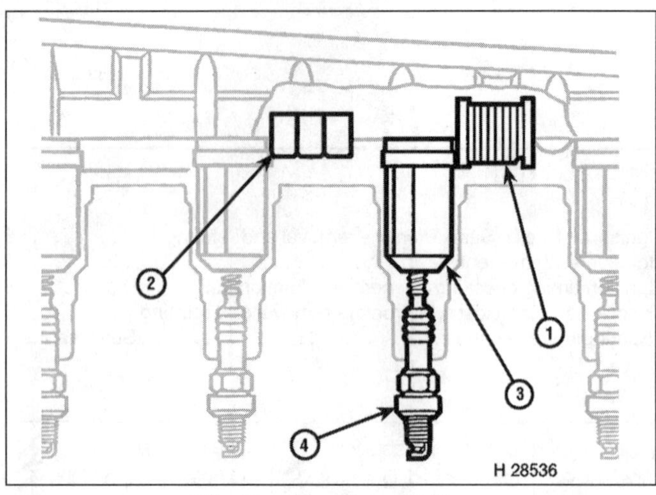

1.7a Direct Ignition cartridge

1 Transformer (12 volts/400 volts)
2 Capacitor
3 Ignition coil
4 Spark plug

1.7b Direct Ignition capacitor (arrowed) located in the cartridge

capacitive discharge method of producing an HT spark. Approximately 400 volts is stored in a capacitor **(see illustrations)**, and at the time of ignition, this voltage is discharged through the primary circuit of the relevant coil. Approximately 40 000 volts is induced in the HT secondary coil, and this is discharged across the spark plug electrodes.

8 Should a fault occur in the system, a fault code is stored in the ECU. This code can only be accessed by a Saab dealer, using dedicated equipment.

9 Note that the starter motor must never be operated with the ignition cartridge disconnected from the spark plugs but still connected to the wiring loom. This can cause irreversible damage to the cartridge.

10 The engine management system controls engine pre-combustion via a knock sensor incorporated into the ignition system. Mounted onto the cylinder block, the sensor detects the high frequency vibrations caused when the engine starts to pre-ignite, or "pink". Under these conditions, the knock sensor sends an electrical signal to the ECU, which in turn retards the ignition advance setting in small steps until the "pinking" ceases. With the Saab Trionic system, the spark plugs themselves are used as knock sensors, instead of employing a separate knock detector in the cylinder block. It achieves this by applying a small, direct current voltage across each spark plug. When two cylinders approach TDC, this voltage causes an ionisation current to flow across the terminals of the spark plug in the cylinder under combustion; a high current indicates that knock is occurring thus indicating which cylinder requires ignition retardation. Sequential control of the fuel injection is achieved in the same manner (see Chapter 4A).

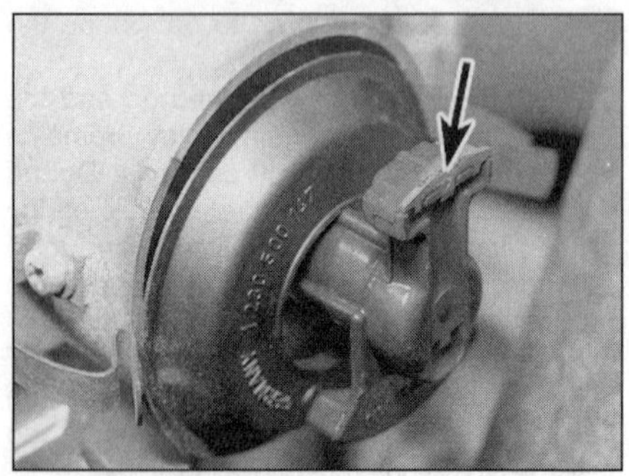

2.4 Rotor arm inside the distributor cap

2 Ignition system - testing

Warning: Voltages produced by an electronic ignition system are considerably higher than those produced by conventional ignition systems. Extreme care must be taken when working on the system with the ignition switched on. Persons with surgically-implanted cardiac pacemaker devices should keep well clear of the ignition circuits, components and test equipment. Always switch off the ignition before disconnecting or connecting any component, and when using a multi-meter to check resistances.

Hall-effect ignition system

1 The components of the Hall-effect ignition system are normally very reliable; most faults are far more likely to be due to loose or dirty connections, or to "tracking" of HT voltage due to dirt, dampness or damaged insulation, than to the failure of any of the system's components. **Always** check all wiring thoroughly before condemning an electrical component, and work methodically to eliminate all other possibilities before deciding that a particular component is faulty.

2 The old practice of checking for a spark by holding the live end of an HT lead a short distance away from the engine is **not** recommended; not only is there a high risk of a powerful electric shock, but the HT coil or amplifier unit may be damaged. Similarly, **never** try to "diagnose" misfires by pulling off one HT lead at a time.

Engine will not start

3 If the engine either will not turn over at all, or only turns very slowly, check the battery and starter motor. Connect a voltmeter across the battery terminals (meter positive probe to battery positive terminal). Disconnect the ignition coil HT lead from the distributor cap, and earth it. Note the voltage reading obtained while turning over the engine on the starter for (no more than) ten seconds. If the reading obtained is less than approximately 9.5 volts, first check the battery, starter motor and charging system as described in Part A of this Chapter.

4 If the engine turns over at normal speed but will not start, check the HT circuit by connecting a timing light (following its manufacturer's instructions) and turning the engine over on the starter motor; if the light flashes, voltage is reaching the spark plugs, so these should be checked first. If the light does not flash, check the HT leads themselves, followed by the distributor cap, carbon brush and rotor arm **(see illustration)**, using the information given in Chapter 1.

5 If there is a spark, check the fuel system for faults, referring to Chapter 4A for further information.

6 If there is still no spark, check the voltage at the ignition HT coil "+" terminal; it should be the same as the battery voltage (ie, at least 11.7 volts). If the voltage at the coil is more than 1 volt less than that at the battery, check the feed from the battery until the fault is found.

7 If the feed to the HT coil is sound, check the coil's primary and secondary winding resistance as described later in this Chapter; renew the coil if faulty, but be careful to check carefully the condition of the LT connections themselves before doing so, to ensure that the fault is not due to dirty or poorly-fastened connectors.

8 If the HT coil is in good condition, the fault is probably within the amplifier unit or Hall generator circuit inside the distributor. Testing of these components should be entrusted to a Saab dealer.

Engine misfires

9 An irregular misfire suggests either a loose connection or intermittent fault on the primary circuit, or an HT lead fault.

10 With the ignition switched off, check carefully through the system, ensuring that all connections are clean and securely fastened.

11 Check that the HT coil, the distributor cap and the HT leads are clean and dry. Check the leads themselves and the spark plugs (by substitution, if necessary), then check the distributor cap, carbon brush and rotor arm as described in Chapter 1.

12 Regular misfiring is almost certainly due to a fault in the distributor cap, HT leads or spark plugs. Use a timing light (paragraph 4 above) to check whether HT voltage is present at all leads.

13 If HT voltage is not present on any particular lead, the fault will be in that lead, or in the distributor cap. If HT is present on all leads, the fault will be in the spark plugs; check and renew them if there is any doubt about their condition.

14 If no HT is present, check the HT coil; its secondary windings may be breaking down under load.

Direct Ignition system

15 If a fault appears in the Direct Ignition system, first check that all wiring is secure and in good condition. If necessary, individual components of the Direct Ignition system may be removed for visual investigation as described later in this Chapter. Coils are best checked by substituting a suspect one with a known good coil, and checking if the misfire is cured.

16 Due to the location of the spark plugs beneath the DI cartridge, it is not possible to easily check the HT circuit for faults. Further testing should be carried out by a Saab dealer, who will have equipment to access fault codes stored in the system ECU.

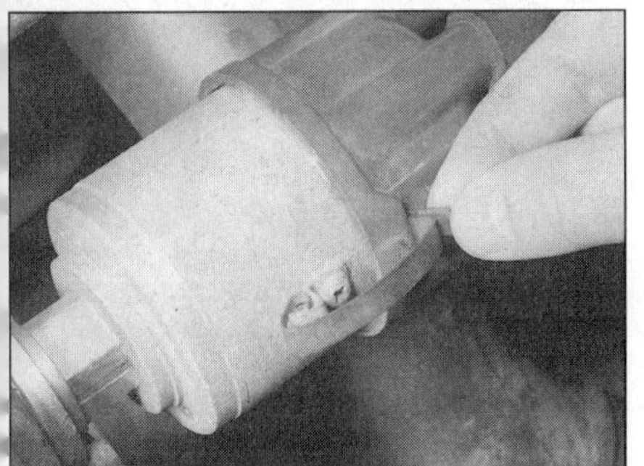

4.1 Releasing the distributor cap clips

3.1 The ignition HT coil is located at the front of the engine compartment, below the power steering fluid reservoir

3 Ignition HT coil (Bosch Motronic) - removal, testing and refitting

Removal

1 The ignition HT coil is located at the front of the engine compartment, below the power steering fluid reservoir **(see illustration)**.

2 Remove the battery from its mounting tray as described in Chapter 5A.

3 Unplug the HT king lead from the top of the distributor.

4 Identify the low-tension leads for position, then disconnect them from the terminals on the coil **(see illustration)**.

5 Unscrew the mounting bracket clamp bolt, and remove the coil from the engine compartment.

Testing

6 Testing of the coil is carried out using a multi-meter set to its resistance function, to check the primary (LT "+" to "-" terminals) and secondary (LT "+" to HT lead terminal) windings for continuity. Compare the results obtained to those given in the Specifications at the start of this Chapter. The resistance of the coil windings will vary slightly according to the coil temperature.

Refitting

7 Refitting is a reversal of removal, but make sure that the mounting clamp bolt is securely tightened, and that the wiring connectors are fitted correctly.

3.4 Disconnect the low-tension leads from the terminals on the HT coil

4 Distributor (Bosch Motronic) - removal and refitting

Removal

1 Mark the spark plug HT leads to aid refitting, and pull them from the distributor cap. If it is required to remove them from the spark plugs, it will be necessary to remove the inspection cover from the centre of the cylinder head. Release the clips from each side of the distributor cap, and place the cap to one side **(see illustration)**. If the clips are tight, use a screwdriver to prise them off carefully.

2 Disconnect the wiring plug for the Hall-effect sensor.

3 Unscrew and remove the distributor flange bolt.

Note: *The distributor flange is not slotted and so the position of the distributor with respect to the cylinder head cannot be adjusted; the basic ignition timing is established by the engine management system.*

4 Withdraw the distributor from the end of the cylinder head. Note that the distributor driveshaft incorporates an off-centre drive dog, which engages a slot in the end of the exhaust camshaft **(see illustrations)**.

5B

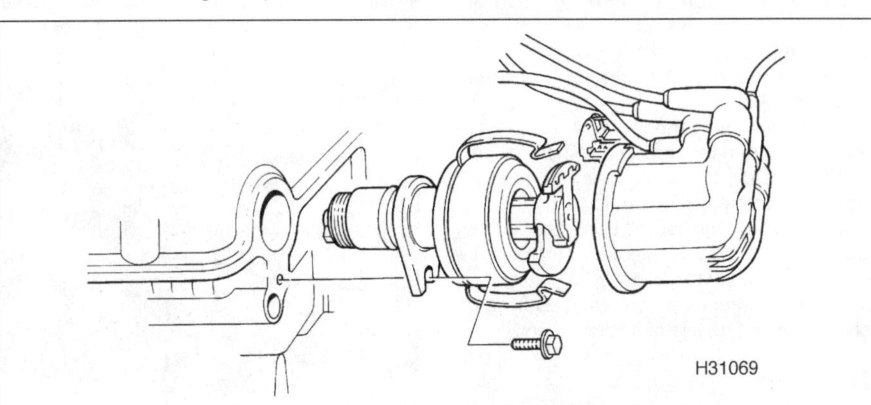

4.4a Withdraw the distributor from the end of the cylinder head

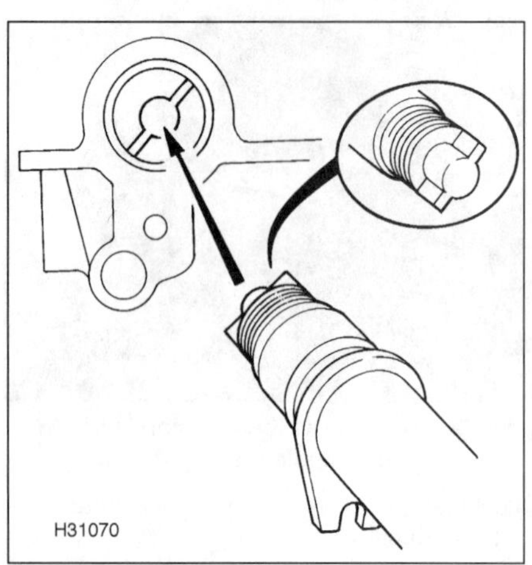

4.4b Note that the distributor driveshaft incorporates an off-centre drive dog, which engages a slot in the end of the exhaust camshaft

Refitting

5 Turn the distributor so that the off centre drive dog lines up with the slot in the end of the camshaft.

6 Slide the distributor into the cylinder head, then insert the flange clamp bolt and tighten it securely.

7 Reconnect the wiring to the Hall-effect sensor.

8 Refit the distributor cap, then reconnect the HT leads.

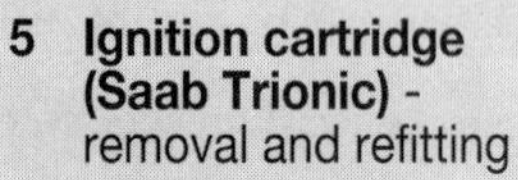

5 Ignition cartridge (Saab Trionic) - removal and refitting

Removal

1 Disconnect the battery negative lead.

2 Unscrew the four screws securing the ignition cartridge to the top of the cylinder head. An Allen key will be required for this **(see illustration)**.

3 Unscrew the bolt and release the cartridge wiring support clip.

4 Where applicable, unscrew the bolt and disconnect the earth lead.

5 Disconnect the system wiring plug, located at the left-hand end of the cartridge **(see illustration)**.

6 Lift the ignition cartridge, at the same time releasing it from the tops of the spark plugs.

7 If necessary, the shroud may be removed from the bottom of the cartridge, by inverting it and removing the screws using an Allen key. Separate the black (lower) shroud from the cartridge **(see illustrations)**.

8 The HT springs may be removed from the shroud by careful use of a screwdriver.

Refitting

9 Refitting is a reversal of removal, but tighten the mounting bolts to the specified torque.

5.2 Removing the ignition cartridge retaining screws (two arrowed)

6 Ignition HT coils (Saab Trionic) - removal and refitting

Removal

1 Remove the shroud from the ignition cartridge as described in Section 5.

2 Carefully remove the HT coils from the upper part of the cartridge.

Refitting

3 Refitting is a reversal of removal.

7 Knock detector (Bosch Motronic) - removal and refitting

Removal

1 The knock detector is located on the rear of the cylinder block, beneath the inlet manifold. First jack up the front of the car, and support on axle stands (see *"Jacking and vehicle support"*).

2 Disconnect the wiring from the knock detector.

3 Unscrew the knock detector from the cylinder block.

Refitting

4 Wipe clean the threads of the knock detector, and the aperture in the cylinder block.

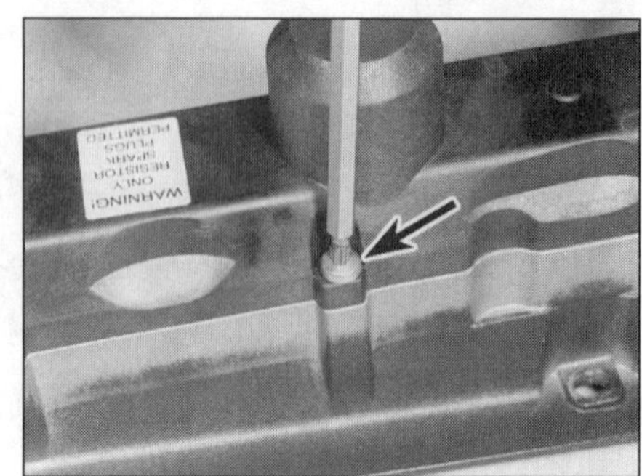

5.7a Unscrew the screws . . .

5.5 Disconnecting the wiring plug from the ignition cartridge

5 Insert the knock detector, and tighten it to the specified torque. **Note:** *It is important to tighten the unit to the correct torque, otherwise it may send incorrect signals to the system ECU.*

6 Reconnect the wiring, and lower the car to the ground.

8 Electronic control unit - removal and refitting

Note: *Refer to the information given in Chapter 4A.*

9 Ignition timing checking - general information

1 On all models, the ignition timing is pre-programmed into the system ECU, and cannot be adjusted. Even checking the basic ignition timing with any accuracy at idle is impractical, as the engine management system is constantly varying the ignition timing to control the engine idle speed, in conjunction with the IAC valve. If the timing is thought to be incorrect, the car should be taken to a Saab dealer, who will have the necessary equipment to extract any fault codes stored in the ECU.

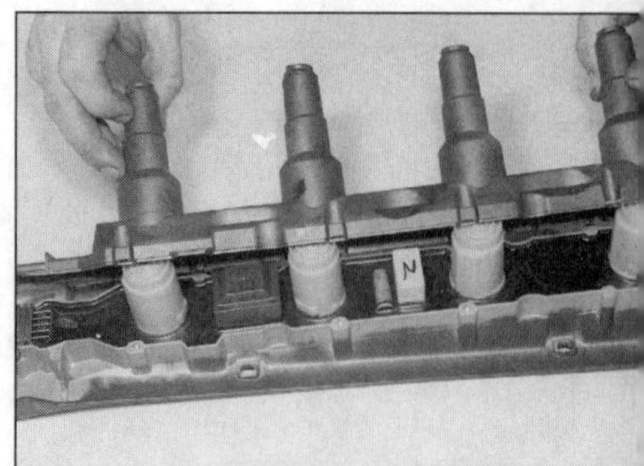

5.7b . . . and separate the black lower shroud from the cartridge

Chapter 6
Clutch

Contents

Degrees of difficulty

Easy, suitable for novice with little experience 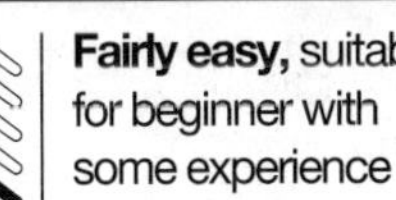	**Fairly easy,** suitable for beginner with some experience 	**Fairly difficult,** suitable for competent DIY mechanic	**Difficult,** suitable for experienced DIY mechanic 	**Very difficult,** suitable for expert DIY or professional

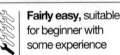

Specifications

System type

1993 to 1998	Single dry plate, operated by self-adjusting cable
From 1998 onwards	Single dry plate, operated by master/slave cylinder hydraulic release system.

Friction disc diameter

2.0 and 2.3 litre non-turbo models	215 mm
2.0 litre Turbo models	228 mm

Hydraulic release mechanism

Slave cylinder stroke	8.0 mm
Master cylinder piston diameter	19.05 mm

Torque wrench settings

	Nm	lbf ft
Clutch cover plate to flywheel	22	16
Clutch pedal pivot to mounting bracket nut	47	35
Clutch pedal/master cylinder mounting bracket to bulkhead nut	24	18
Clutch pedal/master cylinder mounting bracket to bodywork bolt	24	18
Clutch release fork to pivot shaft clamp	25	18
Input shaft seal holder	38	28
Master cylinder securing screws	24	18
Master cylinder to mounting bracket	24	18
Slave cylinder securing screws	10	7
Supply pipe to slave cylinder upper union	15	11
Supply pipe to slave cylinder body	22	16

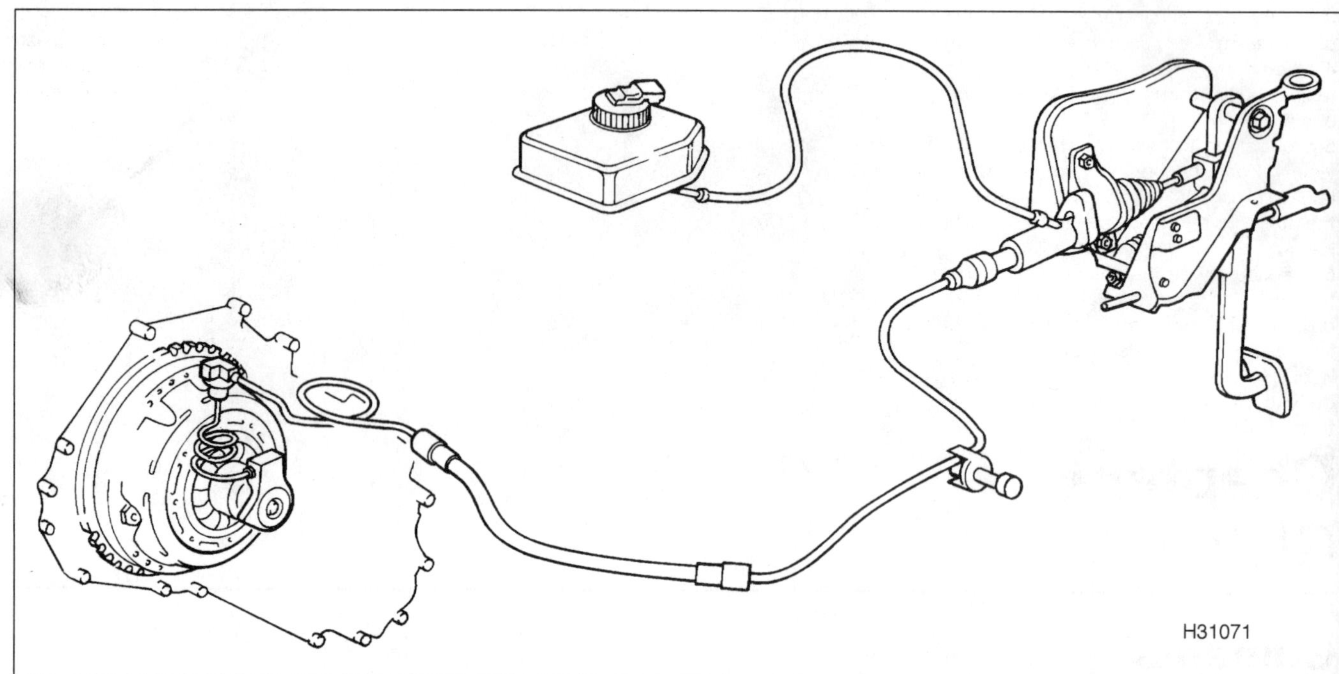

1.1 Hydraulic clutch release system fitted to models built from 1998 onwards

1 General description

1 The clutch system is of single dry plate type, and consists of the following main components: the clutch pedal, the clutch cable, release arm and release bearing, friction disc, and pressure plate with its integral diaphragm spring and cover. On all models built from the beginning of 1998 onwards, a hydraulic clutch release mechanism was fitted in place of the cable release mechanism **(see illustration)**.

2 The friction disc is free to slide along the splines of the transmission input shaft. This is held in position between the flywheel and the pressure plate by the pressure exerted on the pressure plate by the diaphragm spring. Friction lining material is riveted to both sides of the friction disc. Spring cushioning between the friction linings and the hub absorbs transmission shocks, and helps to ensure a smooth take-up of power as the clutch is engaged.

3 The diaphragm spring is mounted on pins, and is held in place in the cover by annular fulcrum rings.

4 The release bearing is located on a guide sleeve at the front of the transmission. The bearing is free to slide on the sleeve, under the action of the release arm that pivots inside the clutch bellhousing.

5 On models fitted with a cable-operated clutch, effort is transmitted from the clutch pedal to the release arm in the transmission by the clutch cable. As wear takes place on the friction disc over a period of time, the increased cable travel is taken up by a self-adjusting mechanism, built into the cable assembly. No periodic adjustment of the clutch cable is specified by the manufacturers.

6 On models with a hydraulically-actuated clutch, effort is transmitted from the clutch pedal to the master cylinder, mounted on the rear of the engine compartment bulkhead, via a push-rod. The master cylinder piston forces hydraulic fluid through a supply pipe to the slave cylinder, which is located inside the transmission casing, mounted concentrically over the transmission input shaft. The fluid forces the piston out of the slave cylinder, thus actuating the release bearing.

7 When the clutch pedal is depressed, the release bearing is forced to slide along the input shaft sleeve, to bear against the centre of the diaphragm spring, thus pushing the centre of the diaphragm spring inwards. The diaphragm spring acts against a circular fulcrum ring in the cover. When the centre of the spring is pushed in, the outside of the spring is pushed out, so allowing the pressure plate to move backwards away from the friction disc.

8 When the clutch pedal is released, the diaphragm spring forces the pressure plate into contact with the friction linings on the friction disc. This simultaneously pushes the friction disc forwards on its splines, forcing it against the flywheel. The friction disc is now firmly sandwiched between the pressure plate and the flywheel, and drive is taken up.

9 The fluid used in the hydraulic clutch system on later models is the same as that used in the braking system, hence fluid is supplied to the master cylinder from a tapping on the brake fluid reservoir. The clutch hydraulic system must be sealed before work is carried out on any of its components and then on completion, topped-up and bled to remove any air bubbles. Details of these procedures are given in Section 8 of this Chapter.

2 Clutch cable - removal and refitting

Removal

1 Working in the engine compartment, remove the battery from its mounting tray as described in Chapter 5A.

2 Unhook the end of the clutch cable from the release arm. Push the release arm towards the engine, if necessary, to aid removal **(see illustration)**.

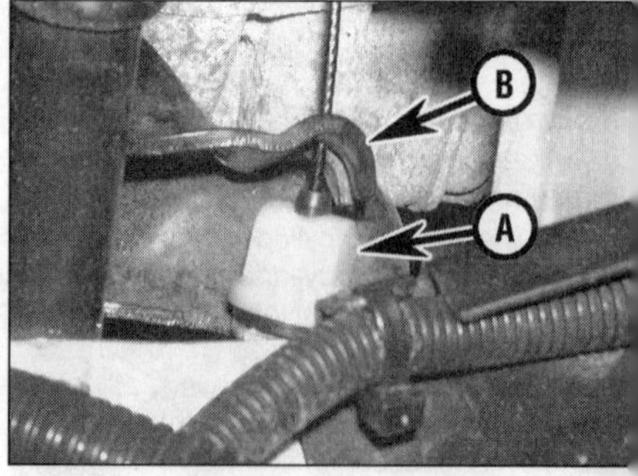

2.2 Unhook the end of the clutch cable (A) from the release arm (B)

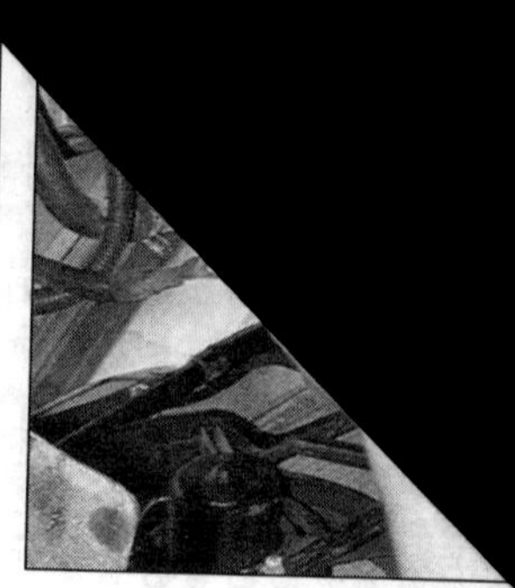

3 Pull the cable damper from the lug on the top of the transmission casing **(see illustration)**.

4 Unbolt the main engine compartment fusebox from the bodywork and move it to one side.

5 Work along the length of the clutch cable visible from the engine compartment and release it from the retaining clips at the rear of the bulkhead and the suspension cross-brace bar.

6 Working inside the vehicle in the driver's footwell, undo the screws and release the diagnostic connector from the underside of the facia then remove the facia lower trim panel.

7 Undo the screws and remove the floor air ducting, then unbolt and the knee shield panel from the facia.

8 Unclip the cover, then remove the securing screws and pivot the fusebox assembly away from the right hand end of the facia moulding.

9 Disconnect and remove the ICE control unit, with reference to Chapter 12.

10 Unclip and remove the air ducting that runs from the heater unit to the driver's right hand face level vent.

11 Reach up behind the facia and unhook the return spring from the clutch pedal, and disconnect the plastic eyelet at the end of the clutch cable from the top of the pedal. Note that the end of the return spring retains the cable end in the pedal.

12 The cable assembly can now be withdrawn into the engine compartment, by pulling it through the bulkhead. Take care not to damage the self adjusting mechanism and bulkhead grommet as the cable is withdrawn.

Refitting

13 Refitting is a reversal of removal. The self-adjusting mechanism must be firmly pressed against the bulkhead when the cable is in position

3 Clutch pedal - removal and refitting

Models with cable-operated clutch

Removal

1 Detach the clutch cable from the top of the clutch pedal, as described in Section 2.

2 Remove the locking spring clip from the right-hand end of the pedal pivot shaft, then unscrew the pedal retaining nut and recover the washer(s).

3 Push the pivot shaft out of the pedal bracket, towards the centre of the vehicle, then lower the pedal and return spring. Note the position of any washers and/or spacers on the pivot shaft, so that they can be refitted in their original positions **(see illustration)**.

4 Withdraw the pedal and return spring from the vehicle. Note the set screw which determines the pedal's neutral position. The

2.3 Pull the cable damper from the lug on the top of the transmission casing

screw is factory set and should not be altered as this will affect the operation of the clutch cable self adjusting mechanism.

Refitting

5 Refitting is a reversal of removal, but before inserting the pedal pivot shaft, smear the surface with a little grease.

Models with hydraulic clutch

Removal

6 Disconnect the battery negative cable and position it away from the terminal.

7 On left hand drive models, unbolt the engine compartment fusebox from its mountings and position it to one side.

8 Apply a proprietary hose clamp to the hose clamp between the fluid reservoir and the master cylinder.

9 Remove all traces of dirt from the outside of the master cylinder and position some cloth beneath the cylinder to catch any spilt fluid.

10 Release the clip and disconnect the supply hose from the top of the master cylinder. Mop up the spilt hydraulic fluid using clean cloths and water.

11 Slide out the retaining clip and free the

ducting, then unbolt the knee shield panel from the facia.

15 Unclip the cover, then remove the securing screws and pivot the fusebox assembly away from the right hand end of the facia moulding.

16 Disconnect and remove the ICE control unit, with reference to Chapter 12.

17 Unclip and remove the air ducting that runs from the heater unit to the driver's right hand face level vent.

18 Release the spring clip and disconnect the master cylinder push-rod from the clutch pedal.

19 Unscrew the nut that secures the clutch pedal pivot to the right hand side of its mounting bracket.

20 Slacken and withdraw the bolt and nut that secures the top of the clutch pedal mounting bracket to the bodywork.

21 From the engine compartment, undo the nut that secures the left hand side of the pedal bracket to the bulkhead.

22 Withdraw the pedal together with its mounting bracket and master cylinder via the underside of the facia, then release the pedal from the bracket.

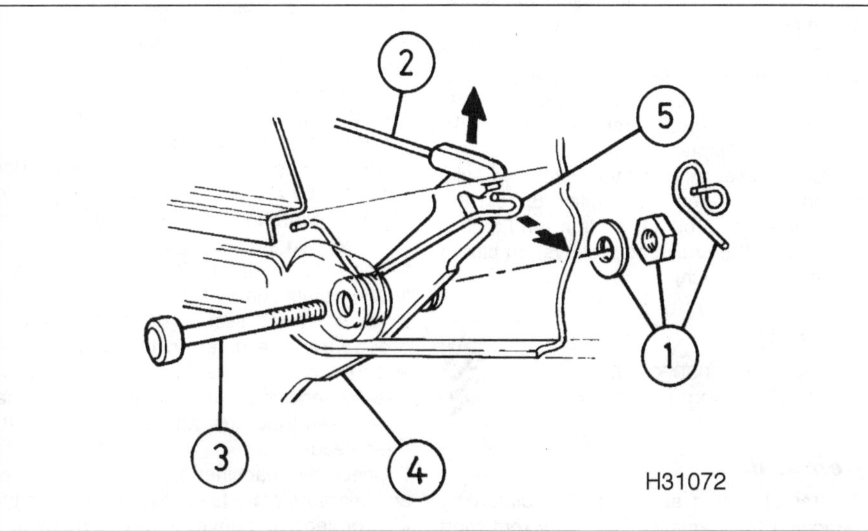

3.3 Clutch pedal components

1 Washer, nut and locking spring clip
2 Clutch cable
3 Pivot shaft
4 Clutch pedal
5 Return spring

4.3 **Unbolt the clutch cover from the flywheel; be prepared to catch the friction disc as the cover assembly is lifted away**

4.7 **With the clutch removed, check the machined surface of the flywheel (arrowed)**

Refitting

23 Offer up the mounting bracket, pedal and master cylinder to the bulkhead. Ensure that the pedal return spring is correctly fitted, then fit the clutch pedal pivot nut, but do not tighten it yet. Insert the bracket to bodywork bolt and nut and tighten to the specified torque.

24 From the engine compartment, fit the mounting bracket to bulkhead securing nuts and tighten them to the specified torque.

25 Reconnect the delivery pipe to the master cylinder and secure it in position with the retaining clip. Likewise, reconnect the fluid supply hose to the port at the top of the master cylinder.

26 Return to the driver's footwell and tighten the clutch pedal pivot bolt to the specified torque.

27 Refit the master cylinder push-rod to the clutch pedal and secure it with the spring clip.

28 Refit all components removed to gain access to the clutch pedal. Where applicable, ensure that the cruise control clutch pedal switch is correctly repositioned, with reference to Chapter 4A.

29 On completion, bleed the clutch hydraulic system with reference to Section 8. Test the operation of the clutch system (and where applicable, the cruise control system clutch pedal cancel switch).

4 Clutch - removal, inspection and refitting

Removal

1 After obtaining access to the clutch by removing the transmission, or by removing and separating the engine/transmission assembly, continue as follows.

2 Note the position of the mark on the flywheel that aligns with the notch in the rim of the clutch cover. Then progressively unscrew the six bolts and spring washers that secure the clutch cover to the flywheel.

3 With all the bolts removed, lift off the clutch assembly. Be prepared to catch the friction disc as the cover assembly is lifted from the flywheel, and note which way round the friction disc is fitted. The greater projecting side of the hub should face away from the flywheel **(see illustration)**.

4 The clutch components can be inspected for wear and damage, as described in Section 5.

Inspection

5 With the clutch assembly removed, clean off all traces of dust using a dry cloth. Although most friction discs now have asbestos-free linings, some do not, and it is wise to take precautions; asbestos dust is harmful, and must not be inhaled.

6 Examine the linings of the friction disc for wear and loose rivets, distortion, cracks, broken torsion springs and worn splines. The surface of the friction linings may be highly glazed, but, as long as the friction material pattern can be clearly seen, this is satisfactory. If there is any sign of oil contamination, indicated by a continuous, or patchy, shiny black discoloration, the plate must be renewed, and the source of the contamination traced and rectified. This will be either a leaking crankshaft oil seal or transmission input shaft oil seal - or both. Renewal procedures are given in Chapters 2A, 2B and 7A, as applicable. The friction disc must also be renewed if the lining thickness has worn down to, or just above, the level of the rivets heads.

7 Check the machined faces of the flywheel and pressure plate **(see illustration)**. If either is grooved, or heavily scored, renewal is necessary. The pressure plate must also be renewed if any cracks are apparent, or if the diaphragm spring is damaged or its pressure suspect.

8 With the clutch removed, it is advisable to check the condition of the release bearing, as described in Section 5.

Refitting

9 Unless the engine and transmission are to be refitted to the vehicle as an assembly, it will prove easier to fit the clutch with the engine in position in the vehicle. This eliminates the need for clutch friction disc centralisation.

10 If applicable, the clutch can be refitted before the engine and transmission are mated and refitted as follows.

11 It is important to ensure that no oil or grease gets on the friction disc linings, or the pressure plate and flywheel faces. It is advisable to refit the clutch assembly with clean hands, and to wipe down the pressure plate and flywheel faces with a clean rag before assembly begins.

12 Place the friction disc against the flywheel, ensuring that it is fitted the correct way round. The greater projecting side of the hub should face away from the flywheel and the stamped lettering should face towards the flywheel **(see illustration)**.

4.12 **Place the friction disc against the flywheel; the stamped lettering 'FLYWHEEL SIDE' should face towards the flywheel**

4.13 Fit the clutch cover retaining bolts and spring washers

5.2 Unscrew the clamp bolt securing the release fork to the release arm pivot shaft

5.3a Pull the release arm pivot shaft up and out of the bellhousing . . .

13 Fit the clutch cover assembly, aligning the mark on the flywheel with the notch in the rim of the clutch cover **(see illustration)**. Insert the six bolts and spring washers (where fitted), and tighten them finger-tight, so that the friction disc is gripped, but can still be moved.

14 The friction disc must now be centralised, so that when the engine and transmission are mated, the transmission input shaft splines will pass through the splines in the friction disc hub.

15 Centralisation can be carried out by inserting a round bar or a long screwdriver through the hole in the centre of the friction disc, so that the end of the bar rests in the spigot bearing in the centre of the crankshaft. Where possible, use a blunt instrument, but if a screwdriver is used, wrap tape around the blade to prevent damage to the bearing surface. Moving the bar sideways or up and down will move the friction disc in whichever direction is necessary to achieve centralisation. With the bar removed, view the friction disc hub, in relation to the hole in the end of the crankshaft and the circle created by the ends of the diaphragm spring fingers. When the hub appears exactly in the centre, all is correct. Alternatively, if a clutch aligning tool can be obtained, this will eliminate all the guesswork, and obviate the need for visual alignment.

16 Tighten the cover retaining bolts gradually in a diagonal sequence, to the specified torque. Remove the alignment tool.

17 The transmission can now be refitted, as described in Chapter 7A or 7B.

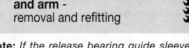

5 Clutch release bearing and arm - removal and refitting

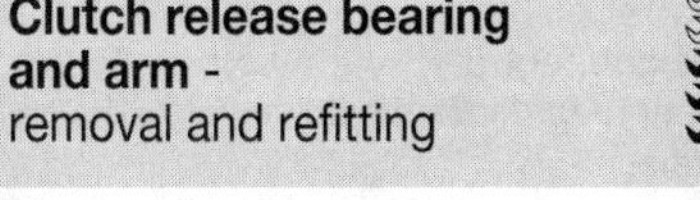

Note: *If the release bearing guide sleeve is removed, a new O-ring should be used on refitting.*

Removal

1 Access to the release bearing can be obtained by removing the transmission as described in Chapter 7A or 7B.

2 Unscrew the clamp bolt securing the release fork to the release arm pivot shaft **(see illustration)**.

3 Pull the release arm pivot shaft up and out of the bellhousing, then pull the release bearing from the input shaft guide sleeve and disengage it from the release fork **(see illustrations)**.

4 Spin the release bearing by hand, and check it for roughness. Hold the outer race, and attempt to move it laterally against the inner race. If any excessive movement or roughness is evident, renew the bearing. If a new clutch has been fitted, it is wise to renew the release bearing as a matter of course.

5 If desired, the release bearing guide sleeve can be removed by unscrewing the three securing bolts, and then the input shaft oil seal can be renewed. Recover the O-ring that fits between the guide sleeve and the bellhousing. Prise the old oil seal from the guide sleeve, and fit a new seal using a tube drift or socket. Fill the space between the lips of the oil seal with lithium-based grease, then refit the guide sleeve, using a new O-ring. The O-ring should be fitted dry.

6 The nylon bushes supporting the release arm pivot shaft can be renewed if necessary, by tapping them from their lugs in the bellhousing using a drift. Drive the new bushes into position, ensuring that their locating tabs engage with the slots in the bellhousing lugs **(see illustrations)**.

Refitting

7 Refitting of the release bearing and arm is a reversal of the removal procedure, remembering the following points.

8 Lightly smear the inner surfaces of the release arm pivot bushes, and the outer surface of the release bearing guide sleeve, with molybdenum disulphide grease.

9 Where applicable, fit the release bearing to the plastic collar, then fit the release bearing and fork together.

5.3b . . . then pull the release bearing from the input shaft guide sleeve and disengage it from the release fork

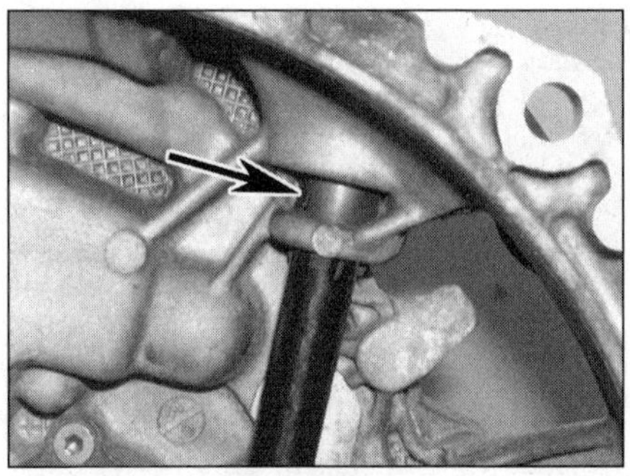
5.6a Release the arm pivot shaft upper . . .

5.6b . . . and lower bushes (arrowed)

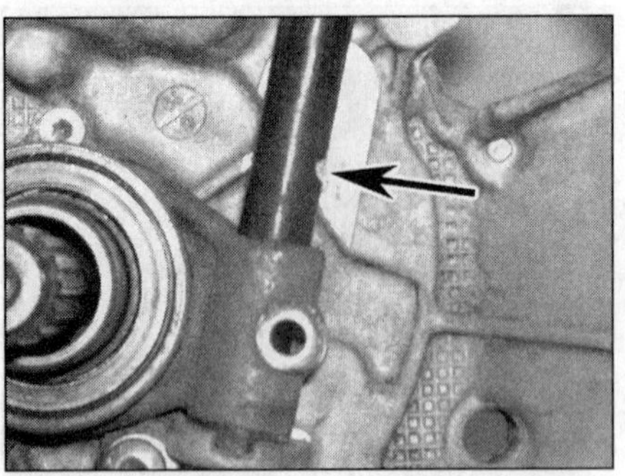

5.10 The notch (arrowed) in the release shaft must engage with the release fork clamp bolt (release shaft withdrawn to show notch)

10 Apply load to the release bearing and release lever simultaneously, so that the release fork is positioned correctly with respect to the notch in the release shaft, then insert and tighten the release fork clamp bolt to the specified torque **(see illustration)**.

11 Refit the transmission to the engine with reference to Chapter 7A or 7B.

6 Clutch slave cylinder - removal and refitting

Removal

1 Unless the complete engine/transmission unit is to be removed from the car and separated for major overhaul (see Chapter 2B), the clutch release cylinder can be reached by removing the transmission only, as described in Chapter 7A or 7B.

2 Wipe clean the outside of the slave cylinder then slacken the union nut and disconnect the hydraulic pipe. Wipe up any spilt fluid with a clean cloth.

3 Unscrew the three retaining bolts and slide the slave cylinder off from the transmission input shaft **(see illustration)**. Remove the sealing ring which is fitted between the cylinder and transmission housing and discard it; a new one must be used on refitting. Whilst the cylinder is removed, take care not to allow any debris to enter the transmission unit.

4 The slave cylinder is a sealed unit and cannot be overhauled. If the cylinder seals have failed or the release bearing is noisy or rough in operation, then the complete unit must be renewed.

Refitting

5 Ensure the slave cylinder and transmission mating surfaces are clean and dry, then fit the new sealing ring to the transmission recess.

6 Lubricate the slave cylinder seal with a smear of transmission oil then carefully ease the cylinder along the input shaft and into position. Ensure the sealing ring is still correctly seated in its groove then refit the slave cylinder retaining bolts and tighten them to the specified torque.

7 Reconnect the hydraulic pipe to the slave cylinder, tightening its union nut to the specified torque.

8 Prime and bleed the slave cylinder with hydraulic fluid, as described in Section 8.

9 Refit the transmission unit as described in Chapter 7A or 7B.

7 Clutch master cylinder - removal and refitting

Removal

1 Disconnect the battery negative cable and position it away from the terminal.

2 On left hand drive models, unbolt the engine compartment fusebox from its mountings and position it to one side.

3 Apply a proprietary hose clamp to the hose clamp between the fluid reservoir and the master cylinder.

4 Remove all traces of dirt from the outside of the master cylinder and position some cloth beneath the cylinder to catch any spilt fluid.

5 Release the clip and disconnect the supply hose from the top of the master cylinder. Mop up the spilt hydraulic fluid using clean cloths and water.

6 Slide out the retaining clip and free the hydraulic delivery pipe from the front of the master cylinder. Plug the pipe end and master cylinder port to minimise fluid loss and prevent the entry of dirt. Recover the sealing ring from the union and discard it; a new one must be used on refitting. Refit the retaining clip to the master cylinder groove, ensuring its is correctly located.

7 Slacken and remove the nut securing the right hand side of the clutch pedal bracket to the rear of the engine compartment bulkhead **(see illustration)**.

8 Working inside the vehicle, in the driver's footwell, undo the screws and release the diagnostic connector from the underside of the facia then remove the facia lower trim panel.

9 Undo the screws and remove the floor air ducting, then unbolt the knee shield panel from the facia.

10 Unclip the cover, then remove the securing screws and pivot the fusebox assembly away from the right hand end of the facia moulding.

11 Disconnect and remove the ICE control unit, with reference to Chapter 12.

12 Unclip and remove the air ducting that runs from the heater unit to the driver's right hand face level vent.

13 Release the spring clip and disconnect the master cylinder push-rod from the clutch pedal.

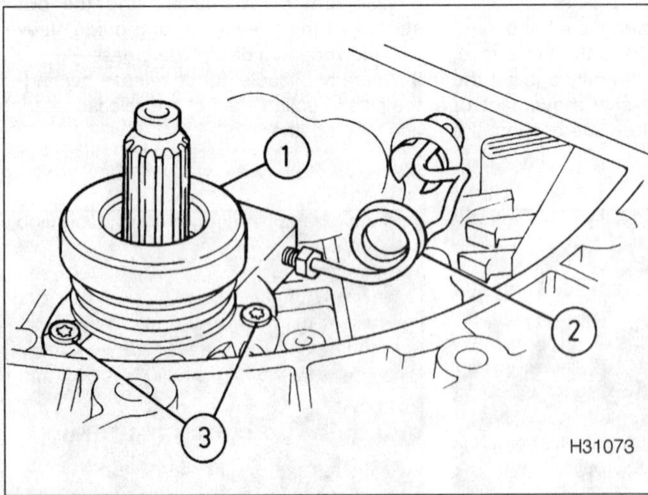

6.3 Slave cylinder

1 Release bearing
2 hydraulic fluid pipe
3 Securing screws

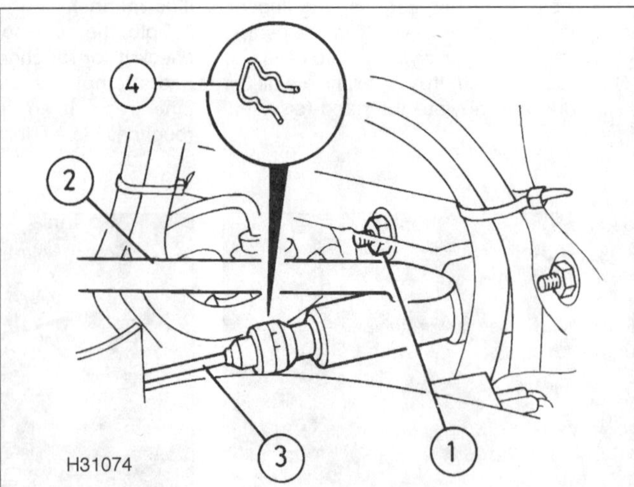

7.7 Remove the nut securing the right hand side of the clutch pedal/master cylinder bracket to the rear of the engine compartment bulkhead

1 Securing nut 2 Supply hose 3 Delivery pipe 4 Clip

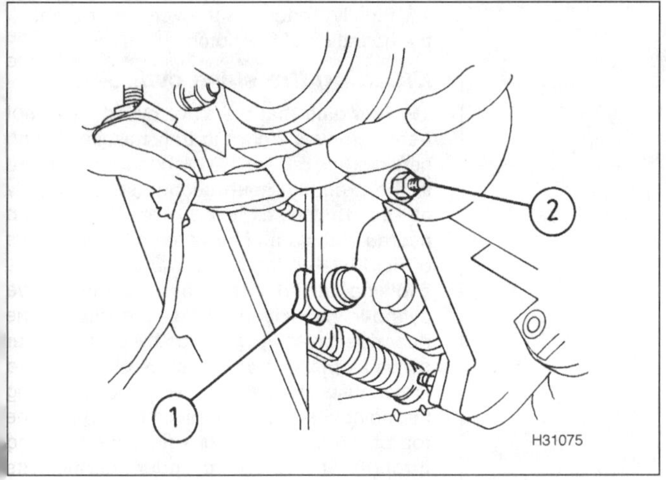

7.14 Clutch pedal to master cylinder connection details
1 *Clutch pedal pivot nut* 2 *Master cylinder push-rod spring clip*

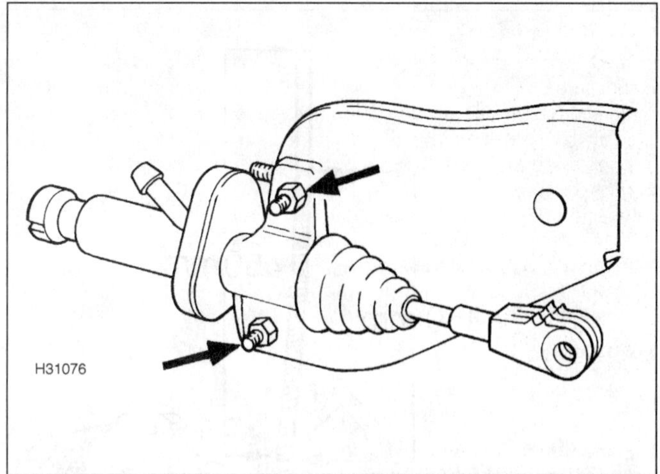

7.15 Undo the nuts (arrowed) and detach the master cylinder from the mounting bracket

14 Unscrew the nut that secures the clutch pedal pivot to the right hand side of its mounting bracket, then withdraw the mounting bracket, together with the master cylinder, from the bulkhead **(see illustration)**.

15 Undo the nuts and detach the master cylinder from the mounting bracket **(see illustration)**. If the master cylinder is faulty it must be renewed; overhaul of the unit is not possible.

Refitting

16 Refit the mater cylinder to the mounting bracket and tighten the securing nuts to the specified torque.

17 Offer up the mounting bracket and master cylinder to the bulkhead and clutch pedal. Ensure that pedal return spring is correctly fitted, then fit the clutch pedal pivot nut, but do not tighten it yet.

18 From the engine compartment, fit the mounting bracket to bulkhead securing nut and tighten it to the specified torque.

19 Reconnect the delivery pipe to the master cylinder and secure it in position with the retaining clip. Likewise, reconnect the fluid supply hose to the port at the top of the master cylinder.

20 Return to the driver's footwell and tighten the clutch pedal pivot bolt to the specified torque.

21 Refit the master cylinder push-rod to the clutch pedal and secure it with the spring clip.

22 Refit all components removed to gain access to the clutch pedal. Where applicable, ensure that the cruise control clutch pedal switch is correctly repositioned, with reference to Chapter 4A.

23 On completion, bleed the clutch hydraulic system with reference to Section 8. Test the operation of the clutch system (and where applicable, the cruise control system clutch pedal cancel switch).

8 Clutch hydraulic system - bleeding

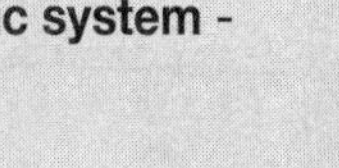

General information

Warning: Hydraulic fluid is poisonous; thoroughly wash off spills from bare skin without delay. Seek immediate medical advice if any fluid is swallowed or gets into the eyes. Certain types of hydraulic fluid are inflammable, and may ignite when brought into contact with hot components. When servicing any hydraulic system, it is safest to assume that the fluid IS inflammable, and to take precautions against the risk of fire as though it is petrol that is being handled. Hydraulic fluid is an effective paint stripper, and will also attack many plastics. If spillage occurs onto painted bodywork or fittings, it should be washed off immediately, using copious quantities of fresh water. It is also hygroscopic (absorbs moisture from the air); excess moisture content lowers the fluid boiling point to an unacceptable level, resulting in a loss of hydraulic pressure. Old fluid may have suffered contamination, and should not be re-used. When topping-up or renewing the fluid, always use the recommended grade, and ensure that it comes from a freshly-opened sealed container.

1 Whenever the clutch hydraulic lines are disconnected for service or repair, a certain amount of air will enter the system. The presence of air in any hydraulic system will cause a degree of elasticity; this will translate into poor pedal feel and reduced travel, leading to an inefficient clutch release action and difficult gear changes. For this reason, the hydraulic system must be bled after repair or servicing, to remove any air bubbles.

2 The clutch hydraulic system is bled by pressurising it externally; the most effective way of achieving this is to use a pressure brake bleeding kit.

3 These are readily available in motor accessory shops and are extremely effective; the following sub-section describes bleeding the clutch system using such a kit.

Bleeding the clutch hydraulic system

Note: *If a new slave cylinder has been fitted, or if you suspect that the hydraulic fluid has been allowed to drain from the existing slave cylinder during servicing or repair, refer to the sub-section entitled 'Bleeding the slave cylinder' first.*

4 Remove the dust cap from the bleed nipple **(see illustration)**.

5 Fit a ring spanner over the bleed nipple head, but do not slacken it at this point. Connect a length of clear plastic hose over the nipple, and insert the other end into a clean container. Pour hydraulic fluid into the

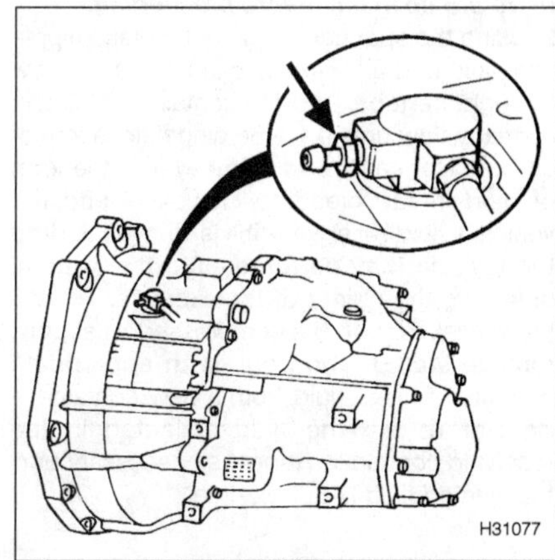

8.4 Clutch hydraulic system bleed nipple (arrowed)

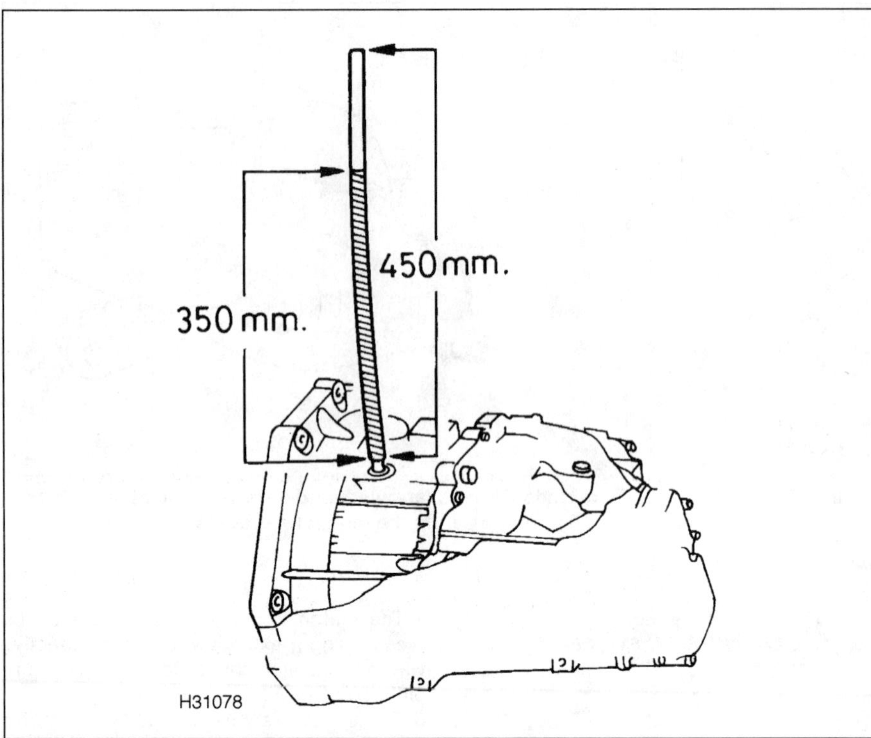

8.20 Fill the hose to a height of 350mm (measured from the bleed nipple) with new brake fluid

container, such that the end of the hose is completely covered.

6 Following the kit manufacturer's instructions, pour hydraulic fluid into the bleeding kit vessel.

7 Unscrew the vehicle's fluid reservoir cap, then connect the bleeding kit fluid supply hose to the reservoir.

8 Connect the pressure hose to a supply of compressed air - a spare tyre is a convenient source.

Caution: Check that the pressure in the tyre does not exceed the maximum quoted by the kit manufacturer, let some air escape to reduce the pressure, if necessary. Gently open the air valve, and allow the air and fluid pressures to equalise. Check that there are no leaks before proceeding.

9 Using the spanner, slacken the bleed nipple until fluid and air bubbles can be seen to flow through the tube, into the container. Maintain a steady flow until the emerging fluid is free of air bubbles; keep a watchful eye on the level of fluid in the bleeding kit vessel and the vehicle's fluid reservoir - if it is allowed to drop too low, air may be forced into the system, defeating the object of the exercise. To refill the vessel, turn off the compressed air supply, remove the lid, and pour in an appropriate quantity of clean fluid from a new container - **do not** re-use the fluid collected in the receiving container. Repeat as necessary until the ejected fluid is bubble-free.

10 On completion, pump the clutch pedal several times to assess its feel and travel. If firm, constant pedal resistance is not felt throughout the pedal stroke, it is probable that air is still present in the system - repeat the bleeding procedure until the pedal feel is restored.

11 Depressurise the bleeding kit, and remove it from the vehicle.

12 If a new slave cylinder has been fitted, or if you suspect that air has entered the existing slave cylinder, proceed as follows: with receiving container still connected, open the bleed nipple, while an assistant fully depresses the clutch pedal and holds it there. Wait for the fluid to flow into the receiving container, then with the clutch pedal at the bottom of its stroke, tighten the bleed nipple, and allow the pedal to return to its rest position. Repeat this sequence until the fluid that flows from the bleed nipple into the receiving container is free from air bubbles. Keep a watchful eye on the level of fluid in the vehicle's fluid reservoir, topping up if necessary.

13 On completion of the bleeding process, tighten the bleed nipple securely, disconnect the receiving container and then refit the nipple dust cap.

14 At this point, the fluid reservoir may well be "over-full"; the excess should be removed using a *clean* pipette to reduce the level to the "MAX" mark.

15 Finally, road-test the vehicle and check the operation of the clutch.

Bleeding the slave cylinder

16 Providing that the slave cylinder has not been removed from the transmission during servicing or repair, the procedure described in the preceding sub-section should cause all air to be expelled from the clutch hydraulic system. If however, a large amount of fluid has drained from the slave cylinder, allowing air to enter, or if a new slave cylinder has been fitted, the procedure described above may not be sufficient to purge all the air from the slave cylinder. This is because the bleed nipple is positioned at the point where the hydraulic fluid enters the top of the slave cylinder - fluid is not forced through the slave cylinder during the bleeding process and such the cylinder is not fully primed with hydraulic fluid. Consequently, some air may remain inside the slave cylinder housing.

17 To overcome this, the slave cylinder must be primed before the transmission is refitted to the transmission, as follows.

18 Take a 450 mm length of 8mm diameter clear plastic hose and fit it to the slave cylinder bleed nipple.

19 Open the bleed nipple then press the release bearing along the input shaft sleeve towards the transmission, so that the piston is pushed fully into the slave cylinder. Catch any fluid ejected from the hose in a container.

20 Hold the hose vertically, then fill it to a height of 350mm (measured from the bleed nipple) with new brake fluid **(see illustration)**.

21 Connect a foot-pump or bicycle pump to the end of the hose, ensuring a good seal. Gradually apply pressure to the hose using the pump, until the brake fluid flows into the slave cylinder. Allow the piston to be pushed out of the slave cylinder to the end of its travel, *but no further* - the resistance felt at the pump should increase when the piston reaches the end of its travel.

22 Press the release bearing back along the input shaft sleeve towards the transmission so that the piston is pushed back fully into the slave cylinder. Allow the air bubbles now flowing through the brake fluid to escape from the end of the plastic hose.

23 Repeat the steps described in paragraphs 21 and 22 inclusive until no more air escapes from the slave cylinder.

24 Leave the piston fully retracted inside the slave cylinder, then disconnect and drain the plastic hose. Refit the transmission as described in Chapter 7A or 7B, without disturbing the slave cylinder. On completion bleed the entire hydraulic system as described in the previous sub-section, paying particular attention to paragraph 12.

Chapter 7 Part A:
Manual transmission

Contents

Degrees of difficulty

Easy, suitable for novice with little experience 

Fairly easy, suitable for beginner with some experience 

Fairly difficult, suitable for competent DIY mechanic

Difficult, suitable for experienced DIY mechanic

Very difficult, suitable for expert DIY or professional

Specifications

General

Type	Transversely-mounted, front-wheel-drive layout, with integral transaxle differential/final drive. Five forward speeds, one reverse, all with synchromesh
Oil type (see caution below*)	See "*Lubricants and fluids*"
Oil capacity	See Chapter 1 Specifications

Caution: During 1997 Model Year, a synthetic transmission fluid was introduced. Transmissions filled with synthetic oil must only be topped up or filled with oil of the same type and grade - do not top up with mineral oil. Where synthetic oil is used, the transmission filler plug will be labelled 'USE ONLY SAAB OIL NO. 87 48 733'

Designation

2.0 and 2.3 litre non-turbo models with B206i, B204I or B234i engines:	
Transmission model	M5N
Transmission type	FM54 501
2.0 litre Turbo models with B204L engines:	
Transmission model	M5NE
Transmission type	FM55 501

Gear ratios (typical):

1st	3.38 : 1
2nd	1.76 : 1
3rd	1.12 : 1
4th	0.89 : 1
5th	0.70 : 1
Reverse	3.17 : 1
Final drive:	
M5N	4.048 : 1
M5NE	3.818 : 1

Torque wrench settings

	Nm	lbf ft
Oil filler, level and drain plugs	60	44
Bellhousing-to-engine block bolts	70	51
Bearing housing-to-differential screws	22	16
Reversing light switch	22	16
Release bearing guide sleeve screws	14	10
Selector rod-to-gear lever bolt	22	16
Selector rod pinch-bolt	20	15
Subframe front mounting bolts	115	85
Subframe centre mounting bolts	190	140
Subframe rear mounting bolts:		
Stage 1	110	81
Stage 2	Angle tighten through 75°	
Transmission-to-subframe mounting bracket nuts	39	29
Left hand engine mounting:		
Mounting to bracket	39	29
Mounting to body	73	54
Bracket to transmission	45	33
Rear engine mounting:		
Bracket to transmission	39	29
Mounting to subframe	39	29

1 General information

The manual transmission is mounted transversely in the engine bay, bolted directly to the engine. This layout has the advantage of providing the shortest possible drive path to the front wheels, as well as locating the transmission in the airflow through the engine bay, optimising cooling.

The unit is cased in aluminium alloy, and has oil filler, drain and level plugs. The case has two mating faces; one to the bellhousing, which is sealed with "liquid gasket" compound, and one to the gearbox end cover, which is sealed with a solid gasket. A "labyrinth" vent at the top of the gearcase allows for air expansion, and permits gases produced by the lubricant to escape. The vent is fitted with a filter plug, that prevents the ingress of water and dirt.

Drive from the crankshaft is transmitted via the clutch to the gearbox input shaft, which is splined to accept the clutch driven plate. All six driving gears (pinions) are mounted on the input shaft; reverse, first and second speed pinions are journalled on sliding contact bearings, and the third, fourth and fifth speed pinions are carried on needle bearings.

The driven gears for all five forward speeds are mounted on the output shaft, again with third, fourth and fifth speed gears carried on needle bearings. Reverse gear is integral with the first/second speed synchromesh sleeve.

The pinions are in constant mesh with their corresponding driven gears, and are free to rotate independently of the gearbox shafts until a speed is selected. The difference in diameter and number of teeth between the pinions and gears provides the required shaft speed reduction and torque multiplication. Drive is then transmitted to the final drive gears/differential through the output shaft.

All gears are fitted with syncromeshes, including reverse. When a speed is selected, the movement of the floor-mounted gear lever is communicated to the gearbox by a selector rod. This in turn actuates a series of selector forks inside the gearbox, which are slotted onto the synchromesh sleeves. The sleeves, which are locked to the gearbox shafts, but can slide axially by means of splined hubs, press baulk rings into contact with the respective gear/pinion. The coned surfaces between the baulk rings and the pinion/gear act as a friction clutch, progressively matching the speed of the synchromesh sleeve (and hence the gearbox shaft) with that of the gear/pinion. The dog teeth on the outside of the baulk ring prevent the synchromesh sleeve ring from meshing with the gear/pinion until their speeds are exactly matched; this allows gearchanges to be carried out smoothly, and greatly reduces the noise and mechanical wear caused by rapid gearchanges.

When reverse gear is engaged, an idler gear is brought into mesh between the reverse pinion and the teeth on the outside of the first/second speed synchromesh sleeve. This arrangement introduces the necessary speed reduction, and also causes the output shaft to rotate in the opposite direction, allowing the vehicle to be driven in reverse.

2 Manual transmission - draining and refilling

General information

1 The gearbox is filled with the correct quantity and grade of oil at manufacture. The level must be checked regularly, and if necessary topped-up, in accordance with the maintenance schedule (see Chapter 1). However, there is no requirement to drain and renew the oil during the normal lifetime of the gearbox, unless repair or overhaul work is carried out.

Draining

2 Take the car on a road test of sufficient length to warm the engine/transmission up to normal operating temperature; this will speed up the draining process, and any sludge and debris will be more likely to be drained out.

3 Park the car on level ground, switch off the ignition, and apply the handbrake firmly. For improved access, jack up the front of the car and support it securely on axle stands (see "*Jacking and vehicle support*"). **Note:** *The car must be lowered to the ground and parked on a level surface, to ensure accuracy when refilling and checking the oil level.*

4 Wipe clean the area around the filler plug, which is situated on the top surface of the transmission (see Chapter 1 for details). Unscrew the plug from the casing, and recover the sealing washer.

5 Position a container with a capacity of at least 2 litres (ideally with a large funnel) under the drain plug. The drain plug is located on the right-hand end of the transmission, under the driveshaft; use a wrench to unscrew the plug from the casing. Note that the drain plug contains a removable magnetic insert, designed to collect the metal fragments produced as the transmission components wear **(see illustrations)**.

2.5a Unscrew the drain plug from the transmission casing

2.5b Note that the drain plug contains a removable magnetic insert

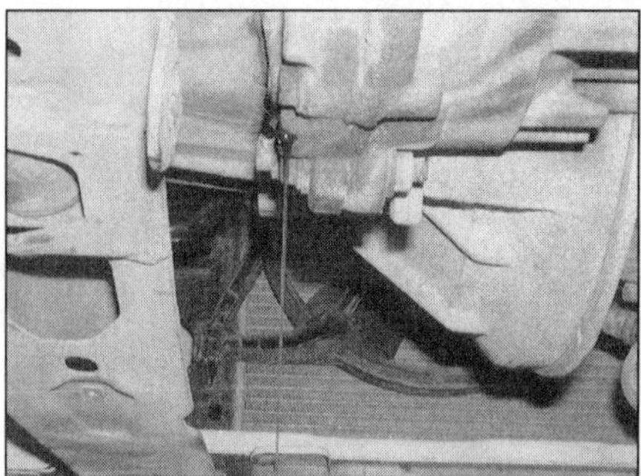
2.6 Allow the transmission oil to drain completely into the container

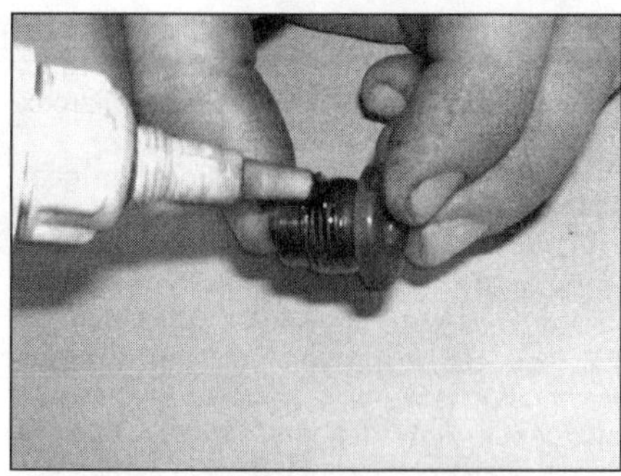
2.7a Coat the threads of the drain plug with locking compound . . .

6 Allow all the oil to drain completely into the container **(see illustration)**. If the oil is still hot, take precautions against scalding. Clean both the filler and drain plugs thoroughly, paying particular attention to the threads. Discard the original sealing washers (where fitted); they should be always renewed whenever they are disturbed.

Refilling

7 When the oil has drained out completely, clean the plug hole threads in the transmission casing. Where applicable, fit a new sealing washer to the drain plug. Coat the threads with thread-locking compound, and tighten it into the transmission casing **(see illustrations)**. If the car was raised for the draining operation, lower it to the ground.
8 When refilling the transmission, allow plenty of time for the oil level to settle completely before attempting to check it. Note that the car must be parked on a flat, level surface when checking the oil level. Use a funnel if necessary to maintain a gradual, constant flow and avoid spillage.
9 Refill the transmission with the specified grade and quantity of oil, then check the oil level as described in Chapter 1. If a large quantity flows out when the level checking plug is removed, refit both the filler and level plugs, then drive the car for a short distance so that the new oil is distributed fully around the transmission components. Re-check the level again upon your return.
10 On completion, fit the filler and level plugs with new sealing washers. Coat their threads with thread-locking compound and tighten them securely.

3 Gearchange linkage - adjustment

1 If the action of the gearchange linkage is stiff, slack or vague, the alignment between the gearchange linkage and the gearbox selector rod may be incorrect. The operations in the following paragraphs describe how to check and, if necessary, adjust this alignment.
2 Park the vehicle, apply the handbrake and switch off the ignition.
3 Locate the alignment hole at the top of the gearbox casing, adjacent to the part number plate. Prise out the plug to expose the alignment hole. Select fourth gear, then take a screwdriver with a shaft diameter of approximately 4 mm, and insert it into the alignment hole; this will lock the gearbox in fourth gear - the screwdriver handle will prevent the screwdriver from falling into the gearbox **(see illustrations)**.
4 Inside the car, remove the gear lever gaiter and mounting frame to expose the gear-change lever housing. Take a screwdriver or drill bit with a shank diameter of approximately 4 mm, and insert it into the alignment hole in the side of the lever housing, to lock the lever in fourth gear - note that the lever can also be locked in third gear, as shown in the photo **(see illustration)**.

2.7b . . . before refitting it to the transmission casing

5 If the screwdriver can be inserted without difficulty, then the gearchange linkage alignment is correct, and hence cannot be blamed for the poor gearchange quality; the best course of action now is to remove the gearchange linkage and inspect it for wear or damage - refer to Section 4 for details.
6 If the screwdriver cannot be inserted into the alignment hole, then the gearchange linkage is incorrectly adjusted.
7 From the engine bay, at the point where the selector rod passes through the bulkhead, slacken the pinch-bolt adjacent to the rubber coupling, to allow movement between the two halves of the selector rod **(see illustration)**.
8 Move the gearchange lever such that the screwdriver shaft can be inserted into the alignment hole in the lever housing; ensure that the lever is still in the 4th gear position.

3.3a Prise the plug from the alignment hole at the top of the transmission casing . . .

3.3b . . . then select fourth gear, and insert a screwdriver into the alignment hole; this will lock the transmission in fourth gear

3.4 Inside the car, insert a drill bit into the alignment hole in the side of the lever housing

9 In the engine bay, tighten the pinch-bolt on the selector rod, observing the correct torque.

10 Remove the screwdriver from the gearbox alignment hole, and fit the plastic plug.

11 Remove the screwdriver from the gear lever housing alignment hole.

12 Refit the gear lever gaiter and mounting frame.

13 Before moving the vehicle, check that the gear lever can be moved from neutral to all six gear positions. Finally, road test the vehicle, and check that all gears can be obtained smoothly and precisely.

4 Gearchange linkage - removal, inspection and refitting

Removal

1 Park the vehicle, switch off the ignition, and apply the handbrake.

2 Referring to Chapter 11, remove the left hand front seat and the gear lever housing console. Unclip the rear passenger air duct from the side of the gear lever housing.

3 Lock the gearchange lever and transmission selector shaft in the 4th gear position, as described in Section 3.

4 From the engine bay, at the point where the selector rod passes through the bulkhead, slacken the pinch-bolt adjacent to the rubber coupling (see Section 3).

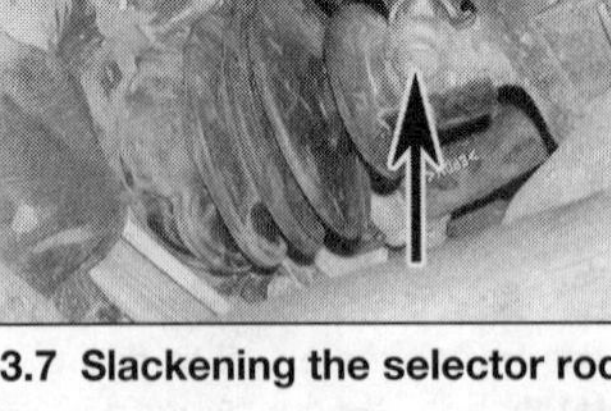

3.7 Slackening the selector rod pinch-bolt

5 Remove the gear lever locking tool, select third gear, then reinsert the locking tool. This will cause the two halves of the selector rod to separate at the coupling in the engine bay.

6 Slacken and remove the four bolts that secure the gearchange lever housing to the floorpan.

7 Lift the housing up as far as possible, without damaging the console trim, and release the ignition lock cables from the housing.

8 Disconnect the ignition cable from the rear of the gear lever housing, then remove the housing by pulling it towards the rear of the vehicle, whilst withdrawing the selector rod through the floorpan aperture.

9 To remove the gear lever, undo the screws and detach the locking plate holder and retaining spring from the underside of the gear lever housing. Prise out the locking plate pivot using a screwdriver, then remove the stop plate. Place the gear lever in the reverse gear position, then undo the screw and separate the selector rod from the base of the gear change lever. At the top of the housing, depress the three clips around the edge of the gear lever's spherical plastic outer bearing and withdraw the lever and bearing assembly from its housing **(see illustration)**.

Inspection

10 It is most likely that any slack found in the mechanism will be caused by worn bushes between the gear lever and the selector rod. Extract the bushes from the gear lever linkage **(see illustration)** and inspect them; if they appear worn or corroded, press them from the gear lever boss and renew them.

Refitting

11 Reassemble the gearchange lever to its housing, then reconnect the lever to the selector rod and tighten the bolt to the specified torque.

12 Press the stop plate into position in the lever housing, then fit the locking plate into position, ensuring that the pivot pins snap into their respective recesses and that the bushings are correctly located.

13 Fit the locking plate holder, then coat the threads of the securing screws with locking fluid and fit them.

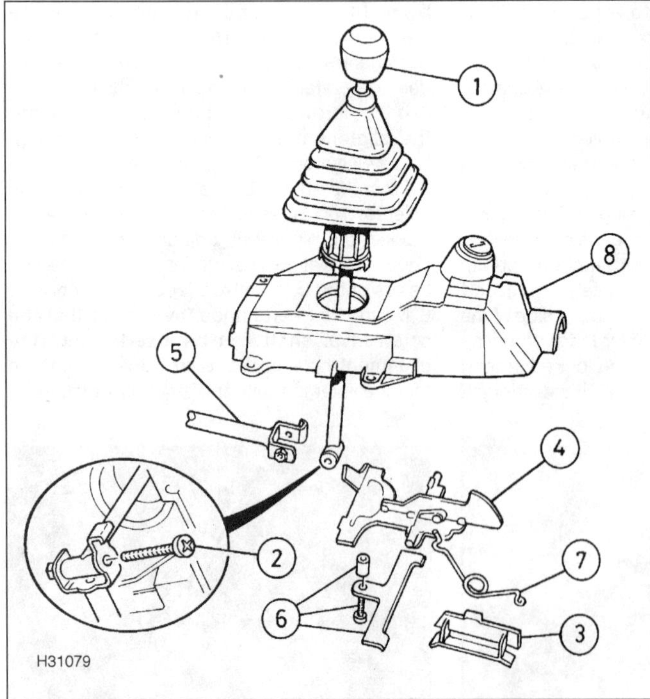

4.9 Gear change lever and housing assembly

1 Gear change lever
2 Gear change lever-to-selector rod screw
3 Stop plate
4 Locking plate
5 Selector rod
6 Screw and collar
7 Locking plate spring
8 Gear change lever housing

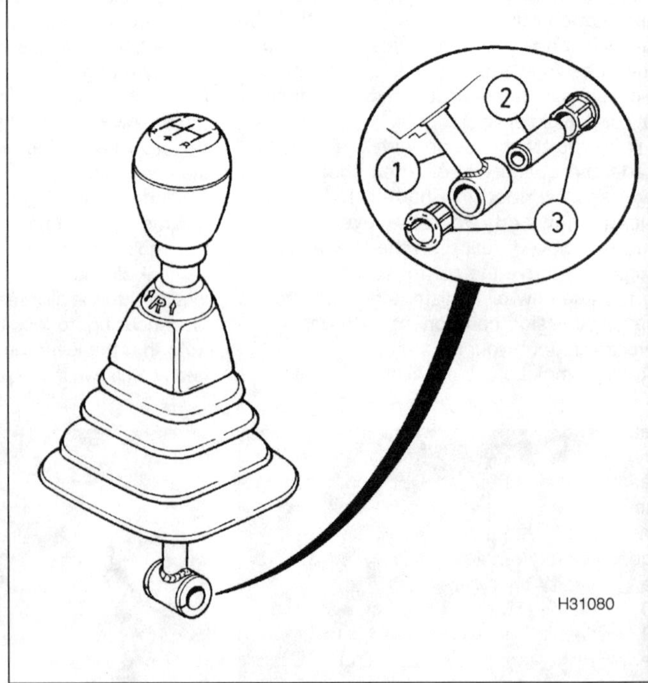

4.10 Gear change lever selector rod bushes

1 Gear change lever *2 Sleeve* *3 Bushes*

14 Fit the locking plate spring, then adjust the position of the locking plate by turning the locking plate holder securing screw, so that the edge of the locking plate is level with the heel in the lever housing. Ensure that the stop does not come into contact with the locking plate **(see illustration)**.

15 Refit the gear lever housing and selector rod assembly to the vehicle by reversing the removal sequence. Reconnect the selector rod to the transmission at the coupling in the engine bay as described in Section 3.

16 On completion, check that the gear lever can be moved from neutral to all six gear positions. Finally, road test the vehicle, and check that all gears can be obtained smoothly and precisely.

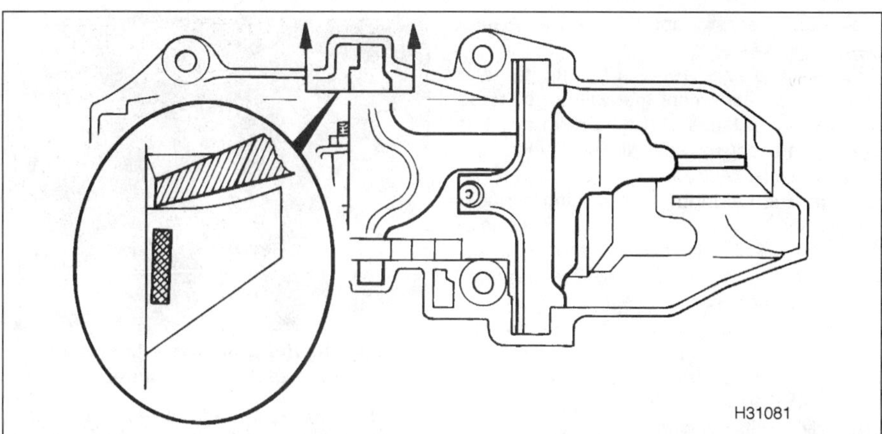

4.14 Adjust the position of the locking plate so that the edge of the locking plate is level with the heel in the lever housing

5 Oil seals - renewal

Right-hand driveshaft oil seal

Note: *This sub-section describes the renewal of the O-ring oil seal in the bearing casing only. Renewal of the driveshaft oil seal is a more complex task, requiring access to a hydraulic press, and as such should be entrusted to a Saab dealer.*

1 Park the vehicle on a level surface, apply the handbrake, and chock the rear wheels.

2 Remove the wheel centre caps, and slacken the wheel bolts.

3 Apply the handbrake, then raise the front of the vehicle, rest it securely on axle stands and remove the roadwheels; refer to *"Jacking and vehicle support"* for guidance.

4 Refer Section 2 and drain the transmission oil. Clean and refit the drain plug as described in Section 2.

5 Working from Chapter 8, remove the right hand driveshaft, and the intermediate driveshaft and bearing assembly.

6 Remove the four retaining screws from the driveshaft bearing housing **(see illustration)**.

7 Carefully prise the bearing housing out of the differential casing. Recover the shims.

8 Extract the O-ring seal from the bearing housing, and discard it.

9 Thoroughly clean the mating surfaces of the bearing housing and differential casing; take precautions to prevent debris entering the bearings of either assembly. If hydraulic press facilities are available, drive out the old driveshaft oil seal and press the new seal squarely into the housing. Fill the cavity of the new seal with driveshaft grease.

10 Lubricate the new O-ring seal with clean oil, and carefully fit it over the driveshaft bearing housing, ensuring that it is seated squarely.

11 Refit the shims, then carefully tap the bearing housing into the differential casing, until it is flush with the surface of the casing.

12 Ensure that the O-ring is seated squarely and not distorted, then refit the five retaining screws into the bearing housing, and tighten them progressively in a diagonal pattern to the correct torque.

13 With reference to Chapter 8, refit the right hand driveshaft and the intermediate drive-shaft and bearing assembly.

14 Refit the roadwheels, and lower the vehicle to the ground. Tighten the roadwheel bolts to the correct torque (see Chapter 1 Specifications), and refit the wheel centre caps/trims.

15 Refer to Section 2 and refill the trans-mission with the correct quantity and grade of oil.

Left-hand driveshaft oil seal

Note: *This sub-section describes the renewal of the O-ring oil seal in the bearing casing only. Renewal of the driveshaft oil seal is a more complex task, requiring access to a hydraulic press, and as such should be entrusted to a Saab dealer.*

16 Park the vehicle on a level surface, apply the handbrake, and chock the rear wheels. Remove the wheel centre caps, and slacken the wheel bolts.

17 Apply the handbrake, then raise the front of the vehicle, rest it securely on axle stands and remove the roadwheels; refer to *"Jacking and vehicle support"* for guidance.

18 Refer to Section 2 and drain the transmission oil. Clean and refit the drain plug as described in Section 2.

19 Working from the relevant section of Chapter 8, disconnect the left-hand driveshaft from the transmission.

20 Place a container beneath the driveshaft housing mating face, then slacken and withdraw the five retaining screws.

21 Carefully prise the bearing housing out of the differential casing.

22 Recover the shims from the driveshaft bearing housing, and then extract the O-ring.

23 Thoroughly clean the mating surfaces of the bearing housing and differential casing; if a cleaning solvent is used, take care to prevent any entering the bearings of either assembly. If hydraulic press facilities are available, drive out the old driveshaft oil seal and press the new seal squarely into the housing.

24 Refit the shims to the differential housing, then lubricate the new O-ring seal with clean engine oil, and carefully fit it over the driveshaft bearing housing, ensuring that it is seated squarely.

25 Refit the shims, then carefully tap the bearing housing into the differential casing, until it is flush with the surface of the casing.

26 Ensure that the O-ring is seated squarely and not distorted, then refit the five retaining screws into the bearing housing, and tighten them progressively and in a diagonal pattern to the correct torque.

27 Refer to Chapter 8, and reconnect the left-hand driveshaft to the transmission.

28 Refit the roadwheels, and lower the vehicle to the ground. Tighten the roadwheel bolts to the correct torque (see Chapter 1 Specifications), and refit the wheel centre caps/trims.

29 Refer to Section 2 and refill the trans-mission with the correct quantity and grade of oil.

Input shaft oil seal

30 Referring to Section 7, remove the trans-mission and rest it securely on a worksurface.

31 Working from Chapter 6, remove the clutch release shaft, fork and bearing. Undo

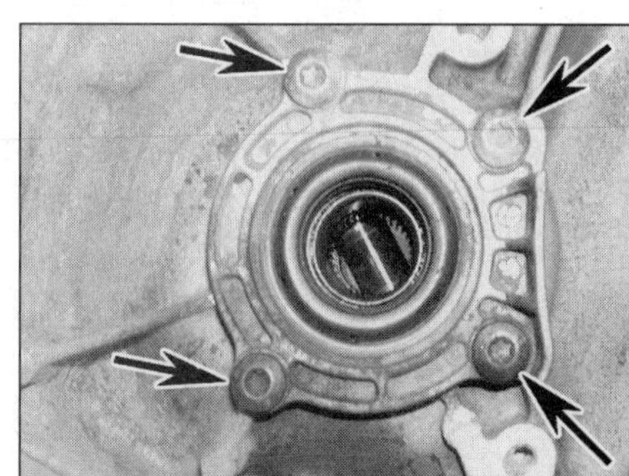

5.6 Remove the four retaining screws (arrowed) from the driveshaft bearing housing

the securing screws and remove the release bearing guide sleeve.

32 Prise the seal from its housing; use a blunt-ended instrument that will not damage the mating surfaces of the housing or input shaft, and cause seal to fail when the transmission is refitted.

33 Examine the input shaft sealing surface, to identify any imperfections that may have caused the seal to fail in the first place. Minor burrs can be removed using fine abrasive paper, but more serious wear or damage will mean that the input shaft has to be renewed.

34 Clean the mating surfaces thoroughly using a clean rag, then lightly lubricate the new oil seal with clean engine oil, and press it squarely into its housing.

35 Refit the clutch release sleeve, shaft, fork and bearing with reference to Chapter 6. Tighten the release bearing guide sleeve screws to the specified torque.

36 Refer to Section 7 and refit the transmission.

Selector rod oil seal

37 Renewal of the selector rod oil seal can only be carried out as part of a complete transmission overhaul and as such, should be entrusted to a Saab dealer.

6 Reversing light switch - testing, removal and refitting

Testing

1 Disconnect the battery negative cable, and position it away from the terminal.

2 Unplug the wiring harness from the reversing light switch at the connector. The switch is located on the rear of the transmission casing **(see illustration)**.

3 Connect the probes of a continuity tester, or a multi-meter set to the resistance function, across the terminals of the reversing light switch.

4 The switch contacts are normally open, so with any gear other than reverse selected, the tester/meter should indicate an open-circuit. When reverse gear is then selected, the switch contacts should close, causing the tester/meter to indicate a short-circuit.

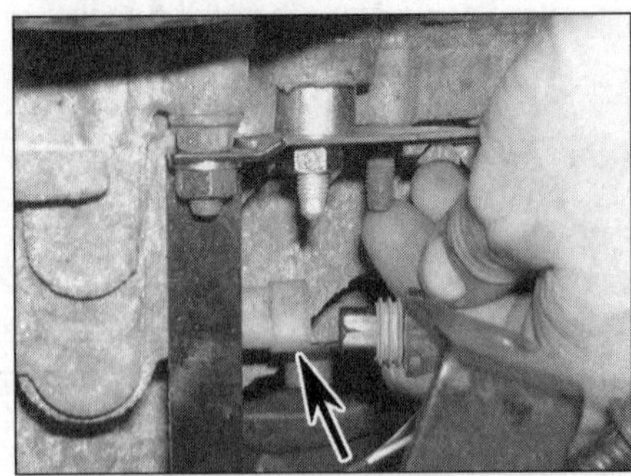

6.2 Unplug the wiring from the reversing light switch at the connector

5 If the switch appears to be constantly open- or short-circuit, or is intermittent in its operation, it should be renewed.

Removal

6 Ensure that the ignition is switched off.

7 Unplug the wiring harness from the reversing light switch at the connector.

8 Using a suitable spanner, unscrew the switch from the endplate, recovering any washers that may be fitted; these **must** be refitted, to ensure that the correct clearance exists between the switch shaft and the reverse gear shaft.

Refitting

9 Refit the switch by reversing the removal procedure, observing the correct torque wrench setting.

7 Manual transmission - removal and refitting

Removal

Note: *Refer to Chapter 2B for details on removal of the engine and transmission as a complete assembly.*

1 Park the vehicle on a level surface, apply the handbrake and chock the rear wheels.

2 Apply the handbrake, then raise the front of the vehicle, rest it securely on axle stands (see "*Jacking and vehicle support*") and remove the front roadwheels.

3 Refer to Section 2 of this Chapter and drain the oil from the transmission. Refit and tighten the drain plug.

4 Referring to Chapter 5A, disconnect both battery cables and then remove the battery from its tray.

5 Unbolt the battery earth cables from the studs on the transmission casing **(see illustration)**. Release the battery positive cable and sheathing from its retaining clips.

6 Unplug the wiring from the reversing light switch at the rear of the transmission casing (Section 6).

7 Release the clutch cable from the transmission as described in Chapter 6. On later models with hydraulic clutch disconnect the hydraulic fluid supply pipe from the slave cylinder.

8 Unplug the lambda sensor wiring from the main engine harness (see Chapter 4A). Release the sensor's wiring from its retaining clips at the front and left hand side of the cylinder head.

9 Remove the air cleaner and intake ducting as described in Chapter 4A, including the intercooler-to-throttle body ducting on Turbo models. Remove the resonator assembly (non-turbo models) or cover panel (Turbo models) from the top of the throttle body.

10 Fit a lifting beam across the top of the engine compartment, in line with the engine lifting eyelets. Remove the rubber grommet from the left hand eyelet and attach lifting beam jib securely to it **(see illustrations)**. Raise the jib until it is just taking the combined weight of the engine and transmission.

11 Separate the gear selector rod at the coupling in the engine bay , as described in Sections 3 and 4. Lock the transmission in fourth gear, and lock the gear change lever in third gear.

12 Unbolt and remove the exhaust system front pipe and catalytic converter (see Chapter 4A).

13 With reference to Chapter 11, remove the spoiler panels from the underside of the front bumper. Remove the securing screws and withdraw the plastic liners from the left hand wheel arch. Also remove the plastic shield from the right hand wheel arch, to expose the crankshaft pulley.

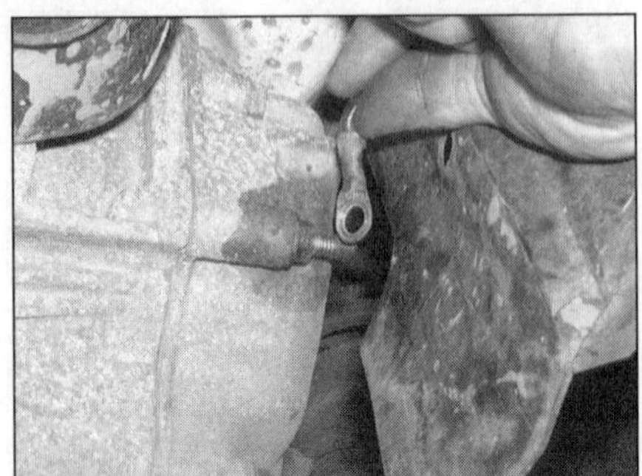

7.5 Unbolt the battery earth cables from the studs on the transmission casing

7.10a Fit a lifting beam across the top of the engine compartment, in line with the engine lifting eyelets

7.10b Remove the rubber grommet from the left hand eyelet (arrowed) and attach lifting beam jib securely to it

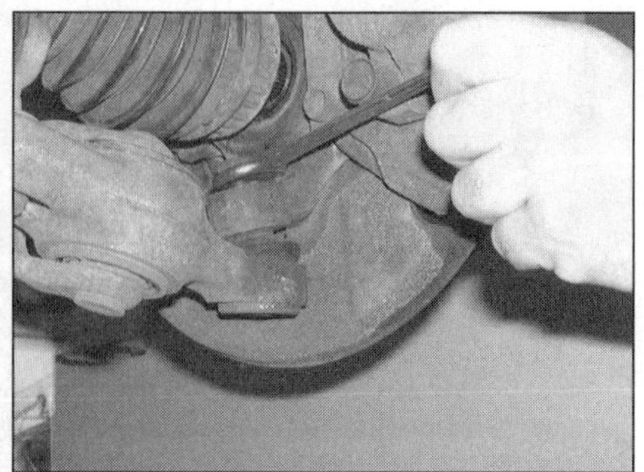
7.15a Unbolt both front suspension lower arm balljoints . . .

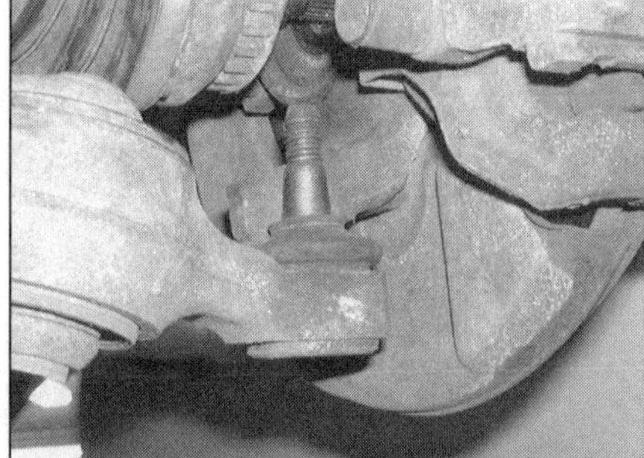
7.15b . . . and separate them from the base of their respective hub carriers

7.16a Removing the left hand driveshaft from the intermediate shaft

7.16b Removing the intermediate shaft

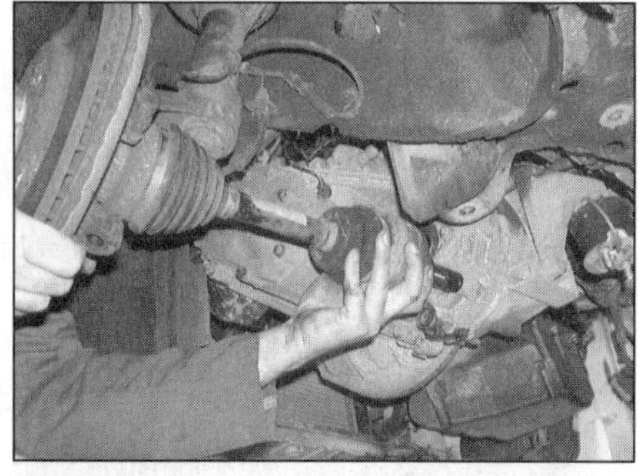
7.16c Removing the right hand driveshaft

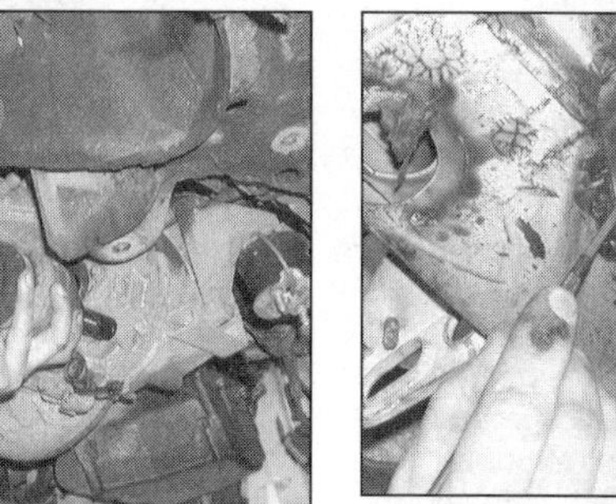
7.18 Mark around the boundary of the suspension subframe, to help achieve correct alignment during refitting

14 Remove the auxiliary drivebelt with reference to Chapter 1.

15 Unbolt both front suspension lower arm balljoints from the base of their respective hub carriers, with reference to Chapter 10. If required, unbolt the ends of the anti-roll bar from the lower arms to increase available clearance **(see illustrations)**.

16 Remove the left hand driveshaft, right hand driveshaft, intermediate shaft and bearing support bracket with reference to Chapter 8 **(see illustrations)**. Note that the alternator lower mounting bolt must be removed to allow the removal of the intermediate driveshaft bearing support bracket.

17 Slacken and remove the nuts that secure the base of the rear engine mounting to the suspension subframe (see Chapter 2A).

18 Mark around the boundary of the suspension subframe, to indicate its fitted position. This will help to achieve the correct alignment during refitting **(see illustration)**.

19 Position a pair of trolley jacks underneath the suspension subframe and raise them until the jack heads rest against the underside of the subframe.

20 Progressively slacken and withdraw each of the six subframe securing bolts. Note that the bolts are of different lengths and diameters - make a note of their fitted positions to aid refitting. Ensure that the lifting beam is taking the weight of the engine/transmission as the unit will tend to pivot towards the rear of the engine compartment as the subframe is removed.

21 Slowly lower the subframe away from the underside of the engine compartment using the trolley jacks. Recover the spacer washers fitted to the two rearmost bolts **(see illustrations)**.

22 Make a final check that any components which would prevent the removal of the transmission from the car have been removed or disconnected. Ensure that components such as the gearchange selector rod and clutch cable are secured so that they cannot be damaged on removal.

23 Position a trolley jack underneath the transmission casing. Raise the jack head so that it is just taking the weight of the transmission.

24 Unbolt and remove the left hand engine/transmission mountings, with reference to Chapter 2A. Lower the lifting beam jib so that the left hand end of the engine and transmission assembly is lowered by approximately 10 cm. This gives enough clearance to allow the transmission to be withdrawn from the engine later.

25 Unbolt the flywheel protection plate from the right hand side of the transmission bellhousing **(see illustration)**.

7.21a Slowly lower the subframe away from the underside of the engine compartment using two trolley jacks . . .

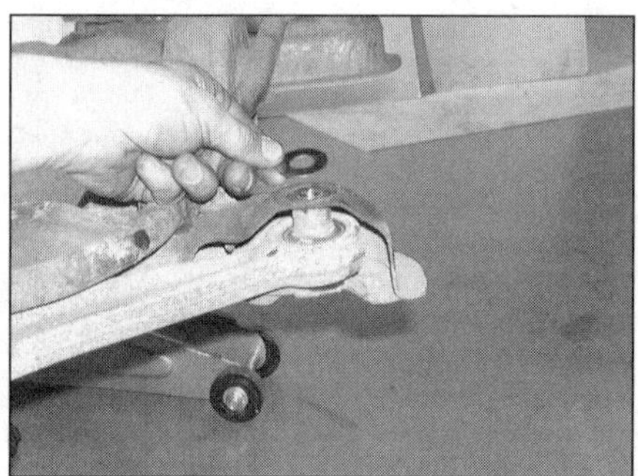
7.21b . . . and recover the spacer washers fitted to the two rearmost bolts

7.25 Unbolt the flywheel protection plate from the right hand side of the transmission bellhousing

7.26a Transmission bellhousing bolts and remove all but the uppermost retaining bolt

7.26b Note that one of the bellhousing bolts (arrowed) is concealed between the starter motor and the intermediate driveshaft

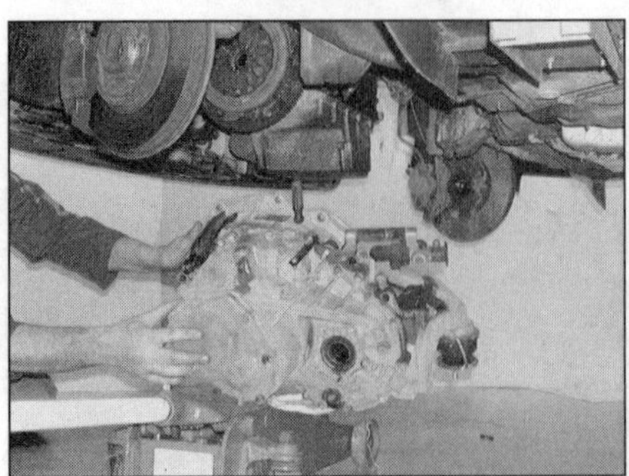

7.29 Slowly lower the transmission assembly from the engine compartment on a trolley jack

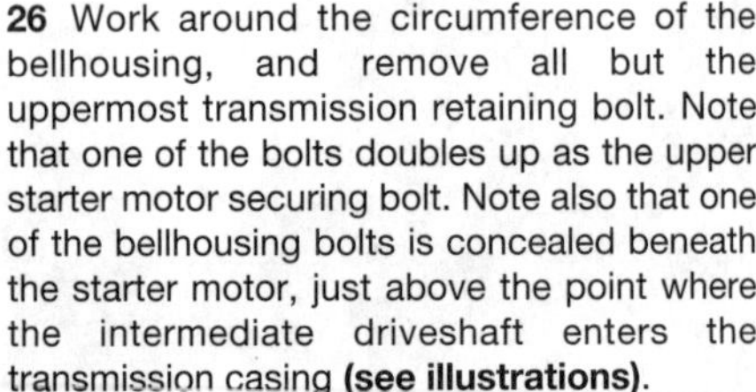

26 Work around the circumference of the bellhousing, and remove all but the uppermost transmission retaining bolt. Note that one of the bolts doubles up as the upper starter motor securing bolt. Note also that one of the bellhousing bolts is concealed beneath the starter motor, just above the point where the intermediate driveshaft enters the transmission casing **(see illustrations)**.

27 Ensure that the trolley jack is taking the weight of the transmission, then remove the last transmission retaining bolt from the bellhousing.

28 Withdraw the transmission from the engine. Do not allow the weight of the unit to bear on the clutch friction plate hub; keep the unit horizontal until the input shaft disengages from the clutch, or damage may result.

29 Slowly lower the transmission assembly from the engine compartment, making sure that it clears the components on the surrounding panels **(see illustration)**. Lower the assembly to the ground and remove it from the underside of the engine compartment.

Refitting

30 Refit the transmission by reversing the removal procedure, noting the following points:

a) *If a new clutch slave cylinder has been fitted, or if hydraulic fluid has been allowed to drain from the existing slave cylinder, the cylinder must be primed and bled* ***before*** *the transmission is refitted; see Chapter 6 for details.*

a) *Apply a smear of high-melting point grease to the transmission input shaft. Do not apply any excessive amount, as there is a possibility of the clutch driven plate being contaminated.*

b) *When refitting the subframe, ensure that the spacer washers are fitted to the two rearmost bolts and observe the alignment markings made during removal. Do not tighten the subframe bolt to their final torque until the full weight of the engine and transmission assembly is resting upon it.*

c) *Observe the specified torque wrench settings (where applicable) when tightening all nuts and bolts after refitting.*

d) *Reconnect the gearchange selector rod with reference to Section 3.*

e) *Ensure that all earthing cables are securely refitted.*

f) *Reconnect the clutch cable with reference to Chapter 6.*

g) *On later models with a hydraulic clutch, reconnect the fluid supply pipe to the slave cylinder and then bleed the clutch hydraulic system.*

h) *On completion, refill the transmission with the specified type and quantity of oil as described in Section 2.*

9 Manual transmission overhaul - general information

The overhaul of a manual transmission is a complex (and often expensive) engineering task for the DIY home mechanic to undertake, which requires access to specialist equipment. It involves dismantling and reassembly of many small components, measuring clearances precisely, and if necessary adjusting them by the selection shims and spacers. Internal transmission components are also often difficult to obtain, and in many instances extremely expensive. Because of this, if the transmission develops a fault or becomes noisy, the best course of action is to have the unit overhauled by a specialist repairer, or to obtain an exchange reconditioned unit.

Nevertheless, it is not impossible for the more experienced mechanic to overhaul the transmission, if the special tools are available and the job is carried out in a deliberate step-by-step manner, to ensure that nothing is overlooked.

The tools necessary for an overhaul include internal and external circlip pliers, bearing pullers, a slide hammer, a set of pin punches, a dial test indicator (dial gauge), and possibly a hydraulic press. In addition, a large, sturdy workbench and a vice will be required.

During dismantling of the transmission, make careful notes of how each component is fitted, to make reassembly easier and accurate.

Before dismantling the transmission, it will help if you have some idea of where the problem lies. Certain problems can be closely related to specific areas in the transmission, which can make component examination and renewal easier. Refer to "*Fault finding*" at the end of this manual for more information.

Chapter 7 Part B:
Automatic transmission

Contents

Degrees of difficulty

Easy, suitable for novice with little experience 	**Fairly easy,** suitable for beginner with some experience 	**Fairly difficult,** suitable for competent DIY mechanic	**Difficult,** suitable for experienced DIY mechanic	**Very difficult,** suitable for expert DIY or professional 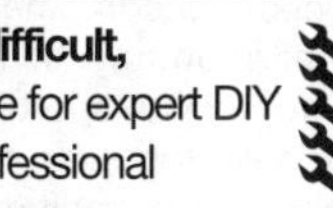

Specifications

General

Type	Four-speed electronically-controlled automatic with three (normal, sport and winter) driving modes
Identification code*:	
2.0 litre models with B204i or B206i engines	FA46 701
2.3 litre models with B234i engines	FA46 801
2.0 litre Turbo models with B204L engines	FA46 901

**The identification code is marked on a plate, attached to the top of the transmission casing*

Lubrication

Fluid type	See "*Lubricants and fluids*"
Fluid capacity (approximate)	See Chapter 1

Adjustments

Selector lever parking lock clearance	0.7 ± 0.3 mm

Torque wrench settings

Torque wrench settings	**Nm**	**lbf ft**
Drain plug	35	26
Engine-to-transmission unit bolts	75	55
Driveplate/lower bellhousing protection plate	7	5
Oil cooler unions	22	16
Fluid temperature sensor	25	18
Fluid temperature sensor cover plate screw	25	18
Input shaft speed sensor bolt	6	4
Output shaft speed sensor bolt	6	4
Transmission range switch:		
Switch to transmission nut/screw	25	18
Lever to range switch shaft nut	8	6
Torque converter-to-driveplate bolts	50	37
Subframe front mounting bolts	115	85
Subframe centre mounting bolts	190	140
Subframe rear mounting bolts:		
Stage 1	110	81
Stage 2	Angle tighten through 75°	
Left hand engine mounting:		
Mounting to bracket	39	29
Mounting to body	73	54
Bracket to transmission	45	33
Rear engine mounting:		
Bracket to transmission	39	29
Mounting to subframe	39	29

1 General information

1 All non-turbo models (and later Turbo models) covered in this manual were offered with the option of a four-speed, electronically-controlled automatic transmission, consisting of a torque converter, an epicyclic geartrain, and hydraulically-operated clutches and brakes. The unit is controlled by the electronic control unit (ECU) via four electrically-operated solenoid valves. The transmission unit has three driving modes: normal (economy), sport and winter modes.

2 The normal (economy) mode is the standard mode for driving in which the transmission shifts up at relatively low engine speeds to combine reasonable performance with economy. If the transmission unit is switched into sport mode, using the button on the selector lever, the transmission shifts up only at high engine speeds, giving improved acceleration and overtaking performance. When the transmission is in sport mode, the indicator light in the instrument panel is illuminated. If the transmission is switched into winter mode, using the button on the selector lever indicator panel, the transmission will select third gear as the vehicle pulls away from a standing start; this helps to maintain traction on very slippery surfaces.

3 The torque converter provides a fluid coupling between engine and transmission, which acts as an automatic clutch, and also provides a degree of torque multiplication when accelerating.

4 The epicyclic geartrain provides either of the four forward or one reverse gear ratios, according to which of its component parts are held stationary or allowed to turn. The components of the geartrain are held or released by brakes and clutches which are activated by the control unit. A fluid pump within the transmission provides the necessary hydraulic pressure to operate the brakes and clutches.

5 Driver control of the transmission is by a seven-position selector lever. The 'drive' D position, allows automatic changing throughout the range of all four gear ratios. An automatic kickdown facility shifts the transmission down a gear if the accelerator pedal is fully depressed. The transmission also has three 'hold' positions, 1 means only the first gear ratio can be selected, 2 allows both the first and second gear ratios position to be automatically selected and 3 allows automatic changing between the first three gear ratios. These 'hold' positions are useful for providing engine braking when travelling down steep gradients. Note, however, that the transmission should *never* be shifted down a position at high engine speeds.

6 Due to the complexity of the automatic transmission, any repair or overhaul work must be left to a Saab dealer with the necessary special equipment for fault diagnosis and repair. The contents of the following Sections are therefore confined to supplying general information, and any service information and instructions that can be used by the owner.

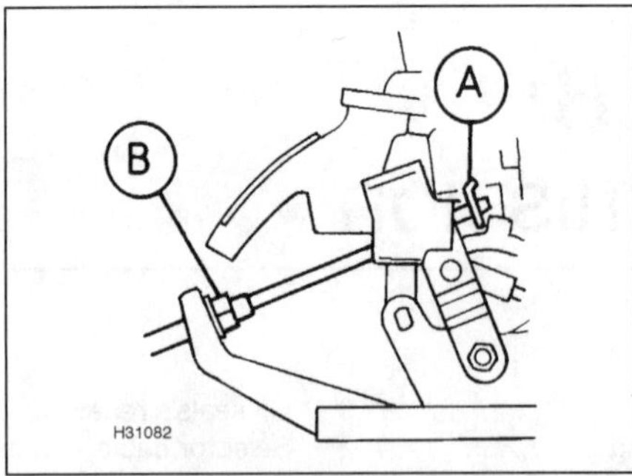

3.4 Remove the locking clip (A) from the end of the selector cable. Fully slacken the cable adjuster nut (B)

2 Automatic transmission fluid - draining and refilling

Refer to the information given in Chapter 1, Section 28.

3 Selector cable - adjustment

Note: *If the battery is disconnected with the selector lever in the 'P' position, the lever will be locked in position. To manually release the lever, carefully prise out the selector lever surround from the top of the centre console then, using a flat-bladed screwdriver, depress the detent lever on the left-hand side of the selector lever.*

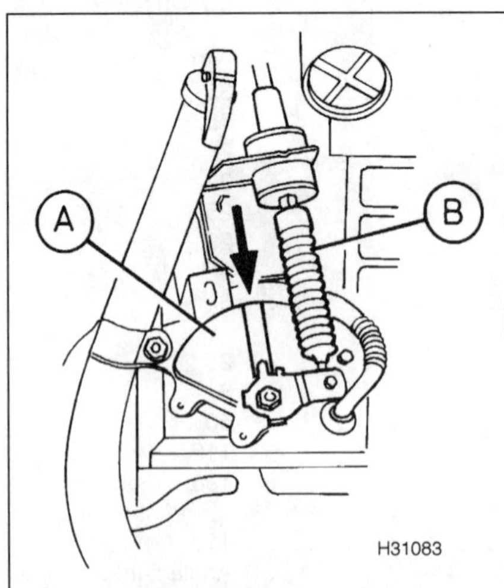

3.6 The arrow on the lever must point between the two parallel indicator lines on the quadrant at the upper surface of the switch body

A Transmission range switch
B Selector cable

1 Operate the selector lever throughout its entire range and check that the transmission engages the correct gear indicated on the selector lever position indicator. If adjustment is necessary, continue as follows.

2 Position the selector lever in the 'N' (neutral) position.

3 With reference to Chapter 11, remove the floor console and rear passenger compartment air ducts from between the front seats, to gain access to the selector lever housing.

4 Remove the locking clip from the end of the selector cable, at the base of the selector lever. Fully slacken the cable adjuster nut, located at the front of the lever housing **(see illustration)**.

5 Working in the engine compartment, to gain access to the transmission end of the selector cable, remove the battery from its mounting plate (see Chapter 5A).

6 Locate the lever on the transmission range switch, to which the selector cable is connected. Position the lever so that the transmission is set in neutral - the arrow on the lever must point between the two parallel indicator lines on the quadrant at the upper surface of the switch body **(see illustration)**.

7 With both the selector lever and transmission correctly positioned, tighten securely the selector cable adjuster nut, located at the front of the lever housing.

8 Refit the locking to the end of the selector cable, at the base of the selector lever.

9 Temporarily refit the battery, then check the operation of the selector lever and, if necessary, repeat the adjustment procedure.

10 On completion, refit the air ducting and floor console with reference to Chapter 11.

4 Selector cable - removal and refitting

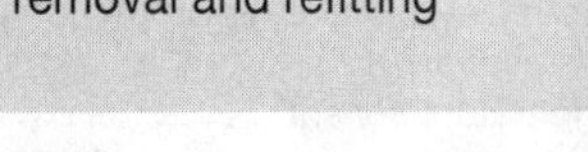

Removal

1 Remove the centre console and rear passenger compartment air ducting, as described in Chapter 11 then position the selector lever in the 'N' (neutral) position.

2 Remove the locking clip and disconnect the selector cable from the base of the selector cable. Fully slacken the selector cable adjuster nut, located at the front of the lever housing **(refer to illustration 3.4)**.

3 Working in the engine compartment, to gain access to the transmission end of the selector cable, remove the battery from its mounting plate (see Chapter 5A).

4 Locate the lever on the transmission range switch, to which the selector cable is connected. Remove the retaining nut and detach the lever from the range switch. Slide

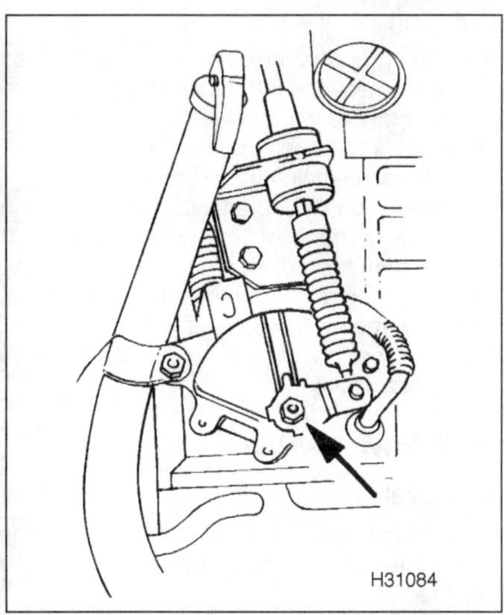

4.4a Remove the transmission range switch lever nut (arrowed) and detach the lever from the switch shaft

off the locking clip and disconnect the selector cable from the lever **(see illustrations)**.

5 Work back along the cable, noting its correct routing, and free it from all the relevant retaining clips. Free the cable grommet from the bulkhead and remove it from the vehicle.

6 Examine the cable, looking for worn end fittings or a damaged outer casing, and for signs of fraying of the inner cable. Check the cable's operation; the inner cable should move smoothly and easily through the outer casing. Remember that a cable that appears serviceable when tested off the car may well be much heavier in operation when curved into its working position. Renew the cable if it shows any signs of excessive wear or any damage.

Refitting

7 Manoeuvre the cable into position, ensuring it is correctly routed and pass it through the bulkhead. Ensure the cable passes through the selector lever housing then locate the grommet securely in the bulkhead.

8 Pass the transmission end of the cable through its mounting bracket and clip the outer cable securely in position. Connect the cable end to the transmission lever then secure it in position with the locking clip. Fit the lever to the transmission range switch, then fit the nut and tighten it securely.

9 From inside the vehicle, secure the outer cable in position in the selector lever housing with the retaining clip.

10 Adjust the selector cable as described in Section 3.

11 On completion, refit the centre console, as described in Chapter 11, and refit all components removed to gain access to the transmission end of the cable.

5 Selector lever assembly - removal and refitting

Note: *Renewal of the sport and winter mode switches is covered in Section 8.*

Removal

1 Remove the centre console, and rear compartment air ducts, as described in Chapter 11, then position the selector lever in the 'N' (neutral) position.

2 Release the indicator plate from the lever housing then disconnect the selector cable from the base of the selector lever and the front of the lever housing, as described in Section 4.

3 Slacken and remove the mounting bolts then manoeuvre the lever assembly away from the floorpan **(see illustration)**.

4 Unplug the mode switch wiring connectors from the side of the housing. Where applicable, free the bulbholder from the indicator panel.

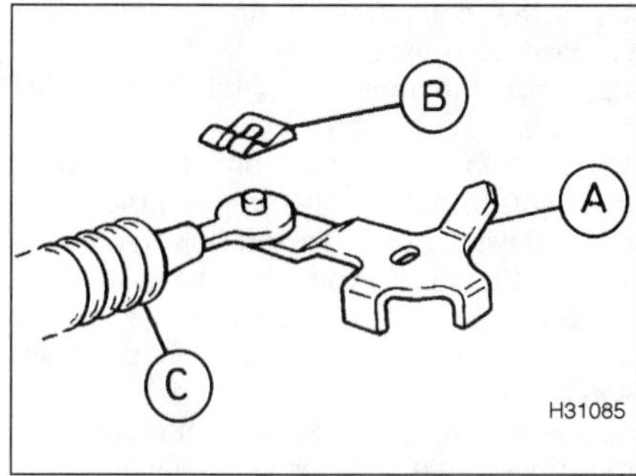

4.4b Slide off the locking clip (C) and disconnect the selector cable (B) from the lever (A)

5 Disconnect the ignition switch/lock cable from the rear of the housing, then remove the housing and lever assembly from the vehicle. Ensure that the selector cable adjuster nut does not fall out.

6 Inspect the selector lever mechanism for signs of wear or damage.

Refitting

7 Check the adjustment of the parking lock mechanism as described in the following sub-Section, before refitting the selector lever housing.

8 Refitting is a reversal of removal; on completion, adjust the selector cable, as described in Section 3, then refit the centre console and air ducts as described in Chapter 11.

Parking lock adjustment

9 Place the selector lever in the 'PARK' position and the ignition switch in the 'OFF' position.

10 Turn the housing over, then using feeler blades, measure the clearance between the locking pin and disc and compare it with the figure given in the Specifications **(see illustration)**.

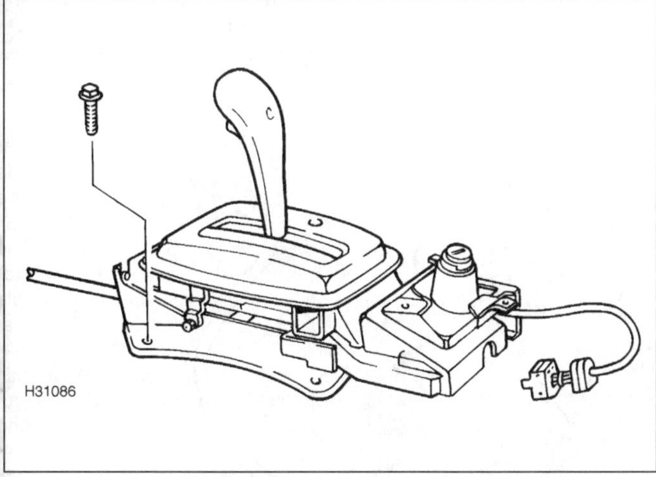

5.3 Remove the mounting bolts then manoeuvre the lever assembly away from the floorpan

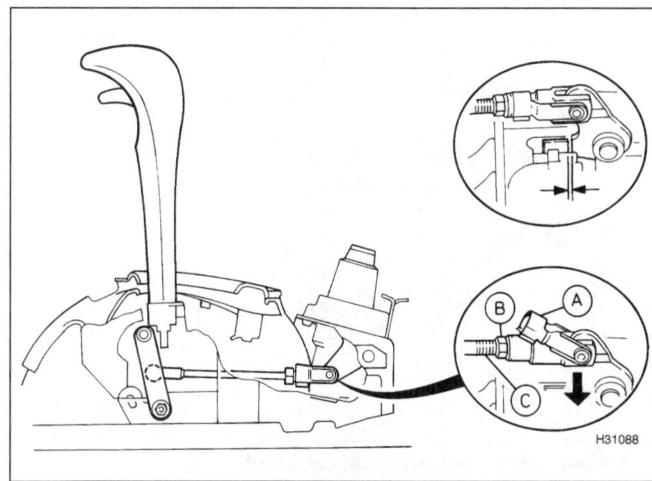

5.10 Using feeler blades, measure the clearance between the locking pin and disc

A Spring clip *B Locknut* *C Linkrod*

11 If the clearance is not as specified, proceed as follows.
12 Place the ignition switch in the 'ON' position.
13 Slacken the nut on the locking mechanism link rod, then release the spring clip and withdraw the linkrod locking pin.
14 Rotate the linkrod end fitting until the correct clearance is achieved.
15 On completion, refit the locking pin and spring clip.
16 Refit the selector lever housing, as described in the previous sub-Section.

6 Oil seals - renewal

Driveshaft oil seals

1 Refer to Chapter 7A.

Torque converter oil seal

2 Remove the transmission as described in Section 9.
3 Carefully slide the torque converter off the transmission shaft whilst being prepared for fluid spillage.
4 Note the correct fitted position of the seal in the oil pump housing then carefully lever the seal out of position taking care not to mark the housing or input shaft.
5 Remove all traces of dirt from the area around the oil seal aperture then press the new seal into position, ensuring its sealing lip is facing inwards.
6 Lubricate the seal with clean transmission fluid then carefully ease the torque converter into position.
7 Refit the transmission (see Section 9).

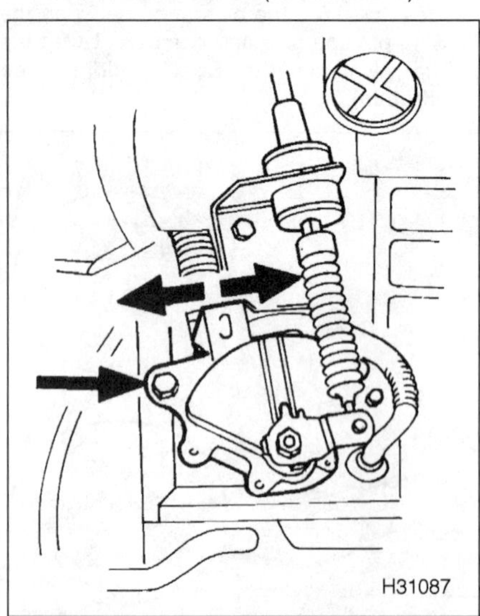

8.8 Slacken the nut (arrowed) and pivot the switch body until the arrow on the lever points between the parallel indicator lines on the upper surface of the switch body

7 Fluid cooler - general information

The transmission fluid cooler is an integral part of the radiator assembly. Refer to Chapter 3 for removal and refitting details, if the cooler is damaged the complete radiator assembly must be renewed.

8 Transmission control system electrical components - removal and refitting

Transmission range switch

General information

1 As well as informing the transmission ECU which gear is currently selected at the selector lever, the transmission range switch also contains contacts which control the operation of the reversing lights relay, and the starter motor inhibitor relay.

Removal

2 Remove the battery from its mounting tray as described in Chapter 5A.
3 Release the power steering fluid hose from its mounting bracket and move it to one side.
4 Undo the securing nut and release the transmission fluid dipstick tube from the side of the transmission range switch.
5 Disconnect the selector cable from the transmission range switch as described in Section 4.
6 Slacken and remove the nuts and screws that secure the transmission range switch in position.
7 Unplug the range switch wiring from the main wiring harness at the two connectors, located on a mounting bracket at the left hand end of the cylinder head. Withdraw the range switch from the transmission selector mechanism shaft and remove it from the engine compartment.

Refitting

8 Refitting is a reversal of removal. Tighten the switch securing nut to the specified torque and on completion, check the adjustment of the selector cable with reference to Section 3. If the arrow on the range switch lever does not point between the parallel indicator lines on the upper surface of the switch body, first ensure that the selector lever is in the 'N' position, then slacken the range switch nut, and pivot the switch body until the arrow and indicator lines are aligned as described above **(see illustration)**.

Kickdown switch

Removal

9 Working in the driver's footwell, remove the trim panel at the base of the A-pillar (see Chapter 11).
10 Lift the accelerator pedal, then peel up the carpet to expose the kickdown switch **(see illustration)**.
11 Unplug the wiring at the connector, then pull the kickdown switch from its mounting recess.

Refitting

12 Refitting is a reversal of removal. Ensure that the switch is pressed fully into its mounting recess and that the wiring is securely reconnected.

Electronic control unit (ECU)

Removal

13 The ECU is located in the front passenger footwell. Prior to removal, disconnect the battery negative terminal.
14 Prise out the retaining clips and remove the undercover from the passenger side of the facia. Remove the glovebox from the facia (see Chapter 11) to gain access to the ECU.
15 Release the retaining clip and disconnect the wiring connector from the ECU. Release the mounting bracket from the body and remove the ECU from the vehicle.

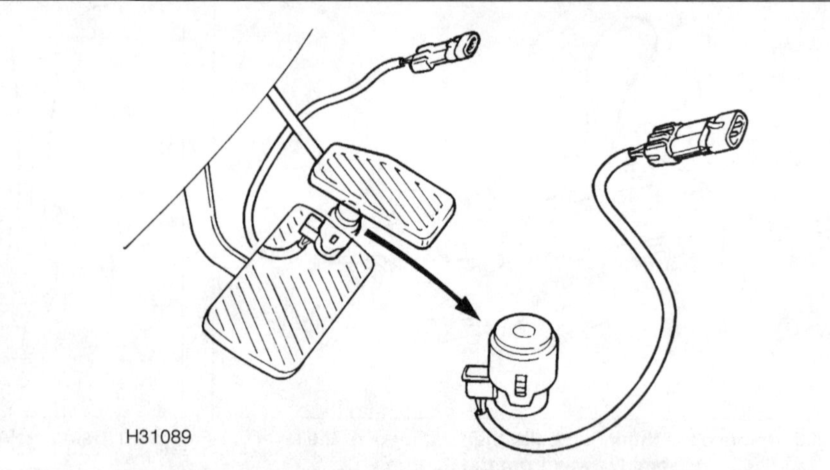

8.10 Lift the accelerator pedal, then peel up the carpet to expose the kickdown switch

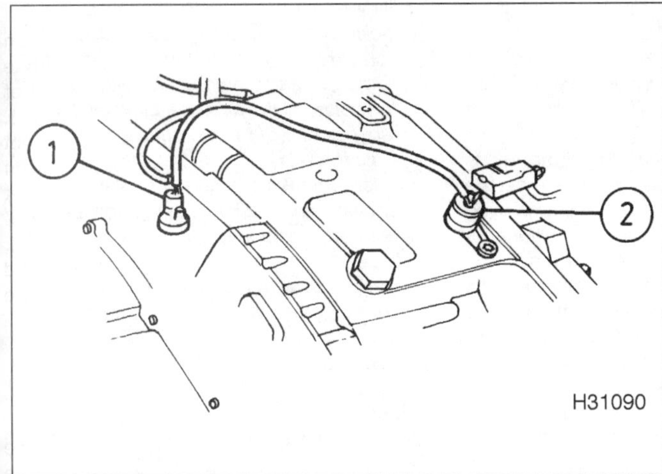

8.17 Automatic transmission input shaft speed sensor (1) and output shaft speed sensor (2) locations

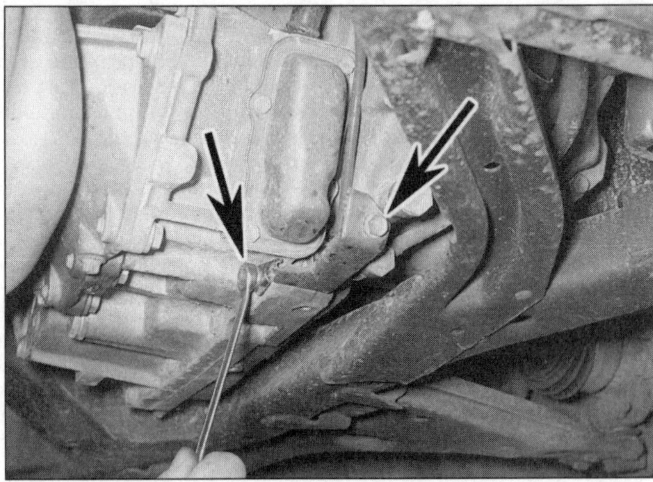

8.27 Undo the retaining bolts (arrowed) and remove the cover plate . . .

Refitting

16 Refitting is the reverse of removal, ensuring that the wiring is securely reconnected.

Transmission input and output shaft speed sensors

Removal

17 The speed sensors are fitted to the top of the transmission unit. The input shaft speed sensor is the front of the two sensors and is nearest to the left-hand end of the transmission. The output shaft sensor is the rear of the two **(see illustration)**.

18 To gain access to the sensors, remove the battery from its mounting plate as described in Chapter 5A. Access can be further improved by unclipping the coolant expansion tank from its mountings and positioning it clear.

19 Disconnect the wiring connector located on a mounting bracket at the left hand end of the cylinder head. Wipe clean the area around the relevant sensor.

20 Undo the retaining bolt and remove the sensor from the transmission. Remove the sealing ring from the sensor and discard it, a new one should be used on refitting.

Refitting

21 Fit the new sealing ring to the sensor groove and lubricate it with a smear of transmission fluid.

22 Ease the sensor into position then refit the retaining bolt and tighten it to the specified torque setting. Reconnect the wiring connector.

23 Refit the battery and clip the expansion tank (where necessary) back into position.

Transmission fluid temperature sensor

Removal

24 The fluid temperature sensor is screwed into the base of the transmission unit, at the front. Before removing the sensor, disconnect the battery negative terminal.

25 Firmly apply the handbrake then jack up the front of the vehicle and support it on axle stands (see "*Jacking and vehicle support*").

26 Trace the wiring back from the sensor, noting its correct routing. Disconnect the wiring connector and free the wiring from its retaining clips.

27 Undo the retaining bolts and remove the cover plate from the sensor **(see illustration)**.

28 Wipe clean the area around the sensor and have a suitable plug ready to minimise fluid loss as the sensor is removed **(see illustration)**.

29 Unscrew the sensor and remove it from the transmission unit along with its sealing washer. Quickly plug the transmission aperture and wipe up any spilt fluid.

Refitting

30 Fit a new sealing washer to the sensor then remove the plug and quickly screw the sensor into the transmission unit. Tighten the sensor to the specified torque and wipe up any spilt fluid. Refit the cover plate and tighten its retaining bolts to the specified torque.

31 Ensure the wiring is correctly routed and retained by all the necessary clips then securely reconnect the wiring connector.

32 Lower the vehicle to the floor and reconnect the battery. Check the transmission fluid level as described in Chapter 1.

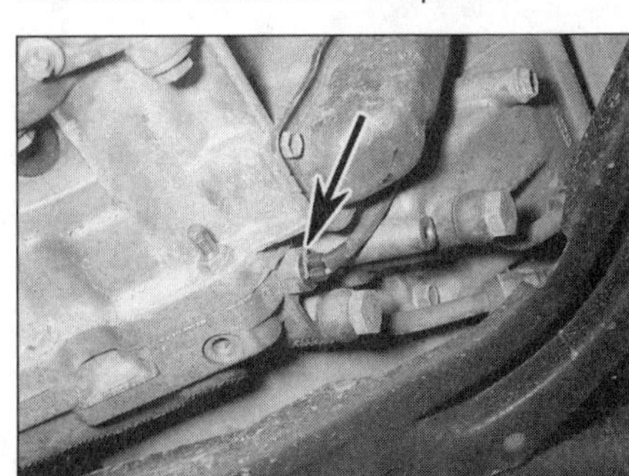

8.28 . . . to gain access to the fluid temperature sensor (arrowed)

9 Automatic transmission - removal and refitting

Note: *New torque converter-to-driveplate bolts and fluid cooler union sealing rings will be required on refitting.*

Removal

1 Chock the rear wheels, apply the handbrake, and place the selector lever in the 'N' (neutral) position. Jack up the front of the vehicle, and securely support it on axle stands (see "*Jacking and vehicle support*"). Remove both front roadwheels then remove the retaining screws and fasteners and (where necessary) remove the undercover panels from beneath the engine/transmission unit.

2 Drain the transmission fluid as described in Chapter 1, then refit the drain plug and tighten it to the specified torque.

3 Remove the battery from its mounting plate as described in Chapter 5A.

4 Disconnect the battery earthing cable(s) from the transmission casing. Release the cabling from the transmission fluid dipstick tube.

5 Withdraw the dipstick and its tube from the transmission casing and plug the open hole, to prevent contamination.

6 Disconnect the breather hose (where fitted) from the top of the transmission unit.

7 Disconnect the selector cable from the transmission as described in Sections 3 and 4.

8 Unplug the transmission control system wiring at the two connectors, located underneath the secondary fusebox, at the left hand side of the engine compartment.

9 Trace the wiring back from the transmission switches and sensors and disconnect the various connectors by lifting their retaining clips. Release the main wiring harness from any clips or ties securing it to the transmission unit.

10 Remove the air cleaner and intake ducting as described in Chapter 4A. On Turbo models, also remove the intercooler to throttle body ducting. Remove the resonator assembly (non-turbo models) or cover panel (Turbo models) from the top of the throttle body.

11 Fit a lifting beam across the top of the engine compartment, in line with the engine lifting eyelets. Remove the rubber grommet from the left hand eyelet and attach lifting beam jib securely to it. Raise the jib until it is just taking the combined weight of the engine and transmission.

12 Unbolt and remove the exhaust system front pipe and catalytic converter (see Chapter 4A).

13 With reference to Chapter 11, remove the spoiler panels from the underside of the front bumper. Remove the securing screws and withdraw the plastic liners from the left hand wheel arch. Also remove the plastic shield from the right hand wheel arch, to expose the crankshaft pulley.

14 Remove the auxiliary drivebelt with reference to Chapter 1.

15 Unbolt both front suspension lower arm balljoints from the base of their respective hub carriers, with reference to Chapter 10. If required, unbolt the ends of the anti-roll bar from the lower arms to increase available clearance.

16 Remove the left hand driveshaft, right hand driveshaft, intermediate shaft and bearing support bracket with reference to Chapter 8. Note that the alternator lower mounting bolt must be removed to allow the removal of the intermediate driveshaft bearing support bracket.

17 Slacken and remove the nuts that secure the base of the rear engine mounting to the suspension subframe.

18 Mark around the boundary of the suspension subframe using a permanent marker pen, to indicate its fitted position. This will help to achieve the correct alignment during refitting.

19 Position a pair of trolley jacks underneath the suspension subframe and raise them until the jack heads rest against the underside of the subframe. Mark around the periphery of the subframe to act as a guide to correct alignment on refitting.

20 Progressively slacken and withdraw each of the six subframe securing bolts. Note that the bolts are of different lengths and diameters - make a note of their fitted positions to aid refitting. Ensure that the lifting beam is taking the weight of the engine/transmission as the unit will tend to pivot towards the rear of the engine compartment as the subframe is removed.

21 Slowly lower the subframe away from the underside of the engine compartment using the trolley jacks. Recover the spacer washers fitted to the two rearmost bolts.

22 Slacken the unions and disconnect the transmission fluid cooler pipes from the front of the transmission casing. Recover the sealing washers.

23 Make a final check that any components which would prevent the removal of the transmission from the car have been removed or disconnected. Ensure that components such as the gear selector cable are secured so that they cannot be damaged on removal.

24 Unbolt the driveplate protection plate from the right hand edge of the underside of the transmission bellhousing, to gain access to the torque converter retaining bolts.

25 Slacken and remove the visible torque converter bolt(s) then, using a socket and extension bar to rotate the crankshaft pulley, undo the remaining bolts securing the torque converter to the driveplate as they become accessible. On all models there is a total of six torque converter securing bolts. Discard the bolts, new ones must be used on refitting.

26 To ensure that the torque converter does not fall out as the transmission is removed, slide the converter along the shaft and fully into the transmission housing.

27 Position a trolley jack underneath the transmission casing. Raise the jack head so that it is just taking the weight of the transmission.

28 Unbolt and remove the left hand engine/transmission mountings, with reference to Chapter 2A. Lower the lifting beam jib so that the left hand end of the engine and transmission assembly is lowered by approximately 10 cm. This gives enough clearance to allow the transmission to be withdrawn from the engine later.

29 Work around the circumference of the bellhousing, and remove all but the uppermost transmission retaining bolts. Note that some of the bolts are threaded in from the right hand side of the bellhousing.

30 Ensure that the trolley jack is taking the weight of the transmission, then remove the last transmission retaining bolt from the bellhousing.

31 Withdraw the transmission from the engine; keep the unit horizontal until the bellhousing is clear of the driveplate and its mounting dowels.

32 Slowly lower the transmission assembly from the engine compartment, making sure that it clears the components on the surrounding panels. Lower the assembly to the ground and remove it from the underside of the engine compartment.

Refitting

33 The transmission is refitted by a reversal of the removal procedure, bearing in mind the following points.

a) Prior to refitting, remove all traces of old locking compound from the torque converter threads by running a tap of the correct thread diameter and pitch down the holes. In the absence of a suitable tap, use one of the old bolts with slots cut in its threads.
b) Prior to refitting, ensure the engine/transmission locating dowels are correctly positioned and apply a smear of molybdenum disulphide grease to the torque converter locating pin and its centring bush in the crankshaft end.
c) Once the transmission and engine are correctly joined, refit the securing bolts, tightening them to the specified torque setting.
d) Fit the new torque converter to driveplate bolts and tighten them lightly only to start then go around and tighten them to the specified torque setting in a diagonal sequence.
e) Tighten all nuts and bolts to the specified torque (where given).
f) Renew the driveshaft oil seals (see Chapter 7A) and refit the driveshafts to the transmission as described in Chapter 8.
g) Fit new sealing rings to the fluid cooler hose unions and ensure both unions are securely retained by their clips.
h) When refitting the subframe, ensure that the spacer washers are fitted to the two rearmost bolts and observe the alignment markings made during removal. Do not tighten the subframe bolt to their final torque until the full weight of the engine and transmission assembly is resting upon it.
i) Ensure that all earthing cables are securely refitted.
j) On completion, refill the transmission with the specified type and quantity of fluid as described in Section 2 and adjust the selector cable as described in Section 3.

10 Automatic transmission overhaul - general information

1 In the event of a fault occurring with the transmission, it is first necessary to determine whether it is of a mechanical or hydraulic nature, and to do this, special test equipment is required. It is therefore essential to have the work carried out by a Saab dealer if a transmission fault is suspected.

2 Do not remove the transmission from the car for possible repair before professional fault diagnosis has been carried out, since most tests require the transmission to be in the vehicle.

Chapter 8
Driveshafts

Contents

Degrees of difficulty

Easy, suitable for novice with little experience 

Fairly easy, suitable for beginner with some experience 

Fairly difficult, suitable for competent DIY mechanic

Difficult, suitable for experienced DIY mechanic 

Very difficult, suitable for expert DIY or professional 

Specifications

General

Driveshaft type	Solid steel shafts with inner and outer universal and constant velocity joints. Intermediate shaft from right-hand side of transmission to driveshaft
Lubrication (overhaul or repair only)	Use only special grease supplied in sachets with gaiter/overhaul kits; joints are otherwise pre-packed with grease and sealed

Torque wrench settings

	Nm	lbf ft
Driveshaft nut	290	214
Roadwheel bolts:		
Alloy	117	86
Steel	100	74
Front suspension lower balljoint to hub carrier/strut	75	55
Front anti-roll bar to lower suspension arm support bar	10	7
Intermediate driveshaft bracket-to-engine bolts	30	22

1 General information

Power is transmitted from the gearbox output to the roadwheels by the driveshafts. The outer joints on all models are of 'constant velocity' (CV) type, consisting of six balls running in axial grooves. The driveshaft outer joints incorporate stub axles which are splined to the hubs located in the front suspension hub carriers/struts. The inner 'universal' joints are designed to move in a smaller arc than the outer CV joints, and can also move axially to allow for movements of the front suspension. There are two types of inner joint according to model. On 2.3 litre, Turbo, and automatic transmission models, the inner joint is of tripod type consisting of a three-armed 'spider' with needle bearings and outer race splined to the driveshaft, and an outer housing with three corresponding grooves for the bearing races to slide in. On 2.0 litre manual transmission models, the inner joint is similar to the CV type joint described earlier, although the outer housing is different to allow for axial movement of the driveshaft.

An intermediate shaft, with its own support bearing, is fitted between the transmission and right-hand driveshaft - a layout which equalises driveshaft angles at all suspension positions, and reduces driveshaft flexing, improving directional stability under hard acceleration.

The universal and CV joints allow smooth transmission of drive to the wheels at all steering and suspension angles. The joints are protected by rubber gaiters, and are packed with grease, to provide permanent lubrication. In the event of wear being detected, the joint can be renewed separate from the driveshaft. The joints do not require additional lubrication, unless they have been renovated or the rubber gaiters have been damaged, allowing the grease to become contaminated. Refer to Chapter 1 for guidance in checking the condition of the driveshaft gaiters.

To check for driveshaft wear, road test the vehicle, driving it slowly in a circle on full steering lock (carry out the test on both left and right lock), while listening for a metallic clicking or knocking sound coming from the front wheels. An assistant in the passenger seat can listen for the sound from the nearside joint. If such a sound is heard, this indicates wear in the outer joint. If vibration proportional to road speed is felt through the car when accelerating or on over-run, there is a possibility of wear in the inner joints. For a more thorough check, remove and dismantle the driveshafts where possible as described in the following Sections. Refer to a Saab dealer for information on the availability of driveshaft components.

2.4 Unscrewing the driveshaft nut

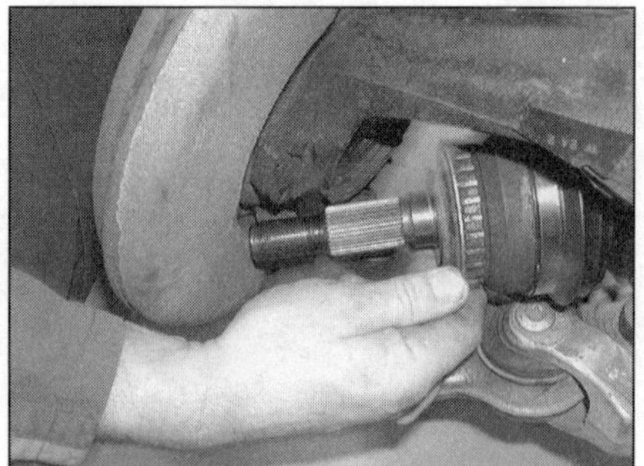
2.8 Removing the driveshaft from the splines in the hub

2.10 Withdrawing the driveshaft from the transmission

2 Driveshaft - removal and refitting

Removal

1 Park the vehicle on a level surface, apply the handbrake and chock the rear wheels.

2 Remove the wheel trim (or wheel centre cap for vehicles fitted with alloy wheels), then loosen the driveshaft nut, bearing in mind the high torque to which this nut is tightened - select a sturdy wrench and close-fitting socket to remove it.

3 Apply the handbrake, then jack up the front of the vehicle and support it on axle stands (see *"Jacking and Vehicle Support"*). Remove the roadwheel.

4 Unscrew and remove the driveshaft nut **(see illustration)**.

5 Unscrew the nut then disconnect the steering track rod end from the steering arm using a balljoint separator tool (see Chapter 10).

6 Unscrew the nut securing the anti-roll bar to the lower suspension arm support bar, and remove the washer and rubber bush.

7 Unscrew the nut then disconnect the lower arm balljoint from the hub carrier/strut using a balljoint separator tool (see Chapter 10). Press the lower suspension arm down as far as possible, and move the hub carrier/strut to one side. Release the arm making sure that the balljoint rubber boot is not damaged by the bottom of the hub carrier/strut (take care not to stretch the brake hoses and brake pad wear warning wiring). **Note:** *Discard the balljoint nut as it must not be re-used. Obtain a new one.*

8 Using a mallet, carefully tap the driveshaft inwards from the splines in the hub while pulling out the bottom of the strut **(see illustration)**.

9 On the right-hand side driveshaft, slide the driveshaft from the intermediate shaft splines. If necessary, use a lever to help release the internal circlip from the groove.

10 On the left-hand side driveshaft, position a container beneath the transmission to catch any spilt oil, then pull out the driveshaft. The internal driveshaft circlip may be tight in the transmission side gears, in which case careful use of a lever against the transmission casing will be required. Lever against a block of wood to prevent damage to the casing, and take care not to damage the oil seal as the driveshaft is being removed **(see illustration)**. **Note:** *On models with a 'universal' joint, take care not to pull the driveshaft spider out of the joint housing.*

Refitting

11 Check the condition of the circlip on the inner end of the driveshaft, and if necessary, renew it **(see illustration)**.

12 Clean the splines on each end of the driveshaft and in the hub, and where applicable wipe clean the oil seal in the transmission casing. Check the oil seal and if necessary renew it as described in Chapter 7A or 7B. Smear a little oil on the lips of the oil seal before fitting the driveshaft.

13 Locate the inner end of the driveshaft in the transmission or onto the intermediate shaft - turn the driveshaft as necessary to engage the splines. Press in the driveshaft until the internal circlip engages the groove. Check that the circlip is engaged by attempting to pull out the driveshaft with only moderate force.

14 Engage the outer end of the driveshaft with the splines in the hub, then press down the lower suspension arm and guide the bottom of the hub carrier/strut onto the balljoint on the lower arm. Screw on the new nut and tighten to the specified torque.

15 Insert the anti-roll bar mounting in the lower arm support bar, then fit the rubber bush and washer and tighten the nut to the specified torque.

2.11 Checking the circlip on the inner end of the driveshaft

16 Insert the steering track rod end in the steering arm and tighten the nut to the specified torque.

17 Screw on the driveshaft nut and tighten just moderately at this stage.

18 Refit the roadwheel, then lower the vehicle to the ground and tighten the bolts to the specified torque.

19 Fully tighten the driveshaft nut to the specified torque.

3 Driveshaft rubber gaiters - renewal

1 A kit containing all of the components needed when renewing the driveshaft gaiters can be obtained from Saab dealers.

2 Refer to Section 2 and remove the driveshaft.

3 Clamp the driveshaft in a soft-jawed vice, and clean the areas around the rubber gaiters.

4 Release the small and large clips holding the gaiter to the driveshaft **(see illustration)**. Where crimped-type clips are fitted, cut off the raised sections using a small hacksaw, and obtain new clips.

5 On CV and Rzeppa joints, slide the gaiter along the driveshaft, away from the joint, then scoop out as much as possible of the grease. Using circlip pliers at the inner end of the joint, open the circlip then slide the joint from the end of the driveshaft **(see illustrations)**. If it is tight, use a hammer and soft drift to tap the joint hub from the splines.

3.4 Remove the clips . . .

3.5a . . . release the rubber gaiter from the joint housing . . .

3.5b . . . then use circlip pliers to open the circlip . . .

3.5c . . . and slide the joint from the end of the driveshaft

6 On 'universal' joints, mark the joint housing in relation to the driveshaft and tripod (spider), then slide off the housing. If necessary, secure the bearing outer races to the spider with adhesive tape. Extract the circlip with circlip pliers, then pull the spider from the splines on the driveshaft **(see illustrations)**. If it is tight, use a puller to remove it.

7 Slide the rubber gaiter from the end of the driveshaft **(see illustration)**.

8 If the joint has been contaminated with water or dirt from the road, clean the component parts thoroughly **(see illustration)**. If necessary, the CV joint may be dismantled as described in the following paragraph. **Note:** *It is not possible to dismantle the Rzeppa type inner joint, and if the contamination cannot be removed, it will be necessary to renew the complete joint.*

9 Rotate the hub and cage inside the housing, and remove the balls one by one. Turn the hub through 90° and withdraw it, then similarly turn the cage through 90° and remove it. Remove the circlip from the hub and check it for wear and damage **(see illustration)**. Thoroughly clean the components in suitable solvent and wipe dry, then reassemble them using a reversal of the dismantling procedure.

10 Clean the driveshaft splines and lightly lubricate them with CV grease.

11 Slide the new gaiter onto the driveshaft together with the small and large retaining clips.

12 On CV and Rzeppa joints, pack the joint with 80g of grease using the grease supplied with the gaiter, making sure that it is worked well into the joint recesses **(see illustration)**. Slide the joint onto the driveshaft splines until the circlip engages with the groove. If necessary, use a mallet to tap the joint into position.

3.6a On 'universal' joints, the spider is retained by a circlip (arrowed)

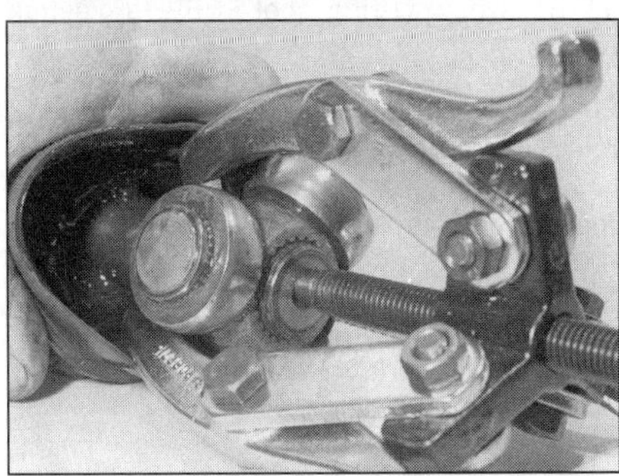
3.6b Using a puller to remove the spider from the driveshaft splines

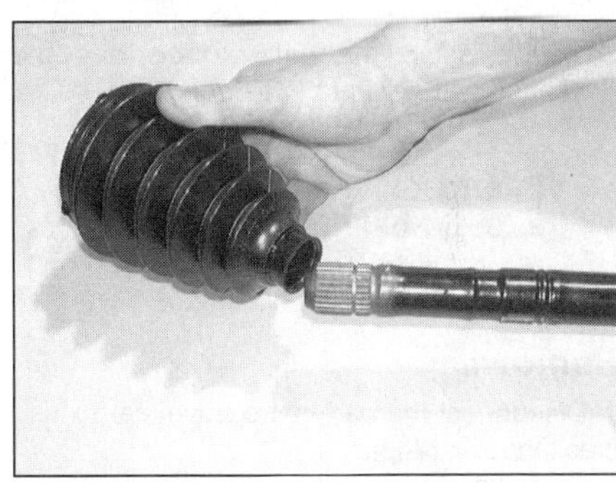
3.7 Removing the outer rubber gaiter

3.8 The outer CV joint

3.9 The retaining circlip (arrowed) is located in the outer joint hub

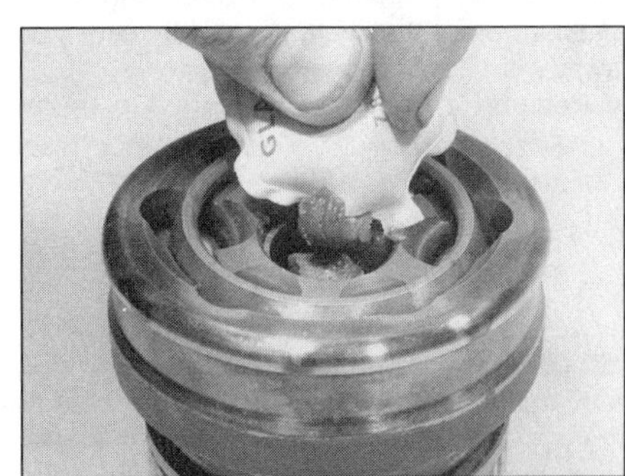
3.12 Pack the CV joint with grease from the service kit

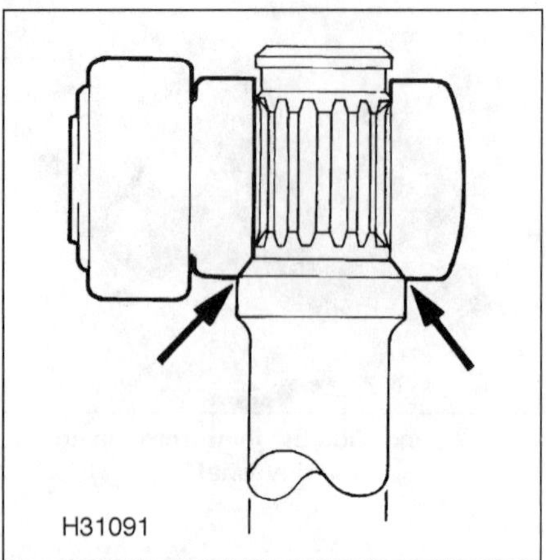

3.13 On 'universal' joints, make sure that the chamfer is located against the inner shoulder on the driveshaft

13 On 'universal' joints locate the spider on the driveshaft splines, chamfered end first, then fit the circlip in the groove **(see illustration)**. Pack the joint housing with 175g of grease using the grease supplied with the gaiter, then slide the housing on the spider making sure it is located in the same position as noted during removal.

14 Slide the gaiter onto the joint housing and fit the retaining clips. Where crimped-type clips are supplied, it may be possible to tighten them by squeezing the raised sections with a pair of pincers **(see illustration)**. Alternatively, plastic cable ties may be used to secure the gaiters.

15 Wipe clean the gaiter, then refit the driveshaft with reference to Section 2.

4 Intermediate driveshaft and support bearing assembly - removal, overhaul and refitting

Removal

1 Disconnect the battery negative (earth) lead (see Chapter 5A).

2 Remove the right-hand driveshaft as described in Section 2.

3 Working under the vehicle, unscrew and remove the alternator lower mounting bolt from the intermediate driveshaft mounting bracket. Move the alternator slightly outwards away from the bracket.

4 Position a container beneath the transmission to catch any escaping oil when the intermediate driveshaft is removed.

5 Unscrew the bolts securing the mounting bracket to the cylinder block.

6 Ease the bracket off of the location dowels, then withdraw the intermediate driveshaft from the transmission side gear, taking care not to damage the oil seal. Withdraw the driveshaft and bracket from under the vehicle.

Overhaul

7 Using circlip pliers, extract the large circlip securing the bearing in the bracket.

8 The intermediate driveshaft and bearing must now be pressed out of the bracket. To do this, use a two-legged puller on the end of the driveshaft.

9 Remove the O-ring seal from the groove in the driveshaft, then extract the circlip.

10 Using the puller, remove the bearing from the driveshaft.

11 Support the bracket with its open end upwards, then locate the new bearing and press or drive it fully in using a metal tube on the outer race. Fit the large circlip to secure the bearing in the bracket.

12 With the intermediate driveshaft mounted in the vice, refit the bearing with bracket onto the driveshaft and press or drive on the bearing inner race until it contacts the shoulder. Make sure that the bracket is fitted the correct way round, and press only on the inner race.

13 Fit the small circlip in the groove, making sure that the concave side faces the bearing.

14 Fit a new O-ring seal in the driveshaft groove.

Refitting

15 Wipe clean the transmission oil seal then smear a little oil on the seal lips. Check that the oil seal is in good condition, and if necessary renew it at this stage with reference to Chapter 7A or 7B.

16 Insert the intermediate driveshaft into the transmission side gear, and engage the splines with each other.

17 Locate the bracket on the dowels, then refit the bolts and tighten to the specified torque.

18 Move the alternator back onto the bracket so that the mounting holes are correctly aligned. Refit the mounting bolt and tighten. If necessary adjust the tension of the alternator drivebelt with reference to Chapter 1.

19 Refit the right-hand driveshaft with reference to Section 2.

3.14 Using a crimping tool to tighten the gaiter clips

20 Reconnect the battery negative (earth) lead (see Chapter 5A).

5 Driveshaft joint - checking and renewal

Checking

1 Road test the vehicle, and listen for a metallic clicking noise from the front as the vehicle is driven slowly in a circle on full-lock. If evident, this indicates wear in the outer constant velocity joint which must be renewed.

2 To check for wear on the inner joint, apply the handbrake then jack up the front of the vehicle and support it on axle stands (see *"Jacking and Vehicle Support"*). Attempt to move the inner end of the driveshaft up and down, then hold the joint with one hand and attempt to rotate the driveshaft with the other.

3 For a more thorough check, the driveshaft can be removed and dismantled as described in Section 3. Thoroughly clean the driveshaft components with paraffin or a suitable solvent, taking care not to remove the alignment marks made during dismantling. Examine the joint components for wear and damage; in particular, check the bearing surfaces for pitting and corrosion. If excessive wear is evident, the joint must be renewed.

Renewal

4 The procedure for renewing the driveshaft joints is given in Section 3 along with the procedure for renewing the rubber gaiters. The gaiters should be renewed as a matter of course, when renewing the joints.

Chapter 9
Braking system

Contents

Degrees of difficulty

Easy, suitable for novice with little experience 	**Fairly easy,** suitable for beginner with some experience 	**Fairly difficult,** suitable for competent DIY mechanic 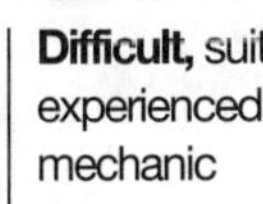	**Difficult,** suitable for experienced DIY mechanic	**Very difficult,** suitable for expert DIY or professional

Specifications

General

Brake system type and layout:		
Footbrake	Diagonally-split dual hydraulic circuits; front left/rear right (primary) and front right/rear left (secondary). Discs fitted front and rear, ventilated at the front. Single-piston, sliding calipers on front and double-piston fixed calipers on rear. Anti-lock Braking System (ABS) fitted as standard on all models with vacuum servo assistance.	
Handbrake	Lever and cable operation, acting on shoes in drums incorporated in rear discs	

Front brakes

Discs:		
Type	Ventilated	
	To model year 1996	**From model year 1997**
Outside diameter	284.0 mm	288.0 mm
Thickness (new disc)	24.0 mm	25.0 mm
Minimum thickness after grinding	22.5 mm	23.5 mm
Minimum wear thickness	21.0 mm	22.0 mm
Maximum runout	0.08 mm	0.08 mm
Maximum variation in disc thickness	0.015 mm	0.015 mm
Calipers:		
Type	Single-piston, floating	
Piston diameter	54.0 mm	57.0 mm
Pads:		
Minimum friction material thickness	5.0 mm	

Rear brakes

Discs:	
Type	Solid
Outside diameter:	
To model year 1996	260.0 mm
From model year 1997	286.0 mm
Thickness (new disc)	10.0 mm
Minimum thickness after grinding	8.5 mm
Minimum wear thickness	8.0 mm
Maximum runout	0.08 mm
Maximum variation in disc thickness	0.015 mm
Handbrake drum inner diameter	160.0 mm
Handbrake drum maximum out-of-round	0.08 mm
Calipers:	
Type	Double-piston, fixed
Piston diameter	35.0 mm
Pads:	
Minimum friction material thickness	5.0 mm
Handbrake:	
Shoe minimum friction material thickness	2.0 mm

Vacuum servo unit

Diameter	229.0 mm

Master cylinder

Diameter	23.81 mm

ABS components

Hydraulic unit:	
Make:	
1994 and 1995 models	Bosch ABS 2E (3-port system)
1996-on models	Bosch ABS 5.3 (4-port system)
Wheel sensors:	
Resistance	1130 ± 115 ohms at 20°C
Clearance between sensor and tooth	0.6 ± 0.3 mm

Torque wrench settings

	Nm	lbf ft
ABS hydraulic unit mounting nut	20	15
Front brake caliper mounting bolt:		
To model year 1996	105	78
From model year 1997	110	81
Rear brake caliper mounting bolt	80	59
Rear brake disc	10	7
Front brake disc	4	3
Front brake caliper guide pin:		
To model year 1996	25	19
From model year 1997	27.5	20.5
Brake pipe union nut	14	10
Front brake hose	40	29
Roadwheel bolts:		
Alloy	117	86
Steel	100	74
Rear hub to axle:		
Stage 1	50	37
Stage 2	Angle-tighten 30°	

1 General information

Braking is achieved by a dual-circuit hydraulic system, assisted by a vacuum servo unit. All models have discs fitted at the front and rear. The front discs are ventilated, to improve cooling and reduce brake fade.

The dual hydraulic circuits are diagonally-split; one circuit operates the front right and rear left brakes, the other operates the front left and rear right brakes. This design ensures that at least 50% of the vehicle's braking capacity will be available, should pressure be lost in one of the hydraulic circuits. Under these circumstances, the diagonal layout should prevent the vehicle from becoming unstable if the brakes are applied when only one circuit is operational.

The front brake calipers are of floating single-piston type - a design which occupies minimal space, and also lessens the amount of heat transferred to the brake fluid, reducing brake fade. Each caliper houses two asbestos-free brake pads, one inboard and one outboard of the disc. During braking, hydraulic pressure forces the piston along its cylinder, and presses the inboard brake pad against the disc. The caliper body reacts to this effort by sliding along its guide pins, bringing the outboard pad into contact with the disc. In this manner, equal pressure is applied to either side of the disc by the brake pads. When braking is ceased, the hydraulic pressure behind the piston drops and the piston is retracted back into the cylinder, releasing the inboard pad from the disc. The caliper body then slides back along its guide pins, and releases the outboard pad.

The rear brake calipers are of fixed double-piston type with two asbestos-free brake pads, one inboard and one outboard of the disc. During braking, hydraulic pressure forces the pistons along their cylinders into contact with each side of the disc. The piston cylinders are smaller in diameter than those in the front caliper; the resulting difference in braking power between front and rear calipers helps to prevent rear wheel lock-up during hard braking. 1994 and 1995 models are fitted with a pressure reducing valve in the rear hydraulic brake lines to each caliper to prevent rear wheel lock-up, however the valves are not fitted to later models.

The master cylinder converts footbrake pedal effort into hydraulic pressure. Its tandem construction incorporates two pistons, one in front of the other, which operate the two hydraulic circuits. Under normal operation, equal pressure is applied to each circuit to provide a balanced braking system, however, if a leak occurs in one of the circuits, the remaining circuit is still operational although increased pedal travel will occur while the inoperative piston moves against its stop.

A constant supply of brake fluid to the master cylinder is maintained by the brake fluid reservoir. It is divided into separate chambers to ensure that a supply of fluid for at least one of the brake circuits is retained in the reservoir, even if the other circuit loses all its fluid through leakage. The reservoir is semi-transparent, to allow visual inspection of the fluid level, and a screw-fit cap allows the level to be topped-up. A level detection switch is incorporated into the filler cap; this causes a light to illuminate on the dashboard when the level of fluid in the reservoir becomes too low.

The vacuum servo unit uses engine manifold vacuum to boost the effort applied to the master cylinder by the brake pedal.

The anti-lock braking system (ABS) prevents wheel lock-up (skidding) under heavy braking, and not only optimises stopping distances, but also allows full steering control to be maintained. By electronically monitoring the speed of each roadwheel in relation to the other wheels, the system can detect when a wheel is about to lock-up, before control is actually lost. The brake fluid pressure applied to that wheel's brake caliper is then decreased and restored ("modulated") several times a second until control is regained (note on pre-1996 models both rear wheels are modulated together). The system components comprise an Electronic Control Unit (ECU), four wheel speed sensors, a hydraulic unit, brake lines and a dashboard-mounted warning light. The four wheel sensors are mounted on the wheel hubs. Each wheel has a rotating toothed disc mounted in the hub; the wheel speed sensors are mounted in close proximity to these discs. The teeth on the surface of the discs excite the sensors, causing them to produce a voltage waveform whose frequency varies with the speed of the discs' rotation. These waveforms are transmitted to the ECU, which uses them to calculate the rotational speed of each wheel. The ECU has a self-diagnostic facility, and will inhibit the operation of the ABS if a fault is detected, lighting the dashboard-mounted warning light. The braking system will then revert to conventional, non-ABS operation. If the nature of the fault is not immediately obvious upon inspection, the vehicle *must* be taken to a Saab dealer, who will have the diagnostic equipment required to interrogate the ABS ECU electronically and pin-point the problem.

2 Hydraulic system - bleeding

Warning: Hydraulic fluid is poisonous; thoroughly wash off spills from bare skin without delay. Seek immediate medical advice if any fluid is swallowed or gets into the eyes. Certain types of hydraulic fluid are inflammable, and may ignite when brought into contact with hot components. When servicing any hydraulic system, it is safest to assume that the fluid IS inflammable, and to take precautions against the risk of fire as though it Is petrol that is being handled. Hydraulic fluid is also an effective paint stripper, and will attack plastics; if any is spilt, it should be washed off immediately, using copious quantities of fresh water. Finally, it is hygroscopic (it absorbs moisture from the air) - old fluid may be contaminated and unfit for further use. When topping-up or renewing the fluid, always use the recommended type, and ensure that it comes from a freshly-opened sealed container.

General

1 The correct operation of any hydraulic system is only possible after removing all air from the components and circuit; this is achieved by bleeding the system.

2 During the bleeding procedure, add only clean, unused hydraulic fluid of the recommended type; never re-use fluid that has already been bled from the system. Ensure that sufficient fluid is available before starting work.

3 If there is any possibility of incorrect fluid being already in the system, the brake components and circuit must be flushed completely with uncontaminated, correct fluid, and new seals should be fitted to the various components.

4 If hydraulic fluid has been lost from the system, or air has entered because of a leak, ensure that the fault is cured before proceeding further.

5 Park the vehicle over an inspection pit or on car ramps. Alternatively, apply the handbrake then jack up the front and rear of the vehicle and support it on axle stands (see *"Jacking and Vehicle Support"*). For improved access with the vehicle jacked up, remove the roadwheels.

6 Check that all pipes and hoses are secure, unions tight and bleed screws closed. Clean any dirt from around the bleed screws.

7 Unscrew the master cylinder reservoir cap, and top the master cylinder reservoir up to the "MAX" level line; refit the cap loosely, and remember to maintain the fluid level at least above the "MIN" level line throughout the procedure, otherwise there is a risk of further air entering the system.

8 There are a number of one-man, do-it-yourself brake bleeding kits currently available from motor accessory shops. It is recommended that one of these kits is used whenever possible, as they greatly simplify the bleeding operation, and also reduce the risk of expelled air and fluid being drawn back into the system. If such a kit is not available, the basic (two-man) method must be used, which is described in detail below.

9 If a kit is to be used, prepare the vehicle as described previously, and follow the kit manufacturer's instructions, as the procedure may vary slightly according to the type being used; generally, they are as outlined below in the relevant sub-section.

10 Whichever method is used, the same sequence must be followed (paragraphs 11 and 12) to ensure the removal of all air from the system.

Bleeding sequence

11 If the system has been only partially disconnected, and suitable precautions were taken to minimise fluid loss, it should only be necessary to bleed that part of the system (ie the primary or secondary circuit).

12 If the complete system is to be bled, then it should be done working in the following sequence:

a) Right-hand front brake.
b) Left-hand front brake.
c) Right-hand rear brake.
d) Left-hand rear brake.

Bleeding - basic (two-man) method

13 Collect together a clean glass jar, a suitable length of plastic or rubber tubing which is a tight fit over the bleed screw, and a ring spanner to fit the screw. The help of an assistant will also be required.

14 Remove the dust cap from the first bleed screw in the sequence. Fit the spanner and tube to the screw, place the other end of the tube in the jar, and pour in sufficient fluid to cover the end of the tube.

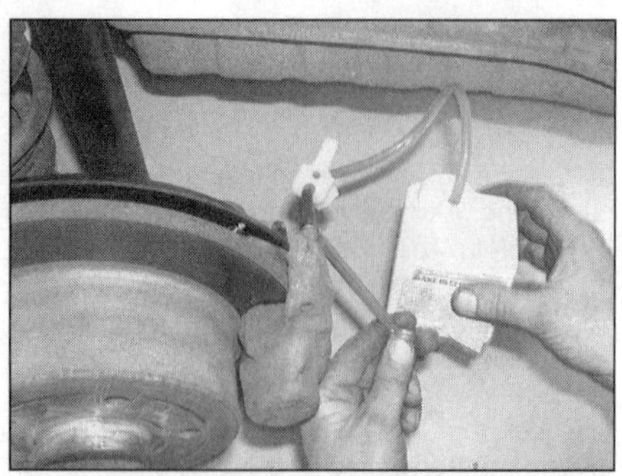

2.22 Using a one-way valve kit to bleed the rear brake circuit

15 Ensure that the master cylinder reservoir fluid level is maintained at least above the "MIN" level mark throughout the procedure.

16 Have the assistant fully depress and release the brake pedal several times to build up initial pressure in the system.

17 Unscrew the bleed screw approximately half a turn then have the assistant slowly depress the brake pedal down to the floor and hold it there. Tighten the bleed screw and have the assistant slowly release the pedal to its rest position.

18 Repeat the procedure given in paragraph 17 until the fluid emerging from the bleed screw is free from air bubbles. After every two or three depressions of the pedal, check the level of fluid in the reservoir and top up if necessary.

19 When no more air bubbles appear, securely tighten the bleed screw, remove the tube and spanner, and refit the dust cap. Do not overtighten the bleed screw.

20 Repeat the procedure on the remaining screws in the sequence, until all air is removed from the system and the brake pedal feels firm again.

Bleeding - using a one-way valve kit

21 As the name implies, these kits consist of a length of tubing with a one-way valve fitted, to prevent expelled air and fluid being drawn back into the system; some kits include a translucent container, which can be positioned so that the air bubbles can be more easily seen flowing from the end of the tube.

22 The kit is connected to the bleed screw, which is then opened **(see illustration)**. The user returns to the driver's seat, depresses the brake pedal with a smooth, steady stroke, and slowly releases it; this is repeated until the expelled fluid is clear of air bubbles.

23 Note that these kits simplify work so much that it is easy to forget the master cylinder reservoir fluid level; ensure that this is maintained at least above the "MIN" level line at all times.

Bleeding - using a pressure-bleeding kit

24 These kits are usually operated by a reservoir of pressurised air contained in the spare tyre. However, note that it will probably be necessary to reduce the pressure to a lower level than normal; refer to the instructions supplied with the kit.

25 By connecting a pressurised, fluid-filled container to the master cylinder reservoir, bleeding can be carried out simply by opening each screw in turn (in the specified sequence), and allowing the fluid to flow out until no more air bubbles can be seen in the expelled fluid.

26 This method has the advantage that the large reservoir of fluid provides an additional safeguard against air being drawn into the system during bleeding.

27 Pressure-bleeding is particularly effective when bleeding "difficult" systems, or when bleeding the complete system at the time of routine fluid renewal.

All methods

28 When bleeding is complete, and firm pedal feel is restored, wipe off any spilt fluid, securely tighten the bleed screws, and refit the dust caps.

29 Check the hydraulic fluid level in the master cylinder reservoir, and top-up if necessary (see *"Weekly checks"*).

30 Discard any hydraulic fluid that has been bled from the system; it will not be fit for re-use.

31 Check the feel of the brake pedal. If it feels at all spongy, air must still be present in the system, and further bleeding is required. Failure to bleed satisfactorily after a reasonable repetition of the bleeding procedure may be due to worn master cylinder seals.

3 Hydraulic pipes and hoses - renewal

Warning: Refer to the warning at the start of Section 2 regarding the safe handling of brake hydraulic fluid.

1 If any pipe or hose is to be renewed, minimise fluid loss by first removing the master cylinder reservoir cap, then tightening it down onto a piece of polythene to obtain an airtight seal. Alternatively, hose clamps can be fitted to flexible hoses to isolate sections of the circuit; metal brake pipe unions can be plugged (if care is taken not to allow dirt into the system) or capped immediately they are disconnected. Place a wad of rag under any union that is to be disconnected, to catch any spilt fluid.

2 If a flexible hose is to be disconnected, unscrew the brake pipe union nut before removing the spring clip which secures the hose to its mounting bracket **(see illustration)**. Where applicable, unscrew the banjo union bolt securing the hose to the caliper and recover the copper washers. When removing the front flexible hose, pull out the spring clip and disconnect it from the strut.

3 To unscrew union nuts, it is preferable to obtain a brake pipe spanner of the correct size; these are available from most motor accessory shops. Failing this, a close-fitting open-ended spanner will be required, though if the nuts are tight or corroded, their flats may be rounded-off if the spanner slips. In such a case, a self-locking wrench is often the only way to unscrew a stubborn union, but it follows that the pipe and the damaged nuts must be renewed on reassembly. Always clean a union and surrounding area before disconnecting it. If disconnecting a component with more than one union, make a careful note of the connections before disturbing any of them.

4 If a brake pipe is to be renewed, it can be obtained, cut to length and with the union nuts and end flares in place, from a dealers parts shop. All that is then necessary is to bend it to shape, following the line of the original, before fitting it to the car. Alternatively, most motor accessory shops can make up brake pipes from kits, but this requires very careful measurement of the original, to ensure that the replacement is of the correct length. The safest answer is usually to take the original to the shop as a pattern.

5 On refitting, do not overtighten the union nuts.

6 When refitting hoses to the calipers, always use new copper washers and tighten the banjo union bolts to the specified torque. Make sure that the hoses are positioned so that they will not touch surrounding bodywork or the roadwheels.

7 Ensure that the pipes and hoses are correctly routed, with no kinks, and that they are secured in the clips or brackets provided. After fitting, remove the polythene from the reservoir, and bleed the hydraulic system as described in Section 2. Wash off any spilt fluid, and check carefully for fluid leaks.

4 Front brake pads - renewal

Warning: Renew BOTH sets of front brake pads at the same time - NEVER renew the pads on only one wheel, as uneven braking may result. Note that although Saab brake pads do not contain asbestos, the dust created by wear of non-genuine pads may be a health hazard. Do not use compressed air to blow out brake dust and debris - use a brush.

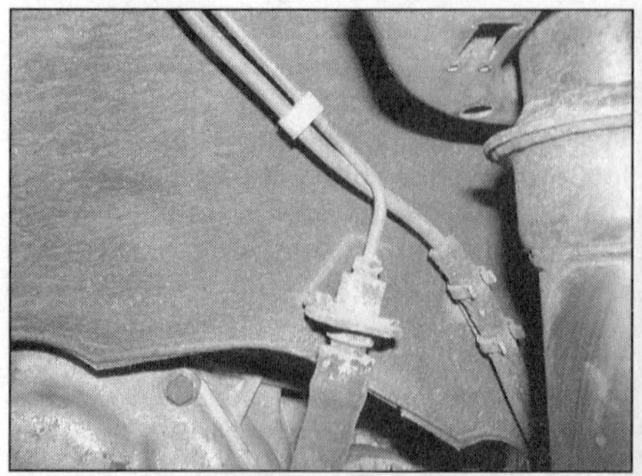

3.2 Front brake pipe and flexible hose under the front wheel arch

4.2 Use a screwdriver to lever off the retaining spring

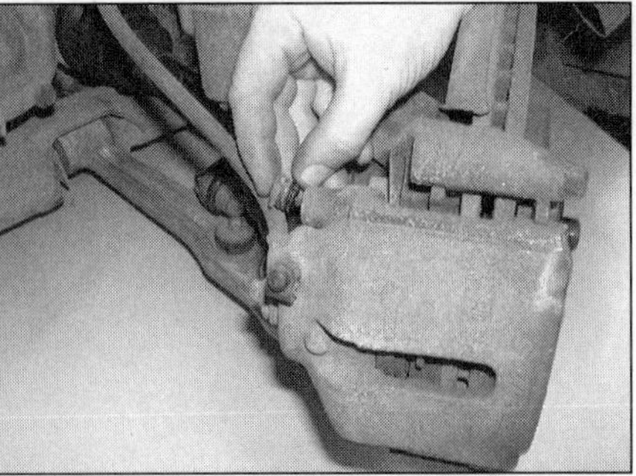

4.3 Remove the dust caps . . .

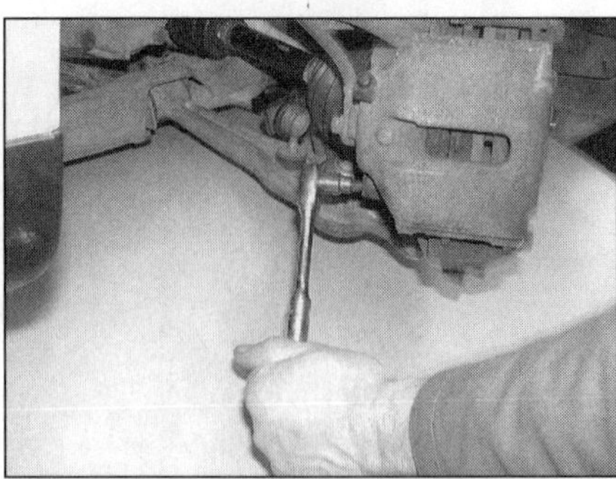

4.4a . . . then unscrew the guide bolts . . .

Avoid inhaling any of the dust; wear an approved filtration mask. Use only proprietary brake cleaner fluid or methylated spirits to clean the brake components, DO NOT use petrol or any other petroleum-based product as this will damage the rubber seals.

1 Apply the handbrake, then jack up the front of the vehicle and support it on axle stands (see (see *"Jacking and vehicle support"*). Remove both front roadwheels.

2 Carefully lever off the retaining spring from the holes on the outer surface of the caliper, noting how the spring is located on the caliper mounting bracket **(see illustration)**.

3 Remove the dust caps from the inner ends of the guide bolts **(see illustration)**.

4 Unscrew the guide bolts from the caliper, and lift the caliper and pads away from the mounting bracket **(see illustrations)**. Tie the caliper to the suspension strut using a suitable piece of wire. Do not allow the caliper to hang unsupported on the flexible brake hose.

5 Remove the inner and outer pads from the caliper piston, noting that the inner one is retained by a spring clip attached to the pad backing plate **(see illustration)**. **Note:** *As from model year 1998, an acoustic wear warning device is fitted to the outer pad, consisting of a metal strip which contacts the brake disc when the thickness of the friction material is less than 3.0 mm. This device causes a scraping noise which warns the driver that the pads are worn excessively.*

6 Brush the dirt and dust from the caliper, but take care not to inhale it. Carefully remove any rust from the edge of the brake disc.

7 Measure the thickness of each brake pad (friction material and backing plate) **(see illustration)**. If either pad is worn at any point to the specified minimum thickness or less, all four pads must be renewed. The pads should also be renewed if any are fouled with oil or grease; there is no satisfactory way of degreasing friction material, once contaminated. If any of the brake pads are worn unevenly, or fouled with oil or grease, trace and rectify the cause before reassembly.

8 If the brake pads are still serviceable, carefully clean them using a clean, fine wire brush or similar, paying particular attention to the sides and back of the metal backing. Where necessary, clean out the grooves in the friction material, and pick out any large embedded particles of dirt or debris. Carefully clean the pad locations in the caliper body/mounting bracket.

9 Prior to fitting the pads, check that the guide bolts are a good fit in the caliper bushes. Brush the dust and dirt from the caliper and piston (see Warning at the beginning of this Section). Apply a little high melting point copper brake grease to the areas on the pad backing plates which contact the caliper and piston. Inspect the dust seal around the piston for damage, and the piston for evidence of fluid leaks, corrosion or damage. If attention to any of these components is necessary, refer to Section 6.

10 If new brake pads are to be fitted, the caliper piston must be pushed back into the cylinder to make room for them. Either use a G-clamp or similar tool, or use suitable pieces of wood as levers. Provided that the master

4.4b . . . and lift the caliper and pads away from the mounting bracket

cylinder reservoir has not been overfilled with hydraulic fluid, there should be no spillage, but keep a careful watch on the fluid level while retracting the piston. If the fluid level rises above the "MAX" level line at any time, the surplus should be syphoned off or ejected via a plastic tube connected to the bleed screw.

Warning: Do not syphon the fluid by mouth, as it is poisonous; use a syringe or an old poultry baster.

11 Check that the cutaway recesses on the caliper piston are positioned horizontally. If necessary, carefully turn the piston to its correct position.

12 Fit the inner pad to the caliper, ensuring that its clip is correctly located in the caliper piston.

13 Fit the outer pad to the caliper mounting bracket, ensuring that its friction material is facing the brake disc **(see illustration)**.

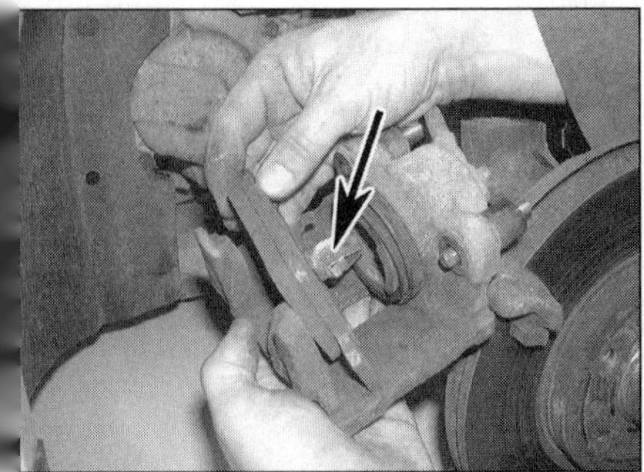

4.5 Removing the inner pad from the caliper - note the retaining spring

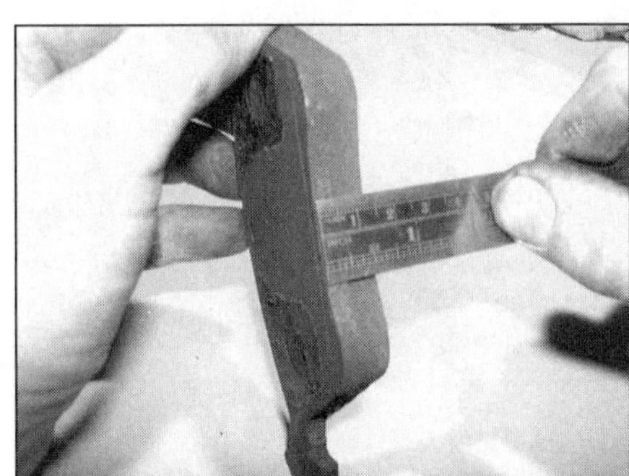

4.7 Measuring the thickness of the front brake pad, including the backing plate

4.13 Locating the outer pad in the caliper mounting bracket

4.14 Locating the caliper and inner pad over the outer pad

5.2 Using a punch to drive out the rear brake pad retaining pins

5.3 Removing the anti-squeal spring

14 Slide the caliper and inner pad into position over the outer pad, and locate it in the mounting bracket **(see illustration)**.

15 Insert the caliper guide bolts, and tighten them to the specified torque setting.

16 Refit the guide bolt dust caps.

17 Refit the retaining spring to the caliper, ensuring that its ends are correctly located in the caliper holes.

18 Depress the brake pedal repeatedly, until normal pedal pressure is restored.

19 Repeat the above procedure on the remaining front brake caliper.

20 Refit the roadwheels, then lower the vehicle to the ground and tighten the roadwheel bolts to the specified torque setting.

21 Check the hydraulic fluid level as described in *"Weekly checks"*.

5 Rear brake pads - renewal

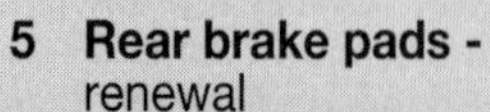

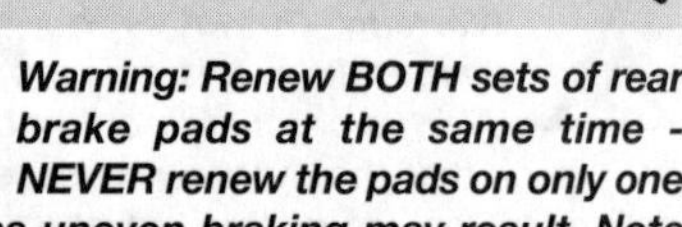

Warning: Renew BOTH sets of rear brake pads at the same time - NEVER renew the pads on only one wheel, as uneven braking may result. Note that the dust created by wear of the pads may contain asbestos, which is a health hazard. Never blow it out with compressed air, and do not inhale any of it. An approved filtering mask should be worn when working on the brakes. DO NOT use petroleum-based solvents to clean brake parts - use brake cleaner or methylated spirit only.

1 Chock the front wheels, then jack up the rear of the vehicle and support on axle stands (see *"Jacking and vehicle support"*). Remove the rear roadwheels.

2 Note how the anti-squeal spring is located, then drive out the upper and lower pad retaining pins from the outside of the caliper using a punch **(see illustration)**.

3 Remove the anti-squeal spring **(see illustration)**.

4 Push the pads away from the disc slightly, then using a pair of pliers or removal tool, withdraw the outer pad from the caliper.

5 Withdraw the inner pad from the caliper **(see illustrations)**.

6 Brush the dirt and dust from the caliper, but take care not to inhale it. Carefully remove any rust from the edge of the brake disc.

7 Measure the thickness of each brake pad (friction material and backing plate). If either pad is worn at any point to the specified minimum thickness or less, all four pads must be renewed. The pads should also be renewed if any are fouled with oil or grease; there is no satisfactory way of degreasing friction material, once contaminated. If any of the brake pads are worn unevenly, or fouled with oil or grease, trace and rectify the cause before reassembly.

8 If the brake pads are still serviceable, clean them using a clean, fine wire brush or similar, paying particular attention to the sides and back of the metal backing. Carefully clean the pad locations in the caliper body/mounting bracket.

9 Prior to fitting the pads, clean and check the pad retaining pins. Brush the dust and dirt from the caliper and piston (see Warning at the beginning of this Section). Apply a little high melting point copper brake grease to the areas on the pad backing plates which contact the caliper and piston. Inspect the dust seal around the piston for damage, and the piston for evidence of fluid leaks, corrosion or damage. If attention to any of these components is necessary, refer to Section 7.

10 If new brake pads are to be fitted, the caliper pistons must be pushed back into the cylinder to make room for them. Either use a G-clamp or similar tool, or use suitable pieces of wood as levers. Provided that the master cylinder reservoir has not been overfilled with hydraulic fluid, there should be no spillage, but keep a careful watch on the fluid level while retracting the pistons. If the fluid level rises above the "MAX" level line at any time, the surplus should be syphoned off or ejected via a plastic tube connected to the bleed screw.

Warning: Do not syphon the fluid by mouth, as it is poisonous; use a syringe or an old poultry baster.

11 Using a steel rule, check that the cutaway recess in the pistons are positioned as shown **(see illustration)**. The recesses must be at the bottom of the caliper. If necessary, carefully turn the pistons to their correct positions.

12 Locate the new pads in the caliper. Ensure that the friction material faces the disc, and check that the pads are free to move.

13 Locate the anti-squeal spring on the pads, then insert the pad retaining pins from the

5.5a Removing the inner rear brake pad

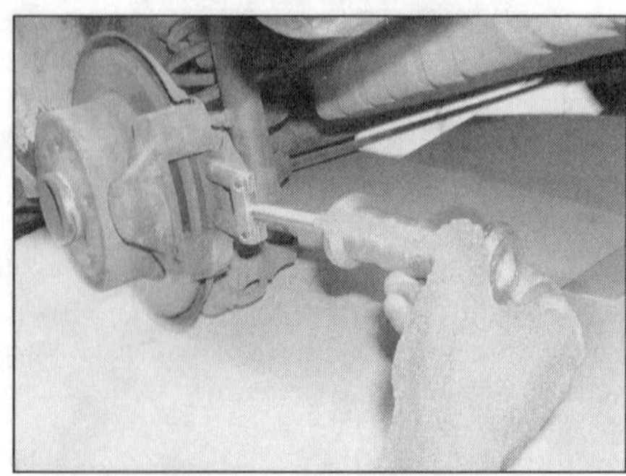
5.5b Using a removal tool to remove the inner rear brake pad

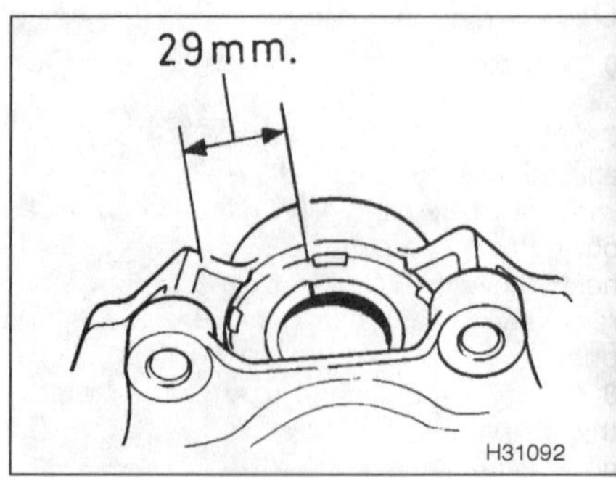

5.11 Correct position of the piston in the rear brake caliper

inside edge of the caliper, while depressing the spring. Tap the pins firmly into the caliper.
14 Depress the brake pedal repeatedly until normal pedal pressure is restored.
15 Repeat the above procedure on the remaining rear brake caliper.
16 Refit the roadwheels, then lower the vehicle to the ground and tighten the roadwheel bolts to the specified torque setting.
17 Check the hydraulic fluid level as described in *"Weekly checks"*.

6 Front brake caliper - removal, overhaul and refitting

Warning: Refer to the warning at the start of Section 2 regarding the safe handling of brake hydraulic fluid, and the warning at the start of Section 4 concerning the dangers of asbestos dust.

Removal

1 Apply the handbrake, then jack up the front of the vehicle and support it on axle stands (see *"Jacking and vehicle support"*). Remove the roadwheel.
2 Minimise fluid loss by first removing the master cylinder reservoir cap, then tightening it down onto a piece of polythene to obtain an airtight seal. Alternatively, use a brake hose clamp, a G-clamp or a similar tool to clamp the flexible hose leading to the brake caliper. ***Caution: The unprotected jaws of a G-clamp should not be used, as they may damage the hose, leading to premature failure.***
3 Clean the area around the caliper brake hose union. Note the fitted angle of the hose (to ensure correct refitting), then unscrew and remove the union bolt and recover the copper sealing washer from each side of the hose union. Discard the washers; new ones must be used on refitting. Plug the hose end and caliper hole, to minimise fluid loss and prevent the ingress of dirt into the hydraulic system.
4 Remove the brake pads as described in Section 4, then remove the caliper from the vehicle.
5 If necessary, unbolt the caliper mounting bracket from the hub carrier/strut.

Overhaul

6 With the caliper on the bench, clean away all external dirt and debris.
7 Withdraw the piston from the caliper body, and remove the dust seal. The piston can be withdrawn by hand, or if necessary pushed out by applying compressed air to the brake hose union hole. Only low pressure should be required, such as is generated by a foot pump.
8 Using a small screwdriver, carefully remove the piston seal from the caliper, taking care not to mark the bore.
9 Remove the guide bolts, then press the guide bushes out of the caliper body.
10 Thoroughly clean all components, using only methylated spirit or clean hydraulic fluid. Never use mineral-based solvents such as petrol or paraffin, which will attack the rubber components of the hydraulic system. Dry the components using compressed air or a clean, lint-free cloth. If available, use compressed air to blow clear the fluid passages (wear eye protection).
11 Check all components, and renew any that are worn or damaged. If the piston and/or cylinder bore are scratched excessively, renew the complete caliper body. Similarly check the condition of the guide bushes and bolts; both bushes and bolts should be undamaged and a reasonably tight sliding fit. If there is any doubt about the condition of any component, renew it. Renew the caliper seals and dust covers as a matter of course; these are available as a repair kit together with assembly grease.
12 On reassembly, ensure that all components are absolutely clean.
13 Lubricate the new seal with the grease supplied, or dip it in clean hydraulic fluid. Locate the seal in the cylinder bore groove, using only the fingers to manipulate it into position.
14 Fill the inner cavity of the dust seal with the grease supplied, or dip it in clean hydraulic fluid, then locate it on the piston.
15 Locate the piston on the caliper so that the cutaway recesses are positioned as described in Section 4. Carefully press the piston fully into the caliper body, twisting the piston from side to side to ensure it enters the internal seal correctly. At the same time, make sure that the inner end of the dust seal enters the groove on the caliper body, and the outer end enters the groove in the piston.
16 Insert the guide bushes and guide bolts in the caliper body, using suitable grease to lubricate them.

Refitting

17 Locate the caliper mounting bracket on the hub carrier/strut, then apply locking fluid to the threads of the mounting bolts, insert them, and tighten securely.
18 Refit the brake pads as described in Section 4, together with the caliper which at this stage will not have the hose attached.
19 Position a new copper sealing washer on each side of the hose union, and connect the brake hose to the caliper. Ensure that the hose is correctly positioned against the caliper body lug, then install the union bolt and tighten securely.
20 Remove the brake hose clamp or the polythene, where fitted, and bleed the hydraulic system as described in Section 2. Note that, providing the precautions described were taken to minimise brake fluid loss, it should only be necessary to bleed the relevant front brake.
21 Refit the roadwheel, then lower the vehicle to the ground and tighten the roadwheel bolts to the specified torque.

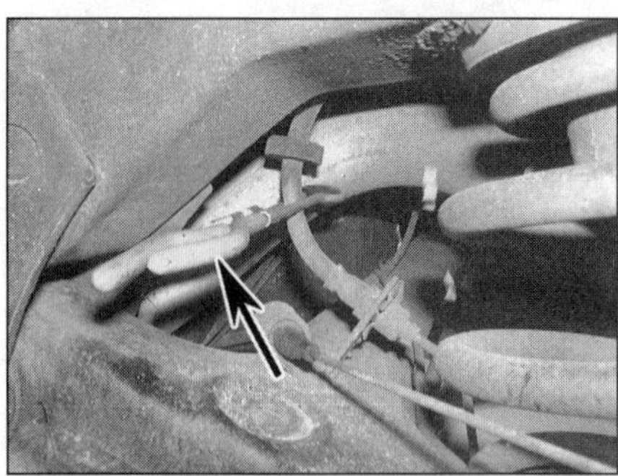

7.2 Brake hose clamp fitted to the flexible hose leading from the body to the brake line on the rear axle

7 Rear brake caliper - removal, overhaul and refitting

Warning: Refer to the warning at the start of Section 2 regarding the safe handling of brake hydraulic fluid, and the warning at the start of Section 4 concerning the dangers of asbestos dust.

Removal

1 Chock the front wheels, then jack up the rear of the vehicle and support on axle stands (see *"Jacking and vehicle support"*). Remove the roadwheel.
2 Minimise fluid loss by first removing the master cylinder reservoir cap, then tightening it down onto a piece of polythene to obtain an airtight seal. Alternatively, use a brake hose clamp, a G-clamp or a similar tool to clamp the flexible hose leading from the body to the brake line on the rear axle **(see illustration)**.
Caution: The unprotected jaws of a G-clamp should not be used, as they may damage the hose, leading to premature failure.
3 Clean the area around the hydraulic line union nut, then loosen the nut **(see illustration)**. Do not fully unscrew the nut at this stage.
4 Remove the brake pads as described in Section 5.

7.3 Unscrewing the hydraulic line union nut from the rear brake caliper

9

7.5 Removing the rear brake caliper mounting bolts

5 Unscrew and remove the mounting bolts securing the caliper to the backplate **(see illustration)**.

6 Fully unscrew the union nut and disconnect the hydraulic line from the caliper, then withdraw the caliper from the disc **(see illustration)**. Tape over or plug the hydraulic line to prevent entry of dust and dirt.

Overhaul

7 With the caliper on the bench, clean away all external dirt and debris.

8 Withdraw the pistons from the caliper body, and remove the dust seals. The pistons can be withdrawn by hand, or if necessary pushed out by applying compressed air to the brake line union hole. Only low pressure should be required, such as is generated by a foot pump. ***Caution: Keep each piston identified for position to ensure correct refitting.***

9 Using a small screwdriver, carefully remove the piston seals from the caliper, taking care not to mark the bores.

10 Thoroughly clean all components, using only methylated spirit or clean hydraulic fluid. Never use mineral-based solvents such as petrol or paraffin, which will attack the rubber components of the hydraulic system. Dry the components using compressed air or a clean, lint-free cloth. If available, use compressed air to blow clear the fluid passages (wear eye protection).

11 Check all components, and renew any that are worn or damaged. If the pistons and/or cylinder bores are scratched excessively, renew the complete caliper body. Renew the caliper seals and dust covers as a matter of course; these are available as a repair kit together with assembly grease.

12 On reassembly, ensure that all components are absolutely clean.

13 Lubricate the new seals with the grease supplied, or dip them in clean hydraulic fluid, then locate them in the cylinder bore grooves, using only the fingers to manipulate them into position.

14 Fill the inner cavities of the dust seals with the grease supplied, or dip them in clean hydraulic fluid, then locate them on the pistons.

15 Working on each piston at a time, locate the piston on the caliper so that the cutaway recesses are positioned as described in Section 5. Carefully press the piston fully into the caliper body, twisting the piston from side to side to ensure it enters the internal seal correctly. At the same time, make sure that the inner end of the dust seal enters the groove on the caliper body, and the outer end enters the groove in the piston.

Refitting

16 With both pistons refitted, locate the caliper over the disc, then insert the hydraulic line and screw in the union nut. Do not fully tighten the nut at this stage.

17 Apply a little locking fluid to the threads of the mounting bolts, then insert them and tighten to the specified torque.

18 Refit the brake pads (see Section 5).

19 Fully tighten the hydraulic union nut.

20 Remove the polythene, where fitted, and bleed the hydraulic system as described in Section 2. Note that, providing the precautions described were taken to minimise brake fluid loss, it should only be necessary to bleed the relevant rear brake.

21 Refit the roadwheel, then lower the vehicle to the ground and tighten the roadwheel bolts to the specified torque.

8 Front brake disc - inspection, removal and refitting

Inspection

1 Apply the handbrake, then jack up the front of the vehicle and support it on axle stands (see "*Jacking and vehicle support*"). Remove both front roadwheels.

2 For an accurate check and for access to each side of the disc, the brake caliper should be unbolted and suspended to one side as described later in this Section. Alternatively, just the brake pads can be removed as described in Section 5.

3 Check that the brake disc securing screw is tight, then fit spacers approximately 10.0 mm thick to each of the roadwheel bolts, and refit and tighten the bolts. This will hold the disc in its normal running position.

4 Rotate the brake disc, and examine it for deep scoring or grooving. Light scoring is normal, but if excessive, the disc should be removed and either renewed or machined (within the specified limits) by an engineering works. The minimum thickness is given in the Specifications at the beginning of this Chapter.

5 Using a dial gauge, or a flat metal block and feeler blades, check that the disc run-out does not exceed the figure given in the Specifications **(see illustration)**.

6 If the disc run-out is excessive, remove the disc as described later, and check that the disc-to-hub surfaces are perfectly clean. Refit the disc and check the run-out again. If the run-out is still excessive, the disc should be renewed.

7 Using a micrometer check that the disc thickness is not less than that given in the Specifications. Take readings at several points around the disc.

8 Repeat the inspection on the other front brake disc.

Removal

9 Remove the roadwheel bolts and spacers used when checking the disc.

10 Remove the disc pads as described in Section 4, then unbolt and remove the front brake caliper and tie it to one side. Also remove the front brake caliper mounting bracket with reference to Section 6.

11 Remove the securing screw and withdraw the disc from the hub **(see illustrations)**.

Refitting

12 Refitting is a reversal of removal, but make sure that the mating faces of the disc

7.6 Removing the rear brake caliper

8.5 Checking the front brake disc with a dial gauge

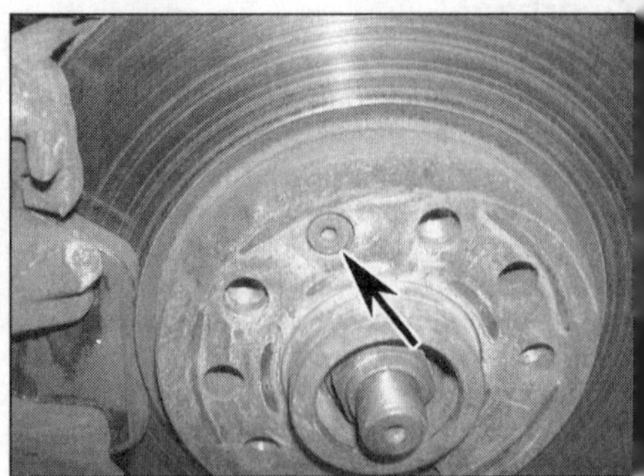

8.11a Front brake disc securing screw

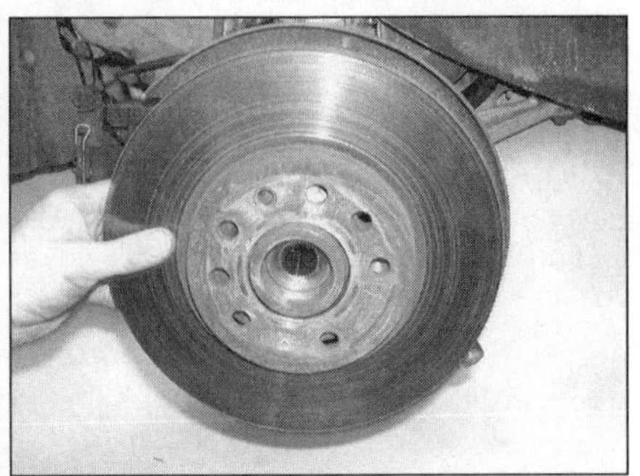
8.11b Removing the front brake disc

9.14a Remove the screw . . .

9.14b . . . and remove the rear brake disc

and hub are perfectly clean, and apply a little locking fluid to the threads of the securing screw before tightening it. If a new disc is being fitted, remove the protective coating from the surface, using an appropriate solvent. Refit the disc pads as described in Section 4, then refit the roadwheel and lower the vehicle to the ground.

9 Rear brake disc - inspection, removal and refitting

Inspection

1 Chock the front wheels, then jack up the rear of the vehicle and support on axle stands (see "*Jacking and vehicle support*"). Remove both rear roadwheels.

2 For an accurate check and for access to each side of the disc, the brake caliper should be unbolted and suspended to one side as described later in this Section. Alternatively, just the brake pads can be removed as described in Section 5.

3 Check that the brake disc securing screw is tight, then fit spacers approximately 10.0 mm thick to each of the roadwheel bolts, and refit and tighten the bolts. This will hold the disc in its normal running position.

4 Rotate the brake disc, and examine it for deep scoring or grooving. Light scoring is normal, but if excessive, the disc should be removed and either renewed or machined (within the specified limits) by an engineering works. The minimum thickness is given in the Specifications at the beginning of this Chapter.

5 Using a dial gauge, or a flat metal block and feeler blades, check that the disc run-out does not exceed the figure given in the Specifications.

6 If the disc run-out is excessive, remove the disc as described later, and check that the disc-to-hub surfaces are perfectly clean. Refit the disc and check the run-out again. If the run-out is still excessive, the disc should be renewed.

7 Using a micrometer check that the disc thickness is not less than that given in the Specifications. Take readings at several points around the disc.

8 Repeat the inspection on the other rear brake disc.

Removal

9 Remove the roadwheel bolts and spacers used when checking the disc.

10 Remove the disc pads as described in Section 4.

11 Carefully release the rear brake hydraulic line from the clip on the rear axle, taking care not to bend the line excessively.

12 Unbolt and remove the rear brake caliper with reference to Section 7, and tie it to one side. A convenient place to secure the caliper on the left-hand side, is to the exhaust system, using a long plastic cable tie.

13 Using a screwdriver through the access hole, back off the handbrake shoe adjustment with reference to Section 15.

14 Remove the securing screw and withdraw the disc from the hub **(see illustrations)**.

Refitting

15 Refitting is a reversal of removal, but make sure that the mating faces of the disc and hub are perfectly clean, and apply a little locking fluid to the threads of the securing screw before tightening it. If a new disc is being fitted, remove the protective coating from the surface, using an appropriate solvent. Refit the rear brake caliper with reference to Section 7 and tighten the mounting bolts to the specified torque. Refit the disc pads as described in Section 4, adjust the handbrake shoes as described in Section 15 and the handbrake cables as described in Section 16. Refit the roadwheel and lower the vehicle to the ground.

10.5 Unhooking the cable return spring

10 Handbrake shoes - inspection, removal and refitting

Warning: The handbrake shoes must be renewed on both rear wheels at the same time to ensure correct operation of the handbrake. Also, the dust created by wear of the shoes may contain asbestos, which is a health hazard. Never blow it out with compressed air, and do not inhale any of it. An approved filtering mask should be worn when working on the brakes. DO NOT use petrol or petroleum-based solvents to clean brake parts; use brake cleaner or methylated spirit only.

Inspection

1 The handbrake operates independently of the footbrake, using brake shoes on the inside of the disc in a similar way to rear drum brake models.

2 Remove the rear brake disc and caliper as described in Section 9.

3 With the disc removed, check that the friction material has not worn down to less than the specified minimum. If any one of the shoes has worn below the specified limit, all four handbrake shoes must be renewed as a set.

Removal

4 With the rear brake disc removed, clean the dust and dirt from the brake shoes and backplate.

5 Unhook the cable return spring from the hole in the backplate and from the cable end fitting **(see illustration)**.

6 Remove the outer cable and grommet from the bracket, and unhook the cable end fitting from the lever **(see illustrations)**.

7 Note the fitted position of all components, and if necessary make a sketch of them.

8 Remove the shoe hold-down pins, springs and cups by depressing the cups and turning them through 90° using a pair of pliers or by inserting a suitable tool through the hole in the

10.6a Remove the outer cable and grommet from the bracket . . .

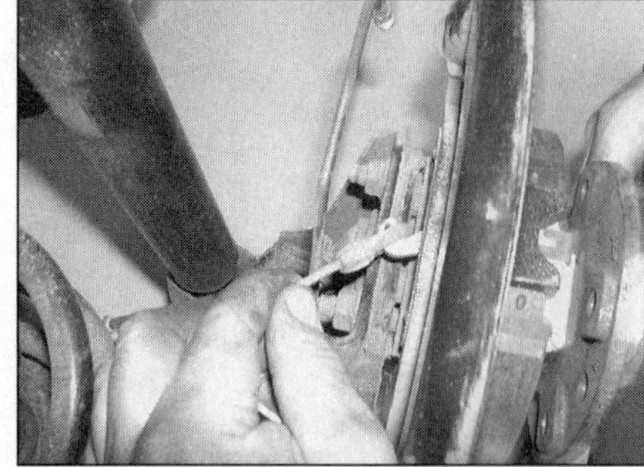

10.6b . . . then unhook the end fitting from the lever

10.8a Depress the hold-down springs and turn the cups through 90° . . .

10.8b . . . then remove the cups and springs . . .

10.8c . . . and remove the pins

hub flange **(see illustrations)**. This is a difficult task due to the strong spring tension and limited access.

9 Unhook the lower return spring, then remove the lower adjuster. Withdraw the shoes and upper expander together, and dismantle them on the bench **(see illustrations)**.

10 If both handbrake assemblies are dismantled at the same time, take care not to mix them up.

11 Dismantle and clean all components, then examine them for wear and damage. Renew worn or damaged components. Make sure that the expander and adjuster are not seized - apply a spot of oil to the expander pivot, and apply a little high melting point grease to the threads of the adjuster before reassembling it. Set the adjuster to its minimum length.

Refitting

12 Prior to installation, clean the backplate thoroughly, and apply a little copper grease to the shoe contact points **(see illustration)**.

13 Assemble the upper expander and shoes together with the return spring and locate them on the backplate at the same time inserting the lever through the rubber dust seal **(see illustration)**.

14 Locate the lower adjuster between the shoes, then refit the return spring.

10.9a Unhook the lower return spring . . .

10.9b . . . and release the lower adjuster . . .

10.9c . . . then remove the shoes and upper expander together

10.9d The upper expander

10.12 Apply a little copper grease to the shoe contact points

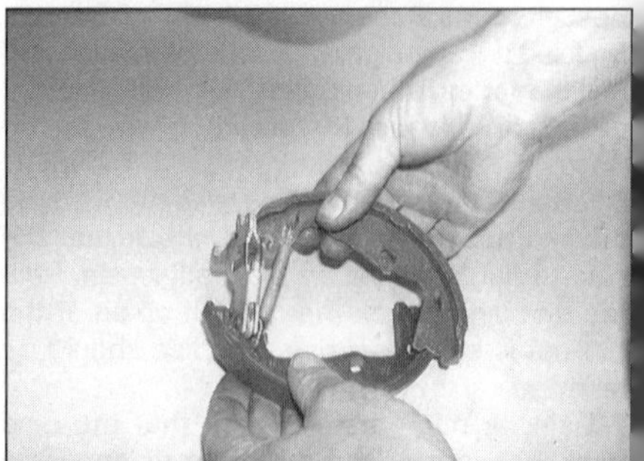

10.13 Assembling the shoes and upper expander

15 Hold the assembly on the backplate and insert the shoe hold-down pins, springs and cups. Depress the cups and turn them through 90° to secure using a pair of pliers.
16 Hook the cable end fitting on the expander lever and locate the cable holder in the bracket.
17 Hook the cable return spring in the backplate hole and on the end fitting.
18 Refit the rear brake disc and caliper as described in Section 9.
19 Adjust the handbrake shoes as described in Section 15, then refit the roadwheels and lower the vehicle to the ground.

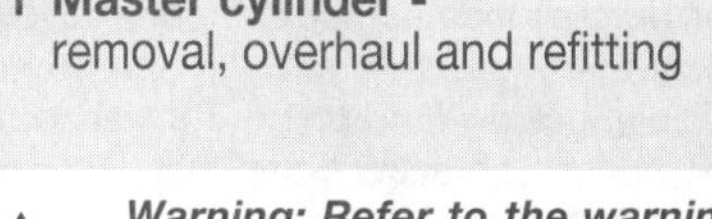

11 Master cylinder - removal, overhaul and refitting

Warning: Refer to the warning at the start of Section 2 regarding the safe handling of brake hydraulic fluid.

Removal

1 Exhaust the vacuum present in the brake servo unit by repeatedly depressing the brake pedal.
2 Disconnect the wiring from the hydraulic fluid level sender on the master cylinder reservoir cap, then remove the cap and syphon the hydraulic fluid from the reservoir.

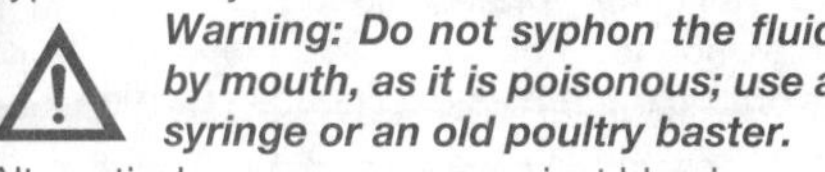

Warning: Do not syphon the fluid by mouth, as it is poisonous; use a syringe or an old poultry baster.

Alternatively, open any convenient bleed screw in the system, and gently pump the brake pedal to expel the fluid through a plastic tube connected to the bleed screw (see Section 2).
3 Place cloth rags beneath the master cylinder to catch spilt fluid.
4 Note the position of the brake lines, then unscrew the union nuts and move the lines to one side so that they are just clear of the master cylinder. Do not bend the brake lines excessively. If available use a split spanner to unscrew the nuts, as they can be very tight. Tape over or plug the outlets of the brake lines and master cylinder.
5 Unscrew the mounting nuts and withdraw the master cylinder from the front of the vacuum servo. Recover the seal. Wrap the master cylinder in cloth rags and remove it from the engine compartment. Take care not to spill fluid on the vehicle paintwork.

Overhaul

6 Before dismantling the master cylinder check on the availability and cost of parts, as it may be more economical to renew the complete unit.
7 Clean all dirt and debris from the exterior of the master cylinder.
8 Using a wide-bladed screwdriver, carefully prise the fluid reservoir from the top of the master cylinder. Prise out the rubber seals **(see illustration)**.
9 Remove the cover and the lock pin from the fluid aperture to the secondary piston.
10 Using circlip pliers, extract the circlip from the mouth of the master cylinder while slightly depressing the piston against the spring tension.
11 Remove the primary and secondary pistons together with their springs, from the master cylinder bore, noting their order of removal. If the pistons are tight, tap the cylinder on the work bench or on a block of wood to release them.
12 Thoroughly clean the master cylinder components with methylated spirit or clean brake fluid, and examine them for wear and damage. In particular, check the bore surfaces and rubber seals. The bore surface must not be pitted or scored, and the rubber seals must not be perished or worn. Clean the fluid entry ports of any rust or sediment.
13 If the cylinder bore is in good condition but the rubber seals are worn excessively, obtain new seals or complete new pistons and seals.
14 Lubricate the seals and bore surface with clean brake fluid. Insert the secondary piston assembly with the slot in line with the top of the cylinder, and then insert the lock pin and cover to hold the piston in place. Make sure that the seal lip is not damaged as it enters the cylinder.
15 Insert the primary piston assembly, again making sure that the seal lip is not damaged as it enters the cylinder.
16 Depress the primary piston, then fit the circlip in the groove in the cylinder mouth. Release the piston.
17 Dip the rubber seals in clean fluid and locate them in the apertures on the top of the master cylinder.
18 Locate the fluid reservoir stubs in the rubber seals, and press firmly until it is fully entered.

Refitting

19 Ensure the mating surfaces are clean and dry then fit the new seal to the rear of the master cylinder.
20 Fit the master cylinder to the studs on the vacuum servo unit, ensuring that the servo unit pushrod enters the master cylinder piston centrally. Fit the retaining nuts and tighten them securely.
21 Remove the tape or plugs, and reconnect the brake lines to the master cylinder. Tighten the union nuts initially with the fingers to prevent cross-threading, then fully tighten them with a spanner.
22 Fill the fluid reservoir with fresh brake fluid up to the MAX level mark.
23 Bleed the hydraulic system as described in Section 2 then refit the filler cap and reconnect the wiring to the hydraulic fluid level sender. Thoroughly check the operation of the braking system before using the vehicle on the road.

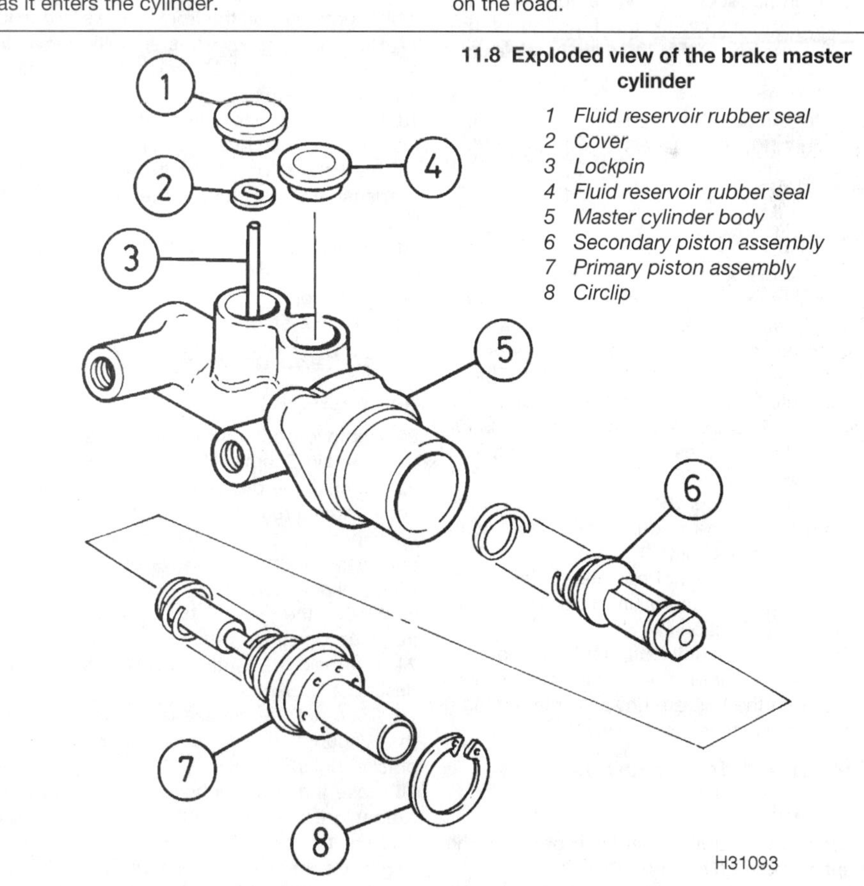

11.8 Exploded view of the brake master cylinder

1 *Fluid reservoir rubber seal*
2 *Cover*
3 *Lockpin*
4 *Fluid reservoir rubber seal*
5 *Master cylinder body*
6 *Secondary piston assembly*
7 *Primary piston assembly*
8 *Circlip*

12 Vacuum servo unit non-return valve - removal, testing and refitting

Removal

1 The non-return valve is located in the hose leading from the vacuum servo unit to the inlet manifold. It cannot be obtained separate to the hose.

2 Carefully ease the hose adapter from the rubber grommet on the front of the servo unit.

3 Unscrew the union nut and disconnect the hose from the inlet manifold.

4 Release the hose from the support and remove from the engine compartment.

Testing

5 Examine the check valve and hose for signs of damage, and renew if necessary. The valve may be tested by blowing through the hose in both directions. Air should flow through the valve in one direction only - when blown through from the servo unit end. Renew the valve and hose complete if necessary.

6 Examine the sealing grommet in the vacuum servo unit for signs of damage or deterioration, and renew as necessary.

Refitting

7 Refitting is a reversal of removal, but tighten the union nut securely. On completion, start the engine and check the function of the brakes; also check that there are no air leaks.

13 Vacuum servo unit - testing, removal and refitting

Testing

1 To test the operation of the servo unit, with the engine off, depress the footbrake several times to exhaust the vacuum. Now start the engine, keeping the pedal firmly depressed. As the engine starts, there should be a noticeable "give" in the brake pedal as the vacuum builds up. Allow the engine to run for at least two minutes, then switch it off. The brake pedal should now feel normal, but further applications should result in the pedal feeling firmer, the pedal stroke decreasing with each application.

2 If the servo does not operate as described, first inspect the servo unit check valve as described in Section 12.

3 If the servo unit still fails to operate satisfactorily, the fault lies within the unit itself. Repairs to the unit are not possible; if faulty, the servo unit must be renewed.

Left-hand drive models

Removal

4 Unbolt the support bar from between the front suspension turrets.

5 Unclip and remove the air induction silencer from above the throttle body as described in Chapter 4A.

6 Remove the brake master cylinder as described in Section 11.

7 Carefully ease the hose adapter from the rubber grommet on the front of the servo unit.

8 For improved access, move the fusebox to one side.

9 Unscrew and remove the mounting nuts and washers securing the vacuum servo unit to the bracket.

10 Ease the rubber gaiter from the bulkhead behind the vacuum servo unit, and pull it towards the servo unit to expose the pedal pushrod.

11 Prise the spring clip from the sleeve, then withdraw the servo unit forwards from the pedal pushrod and remove from the engine compartment.

Refitting

12 Locate the servo unit on the bracket and at the same time engage the sleeve with the pedal pushrod. With all the studs engaged, refit and tighten the mounting nuts and washers.

13 With the pedal pushrod fully engaged, press on the spring clip to secure. Check that the pushrod is engaged by attempting to pull it out of the sleeve.

14 Locate the rubber gaiter on the bulkhead.

15 Refit the fusebox.

16 Press the vacuum hose adapter into the rubber grommet on the front of the servo unit.

17 Refit the brake master cylinder with reference to Section 11, and bleed the brake hydraulic system as described in Section 2.

18 Refit the air induction silencer over the throttle body with reference to Chapter 4A.

19 Refit the support bar between the front suspension turrets and tighten the mounting bolts.

20 On completion, start the engine and check for air leaks at the vacuum hose-to-servo unit connection. Check the operation of the braking system.

Right-hand drive models

Removal

21 Remove both windscreen wiper arms as described in Chapter 12.

22 Remove the plastic cover from the engine compartment rear bulkhead area for access to the wiper linkage. Disconnect the wiring then undo the mounting screws and lift out the wiper linkage assembly.

23 Unbolt the support bar from between the front suspension turrets.

24 Remove the brake master cylinder as described in Section 11.

25 Prise out the access plugs and unscrew the vacuum servo unit upper mounting bracket bolts.

26 Ease the vacuum hose adapter from the rubber grommet in the front of the vacuum servo unit.

27 Inside the vehicle, remove the lower trim panel from the right-hand side of the facia.

28 Extract the spring clip, then pull out the pivot pin securing the pushrod clevis to the brake pedal.

29 Remove the cruise control unit, and position it to one side (refer to Chapter 4A).

30 Withdraw the servo unit and upper mounting bracket from the bulkhead, and remove from the engine compartment.

31 Undo the nuts and remove the bracket from the rear of the servo unit.

Refitting

32 Fit the bracket to the rear of the servo unit, and tighten the nuts.

33 Locate the servo unit and mounting bracket on the bulkhead making sure that the upper bracket locates correctly on the lower bracket.

34 Apply locking fluid to the threads of the upper mounting bracket bolts, then insert and tighten them. Refit the access plugs.

35 Inside the vehicle, connect the pushrod clevis on the pedal, then insert the pivot pin and secure with the spring clip.

36 Adjust the brake stop-light switch with reference to Section 20.

37 Refit the lower trim panel.

38 Press the vacuum hose adapter in the rubber grommet in the front of the vacuum servo unit.

39 Refit the cruise control unit with reference to Chapter 4A.

40 Refit the brake master cylinder with reference to Section 11, and bleed the brake hydraulic system as described in Section 2.

41 Refit the support bar between the front suspension turrets and tighten the mounting bolt.

42 Refit the wiper linkage assembly and tighten the mounting screws. Reconnect the wiring and refit the plastic cover to the rear bulkhead area.

43 Refit the windscreen wiper arms with reference to Chapter 12.

44 On completion, start the engine and check for air leaks at the vacuum hose-to-servo unit connection. Check the operation of the braking system.

14 Vacuum pump - removal and refitting

Removal

1 In order to increase the braking capacity of Turbo automatic models manufactured from model year 1996, an electric vacuum pump is fitted beneath the left-hand front wing behind the wheel arch liner. The pump switches on when the vacuum is less than 0.35 bar, and switches off when the vacuum exceeds 0.4 bar. The pressure is monitored by a pressure sensor located on the bulkhead. The system is only operational with the ignition on and 'D' selected.

2 Apply the handbrake, then jack up the front

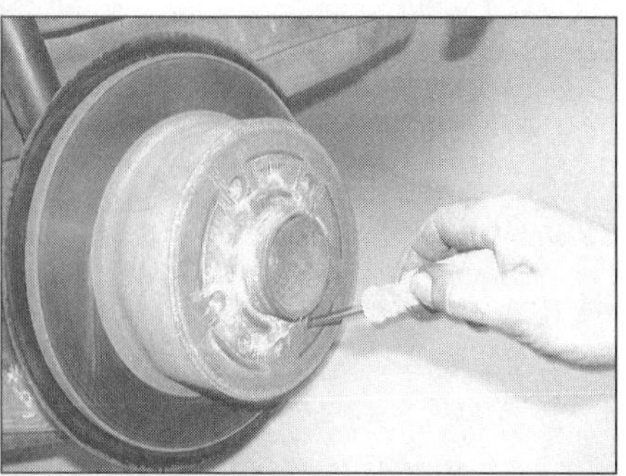

15.3 Use a screwdriver inserted through the hole in the rear disc to turn the handbrake adjuster serrations

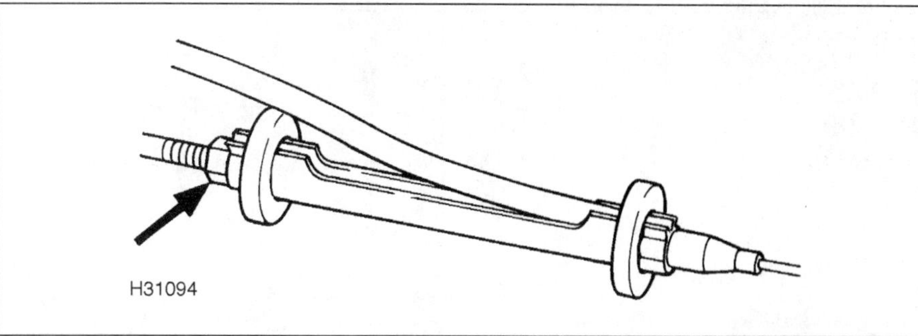

15.6a Handbrake cable equaliser adjustment nut on the single-cable handbrake system

of the vehicle and support it on axle stands (see "*Jacking and vehicle support*"). Remove the left-hand front wheel.

3 Remove the wheel arch liner, and where applicable, the engine undershield.

4 Disconnect the vacuum hose from the pump.

5 Disconnect the wiring.

6 Unscrew the mounting nuts and bolts and withdraw the vacuum pump.

Refitting

7 Refitting is a reversal of removal.

15 Handbrake - adjustment

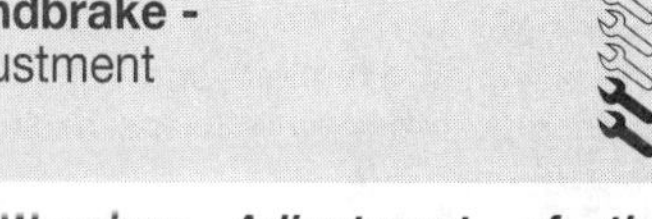

Warning: Adjustment of the handbrake should be carried out after the brake discs have been allowed to cool completely, and not immediately after driving the vehicle, when the discs may still be hot. The expansion of the discs at high temperatures may give rise to an inaccurate adjustment.

1 It is normally only necessary to adjust the handbrake after dismantling or renewing the handbrake shoes or cables. First chock the front wheels, then jack up the rear of the vehicle and support on axle stands (see "*Jacking and vehicle support*"). Remove both rear wheels.

2 Fully release the handbrake lever.

3 Working on each side at a time, adjust the shoe positions as follows. Turn the rear disc/drum until the access hole is positioned over the lower adjuster serrations. Using a screwdriver through the hole, turn the adjuster serrations until the disc/drum is locked **(see illustration)**. Now back off the serrations until the disc/drum is just free to turn. Repeat the adjustment on the remaining disc/drum.

4 Refit the rear wheels and tighten the bolts.

5 Set the handbrake lever on the 3rd to 5th notch on models fitted with a double-cable handbrake system, or on the 6th notch on models fitted with a single-cable handbrake system. Both rear wheels should be locked when attempting to turn them by hand. If only one side is locked, adjust the cable as described in the following paragraphs.

6 Set the handbrake lever on the 2nd notch, then tighten the nut on the equaliser until the rear discs/drums start to bind. On the single-cable handbrake system the equaliser is located on the rear axle, however on the double-cable handbrake system it is located above a heatshield on the underbody, at the front end of the cables **(see illustrations)**.

7 Fully release the handbrake lever, then apply it to the notch position given in paragraph 5. The rear wheels should be locked when attempting to turn them by hand.

8 On completion, lower the vehicle to the ground.

16 Handbrake cables - removal and refitting

Single-cable type

Removal

1 The handbrake cable consists of a single cable from the handbrake lever pull rod to the right-hand rear handbrake shoe operating lever. Near the rear of the cable, an equaliser is fitted together with a short cable extension to the left-hand rear handbrake shoes **(see illustration)**. Chock the front wheels, then jack up the rear of the vehicle and support on axle stands (see *"Jacking and vehicle support"*). Remove both rear wheels.

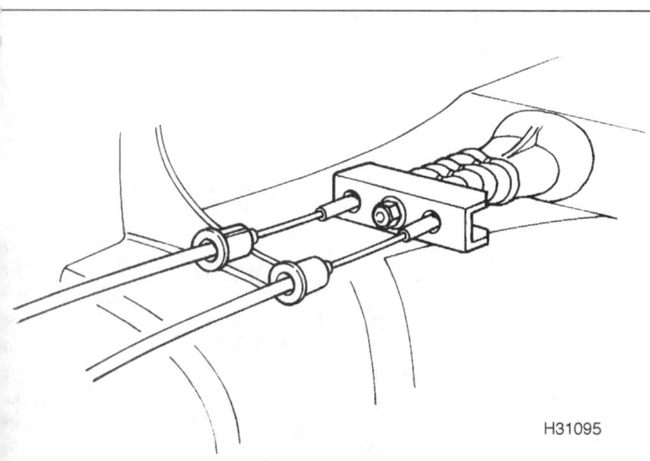

15.6b Handbrake cables, equaliser and adjustment nut on the double-cable handbrake system

15.6c Using a socket and extension to adjust the handbrake cable

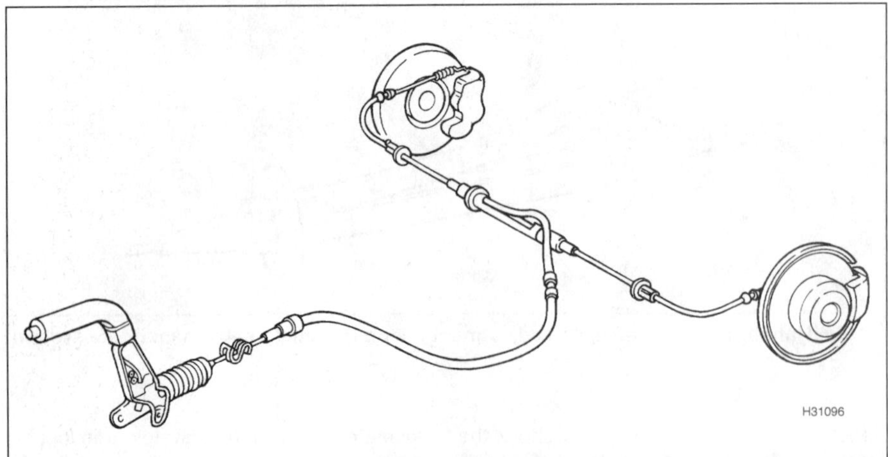

16.1 The single-cable handbrake system

2 Working at the right-hand rear brake, disconnect the return spring from the holes in the backplate and shoe operating lever.

3 Press the front and rear cable guide sleeves from the brackets, and release the cable.

4 Unhook the cable end fitting from the right-hand shoe operating lever.

5 Release the rubber ring, then disconnect the main outer cable from the equaliser bar.

6 Unscrew the nuts and remove the exhaust heatshield from above the rear axle on the left-hand side. Move the panel to one side then remove the cable guide sleeve from the bracket.

7 Unscrew the nuts and lower the exhaust centre heatshield for access to the front end of the handbrake cable. Pull the outer cable from the bracket, then disconnect the inner cable from the handbrake lever pull rod.

8 Pull out the main handbrake cable from in front of the fuel tank.

9 Working at the left-hand rear brake, disconnect the return spring from the holes in the backplate and shoe operating lever.

10 Press the cable guide sleeve from the bracket on the left-hand side of the rear axle, and release the cable.

11 Unhook the short cable end fitting from the left-hand shoe operating lever.

12 Release the rubber ring, then disconnect the short cable adjustment fitting from the equaliser bar **(see illustration)**.

13 Withdraw the cable components from under the vehicle.

14 Measure the length of thread on the adjustment fitting, then unscrew the adjustment nut and disconnect the short cable from the equaliser bar.

Refitting

15 Refitting is a reversal of removal, but finally adjust the handbrake as described in Section 15.

Double-cable type

Removal

16 The handbrake cable consists of two cables from the handbrake lever pull rod to the left- and right-hand handbrake shoe operating levers, joined at the front by an equaliser bar on the inner cables **(see illustration)**. It is not possible to renew the side cables separately. Chock the front wheels, then jack up the rear of the vehicle and support on axle stands (see "*Jacking and vehicle support*"). Remove both rear wheels.

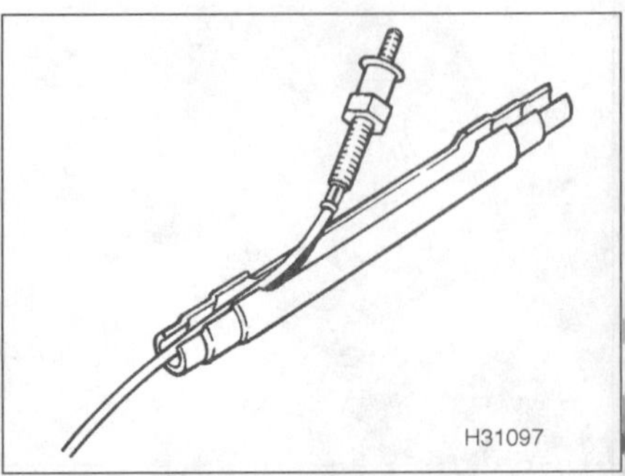

16.12 Disconnecting the short cable adjustment fitting from the equaliser bar (single-cable system)

17 Unscrew the nuts from the underbody and move the centre and rear exhaust heatshields to one side.

18 At the equaliser bar at the front of the cables, measure the length of exposed thread protruding from the adjustment nut to the end of the handbrake lever pull rod. This will act as a guide when refitting the cables.

19 Unscrew the adjusting nut and remove the equaliser from the rear of the pull rod.

20 Support the fuel tank, then unscrew the nut from the left-hand tank strap and unhook the strap.

21 Disconnect the left- and right-hand return springs from the holes in the backplates and shoe operating levers.

22 Remove the rear cable guide sleeves from the brackets, and unhook the cable end fittings from the shoe operating levers on each side **(see illustration)**.

23 Pull the cables from the holes on the rear axle and from the brackets behind the rear heat shield.

24 Release the cables from the front bracket near the cable adjuster.

25 Remove the remaining plastic ties and withdraw the cable components from under the vehicle.

Refitting

26 Refitting is a reversal of removal, but finally adjust the handbrake as described in Section 15.

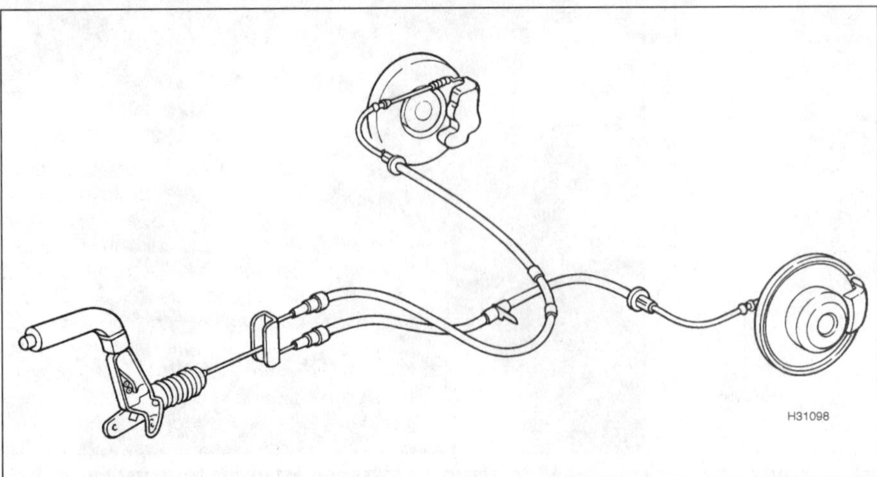

16.16 The double-cable handbrake system

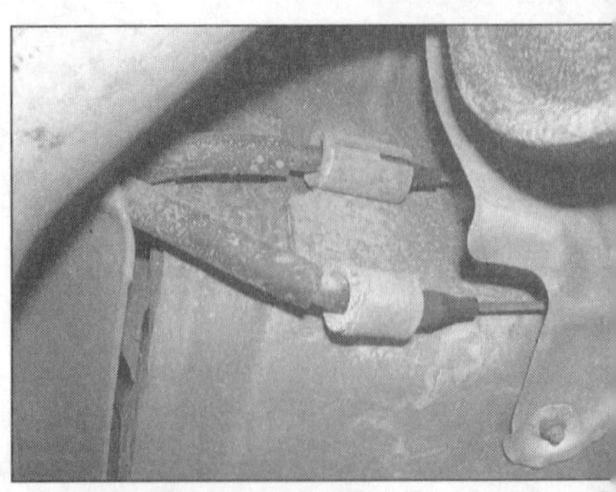

16.22 Handbrake rear cable guide sleeves and brackets

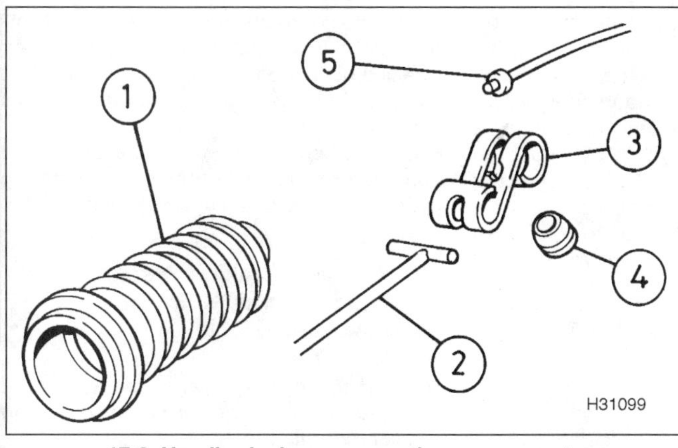

17.6 Handbrake lever connection components

1 Rubber gaiter
2 Pull rod
3 'S' clip
4 Plug
5 Single handbrake cable

17 Handbrake lever - removal and refitting

Removal

1 Chock the front wheels, then jack up the rear of the vehicle and support on axle stands (see *"Jacking and Vehicle Support"*). Remove both rear wheels.

2 Working at each rear wheel brake, disconnect the left- and right-hand return springs from the holes in the backplates and shoe operating levers.

3 Press the rear cable guide sleeves from the brackets on the left- and right-hand side of the rear axle.

4 Press out the front cable guide sleeve, then unhook the rear cable end fittings from the shoe operating levers.

5 Unscrew the nuts and move the exhaust heat shield located in front of the fuel tank.

6 Disconnect the front of the handbrake cable(s) from the lever pull rod. On the single-cable system, prise out the plug and disconnect the 'S' clip from the pull rod **(see illustration)**. On the double-cable system, it will be necessary to unscrew the adjustment nut and slide off the equaliser bar, however, make a note of the number of threads visible as an aid to refitting.

7 Slide the rubber gaiter from the rear of the pull rod.

8 Working inside the vehicle, remove the driver's seat and the centre console as described in Chapter 11.

9 Unscrew and remove the handbrake lever side mounting bolts, and also remove the handbrake warning light switch. Lift the lever assembly from the floor and remove from inside the vehicle.

Refitting

10 Refitting is a reversal of removal, but finally adjust the handbrake as described in Section 15. Tighten the handbrake lever mounting bolts securely.

18 Handbrake "ON" warning light switch - removal, testing and refitting

Removal

1 The handbrake "ON" warning light switch is mounted on the front of the handbrake lever mounting bracket bolted to the floorpan. Refer to Chapter 11 and remove the driver's seat and centre console.

2 Disconnect the wiring from the switch.

3 Unscrew the mounting screw and remove the switch from inside the vehicle.

Testing

4 Connect a multimeter or battery test probe to the wiring contact and switch body.

5 With the switch plunger at rest, there should be continuity and the multimeter should read no resistance, or the test light should light. With the plunger depressed, there should be infinity resistance or the test light should be extinguished.

6 Failure to operate correctly may indicate corroded contacts or ultimately a faulty switch. Check that there is a 12 volt supply to the wiring with the ignition switched on. Renew the switch if necessary.

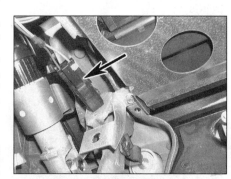

20.1 Stop-light switch

19.2 Brake pedal pushrod and spring clip

Refitting

7 Refitting is a reversal of removal.

19 Brake pedal - removal and refitting

Removal

1 Remove the facia panel as described in Chapter 11.

2 Extract the spring clip, then pull out the pivot pin securing the pushrod clevis to the brake pedal **(see illustration)**.

3 Unhook the return spring from the pedal.

4 Reach up behind the facia and extract the spring clip from the end of the pedal pivot.

5 Unscrew the nut and remove the washer, then remove the pivot pin from the bracket and lower the pedal.

Refitting

6 Refitting is a reversal of removal, but tighten the pivot nut securely.

20 Stop-light switch - removal, testing and refitting

Removal

1 The stop-light switch is mounted on top of the pedal bracket **(see illustration)**. An internal spring tensions the switch plunger so that the contacts are normally closed, however, when the brake pedal is released, the pedal return spring tension is greater than the switch spring, so the contacts are separated when the pedal is in its released position. When the brake pedal is depressed, the switch supplies a current of 12 volts to the central electronic control unit, which then supplies the stop lights with power. The control unit checks the three stop-light bulbs and if necessary displays a warning on the instrument panel. Where a trailer is being towed, current to the trailer stop lights is supplied direct from the stop-light switch.

2 To remove the switch first make sure that the ignition is switched off, then remove the lower trim panel from the facia with reference to Chapter 11.

3 Reach up at the front of the pedal bracket, and disconnect the wiring from the switch.

4 At the end of the stop-light switch body, squeeze together the plastic tangs, and pull the switch back through the mounting bracket.

Testing

5 The switch is a single-pole device, and has normally-closed contacts. The operation of the switch can be tested using either a multimeter (switched to the ohmmeter function), or a continuity tester made up of a flashlight bulb, dry cell battery and two pieces of wire. Connect the meter/tester to the switch connector terminals with the switch in its rest position, and check that the meter reads zero resistance or the tester lights up.

6 Press the switch plunger down, and check that the meter reads infinity resistance (open-circuit) or the tester is extinguished.

7 If the switch does not behave as described, or is intermittent in its operation, then a new switch must be fitted; the unit is not serviceable.

Refitting

8 Refit the brake stop-light switch by reversing the removal procedure.

21 Anti-lock Braking System (ABS) components - general information and fault finding

General information

The Anti-lock Braking System (ABS) is managed by an Electronic Control Unit (ECU), which has the capacity to monitor the status and condition of all the components in the system, including itself. If the ECU detects a fault, it responds by shutting down the ABS and illuminating the dashboard-mounted ABS warning light. Under these circumstances, conventional non-ABS braking is maintained. Note also that the warning light will be illuminated if the power supply to the ABS ECU is disconnected (eg if the supply fuse blows).

If the ABS warning lights indicate a fault, it is very difficult to diagnose problems with the system without the equipment and expertise to electronically "interrogate" the ECU. Therefore, this Section is limited firstly to a list of the basic checks that should be carried out, to establish the integrity of the system, (eg - is there enough brake fluid?, is anything leaking?, etc). Section 22 is limited to a description of the removal and refitting of the ABS wheel sensors and ECU only, as in certain instances, it will be necessary to remove these components to gain access to other assemblies on the vehicle.

If the cause of the fault cannot be immediately identified using the check list described, the *only* course of action open is to take the vehicle to a Saab dealer for examination. Dedicated test equipment is needed to interrogate the ABS ECU, to determine the nature and incidence of the fault. For safety reasons, owners are strongly advised against attempting to diagnose complex problems with the ABS using standard workshop equipment.

Basic fault-finding checks

Brake fluid level

1 Check the brake fluid level (see *"Weekly checks"*). If the level is low, check the complete braking system for signs of leaks. Refer to Chapter 1 and carry out a check of the brake hoses and pipes throughout the vehicle. If no leaks are apparent, remove each roadwheel in turn, and check for leaks at the brake caliper pistons.

Fuses and relays

2 The fuse for the ABS is located beneath a cover on the end of the instrument panel. Remove the cover and pull out the fuse. Visually check the fuse filament; if it is difficult to see whether or not it has blown, use a multimeter or continuity tester to check the electrical continuity of the fuse. If any of the fuses are blown, do not fit a new one, until the fault that caused the fuse to blow has been found and rectified - if necessary, have the vehicle inspected by a Saab dealer.

3 The ABS system relay is located beneath a cover on the left-hand side of the engine compartment. In general, relays are difficult to test conclusively without an electrical specification. However, the metal contacts inside a relay can usually be felt (and often heard) to open or close as it operates - if the relay in question does not behave in this way when the ignition switch is turned on, it may be faulty. It should be noted that this is not a conclusive test, and substitution with a known good relay *of the same type* is the only way to verify the component operation. If any of the relays is suspected of being faulty, it can be renewed by pulling it out of its socket - noting its orientation - and pushing in a new unit.

Electrical connections and earthing points

4 The engine bay is a hostile environment for electrical connections, and even the best seals can sometimes be penetrated. Water, chemicals and air will induce corrosion on the connector's contacts and prevent good continuity, sometimes intermittently. Disconnect the battery negative cable, then check the security and condition of all connectors at the ABS hydraulic unit, situated on the left-hand side of the engine bay.

5 Unplug each connector, and examine the contacts inside. Clean any contacts that are found to be dirty or corroded. Avoid scraping the contacts clean with a blade, as this will accelerate corrosion later. Use a piece of lint-free cloth in conjunction with proprietary cleaning oil to produce a clean, shiny contact surface that will result in good electrical continuity.

6 In addition, check the security and condition of the system electrical earthing point on the side of the hydraulic unit.

22 Anti-lock Braking System (ABS) components - removal and refitting

Note: *If the ABS system is faulty, have it checked by a Saab dealer before removing any component.*

Front wheel sensors (pre-1996 models)

Removal

1 Apply the handbrake, then jack up the front of the vehicle and support it on axle stands (see *"Jacking and vehicle support"*). Remove the roadwheel.

2 Clean the area around the wheel sensor located on a bracket bolted to the hub carrier/strut.

3 Using an Allen key, unscrew the mounting bolt then remove the sensor from the bracket.

4 Release the cable supports, then disconnect the plug located in the engine compartment. Withdraw the sensor from the vehicle.

Refitting

5 Refitting is a reversal of removal.

Front wheel sensors (1996-on models)

Removal

6 Apply the handbrake, then jack up the front of the vehicle and support it on axle stands (see *"Jacking and vehicle support"*). Remove the roadwheel.

Left-hand side

7 Working in the left-hand rear corner of the engine compartment, remove the fusebox and position it to one side without disconnecting the wiring.

8 Disconnect the front wheel sensor wiring at the connector near the fusebox by depressing the catch and releasing it.

9 Release the wiring from the cable tie on the front suspension strut.

10 Disconnect the low fluid warning lamp wiring from the coolant expansion tank, then undo the mounting screws and position the tank to one side.

11 Unscrew the mounting bolt and remove the sensor from the bracket **(see illustration)**.

12 Prise the rubber grommet from the inner wing panel, and release the cable supports. Withdraw the sensor from the vehicle.

Right-hand side

13 Working in the right-hand of the engine compartment, unclip the air cleaner upper casing and position it to one side together with the airflow meter.

22.11 Removing the ABS front left-hand side wheel sensor

14 Release the cable ties, and disconnect the sensor wiring located at the front of the air cleaner.

15 Unscrew the mounting bolt and remove the sensor from the bracket.

16 Prise the rubber grommet from the inner wing panel, and release the cable supports. Withdraw the sensor from the vehicle.

Refitting

17 Refitting is a reversal of removal, however lubricate the rubber grommet with soapy water as an aid to refitting it in the inner wing panel. Renew cable ties as necessary.

Rear wheel sensors

Removal

18 The rear wheel sensors are integral with the rear wheel hubs. First, chock the front wheels, then jack up the rear of the vehicle and support on axle stands (see "*Jacking and vehicle support*"). Remove the roadwheel.

19 Carefully press the brake pads into their cylinders in the caliper until they are clear of the rear brake disc. To do this, use a large pair of pliers on the metal backing plates. Do not use a screwdriver against the friction linings, as this will cause damage.

20 Carefully release the rear brake hydraulic line from the clip on the rear axle, taking care not to bend the line excessively.

21 Unscrew and remove the mounting bolts securing the caliper to the backplate, then withdraw the caliper together with the pads from the disc and tie it to one side. A convenient place to secure the caliper on the left-hand side, is to the exhaust system, using a long plastic cable tie.

22 Using a screwdriver through the access hole, back off the handbrake shoe adjustment (see Section 15).

23 Unhook the handbrake cable return spring from the hole in the backplate and from the cable end fitting.

24 Unhook the handbrake cable end fitting from the handbrake operating lever on the backplate.

25 Undo the securing screw and withdraw the rear disc from the hub.

26 Disconnect the wiring from the wheel sensor on the rear of the hub **(see illustration)**.

22.26 ABS rear wheel sensor wiring

27 Unscrew the mounting nuts and withdraw the hub assembly from the rear axle. At the same time recover the backplate and handbrake shoes, and also the spacer which is located next to the axle. **Note:** *It is recommended that the mounting nuts are renewed.*

Refitting

28 Clean the mounting faces of the rear axle, backplate, spacer and hub then mount the components in the correct order (ie spacer, backplate and hub). Fit and tighten the new nuts to the torque wrench setting and angle given in the Specifications.

29 Reconnect the wiring to the wheel sensor.

30 Refit the rear disc (see Section 9) and adjust the handbrake shoes (see Section 15).

31 Reconnect the handbrake cable and return spring.

32 Refit the brake caliper and pads over the disc, then apply a little locking fluid to the threads of the mounting bolts and insert them. Tighten them to the specified torque.

33 Refit the hydraulic line in the clip.

34 Refit the roadwheel, then lower the vehicle to the ground.

35 Depress the footbrake pedal firmly to set the rear brake pads in their normal running position.

Electronic control unit (pre-1996 models)

Removal

Note: *Treat the ECU with care as it contains delicate electronic components, and do not attempt to connect multi-testers or meters to the multiplug terminals. As a precaution against damage from static electricity, do not touch the terminals.*

36 Disconnect the battery negative (earth) lead (see Chapter 5A).

37 The ABS ECU is mounted on the hydraulic unit located in the left-hand rear of the engine compartment **(see illustration)**. First undo the Torx screw and lift the cover from the unit.

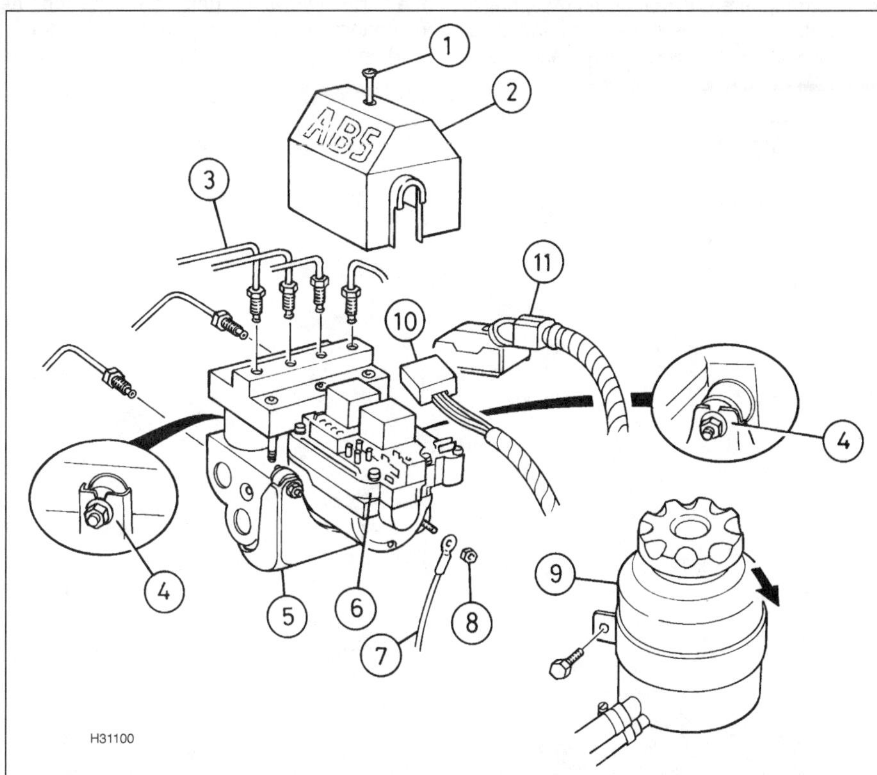

22.37 ABS hydraulic unit and ECU on pre-1996 models

1 Torx screw
2 Cover
3 Hydraulic pipes
4 Hydraulic unit mounting nuts
5 Hydraulic unit body
6 ECU
7 Earth cable
8 Nut
9 Power steering fluid reservoir
10 Small wiring connector
11 Large wiring connector

9

38 Disconnect two multiplugs noting where they are located.
39 Unscrew the mounting bolts and lift the ECU from the hydraulic unit.

Refitting

40 Refitting is a reversal of removal, but on completion, switch on the ignition and check that the warning lamps go out normally.

Electronic control unit (1996-on models)

Removal

Note: *Treat the ECU with care as it contains delicate electronic components, and do not attempt to connect multi-testers or meters to the multiplug terminals. As a precaution against damage from static electricity, do not touch the terminals.*
41 Disconnect the battery negative (earth) lead (see Chapter 5A).
42 The ABS ECU is mounted on the hydraulic unit located in the left-hand rear of the engine compartment. Release the cover then disconnect the two wiring connectors.
43 Undo the retaining screws and lift the ECU from the hydraulic unit. Leave the washers in place on the hydraulic unit.

Refitting

44 Refitting is a reversal of removal, but on completion, switch on the ignition and check that the warning lamps go out normally.
Caution: Make sure that the washers are refitted beneath the retaining screws.

ABS hydraulic unit (pre-1996 models)

Removal

45 Disconnect the battery negative (earth) lead (see Chapter 5A).
46 Unbolt and remove the steady bar from the front suspension top mountings.
47 Undo the Torx screw and lift the cover from the top of the ABS ECU.
48 Disconnect the two multiplugs noting where they are located.
49 Unscrew the nut and disconnect the earth cable from the hydraulic unit.
50 Minimise fluid loss by first removing the master cylinder reservoir cap, then tightening it down onto a piece of polythene to obtain an airtight seal.
51 Identify each hydraulic brake pipe for its location on the hydraulic unit, then unscrew the union nuts and disconnect the pipes. Tape over or plug the apertures and pipe ends.
52 If necessary for improved access, unbolt the power steering fluid reservoir and position it to one side.
53 Unscrew the mounting nuts and remove the ABS hydraulic unit from the engine compartment. Take care not to spill hydraulic fluid on the vehicle paintwork.

Refitting

54 Refitting is a reversal of removal, but finally bleed the hydraulic system as described in Section 2.

ABS hydraulic unit (1996-on models)

Removal

55 Disconnect the battery negative (earth) lead (see Chapter 5A).
56 Working in the left-hand rear corner of the engine compartment, remove the fusebox and position it to one side without disconnecting the wiring.
57 Release the cover then disconnect the two wiring connectors.
58 Minimise fluid loss by first removing the master cylinder reservoir cap, then tightening it down onto a piece of polythene to obtain an airtight seal.
59 Identify each hydraulic brake pipe for its location on the hydraulic unit, then unscrew the union nuts and disconnect the pipes. Tape over or plug the apertures and pipe ends.
60 Unscrew the mounting nuts and remove the ABS hydraulic unit from the engine compartment. Take care not to spill hydraulic fluid on the vehicle paintwork.

Refitting

61 Refitting is a reversal of removal, but finally bleed the hydraulic system as described in Section 2.

Chapter 10
Suspension and steering

Contents

Degrees of difficulty

Easy, suitable for novice with little experience 	**Fairly easy,** suitable for beginner with some experience 	**Fairly difficult,** suitable for competent DIY mechanic	**Difficult,** suitable for experienced DIY mechanic 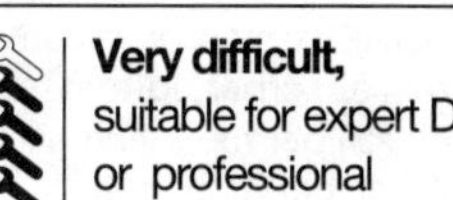	**Very difficult,** suitable for expert DIY or professional

Specifications

General

Front suspension type	Independent with MacPherson struts and anti-roll bar. Struts incorporate gas-filled shock absorbers and coil springs. Lower arms and radius arms.
Rear suspension type	Semi-rigid axle beam, consisting of spring links connected by intermediate section which acts as torsion bar. Two anti-roll bars, one internal and the other external, coil springs and gas-filled shock absorbers
Steering type	Rack-and-pinion, hydraulic power assistance on all models

Coil springs

Front suspension free length	340 to 350 mm (colour coded)
Rear suspension free length	215 mm

Wheel alignment (vehicle unladen):

Front:	
Toe-in	1.5 ± 0.5 mm (measured between inner rims)
Camber	-0.5° ± 0.5°
Castor	2.1° ± 0.5°
Kingpin inclination	13.1°
Rear:	
Toe	1.0 mm toe-out to 3.0 mm toe-in
Camber	-2.0° to -1.4°
Steering angle toe-out on turns:	
Outer wheel	20.0°
Inner wheel	20.9 ± 0.5°

Tyres

Size	6 x 15 or 6.5 x 16
Pressures	See end of "*Weekly checks*"

Power steering

Steering wheel turns, lock to lock:	
Turbo models	3.0 turns
Except Turbo models	3.4 turns

Torque wrench settings

	Nm	lbf ft
Front suspension		
Front suspension lower balljoint to hub carrier/strut	75	55
Front anti-roll bar to lower suspension arm support bar	10	7
Front anti-roll bar to subframe	26	19
Driveshaft nut	290	214
Strut top mounting bolts	18	13
Shock absorber upper nut to strut mounting	90	66
Shock absorber sleeve nut	215	159
Front anti-roll bar link lower nut	10	7
Front anti-roll bar clamp bolts	26	19
Radius arm to subframe:		
Stage 1	100	74
Stage 2	Angle-tighten 75° to 90°	
Radius arm to lower arm	92	68
Lower arm to subframe	115	85
Front suspension lower balljoint	75	55
Subframe centre mounting to underbody	190	140
Subframe front mounting to underbody	115	85
Rear suspension		
Rear axle to body mounting	65	48
Rear hub to spring link:		
Stage 1	50	37
Stage 2	Angle-tighten 30° to 45°	
Rear shock absorber top mounting	20	15
Rear shock absorber bottom mounting	62	46
Outer anti-roll bar mounting	24	18
Inner anti-roll bar mounting:		
Stage 1	60	44
Stage 2	Angle-tighten 60° to 75°	
Tie-down bracket to rear axle	24	18
Steering		
Track rod end to steering arm	60	44
Track rod end/track rod clamp bolts	22	16
Steering gear mounting bolts	24	18
Steering wheel	30	22
Track rod to steering gear	93	69
Power steering pump	20	15
Wheels		
Roadwheel bolts:		
Alloy	117	86
Steel	100	74

1 General information

The front suspension is fully independent, utilising MacPherson struts and an anti-roll bar. The struts incorporate coil springs and gas-filled shock absorbers, and are integral with the hub carriers. The shock absorbers can be renewed separate to the strut. The struts are located on the outer ends of the lower arms by balljoints. The lower arms are supported by radius arms attached to the rear of the subframe. On early models the anti-roll bar locates in the radius arms, however on later models it locates in the lower arms. The front lower suspension arms and radius arms are connected to the subframe by rubber bushes, and the balljoints are integral with the lower arms. The front hubs are located in double race bearings pressed into the hub carriers, and the driveshafts are splined to the hubs and retained by single hub nuts and thrustwashers.

The rear suspension is of semi-rigid type, incorporating trailing arms connected by a crossbar. Two anti-roll bars are fitted between the trailing arms, one internal and the other external. The trailing arms pivot at their front extensions in rubber bushes located on the underbody, and gas-filled shock absorbers are fitted between the rear ends of the arms and mountings on the underbody. The rear coil springs are located between the trailing arms and the underbody, and are supported at their upper ends in polyurethane seats and at the lower ends in rubber seats. The rear hubs and bearings are supplied as integral units which cannot be dismantled, and they are attached to the trailing arms by studs and nuts. Each rear hub incorporates an internal ABS sensor to monitor the wheel speed **(see illustration)**.

A power-assisted, rack-and-pinion steering system is fitted to all models. The steering rack is essentially a hydraulic ram, which is actuated mechanically by a pinion gear, and

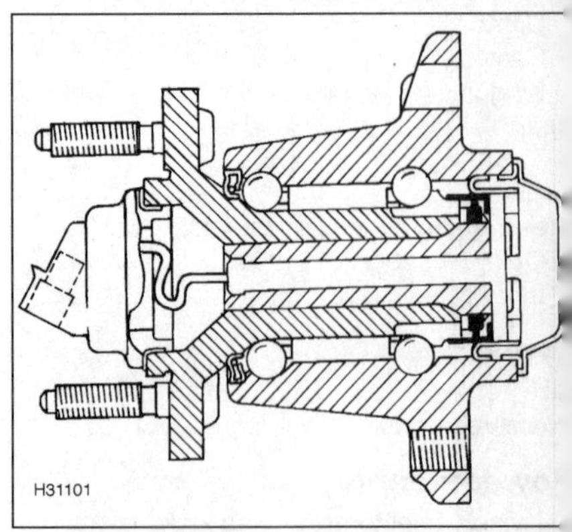

1.2 Cross section of the rear hub and bearing

2.6 Removing the caliper bracket mounting bolts and locking plate

2.13a Unscrew the upper mounting nut . . .

2.13b . . . and lower the strut from under the front wing

hydraulically by pressurised hydraulic fluid, supplied by the power steering pump. The steering column transmits effort applied at the steering wheel to the pinion and a control valve, which manages the supply of hydraulic fluid to the steering rack. When the steering wheel is turned, the valve directs fluid to the appropriate side of the ram, assisting the movement of the rack. The inner ends of the track rods are attached to the rack at the centre of the steering gear, unlike the more conventional method of attaching them to the ends of the rack. The outer ends of the track rods are attached to the steering arms on the struts/hub carriers by balljoints. The power steering pump is mounted externally on the engine, and is driven by the auxiliary drivebelt.

The design and mounting position of the steering column are such that, in the event of a head-on collision, it will absorb impact by crumpling longitudinally, and will also be deflected away from the driver.

2 Front suspension strut/hub carrier - removal, overhaul and refitting

Removal

Note: *Refer to the MOT Section at the rear of the Manual in order to check the shock absorbers before removing them. To ensure even handling, both front shock absorbers must be renewed at the same time.*

1 Before raising the front of the vehicle, prise off the wheel trim for access to the hub nut (driveshaft nut). Loosen the hub nut and the roadwheel bolts.

2 Apply the handbrake, then jack up the front of the vehicle and support it on axle stands (see "*Jacking and vehicle support*"). Remove the roadwheel.

3 Fully unscrew and remove the hub nut.

4 Undo the retaining screw and remove the ABS sensor from the strut/hub carrier.

5 Using a pair of grips, press the inner brake pad a little way into its cylinder so that the pads are clear of the disc.

6 Unscrew the caliper bracket mounting bolts and remove the locking plate, then withdraw the caliper and pads from the disc **(see illustration)**. Tie the caliper to one side taking care not to bend the hydraulic hose excessively.

7 Undo the screw and remove the brake disc.

8 Unbolt and remove the splash guard.

9 Unscrew the nut and disconnect the track rod end from the steering arm on the strut with reference to Section 19.

10 Unscrew the nut and remove the washer securing the anti-roll bar link to the radius arm (early models) or lower arm (later models). Pull out the anti-roll bar and recover the rubber bushes and upper washer.

11 Unscrew the nut from the lower balljoint and use a separator tool to separate the lower arm from the strut/hub carrier. Discard the nut as it is self-locking and must be renewed.

12 Pull out the bottom of the strut and at the same time push the driveshaft through the hub until clear of the splines.

13 Support the strut under the front wing, then unscrew the upper mounting nuts from inside the engine compartment. Lower the strut and remove it from under the front wing **(see illustrations)**.

Overhaul

⚠ ***Warning: Before attempting to dismantle the front suspension strut, the coil spring must be first held in compression, using a suitable tool. Adjustable coil spring compressors are readily-available, and are essential for this operation. DO NOT attempt to dismantle the strut without such a tool, as damage and/or personal injury is likely.***

Note: *A new shock absorber top mounting nut must be used on reassembly.*

14 Support the strut by clamping it in a vice; avoid damaging the surface of the strut by lining the vice jaws with aluminium or wooden blocks.

15 Using the spring compressor, compress the coils of the spring just enough to relieve all pressure from the upper spring seat **(see illustration)**.

16 Unscrew the nut from the top of the shock absorber piston rod while holding the rod with a socket on the hexagon **(see illustrations)**. Discard the nut and obtain a new one.

⚠ ***Warning: Ensure that the upper spring seat has been completely relieved of spring pressure before removing the retaining nut.***

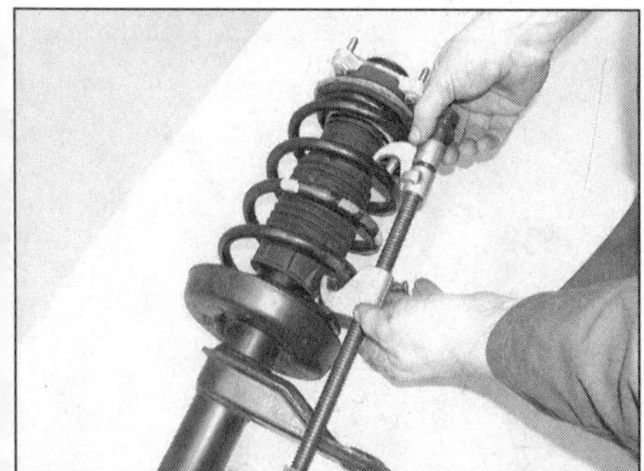
2.15 Compress the front coil spring using a purpose-made coil spring compressor

2.16a Loosen the strut upper nut while holding the rod with a socket

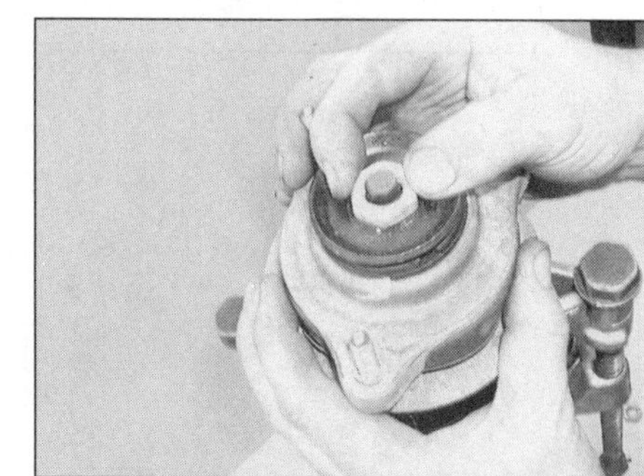
2.16b Removing the strut upper nut

2.17a Remove the cupped washer . . .

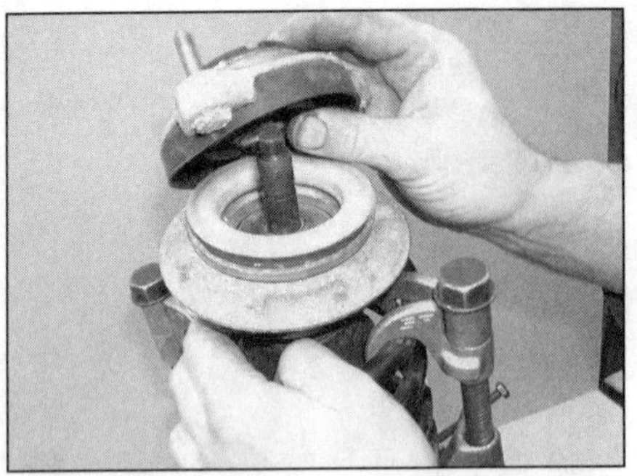
2.17b . . . followed by the top mounting and thrust bearing . . .

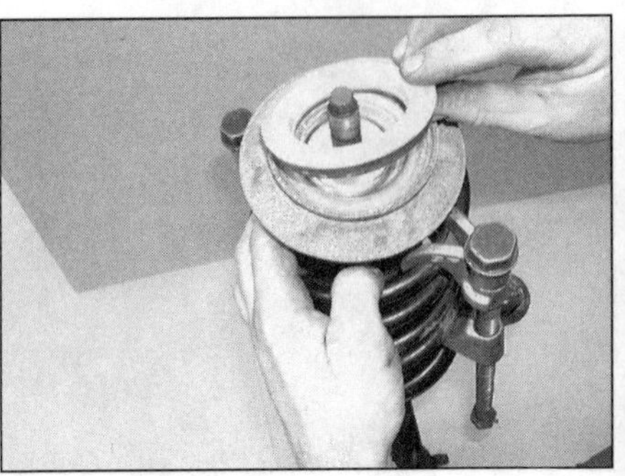
2.17c . . . washer . . .

17 Remove the cupped washer followed by the top mounting, thrust bearing, washer, buffer, and upper spring seat **(see illustrations)**.

18 Remove the coil spring (making sure that the compressor remains firmly attached to it) and the bump stop **(see illustrations)**.

19 To remove the shock absorber, unscrew the sleeve nut. As this is quite large, it may prove better to clamp the nut in a vice and unscrew the strut/hub carrier from it. As a rough guide to tightening the nut to the correct torque on reassembly, mark the nut in relation to the strut before loosening it. With the nut removed, lift out the shock absorber.

20 Clean all the components and examine them for wear and damage. Renew the components as necessary. Check the upper mounting bearing for smooth operation by turning it by hand. Hub bearing renewal is described in Section 6.

21 Insert the shock absorber and secure with the sleeve nut, tightened to the specified torque given in the Specifications.

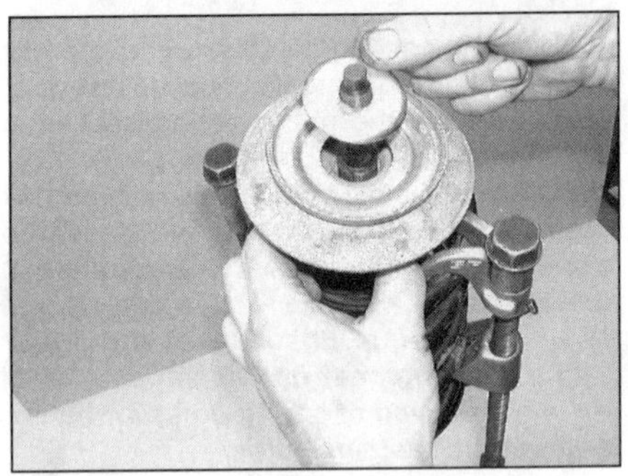
2.17d . . . buffer . . .

22 Locate the bottom end of the coil spring in the strut, making sure its end abuts the location stop.

23 Locate the bump stop onto the piston rod.

24 Fit the upper spring seat on top of the spring, making sure the end stop abuts the end of the spring.

25 Fit the buffer, washer (with its part number facing downwards), thrust bearing, top mounting, and cupped washer.

26 Fit the new nut to the top of the shock absorber piston rod, and tighten it to the specified torque while holding the rod stationary with a spanner on the hexagon.

27 Carefully loosen the spring compressor while at the same time making sure the spring ends located correctly in the upper and lower spring seats. Remove the compressor.

Refitting

28 Locate the strut/hub carrier under the front wing and lift it into position while guiding the mounting studs through the holes in the inner wing. Fit the nuts and progressively tighten to the specified torque.

29 Pull out the bottom of the strut, then engage the hub with the driveshaft splines and slide the hub on until it is possible to screw on the new hub nut a few threads.

30 Locate the bottom of the strut/hub carrier on the balljoint stud and fit the new nut. Tighten the nut to the specified torque.

31 Fit the anti-roll bar link to the radius arm (early models) or lower arm (later models) together with the rubber bushes and washers. Fit and tighten the nut to the specified torque.

32 Reconnect the track rod end to the steering arm on the strut and tighten the nut to the specified torque with reference to Section 19.

33 Refit the splash guard and tighten the bolts securely.

34 Clean the contact faces then refit the brake disc and tighten the screw.

35 Refit the caliper together with the pads over the disc, and tighten the mounting bolts to the specified torque (refer to Chapter 9). Make sure the hydraulic hose is not twisted.

36 Refit the ABS sensor to the strut bracket and tighten the screw securely.

37 Tighten the hub nut moderately at this stage.

38 Refit the roadwheel and lower the vehicle to the ground.

39 Fully tighten the hub nut to the specified torque.

40 Tighten the roadwheel bolts to the specified torque.

41 Refit the wheel trim, then depress the footbrake pedal several times in order to move the brake pads to their normal working position.

3 Front suspension lower arm - removal, overhaul and refitting

Removal

1 Apply the handbrake, then jack up the front of the vehicle and support it on axle stands (see "*Jacking and vehicle support*"). Remove the roadwheel.

2.17e . . . and upper spring seat . . .

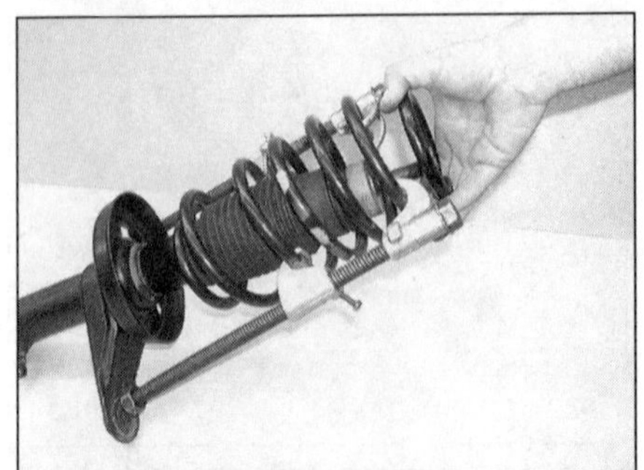
2.18a . . . front coil spring . . .

2.18b . . . and bump stop

3.3a Front suspension lower arm and balljoint nut

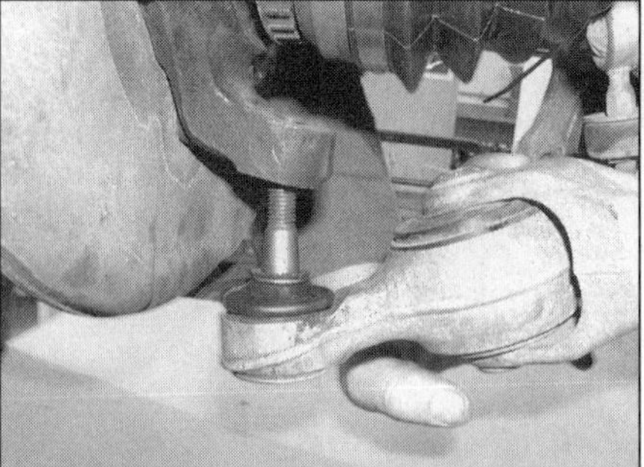

3.3b Separate the lower arm from the strut/hub carrier

3.4 Bolt securing the radius arm to the lower arm

2 Unscrew the nut and remove the washer securing the anti-roll bar link to the radius arm (early models) or lower arm (later models). Pull out the anti-roll bar and recover the rubber bushes and upper washer.
3 Unscrew the nut from the lower balljoint and use a separator tool to separate the lower arm from the strut/hub carrier **(see illustrations)**. Discard the nut as it is self-locking and must be renewed.
4 Using a Torx key, unscrew and remove the bolt securing the radius arm to the lower arm, then lever the radius arm away from the lower arm **(see illustration)**.
5 Unscrew and remove the inner pivot bolt from the front of the subframe, then ease out the lower arm and withdraw from under the vehicle **(see illustration)**.

Overhaul

6 It is not possible to renew the lower balljoint separate to the lower arm, although the balljoint rubber boot may be obtained separately. If the lower balljoint is worn excessively, the lower arm must be renewed complete.
7 Similarly, the inner pivot bush cannot be renewed separate to the arm.
8 If the radius arm location bush in the lower arm is worn, it can be removed using a press and a new one fitted.
9 Check the lower arm for damage and if necessary renew it.

Refitting

10 Locate the lower arm in the subframe and insert the pivot bolt from the front. Hand-tighten the bolt at this stage, as it must be fully tightened with the weight of the vehicle on the front suspension.
11 Press the radius arm onto the lower arm, align the holes, and insert the bolt. Fully tighten the bolt to the specified torque.
12 Locate the lower balljoint stud in the bottom of the strut/hub carrier, then fit the new nut and tighten to the specified torque.
13 Fit the anti-roll bar link to the radius arm (early models) or lower arm (later models) together with the rubber bushes and washers. Fit and tighten the nut to the specified torque.
14 Refit the roadwheel and lower the vehicle to the ground.

4 Front suspension radius arm - removal, overhaul and refitting

Removal

1 Apply the handbrake, then jack up the front of the vehicle and support it on axle stands (see "*Jacking and vehicle support*"). Remove the roadwheel.
2 On early models, unscrew the nut and remove the washer securing the anti-roll bar link to the radius arm. Pull out the anti-roll bar and recover the rubber bushes and upper washer.
3 Unscrew and remove the bolt securing the radius arm to the lower arm, then lever the radius arm away from the lower arm.
4 Unscrew and remove the bolt securing the radius arm to the subframe, then ease out the radius arm and withdraw from under the vehicle **(see illustration)**.

Overhaul

5 Check the inner rubber bush for wear and damage, and if necessary renew it using a press to force out the old bush and insert the new one.
6 Check the radius arm location bush in the lower arm and if necessary renew it by removing the lower arm as described in Section 3.
7 Check the radius arm for damage and if necessary renew it.

Refitting

8 Locate the radius arm inner end in the subframe making sure that the concave side is facing outwards. Insert the bolt, hand-tight at this stage.
9 Locate the outer end of the arm on the lower arm and insert the bolt and nut. Fully tighten both the inner and outer bolts to their specified torque.
10 On early models, locate the anti-roll bar link on the radius arm together with the rubber bushes and washers. Fit and tighten the securing nut.
11 Refit the roadwheel and lower the vehicle to the ground.

3.5 Front suspension lower arm inner pivot bolt

5 Front anti-roll bar - removal, overhaul and refitting

Removal

1 Apply the handbrake, then jack up the front of the vehicle and support it on axle stands (see "*Jacking and vehicle support*"). Remove both roadwheels.
2 The engine assembly must be supported while the subframe is removed. To do this, use a suitable hoist or engine support bar which straddles the engine compartment. Slightly lift the engine assembly so that its weight is supported.
3 Unscrew the clamp bolts connecting the exhaust downpipe to the intermediate section, then separate and lower the front section and suspend it with wire or string from the underbody.

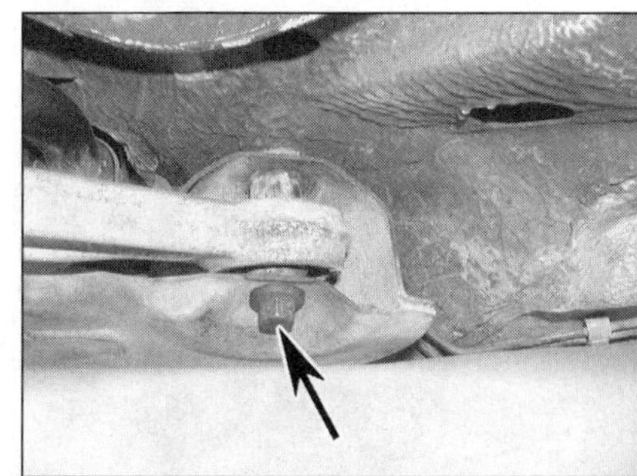

4.4 Bolt securing the radius arm to the subframe

5.7a Unscrew the front anti-roll bar nuts . . .

5.7b . . . and recover the lower washer and rubber mounting

5.11 Front anti-roll bar link nuts

4 Support the subframe using a trolley jack.
5 Loosen the subframe front mounting bolts but do not remove them.
6 At the rear of the subframe, unscrew and remove the four mounting bolts and the two mounting nuts. Lower the subframe as far as possible.
7 Unscrew the nuts securing the anti-roll bar links to the radius arm (early models) or lower arm (later models), and recover the lower washer and rubber mounting **(see illustrations)**.
8 Unscrew the bolts and unhook the mounting clamps.
9 Lift the anti-roll bar and withdraw it from one side. Recover the link upper washers and rubber mountings.
10 Remove the split clamp mounting rubbers from the anti-roll bar.

Overhaul

11 Check the anti-roll bar and mountings for signs of wear and damage. If necessary, unscrew the nuts and remove the side links, then fit new ones and tighten the nuts **(see illustration)**.
12 Check the split clamp mounting rubbers and renew them if necessary.

Refitting

13 Dip the split clamp mounting rubbers in soapy water and locate them on the anti-roll bar.
14 Locate the upper washers and rubber mountings on the links.
15 Check that the mounting rubbers and washers are in place on the links, then insert the anti-roll bar onto the subframe and locate the links in the radius arm (early models) or lower arm (later models).
16 Position the split clamp mounting rubbers and fit the clamps. Insert the clamp mounting bolts hand-tight at this stage.
17 Fit the lower rubber mountings and washers to the anti-roll bar links, then tighten the nuts to the specified torque.
18 Fully tighten the clamp mounting bolts to the specified torque.
19 Raise the subframe and insert the four rear mounting bolts and two nuts. Note that the washers on the rear bolts must contact the underbody. Fully tighten all the subframe mounting bolts and nuts to the specified torque.
20 Reconnect the exhaust downpipe to the intermediate section and fit the clamp. Tighten the clamp bolts to the specified torque as given in Chapter 4A Specifications.
21 Remove the hoist or support bar.
22 Refit the roadwheels and lower the vehicle to the ground.

6.3 Inner circlip securing the front hub bearing in the front suspension strut/hub

6 Front hub bearing - renewal

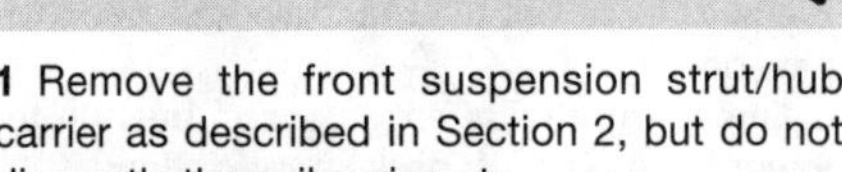

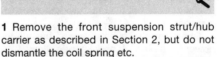

1 Remove the front suspension strut/hub carrier as described in Section 2, but do not dismantle the coil spring etc.
2 Support the hub carrier on its outer point behind the hub flange. This is best achieved on an hydraulic press. Press or drive the hub from the bearings using a metal tube or large socket in contact with the inner end of the hub. **Note:** *The action of pressing out the hub may damage the bearing, therefore it is not recommended that a removed bearing is re-used.*
3 Using circlip pliers, extract the circlips from each side of the hub bearing **(see illustration)**.
4 Support the hub carrier again on its outer point and press or drive out the bearing using a metal tube or large socket in contact with the bearing outer race.
5 Clean the hub and the inside of the hub carrier.
6 Using the circlip pliers, fit the outer circlip to its groove in the hub carrier, positioning the circlip opening at the bottom.
7 Smear some multi-purpose grease on the outer periphery of the bearing and in the hub carrier.
8 Support the outer point of the hub carrier and press or drive in the bearing until it contacts the outer circlip, using a metal tube or large socket on the bearing outer race.
9 Using the circlip pliers, fit the inner circlip to its groove in the hub carrier, positioning the circlip opening at the bottom.
10 Support the inner end of the bearing with a metal tube or large socket on the inner race, then press or drive in the hub from the outside.
11 Refit the front suspension strut/hub carrier as described in Section 2.

7 Rear shock absorber - removal and refitting

Note: *To ensure even handling, both rear shock absorbers must be renewed at the same time.*

Removal

1 Position the rear of the vehicle over an inspection pit or on car ramps. Alternatively, raise and support the rear of the vehicle (see "*Jacking and vehicle support*"), then remove the roadwheel and support the rear axle with an axle stand or trolley jack on the appropriate side.
2 Open the tailgate for access to the rear shock absorber turret. Using a sharp knife, cut open a flap in the trim as shown **(see illustration)**.

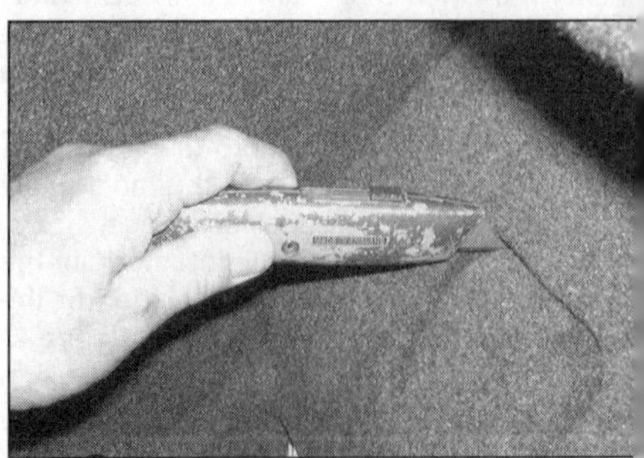

7.2 Access to the shock absorber upper mounting nut is gained by cutting open a flap in the rear luggage compartment

3 Unscrew the rear shock absorber upper mounting nut and recover the washer and rubber bush.
4 Working beneath the vehicle, unscrew and remove the lower mounting bolt **(see illustration)**.
5 Withdraw the rear shock absorber, then remove the remaining rubber bush from the top of the shock absorber.
6 Examine the rubber bushes for wear and damage, and renew them if necessary. Note that the lower bush may be pressed out of the shock absorber and a new one fitted. Dip the new bush in soapy water before pressing it into position.

Refitting

7 Refitting is a reversal of removal, but tighten the mounting bolt/nut to the specified torque.

8 Rear anti-roll bar - removal and refitting

Outer anti-roll bar

Removal

1 Chock the front wheels, then jack up the rear of the vehicle and support on axle stands positioned clear of the rear anti-roll bar (see *"Jacking and vehicle support"*). Remove both rear roadwheels.
2 Unscrew the mounting bolts and lower the anti-roll bar from the rear axle **(see illustration)**.
3 Remove the nut plate from the rear axle flange.
4 Examine the anti-roll bar for damage or distortion and renew it as necessary.

Refitting

5 Refitting is a reversal of removal, but tighten the mounting bolts to the specified torque.

Inner anti-roll bar

Removal

6 Chock the front wheels, then jack up the rear of the vehicle and support on axle stands (see *"Jacking and vehicle support"*). Remove both rear roadwheels.
7 Unscrew and remove the anti-roll bar mounting nuts and bolts located on the outer flanges of the rear axle.
8 Withdraw the anti-roll bar from one side of the rear axle, pulling it through one of the mounting apertures. Release it from the central rubber block at the same time.

Refitting

9 Before refitting the anti-roll bar, smear it with a little grease before sliding it into the rear axle. Check that it is located correctly in the rubber block.
10 Tighten the mounting nuts and bolts to the specified torque and angle.
11 Refit the roadwheels, and lower the vehicle to the ground.

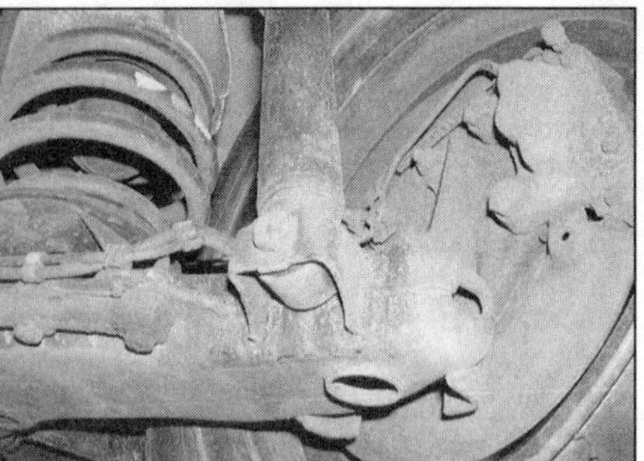

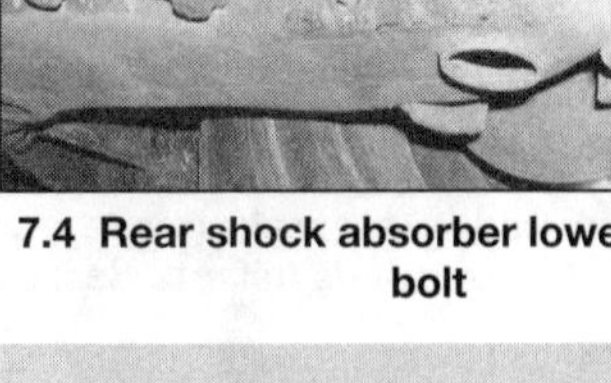

7.4 Rear shock absorber lower mounting bolt

9 Rear coil spring - removal and refitting

Note: *To ensure equal ride heights on each side of the vehicle, both rear coil springs must be renewed at the same time.*

Removal

1 Chock the front wheels, then jack up the rear of the vehicle and support on axle stands (see *"Jacking and Vehicle Support"*). Remove the roadwheel.
2 Position a trolley jack beneath the trailing arm and slightly raise it.
3 Unscrew and remove the rear shock absorber lower mounting bolt.
4 Lower the trailing arm as far as possible and remove the trolley jack.
5 Check for any markings on the rear face of the coil spring - if there are no markings, use a dab of paint to ensure that the spring is refitted the same way around **(see illustration)**.
6 Insert a suitable lever in the shock absorber lower mounting, and lever down the trailing arm sufficient to remove the coil spring.
7 Recover the upper spring seat and bump stop, and the lower spring seat.
8 Clean the spring seat locations on the rear axle and underbody.

Refitting

9 Locate the lower spring seat on the rear axle.
10 Position the upper spring seat in the coil spring.

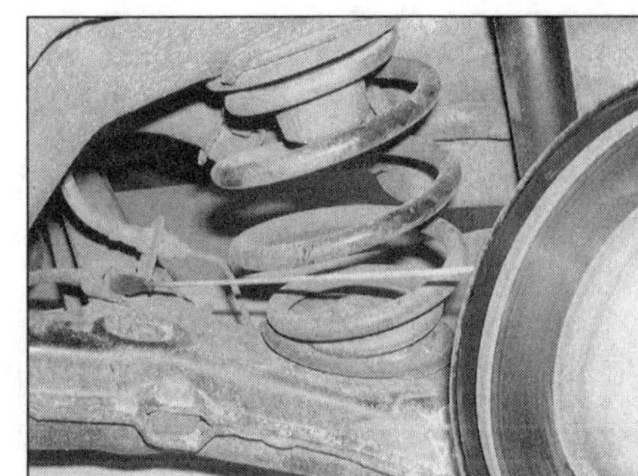

9.5 Rear coil spring

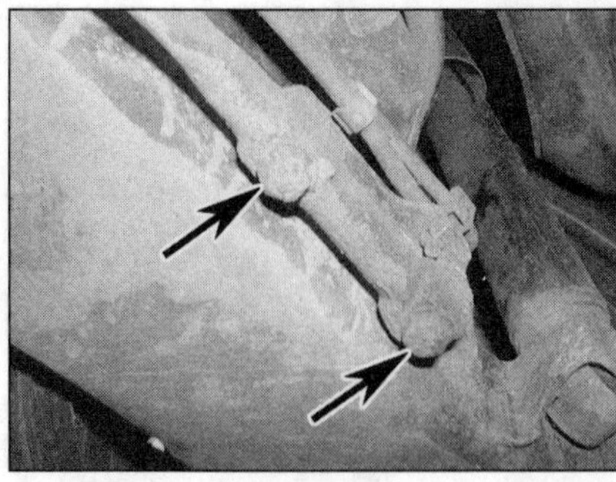

8.2 Mounting bolts for the rear outer anti-roll bar

11 Lever down the trailing arm, then refit the coil spring and upper seat making sure that the marking faces rearwards.
12 Raise the trailing arm with the trolley jack until the shock absorber can be located in its lower mounting. Insert the bolt and tighten to the specified torque.
13 Remove the trolley jack, then refit the roadwheel and lower the vehicle to the ground.

10 Rear axle assembly - removal, overhaul and refitting

Removal

1 Chock the front wheels, then jack up the rear of the vehicle and support on axle stands (see *"Jacking and Vehicle Support"*). Remove both rear roadwheels.
2 Disconnect the wiring from the ABS sensors on both sides, and release the wiring from the trailing arms.
3 Unhook the handbrake cable return springs from the holes in the backplates and from the cable end fittings.
4 Working on each side, press the handbrake cable guide sleeves from the brackets on the rear axle, and release the cables from the handbrake levers on the rear backplates. On the single handbrake cable, release the cable from the equalizer.
5 Remove the exhaust system rear silencer and tailpipe as described in Chapter 4A.
6 Remove the rear outer anti-roll bar as described in Section 8.
7 Before disconnecting the hydraulic line, minimise fluid loss by removing the master cylinder reservoir cap then tightening it down onto a piece of polythene to obtain an airtight seal. Alternatively, use a brake hose clamp, a G-clamp or a similar tool to clamp the flexible hose leading from the body to the brake line on the rear axle.
Caution: The unprotected jaws of a G-clamp should not be used, as they may damage the hose, leading to premature failure.
8 Clean the area around the hydraulic line union nuts, then unscrew the nuts from each rear caliper and flexible hose and remove the

10.14 Rear axle assembly side mounting bolt

hydraulic lines. Tape over or plug the hoses and caliper apertures to prevent the entry of dust and dirt.

9 Pull out the retaining clips and remove the hydraulic hoses from the supports.

10 Using a trolley jack, raise the trailing arm on one side of the rear axle then unscrew and remove the rear shock absorber lower mounting bolt and press the shock absorber out of the mounting.

11 Using a lever, press down the trailing arm and remove the coil spring and seat.

12 Support the rear brake caliper, disc and hub assembly, then unscrew and remove the hub mounting nuts from the inside of the trailing arm and lift off the assembly together with the spacer. Place the assembly to one side. Discard the nuts as new ones must be fitted on reassembly.

13 Repeat the procedure described in paragraphs 5 to 7 inclusive, and remove the hub assembly on the remaining side.

14 Support the middle of the rear axle with the trolley jack, then unscrew and remove the side mounting bolts **(see illustration)**.

15 Withdraw the rear axle from the underbody and remove from under the vehicle.

16 Remove the rear inner anti-roll bar and centre block as described in Section 8.

17 Unbolt the brake hose and handbrake cable support brackets. Also if necessary unbolt the tie-down bracket.

Overhaul

18 Check the rear axle bushes for wear and damage. If necessary, press out the old bushes using suitable metal tubes, a long bolt, nuts and washers.

19 Press in the new bushes using the same method, however note that they must be fitted with their compression holes in the horizontal plane.

Refitting

20 Refit the brake hose and handbrake cable support brackets and the tie-down bracket, and tighten the bolts to the specified torque.

21 Refit the rear inner anti-roll bar and centre block with reference to Section 8.

22 Position the rear axle on a trolley jack beneath the rear of the vehicle, and raise it onto the mountings. Insert the mounting bolts hand-tight at this stage.

23 Using the trolley jack, raise one of the trailing arms until the distance between the edge of the wheel arch and the upper edge of the hub centre is 37 cm. Tighten the rear axle mounting bolt on this side of the rear axle to the specified torque.

24 Locate the lower spring seat on the rear axle.

25 Position the upper spring seat in the coil spring.

26 Lever down the trailing arm, then refit the coil spring and upper seat making sure that the marking faces rearwards (refer to Section 9 if necessary).

27 Raise the trailing arm with the trolley jack until the shock absorber can be located in its lower mounting. Insert the bolt and tighten to the specified torque.

28 Repeat the procedure given in paragraphs 18 to 22 on the remaining side.

29 Locate the rear hub assemblies together with calipers and discs on the trailing arms, and secure with new nuts tightened to the specified torque. Make sure the spacers are positioned between the hubs and trailing arms.

30 Refit the hydraulic hoses to the supports and secure with the retaining clips.

31 Refit the hydraulic lines to each side and tighten the union nuts securely. Remove the hose clamps or polythene.

32 Refit the rear outer anti-roll bar with reference to Section 8 and tighten the mounting bolts to the specified torque.

33 Refit the exhaust system rear silencer and tailpipe with reference to Chapter 4A.

34 Working on each side, locate the handbrake cables in the brackets and connect the end fittings on the levers on the rear backplates. Also refit the equalizer on the single handbrake cable.

35 Reconnect the return springs to the holes in the backplates and cable end fittings.

36 Reconnect the ABS sensor wiring and support it with the clips.

37 Bleed the brake hydraulic system as described in Chapter 9.

38 Refit the rear roadwheels and lower the vehicle to the ground.

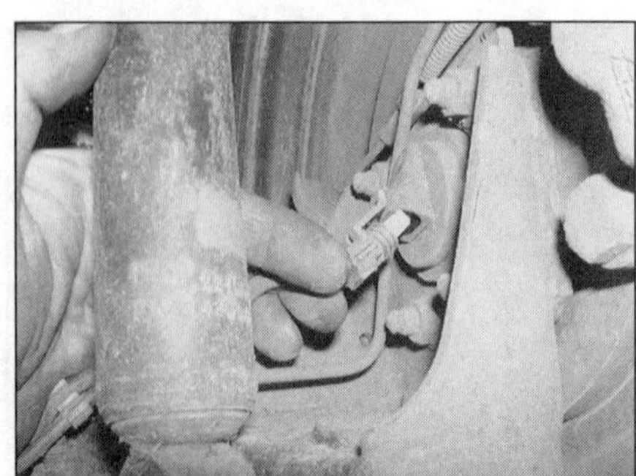

11.2 Disconnecting the wiring from the ABS sensor

11 Rear hub assembly - removal and refitting

Removal

1 Remove the rear brake disc as described in Chapter 9. Take care not to bend the brake line excessively, however, if preferred the line can be disconnected as described in Chapter 9 for the removal of the brake caliper.

2 Disconnect the wiring from the ABS sensor **(see illustration)**.

3 Unhook the handbrake cable return spring from the hole in the backplates and from the cable end fitting.

4 Release the handbrake cable from the lever on the rear backplate, then unhook the cable end fitting.

5 Support the hub and backplate assembly, then unscrew and remove the hub mounting nuts from the inside of the trailing arm and lift off the assembly together with the spacer. Place the assembly to one side. Discard the nuts as new ones must be fitted on reassembly.

6 Separate the hub from the backplate.

Refitting

7 Clean the contact surfaces of the hub, backplate, spacer and trailing arm.

8 Locate the backplate on the hub studs, followed by the spacer, then locate the assembly on the trailing arm and tighten the new nuts to the specified torque. Make sure the spacer is positioned between the hub and trailing arm.

9 Reconnect the handbrake cable end fitting on the backplate lever, then reconnect the return spring.

10 Reconnect the wiring to the ABS sensor.

11 Refit the rear brake disc with reference to Chapter 9. If removed, refit the brake caliper making sure that locking fluid is applied to the threads of the mounting bolts before tightening them.

12 If the brake caliper was removed, bleed the hydraulic system as described in Chapter 9.

12 Steering wheel - removal and refitting

Removal

1 Disconnect the battery negative (earth) lead (see Chapter 5A).

2 Turn the front wheels to the 'straight-ahead' position.

3 Remove the driver's airbag module from the steering wheel as described in Chapter 11.

Caution: Observe the safety instructions meticulously.

4 Disconnect the horn wiring from the steering wheel **(see illustration)**.

12.4 Disconnecting the horn wiring

12.5a Use a long breaker bar to loosen the steering wheel retaining nut

12.5b Removing the steering wheel retaining nut and washer

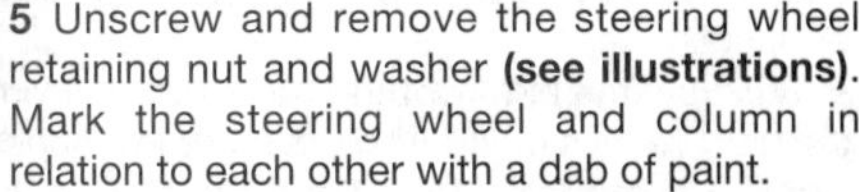

5 Unscrew and remove the steering wheel retaining nut and washer **(see illustrations)**. Mark the steering wheel and column in relation to each other with a dab of paint.

6 Carefully ease the steering wheel from the column splines while feeding the horn and airbag wiring through the hole **(see illustration**.

Caution: Do not use a hammer or mallet to tap the steering wheel from the splines, as this may damage the collapsible inner column. Also take care not to damage the contact roller located over the top of the column.

7 Using adhesive tape, secure the contact spring unit in its central position.

Refitting

8 Remove the adhesive tape from the contact spring unit. If its central position has been lost, first check that the front wheels are pointing straight-ahead, then turn the unit fully clockwise. Now turn the unit back 2.5 turns exactly.

9 Locate the steering wheel on the column splines, with the previously made marks aligned, while feeding the airbag wiring through the hole.

10 Refit the washer and retaining nut and tighten the nut to the specified torque.

11 Reconnect the horn wiring.

12 Refit the driver's airbag module with reference to Chapter 11.

13 Reconnect the battery negative (earth) lead (see Chapter 5A).

14 Have the vehicle electronic control system checked for fault codes by a Saab dealer.

13 Steering column - removal and refitting

Removal

1 Remove the steering wheel as described in Section 12.

2 Undo the crosshead screws and remove the upper and lower shrouds from the steering column.

3 Undo the screws and disconnect the wiring, then remove the contact spring unit. Keep it in its central position using adhesive tape.

4 Remove the combination switch from the steering column with reference to Chapter 12. Remove the stalk switches and cable from the bearing housing.

5 Remove the facia lower trim panel and the air duct **(see illustration)**.

6 Unscrew the bolts and remove the knee protection panel from under the steering column.

7 At the bottom of the steering column, unscrew and remove the clamp bolt and slide the universal joint from the steering gear pinion shaft **(see illustration)**. Mark the shaft and column if necessary to ensure correct refitting.

8 Unscrew and remove the column lower mounting bolt located above the ventilation duct **(see illustration)**.

9 Unscrew and remove the upper mounting nuts located beneath the instrument panel, then withdraw the steering column from the bulkhead bracket.

12.6 Removing the steering wheel while feeding the horn and airbag wiring through the hole

Refitting

10 Locate the steering column on the bulkhead bracket studs, and screw on the nuts loosely at this stage.

11 Engage the universal joint on the bottom of the column with the steering gear pinion shaft, making sure that the bolt hole is aligned with the cut-out in the shaft and the alignment marks are adjacent as previously noted. Tighten the clamp bolt to the specified torque.

12 Insert and tighten the column lower mounting bolt, then fully tighten the upper mounting nuts.

13 Refit the knee protection panel beneath the steering column.

14 Refit the facia lower trim panel.

15 Refit the combination switch to the steering column with reference to Chapter 12. Also refit the stalk switches and cable to the bearing housing.

13.5 Removing the air duct from under the right-hand side of the facia

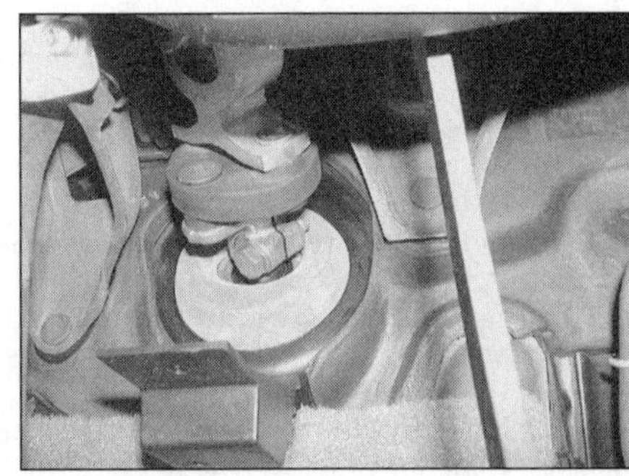

13.7 Steering column lower clamp bolt

13.8 Steering column upper and lower mounting bolts

16 Remove the adhesive tape from the contact spring unit. If its central position has been lost, first check that the front wheels are pointing straight-ahead, then turn the unit fully clockwise. Now turn the unit back 2.5 turns exactly. Tighten the mounting screws, then reconnect the wiring.

17 Refit the upper and lower shrouds, then refit the steering wheel as described in Section 12.

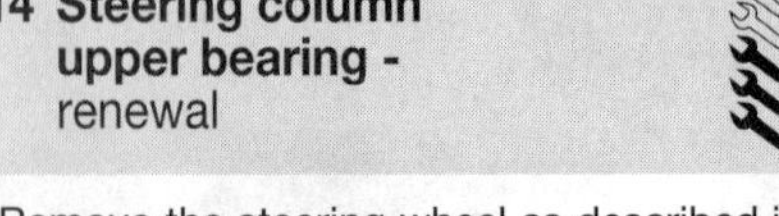

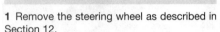

14 Steering column upper bearing - renewal

1 Remove the steering wheel as described in Section 12.

2 Undo the crosshead screws and remove the upper and lower shrouds from the steering column.

3 Undo the screws and disconnect the wiring, then remove the contact spring unit. Keep it in its central position using adhesive tape.

4 Remove the locking ring from the top of the column. Discard the ring as a new one must be fitted on reassembly.

5 Unbolt and remove the bearing housing.

6 Locate the new bearing housing over the top of the column and secure with the mounting bolt.

7 Fit the new locking ring.

8 Remove the adhesive tape from the contact spring unit. If its central position has been lost, first check that the front wheels are pointing straight-ahead, then turn the unit fully clockwise. Now turn the unit back 2.5 turns exactly. Tighten the mounting screws, then reconnect the wiring.

9 Refit the upper and lower shrouds and tighten the screws.

10 Refit the steering wheel as described in Section 12.

15 Power steering hydraulic system - draining, refilling and bleeding

Note: *The power steering hydraulic system must be bled if any part of the system has been disconnected.*

Draining

1 To drain the complete hydraulic system of fluid, position a container (having a capacity of at least one litre) beneath the power steering pump on the right-hand front of the engine. Loosen the clip and disconnect the return hose from the pump. Allow the fluid to drain into the container from the return hose.

2 Secure the container in the engine bay, away from any moving components and direct sources of heat. Start the engine, and allow the hydraulic fluid to be pumped into the container. Turn the steering lock-to-lock several times, to purge the fluid from the steering rack. When the flow of fluid ceases, turn off the engine immediately; **do not** allow the power steering pump to run dry for any length of time.

3 Reconnect the return hose and tighten the clip.

Refilling

4 Remove the fluid reservoir filler cap, and top-up to the maximum level mark with fluid of the specified type and grade; refer to "*Weekly checks*" for guidance.

Bleeding

5 Park the vehicle on a level surface and apply the handbrake.

6 With the engine stopped, slowly move the steering from lock-to-lock several times to purge any trapped air, then top-up the level in the fluid reservoir. Repeat this procedure until the fluid level in the reservoir does not drop any further.

7 Start the engine, then slowly move the steering from lock-to-lock several times to purge out any remaining air in the system. Repeat this procedure until bubbles cease to appear in the fluid reservoir.

8 If an abnormal noise is heard from the pump or fluid pipes when the steering is operated, this is an indication that there is still air in the system. Confirm this by turning the wheels to the straight-ahead position and switching off the engine. If the fluid level in the reservoir rises, then air is present in the system, and further bleeding will be necessary. Repeat the above procedure as necessary.

9 Once all traces of air have been purged from the power steering hydraulic system, stop the engine and allow the system to cool. Finally, check that the fluid level is up to the maximum mark on the reservoir, and top-up if necessary.

16 Steering gear assembly - removal and refitting

Removal

1 Apply the handbrake, then jack up the front of the vehicle and support it on axle stands (see *"Jacking and Vehicle Support"*). Remove both front roadwheels.

2 Drain the hydraulic fluid from the power steering system as described in Section 15, then return the steering to the straight-ahead position.

3 Disconnect the battery negative (earth) lead (see Chapter 5A).

4 On left-hand drive models, remove the main fusebox from the left-hand rear corner of the engine compartment for access to the power steering fluid pipes.

5 Remove the facia lower trim panel.

6 At the bottom of the steering column, unscrew and remove the clamp bolt and slide the universal joint from the steering gear pinion shaft. Mark the shaft and column if necessary to ensure correct refitting.

Caution: Prevent the steering wheel from turning using adhesive tape attached to the facia, otherwise there is a danger of breaking the spring in the contact spring unit.

7 Where fitted, prise the lockplate from the bolts securing the inner ends of the track rods to the steering gear.

8 Unscrew the bolts and remove the track rods from the steering gear. Position them to one side, and recover the mounting plate and washers.

9 Unscrew the nut from the track rod end on the right-hand side (RHD models) or left-hand side (LHD models), then separate the track rod end from the steering arm on the hub carrier using a separator tool. Remove the track rod from the vehicle.

10 Position a container beneath the steering gear to catch spilt fluid. Identify the supply and return hydraulic pipes for location, then unscrew the union nuts and carefully position the pipes to one side. Recover the O-ring seals. Tape over or plug the ends of the pipes and the steering gear apertures to prevent entry of dust and dirt.

11 Unscrew the union nuts and disconnect the internal pipes from the valve body. Recover the O-ring seals. Tape over or plug the pipes and apertures to prevent entry of dust and dirt.

12 Support the steering gear, then unscrew the mounting nuts and bolts and remove the clamps. Note the location of the cable support. Withdraw the steering gear through the wheel housing.

13 Examine the mounting rubbers for wear and damage and renew them if necessary. If a new steering gear is to be fitted, transfer the internal pipes from the old unit and fit new O-ring seals. Tighten the union nuts securely. Check the bulkhead rubber gaiter and renew if necessary.

Refitting

13 Insert the steering gear through the wheel housing and locate it on the bulkhead with the rubber mountings in place. Refit the mounting clamps and cable support and tighten the nuts and bolts to the specified torque.

14 Connect the internal pipes to the valve body using new O-ring seals. Tighten the union nuts securely.

15 Connect the supply and return pipes to the valve body together with new O-ring seals. Tighten the nuts securely.

16 Refit the track rod to the steering arm and tighten the nut to the specified torque.

17 Refit the inner ends of the track rods to the steering gear together with the mounting plate and washers. The mounting plate must be positioned next to the bolt heads, and the washers must be positioned between the

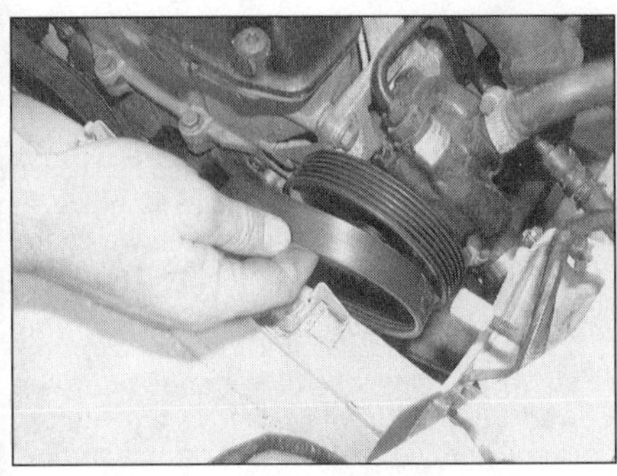

17.3 Removing the auxiliary drivebelt from the power steering pump pulley

track rods and the rack. Tighten the bolts to the specified torque. Where fitted, press the lockplate on the bolt heads to lock them.

18 Engage the universal joint on the bottom of the column with the steering gear pinion shaft, making sure that the bolt hole is aligned with the cut-out in the shaft and the alignment marks are adjacent as previously noted. Tighten the clamp bolt to the specified torque.

19 Refit the facia lower trim panel.

20 On left-hand drive models, refit the main fusebox to the left-hand rear corner of the engine compartment.

21 Reconnect the battery negative (earth) lead.

22 Fill the power steering system with the specified hydraulic fluid and bleed the system with reference to Section 15.

23 Refit the front roadwheels and lower the vehicle to the ground.

24 Have the front wheel alignment checked at the earliest opportunity (see Section 20).

17 Power steering servo pump - removal and refitting

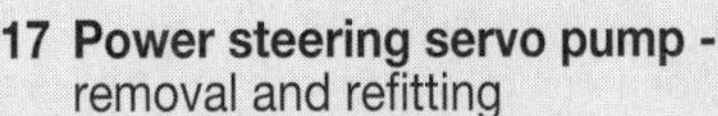

Removal

1 Drain the hydraulic fluid from the power steering system as described in Section 15, then return the steering to the straight-ahead position.

2 Remove the air cleaner from the right-hand corner of the engine compartment (see Chapter 4A).

3 Remove the auxiliary drivebelt from the power steering pump pulley as described in Chapter 1. To do this, lever the automatic tensioner clockwise until a peg or drill bit can be inserted through the special holes to hold the tensioner **(see illustration)**.

4 Unscrew the union nut securing the feed pipe to the pump.

5 Loosen the clip and disconnect the return hose from the pump.

6 Unscrew the mounting bolts, noting that one of them secures the feed pipe support bracket. Access to the bolt at the pulley end is gained through the hole in the pulley **(see illustrations)**.

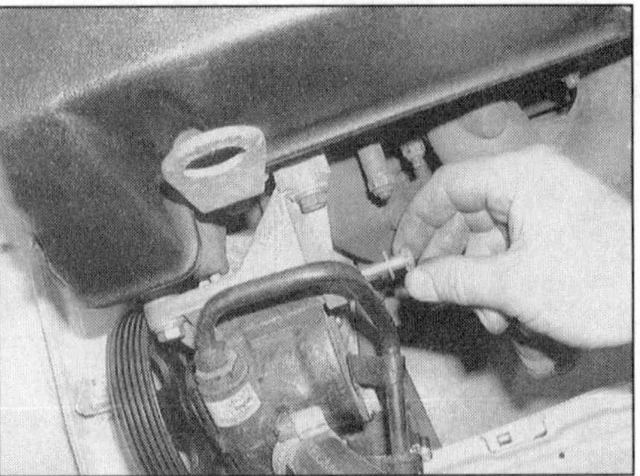

17.6a Unscrew the mounting bolts from the power steering pump

7 Withdraw the pump from the engine **(see illustration)**. Wrap it in cloth rag to prevent fluid dropping onto the vehicle paintwork.

Refitting

8 Locate the pump on the engine, then insert the bolts and tighten them to the specified torque. Make sure the feed pipe support bracket is located on the correct bolt, and locate the union nut in the pump aperture as the bolt is being inserted.

9 Tighten the union nut securing the feed pipe to the pump.

10 Connect the return hose and tighten the clip.

11 Locate the auxiliary drivebelt on the pulleys and release the automatic tensioner (see Chapter 1).

12 Refit the air cleaner (see Chapter 4A).

13 Fill the hydraulic system with fluid and bleed it as described in Section 15.

18 Steering rack rubber gaiter - renewal

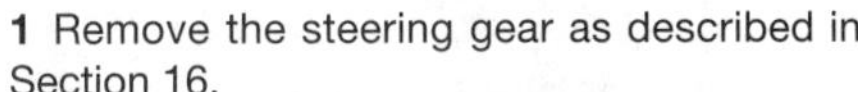

1 Remove the steering gear as described in Section 16.

2 Unscrew the union nuts and remove the internal hydraulic pipes from the steering gear. Recover the O-ring seals.

3 Remove the outer rubber mounting from the end of the steering gear housing opposite to the pinion.

4 Loosen the clips, and slide the rubber gaiter from the end of the housing.

5 Wipe clean the housing, then fit the new gaiter and locate in the grooves. Fit and tighten the retaining clips.

6 Locate the outer rubber mounting on the steering gear housing.

7 Fit the internal hydraulic pipes on the steering gear together with new O-ring seals. With the pipes aligned correctly, tighten the union nuts. Note that the ends which locate in the valve housing are not fitted at this stage.

8 Refit the steering gear with reference to Section 16.

17.6b One of the mounting bolts is accessed through the power steering pump pulley

17.7 Removing the power steering pump from the engine

19 Track rod end - removal and refitting

Removal

1 Apply the handbrake, then jack up the front of the vehicle and support it on axle stands (see *"Jacking and Vehicle Support"*). Remove the roadwheel.

2 Slightly loosen (two or three turns) the clamp bolt securing the track rod end to the adjustment screw. Do not loosen the clamp bolt on the track rod.

3 Unscrew the nut securing the track rod end to the steering arm on the hub carrier **(see illustration)**.

19.3 Unscrew the track rod end securing nut . . .

19.4a . . . then use a separator tool to release the track rod end . . .

19.4b . . . and remove the track rod end from the steering arm

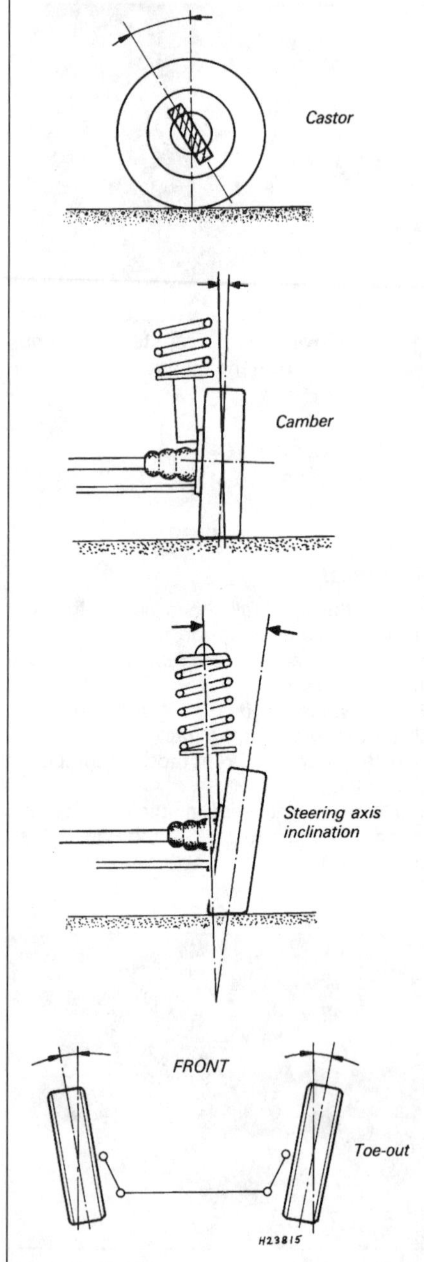

20.2 Wheel alignment and steering angles

4 Using a separator tool, disconnect the track rod end from the steering arm **(see illustrations)**.

5 Using a steel rule or vernier calipers, measure the length of thread visible on the outer end of the adjustment screw. This is necessary to ensure that the track rod end is refitted in exactly the same position.

6 While holding the adjustment screw with a spanner on the flats provided, unscrew and remove the track rod end while counting the number of turns necessary to do so.

Refitting

7 Screw on the track rod end the exact number of turns noted on removal. Check that the length of thread visible is as previously noted.

8 Locate the track rod end stub in the steering arm, then tighten the nut to the specified torque.

9 With the track rod end balljoint housing parallel to the steering arm, tighten the clamp bolt to the specified torque.

10 Refit the roadwheel and lower the vehicle to the ground.

11 Have the front wheel alignment checked at the earliest opportunity (see Section 20).

20 Wheel alignment and steering angles - general information

Front wheel alignment

1 Accurate front wheel alignment is essential to good steering and for even tyre wear. Before considering the steering angles, check that the tyres are correctly inflated, that the front wheels are not buckled, the hub bearings are not worn and that the steering linkage is in good order without slackness or wear at the joints. The fuel tank must be full and the vehicle must be without any passengers.

2 Wheel alignment consists of four factors **(see illustration)**:

Camber, is the angle at which the roadwheels are set from the vertical when viewed from the front or rear of the vehicle. Positive camber is the angle (in degrees) that the wheels are tilted outwards at the top from the vertical. Negative camber is the angle that the wheels are tilted inwards at the top from the vertical. This angle is not adjustable.

Castor, is the angle between the steering axis and a vertical line when viewed from each side of the vehicle. Positive castor is indicated when the steering axis is inclined towards the rear of the vehicle at its upper end. This angle is not adjustable.

Steering axis inclination (kingpin inclination, or swivel pin inclination), is the angle, when viewed from the front or rear of the vehicle, between the vertical and an imaginary line drawn between the upper and lower front suspension strut mountings. This angle is not adjustable.

Toe, is the amount by which the distance between the front inside edges of the roadwheel rim differs from that between the rear inside edges. If the distance between the front edges is less than that at the rear, the wheels are said to toe-in. If the distance between the front inside edges is greater than that at the rear, the wheels toe-out.

3 Owing to the need for precision gauges to measure the small angles of the steering and suspension settings, the checking of camber, castor and steering axis inclination must be carried out by a service station having the necessary equipment. Any deviation from the specified angle will be due to accident damage or gross wear in the suspension mountings.

4 To check the front wheel alignment, first make sure that the lengths of both track-rods are equal when the steering is in the straight-ahead position. To do this, measure the distance between the track rod end and the track rod on each side. The dimension must not be in excess of 52.0 mm, and the dimension must be the same on each side. The flats of the adjustment screws must be positioned centrally between the track rod and track rod end, or within a maximum of 3.0 mm of each other **(see illustration)**. The clamp bolts must be loosened before turning the adjustment screws.

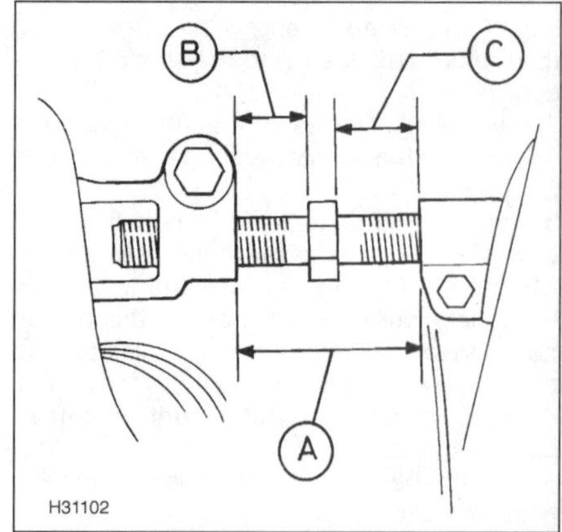

20.4 Track adjustment screw dimensions

A Must not exceed 52.0 mm on each side
B and C Difference between dimension B and C must not exceed 3.0 mm

5 Obtain a tracking gauge. These are available in various forms from accessory stores, or one can be fabricated from a length of steel tubing suitably cranked to clear the sump and transmission, and having a setscrew and locknut at one end.

6 With the gauge, measure the distances between the two wheel inner rims (at hub height) at the rear of the wheel. Push the vehicle forward to rotate the wheel through 180° (half a turn) and measure the distance between the wheel inner rims, again at hub height, at the front of the wheel. This last measurement should differ from the first by the appropriate toe-in which is given in the Specifications. The vehicle must be on level ground.

7 If the toe-in is found to be incorrect, release the clamp bolts and turn the adjustment screws equally and in the same direction. Only turn them a quarter-of-a-turn at a time before re-checking the alignment. Turn the adjustment screws with a spanner on the flats, and after making an adjustment, make sure that the track rod end balljoint housing is parallel to the steering arm. It is important not to allow the track-rods to become unequal in length during adjustment, otherwise the alignment of the steering wheel will become incorrect and tyre scrubbing will occur on turns.

8 On completion tighten the clamp bolts without disturbing the setting. Check that the balljoints are at the centre of their arcs of travel.

Rear wheel alignment

9 The rear wheel toe and camber settings are given for reference only since no adjustment is possible.

Chapter 11
Bodywork and fittings

Contents

Degrees of difficulty

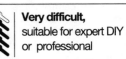

Easy, suitable for novice with little experience 	**Fairly easy,** suitable for beginner with some experience 	**Fairly difficult,** suitable for competent DIY mechanic 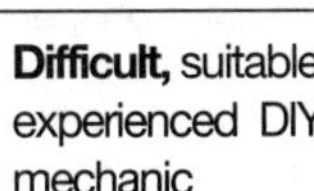	**Difficult,** suitable for experienced DIY mechanic	**Very difficult,** suitable for expert DIY or professional

Specifications

Torque wrench settings	**Nm**	**lbf ft**
Front bumper	39	29
Rear bumper	39	29
Front and rear doors	47	35
Fixed side window (3-door models)	3	2
Rear quarter light (5-door models)	3	2
Front seat	30	22
Front seat belt:		
Reel	45	33
Height adjuster	24	18
Buckle	45	33
Slide rail (3-door)	45	33
Rear seat belt:		
Reel	38	28
Floor anchorage	45	33
Passenger airbag	9	7
Passenger airbag bracket	20	15

1 General information

The vehicle's body is constructed from pressed-steel sections that are either spot-welded or seam-welded together. The overall rigidity of the body is increased by the use of stiffening beams built into the body panels, steel flanges in the window and door openings, and the application of adhesive in fixed glass joints.

The front subframe assembly provides mounting points for the engine/transmission unit and front suspension, and the steering gear is bolted to the bulkhead. The front wings are also bolted on, rather than welded on, allowing accident damage to be repaired easily.

The vehicle's underside is coated with polyester underseal and an anti-corrosion compound. This treatment provides protection against the elements, and also serves as an effective sound insulation layer. The cabin, luggage area and engine compartment are also lined with bituminous felt and other sound-insulating materials, to provide further noise damping.

All models are fitted with electric windows at the front and rear. The window glass is raised and lowered by an electric motor, directly operating a scissor-action regulator.

Central locking is fitted to all models, and is actuated from the driver's or passenger's door lock. It operates the locks on all four doors, the tailgate, and the fuel filler cap. The lock mechanisms are actuated by servo motor units, and the system is controlled by an Electronic Control Unit (ECU).

All models are fitted with a driver's airbag, located in the centre of the steering wheel. Passenger airbags are an optional extra. The front seat belts incorporate automatic tensioners which operate in the event of a front-end collision. The airbags form part of the Supplementary Restraint System (SRS) which is controlled by an Electronic Control Unit (ECU). Sensors, built into the ECU casing and the front of the engine bay, are triggered in the event of a front-end collision, and prompt the ECU to activate the airbag(s) and the seat belt tensioners.

Warning: Section 30 details the special precautions that need to be observed when working on vehicles with an airbag.

2 Maintenance - bodywork and underframe

The general condition of a vehicle's bodywork is the one thing that significantly affects its value. Maintenance is easy, but needs to be regular. Neglect, particularly after minor damage, can lead quickly to further deterioration and costly repair bills. It is important also to keep watch on those parts of the vehicle not immediately visible, for instance the underside, inside all the wheel arches, and the lower part of the engine compartment.

The basic maintenance routine for the bodywork is washing - preferably with a lot of water, from a hose. This will remove all the loose solids which may have stuck to the vehicle. It is important to flush these off in such a way as to prevent grit from scratching the finish. The wheel arches and underframe need washing in the same way, to remove any accumulated mud which will retain moisture and tend to encourage rust. Paradoxically enough, the best time to clean the underframe and wheel arches is in wet weather, when the mud is thoroughly wet and soft. In very wet weather, the underframe is usually cleaned of large accumulations automatically, and this is a good time for inspection.

Periodically, except on vehicles with a wax-based underbody protective coating, it is a good idea to have the whole of the underframe of the vehicle steam-cleaned, engine compartment included, so that a thorough inspection can be carried out to see what minor repairs and renovations are necessary. Steam-cleaning is available at many garages, and is necessary for the removal of the accumulation of oily grime, which sometimes is allowed to become thick in certain areas. If steam-cleaning facilities are not available, there are one or two excellent grease solvents available, which can be brush-applied; the dirt can then be simply hosed off. Note that these methods should not be used on vehicles with wax-based underbody protective coating, or the coating will be removed. Such vehicles should be inspected annually, preferably just prior to Winter, when the underbody should be washed down, and any damage to the wax coating repaired. Ideally, a completely fresh coat should be applied. It would also be worth considering the use of such wax-based protection for injection into door panels, sills, box sections, etc, as an additional safeguard against rust damage, where such protection is not provided by the vehicle manufacturer.

After washing paintwork, wipe off with a chamois leather to give an unspotted clear finish. A coat of clear protective wax polish will give added protection against chemical pollutants in the air. If the paintwork sheen has dulled or oxidised, use a cleaner/polisher combination to restore the brilliance of the shine. This requires a little effort, but such dulling is usually caused because regular washing has been neglected. Care needs to be taken with metallic paintwork, as special non-abrasive cleaner/polisher is required to avoid damage to the finish. Always check that the door and ventilator opening drain holes and pipes are completely clear, so that water can be drained out. Brightwork should be treated in the same way as paintwork. Windscreens and windows can be kept clear of the smeary film which often appears, by the use of proprietary glass cleaner. Never use any form of wax or other body or chromium polish on glass.

3 Maintenance - upholstery and carpets

Mats and carpets should be brushed or vacuum-cleaned regularly, to keep them free of grit. If they are badly stained, remove them from the vehicle for scrubbing or sponging, and make quite sure they are dry before refitting. Seats and interior trim panels can be kept clean by wiping with a damp cloth. If they do become stained (which can be more apparent on light-coloured upholstery), use a little liquid detergent and a soft nail brush to scour the grime out of the grain of the material. Do not forget to keep the headlining clean in the same way as the upholstery. When using liquid cleaners inside the vehicle, do not over-wet the surfaces being cleaned. Excessive damp could get into the seams and padded interior, causing stains, offensive odours or even rot. If the inside of the vehicle gets wet accidentally, it is worthwhile taking some trouble to dry it out properly, particularly where carpets are involved. *Do not leave oil or electric heaters inside the vehicle for this purpose.*

4 Minor body damage - repair

Note: *For more detailed information about bodywork repair, Haynes Publishing produce a book titled "The Car Bodywork Repair Manual". This incorporates information on such aspects as rust treatment, painting and glass-fibre repairs, as well as details on more ambitious repairs involving welding and panel beating.*

Repairs of minor scratches in bodywork

If the scratch is very superficial, and does not penetrate to the metal of the bodywork, repair is very simple. Lightly rub the area of the scratch with a paintwork renovator, or a very fine cutting paste, to remove loose paint from the scratch, and to clear the surrounding bodywork of wax polish. Rinse the area with clean water.

Apply touch-up paint to the scratch using a fine paint brush; continue to apply fine layers of paint until the surface of the paint in the scratch is level with the surrounding paintwork. Allow the new paint at least two weeks to harden, then blend it into the surrounding paintwork by rubbing the scratch area with a paintwork renovator or a very fine cutting paste. Finally, apply wax polish.

Where the scratch has penetrated right through to the metal of the bodywork, causing the metal to rust, a different repair technique is required. Remove any loose rust from the bottom of the scratch with a penknife, then apply rust-inhibiting paint, to prevent the formation of rust in the future. Using a rubber or nylon applicator, fill the scratch with bodystopper paste. If required, this paste can be mixed with cellulose thinners, to provide a very thin paste which is ideal for filling narrow scratches. Before the stopper-paste in the scratch hardens, wrap a piece of smooth cotton rag around the top of a finger. Dip the finger in cellulose thinners, and quickly sweep it across the surface of the stopper-paste in the scratch; this will ensure that the surface of the stopper-paste is slightly hollowed. The scratch can now be painted over as described earlier in this Section.

Repairs of dents in bodywork

When deep denting of the vehicle's bodywork has taken place, the first task is to pull the dent out, until the affected bodywork almost attains its original shape. There is little point in trying to restore the original shape completely, as the metal in the damaged area will have stretched on impact, and cannot be reshaped fully to its original contour. It is better to bring the level of the dent up to a point which is about 3 mm below the level of the surrounding bodywork. In cases where the dent is very shallow anyway, it is not worth trying to pull it out at all. If the underside of the dent is accessible, it can be hammered out gently from behind, using a mallet with a wooden or plastic head. Whilst doing this, hold a suitable block of wood firmly against the outside of the panel, to absorb the impact from the hammer blows and thus prevent a large area of the bodywork from being "belled-out".

Should the dent be in a section of the bodywork which has a double skin, or some other factor making it inaccessible from behind, a different technique is called for. Drill several small holes through the metal inside the area - particularly in the deeper section. Then screw long self-tapping screws into the holes, just sufficiently for them to gain a good purchase in the metal. Now the dent can be pulled out by pulling on the protruding heads of the screws with a pair of pliers.

The next stage of the repair is the removal of the paint from the damaged area, and from an inch or so of the surrounding "sound" bodywork. This is accomplished most easily by using a wire brush or abrasive pad on a power drill, although it can be done just as effectively by hand, using sheets of abrasive paper. To complete the preparation for filling, score the surface of the bare metal with a screwdriver or the tang of a file, or alternatively, drill small holes in the affected area. This will provide a really good "key" for the filler paste.

To complete the repair, see the Section on filling and respraying.

Repairs of rust holes or gashes in bodywork

Remove all paint from the affected area, and from an inch or so of the surrounding "sound" bodywork, using an abrasive pad or a wire brush on a power drill. If these are not available, a few sheets of abrasive paper will do the job most effectively. With the paint removed, you will be able to judge the severity of the corrosion, and therefore decide whether to renew the whole panel (if this is possible) or to repair the affected area. New body panels are not as expensive as most people think, and it is often quicker and more satisfactory to fit a new panel than to attempt to repair large areas of corrosion.

Remove all fittings from the affected area, except those which will act as a guide to the original shape of the damaged bodywork (eg headlamp shells etc). Then, using tin snips or a hacksaw blade, remove all loose metal and any other metal badly affected by corrosion. Hammer the edges of the hole inwards, in order to create a slight depression for the filler paste.

Wire-brush the affected area to remove the powdery rust from the surface of the remaining metal. Paint the affected area with rust-inhibiting paint; if the back of the rusted area is accessible, treat this also.

Before filling can take place, it will be necessary to block the hole in some way. This can be achieved by the use of aluminium or plastic mesh, or aluminium tape.

Aluminium or plastic mesh, or glass-fibre matting is probably the best material to use for a large hole. Cut a piece to the approximate size and shape of the hole to be filled, then position it in the hole so that its edges are below the level of the surrounding bodywork. It can be retained in position by several blobs of filler paste around its periphery.

Aluminium tape should be used for small or very narrow holes. Pull a piece off the roll, trim it to the approximate size and shape required, then pull off the backing paper (if used) and stick the tape over the hole; it can be overlapped if the thickness of one piece is insufficient. Burnish down the edges of the tape with the handle of a screwdriver or similar, to ensure that the tape is securely attached to the metal underneath.

Bodywork repairs - filling and respraying

Before using this Section, see the Sections on dent, deep scratch, rust holes and gash repairs.

Many types of bodyfiller are available, but generally speaking, those proprietary kits which contain a tin of filler paste and a tube of resin hardener are best for this type of repair. A wide, flexible plastic or nylon applicator will be found invaluable for imparting a smooth and well-contoured finish to the surface of the filler.

Mix up a little filler on a clean piece of card or board - measure the hardener carefully (follow the maker's instructions on the pack), otherwise the filler will set too rapidly or too slowly. Using the applicator, apply the filler paste to the prepared area; draw the applicator across the surface of the filler to achieve the correct contour and to level the surface. As soon as a contour that approximates to the correct one is achieved, stop working the paste - if you carry on too long, the paste will become sticky and begin to "pick-up" on the applicator. Continue to add thin layers of filler paste at 20-minute intervals, until the level of the filler is just proud of the surrounding bodywork.

Once the filler has hardened, the excess can be removed using a metal plane or file. From then on, progressively-finer grades of abrasive paper should be used, starting with a 40-grade production paper, and finishing with a 400-grade wet-and-dry paper. Always wrap the abrasive paper around a flat rubber, cork, or wooden block - otherwise the surface of the filler will not be completely flat. During the smoothing of the filler surface, the wet-and-dry paper should be periodically rinsed in water. This will ensure that a very smooth finish is imparted to the filler at the final stage.

At this stage, the "dent" should be surrounded by a ring of bare metal, which in turn should be encircled by the finely "feathered" edge of the good paintwork. Rinse the repair area with clean water, until all of the dust produced by the rubbing-down operation has gone.

Spray the whole area with a light coat of primer - this will show up any imperfections in the surface of the filler. Repair these imperfections with fresh filler paste or bodystopper, and once more smooth the surface with abrasive paper. If bodystopper is used, it can be mixed with cellulose thinners, to form a really thin paste which is ideal for filling small holes. Repeat this spray-and-repair procedure until you are satisfied that the surface of the filler, and the feathered edge of the paintwork, are perfect. Clean the repair area with clean water, and allow to dry fully.

The repair area is now ready for final spraying. Paint spraying must be carried out in a warm, dry, windless and dust-free atmosphere. This condition can be created artificially if you have access to a large indoor working area, but if you are forced to work in the open, you will have to pick your day very carefully. If you are working indoors, dousing the floor in the work area with water will help to settle the dust which would otherwise be in the atmosphere. If the repair area is confined to one body panel, mask off the surrounding panels; this will help to minimise the effects of a slight mis-match in paint colours. Bodywork fittings (eg chrome strips, door handles etc) will also need to be masked off. Use genuine masking tape, and several thicknesses of newspaper, for the masking operations.

Before commencing to spray, agitate the aerosol can thoroughly, then spray a test area (an old tin, or similar) until the technique is mastered. Cover the repair area with a thick coat of primer; the thickness should be built up using several thin layers of paint, rather than one thick one. Using 400 grade wet-and-dry paper, rub down the surface of the primer until it is really smooth. While doing this, the work area should be thoroughly doused with water, and the wet-and-dry paper periodically rinsed in water. Allow to dry before spraying on more paint.

Spray on the top coat, again building up the thickness by using several thin layers of paint. Start spraying in the centre of the repair area, and then, using a circular motion, work outwards until the whole repair area and about 2 inches of the surrounding original paintwork is covered. Remove all masking material 10 to 15 minutes after spraying on the final coat of paint.

Allow the new paint at least two weeks to harden, then, using a paintwork renovator or a very fine cutting paste, blend the edges of the paint into the existing paintwork. Finally, apply wax polish.

Plastic components

With the use of more and more plastic body components by the vehicle manufacturers (eg bumpers. spoilers, and in some cases major body panels), rectification of more serious damage to such items has become a matter of either entrusting repair work to a specialist in this field, or renewing complete components. Repair of such damage by the DIY owner is not really feasible, owing to the cost of the equipment and materials required for effecting such repairs. The basic technique involves making a groove along the line of the crack in the plastic, using a rotary burr in a power drill. The damaged part is then welded back together, using a hot air gun to heat up and fuse a plastic filler rod into the groove. Any excess plastic is then removed, and the area rubbed down to a smooth finish. It is important that a filler rod of the correct plastic is used, as body components can be made of a variety of different types (eg polycarbonate, ABS, polypropylene).

Damage of a less serious nature (abrasions, minor cracks etc) can be repaired by the DIY owner using a two-part epoxy filler repair. Once mixed in equal, this is used in similar fashion to the bodywork filler used on metal panels. The filler is usually cured in twenty to thirty minutes, ready for sanding and painting.

If the owner is renewing a complete component himself, or if he has repaired it with epoxy filler, he will be left with the problem of finding a suitable paint for finishing which is compatible with the type of plastic used. At one time, the use of a universal paint was not possible, owing to the complex range of plastics encountered in body component applications. Standard paints, generally speaking, will not bond to plastic or rubber satisfactorily, but suitable paints to match any plastic or rubber finish, can be obtained from dealers. However, it is now possible to obtain a plastic body parts finishing kit which consists of a pre-primer treatment, a primer and coloured top coat. Full instructions are normally supplied with a kit, but basically, the method of use is to first apply the pre-primer to the component concerned, and allow it to dry for up to 30 minutes. Then the primer is applied, and left to dry for about an hour before finally applying the special-coloured top coat. The result is a correctly-coloured component, where the paint will flex with the plastic or rubber, a property that standard paint does not normally posses.

5 Major body damage - repair

Where serious damage has occurred, or large areas need renewal due to neglect, it means that complete new panels will need welding-in, and this is best left to professionals. If the damage is due to impact, it will also be necessary to check completely the alignment of the bodyshell, and this can only be carried out accurately by a dealer using special jigs. If the body is left misaligned, it is primarily dangerous, as the car will not handle properly, and secondly, uneven stresses will be imposed on the steering, suspension and possibly transmission, causing abnormal wear, or complete failure, particularly to such items as the tyres.

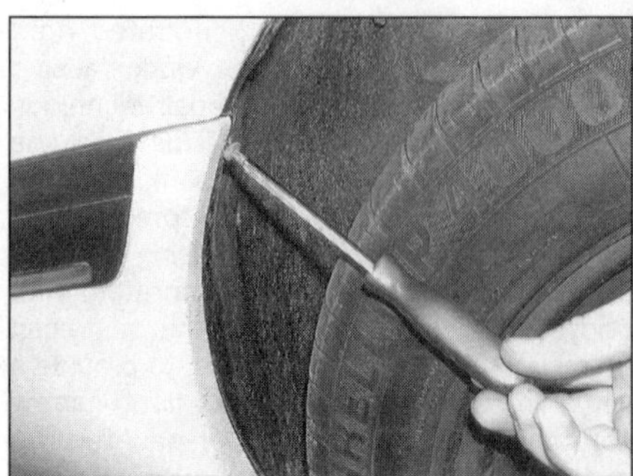

6.3 Removing the screws securing the wheel arch liners to the front bumper

6 Front bumper - removal and refitting

Removal

1 Apply the handbrake, then jack up the front of the vehicle and support it on axle stands (see *"Jacking and Vehicle Support"*).

2 Unbolt and remove the splash shields from under each end of the front bumper.

3 Undo the screws and detach the wheel arch liners from the rear ends of the bumper **(see illustration)**.

4 With the bonnet open, remove the radiator grille as described in Section 8.

5 Lift the wiper arms from the headlamps and unclip the washer tubing from the rear edge of the bumper.

6 Remove the headlights and indicator lamps from both sides of the vehicle with reference to Chapter 12.

7 Unscrew and remove the bolts securing the bumper to the body. The bolts are located in the headlight apertures **(see illustration)**.

8 Disconnect the wiring from the foglights and release the cable ties.

9 Working beneath the middle of the bumper, disconnect the wiring from the ambient temperature sensor **(see illustration)**. Remove the adhesive tape holding the wiring in position.

10 With the aid of an assistant, lift the front bumper and pull it forwards from the brackets in the front wings **(see illustrations)**.

6.7 Removing the front bumper bolts

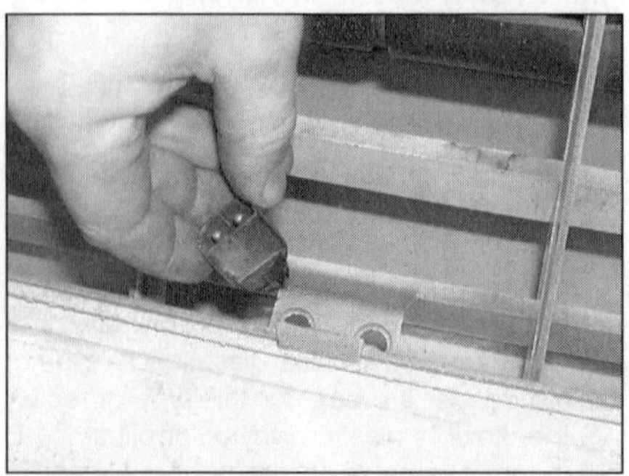

6.9 Disconnecting the wiring from the ambient temperature sensor

6.10a Lifting the front bumper from the car

6.10b The front bumper being removed from the mounting bracket

11 If fitting a new bumper, transfer the number plate, trim insert, spoiler and splash shields to the new unit.

Refitting

12 Lift the bumper into position and locate it in the brackets. Insert the mounting bolts and tighten to the specified torque.
13 Reconnect the wiring to the temperature sensor and attach the wiring to the underside of the bumper with adhesive tape.
14 Reconnect the wiring to the foglights and secure the wiring with new cable ties.
15 Refit the headlights and indicator lamps with reference to Chapter 12.
16 Clip the washer tubing to the rear edge of the bumper. Lower the wiper arms onto the headlights.
17 Refit the radiator grille with reference to Section 8.
18 Refit the wheel arch liners inside the rear edge of the bumper and secure with the screws.
19 Refit the splash shields under each end of the bumper.
20 Lower the vehicle to the ground. If necessary, adjust the headlight alignment (see Chapter 12).

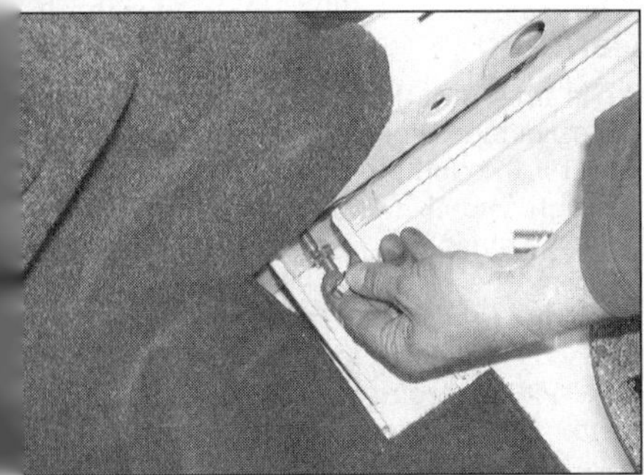

7.4 Removing the rear bumper mounting nuts

7.2 Removing the load securing eyelets in the luggage compartment

7 Rear bumper - removal and refitting

Removal

1 With the tailgate open, release the rubber weatherstrip from the rear valance and inner trim. Do not completely remove it.
2 Unbolt and remove the two load securing eyelets from each side of the luggage compartment **(see illustration)**.
3 Fold the luggage compartment carpet forwards, then undo the plastic nuts and unclip the rear valance trim panel from over the tailgate striker **(see illustration)**.
4 Unscrew and remove the rear bumper mounting nuts **(see illustration)**.
5 At the front ends of the bumper, release the mouldings from the wheel arches **(see illustration)**. On some models two screws secure the mouldings, however, where rivets are used it is possible to pull the mouldings forwards and disconnect them from the wheel arches.
6 With the help of an assistant, pull the bumper rearwards while releasing it from the side brackets **(see illustration)**. Take care not to damage the vehicle paintwork.

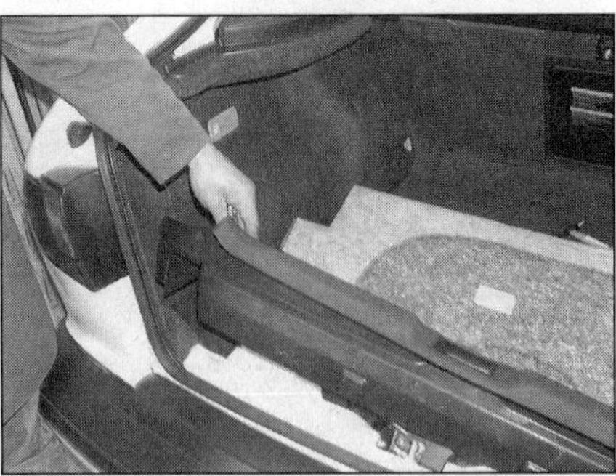

7.3 Removing the rear valance trim panel

Refitting

7 Lift the bumper into position and slide it forwards. Make sure the bumper engages correctly with the side brackets by having the assistant press the sides of the bumper inwards while the bumper is pushed forwards. Check for correct positioning by looking beneath the bumper.
8 Refit and tighten the mounting nuts to the specified torque.
9 Refit the mouldings to the wheel arches.
10 Refit the trim panel and tighten the nuts, then fold the carpet back.
11 Refit the two load securing eyelets and tighten the bolts.
12 Refit the rubber weatherstrip and close the tailgate.

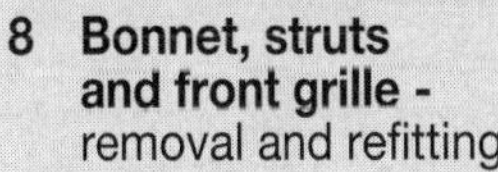

8 Bonnet, struts and front grille - removal and refitting

Bonnet

Warning: It is essential to enlist the help of an assistant for this operation.

Removal

1 With the bonnet open, place some cloth rags or card between the rear edge of the bonnet and the windscreen valance.
2 Disconnect the washer tube from the adapter on the bulkhead cover **(see illustration)**.

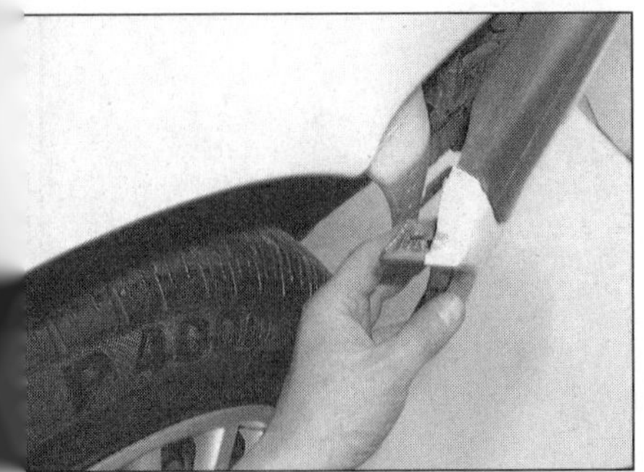

7.5 Releasing the front ends of the rear bumper

7.6 Removing the rear bumper from the rear valance

8.2 Disconnecting the washer tube from the bulkhead adapter

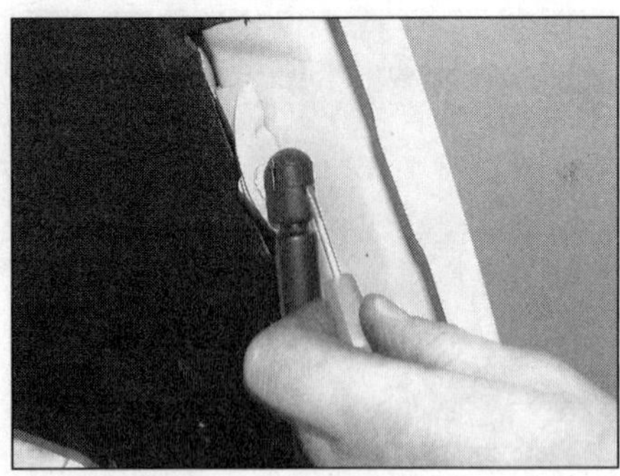
8.4 Disconnecting the struts from the bonnet

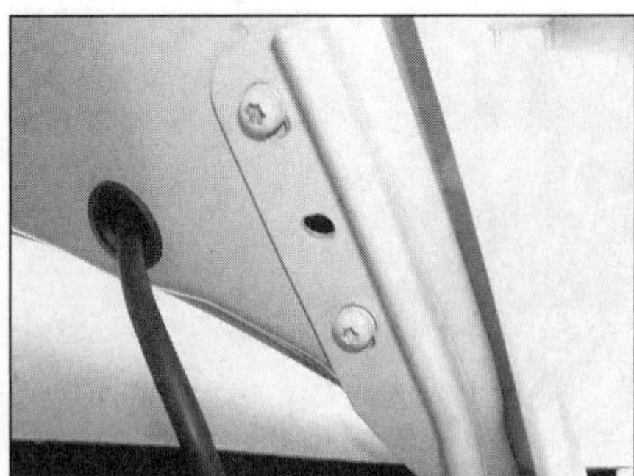
8.6 Bonnet hinge bolts

3 Have the assistant support the bonnet open.

4 Disconnect the struts from the bonnet by prising out the retaining clips with a screwdriver, then pulling off the struts **(see illustration)**. Lower the struts onto the front wings.

5 Using a pencil, mark the position of the hinges on the bonnet.

6 While the assistant supports the bonnet, unscrew and remove the hinge bolts using a Torx key **(see illustration)**. Carefully lift the bonnet from the vehicle and place in a safe position, taking care not to damage the paintwork.

7 If necessary, remove the wiper arms and bulkhead cover, then unbolt and remove the hinges from the body. If a new bonnet is being fitted, transfer the sound insulation and weatherseal to the new unit.

Refitting

8 Refitting is a reversal of removal. When first closing the bonnet, lower it slowly and check that the striker is aligned with the lock **(see illustration)**. Also check that the bonnet is positioned central between the front wings. If necessary, loosen the bolts and reposition the bonnet on the hinges before fully closing the bonnet. Tighten the bolts on completion. Check that the front of the bonnet is level with the front wings, and if necessary screw in or out the rubber stops located in the front corners of the engine compartment.

8.8 Bonnet striker

Struts

Removal

9 Open the bonnet. If removing just one strut, the remaining strut will hold the bonnet up, however if removing both struts an assistant will be required to hold the bonnet open. Alternatively, use a length of wood to prop the bonnet open.

10 Using a screwdriver, prise the spring clip from the top of the strut and disconnect the strut.

11 Disconnect the bottom of the strut by prising out the spring clip.

Refitting

12 Refitting is a reversal of removal.

Front grille

Removal

13 With the bonnet open, depress the retaining clips and release the grille from the engine compartment front crossmember **(see illustration)**.

14 Lift the grille upwards from the two locating holes **(see illustration)**.

Refitting

15 Refitting is a reversal of removal.

9 Bonnet release cable and lever - removal and refitting

Removal

1 With the bonnet open, undo the screw and remove the clamp securing the release cable to the engine compartment front cross-member.

2 Prise out the small rubber plug, then release the bonnet lock spring from the crossmember using a pair of grips to unhook it. With the spring loose, disconnect the cable from it.

3 Withdraw the cable from the clips in the engine compartment.

4 Working inside the vehicle on the driver's side, remove the fusebox cover, lower trim panel, and heater duct then remove the electronic module and relays. Unbolt the fusebox and position it to one side.

5 Fold back the carpet then remove the bonnet release lever using two screwdrivers to prise free the locking tabs at the top and bottom **(see illustration)**.

6 Tie a length of string to the inner end of the cable as an aid to refitting the cable correctly. Withdraw the lever and cable assembly through the bulkhead and remove from the passenger compartment. Untie the string and leave it through the bulkhead.

Refitting

7 Tie the string to the cable and wrap adhesive tape around the end of the cable to assist it through the bulkhead. Pull the cable through into the engine compartment and untie the string.

8 Press the release lever firmly into place inside the vehicle, and reposition the carpet.

9 Insert and tighten the fusebox screws.

10 Refit the electronic module and relays, the heater duct, lower trim panel and fusebox cover.

11 Inside the engine compartment, locate the cable in the clips.

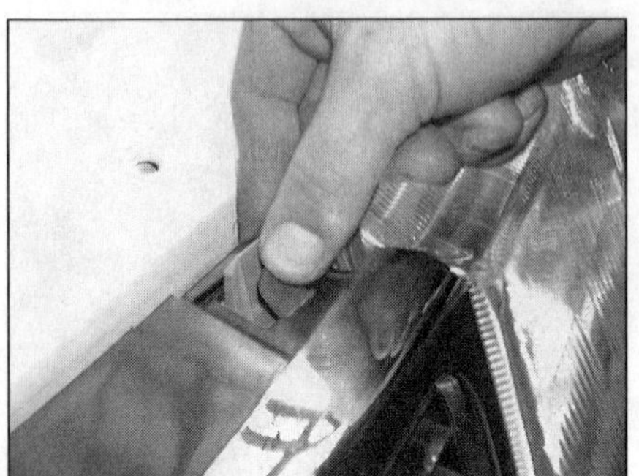
8.13 Depress the retaining clips . . .

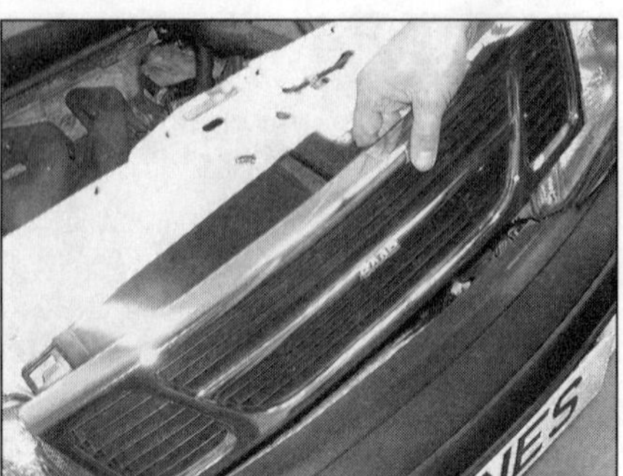
8.14 . . . and lift the front grille upwards from the locating holes

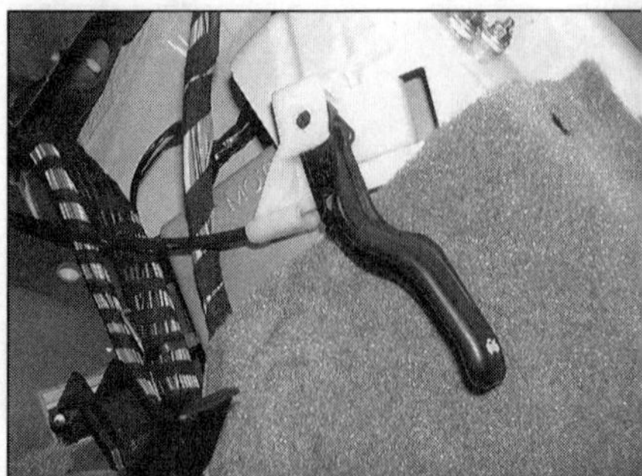
9.5 The bonnet release lever located beneath the right-hand side of the facia

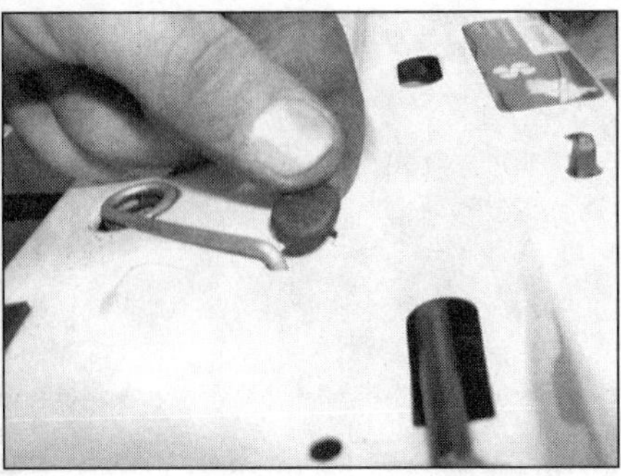

10.1a Remove the rubber plug . . .

12 Attach the cable to the bonnet lock spring, then refit the spring and hook it into the hole. Refit the rubber plug.

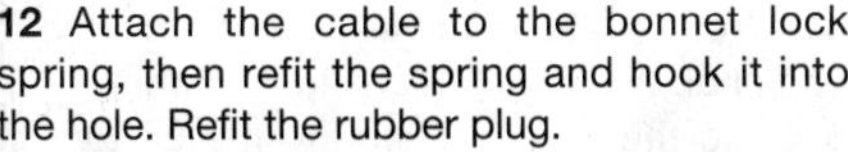

13 Position the outer cable so that there is no free play, then refit the clamp and tighten the screw.

14 Close the bonnet and check that the cable operates the release spring correctly.

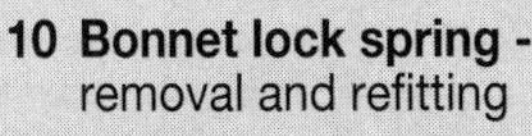

10 Bonnet lock spring - removal and refitting

Removal

1 With the bonnet open, prise out the small rubber plug then release the bonnet lock spring from the engine compartment crossmember using pliers to unhook it **(see illustrations)**.

2 With the spring loose, disconnect the cable from it beneath the crossmember.

11.1 Disconnecting the front door wiring

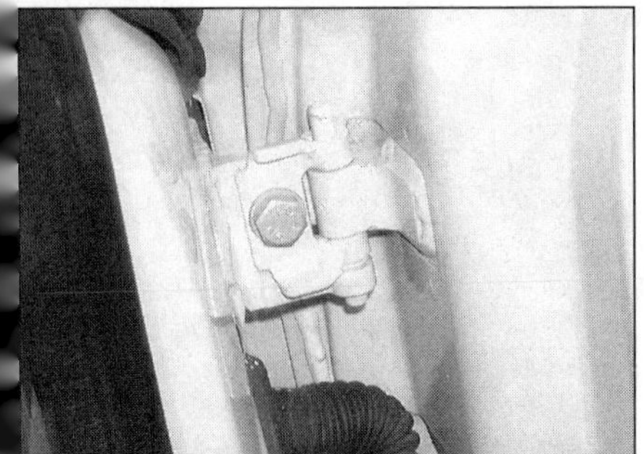

11.3 Front door upper hinge

10.1b . . . and disconnect the bonnet lock spring

3 Withdraw the spring from the crossmember **(see illustration)**.

Refitting

4 Refitting is a reversal of removal, but apply a little grease to the part of the spring which contacts the bonnet striker.

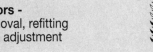

11 Doors - removal, refitting and adjustment

Front

Removal

1 Open the door and disconnect the wiring by depressing and turning the plug and socket located between the door and A-pillar **(see illustration)**.

2 Unbolt the check strap from the A-pillar **(see illustration)**.

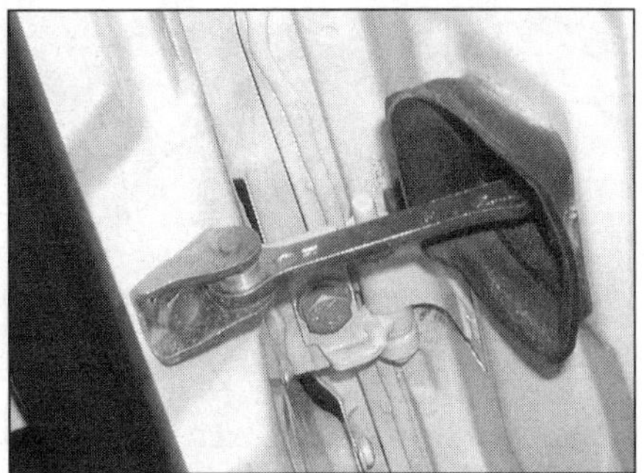

11.2 Front door check strap

11.8 Rear door lower hinge and check strap

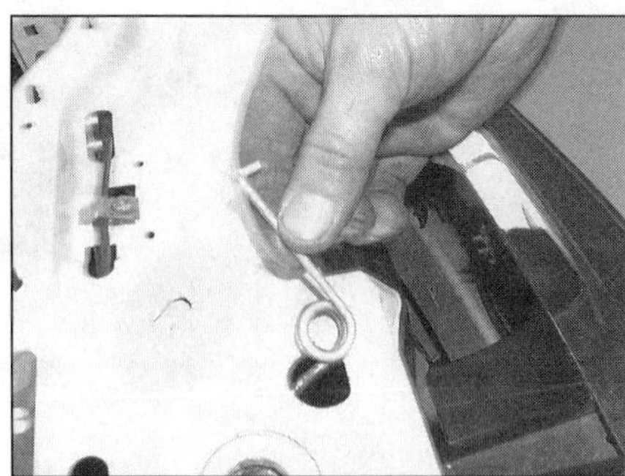

10.3 Removing the bonnet lock spring from the crossmember

3 Mark the position of the hinge plates on the A-pillar brackets in relation to each other **(see illustration)**.

4 With the help of an assistant, unscrew the mounting bolts and withdraw the door from the vehicle. Take care not to damage the paintwork.

Refitting and adjustment

5 Refitting is a reversal of removal, but tighten the mounting bolts to the specified torque. Check that the door lock aligns correctly with the striker on the B-pillar, and that the gap between the door and surrounding bodywork is equal when the door is shut. If necessary, the striker may be adjusted slightly by loosening it. Tighten it on completion. To adjust the vertical position of the door, loosen the hinge bolts, however if there is insufficient downward adjustment, grind off the lower hinge lug to a maximum of 4.0 mm. Rearward adjustment is made with shims fitted between the hinge and pillar.

Rear

Removal

6 Open the front and rear doors on the relevant side.

7 Pull back the sheathing for access to the plug and socket, then disconnect the wiring.

8 Using a suitable drift, drive out the door check bush from below **(see illustration)**.

9 Mark the position of the hinge plates on the B-pillar brackets in relation to each other **(see illustration)**.

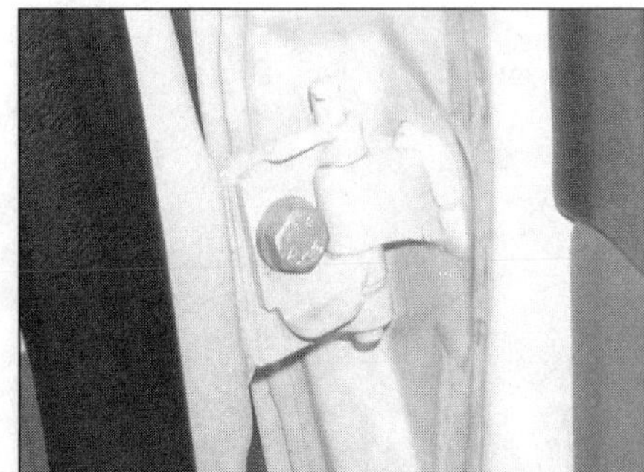

11.9 Rear door upper hinge

11.11 Rear door striker

12.1a Prise out the tailgate opening button . . .

12.1b . . . and disconnect the wiring

10 With the help of an assistant, unscrew the mounting bolts and withdraw the door from the vehicle. Take care not to damage the paintwork.

Refitting and adjustment

11 Refitting is a reversal of removal, but tighten the mounting bolts to the specified torque. Check that the door lock aligns correctly with the striker on the C-pillar, and that the gap between the door and surrounding bodywork is equal when the door is shut. If necessary, the striker may be adjusted slightly by loosening it **(see illustration)**. Tighten it on completion. To adjust the vertical position of the door, loosen the hinge bolts, however if there is insufficient downward adjustment, grind off the lower hinge lug to a maximum of 4.0 mm. Rearward adjustment is made with shims fitted between the hinge and pillar.

12 Door inner trim panel - removal and refitting

Front

Removal

1 Carefully prise the tailgate opening button from the door inner trim panel using a small screwdriver, and disconnect the wiring **(see illustrations)**.

2 Prise the plastic cover from the inner door handle, then undo the screw and unclip the handle from the operating rod **(see illustrations)**.

3 Using a screwdriver inserted at the front of the exterior mirror inner trim panel, carefully prise out the panel and disconnect the wiring from the control switch.

4 Prise the plastic cover from the door pull and undo the screws **(see illustrations)**.

5 Undo the screws securing the bottom of the trim to the door panel **(see illustration)**.

6 Remove the clip from the rear edge of the trim panel by depressing the centre pin **(see illustration)**.

7 Using a wide-bladed screwdriver, carefully prise out the clips securing the trim panel to the door. Take care not to damage the trim panel or break the clips by prising as near to the clip positions as possible.

8 With the clips released, lift the trim panel upwards over the locking button.

9 If necessary carefully pull the membranes from the door inner panel **(see illustrations)**.

Refitting

10 Refitting is a reversal of removal.

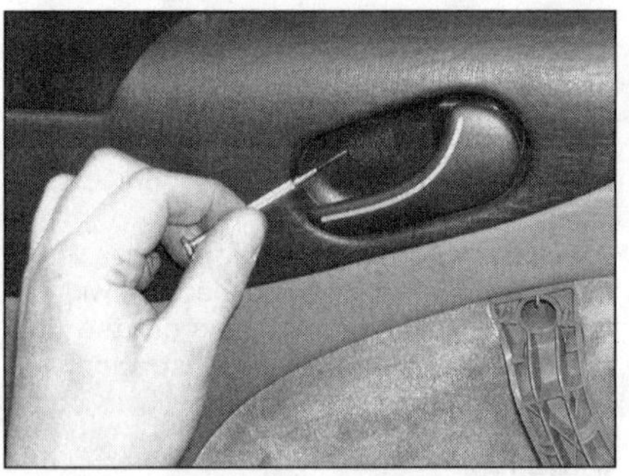

12.2a Prise off the plastic cover . . .

12.2b . . . then undo the screw . . .

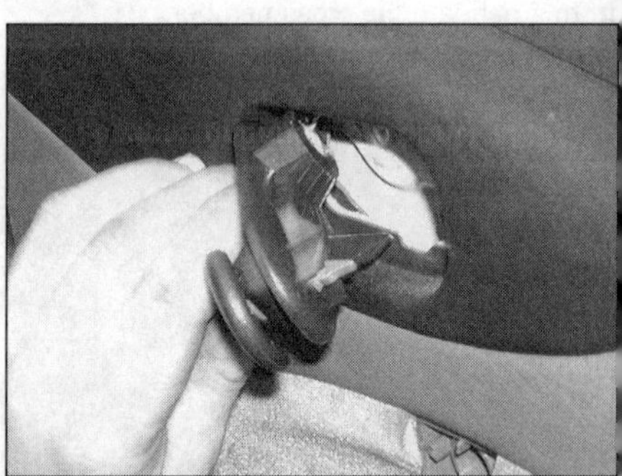

12.2c . . . and disconnect the handle from the operation rod

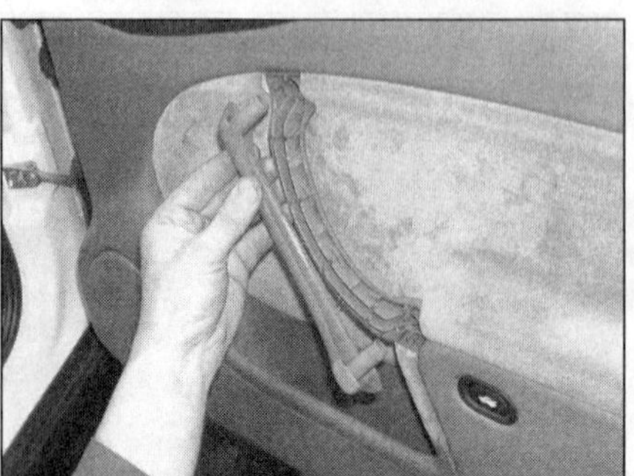

12.4a Remove the plastic cover from the door pull . . .

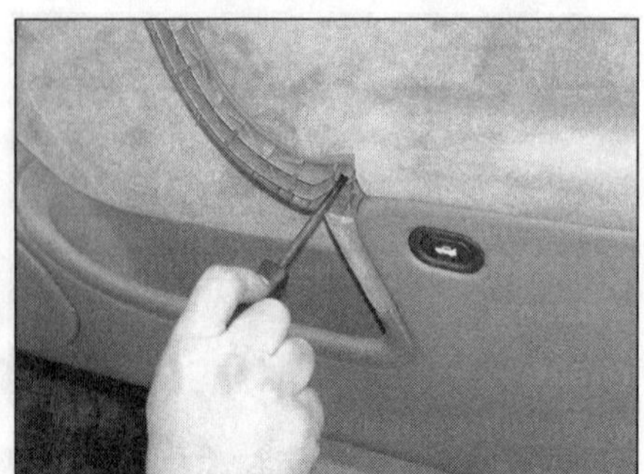

12.4b . . . and undo the screws

12.5 Removing the front door trim panel lower screws

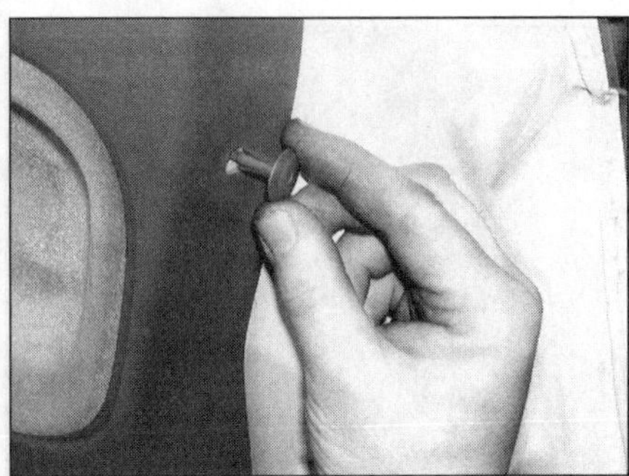
12.6 Removing the clip from the rear edge of the door trim

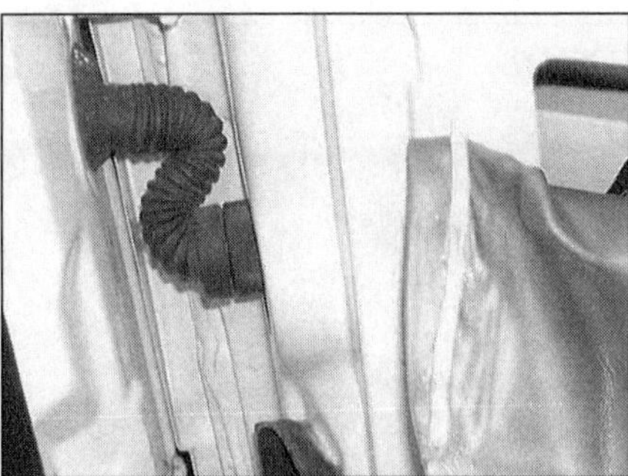
12.9a Removing the front door main membrane . . .

12.9b . . . and lower membrane

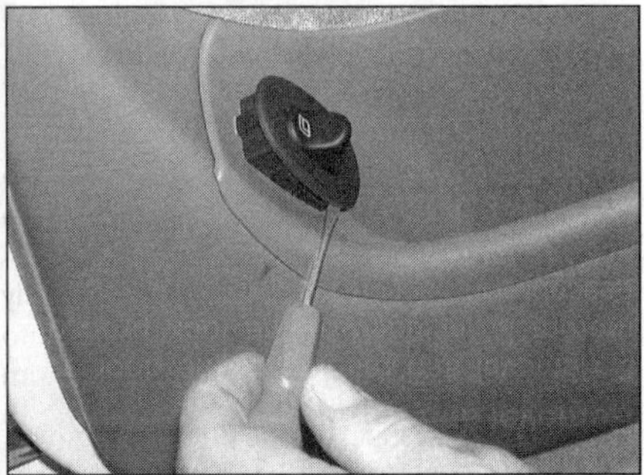
12.11 Removing the electric window lift switch from the rear door trim

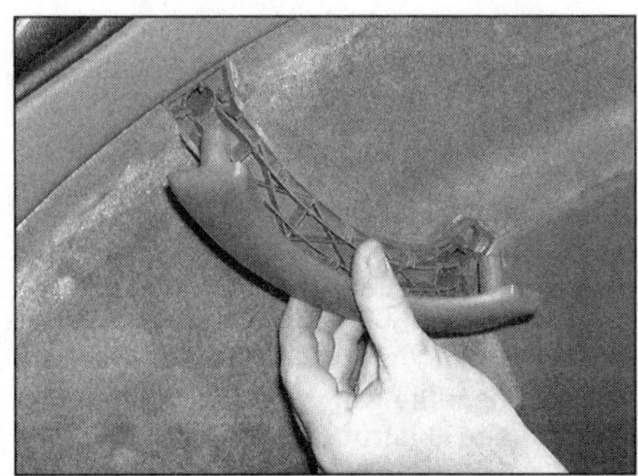
12.12a Prise the plastic cover from the door pull . . .

12.12b . . . then undo the retaining screws

Rear

Removal

11 Carefully prise the electric window lift switch from the door inner trim panel using a small screwdriver, and disconnect the wiring **(see illustration)**.

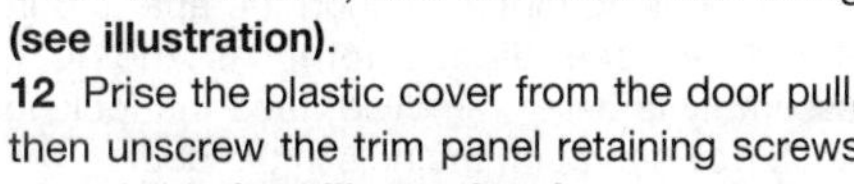

12 Prise the plastic cover from the door pull, then unscrew the trim panel retaining screws now visible **(see illustrations)**.

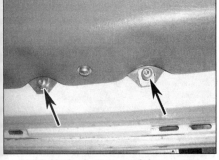

12.13 Undo the two retaining screws arrowed

12.14a Prise off the cover . . .

13 On the lower edge of the trim panel, undo the two retaining screws. Do not unscrew the centre screw as this secures the storage compartment to the trim panel **(see illustration)**.

14 Prise the plastic cover from the inner door handle, then undo the screw and unclip the handle from the operating rod **(see illustrations)**.

15 Using a wide-bladed screwdriver, carefully prise out the clips securing the trim panel to the door. Take care not to damage the trim panel or break the clips by prising as near to the clip positions as possible.

16 With the clips released, lift the trim panel upwards over the locking button.

17 If necessary carefully pull the membranes from the door inner panel **(see illustrations)**.

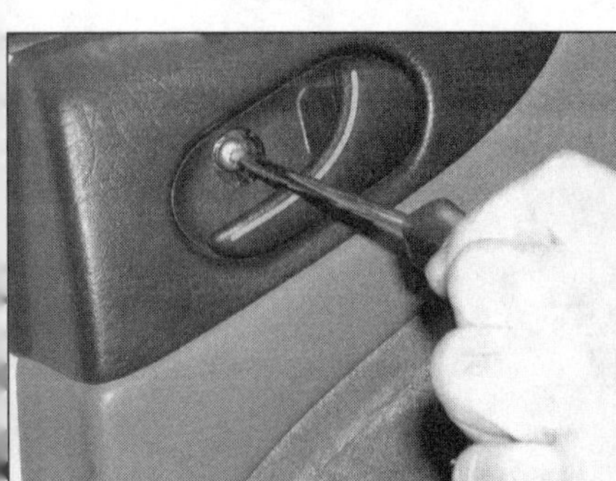
12.14b . . . then undo the screw . . .

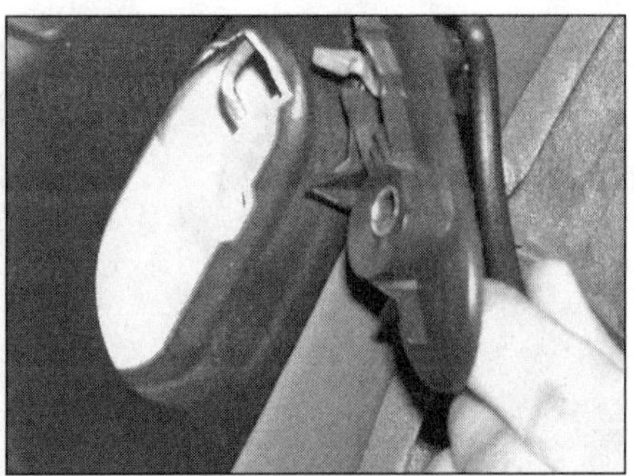
12.14c . . . and unclip the handle from the operating rod

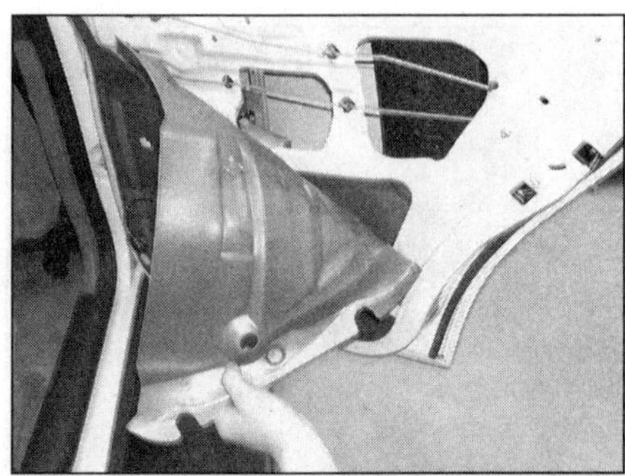
12.17a Removing the rear door main membrane . . .

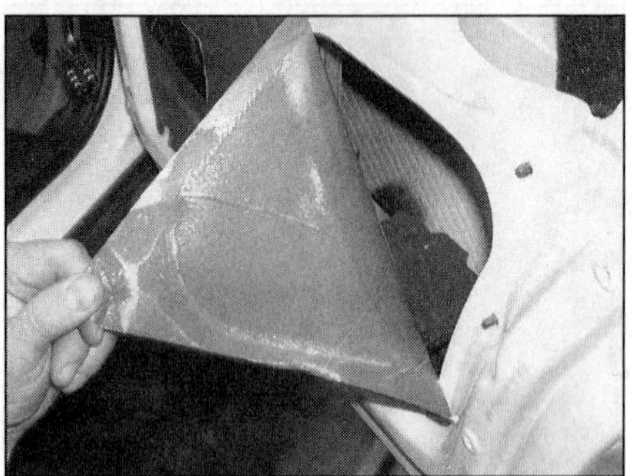

12.17b . . . and lower membrane

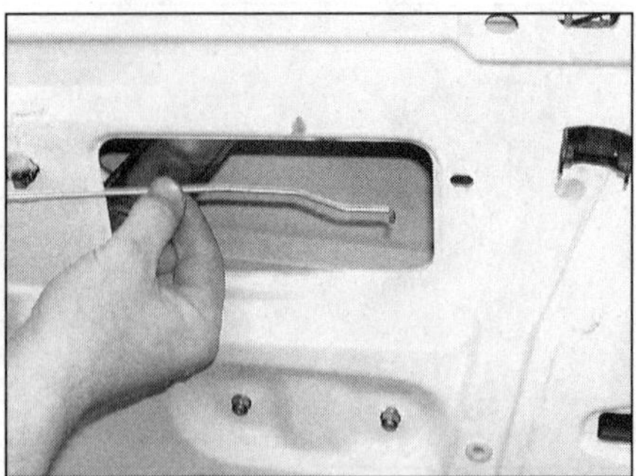

13.4 Disconnecting the operating rod from the lock

13.7 Disconnecting the wiring from the front door central locking

Refitting

18 Refitting is a reversal of removal.

13 Door handle and lock components - removal and refitting

Interior door handle

Removal

1 Prise the plastic cover from the inner door handle, then undo the screw and unclip the handle from the operating rod.

Refitting

2 Refitting is a reversal of removal.

Front door lock

Removal

3 With the window closed, remove the door trim and membranes (see Section 12).

4 Reach inside the door and disconnect the inner handle operating rod from the lock **(see illustration)**. To do this, push up the plastic retainer then release the rod.

5 Unscrew and remove the window rear guide channel lower bolt.

6 Disconnect the lock cylinder operating rod from the lock by pushing up the plastic retainer.

7 Disconnect the central locking wiring from the lock **(see illustration)**.

8 Undo the screws securing the lock to the rear edge of the door, and remove the plate where fitted **(see illustrations)**.

9 Withdraw the door lock complete with central locking motor through the aperture in the door **(see illustration)**. As the lock assembly is being removed, feed the locking knob down through the hole in the door.

10 If necessary, undo the screws and remove the central locking motor from the lock.

Refitting

11 Refitting is a reversal of removal, however before refitting the door trim, make sure that the lock operates correctly.

Rear door lock

Removal

12 With the window closed, remove the door trim and membranes (see Section 12). Also remove the packing from inside the door **(see illustration)**.

13 Reach inside the door and disconnect the inner handle operating rod from the lock **(see illustration)**. To do this, push up the plastic retainer then release the rod.

14 Disconnect the locking knob rod from the lock by pushing up the plastic retainer. If necessary, the complete rod can be removed by removing the crank **(see illustrations)**.

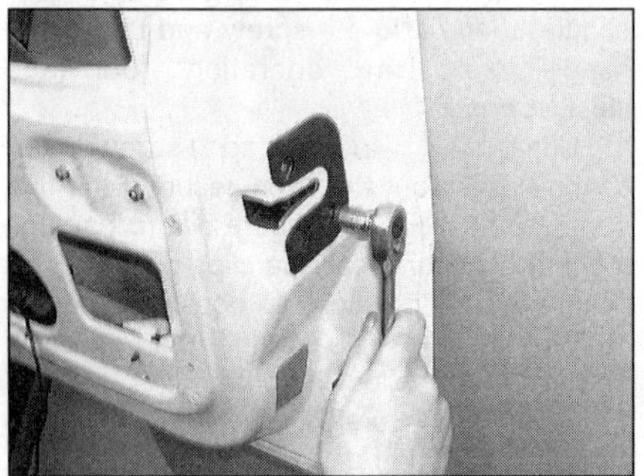

13.8a Undo the screws . . .

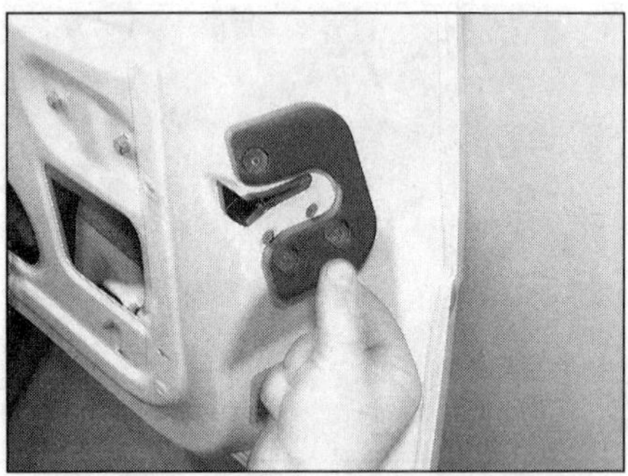

13.8b . . . remove the plate . . .

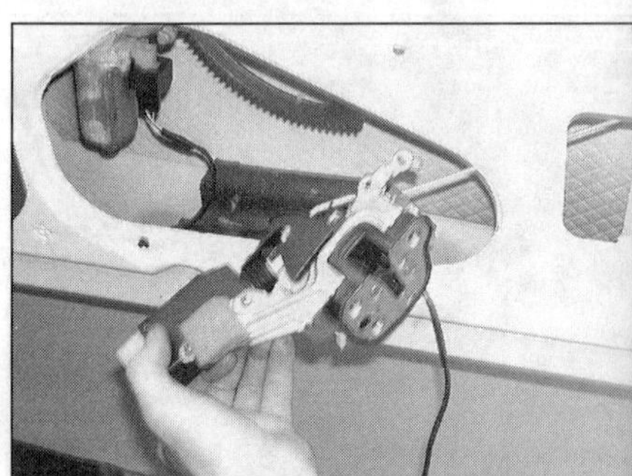

13.9 . . . and withdraw the door lock and central locking motor

13.12 Removing the packing from the rear door

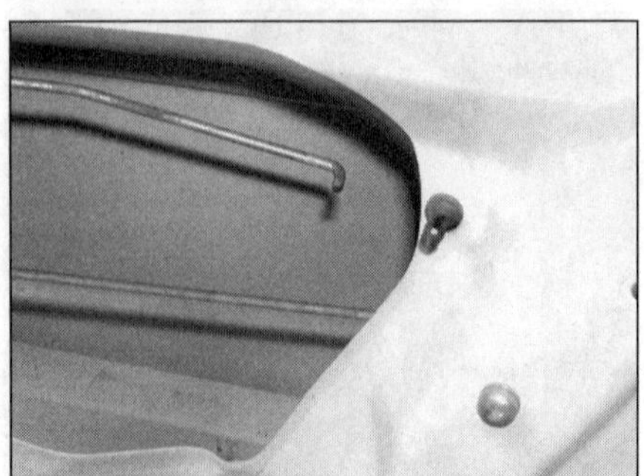

13.13 Disconnecting the inner handle operating rod from the lock

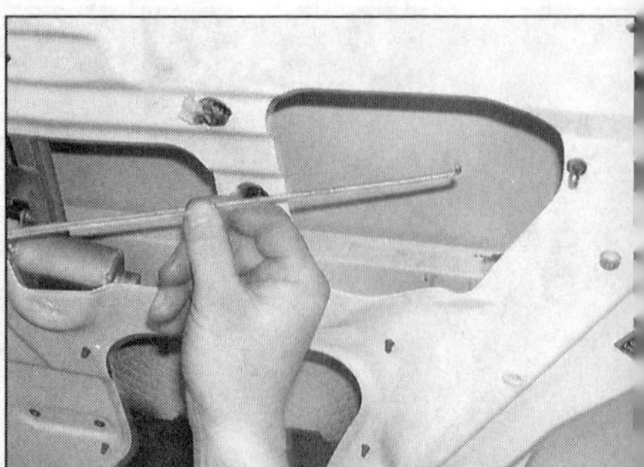

13.14a Disconnect the locking knob rod from the lock . . .

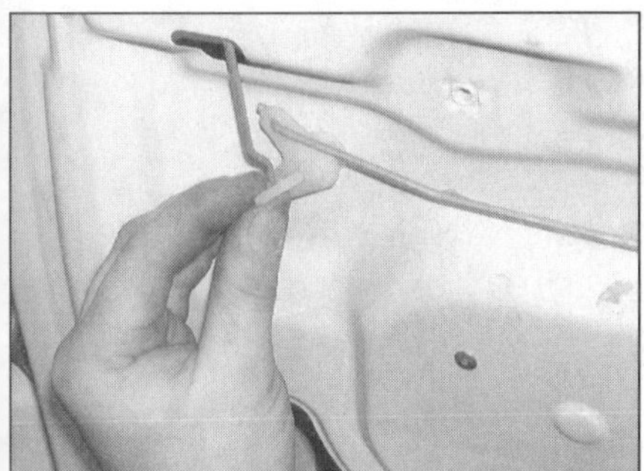

13.14b . . . then remove the crank

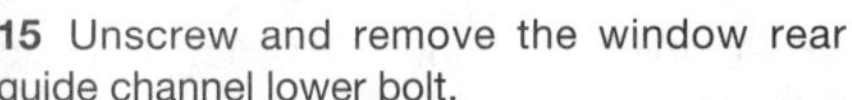

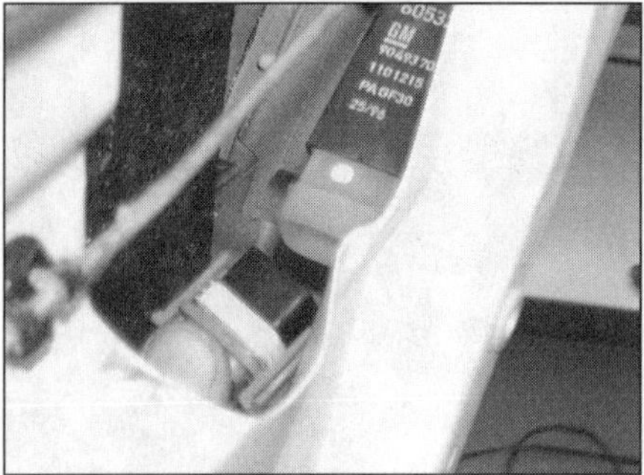

13.16 Disconnecting the central locking wiring from the rear door lock

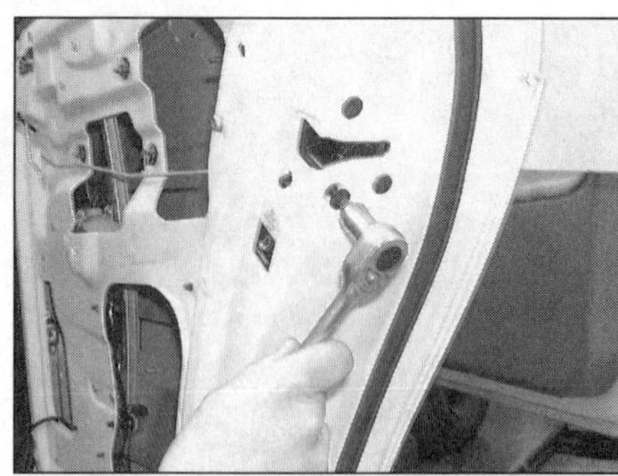

13.17 Undo the rear door lock screws . . .

15 Unscrew and remove the window rear guide channel lower bolt.

16 Disconnect the central locking wiring from the lock **(see illustration)**.

17 Undo the screws securing the lock to the rear edge of the door **(see illustration)**.

18 Withdraw the door lock complete with central locking motor through the aperture in the door **(see illustration)**.

19 If necessary, undo the screws and remove the central locking motor from the lock.

Refitting

20 Refitting is a reversal of removal.

Exterior door handle

Removal

21 With the window closed, remove the door trim and membranes (see Section 12).

22 Reach inside the door and disconnect the inner handle operating rod from the lock. To do this, push up the plastic retainer then release the rod.

23 Unscrew and remove the window rear guide channel lower bolt. On 5-door models, move the channel slightly out but do not disconnect the top of the channel. On 3-door models, pull the channel down slightly then pull it out of the top slot and remove it.

24 Reach inside the door and release the clip securing the microswitch to the rear of the exterior door handle. Position the switch to one side **(see illustration)**.

25 Disconnect the lock cylinder operating rod from the lock.

26 Support the exterior door handle from outside, then unscrew the nut from inside and remove the mounting plate **(see illustration)**.

27 Disconnect the exterior door handle operating rod from the lock.

28 If necessary for improved access, remove the lock completely as described earlier in this Section.

29 Carefully remove the exterior door handle from outside taking care not to damage the paintwork **(see illustration)**.

Refitting

30 Refitting is a reversal of removal.

Lock cylinder

Removal

31 Remove the front door exterior door handle as described earlier in this Section.

32 Insert the ignition key in the lock cylinder.

Driver's side

33 Disconnect the small coiled spring, noting its fitted position to ensure correct refitting, then remove the nylon cylinder **(see illustrations)**.

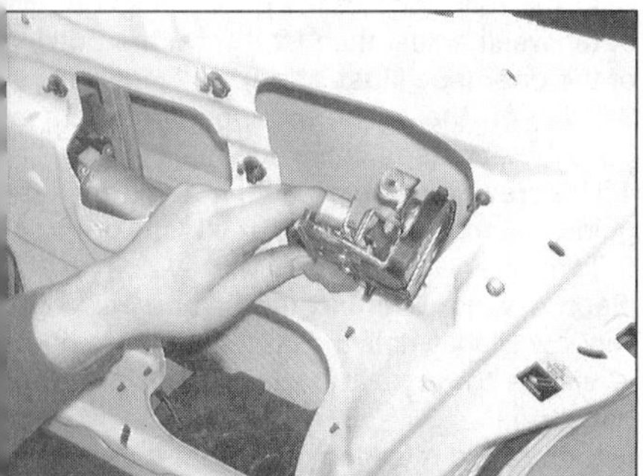

13.18 . . . and withdraw the lock

13.24 Releasing the microswitch clip from the exterior handle

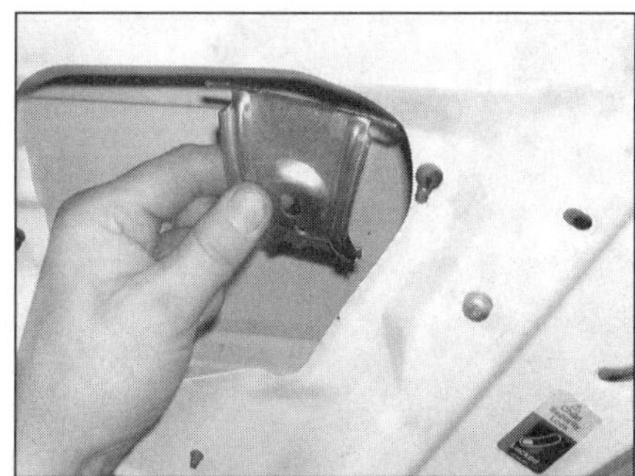

13.26 Removing the rear door exterior handle mounting plate

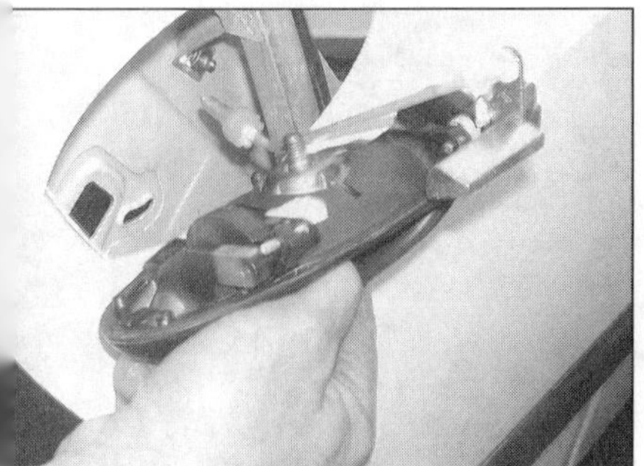

13.29 Removing the exterior handle from the rear door

13.33a Note how the coiled spring is fitted before removing it . . .

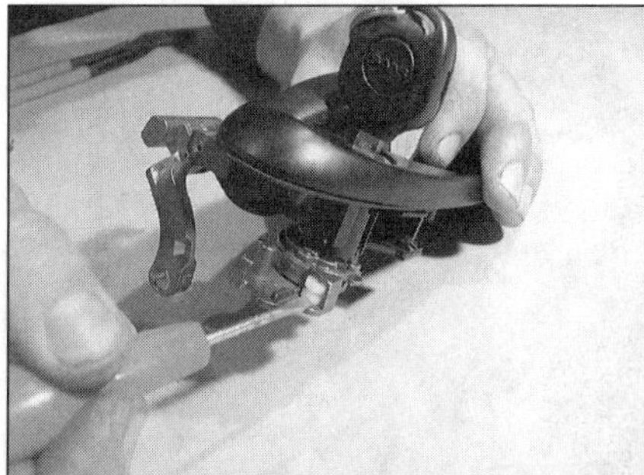

13.33b . . . then remove the nylon cylinder

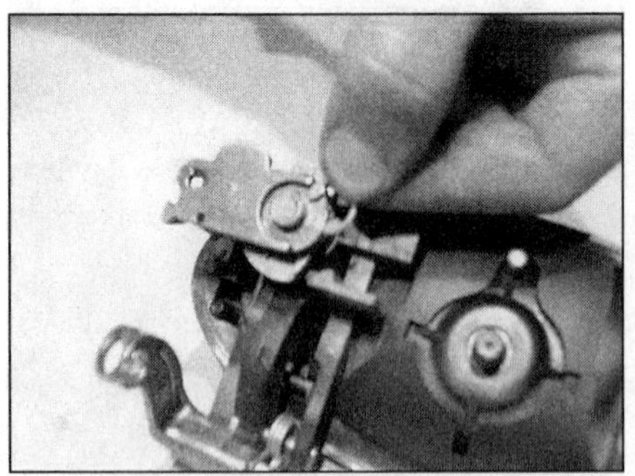
13.34a Extract the circlip . . .

13.34b . . . and casting . . .

13.34c . . . noting the position of the retaining ball

13.35 Remove the large coiled spring and driver . . .

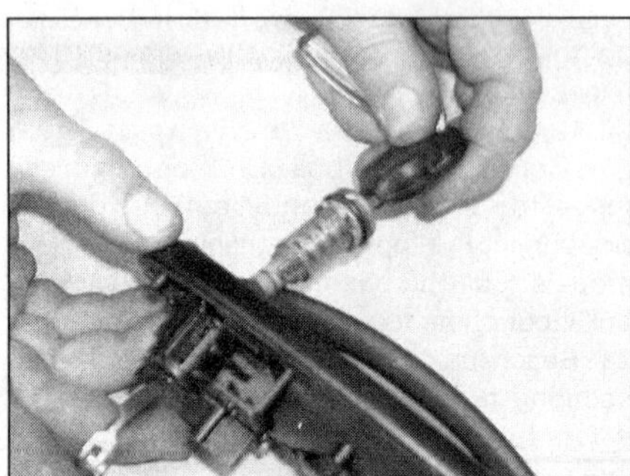
13.36 . . . then rotate the cylinder a quarter turn and withdraw it from the handle

34 Extract the circlip and remove the casting. Note the position of the retaining ball **(see illustrations)**.

35 Remove the large coiled spring and the driver **(see illustration)**.

36 Rotate the cylinder a quarter turn and withdraw it from the handle **(see illustration)**.

Passenger's side

37 Extract the circlip, then remove the driver and spring from the lock cylinder.

38 Rotate the cylinder a quarter turn and withdraw it from the handle.

Refitting

39 Refitting is a reversal of removal. Make sure that the drain hole is fitted at the bottom of the cylinder. On the driver's side, apply a little grease to the retaining ball before refitting it.

14 Door window glass - removal and refitting

Front door

Removal

1 Fully lower the window, then remove the inner door trim panel and membranes as described in Section 12.

2 At the rear edge of the door, press out the outer weatherseal then lift it from the outside of the door **(see illustration)**.

3 Prise off the cover and inner weatherseal from the door **(see illustrations)**.

4 Unscrew and remove the window rear guide channel lower bolt **(see illustration)**.

5 Temporarily reconnect the switch to the electric window lifting motor and raise the window slightly until the bottom of the window is visible through the openings in the door panel.

6 Extract the retaining clips from the channel rollers, then carefully prise the regulator pins from the rollers while supporting the window **(see illustrations)**. The pins are a tight fit in

14.2 Removing the outer weatherseal from the front door

14.3a Prise off the triangular cover . . .

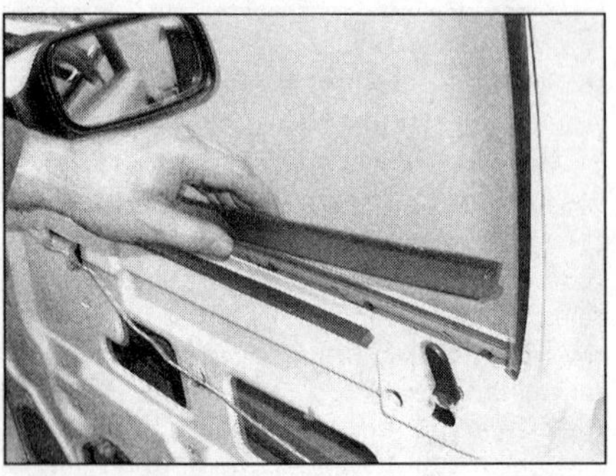
14.3b . . . and the inner weatherseal from the door

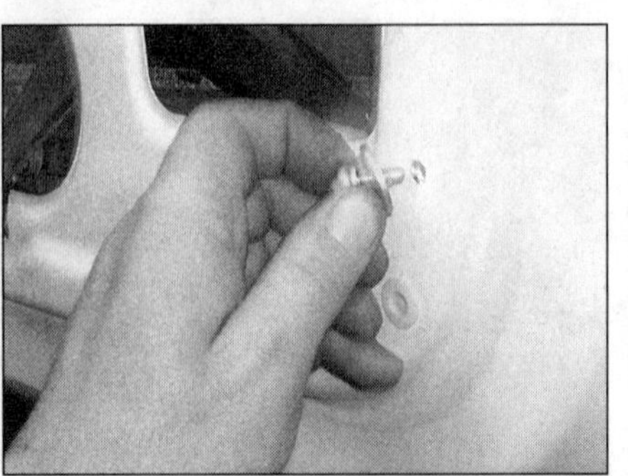
14.4 Removing the front door window rear guide lower bolt

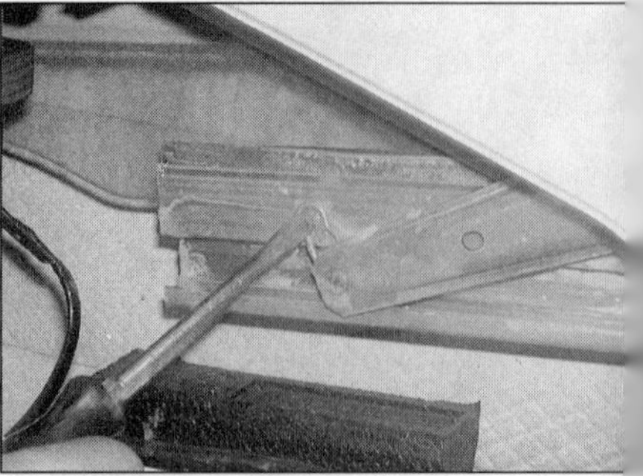
14.6a Extract the retaining clips . . .

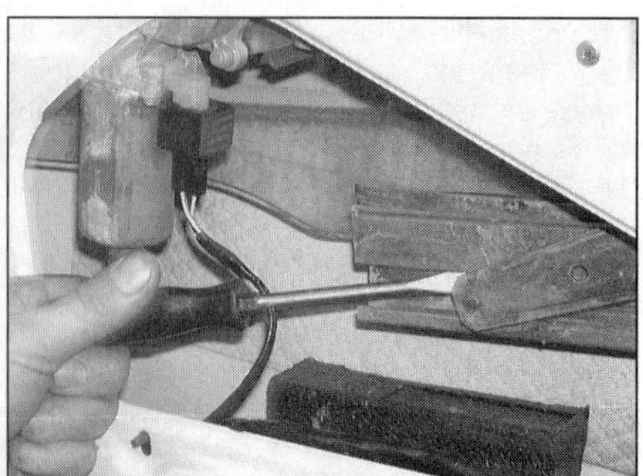
14.6b . . . then prise out the regulator pins from the rollers

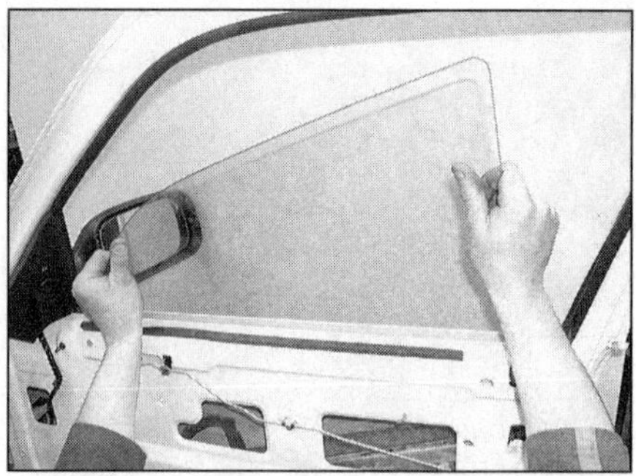
14.7 Lifting the window from the front door

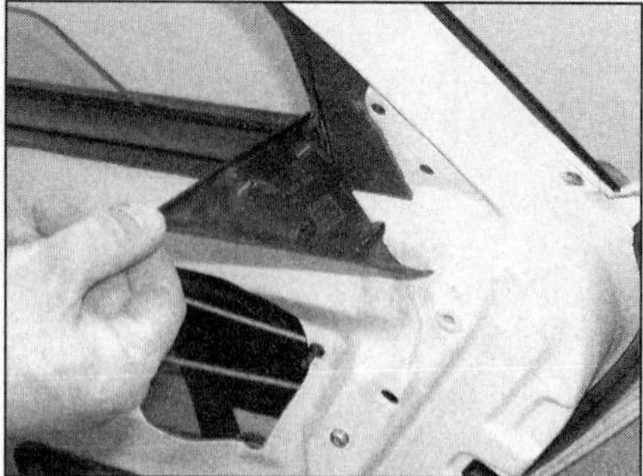
14.18 Removing the triangular trim cover

the rollers so take care not to apply excessive pressure to the glass.

7 Carefully lift the rear of the window and withdraw it from the outside of the door **(see illustration)**.

8 Remove the channel rollers from the glass.

Refitting

9 Lubricate the window glass bottom channel with grease, then locate the rollers in it.

10 Lower the glass into position and locate it in the front and rear guide channels.

11 Press the regulator pins into the rollers then refit the clips.

12 Insert and tighten the window rear guide channel lower bolt.

13 Temporarily reconnect the switch to the electric window lifting motor, then loosen the regulator rearmost adjustment nut and fully raise the window. Now lower the window until it is 3.0 cm from its closed position, and press the window fully to the rear. The top edge of the window should be parallel with the door panel. Tighten the rearmost adjustment nut.

14 Press the inner weatherseal into the door.

15 Refit the outer weatherseal and press the location peg into the hole.

16 Refit the inner door trim panel and membranes (see Section 12).

Rear door

Removal

17 Fully lower the window, then remove the inner door trim panel and membranes as described in Section 12.

18 Using a screwdriver, carefully prise out the triangular trim cover from the door and remove the packing **(see illustration)**.

19 Prise up the inner weatherseal from the door **(see illustration)**.

20 Prise up the outer weatherseal from the door **(see illustration)**.

21 Remove the rubber seal from the rear guide channel **(see illustration)**.

22 Disconnect the inner door handle operating rod from the lock by pushing up the plastic retainer.

23 Unscrew and remove the window rear guide channel lower screw. Remove the outer triangular trim, then disconnect the channel upper end and turn as necessary to remove it **(see illustrations)**.

24 Carefully raise the rear of the glass and release the bottom channel from the regulator. Reposition the glass horizontally, then lift it upwards and remove it from the inside of the door **(see illustrations)**.

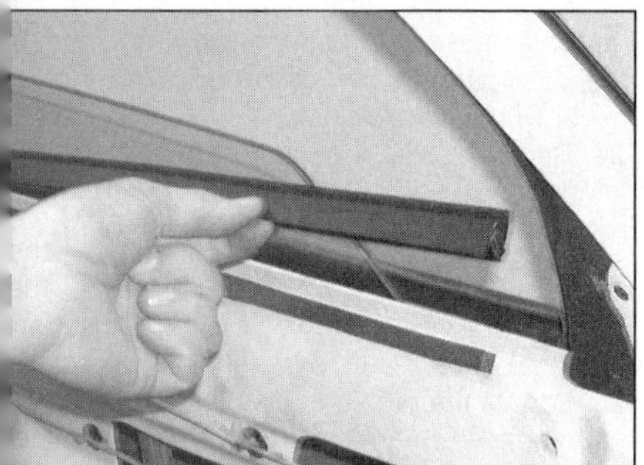
14.19 Removing the inner weatherseal from the rear door

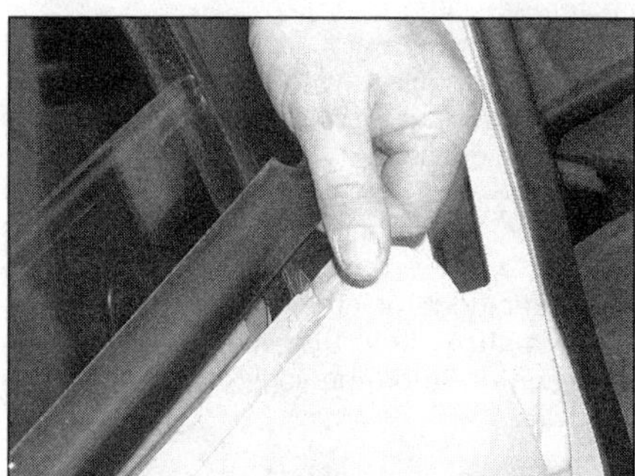
14.20 Removing the outer weatherseal

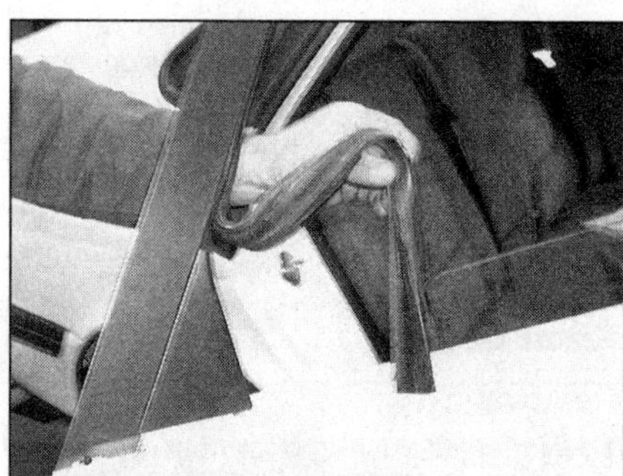
14.21 Removing the rubber seal from the rear guide channel

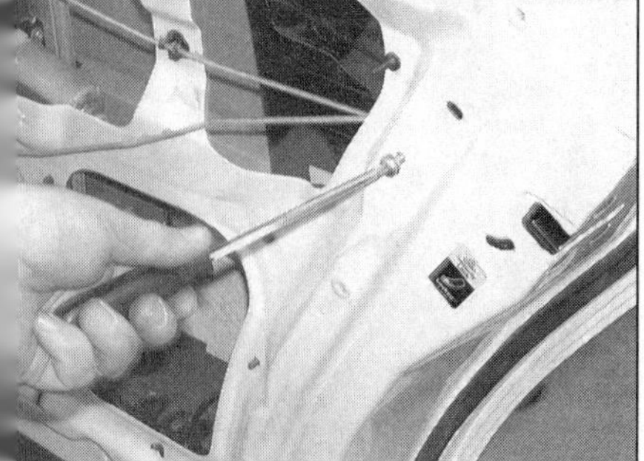
14.23a Remove the guide channel lower screw . . .

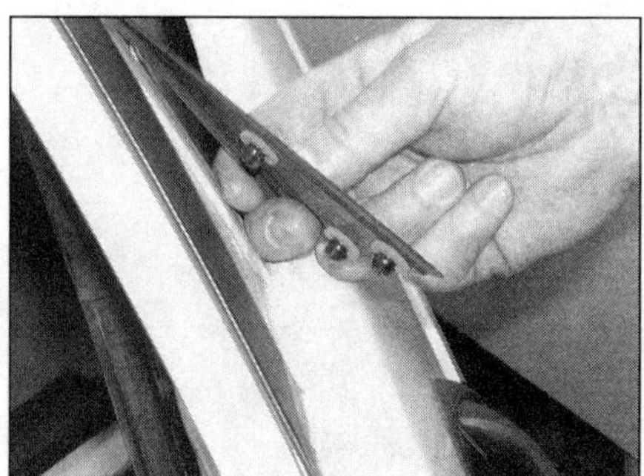
14.23b . . . then remove the triangular trim . . .

14.23c . . . and withdraw the window rear guide channel

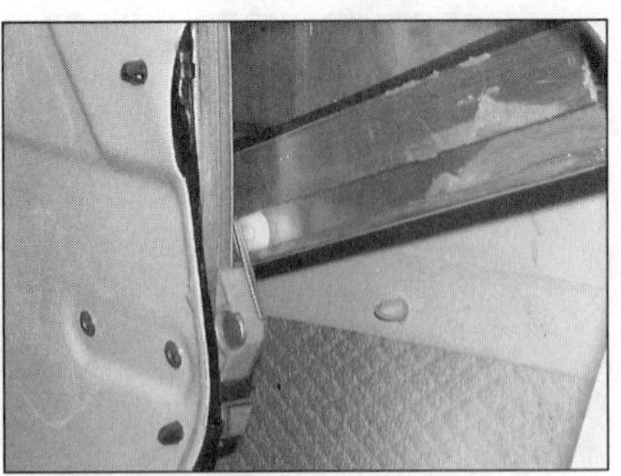

14.24a Release the bottom channel from the regulator . . .

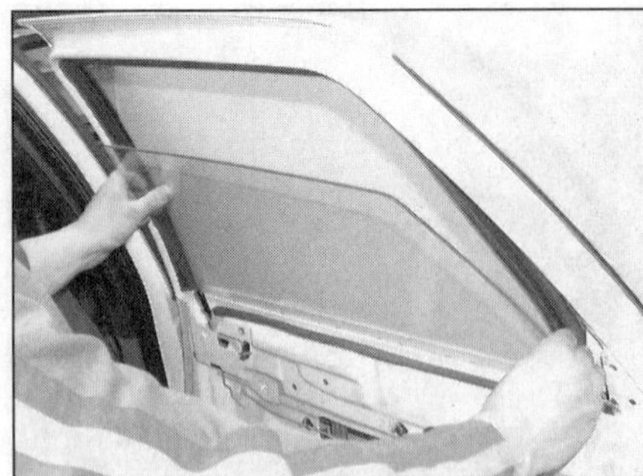

14.24b . . . then withdraw the window from the rear door

Refitting

25 Lubricate the window glass bottom channel with grease.

26 Lower the glass into position and engage the bottom channel with the regulator.

27 Locate the glass in the front guide channel, then refit the rear guide channel and secure with the lower bolt. Make sure the upper end of the channel is correctly located.

28 Reconnect the inner door handle operating rod to the lock and secure with the plastic retainer.

29 Smear some vaseline (petroleum jelly) on the rubber seal, then locate it in the rear guide channel.

30 Refit the inner and outer weatherseals, making sure that they are pressed down firmly.

31 Refit the quarter trim cover and packing, pressing them firmly into place.

32 Refit the inner door trim panel and membranes as described in Section 12.

33 Raise the window and check its operation.

15 Door window regulator - removal and refitting

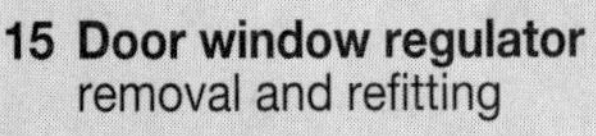

Front door

Removal

1 Remove the inner door trim panel and membranes as described in Section 12.

2 Temporarily reconnect the window operating switch, then lower the window approximately 10 cm and retain in this position using adhesive tape. The window bottom channel and regulator arm ends should now be visible through the apertures in the door inner panel.

3 Prise out the retaining clips from the channel rollers, then carefully prise the regulator pins from the rollers while supporting the window. The pins are a tight fit in the rollers so take care not to apply excessive pressure to the glass.

4 Temporarily reconnect the window operating switch, then operate the motor until the regulator arms are horizontal. This will enable the regulator to be removed more easily through the door aperture.

5 Support the regulator, then drill off the heads of the rivets securing the regulator to the door panel. Tap out the rivets with a small punch.

6 Disconnect the wiring from the electric motor **(see illustration)**.

7 Mark the position of the adjustment channel, then unscrew the retaining nuts.

8 Withdraw the regulator and motor from inside the door.

9 If necessary, unbolt the motor from the regulator. Where one of the retaining bolts is concealed by the regulator, it will be necessary to remove the stator for access to the armature, then turn the armature while pressing down on the segment for access to the bolt.

Refitting

10 If necessary, refit the motor to the regulator and tighten the bolts.

11 Locate the regulator and motor inside the door, then refit the adjustment channel in its previously noted position and tighten the nuts.

12 Reconnect the wiring to the electric motor.

13 Temporarily reconnect the switch then raise the regulator arms slightly.

14 Position the regulator on the door and secure with new rivets.

15 Engage the regulator pins with the window channel rollers and refit the clips.

16 With the adjustment nuts loose, fully raise the window. Now lower the window until it is 3.0 cm from its closed position, and press the window fully to the rear. The top edge of the window should be parallel with the door panel. Tighten the adjustment nuts.

17 Refit the inner door trim panel and membranes with reference to Section 12.

Rear door

Removal

18 Remove the inner door trim panel and membranes as described in Section 12.

19 Prise up the outer weatherseal from the door.

20 Unscrew and remove the window rear guide channel lower bolt.

21 Temporarily reconnect the window operating switch, then lower the window approximately 10 cm and retain in this position using adhesive tape. The window bottom channel and regulator arm ends should now be visible through the apertures in the door inner panel.

22 Disconnect the wiring from the electric motor **(see illustration)**.

23 Support the regulator, then drill off the heads of the rivets securing the regulator to the door panel **(see illustration)**. Tap out the rivets with a small punch.

24 Release the regulator arms from the window bottom channel, then carefully withdraw the regulator and motor through the aperture in the door panel. **Note:** *The motor and regulator cannot be separated.*

Refitting

25 Locate the regulator inside the door panel and engage the arms with the window bottom channel.

26 Position the regulator and secure with new rivets.

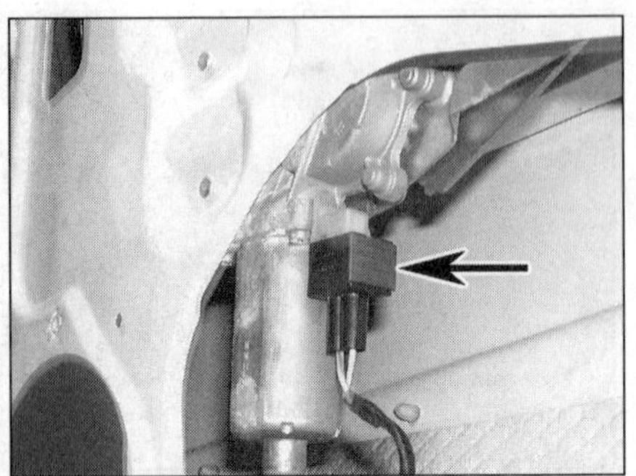

15.6 Wiring plug for the front door electric window

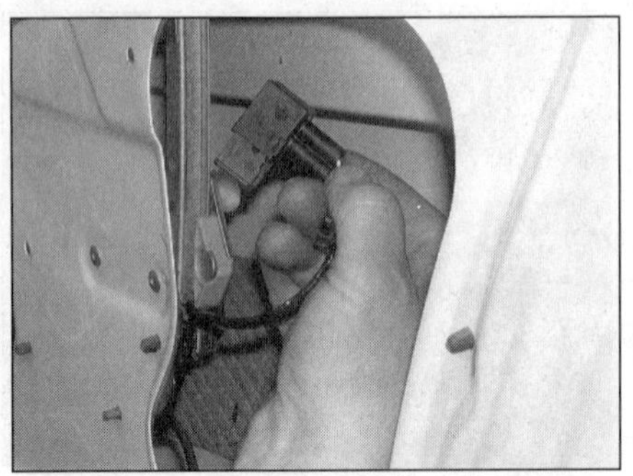

15.22 Disconnecting the wiring from the rear door electric window

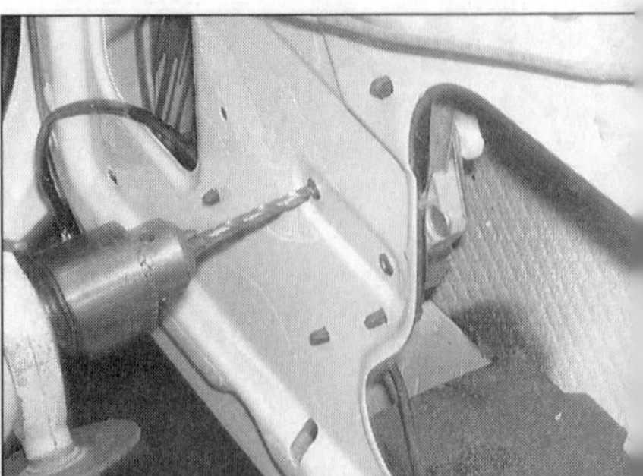

15.23 Drilling out the regulator mounting rivets

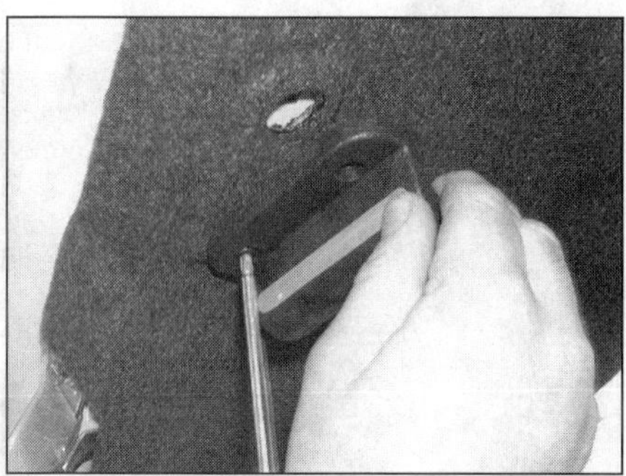

16.4 Removing the grab handle

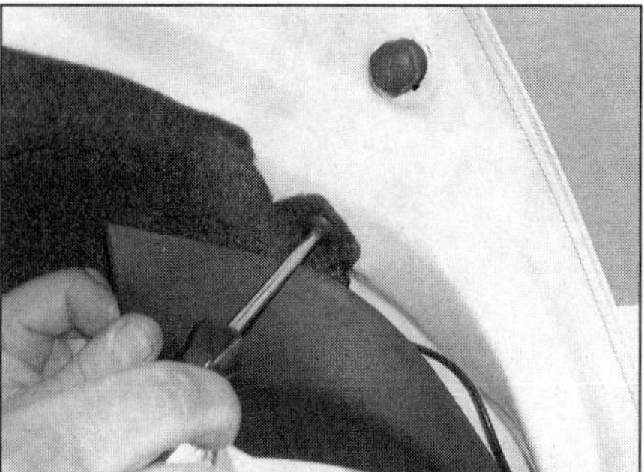

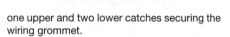

16.5a Undo the screws . . .

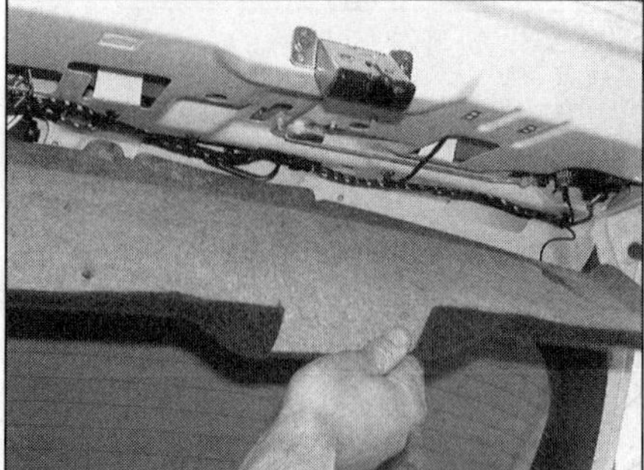

16.5b . . . and remove the trim from the tailgate

27 Reconnect the electric motor wiring.
28 Insert and tighten the window rear guide channel lower bolt.
29 Refit the outer weatherseal to the door.
30 Refit the inner door trim panel and membranes with reference to Section 12.

16 Tailgate and support struts - removal and refitting

Removal

1 Disconnect the battery negative (earth) lead (see Chapter 5A).
2 With the tailgate open, place some cloth rags between the tailgate and the bodywork to prevent any damage.
3 Remove the rear parcel shelf.
4 Using a Torx key, undo the screws and remove the grab handle from the tailgate **(see illustration)**.
5 Using a screwdriver, undo the screws and remove the main trim panel from the inside of the tailgate **(see illustrations)**. Also carefully prise the plastic trim panels from the sides of the tailgate using a screwdriver.
6 Unscrew the central locking motor mounting bolts, then disconnect the lever and wiring and remove the motor.
7 Note the location of the remaining wiring in the tailgate, then disconnect it and release it from the cable ties.
8 At the top of the tailgate, prise out the wiring protector from the inner hole, then use a screwdriver through the hole to release the one upper and two lower catches securing the wiring grommet.
9 Carefully withdraw the wiring through the top of the tailgate.
10 Turn the washer nozzle through 90° and pull it out of the tailgate, then disconnect the tubing.
11 Remove the rubber stop and remove the washer tubing.
12 While an assistant supports the weight of the tailgate, disconnect the struts by prising out the spring clips. Position the struts on the rear body.
13 Extract the circlip from the hinge pins, then use a suitable drift to drive them out **(see illustrations)**.
14 Lift the tailgate from the rear body and place it in a safe position on cloth rags or card to protect the paintwork.

Refitting

15 With the help of an assistant, lift the tailgate into position. Lightly grease the hinge pins then refit them and secure with the circlips.
16 Reconnect the struts and refit the spring clips.
17 Insert the washer tubing and rubber stop, then reconnect the tubing to the nozzle. Insert the nozzle and turn through 90° to secure.
18 Feed the wiring into the tailgate and refit the grommet making sure that the catches are correctly engaged. Refit the wiring protector.
19 Locate the wiring as previously noted and secure with the cable ties.
20 Refit the central locking motor and reconnect the lever and wiring. Insert the bolts and tighten.
21 Refit the trim panels and tighten the screws.
22 Refit the grab handle and tighten the screws.
23 Refit the parcel shelf.
24 Reconnect the battery negative lead (see Chapter 5A).
25 Check that the tailgate closes properly and is located centrally within the body aperture. Adjustment is possible by lowering the headlining and loosening the hinge bolts. Check that the tailgate rests in the rubber buffers located on each side, and if necessary adjust the buffers by removing the trim and loosening the nuts. Check that the striker enters the lock centrally, and if necessary loosen the striker screws to adjust its position.

17 Tailgate/bootlid lock components - removal and refitting

Tailgate lock

Removal

1 Remove the rear parcel shelf.
2 Using a Torx key, undo the screws and remove the grab handle from the tailgate.
3 Using a screwdriver, undo the screws and remove the main trim panel from the inside of the tailgate.
4 Disconnect the operating rod from the crank located near the central locking motor **(see illustration)**. To do this, press off the plastic clip.

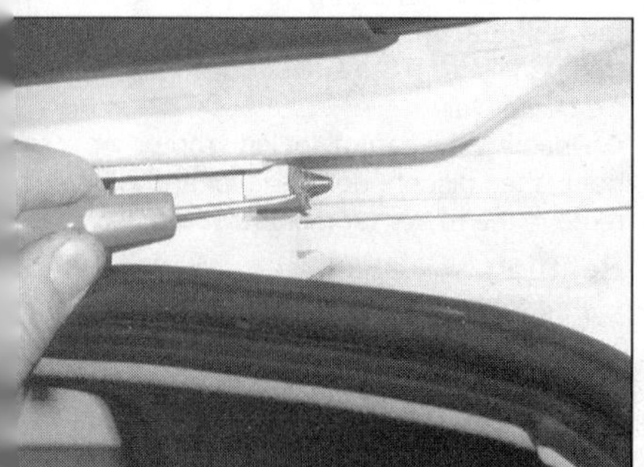

16.13a Extract the circlips . . .

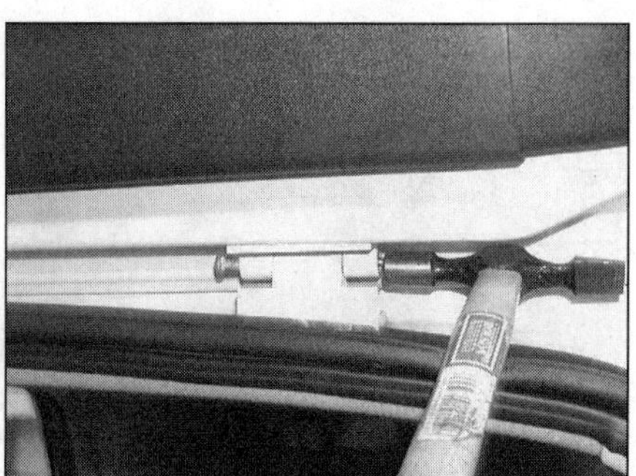

16.13b . . . and drive out the hinge pins

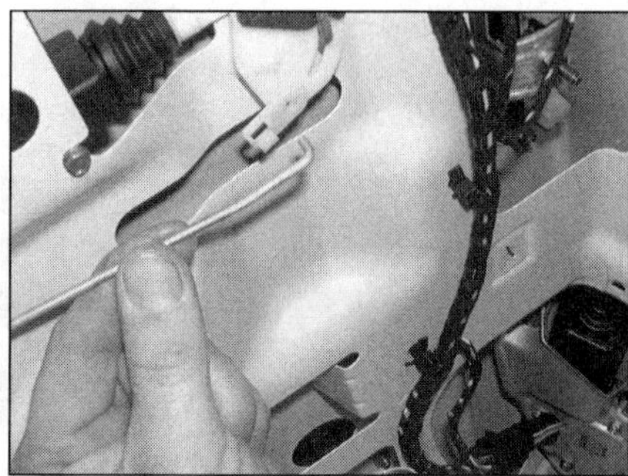

17.4 Disconnecting the operating rod from the crank

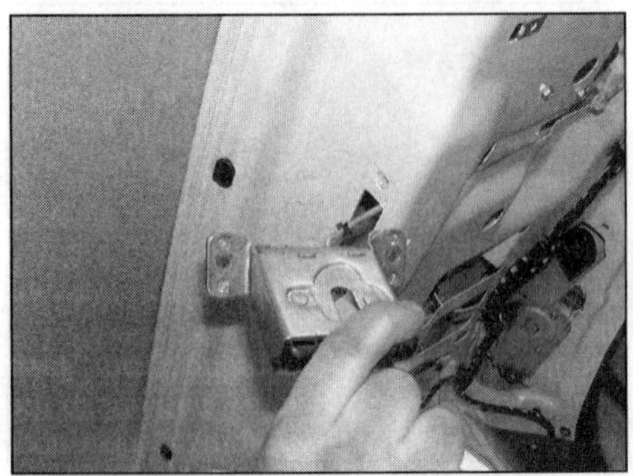

17.5 Removing the tailgate lock

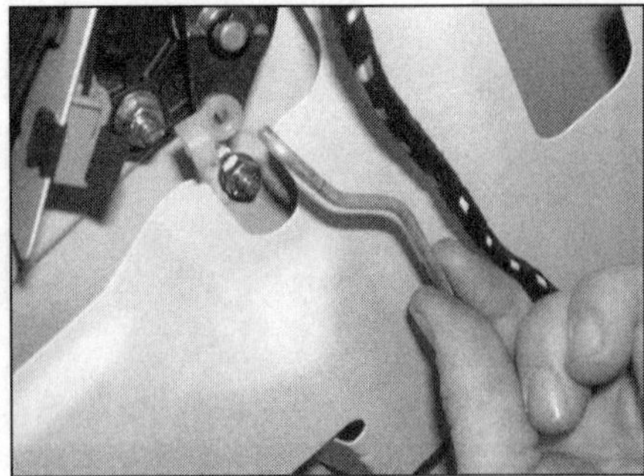

17.11 Disconnecting the operating rod from the tailgate lock cylinder

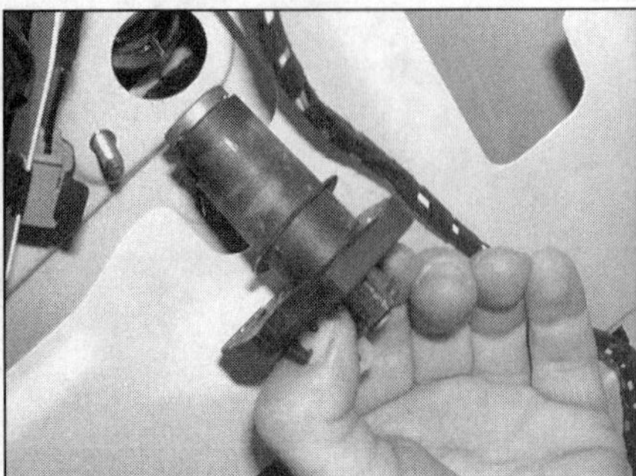

17.13 Removing the tailgate lock cylinder assembly

17.14a Extract the circlip . . .

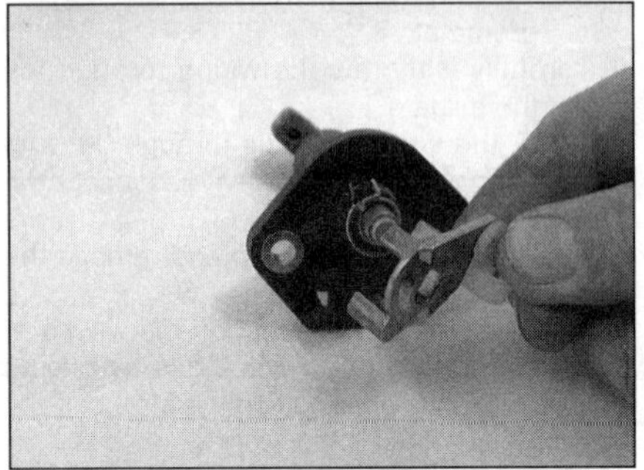

17.14b . . . and remove the lever . . .

17.14c . . . and spring . . .

5 Unscrew the mounting bolts and withdraw the lock together with the operating rod from the hole in the tailgate **(see illustration)**.

6 Disconnect the operating rod.

Refitting

7 Refitting is a reversal of removal.

Tailgate lock cylinder

Removal

8 Remove the rear parcel shelf.

9 Using a Torx key, undo the screws and remove the grab handle from the tailgate.

10 Using a screwdriver, undo the screws and remove the main trim panel from the inside of the tailgate.

11 Press off the plastic clip and disconnect the operating rod from the lock cylinder **(see illustration)**.

12 If necessary, prise off the clip and remove the microswitch.

13 Unscrew the mounting nuts and withdraw the lock cylinder from the tailgate **(see illustration)**.

14 Insert the ignition key into the lock cylinder, then extract the circlip and remove the lever and spring **(see illustrations)**.

15 Press out the cylinder **(see illustration)**.

16 Check the rubber O-ring and if necessary renew it.

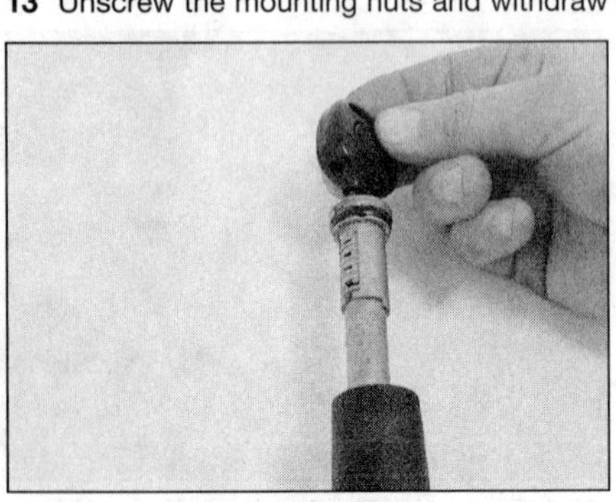

17.15 . . . then remove the cylinder

Refitting

17 Refitting is a reversal of removal. Make sure that the lock cylinder is fitted with the drain hole facing downwards.

Spoiler

Removal

18 Remove the rear parcel shelf.

19 Using a Torx key, undo the screws and remove the grab handle from the tailgate.

20 Using a screwdriver, undo the screws and remove the main trim panel from the inside of the tailgate.

18.4 Tailgate central locking motor

21 Remove the tailgate wiper motor as described in Chapter 12.

22 Unscrew the mounting nuts and remove the spoiler from the tailgate.

Refitting

23 Refitting is a reversal of removal.

18 Central locking servo motors - removal and refitting

Tailgate motors

Removal

1 Remove the rear parcel shelf.

2 Using a Torx key, undo the screws an remove the grab handle from the tailgate.

3 Using a screwdriver, undo the screws an remove the main trim panel from the inside o the tailgate. Also carefully prise the plasti trim panels from the sides of the tailgate usin a screwdriver.

4 Unscrew the central locking motor mountin bolts, then disconnect the lever and wiring an remove the motor **(see illustration)**.

Refitting

5 Refitting is a reversal of removal.

Door motors

Removal and refitting

6 Removal and refitting of the door serv motors is included in the lock procedur described in Section 13.

20.1 Removing the triangular trim

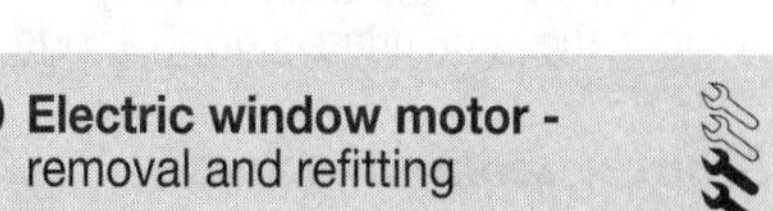

19 Electric window motor - removal and refitting

The procedure for removing and refitting the front door electric window motor is described in Section 15. It is not possible to separate the rear door electric window motor from the regulator.

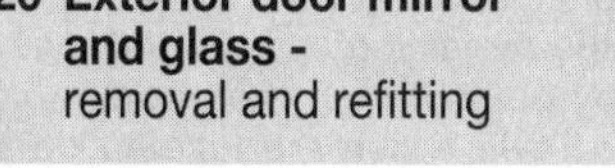

20 Exterior door mirror and glass - removal and refitting

Mirror

Removal

1 With the front door open, prise off the triangular trim cover by inserting a screwdriver beneath the front edge **(see illustration)**. Remove the packing.

2 Disconnect the wiring from the mirror control switch and from the mirror **(see illustrations)**.

3 Undo the mounting screws and withdraw the mirror from the outside of the door **(see illustrations)**.

Refitting

4 Refitting is a reversal of removal.

Glass

Removal

5 Using a wide-bladed screwdriver, prise out the top of the glass until it is released from the clip **(see illustration)**.

6 Disconnect the heater wires **(see illustration)**.

Refitting

7 Reconnect the wiring.

8 Using a wad of cloth rag, press the mirror into position until the clip engages.

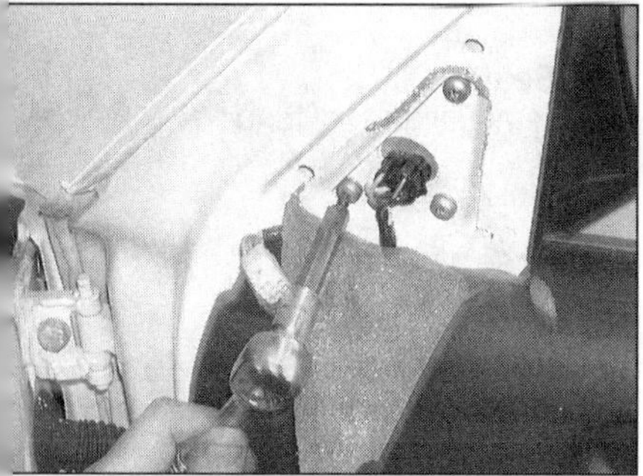

20.3a Undo the mounting screws . . .

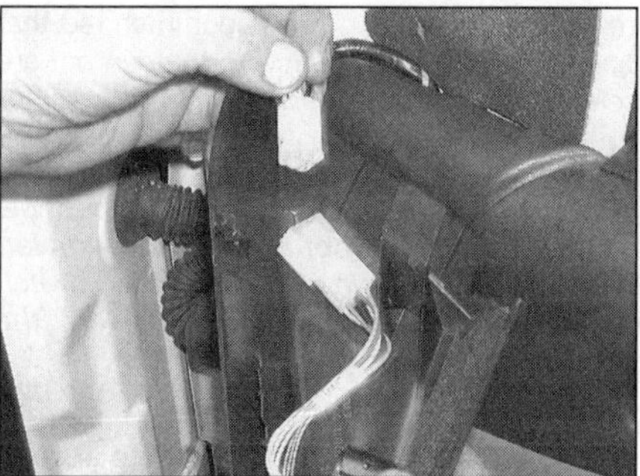

20.2a Disconnect the wiring from the control switch . . .

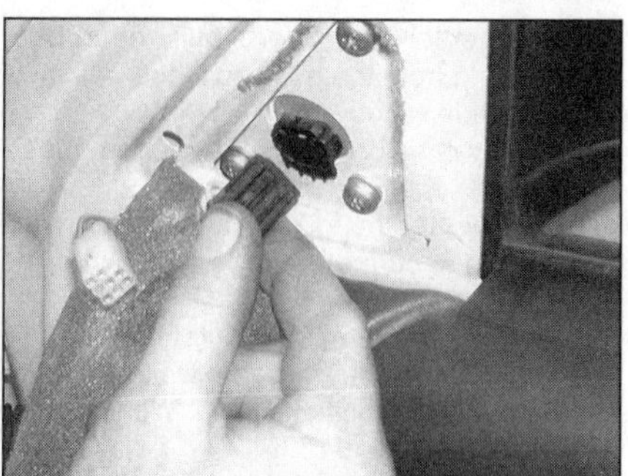

20.2b . . . and from the mirror

21 Windscreen, rear window and fixed windows - general information

Windscreen and rear window

1 The windscreen and rear window glass are bonded in position with a special adhesive. Renewal of such fixed glass is a complex, messy and time-consuming task, which is beyond the scope of the home mechanic; without the benefit of extensive practice, it is difficult to attain a secure, waterproof fit. Furthermore, the task carries a high risk of accidental breakage - this applies especially to the laminated glass windscreen. In view of this, owners are strongly advised to entrust work of this nature to a Saab dealer, or one of the many specialist windscreen fitters.

Fixed side window (3-door models)

Note: *The fixed side window is sealed to the body with butyl tape and is not therefore considered to be a suitable job for the average home mechanic. However, the following information is given for those who may wish to carry out the work themselves.*

Removal

2 With the door open, pull the rubber weatherstrip from the door opening in the vicinity of the fixed side window.

3 Using a wide-bladed screwdriver, carefully prise the trim panel from the top inside of the B-pillar. Lower the panel over the seat belt to the floor.

4 Carefully prise off the kick plate from the bottom of the door opening.

5 Fold the rear seat cushion forwards then fold the rear seat backrest forwards. Unscrew and remove the fastener from the rear of the side trim.

6 Fold the backrest rearwards, then remove the remaining fasteners and withdraw the side trim.

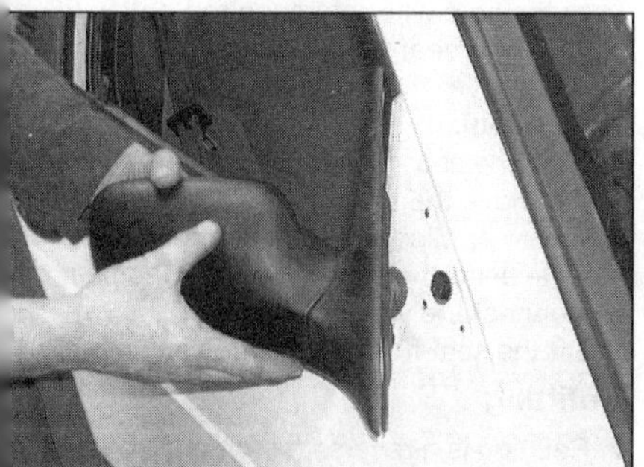

20.3b . . . and withdraw the mirror from the door

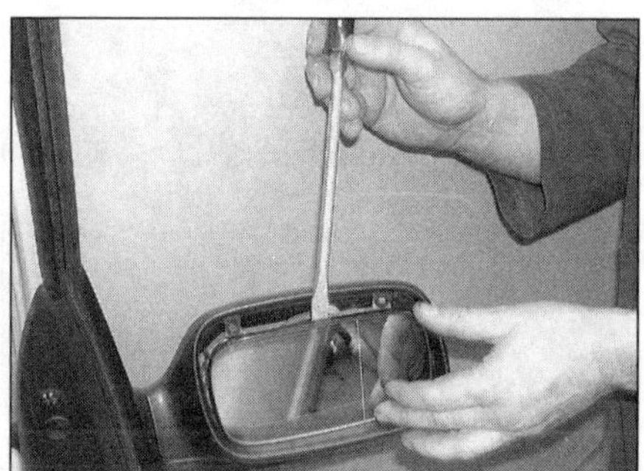

20.5 Prising out the exterior door mirror glass

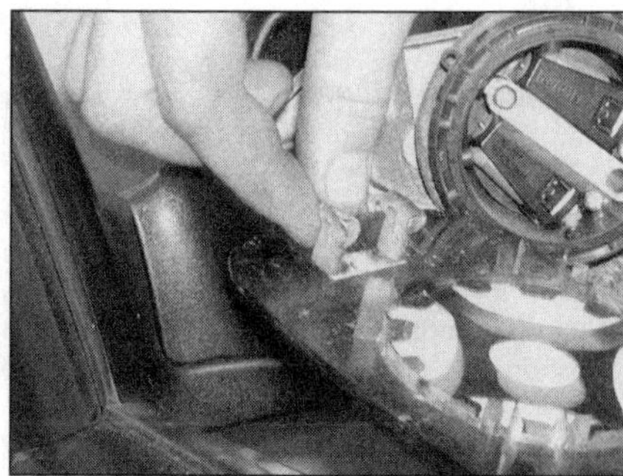

20.6 Disconnecting the heater wires from the exterior door mirror

7 With the tailgate open, pull the rubber weatherstrip from the opening in the vicinity of the fixed side window.

8 Carefully prise off the trim panel from the C-pillar.

9 Pull down the headlining and unscrew the upper nuts securing the side window to the body.

10 Unscrew the remaining nuts then have an assistant support the window while the butyl tape is cut with a suitable knife. Withdraw the window.

Refitting

11 Remove all traces of old tape, then fit new butyl tape around the inside of the fixed window making sure that it is located around the outside of the studs.

12 Locate the window in the body and tighten the mounting nuts to the specified torque.

13 Refit the headlining, trim panels and rubber weatherstrips.

Rear quarter light (5-door models)

Note: *The rear quarter light is sealed to the body with butyl tape and is not therefore considered to be a suitable job for the average home mechanic. However, the following information is given for those who may still wish to carry out the work themselves.*

Removal

14 With the door and tailgate open, pull the rubber weatherstrips from the body openings in the vicinity of the fixed side window.

15 Using a wide-bladed screwdriver, carefully prise the trim panel from the C-pillar.

16 Unscrew the nuts securing the quarter light to the body.

17 Have an assistant support the window while the butyl tape is cut with a suitable knife. Withdraw the quarter light.

Refitting

18 Remove all traces of old tape, then fit new butyl tape around the inside of the quarter light making sure that it is located around the outside of the studs.

19 Locate the quarter light in the body and tighten the mounting nuts to the specified torque.

20 Refit the trim panels and rubber weather-strips.

22 Sunroof assembly - removal and refitting

1 Due to the complexity of the tilt/slide sunroof mechanism, considerable expertise is required to repair, renew or adjust the sunroof components successfully. Removal of the sunroof first requires that the headlining be removed, which is a tedious operation, not to be undertaken lightly (see Section 26). Therefore, this Section is limited to a description of the drive motor assembly removal/refitting, and it is recommended that any other problems related to the sunroof are referred to a Saab dealer.

Drive motor assembly

Note: *If the drive motor is faulty, it is possible to operate the sunroof using a screwdriver. Slide off the cover from the overhead switch panel, and turn the motor shaft with the screwdriver.*

Removal

2 Remove the interior light with reference to Chapter 12.

3 Undo the screws and lower the switch panel from the headlining.

4 Disconnect the motor earth wire.

5 Undo the mounting screws and lower the drive motor from the roof.

Refitting

6 Refitting is a reversal of removal.

23 Body exterior fittings - removal and refitting

Badges and trim mouldings

Removal

1 Side trim panels, rubbing strips, bonnet, bootlid and tailgate emblems are all secured in place by adhesive tape or nuts.

2 To remove the fittings from the bodywork, select an implement to use as a lever that will not damage the paintwork, such as a plastic spatula, or a filling knife wrapped in PVC tape. On items secured with adhesive tape, it will help if heat is applied from a heat gun.

3 Insert the lever between the top edge of the fitting and the bodywork, and carefully prise it away.

4 Progressively pull the lower edge of the fitting away from the bodywork, allowing the adhesive tape to peel off.

5 Clean the bodywork surface, removing all traces of dirt and the remains of any adhesive tape.

Refitting

6 Peel the backing strip from the new fitting. Offer it up to its mounting position, top edge first, and press the stud fixings into their holes. Smooth the lower edge of the fitting into place, then press down on it firmly to ensure that the tape adheres along its whole length.

24.3 Unscrewing the front seat rear mounting bolts

Wheelarch trims

Removal

7 To remove, unscrew the flange nuts from the studs that protrude inside the wheelarch. Pull the trim away from the wheelarch, guiding the stud threads through their mounting holes.

Refitting

8 Clean the surface of the wheelarch before refitting the trim, and brush out any dirt from around the mounting holes, inside the wheelarch.

Front wheelarch liners

Removal

9 The front wheelarch liners are secured by means of screws, nuts, and clips. First apply the handbrake, then jack up the front of the vehicle and support it on axle stands (see *"Jacking and Vehicle Support"*). Remove the front wheel.

10 Undo the screws and nut and remove the mudflap from the rear of the liner.

11 Undo the remaining screws and remove the clips by pressing out their centre pins. Note the screws which are located on the spoiler and bumper.

12 Remove the wheelarch liner from under the wing.

Refitting

13 Refitting is a reversal of removal.

24 Seats - removal and refitting

Front seat

Removal

Note: *If the height adjustment motor is inoperative, or if seat removal is required in order to remove the TCS electronic units, the seat must be removed together with the floor brackets.*

1 Fully lower the seat.

2 On 5-door models, disconnect the seat be[lt] from the seat with reference to Section 25.

3 Slide the seat fully forwards, then unscrew and remove the rear mounting bolts **(see illustration)**.

4 Slide the seat fully to the rear, then unscrew and remove the front mounting bolts.

5 Where applicable, cut free the plastic cable ties securing the wiring beneath the seat then disconnect the wiring at the plug.

6 Lift the seat from inside the vehicle.

Refitting

7 Refitting is a reversal of removal, but tighten the mounting bolts to the specified torque. The inner bolt should be tightened first both at the front and rear.

Rear seat cushion

Removal

8 Fold the rear seat cushion forwards.

9 Extract the circlips from the hinge pins, then use a suitable drift to drive them out **(see illustration)**.

10 Lift the cushion from inside the vehicle.

Refitting

11 Refitting is a reversal of removal. All hinge pins must be fitted from right to left.

Rear seat backrest (40% section)

Removal

12 Move the seat belt to one side and fold the backrest forwards (leave the crossbar in position).

13 Unscrew the nuts from the brackets at the centre of the backrest **(see illustration)**.

14 Withdraw the pivot from the outer bracket and lift out the backrest from inside the vehicle.

Refitting

15 Refitting is a reversal of removal.

Rear seat backrest (60% section)

Removal

16 Remove the 40% section rear seat backrest as described earlier.

17 Move the seat belt to one side and fold the backrest forwards (leave the crossbar in position).

18 Unscrew the nuts and remove the centre seat belt anchorage.

19 Unscrew the nuts and remove the right-hand bracket.

25.14 Front seat belt guide on the B-pillar

25.15 Front seat belt height adjuster on the B-pillar

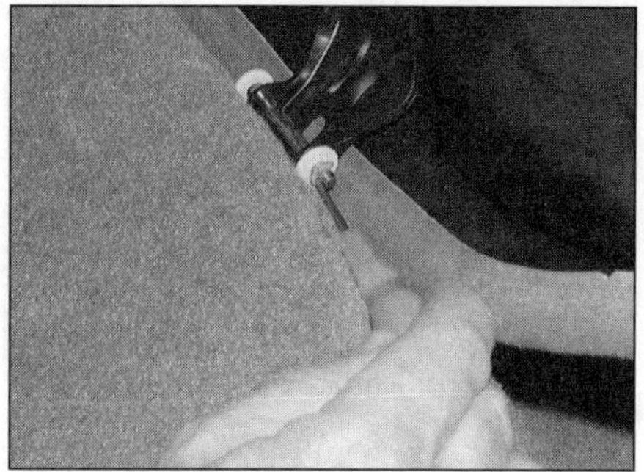

24.9 Extracting the circlips from the rear seat cushion

20 Withdraw the pivot from the outer bracket, then release the fabric tensioner and lift out the backrest from inside the vehicle.

Refitting

21 Refitting is a reversal of removal.

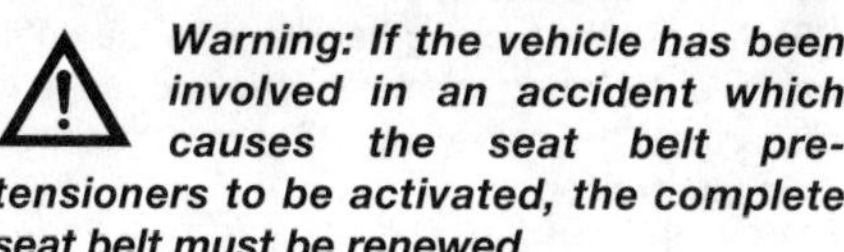

25 Seat belts - removal and refitting

Warning: If the vehicle has been involved in an accident which causes the seat belt pretensioners to be activated, the complete seat belt must be renewed.

Front seat belt (3-door)

Removal

1 Undo the front bolt securing the slide rail to the inner sill panel and slide off the belt.

2 Using a wide-bladed screwdriver, prise the kick plate from the door opening.

3 Pull out the vent, then undo the screw securing the inner trim to the outer trim. Carefully prise off the upper and lower trim panels.

4 Fold the rear seat cushion forwards then fold the rear seat backrest forwards. Unscrew and remove the fastener from the rear of the side trim.

5 Fold the backrest rearwards, then remove the remaining fasteners and withdraw the side trim.

6 Lock the pretensioner on the seat belt reel by engaging the red plastic lever with the safety catch.

25.16 Front seat belt reel and pretensioner

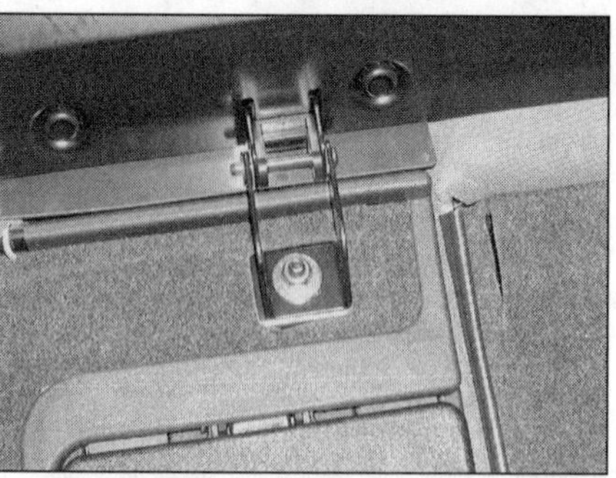

24.13 Rear seat backrest central mounting bracket

7 Drill out the rivet securing the clamp to the pretensioner tube.

8 Unbolt the seat belt guide from the B-pillar.

9 Unscrew the top bolt securing the seat belt height adjuster to the B-pillar, then remove the adjuster.

10 Undo the slide rail rear bolt and remove the rail followed by the reel.

Refitting

11 Refitting is a reversal of removal, but tighten the mounting bolts to the specified torque. Make sure that the red plastic lever is released so that the pretensioner is free to operate in the event of an accident.

Front seat belt (5-door)

Removal

12 Carefully remove the trim panels from the B-pillar using a wide-bladed screwdriver.

13 Lock the pretensioner on the seat belt reel by engaging the red plastic lever with the safety catch. Drill out the rivet securing the clamp to the pretensioner tube.

14 Unbolt the seat belt guide from the B-pillar **(see illustration)**.

15 Unscrew the top bolt securing the seat belt height adjuster to the B-pillar, then remove the adjuster **(see illustration)**.

16 Unscrew the bolt and remove the seat belt reel and pretensioner from the B-pillar **(see illustration)**.

17 Release the front end of the seat belt from the seat by inserting a screwdriver between the trim and depressing the spring tensioned catch. If preferred, the tilt knob and trim can be removed first **(see illustrations)**.

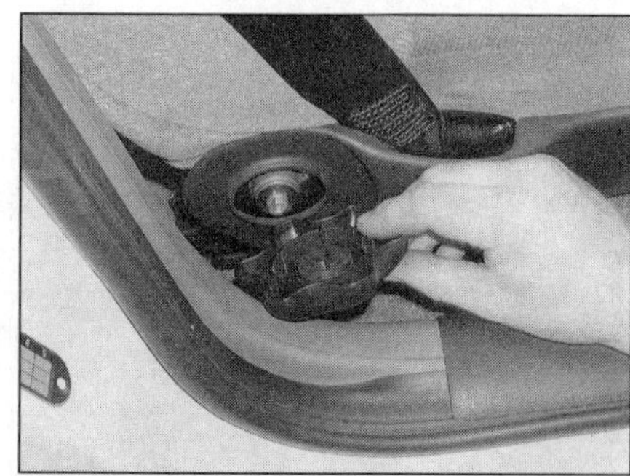

25.17a Remove the tilt knob and trim . . .

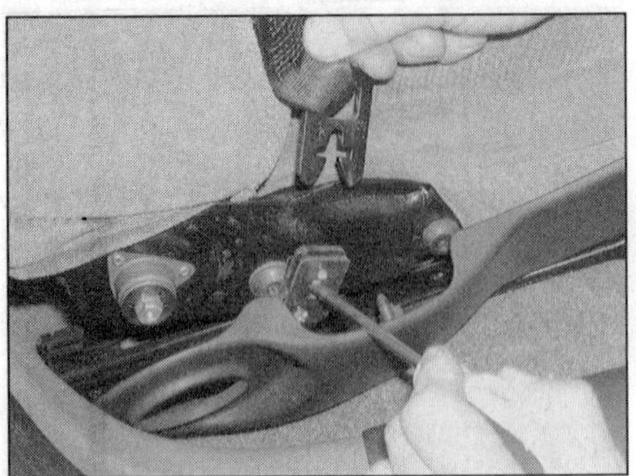

25.17b ... then depress the catch and disconnect the seat belt from the front seat

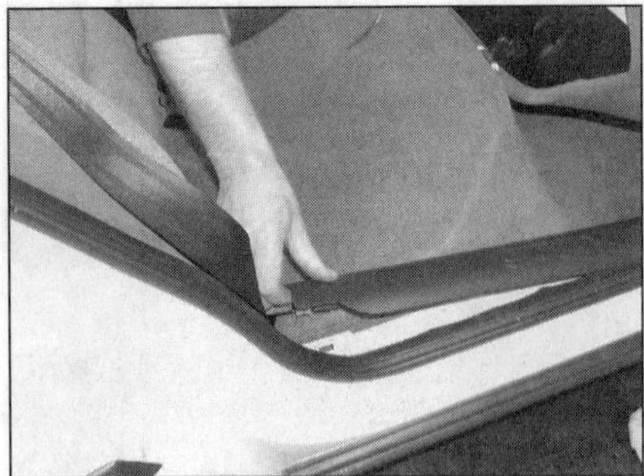

25.21 Remove the rear door kick plate

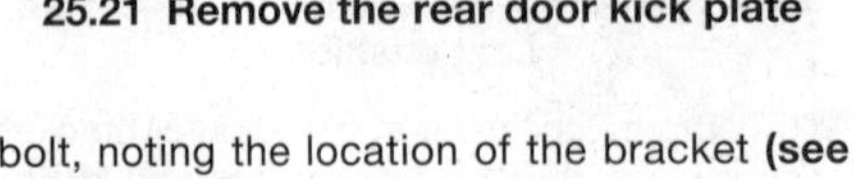

25.22 Rear seat belt lower anchorage bol

18 To remove the buckle, the front seat must be removed as described in Section 24, then the mounting bolt unscrewed.

Refitting

19 Refitting is a reversal of removal, but tighten the mounting bolts to the specified torque. Make sure that the red plastic lever is released so that the pretensioner is free to operate in the event of an accident.

Rear seat belt

Removal

20 The rear seat belt reels are located in the crossbar. First fold the rear seat cushions forwards.

21 On 5-door models, carefully prise up the kick plate from the rear door opening **(see illustration)**.

22 Unscrew the seat belt lower anchorage bolt, noting the location of the bracket **(see illustration)**.

23 Using a Torx key, unscrew the centre belt anchorage bolt **(see illustration)**.

24 Lift out the rear head restraints, then remove the head restraint inserts from the crossbar. To do this, depress the plastic tags with a screwdriver, then use a hammer to tap the inserts up from the crossbar **(see illustrations)**.

25 Prise out the centre plastic cover.

26 Pull out the locking handle from the right-hand side, then remove the cover and disconnect the cable end fitting from the lever **(see illustrations)**.

27 On the left-hand side of the crossbar, undo the screws securing the locking handle, then lift it slightly and disconnect the inner cable, noting how it is fitted to the two levers. Remove the cover and unhook the cable end fitting **(see illustrations)**.

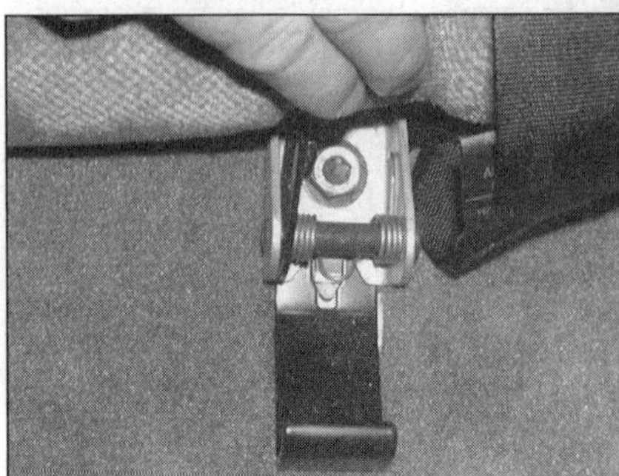

25.23 Rear seat belt centre anchorage an bolt

28 Remove the seat belt cover then unscre the reel mounting bolts and withdraw the re **(see illustration)**.

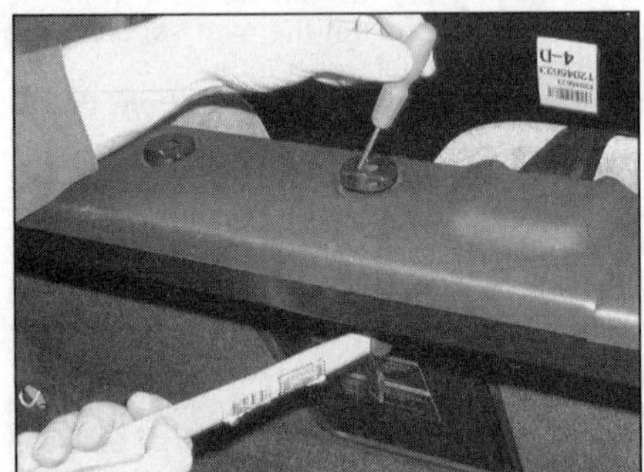

25.24a Depress the plastic tags and tap up the head restraint insert ...

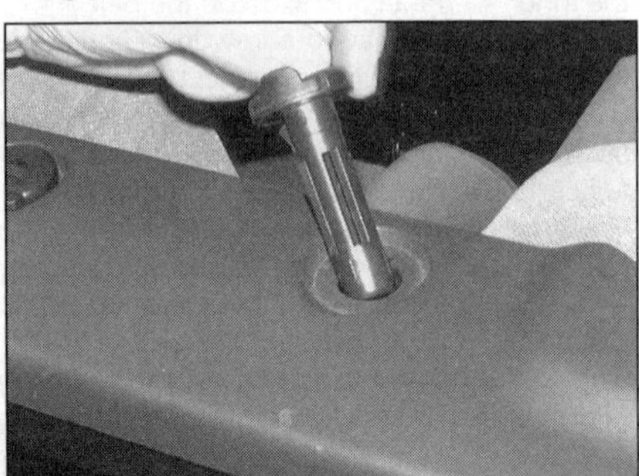

25.24b ... then remove the insert from the crossbar

25.26a Pull out the locking handle ...

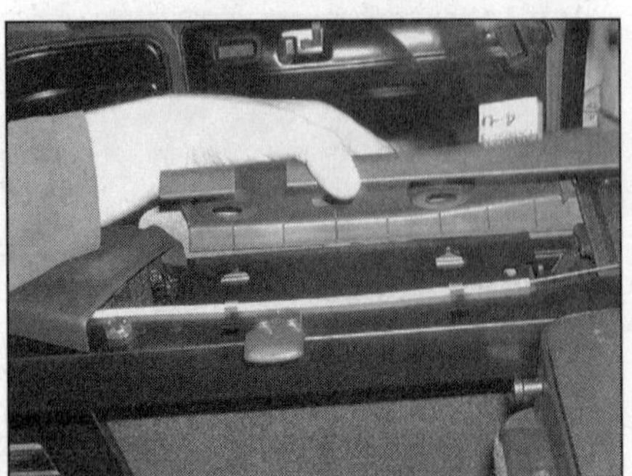

25.26b ... remove the cover ...

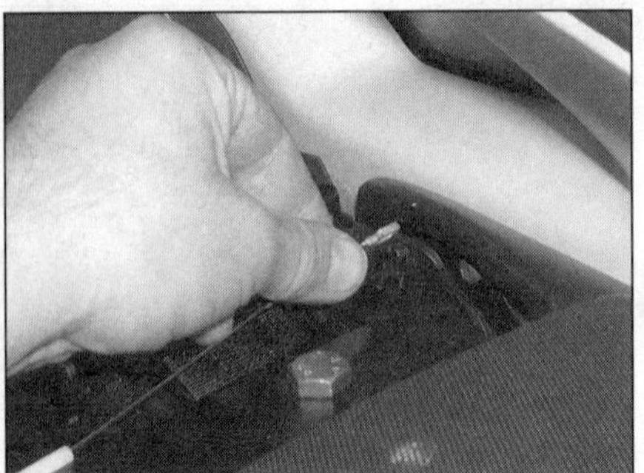

25.26c ... then disconnect the cable end fitting from the lever

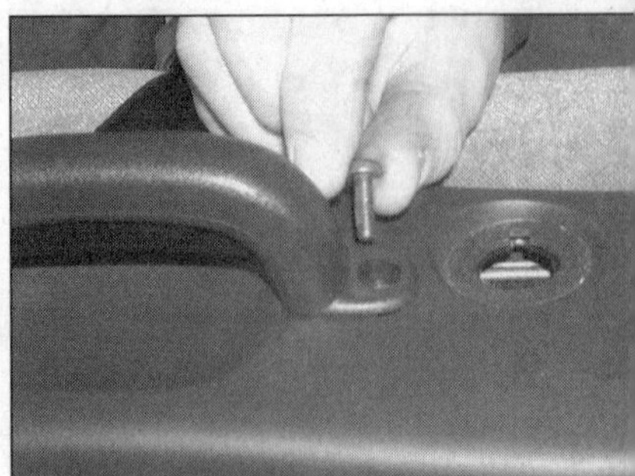

25.27a Undo the screws ...

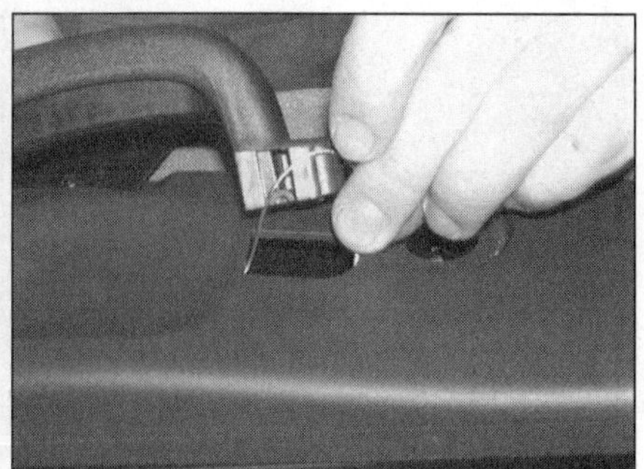
25.27b . . . and disconnect the cable from the locking handle . . .

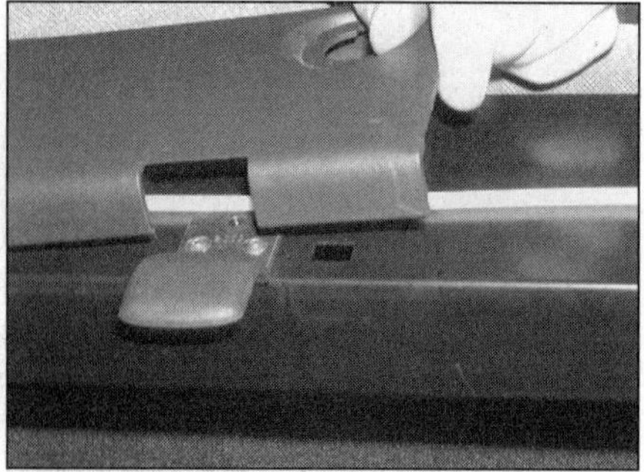
25.27c . . . then lift off the cover . . .

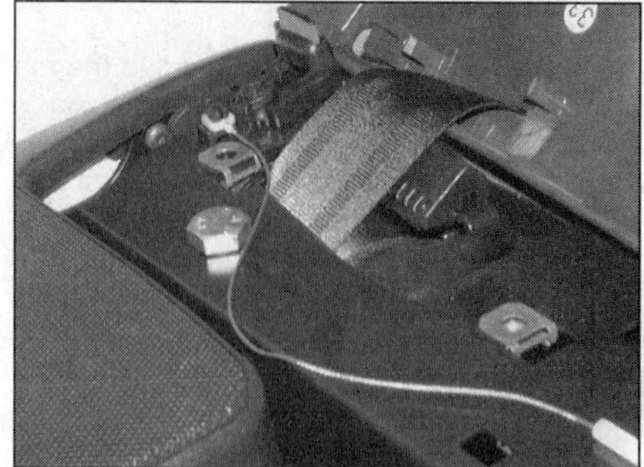
25.27d . . . and disconnect the cable end fitting from the lever

Refitting

29 Refitting is a reversal of removal, but tighten the mounting bolts to the specified torque. When refitting the locking handle, make sure that the inner cable is not trapped between the handle and crossbar.

26 Interior trim panels - removal and refitting

A-pillar trim panels

1 Open the relevant front door, and pull the rubber weatherstrip from the door aperture at the A-pillar.

2 Working from the headlining down, grasp the panel firmly and progressively ease it away from the pillar, allowing the press-studs beneath to disengage one at a time.

3 To refit, offer the panel up to its mounted position, and apply firm pressure over each press-stud until it engages. Press the door aperture weatherstrip back into place.

B-pillar trim panels

3-door models

4 Move the front seat fully forwards, then unscrew the slide rail front bolt and slide off the belt.

5 Pull out the air vent, then undo the screw securing the inner trim panel to the outer panel.

6 Carefully prise off the trim panel. Undo the bolt and remove the height adjuster.

7 Unclip the outer trim panel.

8 Refitting is a reversal of removal.

5-door models

9 Move the front seat fully forwards, then use a wide-bladed screwdriver to prise the kick plates from the front and rear door openings.

10 Pull the rubber weatherstrip from each side of the B-pillar **(see illustration)**.

11 Release the front end of the seat belt from the seat by inserting a screwdriver between the trim and depressing the spring tensioned catch.

12 Prise out the air vent from the upper trim panel, then carefully prise off the upper and lower trim panels. Feed the front seat belt through the hole in the inner trim **(see illustrations)**.

13 Using a screwdriver, prise off the lower trim panel from the B-pillar **(see illustration)**.

14 Unscrew the upper bolt then unhook the height adjuster from the B-pillar.

15 Refitting is a reversal of removal.

25.28 Rear seat belt reel mounting bolt

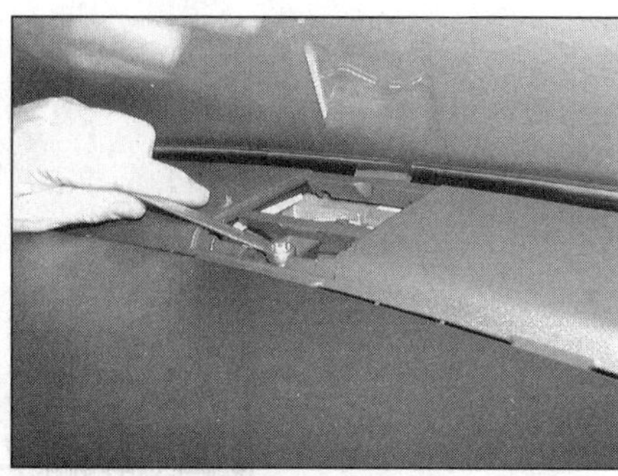
26.10 Removing the rubber weatherstrip from the B-pillar

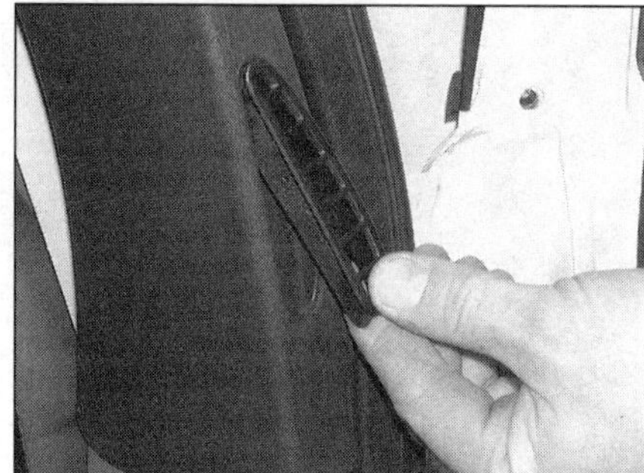
26.12a Remove the air vent . . .

26.12b . . . then use a screwdriver to prise off . . .

26.12c . . . the upper trim panel . . .

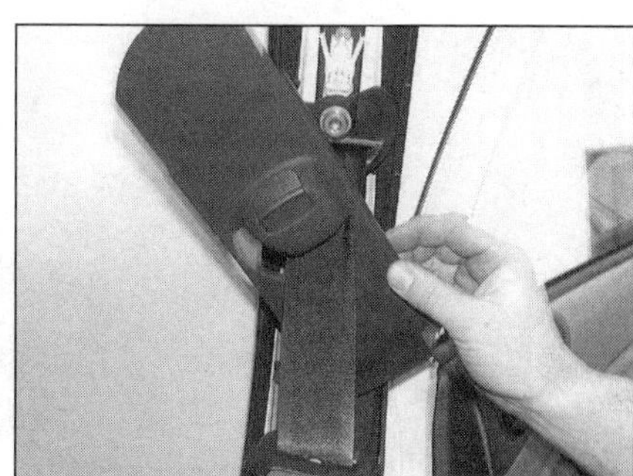
26.12d . . . remove the inner trim panel . . .

C-pillar trim panels

16 Remove the parcel shelf and fold the rear seats forwards together with the crossbar.

17 On 3-door models, carefully prise out the speaker grille using a screwdriver, then undo the screws and remove the speaker frame.

18 Pull the weatherstrip away from the tailgate opening in the vicinity of the C-pillar.

19 On 5-door models, pull the rear door weatherstrip away from the door opening in the vicinity of the C-pillar.

20 Using a wide-bladed screwdriver, carefully prise the trim panel away from the C-pillar.

21 Withdraw the panel from inside the vehicle.

22 Refitting is a reversal of removal.

Luggage compartment side trim panel

23 With the tailgate open, remove the parcel shelf and fold the rear seats forwards.

24 Release the front clips and remove the carpet from the luggage compartment.

25 Unbolt the lashing eyes on each side of the luggage compartment.

26 Remove the clips from the centre of the rear valance trim by pressing in the centre pins.

27 Pull the rear valance trim away and remove.

28 Remove the clips securing the luggage compartment side trim panel to the rear body.

29 Using a screwdriver carefully prise out the speaker grille, then unbolt the speaker frame **(see illustrations)**.

30 Remove the relevant rear seat cushion and backrest as described in Section 24.

31 Bend up the backrest trim tensioner bracket, then remove the side trim panel from inside the vehicle.

32 Refitting is a reversal of removal.

Headlining

33 Open the tailgate and remove the parcel shelf.

34 Undo the screws and remove the sun visors from the front of the headlining.

35 Prise off the cover from the rear view mirror, then undo the screws and remove the mirror **(see illustrations)**.

36 Remove the interior courtesy lights with reference to Chapter 12, then undo the screws and remove the light surrounds.

37 On models with a sunroof, carefully prise out the surround from the sunroof, and disconnect the wiring from the sunroof motor.

38 Pull the rubber weatherstrip from the A-pillars in the vicinity of the windscreen, then prise off the A-pillar trim panels **(see illustration)**.

39 Prise up the covers from the grab handles then undo the screws and remove the handles **(see illustration)**.

40 Remove the trim panels from the B-pillars and C-pillars as described earlier in this Section.

41 Release the clips from the rear edge of the headlining by turning them through 90°.

42 Pull the rubber weatherstrip from the tailgate upper opening and carefully pull down the headlining.

43 Release the tape securing the wiring to the headlining.

44 Withdraw the headlining through the tailgate opening.

45 Refitting is a reversal of removal.

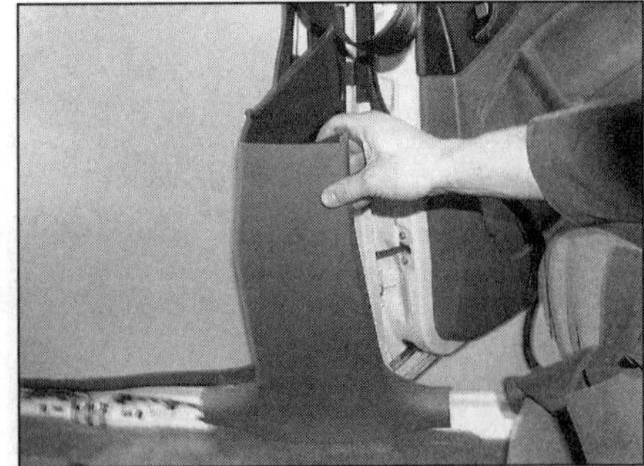

26.13 . . . and prise off the lower trim panel

26.29a Prise out the speaker grille . . .

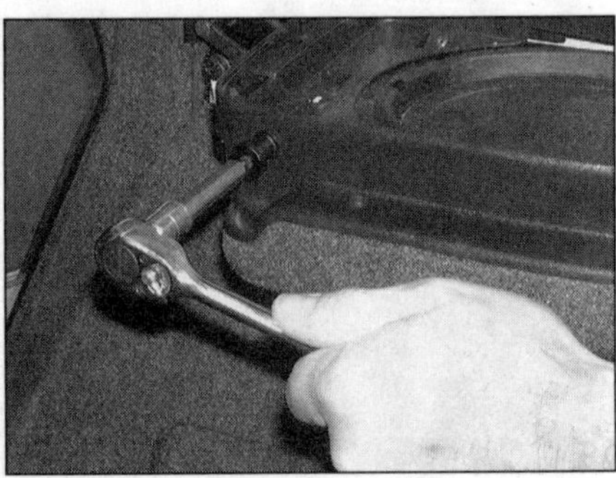

26.29b . . . then unscrew the bolts . . .

26.29c . . . and remove the speaker frame

26.35a Remove the cover . . .

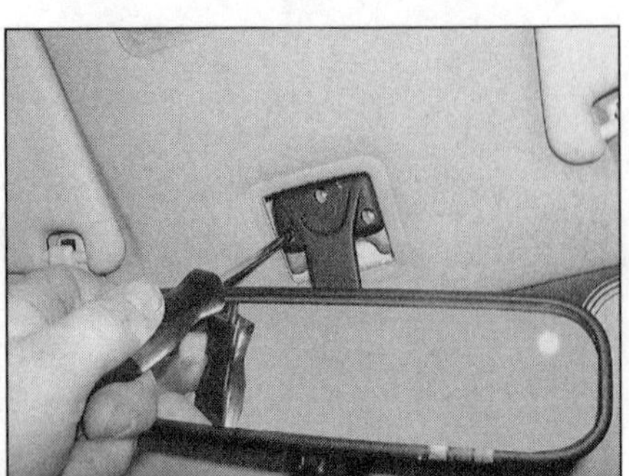

26.35b . . . then undo the screws and remove the rear view mirror

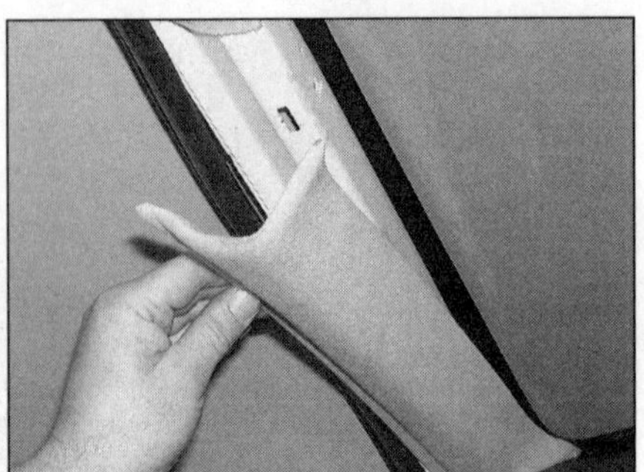

26.38 Removing the A-pillar trim panels

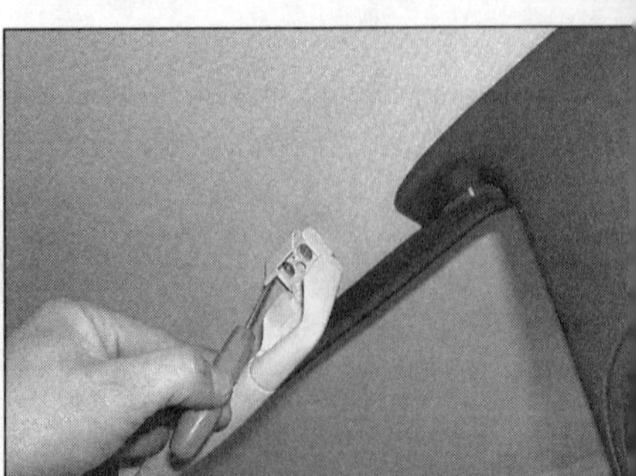

26.39 Removing the grab handles

27.3 Removing the ignition switch cover plate

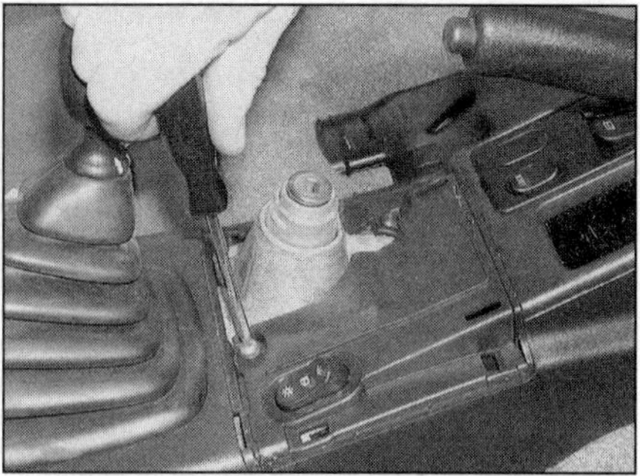

27.5 Undo the centre console front screws . . .

27.6a Remove the ashtray . . .

27 Centre console - removal and refitting

Removal

1 Disconnect the battery negative (earth) lead (see Chapter 5A).

2 With the handbrake lever applied, engage reverse gear and remove the ignition key.

3 Using a screwdriver, carefully prise off the ignition switch cover plate. Insert the screwdriver at the left-hand front of the cover to start with, then ease up the rear edge **(see illustration)**.

4 Disconnect the wiring for the ignition switch lighting.

5 Undo the screws from the front of the centre console rear section **(see illustration)**.

6 Remove the rear ashtray, then undo the screws and remove the housing from the rear section **(see illustrations)**.

27.6b . . . then undo the screws . . .

27.6c . . . and remove the housing

7 Undo the rear nuts then pull the rear section back a little **(see illustration)**.

8 Press out the interior light switch and disconnect the wiring **(see illustrations)**.

9 Prise out the electric window switch module and disconnect the wiring **(see illustrations)**.

10 Lift out the rear section of the centre console and remove from inside the car **(see illustration)**.

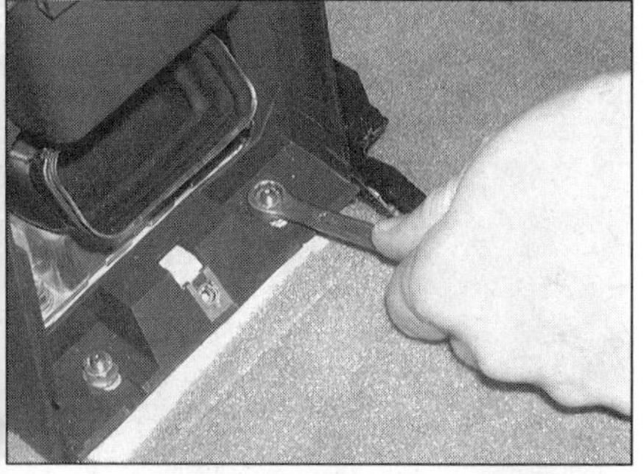

27.7 Removing the rear nuts from the centre console rear section

27.8a Press out the interior light switch . . .

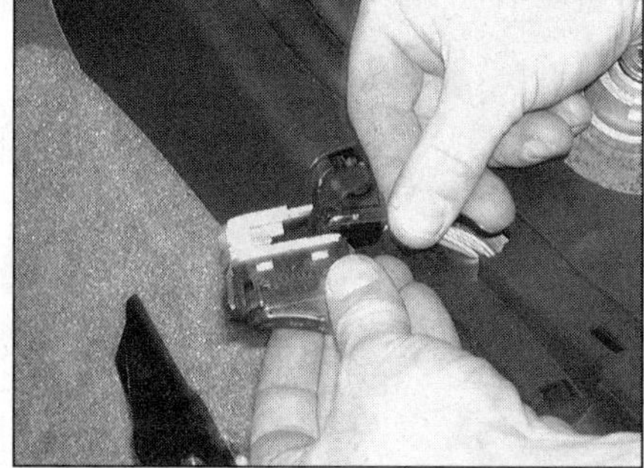

27.8b . . . and disconnect the wiring

27.9a Prise out the electric window switch module . . .

27.9b . . . and disconnect the wiring

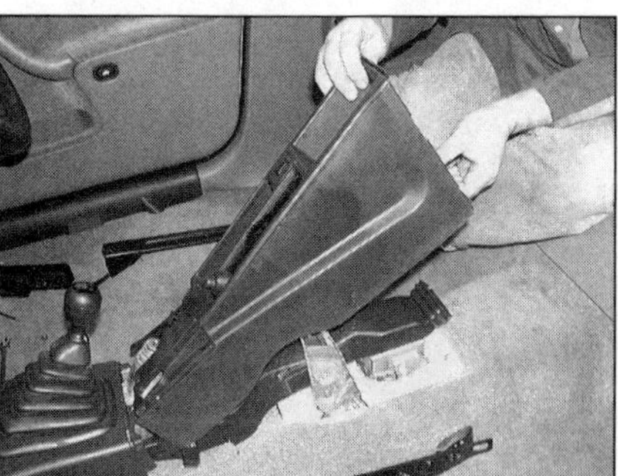

27.10 Removing the rear section of the centre console

27.11 Removing the centre console front trim panels

27.12 Removing the gear lever gaiter

27.14a Press out the heating control panel from behind . . .

11 Undo the screws and remove the front trim panels from each side of the centre console **(see illustration)**.

Manual transmission models

12 Prise out the gear lever gaiter **(see illustration)**.

Air conditioning models

13 Press out the A/C module and disconnect the wiring.

Models without air conditioning

14 Press out the heating control panel from behind, then remove the air distribution shaft **(see illustrations)**.

15 Disconnect the wiring for the air distribution control lighting, fan speed, heated rear window and air recirculation **(see illustration)**.

16 Release the retainer and remove the heating control cable from the control module **(see illustrations)**.

17 Withdraw the heating control panel from inside the car.

All models

18 Disconnect all the wiring from the centre console, noting their locations **(see illustration)**.

19 Release the clips securing the centre console to the facia panel by pressing in the centre pins **(see illustration)**.

20 Withdraw the centre console from inside the car **(see illustration)**.

Refitting

21 Refitting is a reversal of removal.

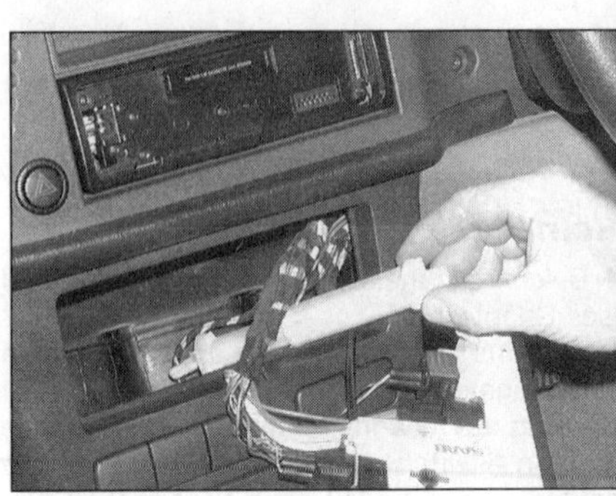
27.14b . . . remove the air distribution shaft . . .

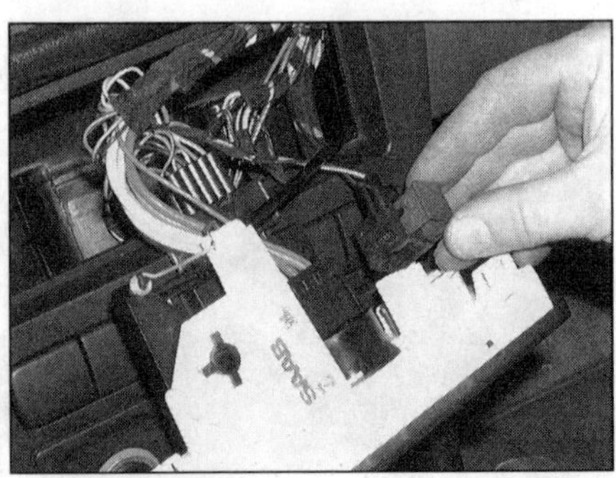

27.15 . . . then disconnect the wiring

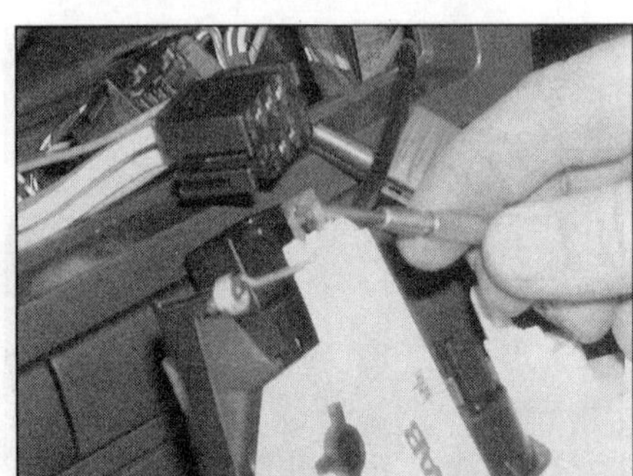
27.16a Release the retainer . . .

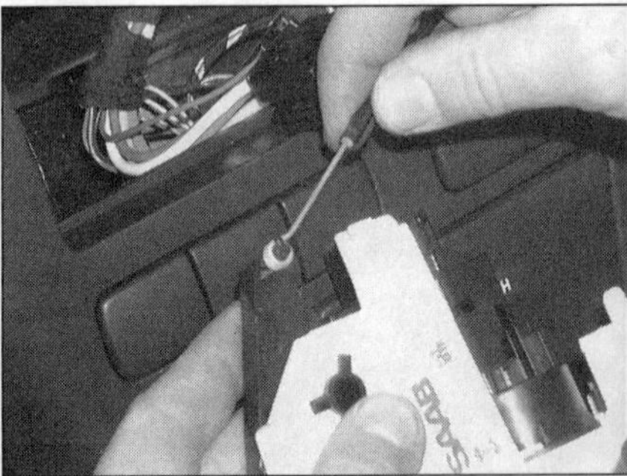

27.16b . . . and disconnect the heating control cable from the module

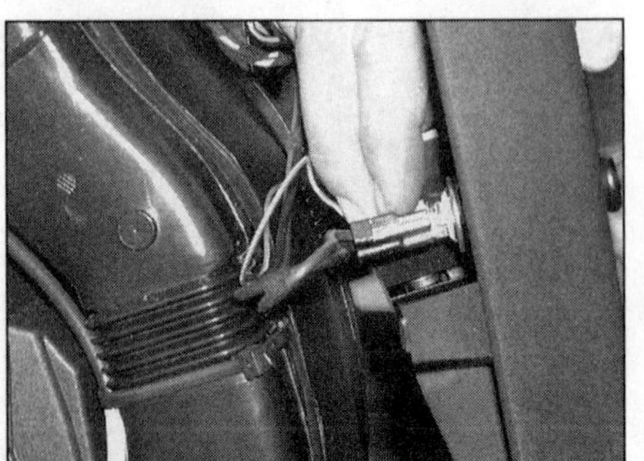
27.18 Disconnecting the wiring from the cigar lighter

27.19 Remove the clips . . .

27.20 . . . and withdraw the centre console from inside the car

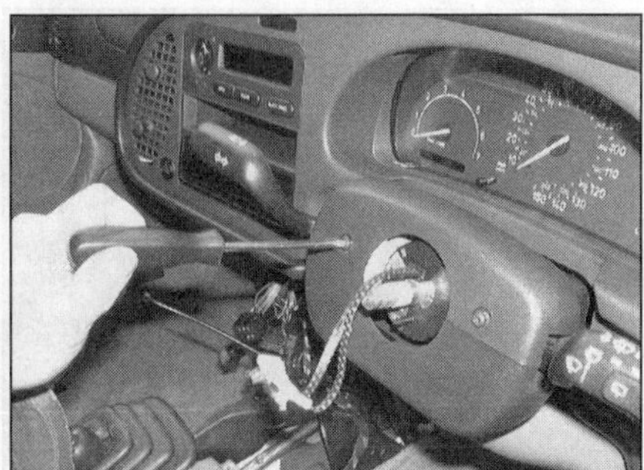
28.7a Undo the upper screws . . .

28.7b . . . and lower screw . . .

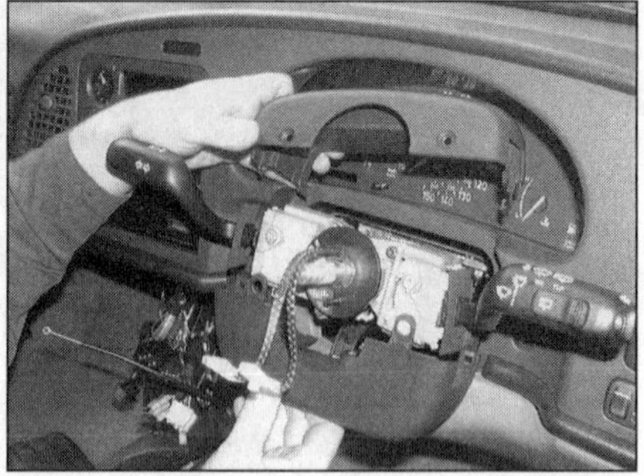
28.7c . . . and remove the steering column shrouds

28 Facia assembly - removal and refitting

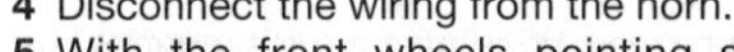

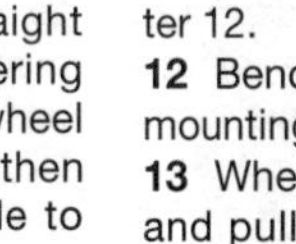

Warning: Observe the safety precautions given in Section 30 when working on or near the airbags.

Removal

1 Disconnect the battery negative (earth) lead (see Chapter 5A).

2 Adjust the steering wheel to its fully extended position.

3 Undo the screws located either side of the steering wheel, and withdraw the airbag module until the wiring connector can be disconnected. Place the module with its upper face pointing upwards in a safe position, making sure that it cannot be tampered with or damaged.

4 Disconnect the wiring from the horn.

5 With the front wheels pointing straight ahead, unscrew and remove the steering wheel retaining nut. Mark the steering wheel hub in relation to the steering column, then rock the steering wheel firmly from side to side until it is released from the splines.

6 Withdraw the steering wheel while feeding the wiring connectors through the hole.

7 Undo the screws and remove the steering column shrouds **(see illustrations)**.

8 Disconnect the wiring from the combination switches on each side of the steering column, then remove the switches by depressing the plastic tabs located on the top and bottom of the switches.

9 Undo the screws and remove the diagnostic socket from under the facia on the driver's side **(see illustration)**.

10 Undo the screws and release the clips then remove the lower trim panel **(see illustrations)**.

11 Remove the radio as described in Chapter 12.

12 Bend back the tabs, and remove the radio mounting box.

13 Where applicable, release the upper clips and pull out the storage compartment **(see illustration)**.

14 Using two M3 screws inserted in the special holes, pull out the auxiliary instrument display panel (SID).

15 Prise out the light switch and headlight beam switch.

16 Remove the instrument panel as described in Chapter 12.

17 With the glovebox open, prise up the covers and undo the mounting screws and bolt **(see illustration)**. Where necessary, release the clips on the front edge and remove the catch.

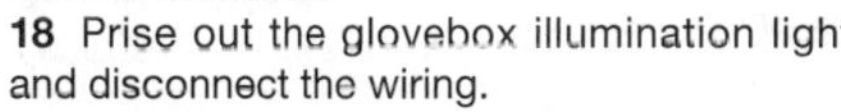

18 Prise out the glovebox illumination light and disconnect the wiring.

19 Withdraw the glovebox from the facia (see Section 29).

20 Pull the rubber weatherstrip away from the A-pillars on each side of the facia.

21 Carefully prise away the trim panels from the A-pillars.

22 Using a screwdriver, prise off the speaker grilles on each side of the facia **(see illustration)**.

23 Slide the sun sensor surround slightly to the rear and lift it off **(see illustration)**.

24 On models with air conditioning and/or an alarm, disconnect the wiring from the sun sensor or alarm.

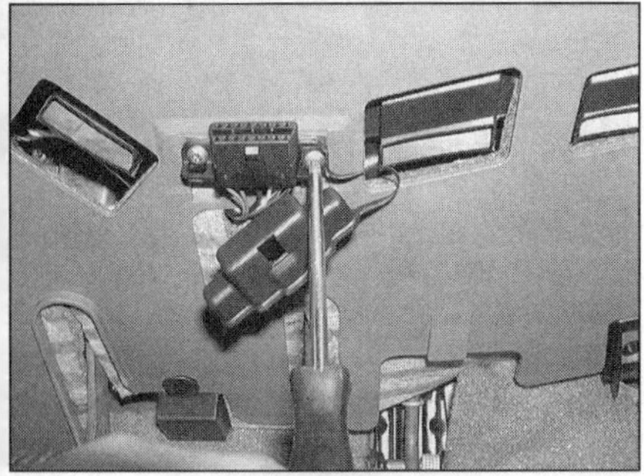
28.9 Removing the diagnostic socket from under the facia

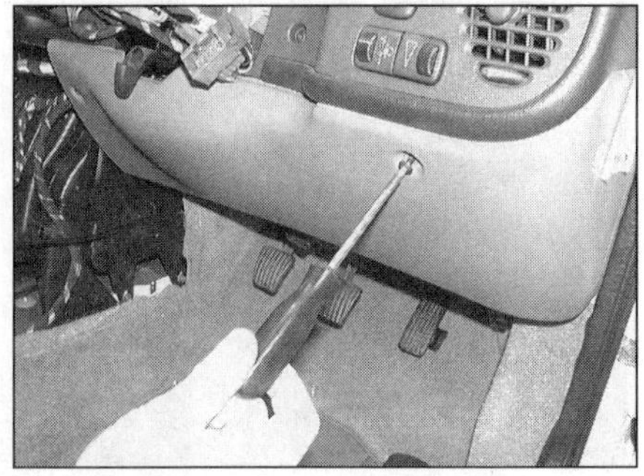
28.10a Undo the screws . . .

28.10b . . . and remove the lower trim panel

28.13 Removing the storage compartment

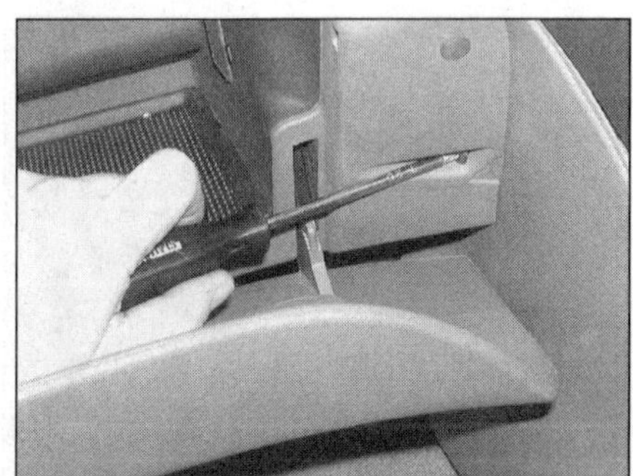
28.17 Undo the mounting screws and remove the glovebox

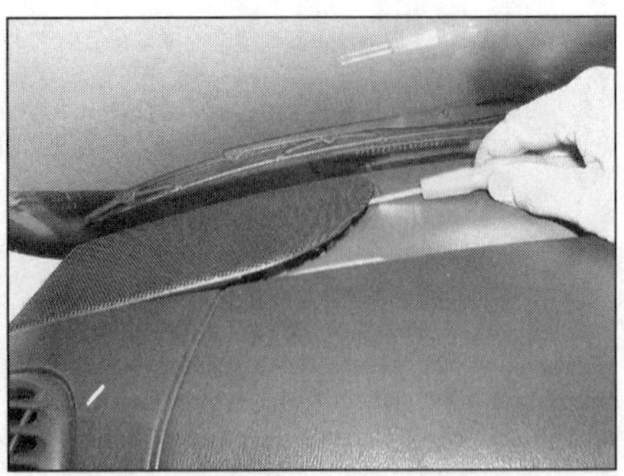
28.22 Prising out the speaker grilles

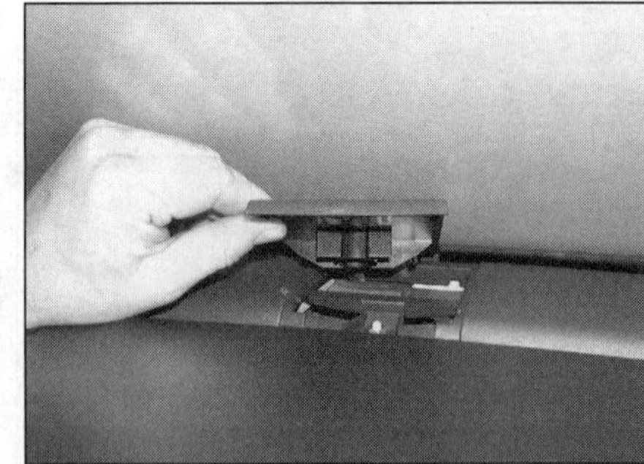
28.23 Removing the sun sensor from the top of the facia

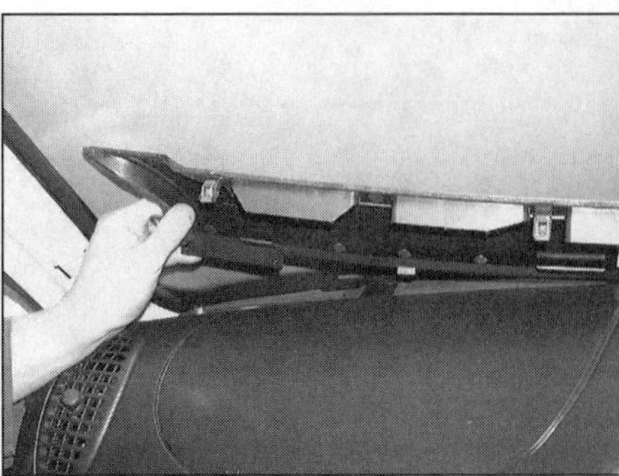
28.25 Removing the defroster panel

25 Unscrew the bolt from the top centre of the facia, then lift the rear edge of the defroster panel, move it sideways, and withdraw **(see illustration)**.

26 Observe the location of the wiring loom on the underside of the facia, and if necessary make notes to ensure correct refitting. Release the cable ties **(see illustration)**.

27 Detach the floor air duct on the left-hand side **(see illustration)**.

28 Undo the screws and remove the fusebox from the right-hand side of the facia **(see illustration)**. Position it to one side, but do not disconnect the wiring.

29 Unscrew and remove the facia mounting bolts located on the A-pillars **(see illustration)**.

30 Remove the centre console as described in Section 27.

31 On models fitted with a passenger airbag, disconnect the wiring from the airbag and unscrew the nut from the stay.

32 Disconnect and remove the air vent ducting from each side.

33 Disconnect the wiring from the speakers on each side of the facia, and release the cable ties.

34 Unscrew the facia mounting bolts located near the top speakers **(see illustration)**.

35 With the help of an assistant, carefully withdraw the facia from the bulkhead and withdraw from the car **(see illustration)**.

Refitting

36 Refitting is a reversal of removal, but refer to Section 30 for details of refitting the airbags. In particular, observe the precautions.

29 Glovebox - removal and refitting

Removal

1 With the glovebox open, undo the lower mounting screws **(see illustrations)**.

2 Release the clips from the front edge of the glovebox by depressing the centre pins **(see illustration)**.

3 Remove the glovebox illumination lamp or alternatively disconnect the wiring **(see illustration)**.

4 Withdraw the glovebox from the facia **(see illustration)**.

5 If necessary, the lid can be removed by

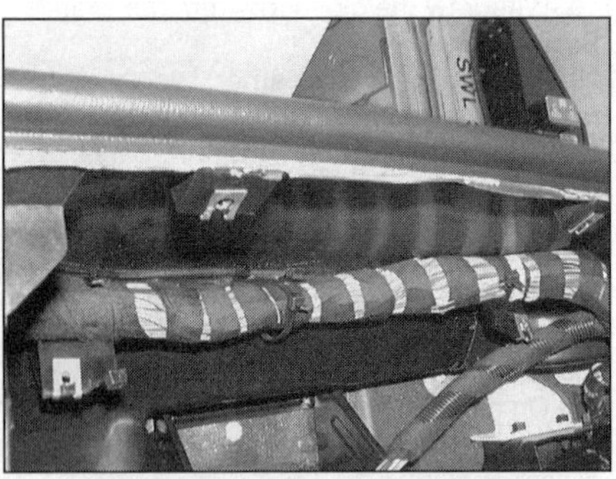
28.26 Wiring loom location on the underside of the facia

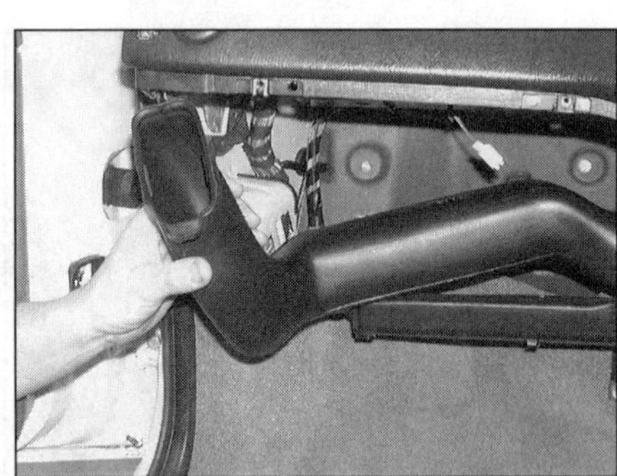
28.27 Removing the air duct on the left-hand side

28.28 Undo the fusebox screws from the right-hand side of the facia

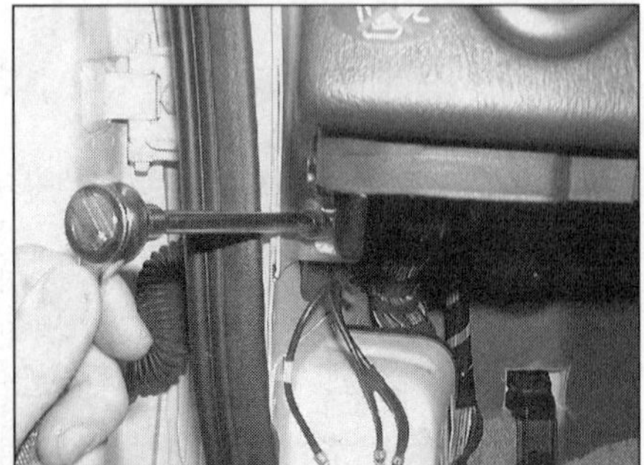
28.29 Unscrewing the facia bolts from the A-pillars

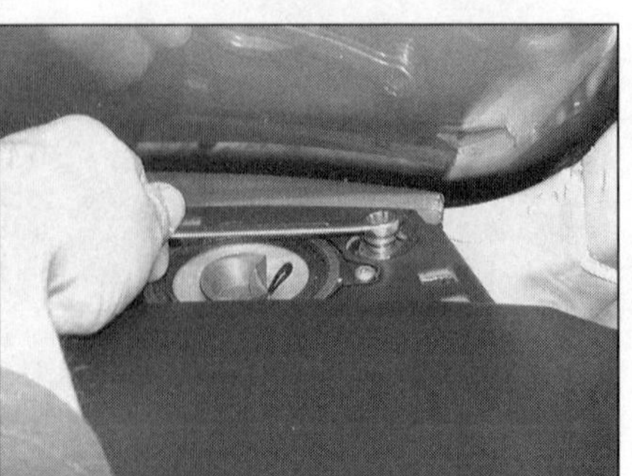
28.34 Unscrewing the facia bolts located near the top speakers

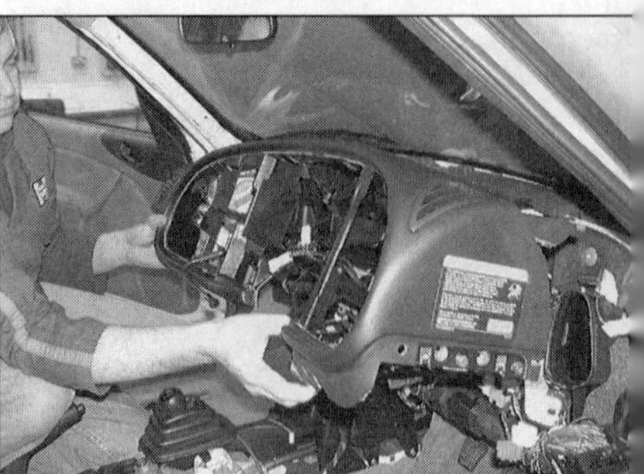
28.35 Withdrawing the facia from the bulkhead

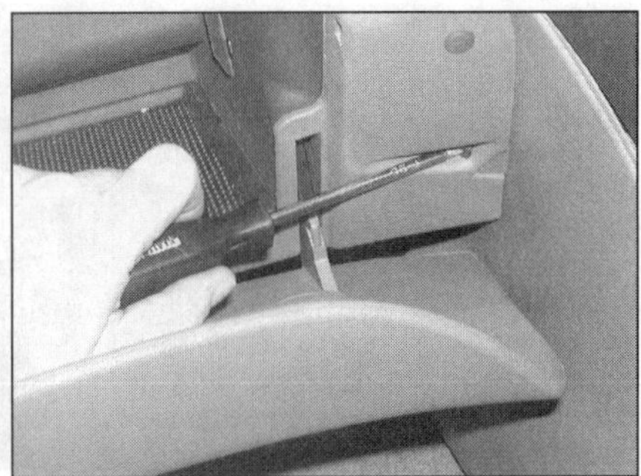

29.1a Unscrewing the glovebox lower right . . .

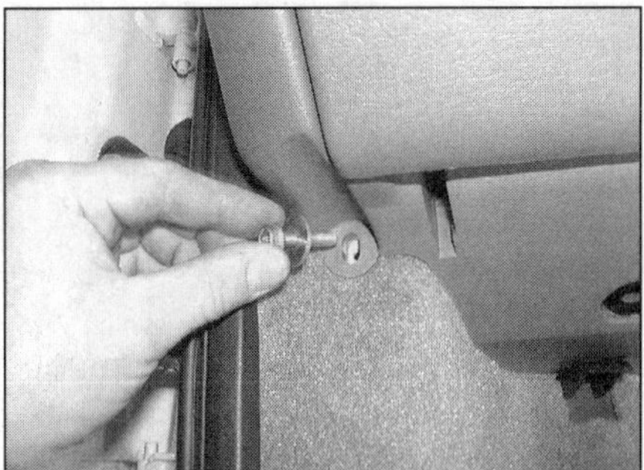

29.1b . . . and lower left mounting screws

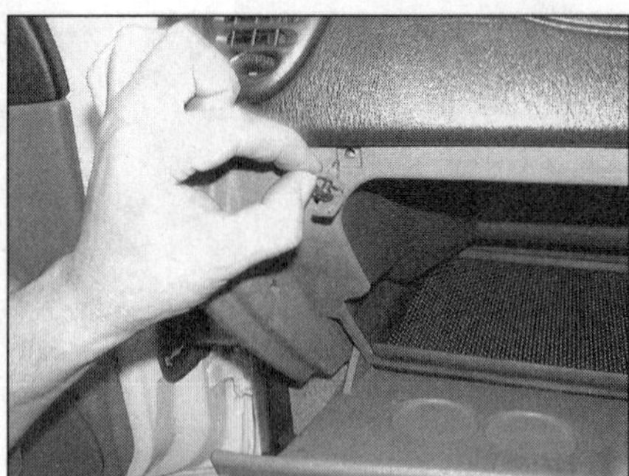

29.2 Removing the glovebox retaining clips

undoing the damper screw, and pressing out the pivot pins.

6 To remove the lock, drill a circle of 2.0 mm holes inside the circle embossed on the rear of the lid and carefully cut out the circle. Take care not to drill more than the thickness of the plastic. Bend back the tabs and remove the lock from the glovebox. Prise off the lock holder.

Refitting

7 Refitting is a reversal of removal. If fitting a new lock, stick the plug supplied with the new lock over the cut circle.

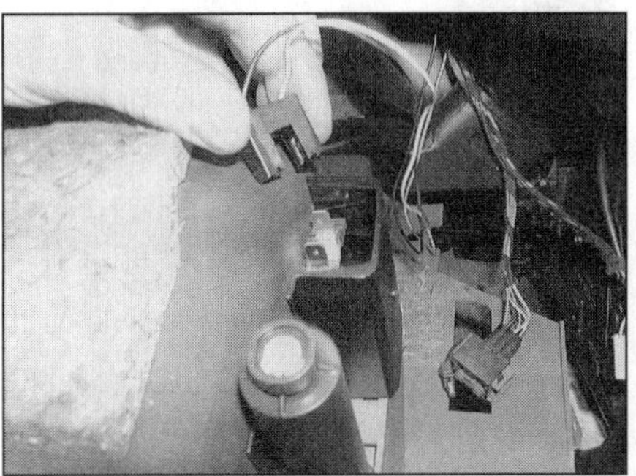

29.3 Disconnecting the wiring from the glovebox illumination lamp

29.4 Withdrawing the glovebox from the facia

30 Supplementary Restraint System (SRS) components - removal and refitting

General information

The operation of the SRS is managed by an Electronic Control Unit (ECU). When the vehicle's ignition switch is turned on, the ECU performs self-test checks of the system's components; if a fault is detected, the ECU records it in memory as a fault 'flag'. Following this, the ECU illuminates the instrument panel-mounted SRS warning light. If this should occur, the vehicle should be taken to a Saab dealer for examination. Dedicated test equipment is needed to interrogate the SRS ECU, firstly to determine the nature and incidence of the fault, and secondly to clear the stored fault 'flag', thus preventing the fault from being displayed by the warning light once the fault has been rectified.

For safety reasons, owners are strongly advised against attempting to diagnose problems with the SRS using standard workshop equipment. The information in this Section is therefore limited to those components in the SRS which must occasionally be removed to gain access to other components on the vehicle.

Warning: A number of additional precautions must be observed when working on vehicles with airbags/SRS:

a) *Disconnect the battery negative cable, and wait* ***at least ten minutes*** *before*

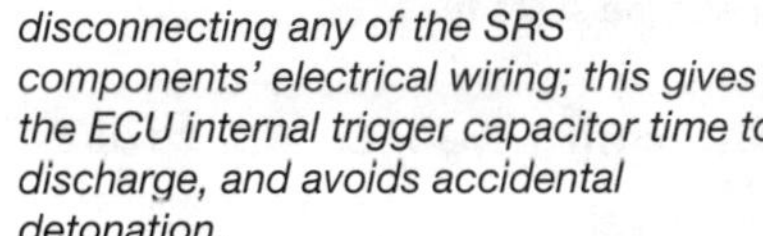

disconnecting any of the SRS components' electrical wiring; this gives the ECU internal trigger capacitor time to discharge, and avoids accidental detonation.

b) ***Do not*** *attempt to splice into any of the electric cables in the SRS wiring harness.*

c) *Avoid hammering or causing any harsh vibration at the front of the vehicle, particularly in the engine bay, as this may trigger the crash sensors and activate the SRS.*

d) *Do not use ohmmeters or any other device capable of supplying current on any of the SRS components, as this may cause accidental detonation.*

e) *Airbags (and seat belt tensioners) are classed as pyrotechnical (explosive) devices, and must be stored and handled according to the relevant laws in the country concerned. In general, do not leave these components disconnected from their electrical wiring any longer than is absolutely necessary; in this state they are unstable, and the risk of accidental detonation is introduced. Rest a disconnected airbag with the metal bracket facing downwards, away from flammable materials - never leave it unattended.*

Driver's airbag

Removal

1 Disconnect the battery negative (earth) lead (see Chapter 5A).

2 Prise out the plugs then undo the screws securing the airbag to the steering wheel. The screws are located on either side of the steering wheel **(see illustrations)**.

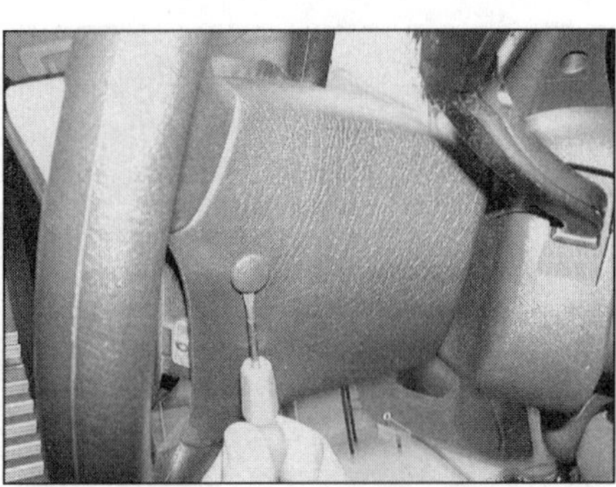

30.2a Prise out the plugs . . .

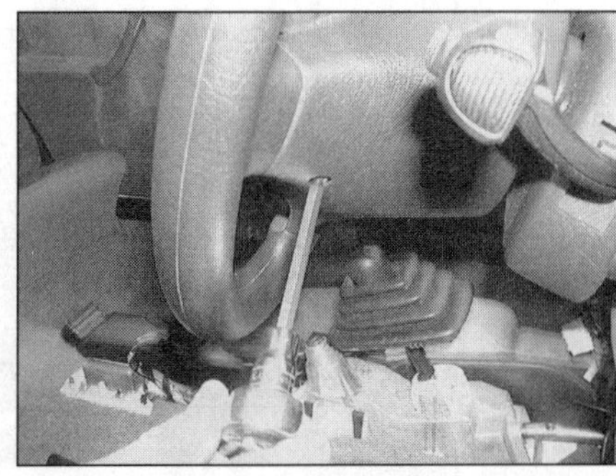

30.2b . . . then undo the screws located on either side of the steering wheel

30.3a Carefully lift the airbag from the steering wheel . . .

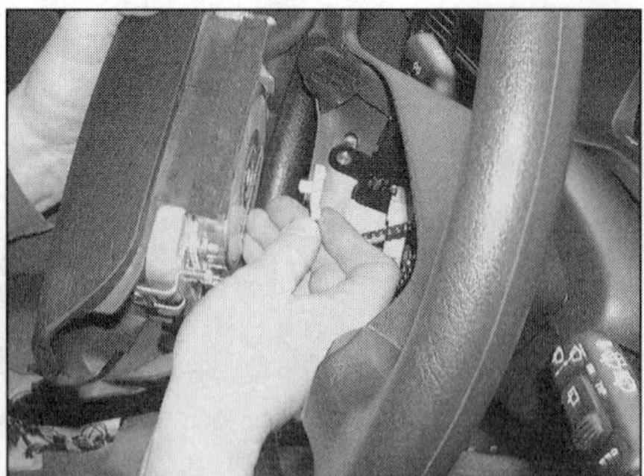
30.3b . . . and disconnect the wiring

30.11 Disconnecting the wiring from the passenger airbag

3 Carefully lift the airbag from the steering wheel sufficient to disconnect the wiring **(see illustrations)**.
4 Rest the airbag in a safe place with the metal bracket facing downwards.

Refitting

5 Locate the airbag over the steering wheel and reconnect the wiring, making sure that it is firmly pressed onto the terminal.
6 Lower the airbag into the steering wheel, then insert and tighten the retaining screws. Refit the rubber plugs.
7 Reconnect the battery negative (earth) lead (see Chapter 5A).
8 Switch on the ignition and check that the SRS warning light goes out. If not, the control unit probably has a fault code stored in it and it will be necessary to have a Saab dealer check the system.

Passenger's airbag

Removal

9 Disconnect the battery negative (earth) lead (see Chapter 5A).
10 Remove the glovebox as described in Section 29.
11 Reach up under the facia and disconnect the wiring from the passenger airbag **(see illustration)**.
12 Unscrew the nut securing the airbag bracket to the bulkhead crossmember.
13 Unscrew the airbag mounting nuts and lift it from the facia **(see illustration)**.
14 Rest the airbag in a safe place with the metal bracket facing downwards.

Refitting

15 Position the airbag in the facia and tighten the nuts to the specified torque. **Note:** *Saab technicians seal the front right and rear left nuts with marking paint.*
16 Refit the airbag bracket nut and tighten to the specified torque.
17 Reconnect the wiring to the airbag.
18 Refit the glovebox with reference to Section 29.
19 Reconnect the battery negative (earth) lead (see Chapter 5A).
20 Switch on the ignition and check that the SRS warning light goes out. If not, the control unit probably has a fault code stored in it and it will be necessary to have a Saab dealer check the system.

Steering wheel contact roller

Removal

21 Disconnect the battery negative (earth) lead (see Chapter 5A).
22 Remove the steering wheel as described in Chapter 10.
23 To prevent damage to the contact roller, use adhesive tape to hold it in its central position.
24 Undo the screws and remove the steering column shrouds.
25 Disconnect the wiring to the contact roller at the two plugs located beneath the steering column.
26 Undo the screws and carefully lift the contact roller over the top of the steering column.

Refitting

27 To prevent damage to the contact roller whilst it is being refitted, use adhesive tape to hold it in its central position.
28 Offer the contact roller over the top of the steering column and reconnect the two wiring plugs.
29 Insert the mounting screws and tighten.
30 Refit the steering column shrouds and tighten the screws.
31 Check that the contact roller is set at its central position as follows. With the front wheels pointing straight ahead, rotate the contact roller fully clockwise. Now turn the contact roller back 21/2 turns.
32 Refit the steering wheel as described in Chapter 10.
33 Reconnect the battery negative (earth) lead (see Chapter 5A).
34 Switch on the ignition and check that the SRS warning light goes out. If not, the control unit probably has a fault code stored in it and it will be necessary to have a Saab dealer check the system.

Electronic control unit (ECU)

Removal

35 Disconnect the battery negative (earth) lead (see Chapter 5A).
36 Remove the rear section of the centre console as described in Section 27.
37 Disconnect the wiring from the ECU.
38 Unscrew the nuts and remove the ECU from inside the car **(see illustration)**.

Refitting

39 Refitting is a reversal of removal.

30.13 Passenger's airbag viewed from under the facia

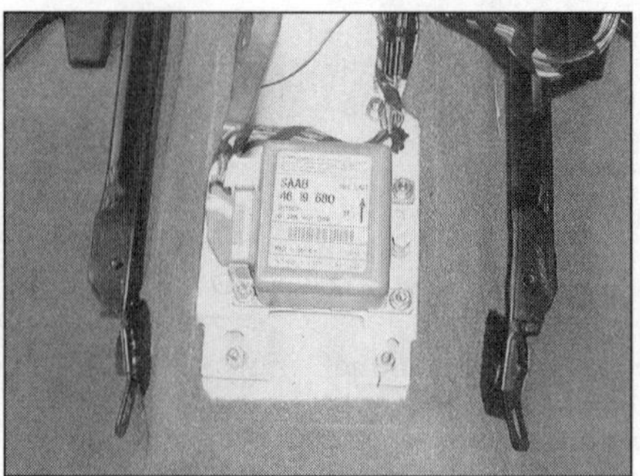

30.38 SRS ECU located under the centre console rear section

Chapter 12
Body electrical system

Contents

Degrees of difficulty

Easy, suitable for novice with little experience 	**Fairly easy,** suitable for beginner with some experience 	**Fairly difficult,** suitable for competent DIY mechanic 	**Difficult,** suitable for experienced DIY mechanic	**Very difficult,** suitable for expert DIY or professional

Specifications

System type	12-volt negative earth
Bulb ratings	**Watts**
Headlights	60/55
Front foglights	55
Illumination for ashtray, cigarette lighter and seat belt warning	1.2
Tail lights	5
Rear foglight, reversing light	21
Stop/tail lights	21/5
Front and rear direction indicators	21
Number plate light, make-up lights	5
Interior dome light, luggage compartment light, glove compartment light	10
Side repeater light, high-level stop light, side lights	5

1 General information and precautions

General information

The electrical system is of the 12-volt negative earth type and comprises a 12-volt battery, an alternator with integral voltage regulator, a starter motor and related electrical accessories, components and wiring.

Most models are fitted with an anti-theft alarm system consisting of sensors on the doors, tailgate and bonnet. A glass breakage sensor is also fitted in the interior light on the front of the headlining. The system is controlled by a central electronic control module which operates the warning horn.

While some repair procedures are given, the usual course of action is to renew a defective component. The owner whose interest extends beyond mere component renewal should obtain a copy of the *Automotive Electrical & Electronic Systems Manual*, available from the publishers of this Manual.

Precautions

It is necessary to take extra care when working on the electrical system to avoid damage to semi-conductor devices (diodes and transistors) and to avoid the risk of personal injury. Certain procedures must be followed when removing the SRS components; refer to Chapter 11 for more information. In addition to the precautions given in *"Safety first!"* at the beginning of this Manual, observe the following when working on the system:

a) *Always remove rings, watches, etc. before working on the electrical system. Even with the battery disconnected, capacitive discharge could occur if a component's live terminal is earthed through a metal object. This could cause a shock or nasty burn.*
b) *Do not reverse the battery connections. Components such as the alternator, fuel injection/ignition system ECU, or any other having semi-conductor circuitry could be irreparably damaged.*
c) *Do not allow the engine to turn the alternator when the alternator is not connected.*
d) *Always ensure that the battery negative lead is disconnected when working on the electrical system.*
e) *Before using electric-arc welding equipment on the vehicle, disconnect the battery, alternator and components such as the fuel injection/ignition system ECU to protect them.*

2 Electrical fault-finding - general information

Note: *Refer to the precautions given in "Safety first!" and in Section 1 of this Chapter before starting work. The following tests relate to testing of the main electrical circuits, and should not be used to test delicate electronic circuits (such as anti-lock braking systems), particularly where an electronic control unit (ECU) is involved.*

General

1 A typical electrical circuit consists of an electrical component, any switches, relays, motors, fuses, fusible links or circuit breakers related to that component, and the wiring and connectors which link the component to both the battery and the chassis. To help to pinpoint a problem in an electrical circuit, wiring diagrams are included at the end of this manual.

2 Before attempting to diagnose an electrical fault, first study the appropriate wiring diagram, to obtain a more complete understanding of the components included in the particular circuit concerned. The possible sources of a fault can be narrowed down by noting whether other components related to the circuit are operating properly. If several components or circuits fail at one time, the problem is likely to be related to a shared fuse or earth connection.

3 Electrical problems usually stem from simple causes, such as loose or corroded connections, a faulty earth connection, a blown fuse, a melted fusible link, or a faulty relay (refer to Section 3 for details of testing relays). Visually inspect the condition of all fuses, wires and connections in a problem circuit before testing the components. Use the wiring diagrams to determine which terminal connections will need to be checked, in order to pinpoint the trouble-spot.

4 The basic tools required for electrical fault-finding include: a circuit tester or voltmeter (a 12-volt bulb with a set of test leads can also be used for certain tests), a self-powered test light (sometimes known as a continuity tester), an ohmmeter (to measure resistance), a battery and set of test leads, and a jumper wire, preferably with a circuit breaker or fuse incorporated, which can be used to bypass suspect wires or electrical components. Before attempting to locate a problem with test instruments, use the wiring diagram to determine where to make the connections.

5 To find the source of an intermittent wiring fault (usually due to a poor or dirty connection, or damaged wiring insulation), an integrity test can be performed on the wiring, which involves moving the wiring by hand, to see if the fault occurs as the wiring is moved. It should be possible to narrow down the source of the fault to a particular section of wiring. This method of testing can be used in conjunction with any of the tests described in the following sub-Sections.

6 Apart from problems due to poor connections, two basic types of fault can occur in an electrical circuit - open-circuit, or short-circuit.

7 Open-circuit faults are caused by a break somewhere in the circuit, which prevents current from flowing. An open-circuit fault will prevent a component from working, but will not cause the relevant circuit fuse to blow.

8 Short-circuit faults are caused by a "short" somewhere in the circuit, which allows the current flowing in the circuit to "escape" along an alternative route, usually to earth. Short-circuit faults are normally caused by a breakdown in wiring insulation, which allows a feed wire to touch either another wire, or an earthed component such as the bodyshell. A short-circuit fault will normally cause the relevant circuit fuse to blow. **Note:** *A short-circuit that occurs in the wiring between a circuit's battery supply and its fuse will not cause the fuse in that particular circuit to blow. This part of the circuit is unprotected - bear this in mind when fault-finding on the vehicle's electrical system.*

Finding an open-circuit

9 To check for an open-circuit, connect one lead of a circuit tester or voltmeter to either the negative battery terminal or a known good earth.

10 Connect the other lead to a connector in the circuit being tested, preferably nearest to the battery or fuse.

11 Switch on the circuit, bearing in mind that some circuits are live only when the ignition switch is moved to a particular position.

12 If voltage is present (indicated either by the tester bulb lighting or a voltmeter reading, as applicable), this means that the section of the circuit between the relevant connector and the battery is problem-free.

13 Continue to check the remainder of the circuit in the same fashion.

14 When a point is reached at which no voltage is present, the problem must lie between that point and the previous test point with voltage. Most problems can be traced to a broken, corroded or loose connection.

Finding a short-circuit

15 To check for a short-circuit, first disconnect the load(s) from the circuit (loads are the components which draw current from a circuit, such as bulbs, motors, heating elements, etc).

16 Remove the relevant fuse from the circuit, and connect a circuit tester or voltmeter to the fuse connections.

17 Switch on the circuit, bearing in mind that some circuits are live only when the ignition switch is moved to a particular position.

18 If voltage is present (indicated either by the tester bulb lighting or a voltmeter reading, as applicable), this means that there is a short-circuit.

19 If no voltage is present, but the fuse still blows with the load(s) connected, this indicates an internal fault in the load(s).

Finding an earth fault

20 The battery negative terminal is connected to "earth" - the metal of the engine/ transmission and the car body - and most systems are wired so that they only receive a positive feed, the current returning via the metal of the car body. This means that the component mounting and the body form part of that circuit. Loose or corroded mountings can therefore cause a range of electrical faults, ranging from total failure of a circuit, to a puzzling partial fault. In particular, lights may shine dimly (especially when another circuit sharing the same earth point is in operation), motors (eg wiper motors or the radiator cooling fan motor) may run slowly, and the operation of one circuit may have an apparently-unrelated effect on another. Note that on many vehicles, earth straps are used between certain components, such as the engine/transmission and the body, usually where there is no metal-to-metal contact between components, due to flexible rubber mountings, etc.

21 To check whether a component is properly earthed, disconnect the battery, and connect one lead of an ohmmeter to a known good earth point. Connect the other lead to the wire or earth connection being tested. The resistance reading should be zero; if not, check the connection as follows.

22 If an earth connection is thought to be faulty, dismantle the connection, and clean back to bare metal both the bodyshell and the wire terminal, or the component's earth connection mating surface. Be careful to remove all traces of dirt and corrosion, then use a knife to trim away any paint, so that a clean metal-to-metal joint is made. On reassembly, tighten the joint fasteners securely; if a wire terminal is being refitted, use serrated washers between the terminal and the bodyshell, to ensure a clean and secure connection. When the connection is remade, prevent the onset of corrosion in the future by applying a coat of petroleum jelly or silicone-based grease, or by spraying on (at regular intervals) a proprietary ignition sealer or a water-dispersant lubricant.

3 Fuses and relays - general information

Fuses

1 Fuses are designed to break an electrical circuit when a predetermined current limit is reached, in order to protect the components and wiring which could be damaged by excessive current flow. Any excessive current flow will be due to a fault in the circuit, usually a short-circuit (see Section 2).

3.3a The facia fusebox

3.3b The fusebox located in the left-hand rear of the engine compartment

2 The fuses are located either in the fusebox located on the right-hand end of the facia, or in the fusebox located in the left-hand rear of the engine compartment. The engine compartment fusebox also includes the main relays.

3 Access to the facia fusebox is gained by opening the right-hand front door and releasing the plastic cover. The engine compartment fusebox is opened by opening the bonnet and lifting the plastic cover **(see illustrations)**.

4 To remove a fuse, use the plastic tool provided in the fusebox to pull the fuse from its socket **(see illustration)**.

5 Inspect the fuse from the side, through the transparent plastic body - a blown fuse can be recognised by its melted or broken wire.

6 Spare fuses are provided in the blank terminal positions in the fusebox.

7 Before renewing a blown fuse, trace and rectify the cause, and always use a fuse of the correct rating.

Caution: Never substitute a fuse of a higher rating, or make temporary repairs using wire or metal foil; more serious damage, or even a fire, could result.

8 Note that the fuses are colour-coded, as described below - refer to the wiring diagrams for details of the fuse ratings and the circuits protected.

Colour	Rating
Brown	5A
Red	10A
Blue	15A
Yellow	20A
Clear	25A
Green	30A

9 In addition to the system fuses, fusible links are also located next to the battery and also in the fusebox at the rear of the engine compartment. There are four fusible links in each location, and their purpose is to protect certain areas of the car's electrical wiring, each including more than one electrical component. They will not blow as the result of a fault in a single component. Their ratings are as follows:

Colour	Rating
Orange	40A (maximum)
Blue	60A (maximum)

Relays

10 A relay is an electrically-operated mechanical switch, which is used for the following reasons:

a) A relay can switch a heavy current remotely from the circuit in which the current is flowing, therefore allowing the use of lighter-gauge wiring and switch contacts.

b) A relay can receive more than one control input, unlike a mechanically-operated switch.

c) A relay can have a timer function, although on the Saab models in this Manual this function is carried out by the ICE Control module.

11 The main relays are located in the fusebox at the left-hand rear corner of the engine compartment. Lift off the cover for access to the relays. Additional relays are located beneath the right-hand side of the facia **(see illustration)**.

12 If a circuit or system that is controlled by a relay develops a fault and the performance of the relay is in doubt, switch on the system in question. *In general*, if the relay is functioning, it should be possible to hear it "click" as it is energised. If this is found to be the case, then it is probable that the fault lies with the system's components or wiring. If the relay cannot be heard to energise, then either the relay is not receiving a main supply or switching voltage, or the relay itself is faulty. Verification can be carried out by the substitution of a known good unit, but be careful - while some relays are identical in appearance and operation, others look similar but perform different functions - ensure that the substitute relay is of exactly the same type.

13 To remove a relay, first ensure that the relevant circuit is switched off. The relay can then simply be pulled out from the socket, and pushed back into position **(see illustration)**.

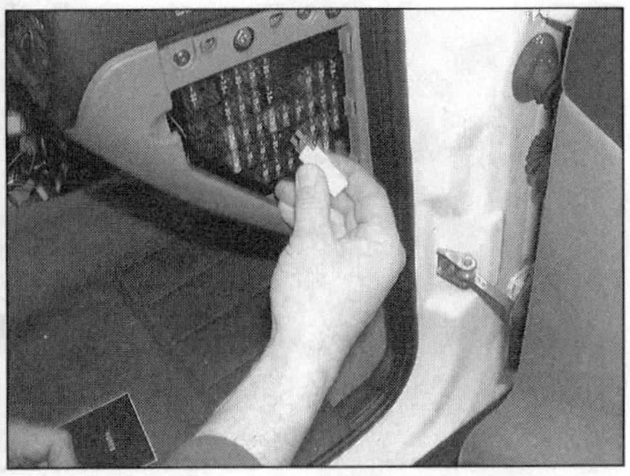

3.4 Removing a fuse with the plastic tool provided

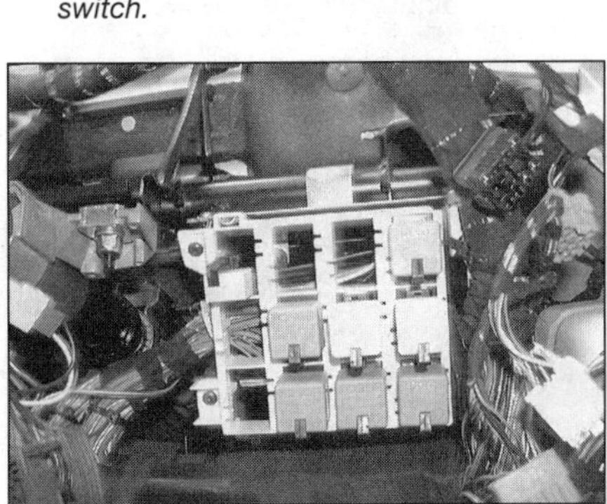

3.11 Additional relays located beneath the right-hand side of the facia

3.13 Removing a relay

4.4a Depress the tabs to remove the combination switch . . .

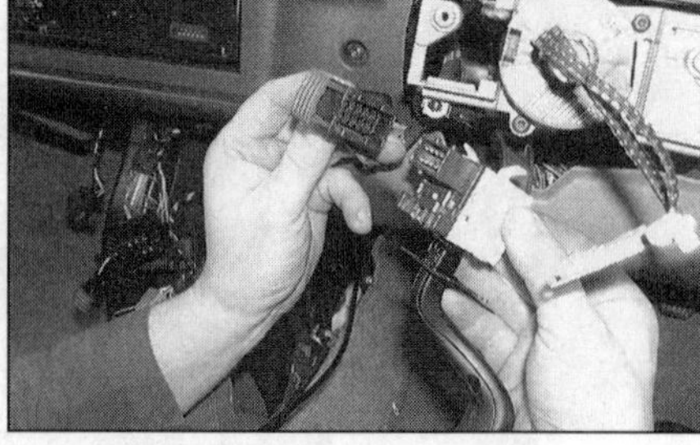
4.4b . . . then disconnect the wiring

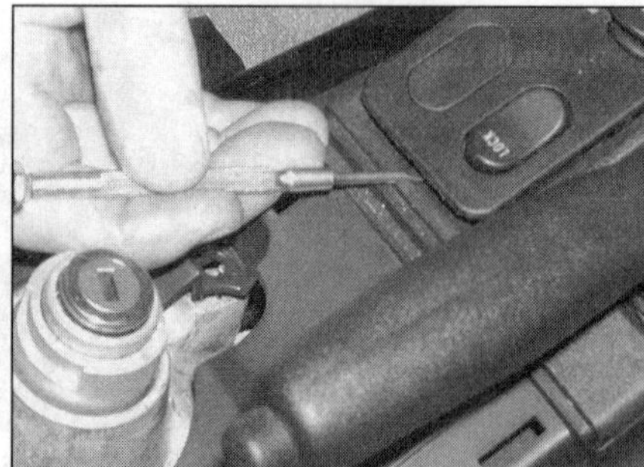
4.6 Prise out the electric window control switch with a screwdriver . . .

4 Switches and controls - removal and refitting

Ignition switch and lock

1 The ignition switch and lock is incorporated in the gearchange assembly between the front seats. Refer to Chapter 7A or 7B for more information.

Steering column combination switch

Removal

2 Remove the steering wheel (See Chapter 10).
3 Undo the screws and remove the steering column shrouds.
4 Remove the switch by depressing the top and bottom plastic tabs, then disconnect the wiring **(see illustrations)**.

Refitting

5 Refitting is a reversal of removal.

Electric window control switch

Removal

6 Using a screwdriver, carefully prise up the front of the switch from the centre console **(see illustration)**.
7 Disconnect the wiring **(see illustration)**.

Refitting

8 Refitting is a reversal of removal.

Headlight height adjustment switch

Removal

9 Using a screwdriver, carefully prise the switch from the facia panel. If it is tight, remove the lower trim panel and press the switch out from behind **(see illustration)**.
10 Disconnect the wiring **(see illustration)**.

Refitting

11 Refitting is a reversal of removal.

Interior lighting control switch

Removal

12 Using a screwdriver, carefully prise the switch from the centre console rear section. If it is tight, temporarily slide the rear section slightly to the rear and press out the switch from below **(see illustration)**.
13 Disconnect the wiring **(see illustration)**.

Refitting

14 Refitting is a reversal of removal.

Instrument illumination rheostat

Removal

15 Using a screwdriver, carefully prise the switch from the facia panel. If it is tight, remove the lower trim panel and press the switch out from behind **(see illustration)**.

4.7 . . . then disconnect the wiring

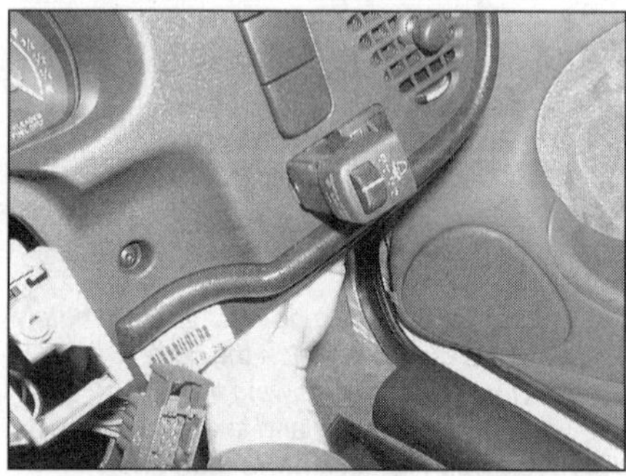
4.9 Press out the headlight height adjustment switch . . .

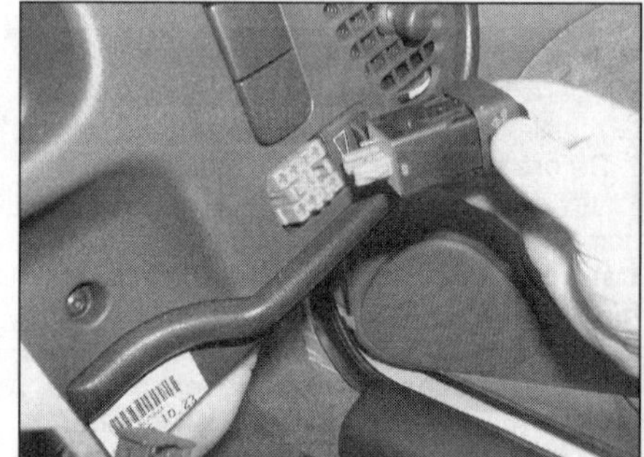
4.10 . . . and disconnect the wiring

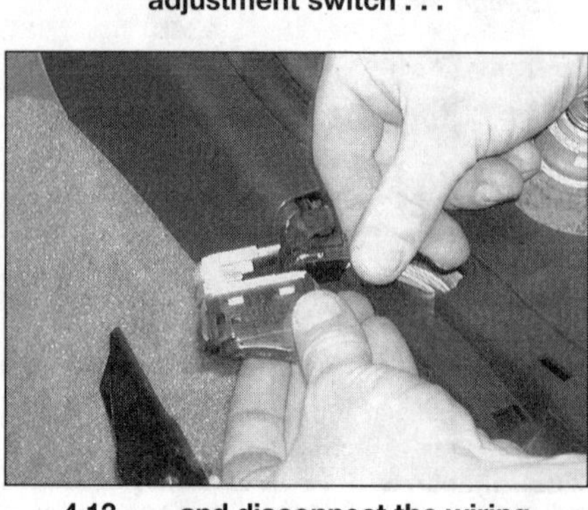
4.12 Remove the interior lighting control switch . . .

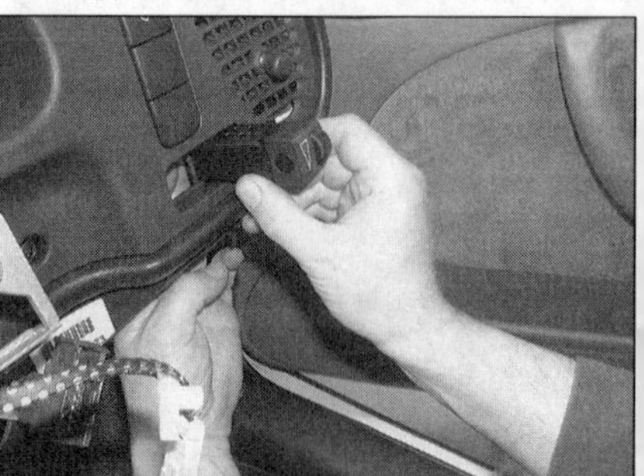
4.13 . . . and disconnect the wiring

4.15 Removing the instrument illumination rheostat

4.18 Removing the rear foglight switch

4.21 Remove the lighting switch . . .

4.22 . . . and disconnect the wiring

4.25 Brake stop-light switch

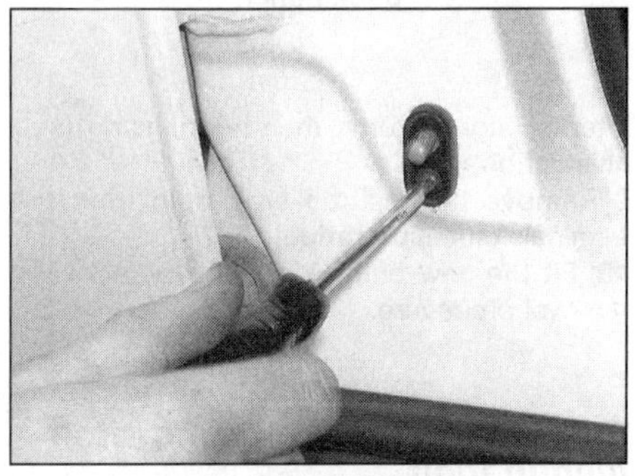
4.34a Undo the screw . . .

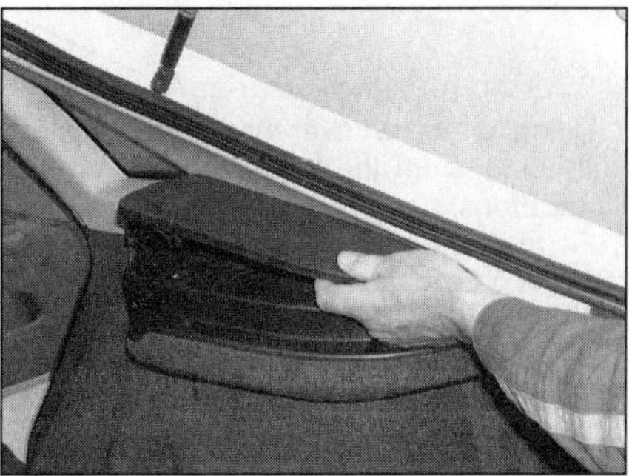
4.34b . . . and withdraw the door courtesy light switch

16 Disconnect the wiring.

Refitting

17 Refitting is a reversal of removal.

Rear foglight switch

Removal

18 Using a screwdriver, carefully prise the switch from the facia panel. If it is tight, remove the lower trim panel and press the switch out from behind **(see illustration)**.
19 Disconnect the wiring.

Refitting

20 Refitting is a reversal of removal.

Lighting switch

Removal

21 Carefully prise the switch from the facia using a screwdriver **(see illustration)**.
22 Disconnect the wiring **(see illustration)**.

Refitting

23 Refitting is a reversal of removal.

Brake stop-light switch

Removal

24 To remove the switch first make sure that the ignition is switched off, then remove the lower trim panel from the facia with reference to Chapter 11.
25 Reach up at the front of the pedal bracket, and disconnect the wiring from the switch **(see illustration)**.
26 At the end of the stop-light switch body, squeeze together the plastic tangs, and pull the switch back through the mounting bracket.

Refitting

27 Refitting is a reversal of removal.

Hazard warning light switch

Removal

28 Carefully prise the switch from the facia using a screwdriver.
29 Disconnect the wiring.

Refitting

30 Refitting is a reversal of removal.

Electric door mirror switch

Removal

31 Carefully prise the switch from the triangular cover on the front door.
32 Disconnect the wiring.

Refitting

33 Refitting is a reversal of removal.

Door courtesy light switch

Removal

34 With the door open, undo the screw and withdraw the switch from the door pillar **(see illustrations)**.
35 Disconnect the wiring, making sure that it does not drop back into the bodywork.

Tape the wiring to the door, to prevent it falling back into the door pillar. Alternatively, tie a length of string to the wiring to retrieve it.

Refitting

36 Refitting is a reversal of removal.

5 Interior light bulbs - renewal

Instrument panel

1 Remove the instrument panel as described in Section 9.
2 Undo the screws and lift the back panel and module from the instrument panel. Carefully disconnect the wiring plugs **(see illustrations)**.

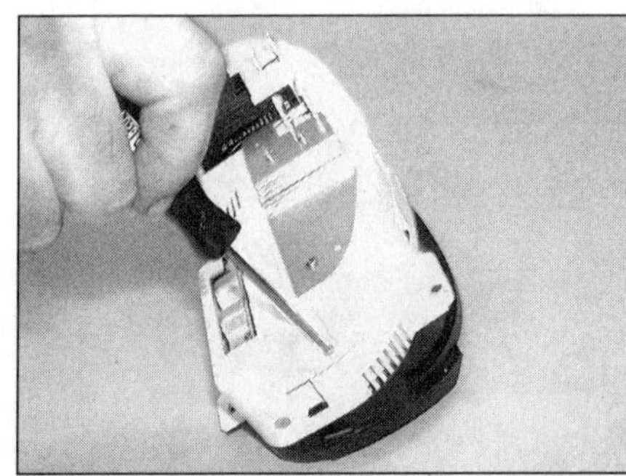
5.2a Undo the screws and lift the back panel . . .

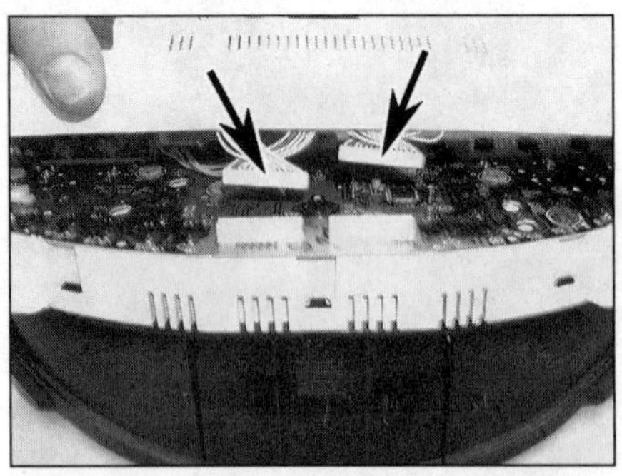
5.2b . . . then disconnect the wiring plugs

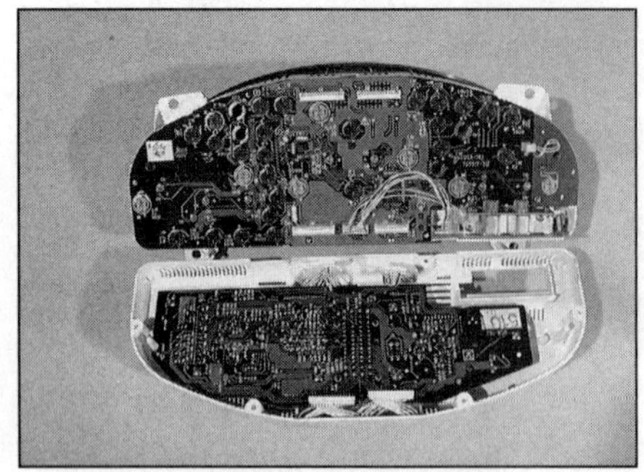
5.2c Instrument panel main console and back panel

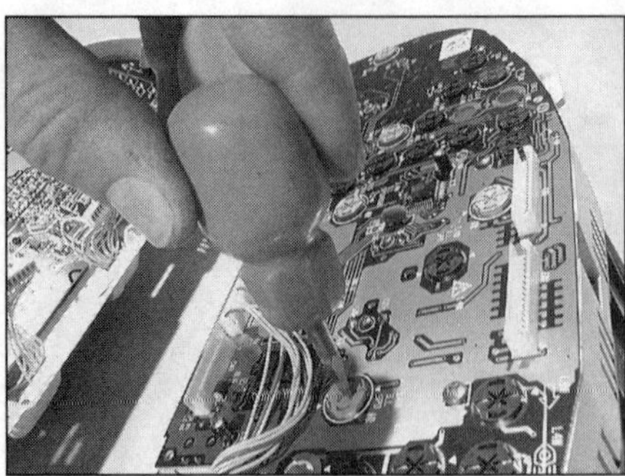
5.3a Unscrew the bulbholder . . .

3 Using a screwdriver undo the relevant bulbholder from the instrument panel **(see illustrations)**.

4 Fit the new bulb using a reversal of the removal procedure.

Clock/SID module

5 Remove the clock/SID module as described in Section 10.

6 Using a screwdriver or curved pair of pliers, twist the bulbholder and remove the bulb **(see illustrations)**.

7 Fit the new bulb using a reversal of the removal procedure.

Interior lights

8 Using a screwdriver carefully prise the interior light from the headlining **(see illustrations)**.

9 Remove the festoon type bulb from the terminals **(see illustration)**.

10 Fit the new bulb using a reversal of the removal procedure.

Electric window control switch illumination

11 Remove the electric window control switch as described in Section 4.

12 Using a screwdriver, twist the bulbholder anticlockwise to remove it **(see illustration)**.

13 Fit the new bulb using a reversal of the removal procedure.

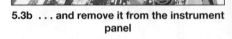

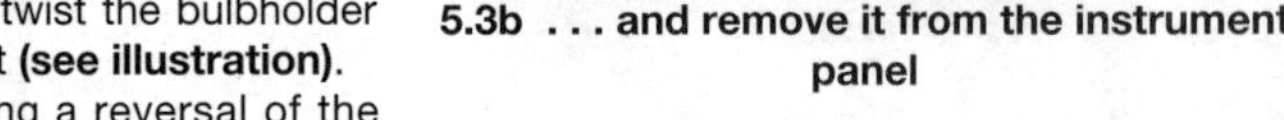
5.3b . . . and remove it from the instrument panel

5.6a Unscrew the bulbholder . . .

5.6b . . . and remove it from the clock/SID module

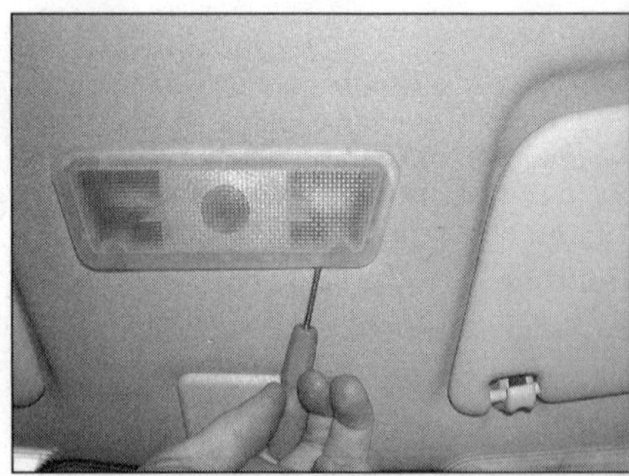
5.8a Carefully prise away the interior light . . .

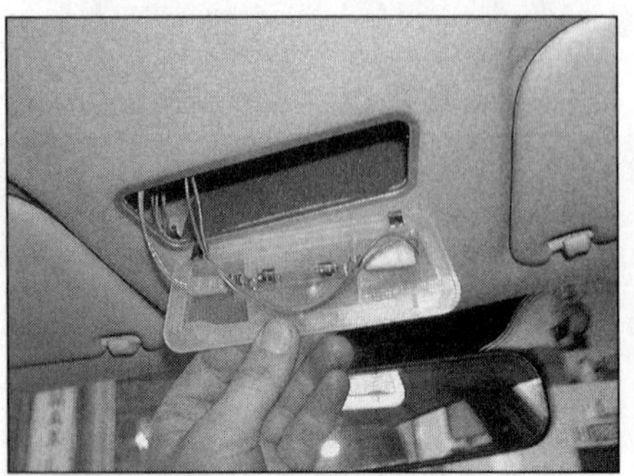
5.8b . . . and remove it from the headlining

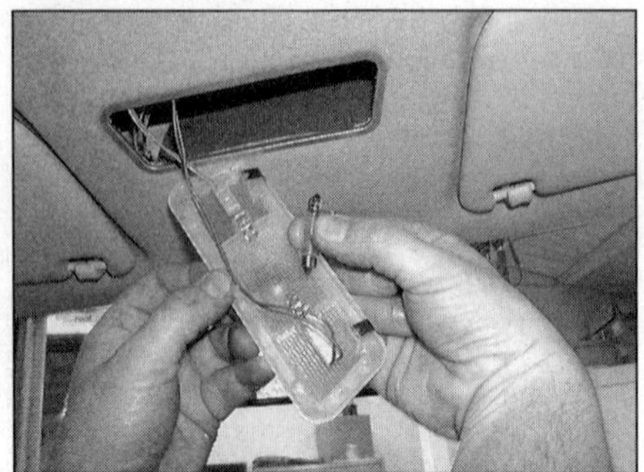
5.9 Removing the festoon type bulb

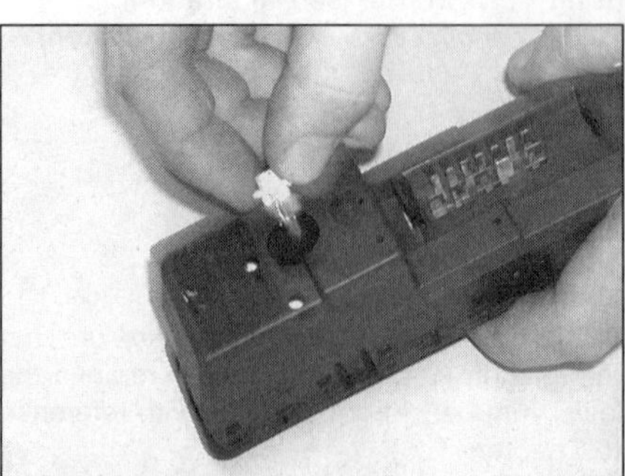
5.12 Removing the illumination bulbholder from the electric window control switch

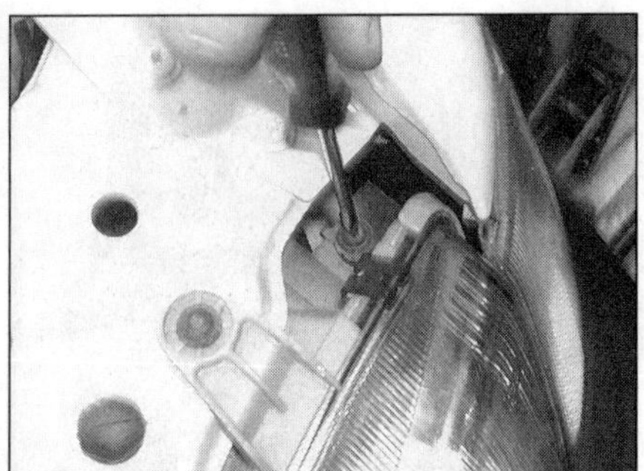
6.3 Loosen the direction indicator unit retaining screw . . .

6.4 . . . then withdraw the unit and disconnect the wiring

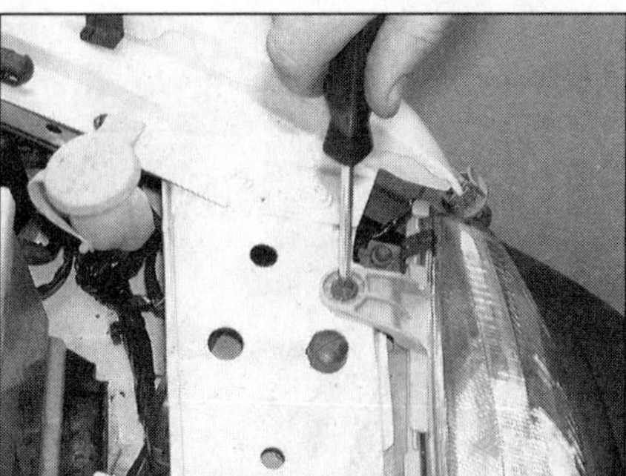
6.5a Unscrew the upper mounting screw . . .

6 Exterior light units - removal and refitting

Headlight

Removal

1 With the bonnet open, remove the radiator grille as described in Chapter 11, Section 8.
2 Lift the wiper arms from the headlamps.
3 Through the aperture at the rear of the headlight, loosen only the bolt securing the direction indicator unit to the headlight **(see illustration)**. The bolt does not have to be completely removed.
4 Withdraw the direction indicator light unit and disconnect the wiring plug **(see illustration)**.
5 Undo the headlight mounting screws **(see illustrations)**.
6 Carefully lift the headlight unit from the front of the car and disconnect the wiring from the main beam and parking light bulbs **(see illustrations)**.

Refitting

7 Refitting is a reversal of removal.

Front direction indicator light

Removal

8 With the bonnet open, use a socket through the aperture at the rear of the headlight to loosen only the bolt securing the direction indicator unit to the headlight. The bolt does not have to be completely removed.
9 Withdraw the direction indicator light unit.
10 Disconnect the bulb wiring plug.
11 If necessary, remove the bulbholder and bulb.

Refitting

12 Refitting is a reversal of removal.

Side repeater light

Removal

13 Carefully press the light forwards against the tension of the plastic clip, then release the rear of the light from the front wing **(see illustration)**.
14 Twist the bulbholder and remove the light unit.

Refitting

15 Refitting is a reversal of removal.

Rear light cluster

16 With the tailgate open, open the carpet flap behind the rear light cluster.
17 Disconnect the wiring from the bulbholder.
18 Unscrew the nuts and withdraw the cluster from the rear wing **(see illustration)**.

6.5b . . . and lower mounting screw

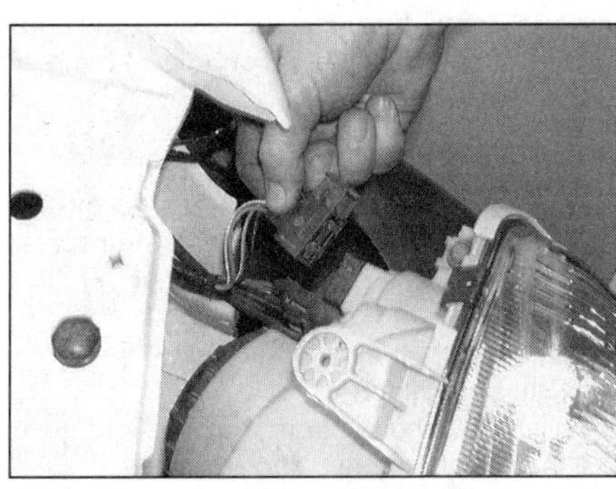
6.6a Disconnect the wiring from the main beam . . .

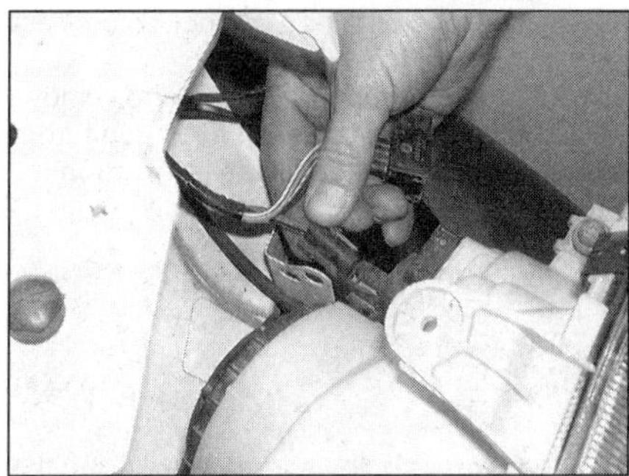
6.6b . . . and parking light bulbs . . .

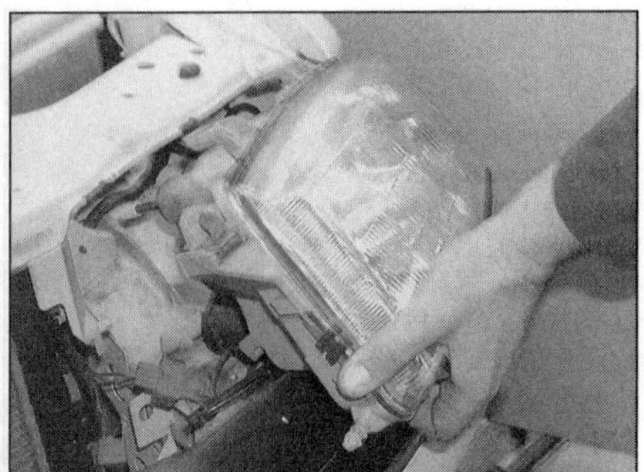
6.6c . . . and withdraw the headlight from the car

6.13 Removing the side repeater light

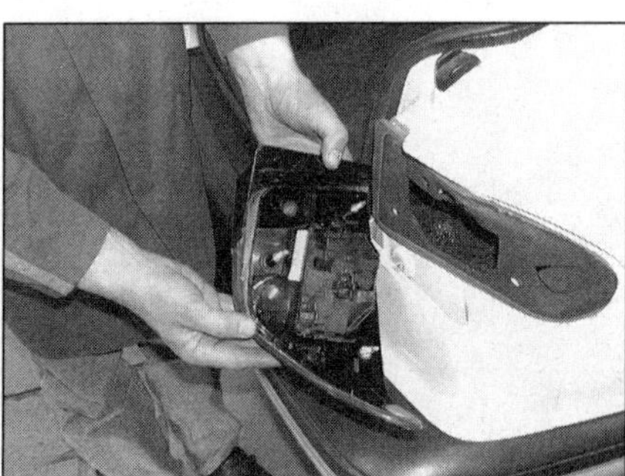
6.18 Removing the rear light cluster

6.23a Undo the screws from the number plate light . . .

6.23b . . . and lower it from the tailgate

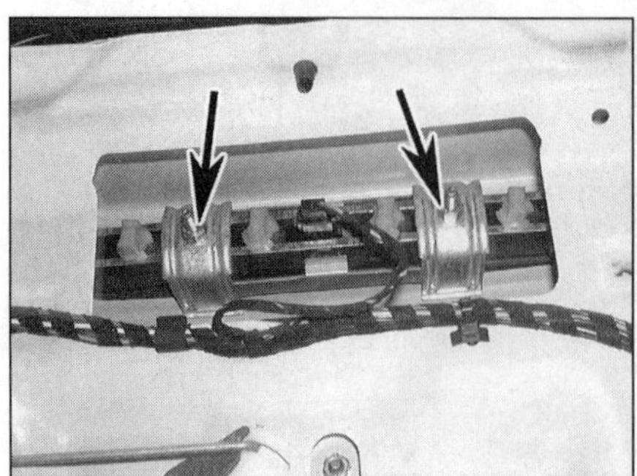

6.29 High level stop light mounting nuts and clamps

19 Refitting is a reversal of removal.

Front foglight

20 Reach up behind the front bumper and disconnect the wiring for the front foglight.
21 Unscrew the mounting bolts and withdraw the foglight from the front bumper.
22 Refitting is a reversal of removal.

Number plate light

23 Undo the screws and lower the number plate light from the tailgate **(see illustrations)**.
24 Disconnect the wiring.
25 Refitting is a reversal of removal.

High level stop light

26 With the tailgate open, use a Torx key to undo the screws and remove the grab handle from the tailgate.
27 Using a screwdriver, undo the screws and remove the main trim panel from the inside of the tailgate.
28 Reach up into the tailgate, then disconnect the wiring.
29 Unscrew the mounting nuts and remove the clamps, then withdraw the light unit from the outside of the tailgate **(see illustration)**.
30 Refitting is a reversal of removal.

7 Exterior light bulbs - renewal

1 Whenever a bulb is renewed, note the following points:

a) Remember that, if the light has just been in use, the bulb may be extremely hot.
b) Do not touch the bulb glass with the fingers, as this can result in early failure or a dull reflector.
c) Always check the bulb contacts and holder, ensuring that there is clean metal-to metal contact between the bulb and its live(s) and earth. Clean off any corrosion or dirt before fitting a new bulb.
d) Ensure that the new bulb is of the correct rating.

Headlight main beam

2 With the bonnet open, unscrew the plastic cover from the rear of the headlight.
3 Disconnect the wiring from the main beam bulb.
4 Release the spring clip and remove the bulb. Use a tissue or clean cloth to prevent touching the bulb.
5 Fit the new bulb using a reversal of the removal procedure, but make sure that the bulb location lugs engage correctly in the rear of the headlight.

Front sidelight

6 The front sidelight bulb is located on the main beam headlight assembly. First unscrew the plastic cover from the rear of the headlight.
7 Disconnect the wiring from the front sidelight bulbholder.
8 Pull the bulbholder from the headlight, then pull the bulb from the bulbholder.
9 Fit the new bulb using a reversal of the removal procedure.

Front direction indicator

10 With the bonnet open, use a socket through the aperture at the rear of the headlight to loosen only the bolt securing the direction indicator unit to the headlight. The bolt does not have to be completely removed.
11 Withdraw the direction indicator light unit.
12 Twist the bulbholder anticlockwise and remove it, then depress and twist the bulb to remove it from the bulbholder.
13 Fit the new bulb using a reversal of the removal procedure.

Side repeater lights

14 Carefully press the light forwards against the tension of the plastic clip, then release the rear of the light from the front wing **(see illustration)**.
15 Twist the bulbholder and remove the lens unit, then pull out the wedge-type bulb **(see illustrations)**. Do not allow the wiring to drop into the space behind the wing.
16 Fit the new bulb using a reversal of the removal procedure.

Rear light cluster

17 With the tailgate open, prise open the carpet flap from over the rear light cluster.
18 Squeeze together the locking tabs and remove the bulbholder from the cluster.
19 Depress and twist the relevant bulb and remove it from the bulbholder.
20 Fit the new bulb using a reversal of the removal procedure.

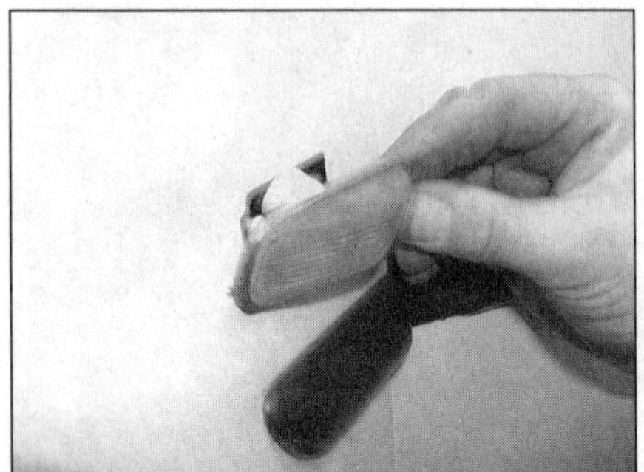

7.14 Remove the side repeater light . . .

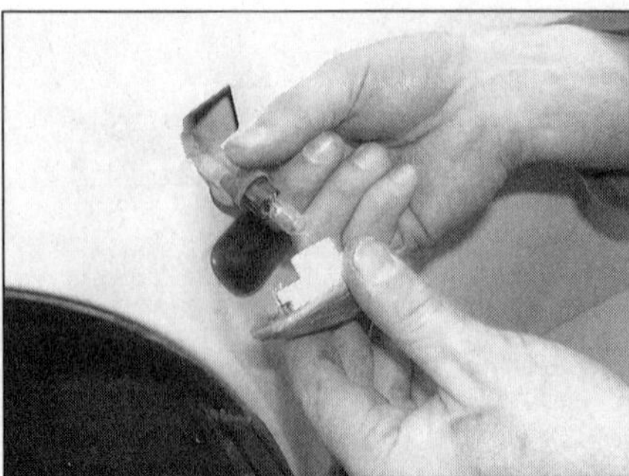

7.15a . . . twist the bulbholder to remove it from the lens unit

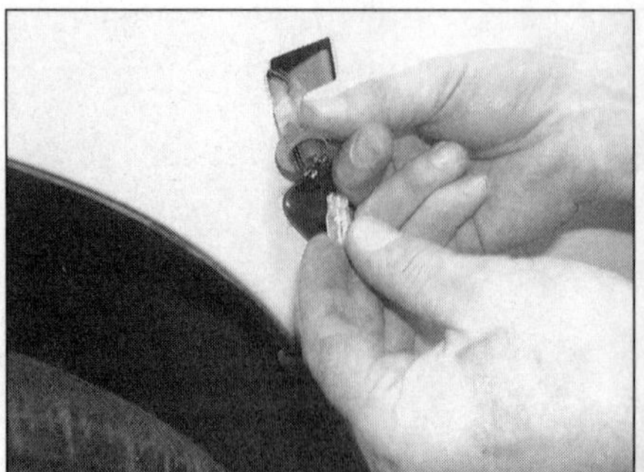

7.15b . . . and pull out the wedge-type bulb

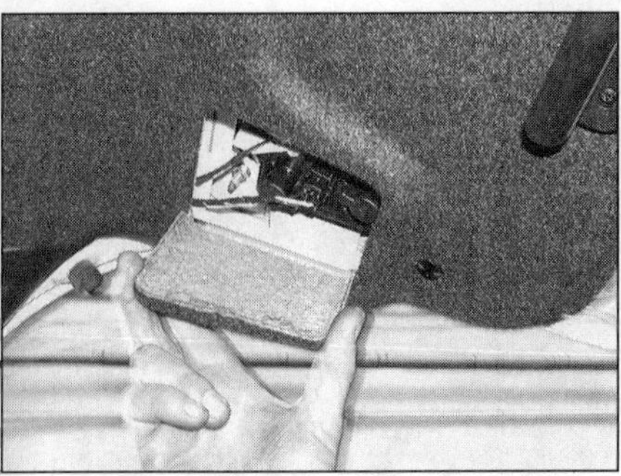

7.21 Prise open the carpet flap . . .

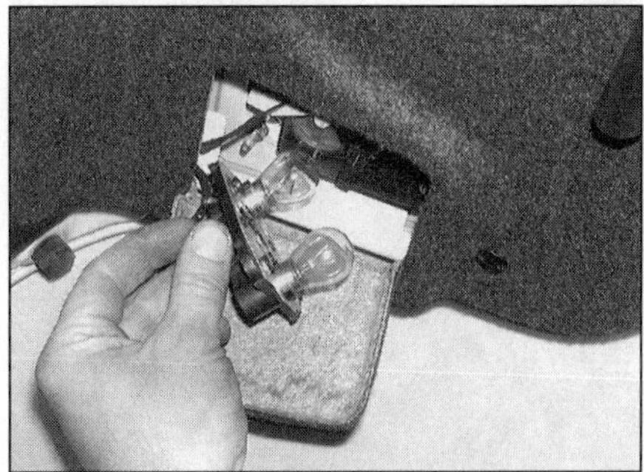

7.22 . . . and withdraw the reversing and rear fog light bulbholder . . .

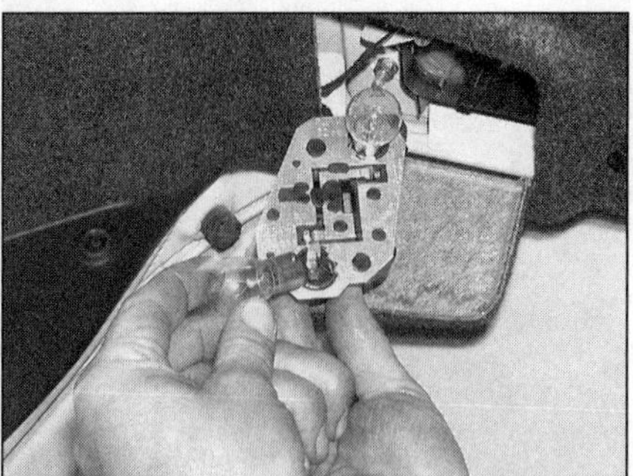

7.23 . . . then remove the relevant bulb

Reversing and rear foglights

21 With the tailgate open, prise open the carpet flap from over the reversing and rear foglights **(see illustration)**.

22 Release the clip and pull the bulbholder from the light **(see illustration)**.

23 Depress and twist the relevant bulb and remove it from the bulbholder **(see illustration)**.

24 Fit the new bulb using a reversal of the removal procedure.

Front foglight

25 Undo the screws and remove the cover from the bottom of the front foglight. Recover the seal.

26 Disconnect the wiring.

27 Twist the bulbholder and remove from the foglight.

28 Fit the new bulb using a reversal of the removal procedure.

Number plate light

29 Undo the screws and lower the number plate light from the tailgate **(see illustrations)**.

30 Remove the festoon type bulb from the terminals **(see illustration)**.

31 Fit the new bulb using a reversal of the removal procedure, but make sure that the terminals are tensioned sufficiently to hold the bulb securely.

High level stop light

32 With the tailgate open, use a Torx key to undo the screws and remove the grab handle from the tailgate.

33 Using a screwdriver, undo the screws and remove the main trim panel from the inside of the tailgate.

34 Reach up inside the tailgate and twist the high level stop light bulbholder anticlockwise to remove it **(see illustration)**.

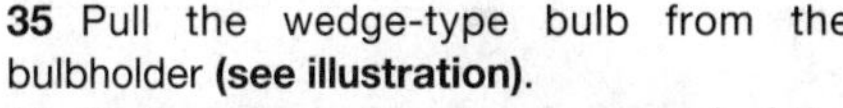

35 Pull the wedge-type bulb from the bulbholder **(see illustration)**.

36 Fit the new bulb using a reversal of the removal procedure.

8 Headlight beam adjustment - general information

1 Accurate adjustment of the headlight beam is only possible using optical beam-setting equipment, and this work should therefore be carried out by a Saab dealer or suitably-equipped workshop. In an emergency, it is possible to adjust the headlights by turning the knobs located on the rear of the headlight **(see illustration)**.

2 Most models have a headlight beam adjustment control, which allows the aim of

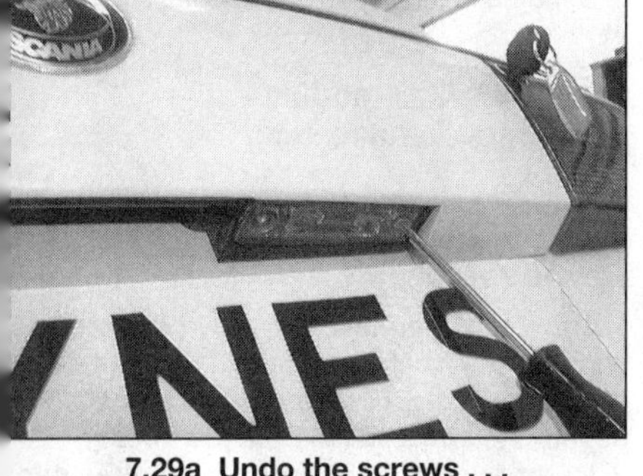

7.29a Undo the screws . . .

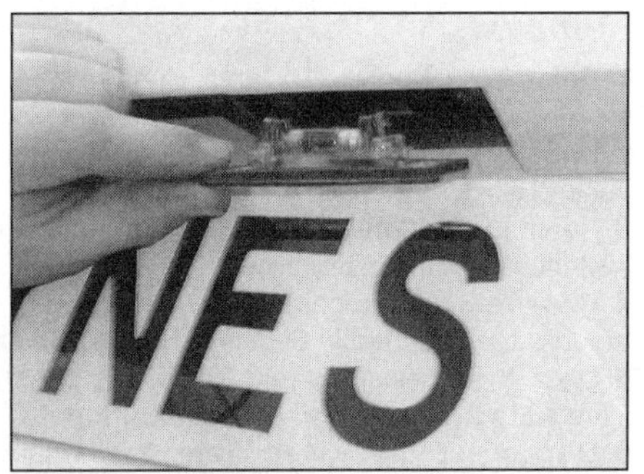

7.29b . . . and lower the number plate light . . .

7.30 . . . then remove the festoon type bulb

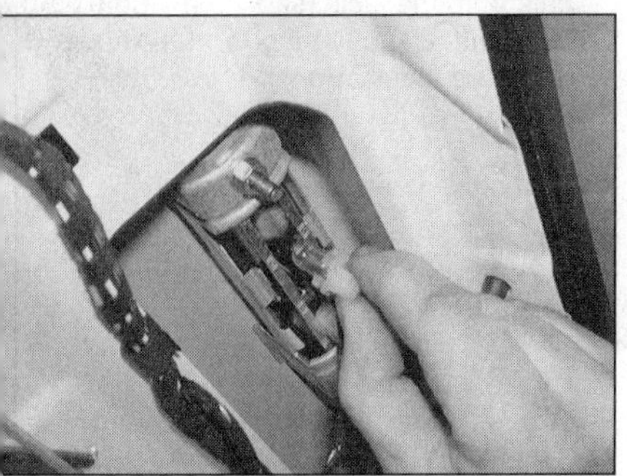

7.34 Remove the high level stop light bulbholder . . .

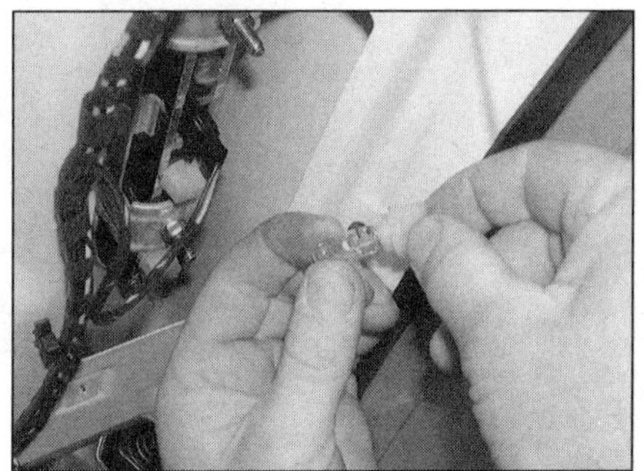

7.35 . . . then pull the wedge-type bulb from the bulbholder

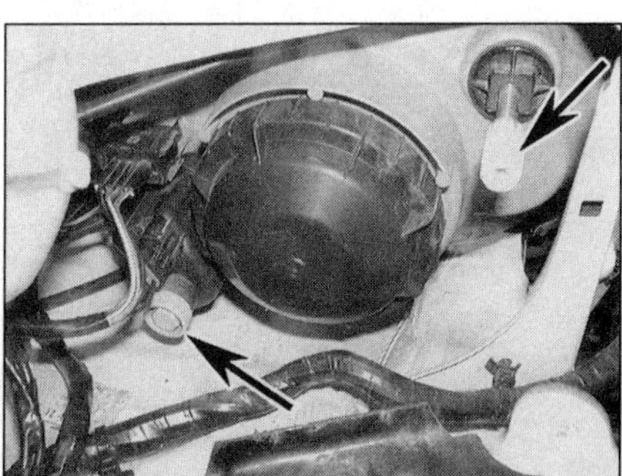

8.1 Headlight beam adjustment knobs on the rear of the headlight

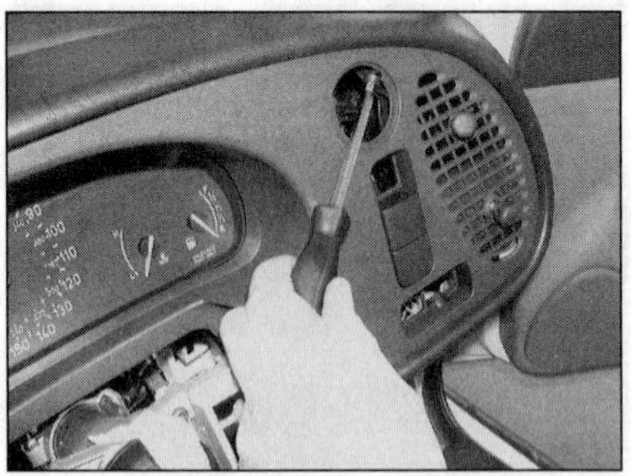
9.5a Undo the screws . . .

9.5b . . . and remove the instrument panel surround

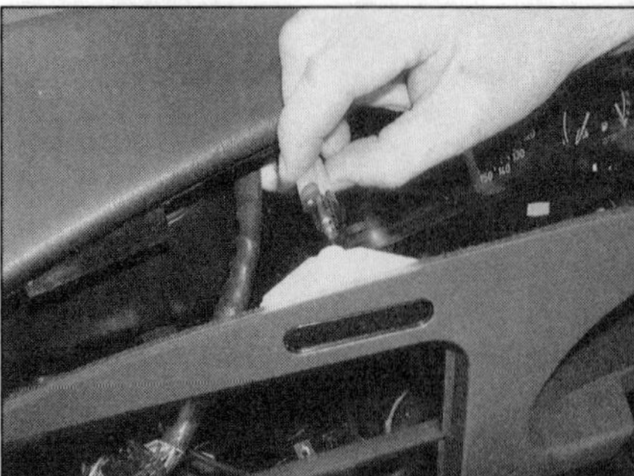
9.6 Disconnecting the wiring from the small display panel

9.7 Undo the screws . . .

9.8a . . . then withdraw the instrument panel . . .

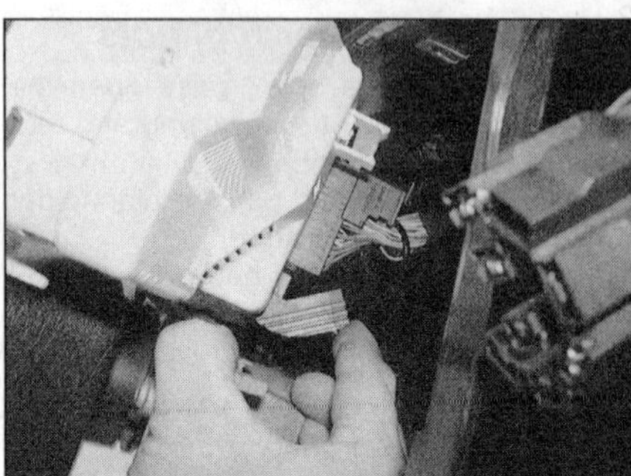
9.8b . . . and disconnect the wiring

the headlights to be adjusted to compensate for variation in the vehicle's payload. The aim is altered by means of facia-mounted switch, which controls electric adjuster motors located in the rear of the headlight assemblies. The switch should be positioned as follows, according to the load being carried in the vehicle:

Switch position	Vehicle load
0	*Up to 3 occupants (no more than one in the rear seat), no luggage.*
1	*Up to 3 occupants in rear seats, up to 30 kg in luggage.*
2	*Up to 3 occupants in rear seats, up to 80 kg in luggage.*
3	*Up to 5 occupants, luggage area full - or up to 5 occupants, luggage area full, towing caravan/trailer.*

10.2 Using two M4 screws to withdraw the SID unit

9 Instrument panel - removal and refitting

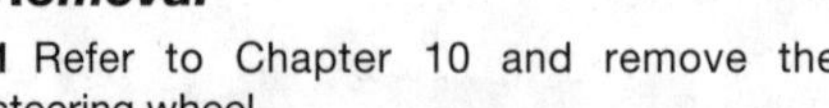

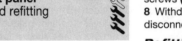

Removal

1 Refer to Chapter 10 and remove the steering wheel.
2 Undo the screws and remove the steering column shrouds.
3 Refer to Section 4 and remove all of the switches from the instrument panel surround.
4 Remove the radio/cassette player and SID module as described in Sections 16 and 10.
5 Undo the screws and remove the surround - there are 9 screws in all **(see illustrations)**.
6 Disconnect the wiring from the small display panel at the top of the surround **(see illustration)**.

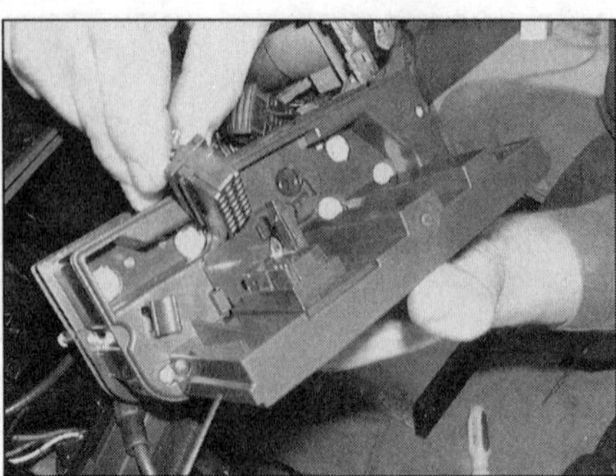
10.3 Disconnecting the wiring from the SID unit

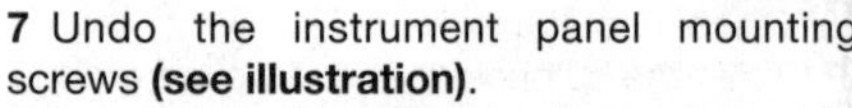

7 Undo the instrument panel mounting screws **(see illustration)**.
8 Withdraw the instrument panel sufficient to disconnect the wiring **(see illustrations)**.

Refitting

9 Refitting is a reversal of removal.

10 Clock/SID module - removal and refitting

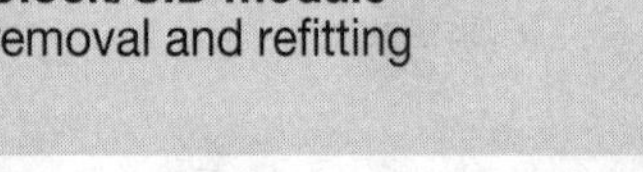

Removal

1 The Saab Information Display (SID) module and clock is located in the centre of the facia above the radio. First disconnect the battery negative (earth) lead (see Chapter 5A).
2 Insert two M4 screws in the two removal holes on the face of the module, then ease the module from the facia **(see illustration)**.
3 Disconnect the wiring and remove the module **(see illustration)**.

Refitting

4 Refitting is a reversal of removal.

11 Cigarette lighter - removal and refitting

Removal

1 Remove the centre console as described in Chapter 11.

11.3 Disconnecting the wiring from the cigarette lighter

2 Undo the screws and remove the front trim panel from the side of the centre console.
3 Disconnect the wiring from the rear of the cigarette lighter **(see illustration)**.
4 Remove the illumination ring, then remove the cigarette lighter from the centre console.

Refitting

5 Refitting is a reversal of removal.

12 Horn - removal and refitting

Removal

1 Remove the radiator grille as described in Chapter 11, Section 8.
2 Disconnect the wiring from the horn **(see illustration)**.

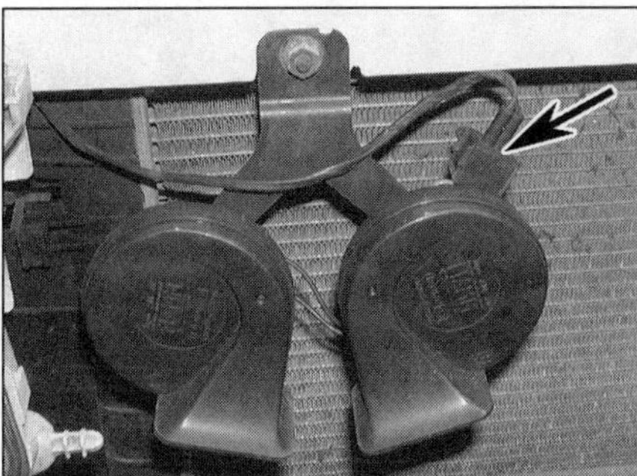

12.2 Horn and wiring connector

3 Unscrew the bracket mounting bolt and lift the horn assembly from the front cross-member.

Refitting

4 Refitting is a reversal of removal.

13 Windscreen, tailgate and headlight wiper arms - removal and refitting

Windscreen wiper arm

Removal

1 Make sure that the windscreen wipers are at their rest positions. Use a piece of tape to mark the position on the windscreen.
2 Using a screwdriver, prise up the cover from the windscreen wiper arm **(see illustrations)**.
3 Unscrew the nut securing the wiper arm to the shaft **(see illustration)**.
4 Ease the arm from the shaft by carefully rocking it side to side **(see illustration)**.

Refitting

5 Refitting is a reversal of removal.

Tailgate wiper arm

Removal

6 Make sure that the windscreen wipers are at their rest positions. Use a piece of tape to mark the position on the windscreen.
7 Lift up the cover at the base of the tailgate wiper arm.
8 Unscrew the nut securing the wiper arm to the shaft **(see illustration)**.
9 Ease the arm from the shaft by carefully rocking it side to side **(see illustration)**.

Refitting

10 Refitting is a reversal of removal.

Headlight wiper arm

Removal

11 Note the rest position of the headlight wiper arms. Use a piece of tape to mark the position on the headlight.
12 Using a screwdriver, prise up the cover from the arm.
13 Unscrew the nut securing the wiper arm to the shaft **(see illustration)**.
14 Ease the arm from the shaft by rocking it side to side, then disconnect the washer tubing. Remove the arm **(see illustrations)**.

13.2a Insert a screwdriver . . .

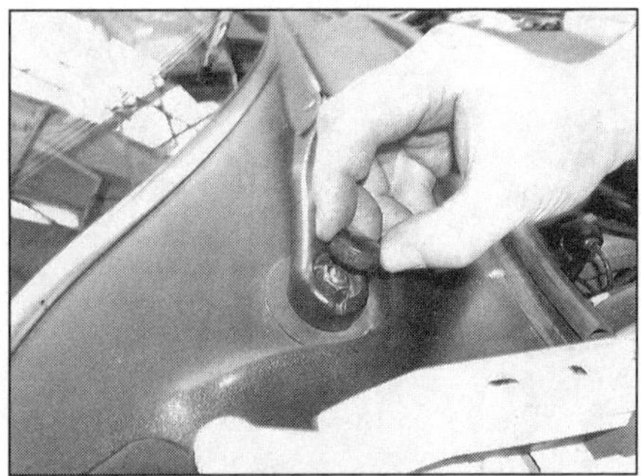

13.2b . . . and lift the cover from the windscreen wiper arm

13.3 Unscrew the nut . . .

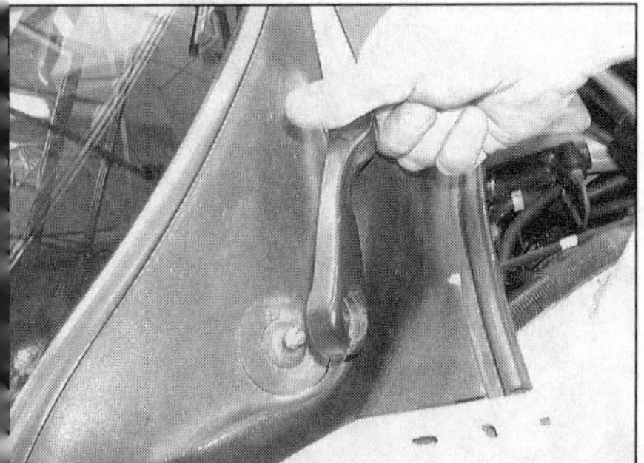

13.4 . . . and ease the wiper arm from the shaft

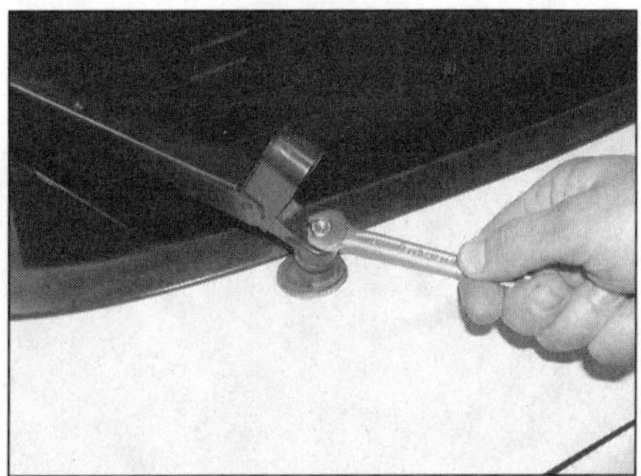

13.8 Unscrew the nut . . .

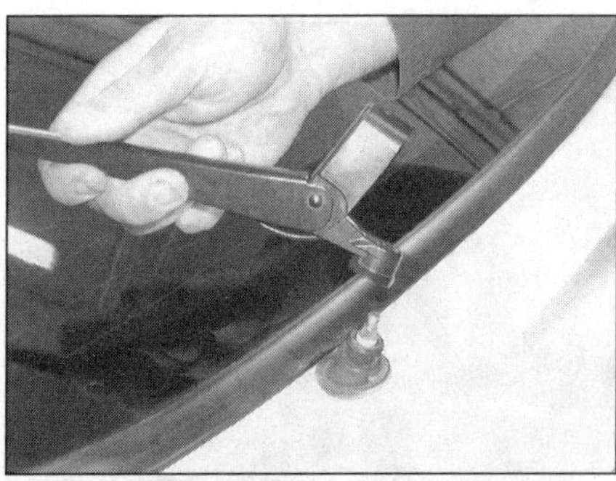

13.9 . . . and ease the wiper arm from the shaft

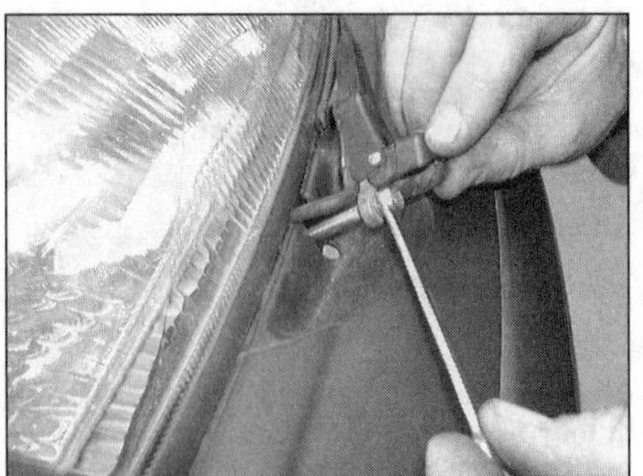
13.13 Unscrew the nut . . .

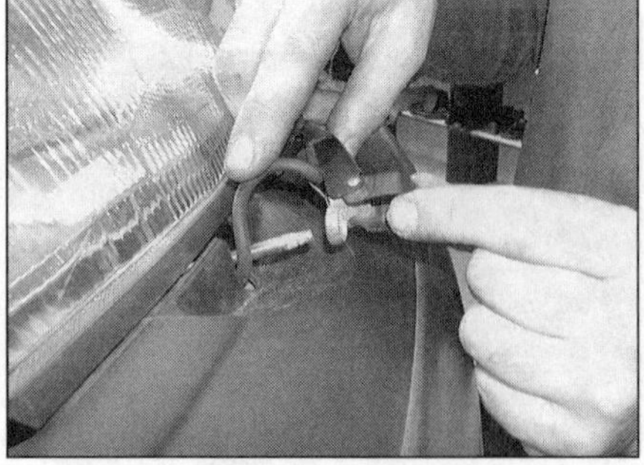
13.14a . . . then ease the arm from the shaft . . .

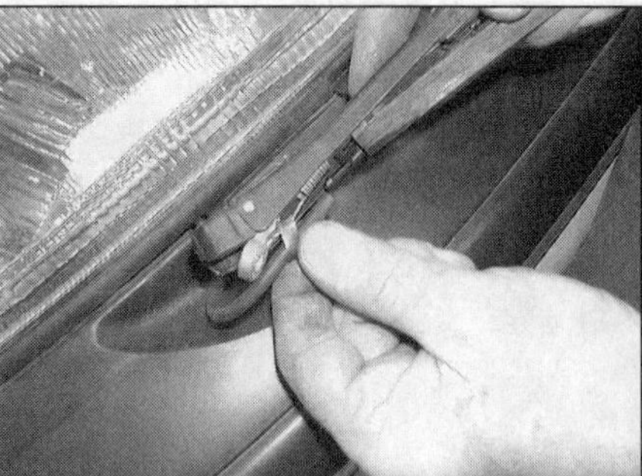
13.14b . . . and disconnect the washer tubing

Refitting

15 Refitting is a reversal of removal.

14 Windscreen, tailgate and headlight wiper motor and linkage - removal and refitting

Windscreen wiper motor and linkage

Removal

1 Make sure that the windscreen wipers are at their rest positions. Use a piece of tape to mark the position on the windscreen.

2 Using a screwdriver, prise the cover from the windscreen wiper arm.

3 Unscrew the nut securing the wiper arm to the shaft.

4 Ease the arm from the shaft by carefully rocking it side to side.

5 Pull the weatherstrip from the bulkhead **(see illustration)**.

6 Lift up the bulkhead cover and disconnect the washer tube from the adapter **(see illustration)**.

7 Disconnect the wiring from the wiper motor **(see illustration)**.

8 Unscrew the mounting bolts and lift the wiper motor and linkage from the bulkhead **(see illustration)**.

Refitting

9 Refitting is a reversal of removal.

Tailgate wiper motor assembly

Removal

10 With the tailgate open, remove the rear parcel shelf.

11 Using a Torx key, undo the screws and remove the grab handle from the tailgate.

12 Using a screwdriver, undo the screws and remove the main trim panel from the inside of the tailgate

13 Remove the wiper arm (see Section 13).

14 Disconnect the wiring from the wiper motor **(see illustration)**.

15 Unscrew the mounting bolts and lower the wiper motor from the tailgate, while guiding the shaft through the rubber grommet **(see illustrations)**.

16 If necessary, remove the grommet.

Refitting

17 Refitting is a reversal of removal.

Headlight wiper motor assembly

Removal

18 Remove the headlight unit as described in Section 6.

19 Remove the wiper arm as described in Section 13.

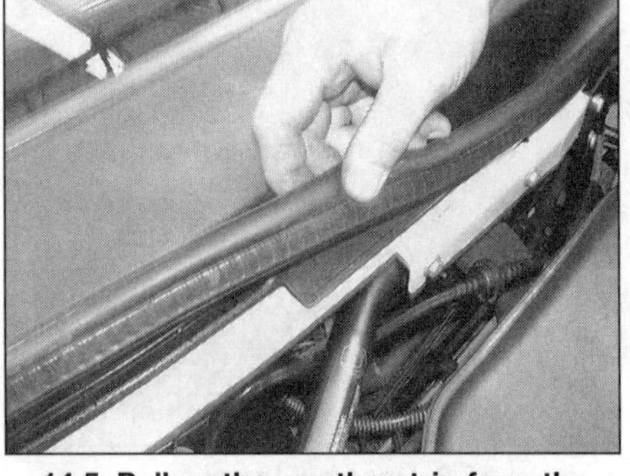
14.5 Pull up the weatherstrip from the bulkhead . . .

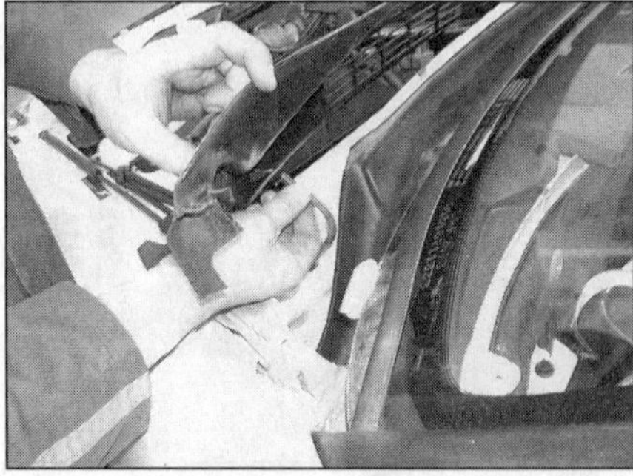
14.6 . . . then lift the cover and disconnect the washer tube . . .

14.7 . . . disconnect the wiring . . .

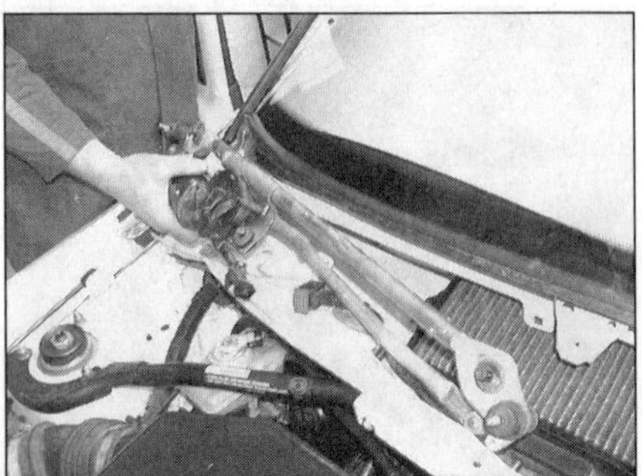
14.8 . . . and unbolt the wiper motor and linkage

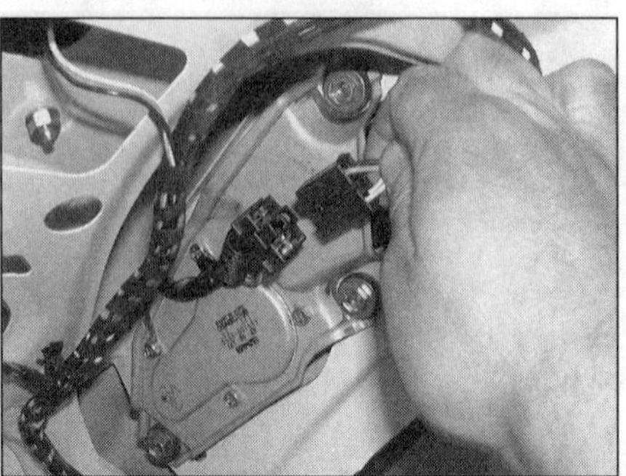
14.14 Disconnect the wiring from the tailgate wiper motor . . .

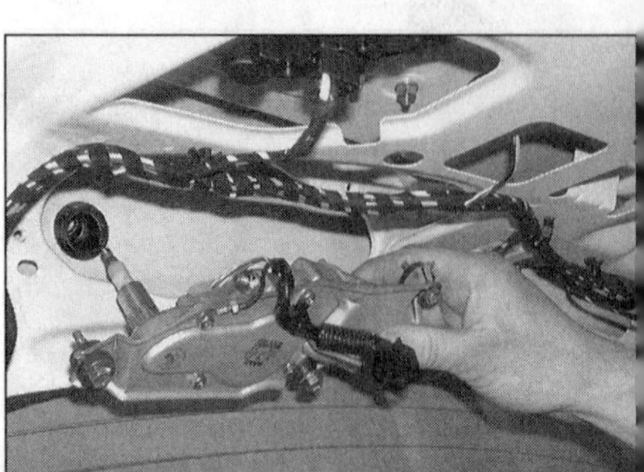
14.15a . . . then unscrew the bolts and lower the wiper motor from the tailgate

14.15b Wiper motor assembly removed from the tailgate

14.20 Headlight wiper motor assembly with the headlight removed

20 Disconnect the wiring from the motor **(see illustration)**.

21 Unscrew the mounting nuts and withdraw the wiper motor assembly from the front valance.

Refitting

22 Refitting is a reversal of removal.

15 Windscreen, tailgate and headlight washer system - removal and refitting

Removal

1 The washer fluid reservoir and pump are located beneath the front left-hand wing. For access to them, remove the wheel arch liner and the front bumper.

2 To remove the pump, position a container beneath the reservoir, then disconnect the pump wiring and washer tubes and allow the fluid to drain. Pull the pump out of the reservoir then remove the bush.

3 To remove the reservoir, first remove the pump. Unscrew the nut and disconnect the upper filler neck from the reservoir, then unscrew the mounting bolts and remove the reservoir.

Refitting

4 Refitting is a reversal of removal.

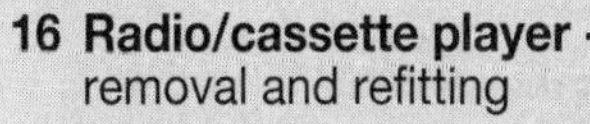

16 Radio/cassette player - removal and refitting

Note: *On models with a security-coded radio/cassette player, once the battery has been disconnected, the unit cannot be re-activated until the appropriate security code has been entered. Do not remove the unit unless the appropriate code is known.*

Removal

1 The standard radio is retained by DIN fixings, and two DIN removal tools will be required to release the retaining clips. The tools are available from car accessory shops, and are inserted into the holes on each side of the radio until they are felt to engage with the retaining strips. Non-standard radios may be retained by other means, but the method of removal is similar. On the project car, two lengths of plastic cable tie were inserted through holes at the top of the radio in order to release the retaining clips **(see illustration)**.

2 With the clips released, carefully withdraw the radio from the facia.

3 Disconnect the wiring and aerial cable from the rear of the radio **(see illustrations)**.

4 If necessary, the radio mounting box can be removed from the facia by bending up the retaining tabs **(see illustration)**.

Refitting

5 Refitting is a reversal of removal.

17 Loudspeakers - removal and refitting

Facia-mounted speaker

Removal

1 Using a screwdriver carefully prise out the grille from the relevant speaker.

2 Using a Torx key, undo the screws securing the speaker in the facia, and carefully lift it out **(see illustration)**.

3 Disconnect the wiring and tape it to the facia to prevent it dropping down inside.

Refitting

4 Refitting is a reversal of removal.

Front door mounted speaker

Removal

5 Remove the door inner trim panel as described in Chapter 11.

6 Undo the mounting screws, then withdraw the speaker and disconnect the wiring.

16.1 On this type of radio, insert two lengths of plastic cable tie to release it

16.3a Disconnecting the wiring . . .

16.3b . . . and aerial cable

16.4 Removing the radio mounting box

17.2 Facia-mounted speaker

Refitting

7 Refitting is a reversal of removal.

Rear speaker

Removal

8 With the tailgate open, remove the parcel shelf.
9 Using a screwdriver carefully prise out the speaker grille.
10 Undo the screws and remove the speaker frame.
11 Undo the screws and lift out the speaker, then disconnect the wiring.

Refitting

12 Refitting is a reversal of removal.

18 Aerial - removal and refitting

Removal

1 With the tailgate open, unclip the left-hand side luggage compartment interior trim and bend it to one side. Note that it will also be necessary to unscrew the rear speaker grille support screws.
2 To remove the fixed aerial, disconnect the aerial cable then unscrew the bottom mounting bolt. At the top of the aerial, unscrew the collar and remove the adapter, then withdraw the aerial downwards from inside the luggage compartment.
3 To remove the electric aerial, unscrew the bottom mounting nut and also the two bracket screws. At the top of the aerial, unscrew the collar and remove the adapter, then lower the aerial and bracket into the luggage compartment and disconnect the cable. If necessary, the motor can be removed from the bracket.

Refitting

4 Refitting is a reversal of removal.

19 Heated front seat components - general information

Certain models are fitted with thermostatically-regulated heated front seats. Individual control switches are provided for each seat, which allow the heating element temperature to be set to one of three levels, or switched off completely.

Two heating elements are fitted to each seat - one in the backrest, and one in the seat cushion. Access to the heating elements can only be gained by removing the upholstery from the seat - this is an operation which should be entrusted to a Saab dealer.

20 Integrated Central Electronics Control module - removal and refitting

Removal

1 Disconnect the battery negative (earth) lead (see Chapter 5A).
2 With the front driver's door open, unclip the cover from the fusebox on the end of the facia.
3 Remove the lower facia trim panel with reference to Chapter 11.
4 On left-hand drive models, remove the air duct for access to the relay holder.
5 Undo the relay holder mounting screws, and move the holder to one side.
6 Disconnect the wiring plug, then undo the screws and remove the module.

Refitting

7 Refitting is a reversal of removal.

21 Anti-theft alarm system components - removal and refitting

Electronic control module

Removal

1 Disconnect the battery negative (earth) lead (see Chapter 5A).
2 Raise the front left-hand seat to its highest position.
3 Carefully prise out the kick plate from the bottom of the front door opening.
4 Lift up the carpet just in front of the B-pillar for access to the electronic control module.
5 On 3-door models, unscrew and remove the seat belt anchor bolt from the floor.
6 Unscrew the plastic nuts and lift the module from the floor.
7 Disconnect the wiring and remove the module from inside the car.

Refitting

8 Refitting is a reversal of removal.

Glass breakage sensor

Removal

9 Remove the interior light from the front of the headlining as described in Section 5.
10 On the rear of the light unit, disconnect the wiring.

Refitting

11 Refitting is a reversal of removal.

Warning LED on top of the facia

Removal

12 Slide the LED panel to the rear and lift it up from the facia.
13 Disconnect the wiring and remove the LED.

Refitting

14 Refitting is a reversal of removal.

Bonnet switch

Removal

15 With the bonnet open, slide the bonnet switch up from its location on the fusebox in the left-hand rear of the engine compartment.
16 Disconnect the wiring.

Refitting

17 Refitting is a reversal of removal.

Horn

Removal

18 Disconnect the battery negative (earth) lead (see Chapter 5A).
19 Working beneath the front left-hand wheel arch, remove the rear section of the wheel arch liner.
20 Unscrew the mounting nut, then disconnect the wiring.

Refitting

21 Refitting is a reversal of removal.

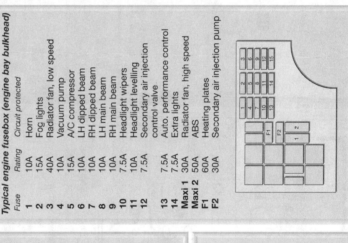

Key to symbols

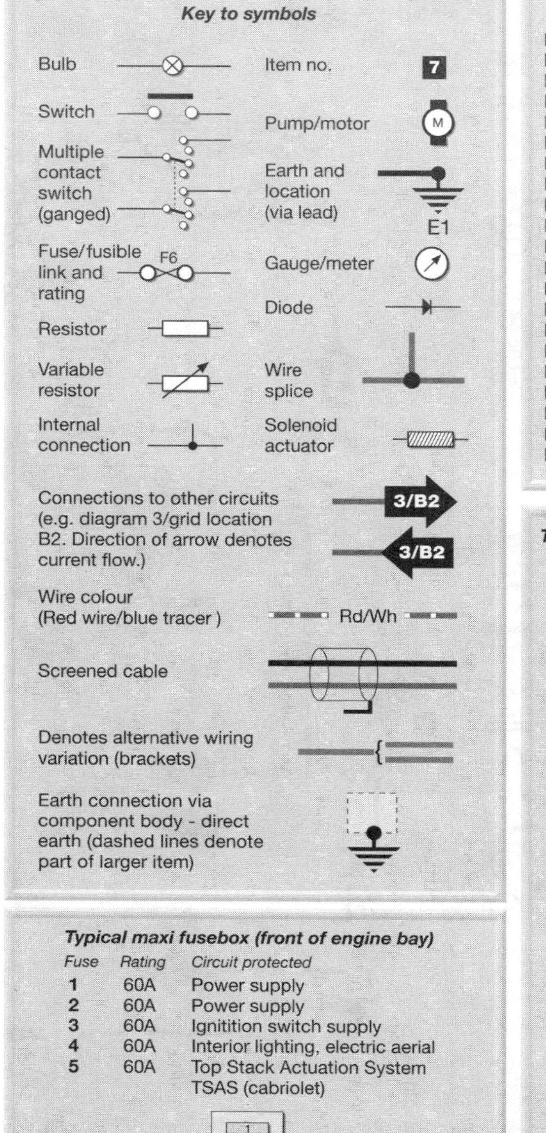

Typical maxi fusebox (front of engine bay)

Fuse	Rating	Circuit protected
1	60A	Power supply
2	60A	Power supply
3	60A	Ignitition switch supply
4	60A	Interior lighting, electric aerial
5	60A	Top Stack Actuation System TSAS (cabriolet)

Earth locations

E1	Behind battery on structural member
E2	In luggage compartment next to rear light
E3	Centre console between front seats
E4	On bracket on engine
E5	On bracket on engine
E6	On bracket on engine
E7	LH front seat member
E8	RH front seat member
E9	On gearbox
E10	Electric aerial bracket
E11	LH structural member behind battery
E12	RH front structural member in engine bay
E13	Base of LH 'A' pillar
E14	Base of LH 'A' pillar
E15	Base of RH 'A' pillar
E16	Base of RH 'A' pillar
E17	Below dash panel LH 'A' pillar
E18	On LH secondary 'B' pillar
E19	Base of RH 'A' pillar
E20	Base of RH 'A' pillar
E21	Base of RH 'A' pillar

Typical engine fusebox (engine bay bulkhead)

Fuse	Rating	Circuit protected
1	10A	Horn
2	15A	Fog lights
3	40A	Radiator fan, low speed
4	10A	Vacuum pump
5	15A	A/C compressor
6	10A	LH dipped beam
7	10A	RH dipped beam
8	10A	LH main beam
9	10A	RH main beam
10	7.5A	Headlight wipers
11	10A	Headlight levelling
12	7.5A	Secondary air injection control valve
13	7.5A	Auto. performance control
14	7.5A	Extra lights
Maxi 1	30A	Radiator fan, high speed
Maxi 2	50A	ABS
F1	60A	Heating plates
F2	30A	Secondary air injection pump

Typical passenger compartment fusebox

Fuse	Rating	Circuit protected
1	30A	Heated rear window
2	15A	Direction indicators
3	30A	Heater blower
4	7.5A	Interior lighting, electric aerial
5	30A	RH power seat
6	30A	Cigar lighter
7	30A	Rear electric windows
	7.5A	Rear electric windows (cabriolet)
8	15A	Rear window wiper
9	15A	Transmission control module
10	30A	Sensonic
11	7.5A	Radio
12	15A	Brake lights
13	15A	Radio, data link connector
14	30A	Front electric windows
15	20A	Daytime driving lights
16	30A	LH power seat
16B	30A	Fuel injection relay
17	15A	Instruments, alarm, trionic, motronic, transmission control, sensonic
18	10A	Airbag
19	15A	ABS, A/C relay, secondary air injection pump relay
20	20A	Heated seats, central locking
21	10A	A/C, automatic climate control, integrated central electronics
22	15A	Cruise control
23	20A	Alarm, mobile phone
24	-	-
25	15A	Central locking system (boot lid) Amplifier
26	7.5A	Electrically heated rear seat
27	15A	Main/dip beam, automatic climate control
28	30A	Traction control, motronic, trionic
29	10A	RH parking lights, rheostat, number plate illumination
30	10A	LH parking lights
31	20A	Windscreen wipers, reversing lights, headlight levelling
32	15A	Fuel pump
33	15A	Direction indicators, heated rear seat
34	10A	Instruments, transmission module
35	10A	Integrated central electronics
36	10A	Starter motor relay
37	10A	Rear foglights
38	25A	Oxygen sensors
39	-	-

Standard terminal identification (typical)

15	Ignition switch 'ignition' position
30	Battery +ve
31	Earth
50	Ignition switch 'start' position
85	Relay winding input
86	Relay winding earth
87	Relay output
87a	Relay output

H31161

Diagram 1 : Information for wiring diagrams - typical

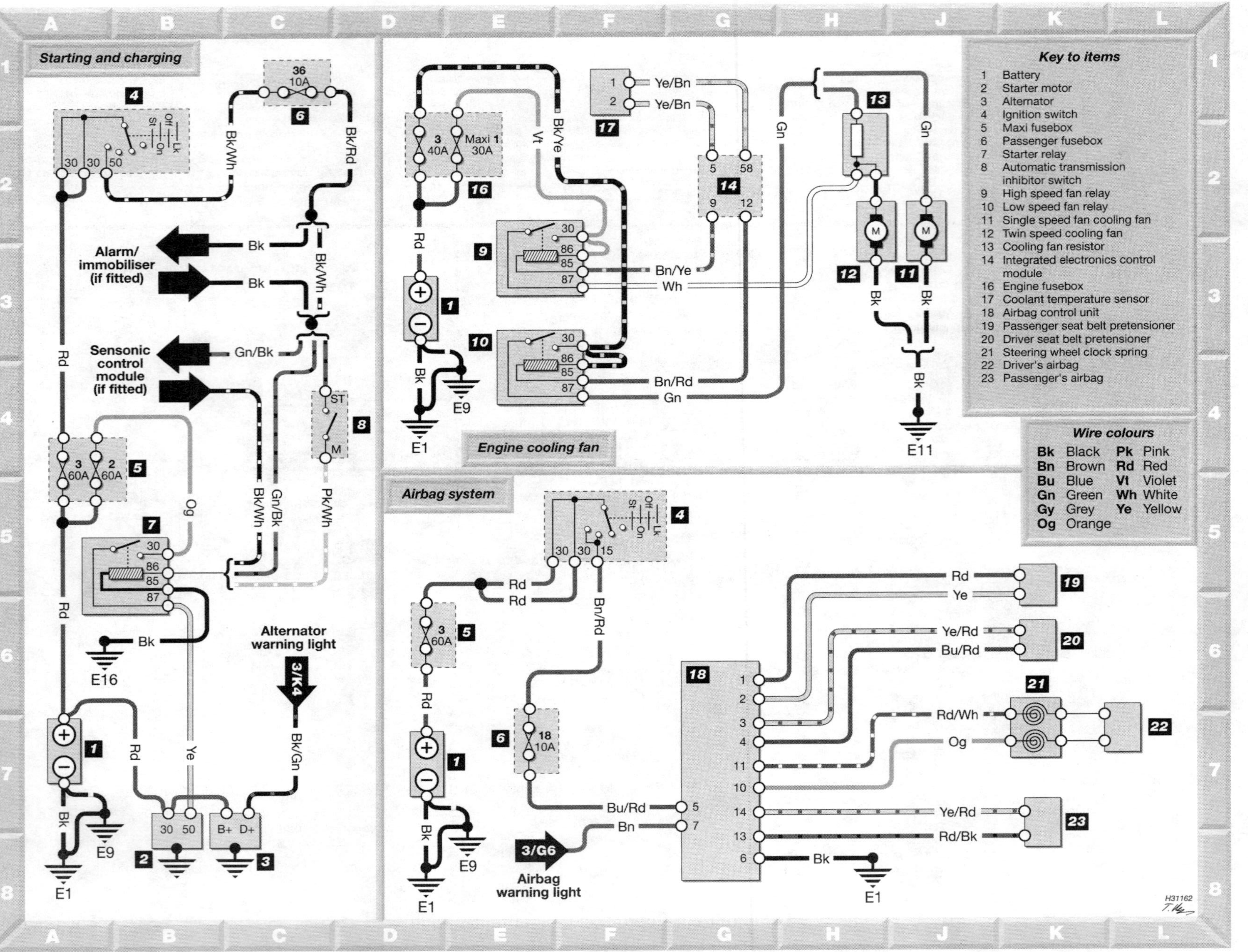

Diagram 2 : Typical starting, charging, engine cooling fan and airbag system

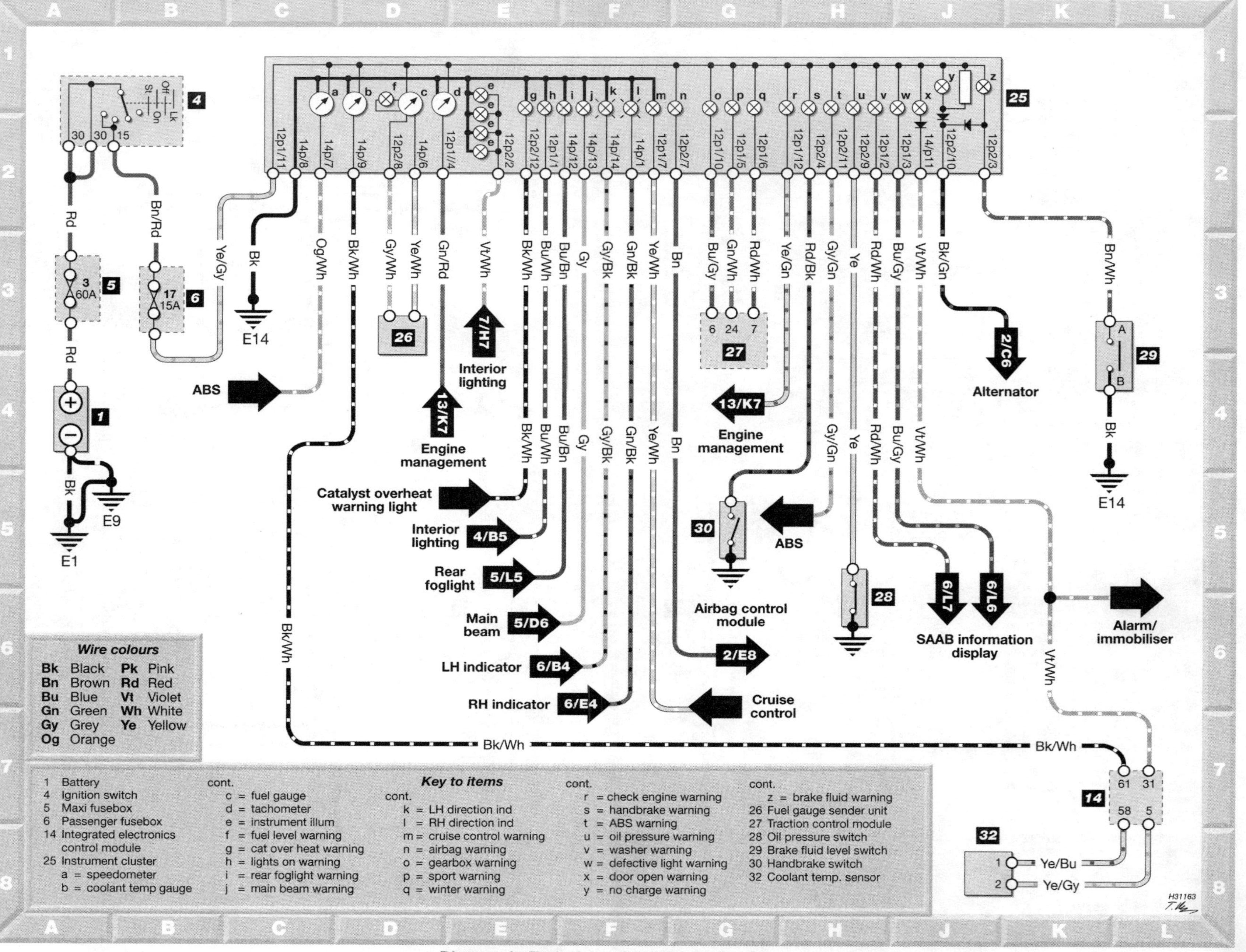
Alternator
Alarm/ immobiliser
SAAB information display
Engine management
Airbag control module
Cruise control
ABS
Interior lighting
Catalyst overheat warning light
Rear foglight
Main beam
LH indicator
RH indicator
H31163

Wire colours
Bk Black
Bn Brown
Bu Blue
Gn Green
Gy Grey
Og Orange
Pk Pink
Rd Red
Vt Violet
Wh White
Ye Yellow

Key to items
1 Battery
4 Ignition switch
5 Maxi fusebox
6 Passenger fusebox
14 Integrated electronics control module
25 Instrument cluster
a = speedometer
b = coolant temp gauge
c = fuel gauge
d = tachometer
e = instrument illum
f = fuel level warning
g = cat over heat warning
h = lights on warning
i = rear foglight warning
j = main beam warning
k = LH direction ind
l = RH direction ind
m = cruise control warning
n = airbag warning
o = gearbox warning
p = sport warning
q = winter warning
r = check engine warning
s = handbrake warning
t = ABS warning
u = oil pressure warning
v = washer warning
w = defective light warning
x = door open warning
y = no charge warning
z = brake fluid warning
26 Fuel gauge sender unit
27 Traction control module
28 Oil pressure switch
29 Brake fluid level switch
30 Handbrake switch
32 Coolant temp. sensor

Diagram 3 : Typical warning lights and gauges

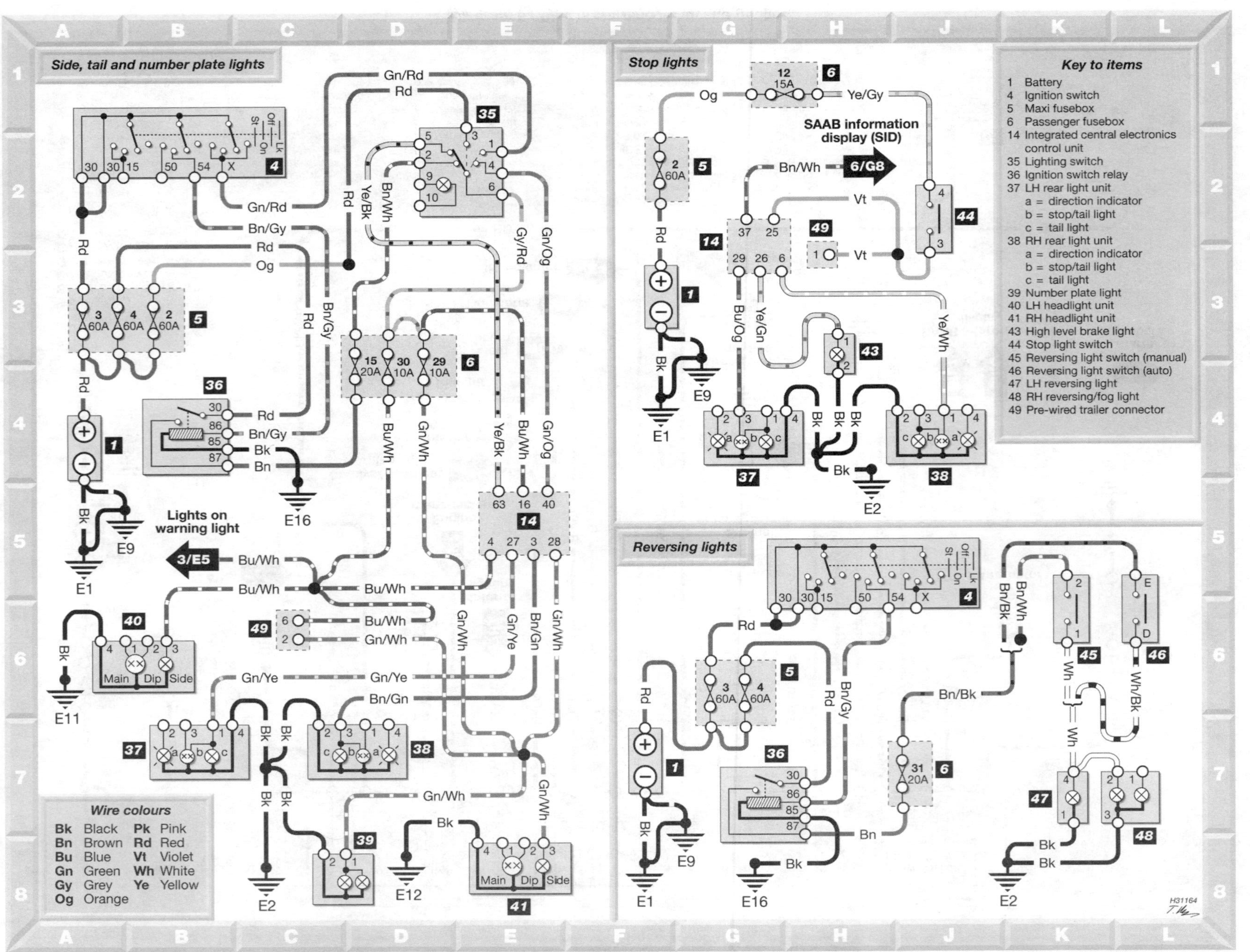

Side, tail and number plate lights
Lights on warning light
3/E5
Stop lights
SAAB information display (SID)
6/G8
Reversing lights
Key to items
1 Battery
4 Ignition switch
5 Maxi fusebox
6 Passenger fusebox
14 Integrated central electronics control unit
35 Lighting switch
36 Ignition switch relay
37 LH rear light unit
a = direction indicator
b = stop/tail light
c = tail light
38 RH rear light unit
a = direction indicator
b = stop/tail light
c = tail light
39 Number plate light
40 LH headlight unit
41 RH headlight unit
43 High level brake light
44 Stop light switch
45 Reversing light switch (manual)
46 Reversing light switch (auto)
47 LH reversing light
48 RH reversing/fog light
49 Pre-wired trailer connector
Wire colours
Bk Black
Bn Brown
Bu Blue
Gn Green
Gy Grey
Og Orange
Pk Pink
Rd Red
Vt Violet
Wh White
Ye Yellow
H31164

Diagram 4 : Typical side, tail, number plate, stop and reversing lights

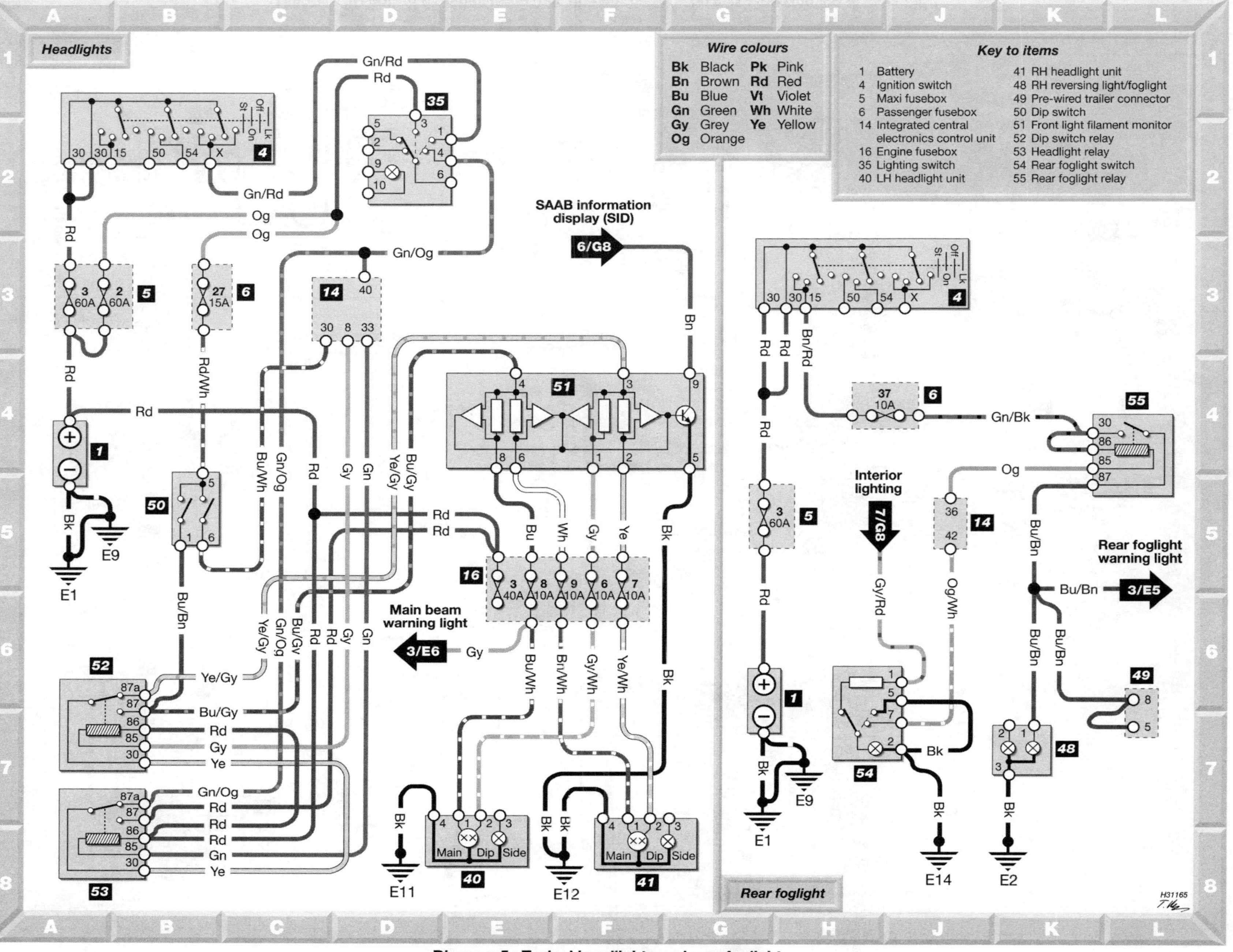
Headlights
Wire colours
Bk Black
Bn Brown
Bu Blue
Gn Green
Gy Grey
Og Orange
Pk Pink
Rd Red
Vt Violet
Wh White
Ye Yellow
Key to items
1 Battery
4 Ignition switch
5 Maxi fusebox
6 Passenger fusebox
14 Integrated central electronics control unit
16 Engine fusebox
35 Lighting switch
40 LH headlight unit
41 RH headlight unit
48 RH reversing light/foglight
49 Pre-wired trailer connector
50 Dip switch
51 Front light filament monitor
52 Dip switch relay
53 Headlight relay
54 Rear foglight switch
55 Rear foglight relay
SAAB information display (SID)
Main beam warning light
Interior lighting
Rear foglight warning light
Rear foglight
H31165

Diagram 5 : Typical headlights and rear foglight

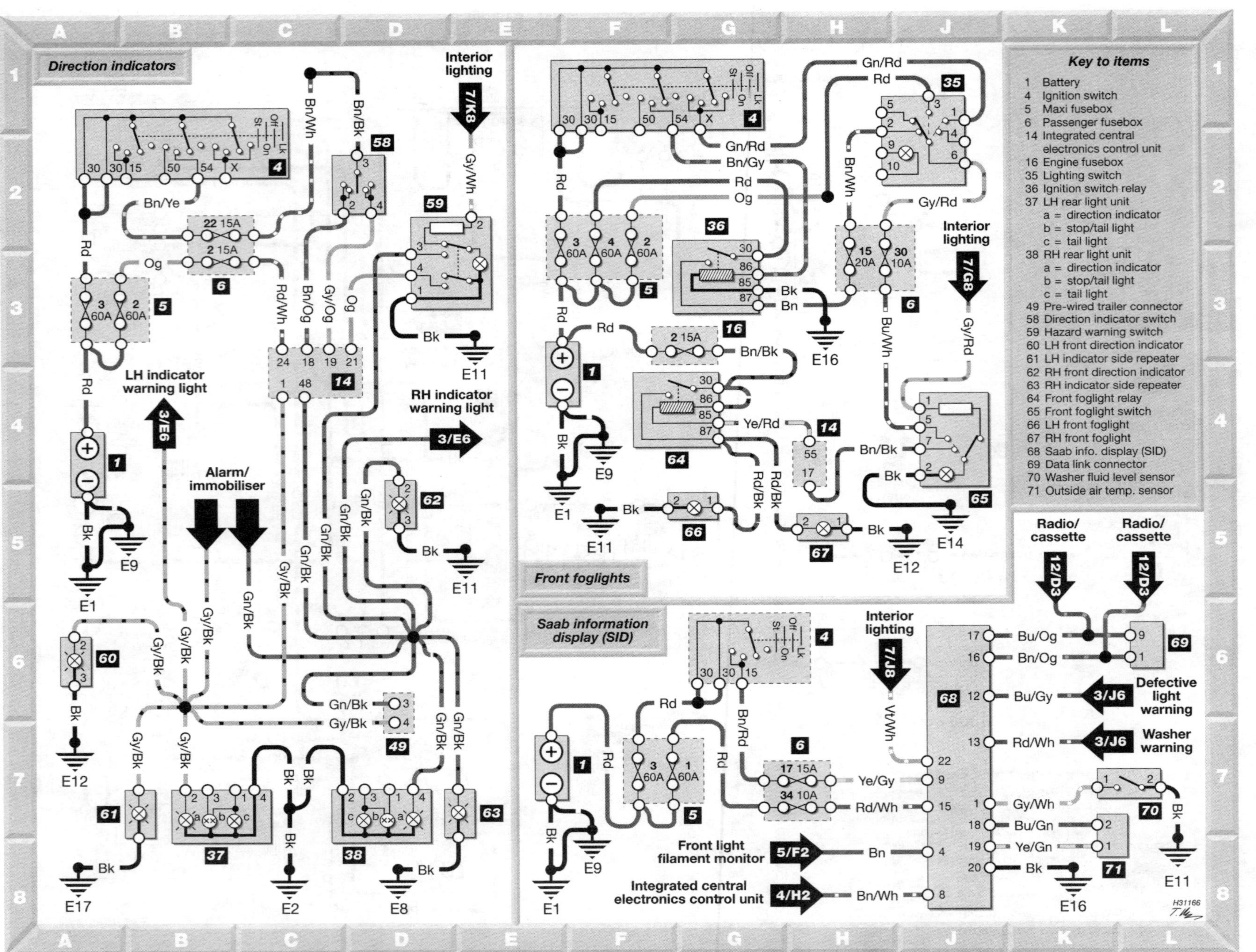

Direction indicators
Interior lighting
LH indicator warning light
RH indicator warning light
Alarm/ immobiliser
Front foglights
Saab information display (SID)
Radio/ cassette
Radio/ cassette
Defective light warning
Washer warning
Front light filament monitor
Integrated central electronics control unit
Key to items
1 Battery
4 Ignition switch
5 Maxi fusebox
6 Passenger fusebox
14 Integrated central electronics control unit
16 Engine fusebox
35 Lighting switch
36 Ignition switch relay
37 LH rear light unit
a = direction indicator
b = stop/tail light
c = tail light
38 RH rear light unit
a = direction indicator
b = stop/tail light
c = tail light
49 Pre-wired trailer connector
58 Direction indicator switch
59 Hazard warning switch
60 LH front direction indicator
61 LH indicator side repeater
62 RH front direction indicator
63 RH indicator side repeater
64 Front foglight relay
65 Front foglight switch
66 LH front foglight
67 RH front foglight
68 Saab info. display (SID)
69 Data link connector
70 Washer fluid level sensor
71 Outside air temp. sensor
H31166

Diagram 6 : Typical direction indicators, front foglights and Saab information display (SID)

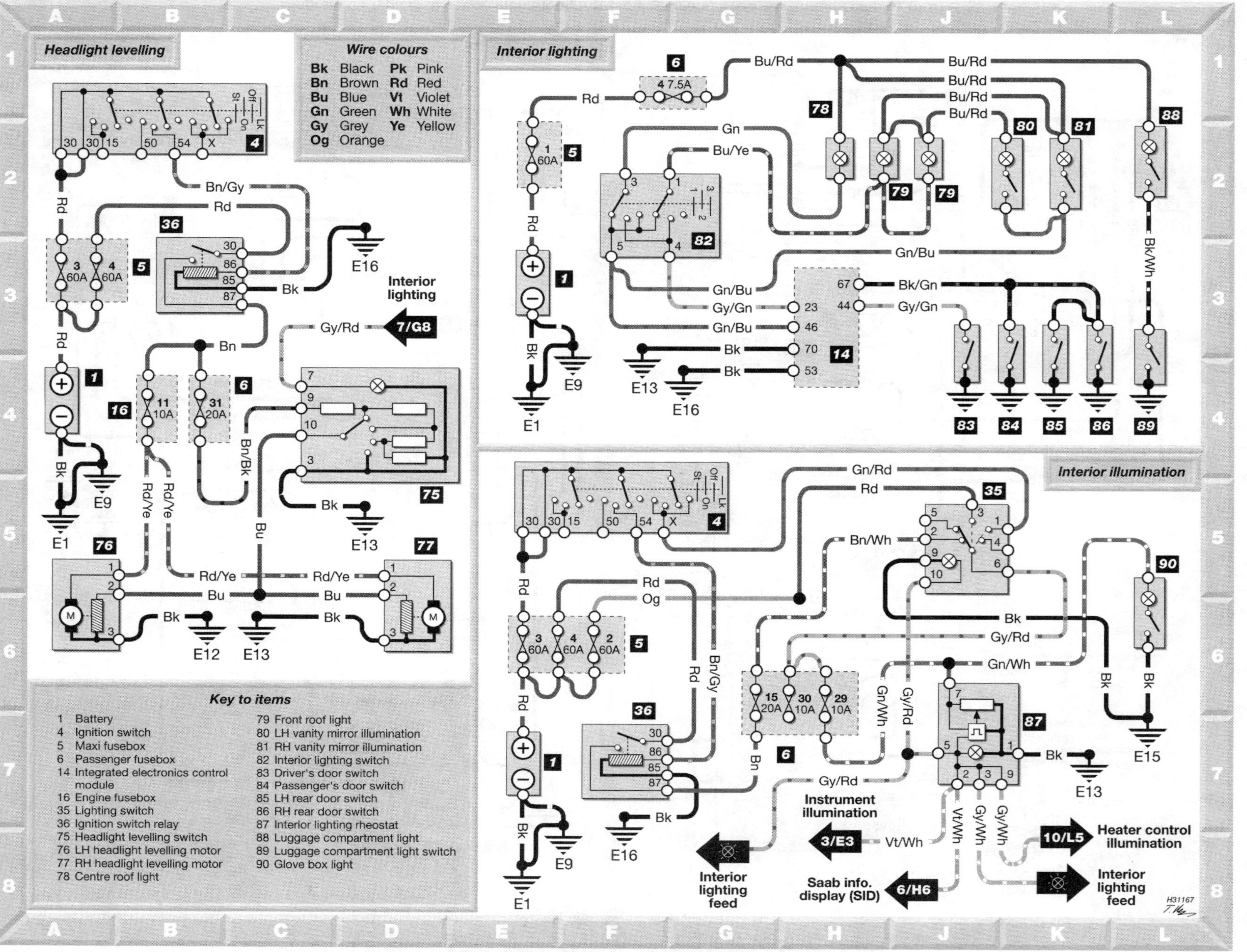
Headlight levelling
Wire colours
Bk Black
Bn Brown
Bu Blue
Gn Green
Gy Grey
Og Orange
Pk Pink
Rd Red
Vt Violet
Wh White
Ye Yellow
Interior lighting
Interior illumination
Interior lighting 7/G8
Key to items
1 Battery
4 Ignition switch
5 Maxi fusebox
6 Passenger fusebox
14 Integrated electronics control module
16 Engine fusebox
35 Lighting switch
36 Ignition switch relay
75 Headlight levelling switch
76 LH headlight levelling motor
77 RH headlight levelling motor
78 Centre roof light
79 Front roof light
80 LH vanity mirror illumination
81 RH vanity mirror illumination
82 Interior lighting switch
83 Driver's door switch
84 Passenger's door switch
85 LH rear door switch
86 RH rear door switch
87 Interior lighting rheostat
88 Luggage compartment light
89 Luggage compartment light switch
90 Glove box light
Instrument illumination 3/E3
Heater control illumination 10/L5
Interior lighting feed
Saab info. display (SID) 6/H6
Interior lighting feed
H31167

Diagram 7 : Typical headlight levelling, interior lighting and illumination

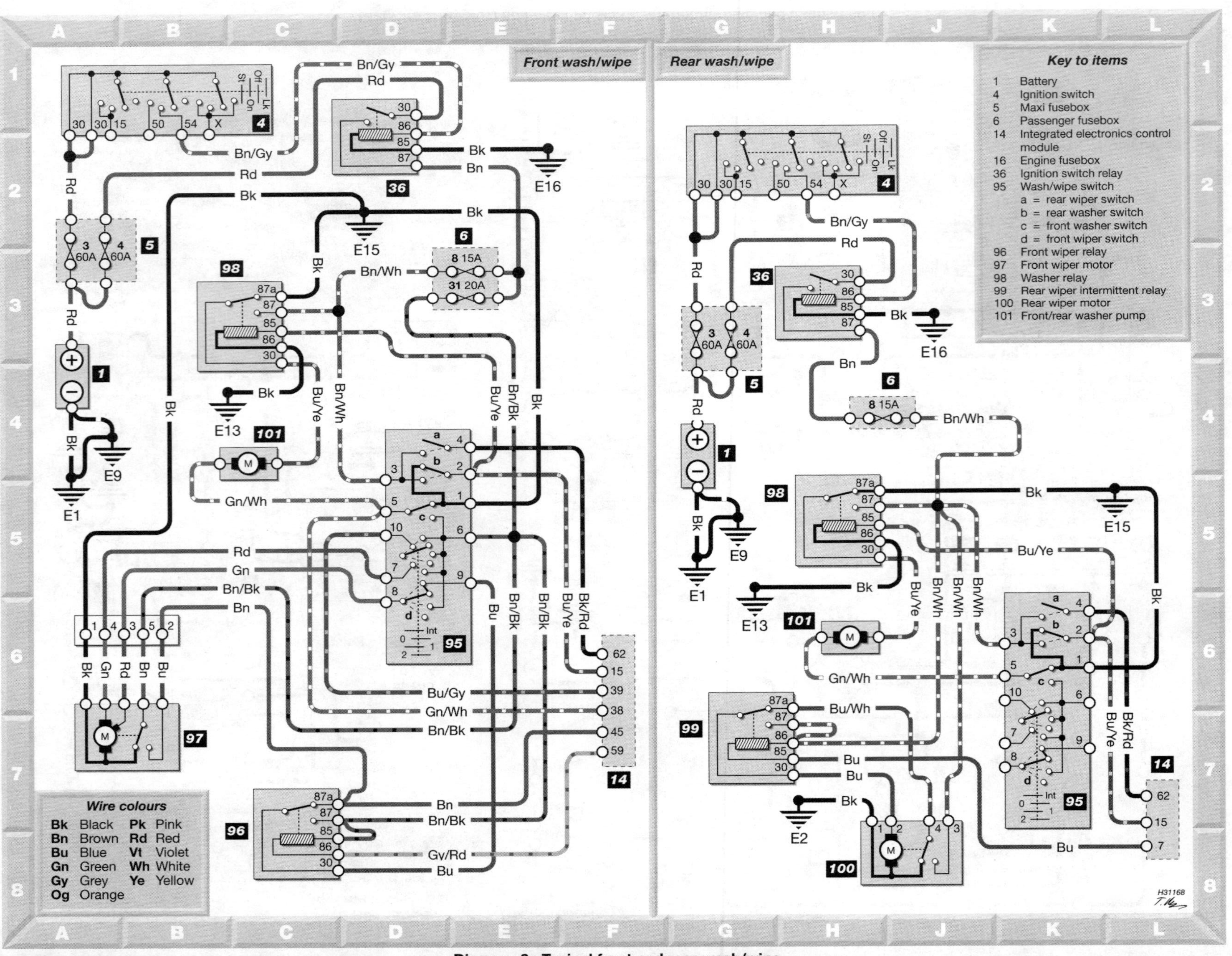

Front wash/wipe
Rear wash/wipe
Key to items
1 Battery
4 Ignition switch
5 Maxi fusebox
6 Passenger fusebox
14 Integrated electronics control module
16 Engine fusebox
36 Ignition switch relay
95 Wash/wipe switch
a = rear wiper switch
b = rear washer switch
c = front washer switch
d = front wiper switch
96 Front wiper relay
97 Front wiper motor
98 Washer relay
99 Rear wiper intermittent relay
100 Rear wiper motor
101 Front/rear washer pump
Wire colours
Bk Black
Bn Brown
Bu Blue
Gn Green
Gy Grey
Og Orange
Pk Pink
Rd Red
Vt Violet
Wh White
Ye Yellow
H31168

Diagram 8 : Typical front and rear wash/wipe

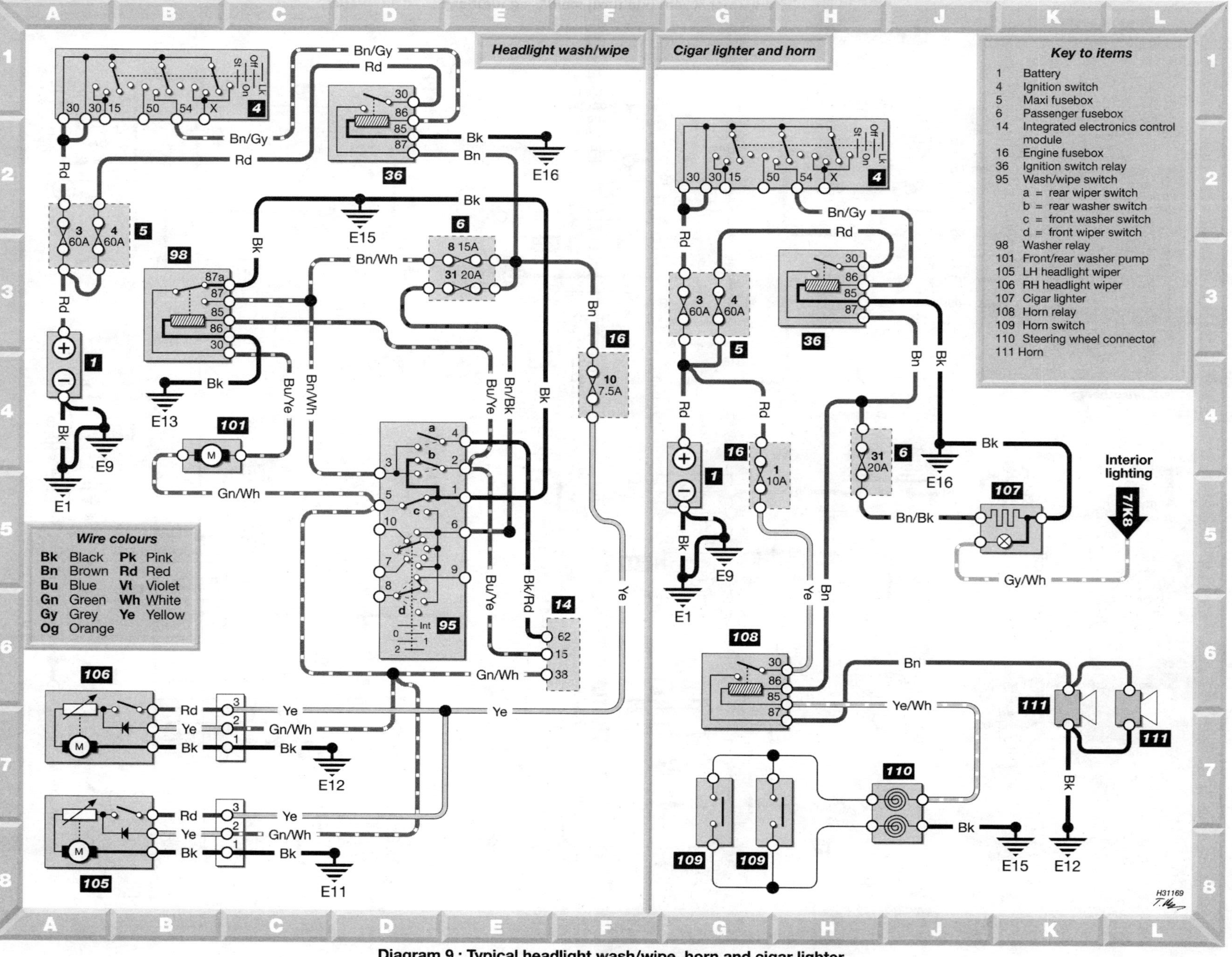

Diagram 9 : Typical headlight wash/wipe, horn and cigar lighter

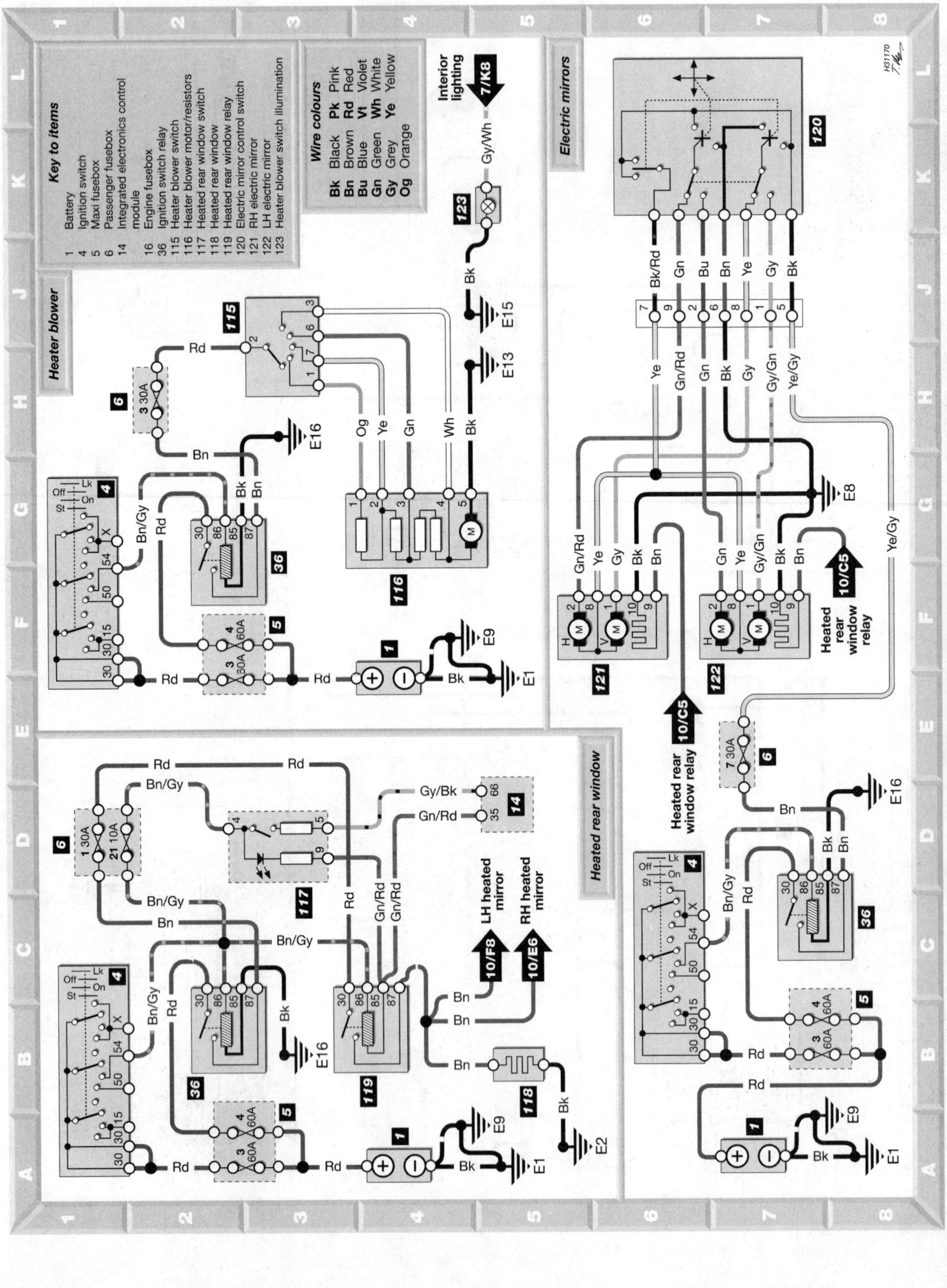

Key to items

1	Battery
4	Ignition switch
5	Maxi fusebox
6	Passenger fusebox
14	Integrated electronics control module
16	Engine fusebox
36	Ignition switch relay
115	Heater blower switch
116	Heater blower motor/resistors
117	Heated rear window switch
118	Heated rear window
119	Heated rear window relay
120	Electric mirror control switch
121	RH electric mirror
122	LH electric mirror
123	Heater blower switch illumination

Wire colours

Bk	Black	**Pk**	Pink
Bn	Brown	**Rd**	Red
Bu	Blue	**Vt**	Violet
Gn	Green	**Wh**	White
Gy	Grey	**Ye**	Yellow
Og	Orange		

Heater blower

Heated rear window

Electric mirrors

H31170

Diagram 10 : Typical heater blower, heated rear window and electric mirrors

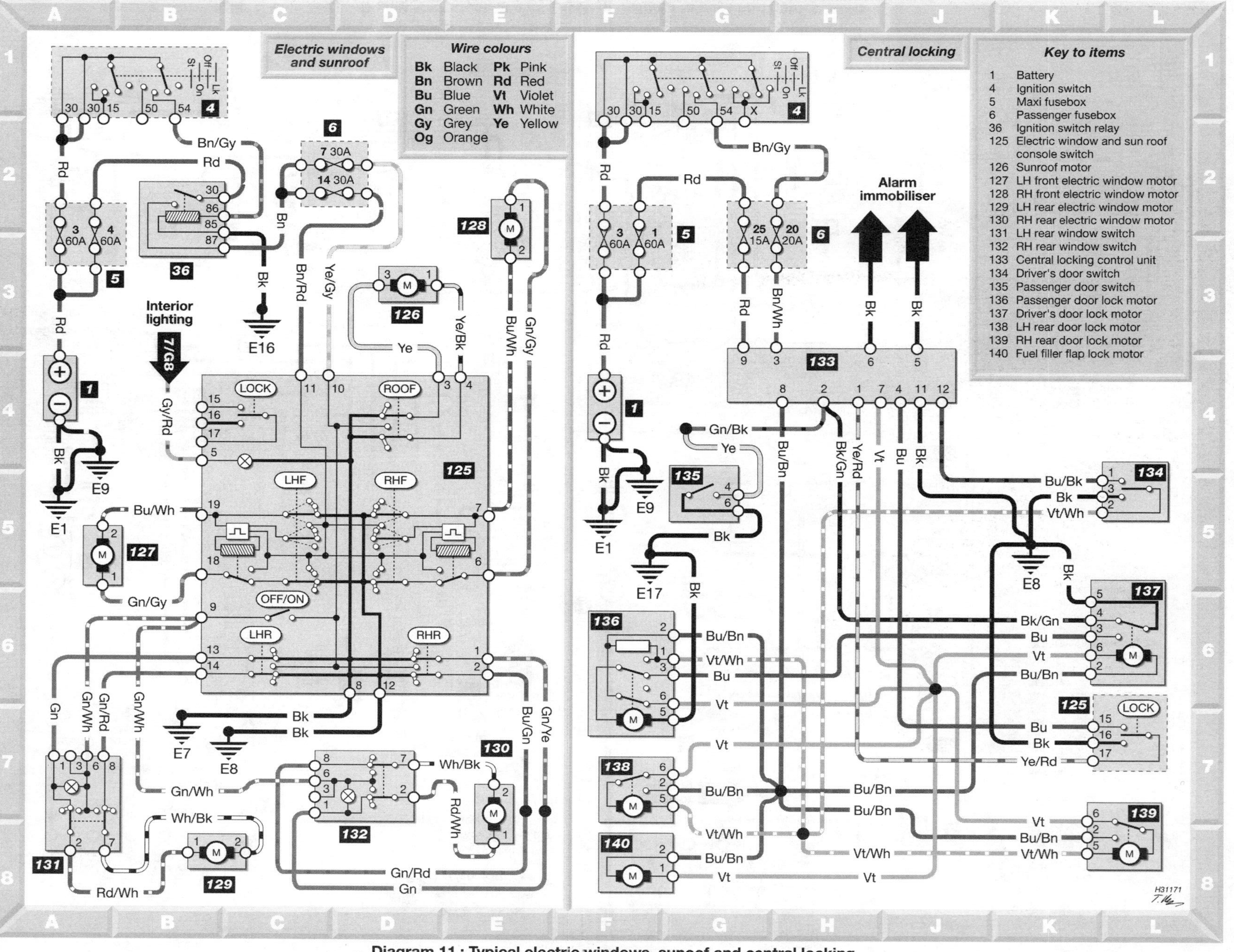

Diagram 11 : Typical electric windows, sunoof and central locking

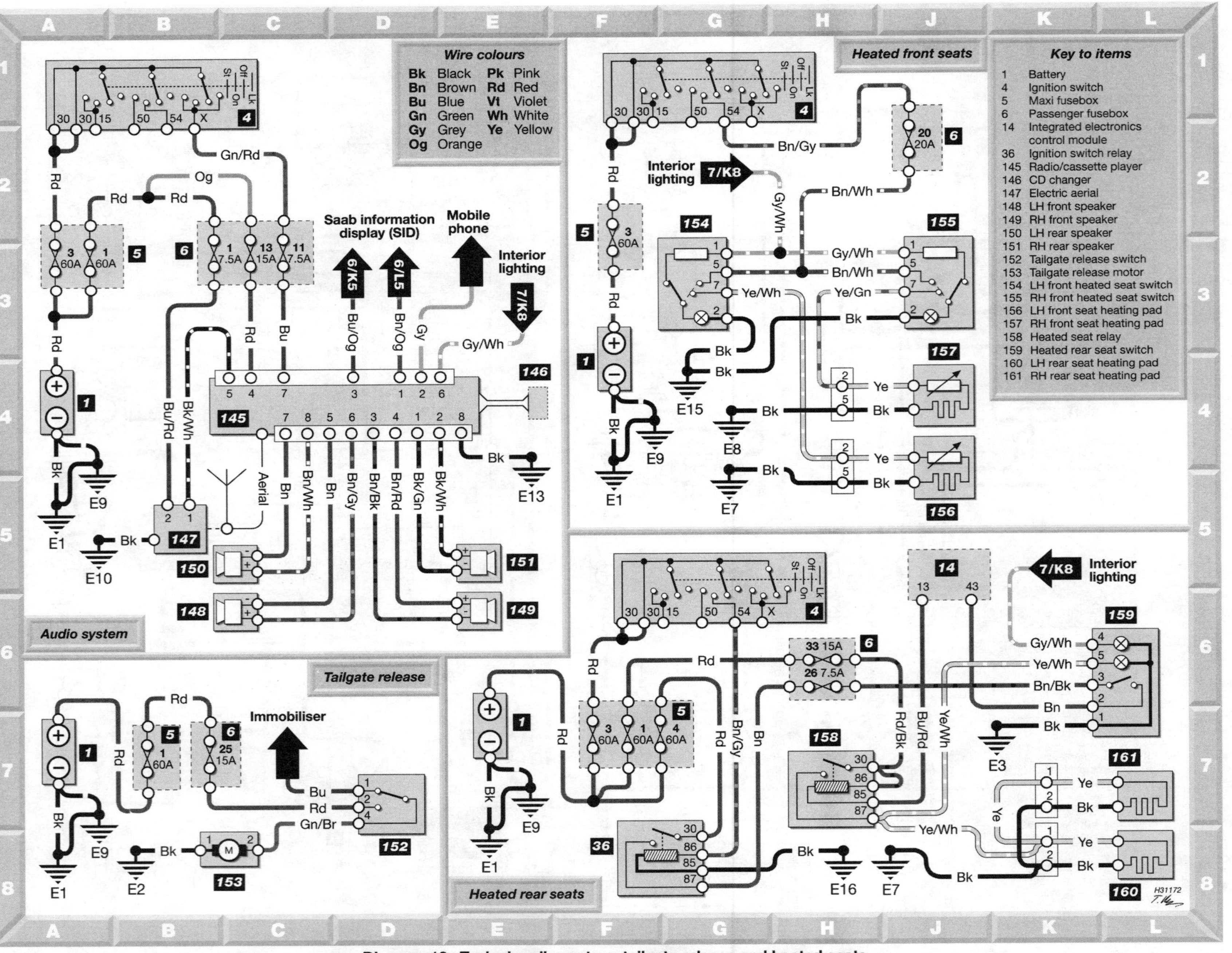

Wire colours
Bk Black
Bn Brown
Bu Blue
Gn Green
Gy Grey
Og Orange
Pk Pink
Rd Red
Vt Violet
Wh White
Ye Yellow
Key to items
1 Battery
4 Ignition switch
5 Maxi fusebox
6 Passenger fusebox
14 Integrated electronics control module
36 Ignition switch relay
145 Radio/cassette player
146 CD changer
147 Electric aerial
148 LH front speaker
149 RH front speaker
150 LH rear speaker
151 RH rear speaker
152 Tailgate release switch
153 Tailgate release motor
154 LH front heated seat switch
155 RH front heated seat switch
156 LH front seat heating pad
157 RH front seat heating pad
158 Heated seat relay
159 Heated rear seat switch
160 LH rear seat heating pad
161 RH rear seat heating pad
Audio system
Tailgate release
Heated front seats
Heated rear seats
Saab information display (SID)
Mobile phone
Interior lighting
Immobiliser
Aerial
H31172

Diagram 12 : Typical audio system, tailgate release and heated seats

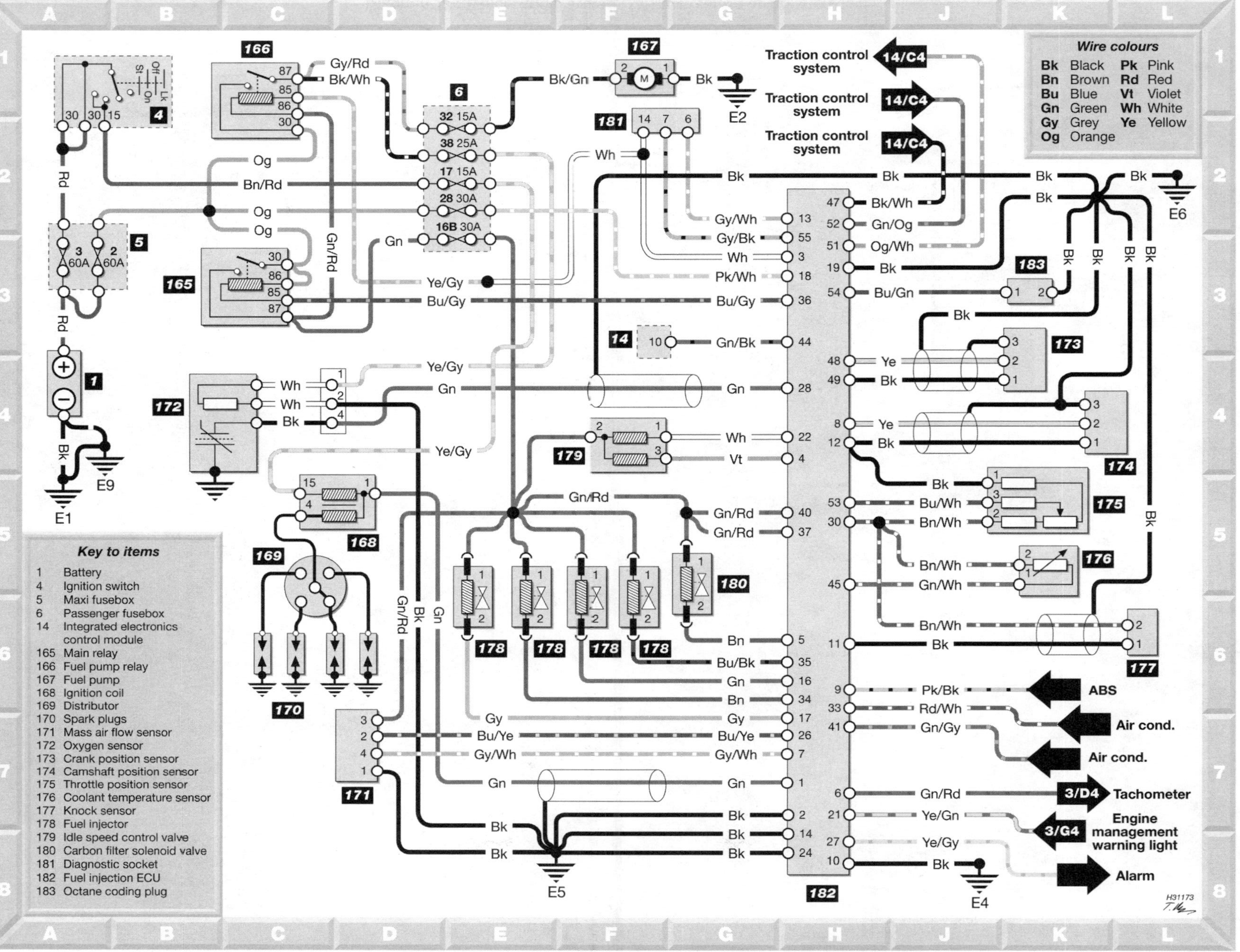

Wire colours
Bk Black
Bn Brown
Bu Blue
Gn Green
Gy Grey
Og Orange
Pk Pink
Rd Red
Vt Violet
Wh White
Ye Yellow
Key to items
1 Battery
4 Ignition switch
5 Maxi fusebox
6 Passenger fusebox
14 Integrated electronics control module
165 Main relay
166 Fuel pump relay
167 Fuel pump
168 Ignition coil
169 Distributor
170 Spark plugs
171 Mass air flow sensor
172 Oxygen sensor
173 Crank position sensor
174 Camshaft position sensor
175 Throttle position sensor
176 Coolant temperature sensor
177 Knock sensor
178 Fuel injector
179 Idle speed control valve
180 Carbon filter solenoid valve
181 Diagnostic socket
182 Fuel injection ECU
183 Octane coding plug
Traction control system
14/C4
ABS
Air cond.
Tachometer
3/D4
Engine management warning light
3/G4
Alarm
E1
E2
E4
E5
E6
E9
H31173

Diagram 13 : Typical Motronic engine management system

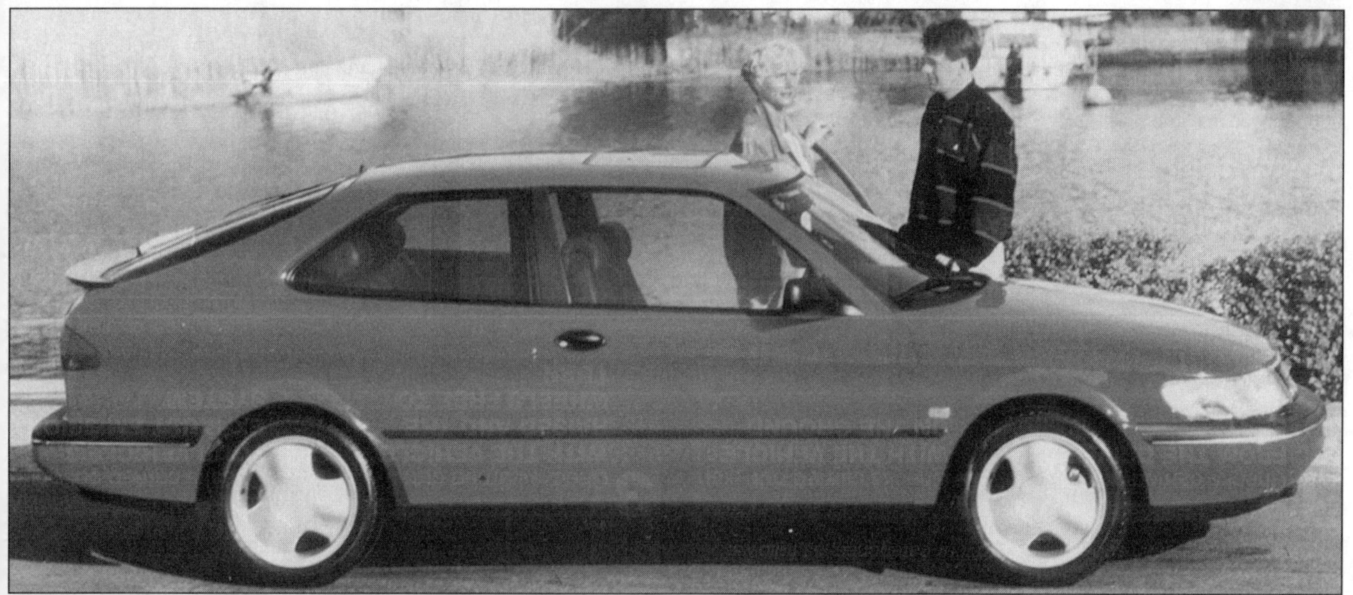

Dimensions and weights

Note: *All figures are approximate, and vary according to model. Refer to manufacturer's data for exact figures.*

Dimensions

Overall length (including bumpers)	4637 mm
Overall width (excluding wing mirrors)	1711 mm
Overall height:	
Hatchback and Coupe	1436 mm
Cabriolet*	2200 mm
**Maximum clearance required when soft top is operated.*	
Wheelbase	2600 mm
Track width:	
Front	1446 mm
Rear	1443 mm
Ground clearance (typical)	130 mm
Turning circle diameter:	
Wall to wall	11.1 m
Kerb to kerb	10.5 m
Front overhang*	1007 mm
Rear overhang*	1030 mm
**Measure from centre of roadwheel to tip of bumper*	
Boot length:	
3 and 5 door, rear seat upright	973 mm
3 and 4 door, rear seat folded	1690 mm
Cabriolet, rear seat upright	734 mm

Weights

Kerb weight	1300 - 1550 kg
Maximum axle load, front	1030 kg
Maximum axle load, rear:	
1994-1995	1880 kg
1996 on	1930 kg
Maximum roof rack load	100 kg
Maximum towing weight:	
Unbraked trailer	750 kg
Braked trailer	1600 kg

Conversion factors

Length (distance)

Inches (in)	x 25.4	= Millimetres (mm)	x 0.0394	= Inches (in)
Feet (ft)	x 0.305	= Metres (m)	x 3.281	= Feet (ft)
Miles	x 1.609	= Kilometres (km)	x 0.621	= Miles

Volume (capacity)

Cubic inches (cu in; in^3)	x 16.387	= Cubic centimetres (cc; cm^3)	x 0.061	= Cubic inches (cu in; in^3)
Imperial pints (Imp pt)	x 0.568	= Litres (l)	x 1.76	= Imperial pints (Imp pt)
Imperial quarts (Imp qt)	x 1.137	= Litres (l)	x 0.88	= Imperial quarts (Imp qt)
Imperial quarts (Imp qt)	x 1.201	= US quarts (US qt)	x 0.833	= Imperial quarts (Imp qt)
US quarts (US qt)	x 0.946	= Litres (l)	x 1.057	= US quarts (US qt)
Imperial gallons (Imp gal)	x 4.546	= Litres (l)	x 0.22	= Imperial gallons (Imp gal)
Imperial gallons (Imp gal)	x 1.201	= US gallons (US gal)	x 0.833	= Imperial gallons (Imp gal)
US gallons (US gal)	x 3.785	= Litres (l)	x 0.264	= US gallons (US gal)

Mass (weight)

Ounces (oz)	x 28.35	= Grams (g)	x 0.035	= Ounces (oz)
Pounds (lb)	x 0.454	= Kilograms (kg)	x 2.205	= Pounds (lb)

Force

Ounces-force (ozf; oz)	x 0.278	= Newtons (N)	x 3.6	= Ounces-force (ozf; oz)
Pounds-force (lbf; lb)	x 4.448	= Newtons (N)	x 0.225	= Pounds-force (lbf; lb)
Newtons (N)	x 0.1	= Kilograms-force (kgf; kg)	x 9.81	= Newtons (N)

Pressure

Pounds-force per square inch (psi; lbf/in^2; lb/in^2)	x 0.070	= Kilograms-force per square centimetre (kgf/cm^2; kg/cm^2)	x 14.223	= Pounds-force per square inch (psi; lbf/in^2; lb/in^2)
Pounds-force per square inch (psi; lbf/in^2; lb/in^2)	x 0.068	= Atmospheres (atm)	x 14.696	= Pounds-force per square inch (psi; lbf/in^2; lb/in^2)
Pounds-force per square inch (psi; lbf/in^2; lb/in^2)	x 0.069	= Bars	x 14.5	= Pounds-force per square inch (psi; lbf/in^2; lb/in^2)
Pounds-force per square inch (psi; lbf/in^2; lb/in^2)	x 6.895	= Kilopascals (kPa)	x 0.145	= Pounds-force per square inch (psi; lbf/in^2; lb/in^2)
Kilopascals (kPa)	x 0.01	= Kilograms-force per square centimetre (kgf/cm^2; kg/cm^2)	x 98.1	= Kilopascals (kPa)
Millibar (mbar)	x 100	= Pascals (Pa)	x 0.01	= Millibar (mbar)
Millibar (mbar)	x 0.0145	= Pounds-force per square inch (psi; lbf/in^2; lb/in^2)	x 68.947	= Millibar (mbar)
Millibar (mbar)	x 0.75	= Millimetres of mercury (mmHg)	x 1.333	= Millibar (mbar)
Millibar (mbar)	x 0.401	= Inches of water (inH_2O)	x 2.491	= Millibar (mbar)
Millimetres of mercury (mmHg)	x 0.535	= Inches of water (inH_2O)	x 1.868	= Millimetres of mercury (mmHg)
Inches of water (inH_2O)	x 0.036	= Pounds-force per square inch (psi; lbf/in^2; lb/in^2)	x 27.68	= Inches of water (inH_2O)

Torque (moment of force)

Pounds-force inches (lbf in; lb in)	x 1.152	= Kilograms-force centimetre (kgf cm; kg cm)	x 0.868	= Pounds-force inches (lbf in; lb in)
Pounds-force inches (lbf in; lb in)	x 0.113	= Newton metres (Nm)	x 8.85	= Pounds-force inches (lbf in; lb in)
Pounds-force inches (lbf in; lb in)	x 0.083	= Pounds-force feet (lbf ft; lb ft)	x 12	= Pounds-force inches (lbf in; lb in)
Pounds-force feet (lbf ft; lb ft)	x 0.138	= Kilograms-force metres (kgf m; kg m)	x 7.233	= Pounds-force feet (lbf ft; lb ft)
Pounds-force feet (lbf ft; lb ft)	x 1.356	= Newton metres (Nm)	x 0.738	= Pounds-force feet (lbf ft; lb ft)
Newton metres (Nm)	x 0.102	= Kilograms-force metres (kgf m; kg m)	x 9.804	= Newton metres (Nm)

Power

Horsepower (hp)	x 745.7	= Watts (W)	x 0.0013	= Horsepower (hp)

Velocity (speed)

Miles per hour (miles/hr; mph)	x 1.609	= Kilometres per hour (km/hr; kph)	x 0.621	= Miles per hour (miles/hr; mph)

Fuel consumption*

Miles per gallon, Imperial (mpg)	x 0.354	= Kilometres per litre (km/l)	x 2.825	= Miles per gallon, Imperial (mpg)
Miles per gallon, US (mpg)	x 0.425	= Kilometres per litre (km/l)	x 2.352	= Miles per gallon, US (mpg)

Temperature

Degrees Fahrenheit = (°C x 1.8) + 32

Degrees Celsius (Degrees Centigrade; °C) = (°F - 32) x 0.56

** It is common practice to convert from miles per gallon (mpg) to litres/100 kilometres (l/100km), where mpg x l/100 km = 282*

Spare parts are available from many sources, including maker's appointed garages, accessory shops, and motor factors. To be sure of obtaining the correct parts, it will sometimes be necessary to quote the vehicle identification number. If possible, it can also be useful to take the old parts along for positive identification. Items such as starter motors and alternators may be available under a service exchange scheme - any parts returned should be clean.

Our advice regarding spare parts is as follows.

Officially appointed garages

This is the best source of parts which are peculiar to your car, and which are not otherwise generally available (eg, badges, interior trim, certain body panels, etc). It is also the only place at which you should buy parts if the vehicle is still under warranty.

Accessory shops

These are very good places to buy materials and components needed for the maintenance of your car (oil, air and fuel filters, light bulbs, drivebelts, greases, brake pads, tough-up paint, etc). Components of this nature sold by a reputable shop are of the same standard as those used by the car manufacturer.

Besides components, these shops also sell tools and general accessories, usually have convenient opening hours, charge lower prices, and can often be found close to home. Some accessory shops have parts counters where components needed for almost any repair job can be purchased or ordered.

Motor factors

Good factors will stock all the more important components which wear out comparatively quickly, and can sometimes supply individual components needed for the overhaul of a larger assembly (eg, brake seals and hydraulic parts, bearing shells, pistons, valves). They may also handle work such as cylinder block reboring, crankshaft regrinding, etc.

Tyre and exhaust specialists

These outlets may be independent, or members of a local or national chain. They frequently offer competitive prices when compared with a main dealer or local garage, but it will pay to obtain several quotes before making a decision. When researching prices, also ask what 'extras' may be added - for instance fitting a new valve and balancing the wheel are both commonly charged on top of the price of a new tyre.

Other sources

Beware of parts or materials obtained from market stalls, car boot sales or similar outlets. Such items are not invariably sub-standard, but there is little chance of compensation if they do prove unsatisfactory. In the case of safety-critical components such as brake pads, there is the risk not only of financial loss, but also of an accident causing injury or death.

Second-hand components or assemblies obtained from a car breaker can be a good buy in some circumstances, but his sort of purchase is best made by the experienced DIY mechanic.

Vehicle identification

Modifications are a continuing and unpublicised process in vehicle manufacture, quite apart from major model changes. Spare parts manuals and lists are compiled upon a numerical basis, the individual vehicle identification numbers being essential to correct identification of the component concerned.

When ordering spare parts, always give as much information as possible. Quote the car model, year of manufacture, body and engine numbers as appropriate.

The *Vehicle Identification Number (VIN)* or *chassis number* appears in several places on the vehicle:

a) *On a metal plate riveted to the crossmember at the front right hand side of the engine compartment* ***(see illustration)***
b) *Stamped on the bulkhead at the rear of the engine compartment*
c) *Printed on a plate, attached to the top of the facia, behind the windscreen*

The *Engine number* is stamped on the front left-hand side of the cylinder block.

The *Transmission number* is printed on a plate, attached to the front/top of the transmission casing.

The *Body number* is stamped on a metal plate riveted to the crossmember at the front left hand side of the engine compartment.

The *Paint codes* are printed on a label attached to the trailing edge of the passenger door, next to the tyre pressure chart.

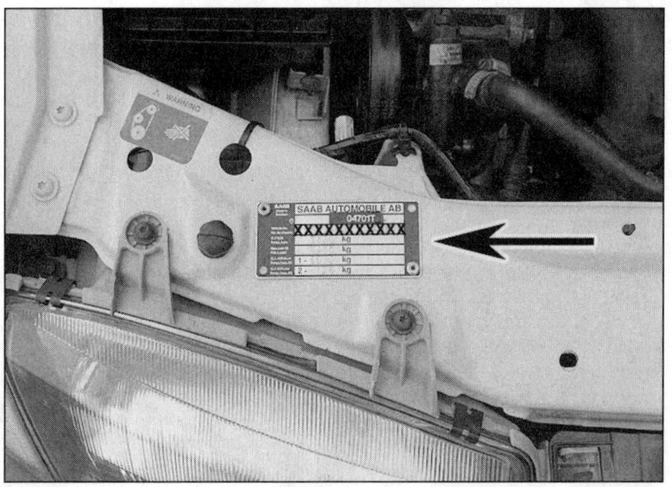

Vehicle Identification Number (VIN) stamped on a plate riveted to the engine compartment front crossmember

Whenever servicing, repair or overhaul work is carried out on the car or its components, observe the following procedures and instructions. This will assist in carrying out the operation efficiently and to a professional standard of workmanship.

Joint mating faces and gaskets

When separating components at their mating faces, never insert screwdrivers or similar implements into the joint between the faces in order to prise them apart. This can cause severe damage which results in oil leaks, coolant leaks, etc upon reassembly. Separation is usually achieved by tapping along the joint with a soft-faced hammer in order to break the seal. However, note that this method may not be suitable where dowels are used for component location.

Where a gasket is used between the mating faces of two components, a new one must be fitted on reassembly; fit it dry unless otherwise stated in the repair procedure. Make sure that the mating faces are clean and dry, with all traces of old gasket removed. When cleaning a joint face, use a tool which is unlikely to score or damage the face, and remove any burrs or nicks with an oilstone or fine file.

Make sure that tapped holes are cleaned with a pipe cleaner, and keep them free of jointing compound, if this is being used, unless specifically instructed otherwise.

Ensure that all orifices, channels or pipes are clear, and blow through them, preferably using compressed air.

Oil seals

Oil seals can be removed by levering them out with a wide flat-bladed screwdriver or similar implement. Alternatively, a number of self-tapping screws may be screwed into the seal, and these used as a purchase for pliers or some similar device in order to pull the seal free.

Whenever an oil seal is removed from its working location, either individually or as part of an assembly, it should be renewed.

The very fine sealing lip of the seal is easily damaged, and will not seal if the surface it contacts is not completely clean and free from scratches, nicks or grooves. If the original sealing surface of the component cannot be restored, and the manufacturer has not made provision for slight relocation of the seal relative to the sealing surface, the component should be renewed.

Protect the lips of the seal from any surface which may damage them in the course of fitting. Use tape or a conical sleeve where possible. Lubricate the seal lips with oil before fitting and, on dual-lipped seals, fill the space between the lips with grease.

Unless otherwise stated, oil seals must be fitted with their sealing lips toward the lubricant to be sealed.

Use a tubular drift or block of wood of the appropriate size to install the seal and, if the seal housing is shouldered, drive the seal down to the shoulder. If the seal housing is unshouldered, the seal should be fitted with its face flush with the housing top face (unless otherwise instructed).

Screw threads and fastenings

Seized nuts, bolts and screws are quite a common occurrence where corrosion has set in, and the use of penetrating oil or releasing fluid will often overcome this problem if the offending item is soaked for a while before attempting to release it. The use of an impact driver may also provide a means of releasing such stubborn fastening devices, when used in conjunction with the appropriate screwdriver bit or socket. If none of these methods works, it may be necessary to resort to the careful application of heat, or the use of a hacksaw or nut splitter device.

Studs are usually removed by locking two nuts together on the threaded part, and then using a spanner on the lower nut to unscrew the stud. Studs or bolts which have broken off below the surface of the component in which they are mounted can sometimes be removed using a stud extractor. Always ensure that a blind tapped hole is completely free from oil, grease, water or other fluid before installing the bolt or stud. Failure to do this could cause the housing to crack due to the hydraulic action of the bolt or stud as it is screwed in.

When tightening a castellated nut to accept a split pin, tighten the nut to the specified torque, where applicable, and then tighten further to the next split pin hole. Never slacken the nut to align the split pin hole, unless stated in the repair procedure.

When checking or retightening a nut or bolt to a specified torque setting, slacken the nut or bolt by a quarter of a turn, and then retighten to the specified setting. However, this should not be attempted where angular tightening has been used.

For some screw fastenings, notably cylinder head bolts or nuts, torque wrench settings are no longer specified for the latter stages of tightening, "angle-tightening" being called up instead. Typically, a fairly low torque wrench setting will be applied to the bolts/nuts in the correct sequence, followed by one or more stages of tightening through specified angles.

Locknuts, locktabs and washers

Any fastening which will rotate against a component or housing during tightening should always have a washer between it and the relevant component or housing.

Spring or split washers should always be renewed when they are used to lock a critical component such as a big-end bearing retaining bolt or nut. Locktabs which are folded over to retain a nut or bolt should always be renewed.

Self-locking nuts can be re-used in non-critical areas, providing resistance can be felt when the locking portion passes over the bolt or stud thread. However, it should be noted that self-locking stiffnuts tend to lose their effectiveness after long periods of use, and should then be renewed as a matter of course.

Split pins must always be replaced with new ones of the correct size for the hole.

When thread-locking compound is found on the threads of a fastener which is to be re-used, it should be cleaned off with a wire brush and solvent, and fresh compound applied on reassembly.

Special tools

Some repair procedures in this manual entail the use of special tools such as a press, two or three-legged pullers, spring compressors, etc. Wherever possible, suitable readily-available alternatives to the manufacturer's special tools are described, and are shown in use. In some instances, where no alternative is possible, it has been necessary to resort to the use of a manufacturer's tool, and this has been done for reasons of safety as well as the efficient completion of the repair operation. Unless you are highly-skilled and have a thorough understanding of the procedures described, never attempt to bypass the use of any special tool when the procedure described specifies its use. Not only is there a very great risk of personal injury, but expensive damage could be caused to the components involved.

Environmental considerations

When disposing of used engine oil, brake fluid, antifreeze, etc, give due consideration to any detrimental environmental effects. Do not, for instance, pour any of the above liquids down drains into the general sewage system, or onto the ground to soak away. Many local council refuse tips provide a facility for waste oil disposal, as do some garages. If none of these facilities are available, consult your local Environmental Health Department, or the National Rivers Authority, for further advice.

With the universal tightening-up of legislation regarding the emission of environmentally-harmful substances from motor vehicles, most vehicles have tamperproof devices fitted to the main adjustment points of the fuel system. These devices are primarily designed to prevent unqualified persons from adjusting the fuel/air mixture, with the chance of a consequent increase in toxic emissions. If such devices are found during servicing or overhaul, they should, wherever possible, be renewed or refitted in accordance with the manufacturer's requirements or current legislation.

OIL CARE
FOLLOW THE CODE
OIL BANK LINE
0800 66 33 66

Note: It is antisocial and illegal to dump oil down the drain. To find the location of your local oil recycling bank, call this number free.

The jack supplied with the vehicle tool kit should only be used for changing the roadwheels - see *"Wheel changing"* at the front of this manual. When carrying out any other kind of work, raise the vehicle using a hydraulic trolley jack, and always supplement the jack with axle stands positioned under the vehicle jacking points.

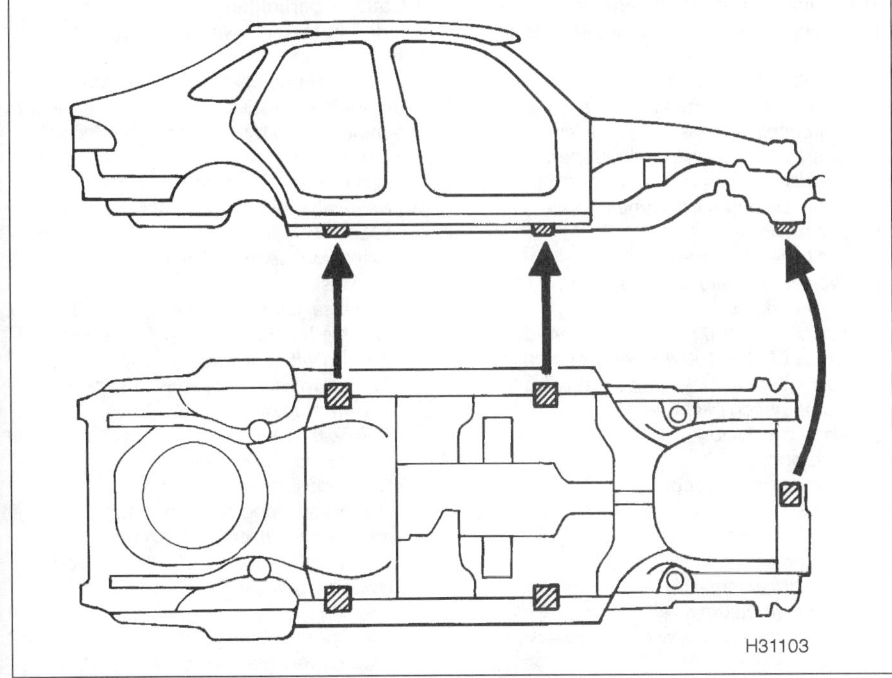

Jacking points for hydraulic jack (arrowed)

When using a trolley jack or axle stands, always position the jack head or axle stand head under, or adjacent to one of the relevant wheel changing jacking points under the sills. Use a block of wood between the jack or axle stand and the sill - the block of wood should have a groove cut into it, in which the welded flange of the sill will locate **(see illustrations)**.

Do **not** attempt to jack the vehicle under the rear axle, floorpan, engine sump, automatic transmission sump, or any of the suspension components.

The jack supplied with the vehicle locates in the jacking points on the underside of the sills - see *"Wheel changing"* at the front of this manual. Ensure that the jack head is correctly engaged before attempting to raise the vehicle.

Never work under, around, or near a raised vehicle, unless it is adequately supported in at least two places.

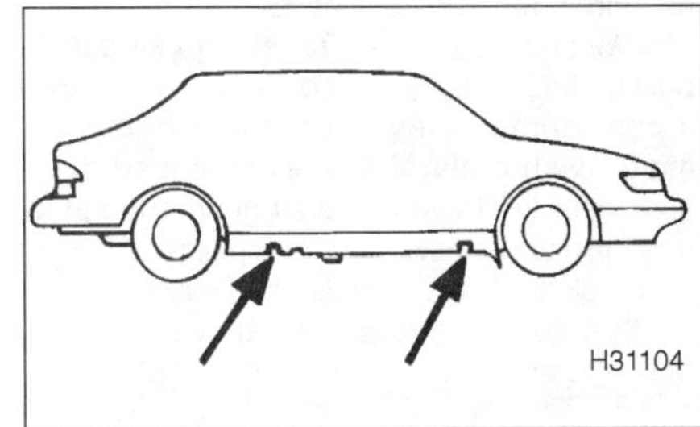

Wheel changing jacking points (arrowed)

Radio/cassette unit anti-theft system - precautions

The radio/cassette unit fitted may be equipped with a built-in security code, to deter thieves. If the power source to the unit is cut, the anti-theft system will activate. Even if the power source is immediately reconnected, the radio/cassette unit will not function until the correct security code has been entered. Therefore if you do not know the correct security code for the unit, **do not** disconnect the battery negative lead, or remove the radio/cassette unit from the vehicle.

If the security code is lost or forgotten, seek the advice of your Saab dealer. On presentation of proof of ownership, a Saab dealer will be able to provide you with a new security code.

Introduction

A selection of good tools is a fundamental requirement for anyone contemplating the maintenance and repair of a motor vehicle. For the owner who does not possess any, their purchase will prove a considerable expense, offsetting some of the savings made by doing-it-yourself. However, provided that the tools purchased meet the relevant national safety standards and are of good quality, they will last for many years and prove an extremely worthwhile investment.

To help the average owner to decide which tools are needed to carry out the various tasks detailed in this manual, we have compiled three lists of tools under the following headings: *Maintenance and minor repair*, *Repair and overhaul*, and *Special*. Newcomers to practical mechanics should start off with the *Maintenance and minor repair* tool kit, and confine themselves to the simpler jobs around the vehicle. Then, as confidence and experience grow, more difficult tasks can be undertaken, with extra tools being purchased as, and when, they are needed. In this way, a *Maintenance and minor repair* tool kit can be built up into a *Repair and overhaul* tool kit over a considerable period of time, without any major cash outlays. The experienced do-it-yourselfer will have a tool kit good enough for most repair and overhaul procedures, and will add tools from the *Special* category when it is felt that the expense is justified by the amount of use to which these tools will be put.

Maintenance and minor repair tool kit

The tools given in this list should be considered as a minimum requirement if routine maintenance, servicing and minor repair operations are to be undertaken. We recommend the purchase of combination spanners (ring one end, open-ended the other); although more expensive than open-ended ones, they do give the advantages of both types of spanner.

- ☐ *Combination spanners:*
  Metric - 8 to 19 mm inclusive
- ☐ *Adjustable spanner - 35 mm jaw (approx.)*
- ☐ *Spark plug spanner (with rubber insert) - petrol models*
- ☐ *Spark plug gap adjustment tool - petrol models*
- ☐ *Set of feeler gauges*
- ☐ *Brake bleed nipple spanner*
- ☐ *Screwdrivers:*
  Flat blade - 100 mm long x 6 mm dia
  Cross blade - 100 mm long x 6 mm dia
  Torx - various sizes (not all vehicles)
- ☐ *Combination pliers*
- ☐ *Hacksaw (junior)*
- ☐ *Tyre pump*
- ☐ *Tyre pressure gauge*
- ☐ *Oil can*
- ☐ *Oil filter removal tool*
- ☐ *Fine emery cloth*
- ☐ *Wire brush (small)*
- ☐ *Funnel (medium size)*
- ☐ *Sump drain plug key (not all vehicles)*

Repair and overhaul tool kit

These tools are virtually essential for anyone undertaking any major repairs to a motor vehicle, and are additional to those given in the *Maintenance and minor repair* list. Included in this list is a comprehensive set of sockets. Although these are expensive, they will be found invaluable as they are so versatile - particularly if various drives are included in the set. We recommend the half-inch square-drive type, as this can be used with most proprietary torque wrenches.

The tools in this list will sometimes need to be supplemented by tools from the *Special* list:

- ☐ *Sockets (or box spanners) to cover range in previous list (including Torx sockets)*
- ☐ *Reversible ratchet drive (for use with sockets)*
- ☐ *Extension piece, 250 mm (for use with sockets)*
- ☐ *Universal joint (for use with sockets)*
- ☐ *Flexible handle or sliding T "breaker bar" (for use with sockets)*
- ☐ *Torque wrench (for use with sockets)*
- ☐ *Self-locking grips*
- ☐ *Ball pein hammer*
- ☐ *Soft-faced mallet (plastic or rubber)*
- ☐ *Screwdrivers:*
  Flat blade - long & sturdy, short (chubby), and narrow (electrician's) types
  Cross blade – long & sturdy, and short (chubby) types
- ☐ *Pliers:*
  Long-nosed
  Side cutters (electrician's)
  Circlip (internal and external)
- ☐ *Cold chisel - 25 mm*
- ☐ *Scriber*
- ☐ *Scraper*
- ☐ *Centre-punch*
- ☐ *Pin punch*
- ☐ *Hacksaw*
- ☐ *Brake hose clamp*
- ☐ *Brake/clutch bleeding kit*
- ☐ *Selection of twist drills*
- ☐ *Steel rule/straight-edge*
- ☐ *Allen keys (inc. splined/Torx type)*
- ☐ *Selection of files*
- ☐ *Wire brush*
- ☐ *Axle stands*
- ☐ *Jack (strong trolley or hydraulic type)*
- ☐ *Light with extension lead*
- ☐ *Universal electrical multi-meter*

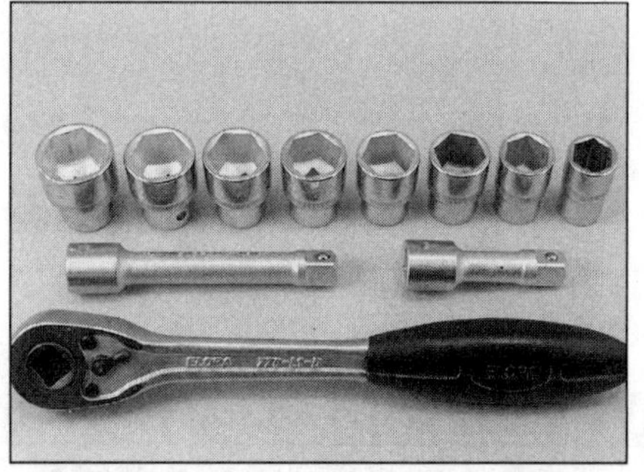

Sockets and reversible ratchet drive

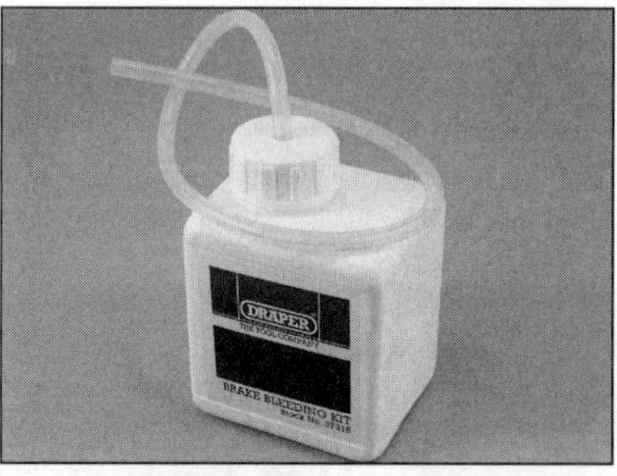

Brake bleeding kit

Torx key, socket and bit

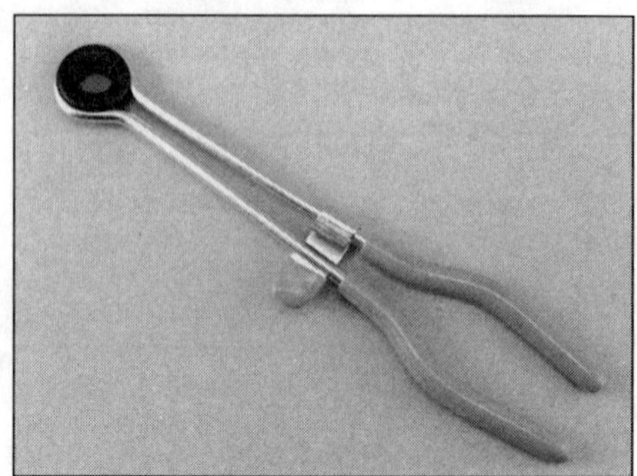

Hose clamp

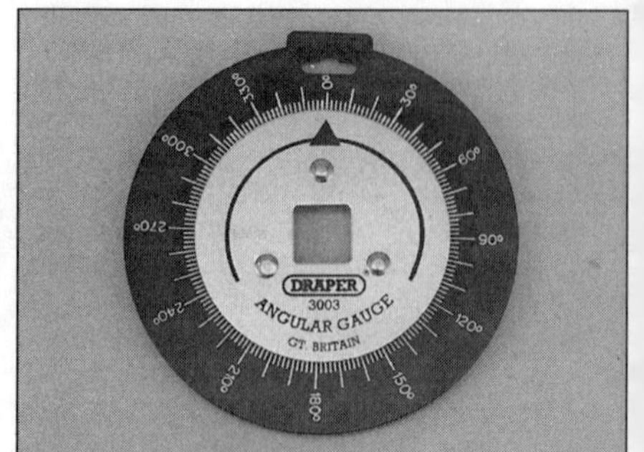

Angular-tightening gauge

Special tools

The tools in this list are those which are not used regularly, are expensive to buy, or which need to be used in accordance with their manufacturers' instructions. Unless relatively difficult mechanical jobs are undertaken frequently, it will not be economic to buy many of these tools. Where this is the case, you could consider clubbing together with friends (or joining a motorists' club) to make a joint purchase, or borrowing the tools against a deposit from a local garage or tool hire specialist. It is worth noting that many of the larger DIY superstores now carry a large range of special tools for hire at modest rates.

The following list contains only those tools and instruments freely available to the public, and not those special tools produced by the vehicle manufacturer specifically for its dealer network. You will find occasional references to these manufacturers' special tools in the text of this manual. Generally, an alternative method of doing the job without the vehicle manufacturers' special tool is given. However, sometimes there is no alternative to using them. Where this is the case and the relevant tool cannot be bought or borrowed, you will have to entrust the work to a dealer.

- ☐ *Angular-tightening gauge*
- ☐ *Valve spring compressor*
- ☐ *Valve grinding tool*
- ☐ *Piston ring compressor*
- ☐ *Piston ring removal/installation tool*
- ☐ *Cylinder bore hone*
- ☐ *Balljoint separator*
- ☐ *Coil spring compressors (where applicable)*
- ☐ *Two/three-legged hub and bearing puller*
- ☐ *Impact screwdriver*
- ☐ *Micrometer and/or vernier calipers*
- ☐ *Dial gauge*
- ☐ *Stroboscopic timing light*
- ☐ *Dwell angle meter/tachometer*
- ☐ *Fault code reader*
- ☐ *Cylinder compression gauge*
- ☐ *Hand-operated vacuum pump and gauge*
- ☐ *Clutch plate alignment set*
- ☐ *Brake shoe steady spring cup removal tool*
- ☐ *Bush and bearing removal/installation set*
- ☐ *Stud extractors*
- ☐ *Tap and die set*
- ☐ *Lifting tackle*
- ☐ *Trolley jack*

Buying tools

Reputable motor accessory shops and superstores often offer excellent quality tools at discount prices, so it pays to shop around.

Remember, you don't have to buy the most expensive items on the shelf, but it is always advisable to steer clear of the very cheap tools. Beware of 'bargains' offered on market stalls or at car boot sales. There are plenty of good tools around at reasonable prices, but always aim to purchase items which meet the relevant national safety standards. If in doubt, ask the proprietor or manager of the shop for advice before making a purchase.

Care and maintenance of tools

Having purchased a reasonable tool kit, it is necessary to keep the tools in a clean and serviceable condition. After use, always wipe off any dirt, grease and metal particles using a clean, dry cloth, before putting the tools away. Never leave them lying around after they have been used. A simple tool rack on the garage or workshop wall for items such as screwdrivers and pliers is a good idea. Store all normal spanners and sockets in a metal box. Any measuring instruments, gauges, meters, etc, must be carefully stored where they cannot be damaged or become rusty.

Take a little care when tools are used. Hammer heads inevitably become marked, and screwdrivers lose the keen edge on their blades from time to time. A little timely attention with emery cloth or a file will soon restore items like this to a good finish.

Working facilities

Not to be forgotten when discussing tools is the workshop itself. If anything more than routine maintenance is to be carried out, a suitable working area becomes essential.

It is appreciated that many an owner-mechanic is forced by circumstances to remove an engine or similar item without the benefit of a garage or workshop. Having done this, any repairs should always be done under the cover of a roof.

Wherever possible, any dismantling should be done on a clean, flat workbench or table at a suitable working height.

Any workbench needs a vice; one with a jaw opening of 100 mm is suitable for most jobs. As mentioned previously, some clean dry storage space is also required for tools, as well as for any lubricants, cleaning fluids, touch-up paints etc, which become necessary.

Another item which may be required, and which has a much more general usage, is an electric drill with a chuck capacity of at least 8 mm. This, together with a good range of twist drills, is virtually essential for fitting accessories.

Last, but not least, always keep a supply of old newspapers and clean, lint-free rags available, and try to keep any working area as clean as possible.

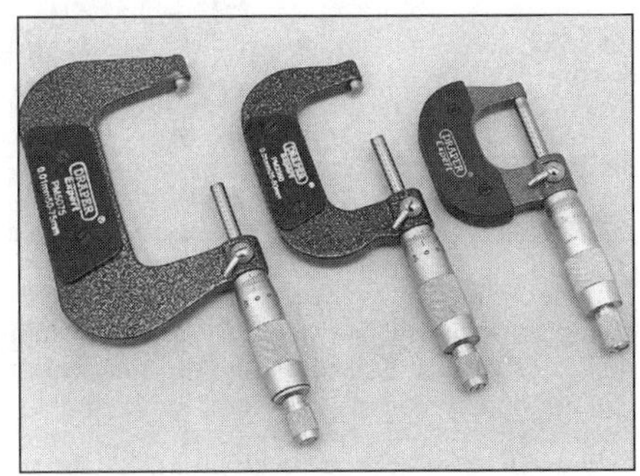

Micrometers

Dial test indicator ("dial gauge")

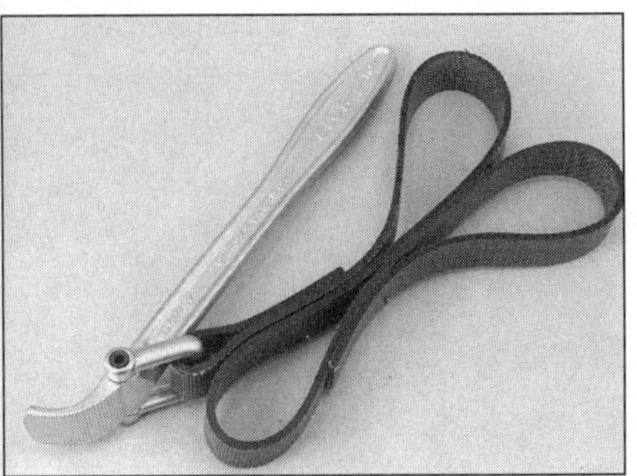

Strap wrench

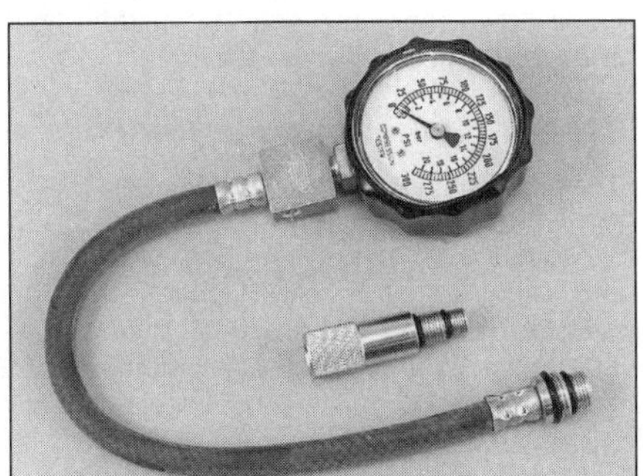

Compression tester

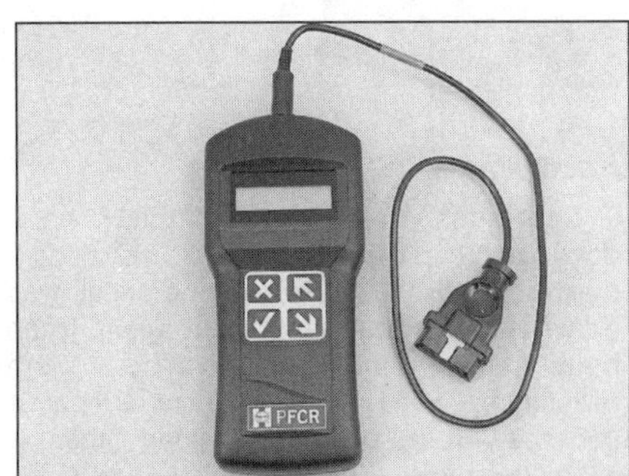

Fault code reader

This is a guide to getting your vehicle through the MOT test. Obviously it will not be possible to examine the vehicle to the same standard as the professional MOT tester. However, working through the following checks will enable you to identify any problem areas before submitting the vehicle for the test.

Where a testable component is in borderline condition, the tester has discretion in deciding whether to pass or fail it. The basis of such discretion is whether the tester would be happy for a close relative or friend to use the vehicle with the component in that condition. If the vehicle presented is clean and evidently well cared for, the tester may be more inclined to pass a borderline component than if the vehicle is scruffy and apparently neglected.

It has only been possible to summarise the test requirements here, based on the regulations in force at the time of printing. Test standards are becoming increasingly stringent, although there are some exemptions for older vehicles. For full details obtain a copy of the Haynes publication Pass the MOT! (available from stockists of Haynes manuals).

An assistant will be needed to help carry out some of these checks.

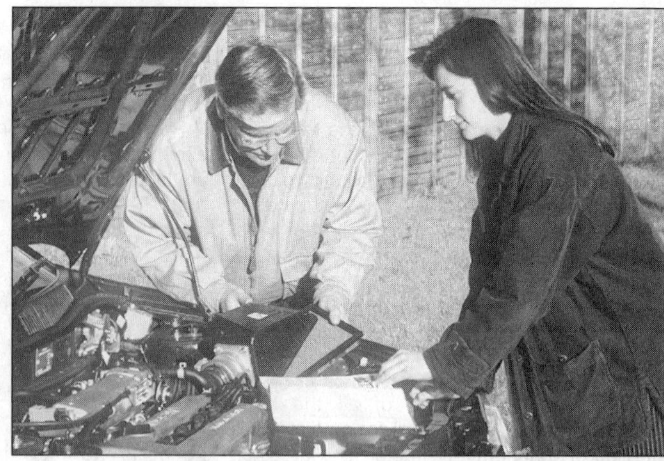

The checks have been sub-divided into four categories, as follows:

1 Checks carried out **FROM THE DRIVER'S SEAT**

2 Checks carried out **WITH THE VEHICLE ON THE GROUND**

3 Checks carried out **WITH THE VEHICLE RAISED AND THE WHEELS FREE TO TURN**

4 Checks carried out on **YOUR VEHICLE'S EXHAUST EMISSION SYSTEM**

1 Checks carried out FROM THE DRIVER'S SEAT

Handbrake

☐ Test the operation of the handbrake. Excessive travel (too many clicks) indicates incorrect brake or cable adjustment.

☐ Check that the handbrake cannot be released by tapping the lever sideways. Check the security of the lever mountings.

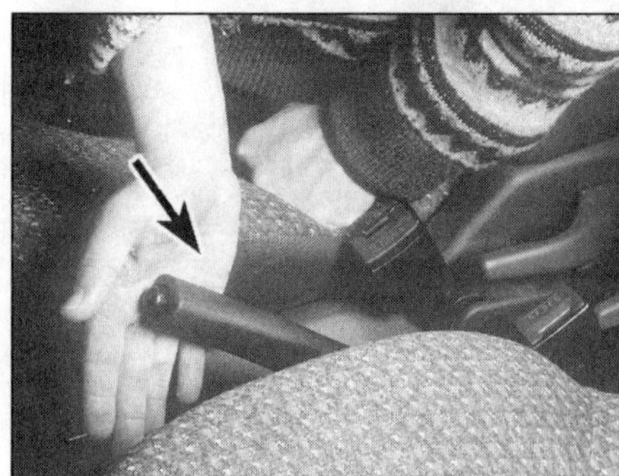

Footbrake

☐ Depress the brake pedal and check that it does not creep down to the floor, indicating a master cylinder fault. Release the pedal, wait a few seconds, then depress it again. If the pedal travels nearly to the floor before firm resistance is felt, brake adjustment or repair is necessary. If the pedal feels spongy, there is air in the hydraulic system which must be removed by bleeding.

☐ Check that the brake pedal is secure and in good condition. Check also for signs of fluid leaks on the pedal, floor or carpets, which would indicate failed seals in the brake master cylinder.

☐ Check the servo unit (when applicable) by operating the brake pedal several times, then keeping the pedal depressed and starting the engine. As the engine starts, the pedal will move down slightly. If not, the vacuum hose or the servo itself may be faulty.

Steering wheel and column

☐ Examine the steering wheel for fractures or looseness of the hub, spokes or rim.

☐ Move the steering wheel from side to side and then up and down. Check that the steering wheel is not loose on the column, indicating wear or a loose retaining nut. Continue moving the steering wheel as before, but also turn it slightly from left to right.

☐ Check that the steering wheel is not loose on the column, and that there is no abnormal

movement of the steering wheel, indicating wear in the column support bearings or couplings.

Windscreen and mirrors

☐ The windscreen must be free of cracks or other significant damage within the driver's field of view. (Small stone chips are acceptable.) Rear view mirrors must be secure, intact, and capable of being adjusted.

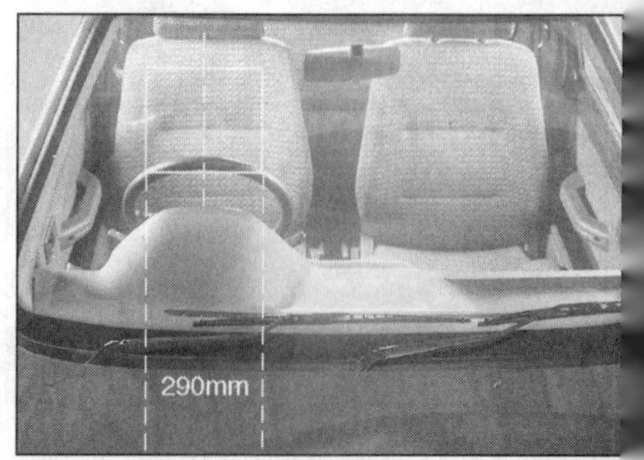

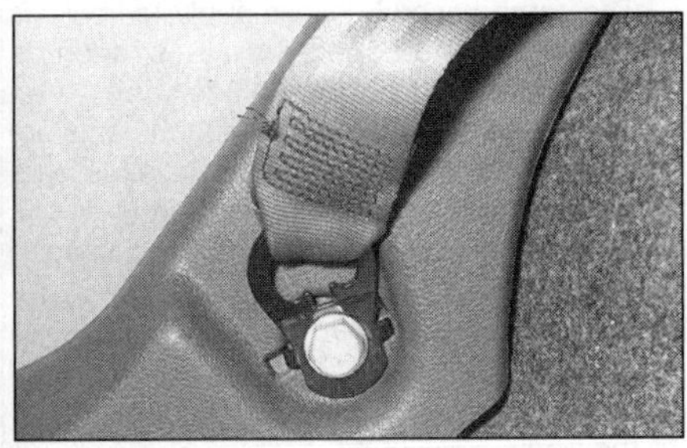

Seat belts and seats

Note: *The following checks are applicable to all seat belts, front and rear.*

☐ Examine the webbing of all the belts (including rear belts if fitted) for cuts, serious fraying or deterioration. Fasten and unfasten each belt to check the buckles. If applicable, check the retracting mechanism. Check the security of all seat belt mountings accessible from inside the vehicle.

☐ The front seats themselves must be securely attached and the backrests must lock in the upright position.

Doors

☐ Both front doors must be able to be opened and closed from outside and inside, and must latch securely when closed.

2 Checks carried out WITH THE VEHICLE ON THE GROUND

Vehicle identification

☐ Number plates must be in good condition, secure and legible, with letters and numbers correctly spaced – spacing at (A) should be twice that at (B).

☐ The VIN plate and/or homologation plate must be legible.

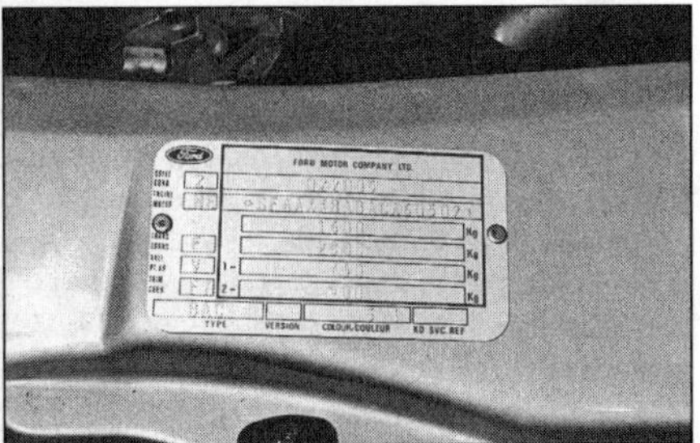

Electrical equipment

☐ Switch on the ignition and check the operation of the horn.

☐ Check the windscreen washers and wipers, examining the wiper blades; renew damaged or perished blades. Also check the operation of the stop-lights.

☐ Check the operation of the sidelights and number plate lights. The lenses and reflectors must be secure, clean and undamaged.

☐ Check the operation and alignment of the headlights. The headlight reflectors must not be tarnished and the lenses must be undamaged.

☐ Switch on the ignition and check the operation of the direction indicators (including the instrument panel tell-tale) and the hazard warning lights. Operation of the sidelights and stop-lights must not affect the indicators - if it does, the cause is usually a bad earth at the rear light cluster.

☐ Check the operation of the rear foglight(s), including the warning light on the instrument panel or in the switch.

Footbrake

☐ Examine the master cylinder, brake pipes and servo unit for leaks, loose mountings, corrosion or other damage.

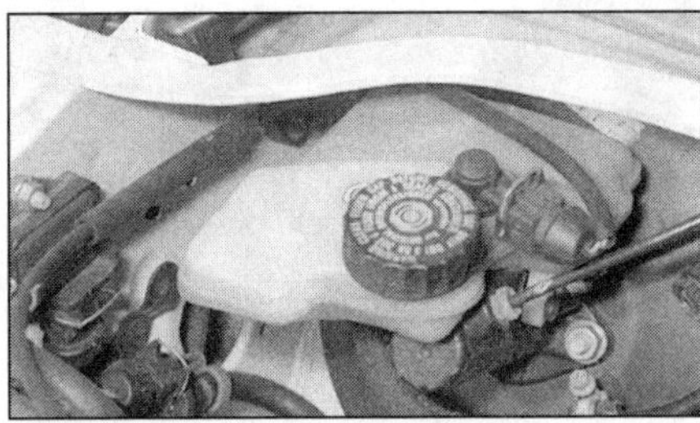

☐ The fluid reservoir must be secure and the fluid level must be between the upper (**A**) and lower (**B**) markings.

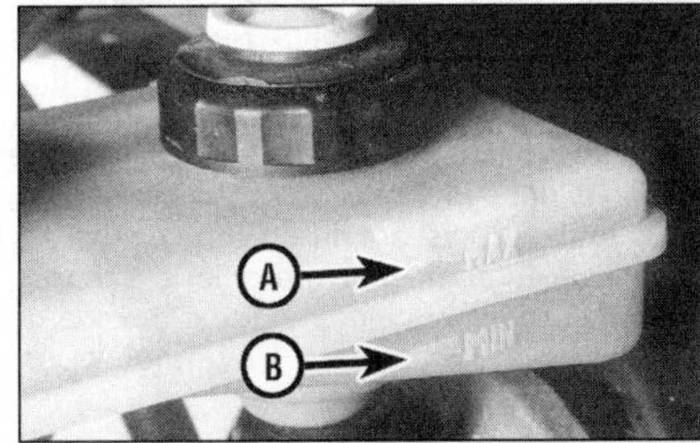

☐ Inspect both front brake flexible hoses for cracks or deterioration of the rubber. Turn the steering from lock to lock, and ensure that the hoses do not contact the wheel, tyre, or any part of the steering or suspension mechanism. With the brake pedal firmly depressed, check the hoses for bulges or leaks under pressure.

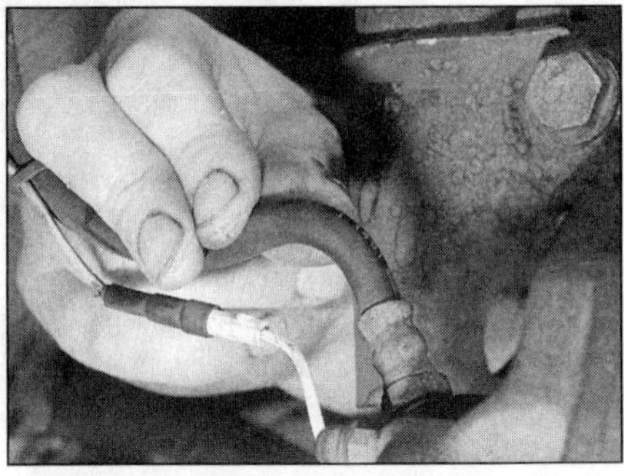

Steering and suspension

☐ Have your assistant turn the steering wheel from side to side slightly, up to the point where the steering gear just begins to transmit this movement to the roadwheels. Check for excessive free play between the steering wheel and the steering gear, indicating wear or insecurity of the steering column joints, the column-to-steering gear coupling, or the steering gear itself.

☐ Have your assistant turn the steering wheel more vigorously in each direction, so that the roadwheels just begin to turn. As this is done, examine all the steering joints, linkages, fittings and attachments. Renew any component that shows signs of wear or damage. On vehicles with power steering, check the security and condition of the steering pump, drivebelt and hoses.

☐ Check that the vehicle is standing level, and at approximately the correct ride height.

Shock absorbers

☐ Depress each corner of the vehicle in turn, then release it. The vehicle should rise and then settle in its normal position. If the vehicle continues to rise and fall, the shock absorber is defective. A shock absorber which has seized will also cause the vehicle to fail.

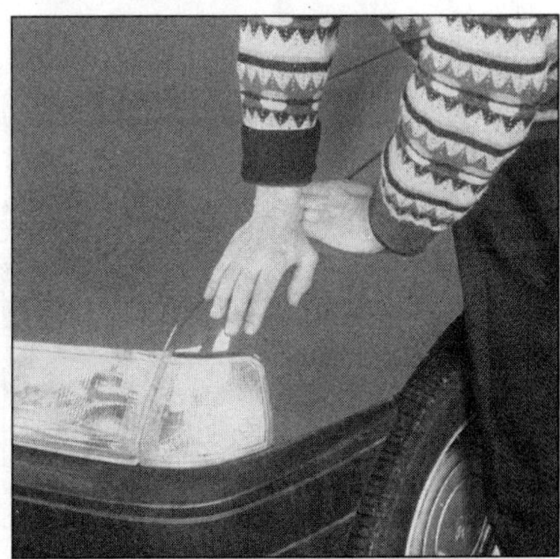

Exhaust system

☐ Start the engine. With your assistant holding a rag over the tailpipe, check the entire system for leaks. Repair or renew leaking sections.

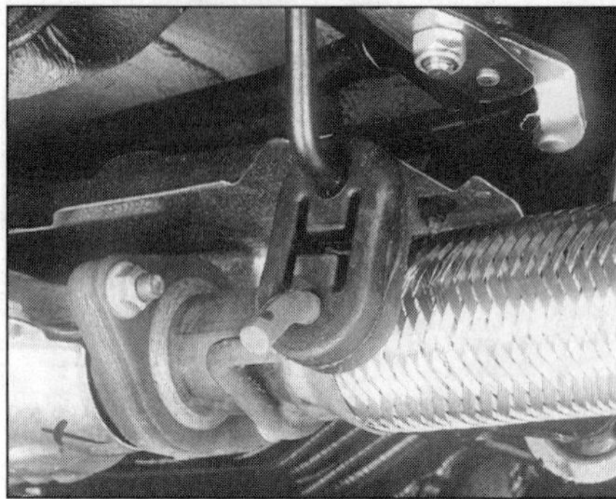

3 Checks carried out WITH THE VEHICLE RAISED AND THE WHEELS FREE TO TURN

Jack up the front and rear of the vehicle, and securely support it on axle stands. Position the stands clear of the suspension assemblies. Ensure that the wheels are clear of the ground and that the steering can be turned from lock to lock.

Steering mechanism

☐ Have your assistant turn the steering from lock to lock. Check that the steering turns smoothly, and that no part of the steering mechanism, including a wheel or tyre, fouls any brake hose or pipe or any part of the body structure.

☐ Examine the steering rack rubber gaiters for damage or insecurity of the retaining clips. If power steering is fitted, check for signs of damage or leakage of the fluid hoses, pipes or connections. Also check for excessive stiffness or binding of the steering, a missing split pin or locking device, or severe corrosion of the body structure within 30 cm of any steering component attachment point.

Front and rear suspension and wheel bearings

☐ Starting at the front right-hand side, grasp the roadwheel at the 3 o'clock and 9 o'clock positions and shake it vigorously. Check for free play or insecurity at the wheel bearings, suspension balljoints, or suspension mountings, pivots and attachments.

☐ Now grasp the wheel at the 12 o'clock and 6 o'clock positions and repeat the previous inspection. Spin the wheel, and check for roughness or tightness of the front wheel bearing.

☐ If excess free play is suspected at a component pivot point, this can be confirmed by using a large screwdriver or similar tool and levering between the mounting and the component attachment. This will confirm whether the wear is in the pivot bush, its retaining bolt, or in the mounting itself (the bolt holes can often become elongated).

☐ Carry out all the above checks at the other front wheel, and then at both rear wheels.

Springs and shock absorbers

☐ Examine the suspension struts (when applicable) for serious fluid leakage, corrosion, or damage to the casing. Also check the security of the mounting points.

☐ If coil springs are fitted, check that the spring ends locate in their seats, and that the spring is not corroded, cracked or broken.

☐ If leaf springs are fitted, check that all leaves are intact, that the axle is securely attached to each spring, and that there is no deterioration of the spring eye mountings, bushes, and shackles.

☐ The same general checks apply to vehicles fitted with other suspension types, such as torsion bars, hydraulic displacer units, etc. Ensure that all mountings and attachments are secure, that there are no signs of excessive wear, corrosion or damage, and (on hydraulic types) that there are no fluid leaks or damaged pipes.

☐ Inspect the shock absorbers for signs of serious fluid leakage. Check for wear of the mounting bushes or attachments, or damage to the body of the unit.

Driveshafts (fwd vehicles only)

☐ Rotate each front wheel in turn and inspect the constant velocity joint gaiters for splits or damage. Also check that each driveshaft is straight and undamaged.

Braking system

☐ If possible without dismantling, check brake pad wear and disc condition. Ensure that the friction lining material has not worn excessively, (A) and that the discs are not fractured, pitted, scored or badly worn (B).

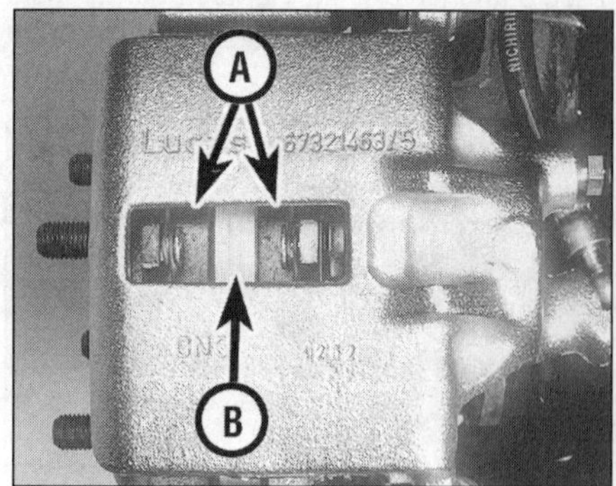

☐ Examine all the rigid brake pipes underneath the vehicle, and the flexible hose(s) at the rear. Look for corrosion, chafing or insecurity of the pipes, and for signs of bulging under pressure, chafing, splits or deterioration of the flexible hoses.

☐ Look for signs of fluid leaks at the brake calipers or on the brake backplates. Repair or renew leaking components.

☐ Slowly spin each wheel, while your assistant depresses and releases the footbrake. Ensure that each brake is operating and does not bind when the pedal is released.

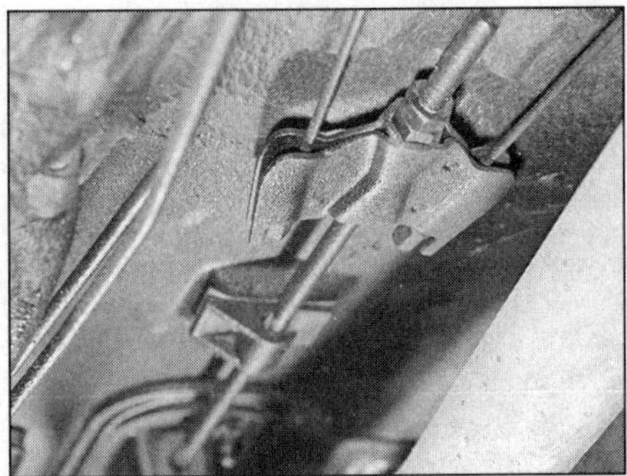

☐ Examine the handbrake mechanism, checking for frayed or broken cables, excessive corrosion, or wear or insecurity of the linkage. Check that the mechanism works on each relevant wheel, and releases fully, without binding.

☐ It is not possible to test brake efficiency without special equipment, but a road test can be carried out later to check that the vehicle pulls up in a straight line.

Fuel and exhaust systems

☐ Inspect the fuel tank (including the filler cap), fuel pipes, hoses and unions. All components must be secure and free from leaks.

☐ Examine the exhaust system over its entire length, checking for any damaged, broken or missing mountings, security of the retaining clamps and rust or corrosion.

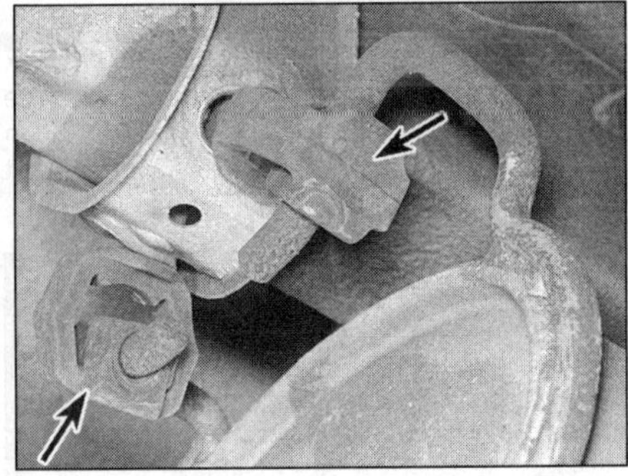

Wheels and tyres

☐ Examine the sidewalls and tread area of each tyre in turn. Check for cuts, tears, lumps, bulges, separation of the tread, and exposure of the ply or cord due to wear or damage. Check that the tyre bead is correctly seated on the wheel rim, that the valve is sound and properly seated, and that the wheel is not distorted or damaged.

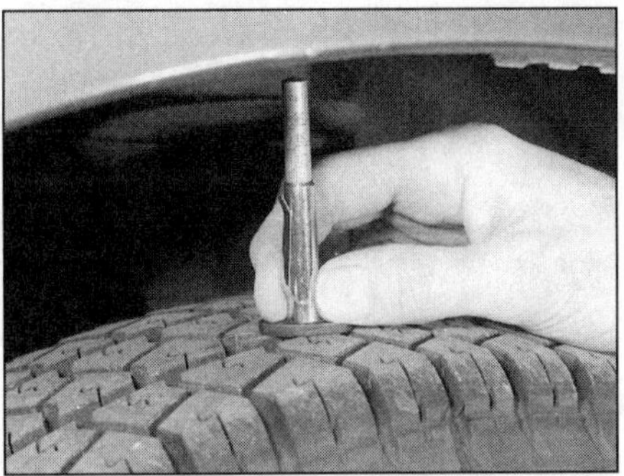

☐ Check that the tyres are of the correct size for the vehicle, that they are of the same size and type on each axle, and that the pressures are correct.

☐ Check the tyre tread depth. The legal minimum at the time of writing is 1.6 mm over at least three-quarters of the tread width. Abnormal tread wear may indicate incorrect front wheel alignment.

Body corrosion

☐ Check the condition of the entire vehicle structure for signs of corrosion in load-bearing areas. (These include chassis box sections, side sills, cross-members, pillars, and all suspension, steering, braking system and seat belt mountings and anchorages.) Any corrosion which has seriously reduced the thickness of a load-bearing area is likely to cause the vehicle to fail. In this case professional repairs are likely to be needed.

☐ Damage or corrosion which causes sharp or otherwise dangerous edges to be exposed will also cause the vehicle to fail.

4 Checks carried out on **YOUR VEHICLE'S EXHAUST EMISSION SYSTEM**

Petrol models

☐ Have the engine at normal operating temperature, and make sure that it is in good tune (ignition system in good order, air filter element clean, etc).

☐ Before any measurements are carried out, raise the engine speed to around 2500 rpm, and hold it at this speed for 20 seconds. Allow the engine speed to return to idle, and watch for smoke emissions from the exhaust tailpipe. If the idle speed is obviously much too high, or if dense blue or clearly-visible black smoke comes from the tailpipe for more than 5 seconds, the vehicle will fail. As a rule of thumb, blue smoke signifies oil being burnt (engine wear) while black smoke signifies unburnt fuel (dirty air cleaner element, or other carburettor or fuel system fault).

☐ An exhaust gas analyser capable of measuring carbon monoxide (CO) and hydrocarbons (HC) is now needed. If such an instrument cannot be hired or borrowed, a local garage may agree to perform the check for a small fee.

CO emissions (mixture)

☐ At the time of writing, the maximum CO level at idle is 3.5% for vehicles first used after August 1986 and 4.5% for older vehicles. From January 1996 a much tighter limit (around 0.5%) applies to catalyst-equipped vehicles first used from August 1992. If the CO level cannot be reduced far enough to pass the test (and the fuel and ignition systems are otherwise in good condition) then the carburettor is badly worn, or there is some problem in the fuel injection system or catalytic converter (as applicable).

HC emissions

☐ With the CO emissions within limits, HC emissions must be no more than 1200 ppm (parts per million). If the vehicle fails this test at idle, it can be re-tested at around 2000 rpm; if the HC level is then 1200 ppm or less, this counts as a pass.

☐ Excessive HC emissions can be caused by oil being burnt, but they are more likely to be due to unburnt fuel.

Diesel models

☐ The only emission test applicable to Diesel engines is the measuring of exhaust smoke density. The test involves accelerating the engine several times to its maximum unloaded speed.

Note: *It is of the utmost importance that the engine timing belt is in good condition before the test is carried out.*

☐ Excessive smoke can be caused by a dirty air cleaner element. Otherwise, professional advice may be needed to find the cause.

Engine

- ☐ Engine fails to rotate when attempting to start
- ☐ Starter motor turns engine slowly
- ☐ Engine rotates, but will not start
- ☐ Engine difficult to start when cold
- ☐ Engine difficult to start when hot
- ☐ Starter motor noisy or excessively-rough in engagement
- ☐ Engine starts, but stops immediately
- ☐ Engine idles erratically
- ☐ Engine misfires at idle speed
- ☐ Engine misfires throughout the driving speed range
- ☐ Engine stalls
- ☐ Engine hesitates on acceleration
- ☐ Engine lacks power
- ☐ Engine backfires
- ☐ Oil pressure warning light illuminated with engine running
- ☐ Engine runs-on after switching off
- ☐ Engine noises

Cooling system

- ☐ Overheating
- ☐ Overcooling
- ☐ External coolant leakage
- ☐ Internal coolant leakage
- ☐ Corrosion

Fuel and exhaust systems

- ☐ Excessive fuel consumption
- ☐ Fuel leakage and/or fuel odour
- ☐ Excessive noise or fumes from exhaust system

Clutch

- ☐ Pedal travels to floor - no pressure or very little resistance
- ☐ Clutch fails to disengage (unable to select gears)
- ☐ Clutch slips (engine speed increases, with no increase in vehicle speed)
- ☐ Judder as clutch is engaged
- ☐ Noise when depressing or releasing clutch pedal

Manual transmission

- ☐ Difficulty engaging gears
- ☐ Jumps out of gear
- ☐ Vibration
- ☐ Noisy in neutral with engine running
- ☐ Noisy in one particular gear
- ☐ Lubricant leaks

Automatic transmission

- ☐ Fluid leakage
- ☐ Transmission fluid brown, or has burned smell
- ☐ General gear selection problems
- ☐ Transmission will not downshift (kickdown) with accelerator pedal fully depressed
- ☐ Engine will not start in any gear, or starts in gears other than Park or Neutral
- ☐ Transmission slips, shifts roughly, is noisy, or has no drive in forward or reverse gears

Driveshafts

- ☐ Clicking or knocking noise on turns (at slow speed on full-lock)
- ☐ Vibration when accelerating or decelerating

Braking system

- ☐ Vehicle pulls to one side under braking
- ☐ Noise (grinding or high-pitched squeal) when brakes applied
- ☐ Brake pedal feels spongy when depressed
- ☐ Excessive brake pedal travel
- ☐ Excessive brake pedal effort required to stop vehicle
- ☐ Judder felt through brake pedal or steering wheel when braking
- ☐ Brakes binding
- ☐ Rear wheels locking under normal braking

Suspension and steering systems

- ☐ Vehicle pulls to one side
- ☐ Wheel wobble and vibration
- ☐ Excessive pitching and/or rolling around corners, or during braking
- ☐ Wandering or general instability
- ☐ Excessively-stiff steering
- ☐ Excessive play in steering
- ☐ Lack of power assistance
- ☐ Tyre wear excessive

Electrical system

- ☐ Battery will not hold a charge for more than a few days
- ☐ Ignition/no-charge warning light remains illuminated with engine running
- ☐ Ignition/no-charge warning light fails to come on
- ☐ Lights inoperative
- ☐ Instrument readings inaccurate or erratic
- ☐ Horn inoperative, or unsatisfactory in operation
- ☐ Windscreen/tailgate wipers inoperative, or unsatisfactory in operation
- ☐ Windscreen/tailgate washers inoperative, or unsatisfactory in operation
- ☐ Electric windows inoperative, or unsatisfactory in operation
- ☐ Central locking system inoperative, or unsatisfactory in operation

Introduction

The vehicle owner who does his or her own maintenance according to the recommended service schedules should not have to use this section of the manual very often. Modern component reliability is such that, provided those items subject to wear or deterioration are inspected or renewed at the specified intervals, sudden failure is comparatively rare. Faults do not usually just happen as a result of sudden failure, but develop over a period of time. Major mechanical failures in particular are usually preceded by characteristic symptoms over hundreds or even thousands of miles. Those components which do occasionally fail without warning are often small and easily carried in the vehicle.

With any fault-finding, the first step is to decide where to begin investigations. Sometimes this is obvious, but on other occasions, a little detective work will be necessary. The owner who makes half a dozen haphazard adjustments or replacements may be successful in curing a fault (or its symptoms), but will be none the wiser if the fault recurs, and ultimately may have spent more time and money than was necessary. A calm and logical approach will be found to be more satisfactory in the long run. Always take into account any warning signs or abnormalities that may have been noticed in the period preceding the fault - power loss, high or low gauge readings, unusual smells, etc - and remember that failure of components such as fuses or spark plugs may only be pointers to some underlying fault.

The pages which follow provide an easy-reference guide to the more common problems which may occur during the operation of the vehicle. These problems and their possible causes are grouped under headings denoting various components or systems, such as Engine, Cooling system, etc. The Chapter and/or Section which deals with the problem is also shown in brackets. Whatever the fault, certain basic principles apply. These are as follows:

Verify the fault. This is simply a matter of being sure that you know what the symptoms are before starting work. This is particularly important if you are investigating a fault for someone else, who may not have described it very accurately.

Don't overlook the obvious. For example, if the vehicle won't start, is there fuel in the tank? (Don't take anyone else's word on this particular point, and don't trust the fuel gauge either!) If an electrical fault is indicated, look for loose or broken wires before digging out the test gear.

Cure the disease, not the symptom. Substituting a flat battery with a fully-charged one will get you off the hard shoulder, but if the underlying cause is not attended to, the new battery will go the same way. Similarly, changing oil-fouled spark plugs for a new set will get you moving again, but remember that the reason for the fouling (if it wasn't simply an incorrect grade of plug) will have to be established and corrected.

Don't take anything for granted. Particularly, don't forget that a 'new' component may itself be defective (especially if it's been rattling around in the boot for months), and don't leave components out of a fault diagnosis sequence just because they are new or recently-fitted. When you do finally diagnose a difficult fault, you'll probably realise that all the evidence was there from the start.

1 Engine

Engine fails to rotate when attempting to start

- ☐ Battery terminal connections loose or corroded (*"Weekly checks"*).
- ☐ Battery discharged or faulty (Chapter 5A).
- ☐ Broken, loose or disconnected wiring in the starting circuit (Chapter 5A).
- ☐ Defective starter solenoid or switch (Chapter 5A).
- ☐ Defective starter motor (Chapter 5A).
- ☐ Starter pinion or flywheel/driveplate ring gear teeth loose or broken (Chapters 2A or 5A).
- ☐ Engine earth cable broken or disconnected (Chapter 2A).

Starter motor turns engine slowly

- ☐ Partially-discharged battery (recharge, use jump leads, or push start) (Chapter 5A).
- ☐ Battery terminals loose or corroded (*"Weekly checks"*).
- ☐ Battery earth to body defective (Chapter 5A).
- ☐ Engine earth strap loose (Chapter 2A).
- ☐ Starter motor (or solenoid) wiring loose (Chapter 5A).
- ☐ Starter motor internal fault (Chapter 5A).

Engine rotates, but will not start

- ☐ Fuel tank empty.
- ☐ Battery discharged (engine rotates slowly) (Chapter 5A).
- ☐ Battery terminal connections loose or corroded (*"Weekly checks"*).
- ☐ Ignition components damp or damaged (Chapters 1 and 5B).
- ☐ Broken, loose or disconnected wiring in the ignition circuit (Chapters 1 and 5B).
- ☐ Worn, faulty or incorrectly-gapped spark plugs (Chapter 1).
- ☐ Fuel injection system fault (Chapter 4A).
- ☐ Major mechanical failure (eg broken timing chain) (Chapter 2A).

Engine difficult to start when cold

- ☐ Battery discharged (Chapter 5A).
- ☐ Battery terminal connections loose or corroded (*"Weekly checks"*).
- ☐ Worn, faulty or incorrectly-gapped spark plugs (Chapter 1).
- ☐ Fuel injection system fault (Chapter 4A).
- ☐ Other ignition system fault (Chapters 1 and 5B).
- ☐ Low cylinder compressions (Chapter 2A).

Engine difficult to start when hot

- ☐ Air filter element dirty or clogged (Chapter 1).
- ☐ Fuel injection system fault (Chapter 4A).
- ☐ Low cylinder compressions (Chapter 2A).

Starter motor noisy or excessively-rough in engagement

- ☐ Starter pinion or flywheel/driveplate ring gear teeth loose or broken (Chapters 2A or 5A).
- ☐ Starter motor mounting bolts loose or missing (Chapter 5A).
- ☐ Starter motor internal components worn or damaged (Chapter 5A).

Engine starts, but stops immediately

- ☐ Loose or faulty electrical connections in the ignition circuit (Chapters 1 and 5B).
- ☐ Vacuum leak at the throttle body or inlet manifold (Chapter 4A).
- ☐ Fuel injection system fault (Chapter 4A).

Engine idles erratically

- ☐ Incorrectly-adjusted idle speed (Chapter 4A).
- ☐ Air filter element clogged (Chapter 1).
- ☐ Vacuum leak at the throttle body, inlet manifold or associated hoses (Chapter 4A or 4B).
- ☐ Worn, faulty or incorrectly-gapped spark plugs (Chapter 1).
- ☐ Uneven or low cylinder compressions (Chapter 2A).
- ☐ Camshaft lobes worn (Chapter 2A).
- ☐ Fuel injection system fault (Chapter 4A).

Engine misfires at idle speed

- ☐ Worn, faulty or incorrectly-gapped spark plugs (Chapter 1).
- ☐ Faulty spark plug HT leads or DI cartridge as applicable (Chapter 1).
- ☐ Vacuum leak at the throttle body, inlet manifold or associated hoses (Chapter 4A or 4B).
- ☐ Fuel injection system fault (Chapter 4A).
- ☐ Distributor cap cracked or tracking internally, where applicable (Chapter 1).
- ☐ Uneven or low cylinder compressions (Chapter 2A).
- ☐ Disconnected, leaking, or perished crankcase ventilation hoses (Chapter 4B).

Engine misfires throughout the driving speed range

- ☐ Fuel filter choked (Chapter 1).
- ☐ Fuel pump faulty, or delivery pressure low (Chapter 4A).
- ☐ Fuel tank vent blocked, or fuel pipes restricted (Chapter 4A).
- ☐ Vacuum leak at the throttle body, inlet manifold or associated hoses (Chapter 4A).
- ☐ Worn, faulty or incorrectly-gapped spark plugs (Chapter 1).
- ☐ Faulty spark plug HT leads or DI cartridge, as applicable (Chapter 1).
- ☐ Distributor cap cracked or tracking internally, where applicable (Chapter 1).
- ☐ Faulty ignition coil (Chapter 5B).
- ☐ Uneven or low cylinder compressions (Chapter 2A).
- ☐ Fuel injection system fault (Chapter 4A).

Engine stalls

- ☐ Vacuum leak at the throttle body, inlet manifold or associated hoses (Chapter 4A or 4B).
- ☐ Fuel filter choked (Chapter 1).
- ☐ Fuel pump faulty, or delivery pressure low (Chapter 4A).
- ☐ Fuel tank vent blocked, or fuel pipes restricted (Chapter 4A).
- ☐ Fuel injection system fault (Chapter 4A).

Engine (continued)

Engine hesitates on acceleration

- ☐ Worn, faulty or incorrectly-gapped spark plugs (Chapter 1).
- ☐ Vacuum leak at the throttle body, inlet manifold or associated hoses (Chapter 4A or 4B).
- ☐ Fuel injection system fault (Chapter 4A).

Engine lacks power

- ☐ Fuel filter choked (Chapter 1).
- ☐ Fuel pump faulty, or delivery pressure low (Chapter 4A).
- ☐ Uneven or low cylinder compressions (Chapter 2A).
- ☐ Worn, faulty or incorrectly-gapped spark plugs (Chapter 1).
- ☐ Vacuum leak at the throttle body, inlet manifold or associated hoses (Chapter 4A or 4B).
- ☐ Fuel injection system fault (Chapter 4A).
- ☐ Faulty turbocharger, where applicable (Chapter 4A).
- ☐ Brakes binding (Chapters 1 and 9).
- ☐ Clutch slipping (Chapter 6).

Engine backfires

- ☐ Vacuum leak at the throttle body, inlet manifold or associated hoses (Chapter 4A or 4B).
- ☐ Fuel injection system fault (Chapter 4A).

Oil pressure warning light illuminated with engine running

- ☐ Low oil level, or incorrect oil grade ("*Weekly checks*").
- ☐ Faulty oil pressure sensor (Chapter 2A).
- ☐ Worn engine bearings and/or oil pump (Chapter 2A or 2B).
- ☐ Excessively high engine operating temperature (Chapter 3).
- ☐ Oil pressure relief valve defective (Chapter 2A).
- ☐ Oil pick-up strainer clogged (Chapter 2A).

Note: *Low oil pressure in a high-mileage engine at tick-over is not necessarily a cause for concern. Sudden pressure loss at speed is far more significant. In any event, check the gauge or warning light sender before condemning the engine.*

Engine runs-on after switching off

- ☐ Excessive carbon build-up in engine (Chapter 2A or 2B).
- ☐ Excessively high engine operating temperature (Chapter 3).

Engine noises

Pre-ignition (pinking) or knocking during acceleration or under load

- ☐ Ignition timing incorrect/ignition system fault (Chapters 1 and 5B).
- ☐ Incorrect grade of spark plug (Chapter 1).
- ☐ Incorrect grade of fuel (Chapter 4A).
- ☐ Vacuum leak at throttle body, inlet manifold or associated hoses (Chapter 4A or 4B).
- ☐ Excessive carbon build-up in engine (Chapter 2A or 2B).
- ☐ Fuel injection system fault (Chapter 4A).

Whistling or wheezing noises

- ☐ Leaking inlet manifold or throttle body gasket (Chapter 4A).
- ☐ Leaking exhaust manifold gasket (Chapter 4A).
- ☐ Leaking vacuum hose (Chapters 4A, 4B and 9).
- ☐ Blowing cylinder head gasket (Chapter 2A).

Tapping or rattling noises

- ☐ Worn valve gear, timing chain, camshaft or hydraulic tappets (Chapter 2A).
- ☐ Ancillary component fault (water pump, alternator, etc) (Chapters 3, 5A, etc).

Knocking or thumping noises

- ☐ Worn big-end bearings (regular heavy knocking, perhaps less under load) (Chapter 2B).
- ☐ Worn main bearings (rumbling and knocking, perhaps worsening under load) (Chapter 2B).
- ☐ Piston slap (most noticeable when cold) (Chapter 2B).
- ☐ Ancillary component fault (water pump, alternator, etc) (Chapters 3, 5A, etc).

2 Cooling system

Overheating

- ☐ Auxiliary drivebelt broken - or, where applicable, incorrectly adjusted (Chapter 1).
- ☐ Insufficient coolant in system ("*Weekly checks*").
- ☐ Thermostat faulty (Chapter 3).
- ☐ Radiator core blocked, or grille restricted (Chapter 3).
- ☐ Electric cooling fan or thermostatic switch faulty (Chapter 3).
- ☐ Pressure cap faulty (Chapter 3).
- ☐ Ignition timing incorrect, or ignition system fault (Chapters 1 and 5B).
- ☐ Inaccurate temperature gauge sender unit (Chapter 3).
- ☐ Airlock in cooling system (Chapter 1).

Overcooling

- ☐ Thermostat faulty (Chapter 3).
- ☐ Inaccurate temperature gauge sender unit (Chapter 3).

External coolant leakage

- ☐ Deteriorated or damaged hoses or hose clips (Chapter 1).
- ☐ Radiator core or heater matrix leaking (Chapter 3).
- ☐ Pressure cap faulty (Chapter 3).
- ☐ Water pump internal seal leaking (Chapter 3).
- ☐ Water pump-to-block O-ring or housing gasket leaking (Chapter 3).
- ☐ Boiling due to overheating (Chapter 3).
- ☐ Core plug leaking (Chapter 2B).

Internal coolant leakage

- ☐ Leaking cylinder head gasket (Chapter 2A).
- ☐ Cracked cylinder head or cylinder block (Chapter 2A or 2B).

Corrosion

- ☐ Infrequent draining and flushing (Chapter 1).
- ☐ Incorrect coolant mixture or inappropriate coolant type ("*Weekly checks*").

3 Fuel and exhaust systems

Excessive fuel consumption

- ☐ Air filter element dirty or clogged (Chapter 1).
- ☐ Fuel injection system fault (Chapter 4A).
- ☐ Ignition timing incorrect or ignition system fault (Chapters 1 and 5B).
- ☐ Brakes binding (Chapter 9).
- ☐ Tyres under-inflated ("*Weekly checks*").

Fuel leakage and/or fuel odour

- ☐ Damaged fuel tank, pipes or connections (Chapters 1 and 4A).

Excessive noise or fumes from exhaust system

- ☐ Leaking exhaust system or manifold joints (Chapters 1 and 4A).
- ☐ Leaking, corroded or damaged silencers or pipe (Chapters 1 and 4A).
- ☐ Broken mountings causing body or suspension contact (Chapter 4A).

4 Clutch

Pedal travels to floor - no pressure or very little resistance

- ☐ Broken/worn clutch cable (Chapter 6).
- ☐ Broken clutch release bearing or fork (Chapter 6).
- ☐ Broken diaphragm spring in clutch pressure plate (Chapter 6).

Clutch fails to disengage (unable to select gears)

- ☐ Broken/worn clutch cable (Chapter 6).
- ☐ Clutch disc sticking on gearbox input shaft splines (Chapter 6).
- ☐ Clutch disc sticking to flywheel or pressure plate (Chapter 6).
- ☐ Faulty pressure plate assembly (Chapter 6).
- ☐ Clutch release mechanism worn or incorrectly assembled (Chapter 6).

Clutch slips (engine speed increases, with no increase in vehicle speed)

- ☐ Clutch disc linings excessively worn (Chapter 6).
- ☐ Clutch disc linings contaminated with oil or grease (Chapter 6).
- ☐ Faulty pressure plate or weak diaphragm spring (Chapter 6).

Judder as clutch is engaged

- ☐ Clutch disc linings contaminated with oil or grease (Chapter 6).
- ☐ Clutch disc linings excessively worn (Chapter 6).
- ☐ Faulty or distorted pressure plate or diaphragm spring (Chapter 6).
- ☐ Worn or loose engine or gearbox mountings (Chapter 2A or 2B).
- ☐ Clutch disc hub or gearbox input shaft splines worn (Chapter 6).

Noise when depressing or releasing clutch pedal

- ☐ Worn clutch release bearing (Chapter 6).
- ☐ Worn or dry clutch pedal bushes (Chapter 6).
- ☐ Faulty pressure plate assembly (Chapter 6).
- ☐ Pressure plate diaphragm spring broken (Chapter 6).
- ☐ Broken clutch disc cushioning springs (Chapter 6).

5 Manual transmission

Difficulty engaging gears

- ☐ Clutch fault (Chapter 6).
- ☐ Worn or damaged gear linkage (Chapter 7A).
- ☐ Incorrectly-adjusted gear linkage (Chapter 7A).
- ☐ Worn synchroniser units (Chapter 7A).*

Jumps out of gear

- ☐ Worn or damaged gear linkage (Chapter 7A).
- ☐ Incorrectly-adjusted gear linkage (Chapter 7A).
- ☐ Worn synchroniser units (Chapter 7A).*
- ☐ Worn selector forks (Chapter 7A).*

Vibration

- ☐ Lack of oil (Chapter 1).
- ☐ Worn bearings (Chapter 7A).*

Noisy in neutral with engine running

- ☐ Input shaft bearings worn (noise apparent with clutch pedal released, but not when depressed) (Chapter 7A).*
- ☐ Clutch release bearing worn (noise apparent with clutch pedal depressed, possibly less when released) (Chapter 6).

Noisy in one particular gear

- ☐ Worn, damaged or chipped gear teeth (Chapter 7A).*

Lubricant leaks

- ☐ Leaking oil seal (Chapter 7A).
- ☐ Leaking housing joint (Chapter 7A).*

**Although the corrective action necessary to remedy the symptoms described is beyond the scope of this manual, the above information should be helpful in isolating the cause of the condition, so that the owner can communicate clearly with a professional mechanic.*

6 Automatic transmission

Note: *Due to the complexity of the automatic transmission, it is difficult for the home mechanic to properly diagnose and service this unit. For problems other than the following, the vehicle should be taken to a dealer service department or automatic transmission specialist.*

Fluid leakage

- ☐ Automatic transmission fluid is usually deep red in colour. Fluid leaks should not be confused with engine oil, which can easily be blown onto the transmission by air flow.
- ☐ To determine the source of a leak, first remove all built-up dirt and grime from the transmission housing and surrounding areas, using a degreasing agent or by steam-cleaning. Drive the vehicle at low speed, so that air flow will not blow the leak far from its source. Raise and support the vehicle, and determine where the leak is coming from. The following are common areas of leakage.

a) Fluid pan (transmission "sump").
b) Dipstick tube (Chapter 1).
c) Transmission-to-fluid cooler fluid pipes/unions (Chapter 7B).

Transmission fluid brown, or has burned smell

- ☐ Transmission fluid level low, or fluid in need of renewal (Chapter 1).

General gear selection problems

- ☐ The most likely cause of gear selection problems is a faulty or poorly-adjusted gear selector mechanism. The following are common problems associated with a faulty selector mechanism.

a) Engine starting in gears other than Park or Neutral.
b) Indicator on gear selector lever pointing to a gear other than the one actually being used.
c) Vehicle moves when in Park or Neutral.
d) Poor gear shift quality, or erratic gear changes.

- ☐ Refer any problems to a Saab dealer, or an automatic transmission specialist.

Transmission will not downshift (kickdown) with accelerator pedal fully depressed

- ☐ Low transmission fluid level (Chapter 1).
- ☐ Incorrect selector cable adjustment (Chapter 7B).

Engine will not start in any gear, or starts in gears other than Park or Neutral

- ☐ Incorrect starter inhibitor switch adjustment - where applicable (Chapter 7B).
- ☐ Incorrect selector cable adjustment (Chapter 7B).

Transmission slips, shifts roughly, is noisy, or has no drive in forward or reverse gears

- ☐ There are many probable causes for the above problems, but the home mechanic should be concerned with only one possibility - incorrect transmission fluid level. Before taking the vehicle to a dealer or transmission specialist, check the fluid level and condition of the fluid as described in Chapter 1. Correct the fluid level as necessary, or change the fluid and filter if needed. If the problem persists, professional help will be necessary.

7 Driveshafts

Clicking or knocking noise on turns (at slow speed on full-lock)

- ☐ Lack of constant velocity joint lubricant, possibly due to damaged gaiter (Chapter 8).
- ☐ Worn outer constant velocity joint (Chapter 8).

Vibration when accelerating or decelerating

- ☐ Worn inner constant velocity joint (Chapter 8).
- ☐ Bent or distorted driveshaft (Chapter 8).

8 Braking system

Note: *Before assuming that a brake problem exists, make sure that the tyres are in good condition and correctly inflated, that the front wheel alignment is correct, and that the vehicle is not loaded with weight in an unequal manner. Apart from checking the condition of all pipe and hose connections, any faults occurring on the anti-lock braking system should be referred to a Saab dealer for diagnosis.*

Vehicle pulls to one side under braking

- ☐ Worn, defective, damaged or contaminated front or rear brake pads on one side (Chapters 1 and 9).
- ☐ Seized or partially-seized front or rear brake caliper piston (Chapter 9).
- ☐ A mixture of brake pad lining materials fitted between sides (Chapter 9).
- ☐ Brake caliper mounting bolts loose (Chapter 9).
- ☐ Worn or damaged steering or suspension components (Chapters 1 and 10).

Noise (grinding or high-pitched squeal) when brakes applied

- ☐ Brake pad friction lining material worn down to metal backing (Chapters 1 and 9).
- ☐ Excessive corrosion of brake disc - may be apparent after the vehicle has been standing for some time (Chapters 1 and 9).

Brake pedal feels spongy when depressed

- ☐ Air in hydraulic system (Chapter 9).
- ☐ Deteriorated flexible rubber brake hoses (Chapters 1 and 9).
- ☐ Master cylinder mountings loose (Chapter 9).
- ☐ Faulty master cylinder (Chapter 9).

Excessive brake pedal travel

- ☐ Faulty master cylinder (Chapter 9).
- ☐ Air in hydraulic system (Chapter 9).
- ☐ Faulty vacuum servo unit (Chapter 9).

Excessive brake pedal effort required to stop vehicle

- ☐ Air in hydraulic system (Chapter 9).
- ☐ Brake fluid requires renewal (Chapter 1).
- ☐ Faulty vacuum servo unit (Chapter 9).
- ☐ Disconnected, damaged or insecure brake servo vacuum hose (Chapters 1 and 9).
- ☐ Primary or secondary hydraulic circuit failure (Chapter 9).
- ☐ Seized brake caliper piston(s) (Chapter 9).
- ☐ Brake pads incorrectly fitted (Chapter 9).
- ☐ Incorrect grade of brake pads fitted (Chapter 9).
- ☐ Brake pads contaminated (Chapter 9).

Judder felt through brake pedal or steering wheel when braking

- ☐ Excessive run-out or distortion of brake disc(s) (Chapter 9).
- ☐ Brake pad linings worn (Chapters 1 and 9).
- ☐ Brake caliper mounting bolts loose (Chapter 9).
- ☐ Wear in suspension or steering components or mountings (Chapters 1 and 10).

Brakes binding

- ☐ Seized brake caliper piston(s) (Chapter 9).
- ☐ Incorrectly-adjusted handbrake mechanism (Chapter 9).
- ☐ Faulty master cylinder (Chapter 9).

Rear wheels locking under normal braking

- ☐ Seized brake caliper piston(s) (Chapter 9).
- ☐ Faulty brake pressure regulator (Chapter 9).

9 Suspension and steering

Note: *Before diagnosing suspension or steering faults, be sure that the trouble is not due to incorrect tyre pressures, mixtures of tyre types, or binding brakes.*

Vehicle pulls to one side

- ☐ Defective tyre ("*Weekly checks*").
- ☐ Excessive wear in suspension or steering components (Chapters 1 and 10).
- ☐ Incorrect front wheel alignment (Chapter 10).
- ☐ Accident damage to steering or suspension components (Chapters 1 and 10).

Wheel wobble and vibration

- ☐ Front roadwheels out of balance (vibration felt mainly through the steering wheel) ("*Weekly checks*").
- ☐ Rear roadwheels out of balance (vibration felt throughout the vehicle) ("*Weekly checks*").
- ☐ Roadwheels damaged or distorted ("*Weekly checks*").
- ☐ Faulty or damaged tyre ("*Weekly checks*").
- ☐ Worn steering or suspension joints, bushes or components (Chapters 1 and 10).
- ☐ Wheel bolts loose.

Excessive pitching and/or rolling around corners, or during braking

- ☐ Defective shock absorbers (Chapters 1 and 10).
- ☐ Broken or weak coil spring and/or suspension component (Chapters 1 and 10).
- ☐ Worn or damaged anti-roll bar or mountings (Chapter 10).

Wandering or general instability

- ☐ Incorrect front wheel alignment (Chapter 10).
- ☐ Worn steering or suspension joints, bushes or components (Chapters 1 and 10).
- ☐ Roadwheels out of balance ("*Weekly checks*").
- ☐ Faulty or damaged tyre ("*Weekly checks*").
- ☐ Wheel bolts loose.
- ☐ Defective shock absorbers (Chapters 1 and 10).

Excessively-stiff steering

- ☐ Lack of steering gear lubricant (Chapter 10).
- ☐ Seized track rod end balljoint or suspension balljoint (Chapters 1 and 10).
- ☐ Broken or incorrectly adjusted auxiliary drivebelt (Chapter 1).
- ☐ Incorrect front wheel alignment (Chapter 10).
- ☐ Steering rack or column bent or damaged (Chapter 10).

Suspension and steering (continued)

Excessive play in steering

- ☐ Worn steering column universal joint(s) (Chapter 10).
- ☐ Worn steering track rod end balljoints (Chapters 1 and 10).
- ☐ Worn rack-and-pinion steering gear (Chapter 10).
- ☐ Worn steering or suspension joints, bushes or components (Chapters 1 and 10).

Lack of power assistance

- ☐ Broken or incorrectly-adjusted auxiliary drivebelt (Chapter 1).
- ☐ Incorrect power steering fluid level ("*Weekly checks*").
- ☐ Restriction in power steering fluid hoses (Chapter 1).
- ☐ Faulty power steering pump (Chapter 10).
- ☐ Faulty rack-and-pinion steering gear (Chapter 10).

Tyre wear excessive

Tyres worn on inside or outside edges

- ☐ Tyres under-inflated (wear on both edges) ("*Weekly checks*").
- ☐ Incorrect camber or castor angles (wear on one edge only) (Chapter 10).
- ☐ Worn steering or suspension joints, bushes or components (Chapters 1 and 10).
- ☐ Excessively-hard cornering.
- ☐ Accident damage.

Tyre treads exhibit feathered edges

- ☐ Incorrect toe setting (Chapter 10).

Tyres worn in centre of tread

- ☐ Tyres over-inflated ("*Weekly checks*").

Tyres worn on inside and outside edges

- ☐ Tyres under-inflated ("*Weekly checks*").
- ☐ Worn shock absorbers (Chapters 1 and 10).

Tyres worn unevenly

- ☐ Tyres out of balance ("*Weekly checks*").
- ☐ Excessive wheel or tyre run-out ("*Weekly checks*").
- ☐ Worn shock absorbers (Chapters 1 and 10).
- ☐ Faulty tyre ("*Weekly checks*").

10 Electrical system

Note: *For problems associated with the starting system, refer to the faults listed under "Engine" earlier in this Section.*

Battery will not hold a charge for more than a few days

- ☐ Battery defective internally (Chapter 5A).
- ☐ Battery electrolyte level low - where applicable (Chapter 5A).
- ☐ Battery terminal connections loose or corroded ("*Weekly checks*").
- ☐ Auxiliary drivebelt worn (Chapter 1).
- ☐ Alternator not charging at correct output (Chapter 5A).
- ☐ Alternator or voltage regulator faulty (Chapter 5A).
- ☐ Short-circuit causing continual battery drain (Chapters 5A and 12).

Ignition/no-charge warning light remains illuminated with engine running

- ☐ Auxiliary drivebelt broken or worn (Chapter 1).
- ☐ Alternator brushes worn, sticking, or dirty (Chapter 5A).
- ☐ Alternator brush springs weak or broken (Chapter 5A).
- ☐ Internal fault in alternator or voltage regulator (Chapter 5A).
- ☐ Broken, disconnected, or loose wiring in charging circuit (Chapter 5A).

Ignition/no-charge warning light fails to come on

- ☐ Warning light bulb blown (Chapter 12).
- ☐ Broken, disconnected, or loose wiring in warning light circuit (Chapter 12).
- ☐ Alternator faulty (Chapter 5A).

Lights inoperative

- ☐ Bulb blown (Chapter 12).
- ☐ Corrosion of bulb or bulbholder contacts (Chapter 12).
- ☐ Blown fuse (Chapter 12).
- ☐ Faulty relay (Chapter 12).
- ☐ Broken, loose, or disconnected wiring (Chapter 12).
- ☐ Faulty switch (Chapter 12).

Instrument readings inaccurate or erratic

Instrument readings increase with engine speed

- ☐ Faulty voltage regulator (Chapter 12).

Fuel or temperature gauges give no reading

- ☐ Faulty gauge sender unit (Chapters 3 and 4).
- ☐ Wiring open-circuit (Chapter 12).
- ☐ Faulty gauge (Chapter 12).

Fuel or temperature gauges give continuous maximum reading

- ☐ Faulty gauge sender unit (Chapters 3 and 4).
- ☐ Wiring short-circuit (Chapter 12).
- ☐ Faulty gauge (Chapter 12).

Horn inoperative, or unsatisfactory in operation

Horn operates all the time

- ☐ Horn contacts permanently bridged or horn push stuck down (Chapter 12).

Horn fails to operate

- ☐ Blown fuse (Chapter 12).
- ☐ Cable or cable connections loose, broken or disconnected (Chapter 12).
- ☐ Faulty horn (Chapter 12).

Horn emits intermittent or unsatisfactory sound

- ☐ Cable connections loose (Chapter 12).
- ☐ Horn mountings loose (Chapter 12).
- ☐ Faulty horn (Chapter 12).

Windscreen/tailgate wipers inoperative, or unsatisfactory in operation

Wipers fail to operate, or operate very slowly

- ☐ Wiper blades stuck to screen, or linkage seized or binding ("*Weekly checks*" and Chapter 12).
- ☐ Blown fuse (Chapter 12).
- ☐ Cable or cable connections loose, broken or disconnected (Chapter 12).
- ☐ Faulty relay (Chapter 12).
- ☐ Faulty wiper motor (Chapter 12).

Wiper blades sweep over too large or too small an area of the glass

- ☐ Wiper arms incorrectly positioned on spindles (Chapter 12).
- ☐ Excessive wear of wiper linkage (Chapter 12).
- ☐ Wiper motor or linkage mountings loose or insecure (Chapter 12).

Wiper blades fail to clean the glass effectively

- ☐ Wiper blade rubbers worn or perished ("*Weekly checks*").
- ☐ Wiper arm tension springs broken, or arm pivots seized (Chapter 12).
- ☐ Insufficient windscreen washer additive to adequately remove road film ("*Weekly checks*").

Electrical system (continued)

Windscreen/tailgate washers inoperative, or unsatisfactory in operation

One or more washer jets inoperative

- ☐ Blocked washer jet.
- ☐ Disconnected, kinked or restricted fluid hose (Chapter 12).
- ☐ Insufficient fluid in washer reservoir ("*Weekly checks*").

Washer pump fails to operate

- ☐ Broken or disconnected wiring or connections (Chapter 12).
- ☐ Blown fuse (Chapter 12).
- ☐ Faulty washer switch (Chapter 12).
- ☐ Faulty washer pump (Chapter 12).

Washer pump runs for some time before fluid is emitted from jets

- ☐ Faulty one-way valve in fluid supply hose (Chapter 12).

Electric windows inoperative, or unsatisfactory in operation

Window glass will only move in one direction

- ☐ Faulty switch (Chapter 12).

Window glass slow to move

- ☐ Regulator seized or damaged, or in need of lubrication (Chapter 11).
- ☐ Door internal components or trim fouling regulator (Chapter 11).
- ☐ Faulty motor (Chapter 11).

Window glass fails to move

- ☐ Blown fuse (Chapter 12).
- ☐ Regulator seized or jammed (Chapter 12)
- ☐ Faulty relay (Chapter 12).
- ☐ Broken or disconnected wiring or connections (Chapter 12).
- ☐ Faulty motor (Chapter 11).

Central locking system inoperative, or unsatisfactory in operation

Complete system failure

- ☐ Blown fuse (Chapter 12).
- ☐ Faulty relay (Chapter 12).
- ☐ Broken or disconnected wiring or connections (Chapter 12).

A

ABS (Anti-lock brake system) A system, usually electronically controlled, that senses incipient wheel lockup during braking and relieves hydraulic pressure at wheels that are about to skid.
Air bag An inflatable bag hidden in the steering wheel (driver's side) or the dash or glovebox (passenger side). In a head-on collision, the bags inflate, preventing the driver and front passenger from being thrown forward into the steering wheel or windscreen.
Air cleaner A metal or plastic housing, containing a filter element, which removes dust and dirt from the air being drawn into the engine.
Air filter element The actual filter in an air cleaner system, usually manufactured from pleated paper and requiring renewal at regular intervals.

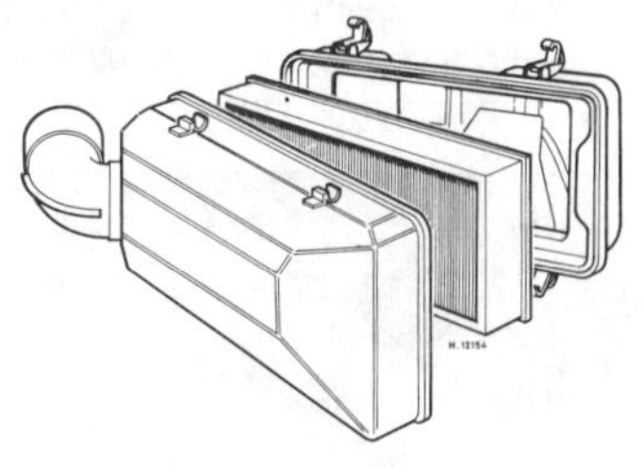

Air filter

Allen key A hexagonal wrench which fits into a recessed hexagonal hole.
Alligator clip A long-nosed spring-loaded metal clip with meshing teeth. Used to make temporary electrical connections.
Alternator A component in the electrical system which converts mechanical energy from a drivebelt into electrical energy to charge the battery and to operate the starting system, ignition system and electrical accessories.
Ampere (amp) A unit of measurement for the flow of electric current. One amp is the amount of current produced by one volt acting through a resistance of one ohm.
Anaerobic sealer A substance used to prevent bolts and screws from loosening. Anaerobic means that it does not require oxygen for activation. The Loctite brand is widely used.
Antifreeze A substance (usually ethylene glycol) mixed with water, and added to a vehicle's cooling system, to prevent freezing of the coolant in winter. Antifreeze also contains chemicals to inhibit corrosion and the formation of rust and other deposits that would tend to clog the radiator and coolant passages and reduce cooling efficiency.
Anti-seize compound A coating that reduces the risk of seizing on fasteners that are subjected to high temperatures, such as exhaust manifold bolts and nuts.
Asbestos A natural fibrous mineral with great heat resistance, commonly used in the composition of brake friction materials. Asbestos is a health hazard and the dust created by brake systems should never be inhaled or ingested.
Axle A shaft on which a wheel revolves, or which revolves with a wheel. Also, a solid beam that connects the two wheels at one end of the vehicle. An axle which also transmits power to the wheels is known as a live axle.
Axleshaft A single rotating shaft, on either side of the differential, which delivers power from the final drive assembly to the drive wheels. Also called a driveshaft or a halfshaft.

B

Ball bearing An anti-friction bearing consisting of a hardened inner and outer race with hardened steel balls between two races.
Bearing The curved surface on a shaft or in a bore, or the part assembled into either, that permits relative motion between them with minimum wear and friction.

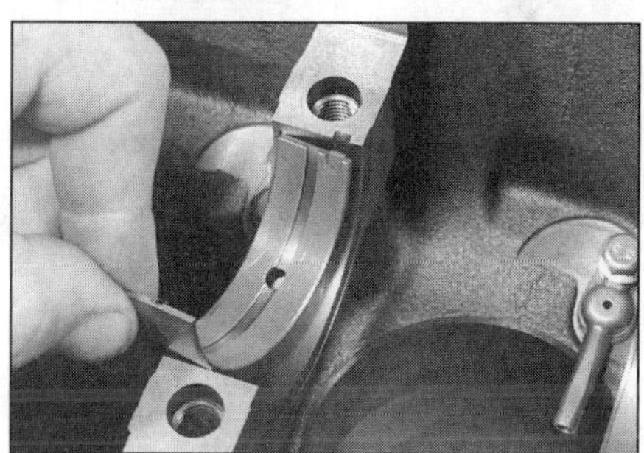

Bearing

Big-end bearing The bearing in the end of the connecting rod that's attached to the crankshaft.
Bleed nipple A valve on a brake wheel cylinder, caliper or other hydraulic component that is opened to purge the hydraulic system of air. Also called a bleed screw.
Brake bleeding Procedure for removing air from lines of a hydraulic brake system.

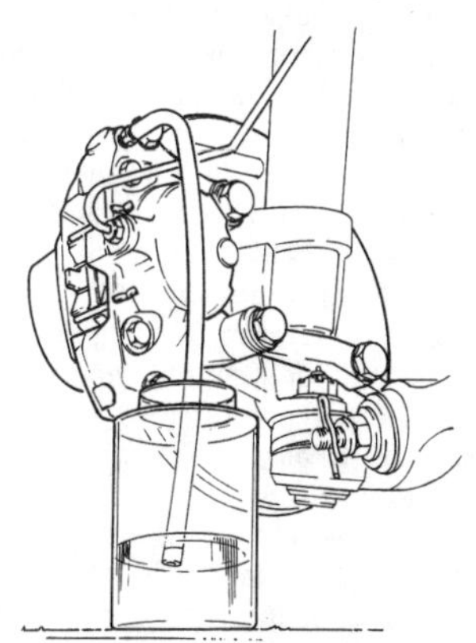

Brake bleeding

Brake disc The component of a disc brake that rotates with the wheels.
Brake drum The component of a drum brake that rotates with the wheels.
Brake linings The friction material which contacts the brake disc or drum to retard the vehicle's speed. The linings are bonded or riveted to the brake pads or shoes.
Brake pads The replaceable friction pads that pinch the brake disc when the brakes are applied. Brake pads consist of a friction material bonded or riveted to a rigid backing plate.
Brake shoe The crescent-shaped carrier to which the brake linings are mounted and which forces the lining against the rotating drum during braking.
Braking systems For more information on braking systems, consult the *Haynes Automotive Brake Manual*.
Breaker bar A long socket wrench handle providing greater leverage.
Bulkhead The insulated partition between the engine and the passenger compartment.

C

Caliper The non-rotating part of a disc-brake assembly that straddles the disc and carries the brake pads. The caliper also contains the hydraulic components that cause the pads to pinch the disc when the brakes are applied. A caliper is also a measuring tool that can be set to measure inside or outside dimensions of an object.
Camshaft A rotating shaft on which a series of cam lobes operate the valve mechanisms. The camshaft may be driven by gears, by sprockets and chain or by sprockets and a belt.
Canister A container in an evaporative emission control system; contains activated charcoal granules to trap vapours from the fuel system.

Canister

Carburettor A device which mixes fuel with air in the proper proportions to provide a desired power output from a spark ignition internal combustion engine.
Castellated Resembling the parapets along the top of a castle wall. For example, a castellated balljoint stud nut.
Castor In wheel alignment, the backward or forward tilt of the steering axis. Castor is positive when the steering axis is inclined rearward at the top.

Catalytic converter A silencer-like device in the exhaust system which converts certain pollutants in the exhaust gases into less harmful substances.

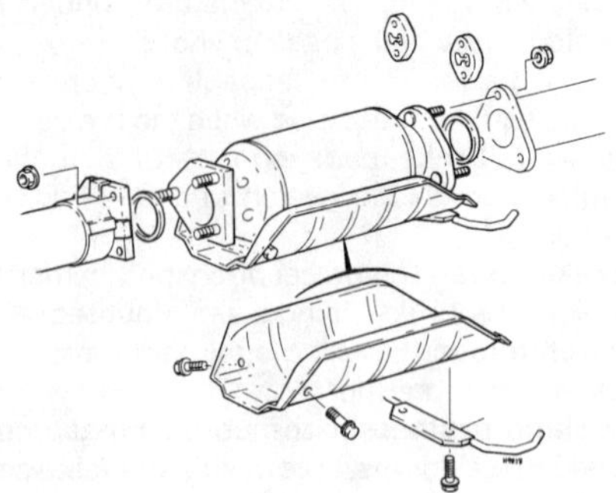

Catalytic converter

Circlip A ring-shaped clip used to prevent endwise movement of cylindrical parts and shafts. An internal circlip is installed in a groove in a housing; an external circlip fits into a groove on the outside of a cylindrical piece such as a shaft.

Clearance The amount of space between two parts. For example, between a piston and a cylinder, between a bearing and a journal, etc.

Coil spring A spiral of elastic steel found in various sizes throughout a vehicle, for example as a springing medium in the suspension and in the valve train.

Compression Reduction in volume, and increase in pressure and temperature, of a gas, caused by squeezing it into a smaller space.

Compression ratio The relationship between cylinder volume when the piston is at top dead centre and cylinder volume when the piston is at bottom dead centre.

Constant velocity (CV) joint A type of universal joint that cancels out vibrations caused by driving power being transmitted through an angle.

Core plug A disc or cup-shaped metal device inserted in a hole in a casting through which core was removed when the casting was formed. Also known as a freeze plug or expansion plug.

Crankcase The lower part of the engine block in which the crankshaft rotates.

Crankshaft The main rotating member, or shaft, running the length of the crankcase, with offset "throws" to which the connecting rods are attached.

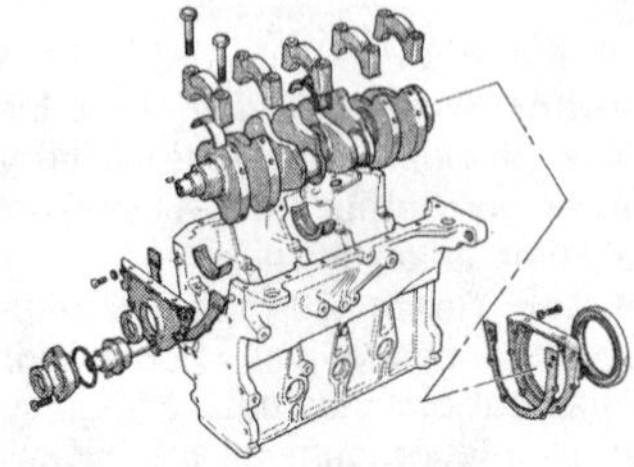

Crankshaft assembly

Crocodile clip See Alligator clip

D

Diagnostic code Code numbers obtained by accessing the diagnostic mode of an engine management computer. This code can be used to determine the area in the system where a malfunction may be located.

Disc brake A brake design incorporating a rotating disc onto which brake pads are squeezed. The resulting friction converts the energy of a moving vehicle into heat.

Double-overhead cam (DOHC) An engine that uses two overhead camshafts, usually one for the intake valves and one for the exhaust valves.

Drivebelt(s) The belt(s) used to drive accessories such as the alternator, water pump, power steering pump, air conditioning compressor, etc. off the crankshaft pulley.

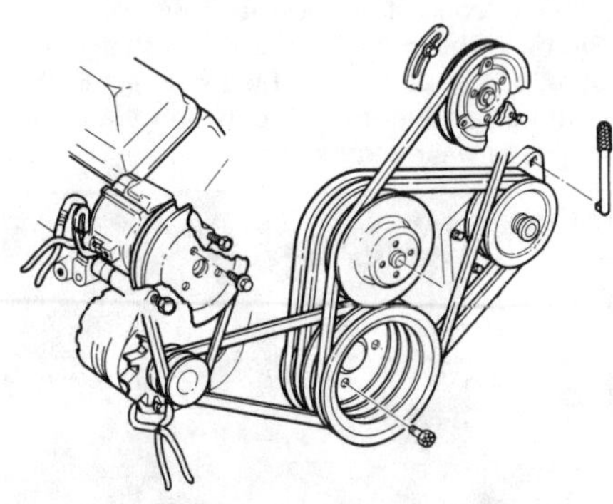

Accessory drivebelts

Driveshaft Any shaft used to transmit motion. Commonly used when referring to the axleshafts on a front wheel drive vehicle.

Drum brake A type of brake using a drum-shaped metal cylinder attached to the inner surface of the wheel. When the brake pedal is pressed, curved brake shoes with friction linings press against the inside of the drum to slow or stop the vehicle.

E

EGR valve A valve used to introduce exhaust gases into the intake air stream.

Electronic control unit (ECU) A computer which controls (for instance) ignition and fuel injection systems, or an anti-lock braking system. For more information refer to the *Haynes Automotive Electrical and Electronic Systems Manual.*

Electronic Fuel Injection (EFI) A computer controlled fuel system that distributes fuel through an injector located in each intake port of the engine.

Emergency brake A braking system, independent of the main hydraulic system, that can be used to slow or stop the vehicle if the primary brakes fail, or to hold the vehicle stationary even though the brake pedal isn't depressed. It usually consists of a hand lever that actuates either front or rear brakes mechanically through a series of cables and linkages. Also known as a handbrake or parking brake.

Endfloat The amount of lengthwise movement between two parts. As applied to a crankshaft, the distance that the crankshaft can move forward and back in the cylinder block.

Engine management system (EMS) A computer controlled system which manages the fuel injection and the ignition systems in an integrated fashion.

Exhaust manifold A part with several passages through which exhaust gases leave the engine combustion chambers and enter the exhaust pipe.

F

Fan clutch A viscous (fluid) drive coupling device which permits variable engine fan speeds in relation to engine speeds.

Feeler blade A thin strip or blade of hardened steel, ground to an exact thickness, used to check or measure clearances between parts.

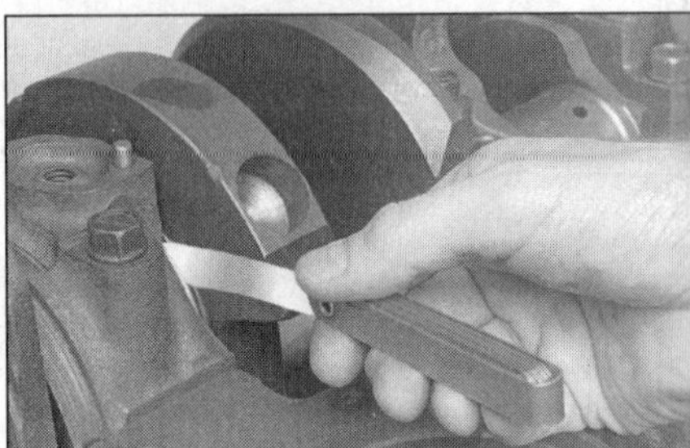

Feeler blade

Firing order The order in which the engine cylinders fire, or deliver their power strokes, beginning with the number one cylinder.

Flywheel A heavy spinning wheel in which energy is absorbed and stored by means of momentum. On cars, the flywheel is attached to the crankshaft to smooth out firing impulses.

Free play The amount of travel before any action takes place. The "looseness" in a linkage, or an assembly of parts, between the initial application of force and actual movement. For example, the distance the brake pedal moves before the pistons in the master cylinder are actuated.

Fuse An electrical device which protects a circuit against accidental overload. The typical fuse contains a soft piece of metal which is calibrated to melt at a predetermined current flow (expressed as amps) and break the circuit.

Fusible link A circuit protection device consisting of a conductor surrounded by heat-resistant insulation. The conductor is smaller than the wire it protects, so it acts as the weakest link in the circuit. Unlike a blown fuse, a failed fusible link must frequently be cut from the wire for replacement.

G

Gap The distance the spark must travel in jumping from the centre electrode to the side electrode in a spark plug. Also refers to the spacing between the points in a contact breaker assembly in a conventional points-type ignition, or to the distance between the reluctor or rotor and the pickup coil in an electronic ignition.

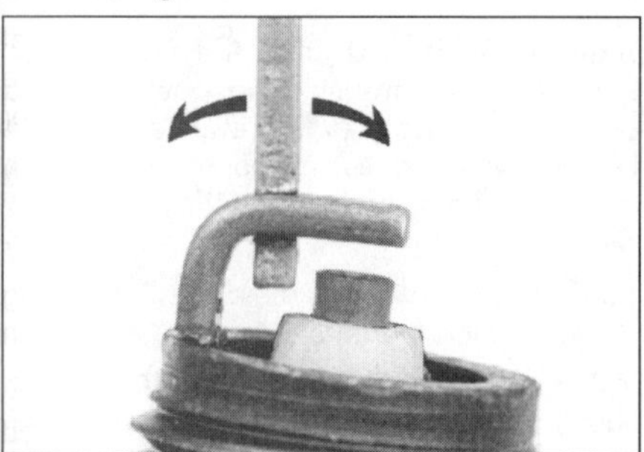

Adjusting spark plug gap

Gasket Any thin, soft material - usually cork, cardboard, asbestos or soft metal - installed between two metal surfaces to ensure a good seal. For instance, the cylinder head gasket seals the joint between the block and the cylinder head.

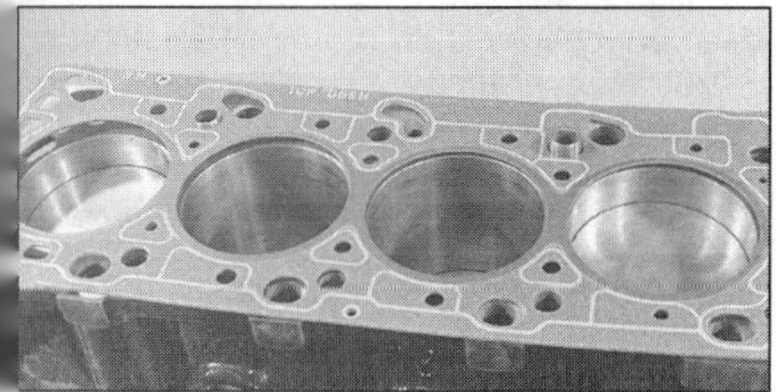

Gasket

Gauge An instrument panel display used to monitor engine conditions. A gauge with a movable pointer on a dial or a fixed scale is an analogue gauge. A gauge with a numerical readout is called a digital gauge.

H

Halfshaft A rotating shaft that transmits power from the final drive unit to a drive wheel, usually when referring to a live rear axle.
Harmonic balancer A device designed to reduce torsion or twisting vibration in the crankshaft. May be incorporated in the crankshaft pulley. Also known as a vibration damper.
Hone An abrasive tool for correcting small irregularities or differences in diameter in an engine cylinder, brake cylinder, etc.
Hydraulic tappet A tappet that utilises hydraulic pressure from the engine's lubrication system to maintain zero clearance (constant contact with both camshaft and valve stem). Automatically adjusts to variation in valve stem length. Hydraulic tappets also reduce valve noise.

I

Ignition timing The moment at which the spark plug fires, usually expressed in the number of crankshaft degrees before the piston reaches the top of its stroke.
Inlet manifold A tube or housing with passages through which flows the air-fuel mixture (carburettor vehicles and vehicles with throttle body injection) or air only (port fuel-injected vehicles) to the port openings in the cylinder head.

J

Jump start Starting the engine of a vehicle with a discharged or weak battery by attaching jump leads from the weak battery to a charged or helper battery.

L

Load Sensing Proportioning Valve (LSPV) A brake hydraulic system control valve that works like a proportioning valve, but also takes into consideration the amount of weight carried by the rear axle.
Locknut A nut used to lock an adjustment nut, or other threaded component, in place. For example, a locknut is employed to keep the adjusting nut on the rocker arm in position.
Lockwasher A form of washer designed to prevent an attaching nut from working loose.

M

MacPherson strut A type of front suspension system devised by Earle MacPherson at Ford of England. In its original form, a simple lateral link with the anti-roll bar creates the lower control arm. A long strut - an integral coil spring and shock absorber - is mounted between the body and the steering knuckle. Many modern so-called MacPherson strut systems use a conventional lower A-arm and don't rely on the anti-roll bar for location.
Multimeter An electrical test instrument with the capability to measure voltage, current and resistance.

N

NOx Oxides of Nitrogen. A common toxic pollutant emitted by petrol and diesel engines at higher temperatures.

O

Ohm The unit of electrical resistance. One volt applied to a resistance of one ohm will produce a current of one amp.
Ohmmeter An instrument for measuring electrical resistance.
O-ring A type of sealing ring made of a special rubber-like material; in use, the O-ring is compressed into a groove to provide the sealing action.
Overhead cam (ohc) engine An engine with the camshaft(s) located on top of the cylinder head(s).
Overhead valve (ohv) engine An engine with the valves located in the cylinder head, but with the camshaft located in the engine block.
Oxygen sensor A device installed in the engine exhaust manifold, which senses the oxygen content in the exhaust and converts this information into an electric current. Also called a Lambda sensor.

P

Phillips screw A type of screw head having a cross instead of a slot for a corresponding type of screwdriver.
Plastigage A thin strip of plastic thread, available in different sizes, used for measuring clearances. For example, a strip of Plastigage is laid across a bearing journal. The parts are assembled and dismantled; the width of the crushed strip indicates the clearance between journal and bearing.

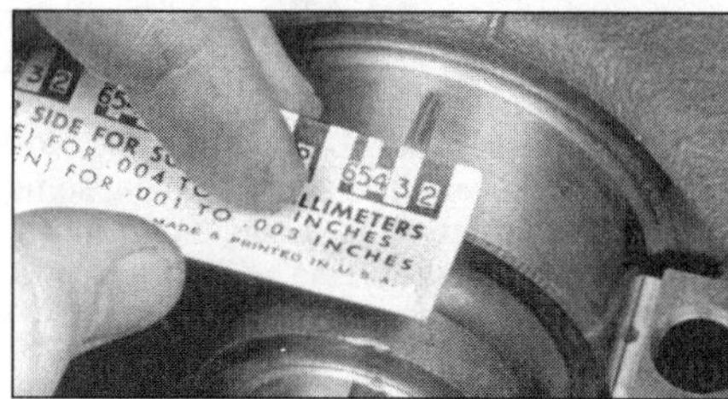

Plastigage

Propeller shaft The long hollow tube with universal joints at both ends that carries power from the transmission to the differential on front-engined rear wheel drive vehicles.
Proportioning valve A hydraulic control valve which limits the amount of pressure to the rear brakes during panic stops to prevent wheel lock-up.

R

Rack-and-pinion steering A steering system with a pinion gear on the end of the steering shaft that mates with a rack (think of a geared wheel opened up and laid flat). When the steering wheel is turned, the pinion turns, moving the rack to the left or right. This movement is transmitted through the track rods to the steering arms at the wheels.
Radiator A liquid-to-air heat transfer device designed to reduce the temperature of the coolant in an internal combustion engine cooling system.
Refrigerant Any substance used as a heat transfer agent in an air-conditioning system. R-12 has been the principle refrigerant for many years; recently, however, manufacturers have begun using R-134a, a non-CFC substance that is considered less harmful to the ozone in the upper atmosphere.
Rocker arm A lever arm that rocks on a shaft or pivots on a stud. In an overhead valve engine, the rocker arm converts the upward movement of the pushrod into a downward movement to open a valve.

Rotor In a distributor, the rotating device inside the cap that connects the centre electrode and the outer terminals as it turns, distributing the high voltage from the coil secondary winding to the proper spark plug. Also, that part of an alternator which rotates inside the stator. Also, the rotating assembly of a turbocharger, including the compressor wheel, shaft and turbine wheel.

Runout The amount of wobble (in-and-out movement) of a gear or wheel as it's rotated. The amount a shaft rotates "out-of-true." The out-of-round condition of a rotating part.

S

Sealant A liquid or paste used to prevent leakage at a joint. Sometimes used in conjunction with a gasket.

Sealed beam lamp An older headlight design which integrates the reflector, lens and filaments into a hermetically-sealed one-piece unit. When a filament burns out or the lens cracks, the entire unit is simply replaced.

Serpentine drivebelt A single, long, wide accessory drivebelt that's used on some newer vehicles to drive all the accessories, instead of a series of smaller, shorter belts. Serpentine drivebelts are usually tensioned by an automatic tensioner.

Serpentine drivebelt

Shim Thin spacer, commonly used to adjust the clearance or relative positions between two parts. For example, shims inserted into or under bucket tappets control valve clearances. Clearance is adjusted by changing the thickness of the shim.

Slide hammer A special puller that screws into or hooks onto a component such as a shaft or bearing; a heavy sliding handle on the shaft bottoms against the end of the shaft to knock the component free.

Sprocket A tooth or projection on the periphery of a wheel, shaped to engage with a chain or drivebelt. Commonly used to refer to the sprocket wheel itself.

Starter inhibitor switch On vehicles with an automatic transmission, a switch that prevents starting if the vehicle is not in Neutral or Park.

Strut See MacPherson strut.

T

Tappet A cylindrical component which transmits motion from the cam to the valve stem, either directly or via a pushrod and rocker arm. Also called a cam follower.

Thermostat A heat-controlled valve that regulates the flow of coolant between the cylinder block and the radiator, so maintaining optimum engine operating temperature. A thermostat is also used in some air cleaners in which the temperature is regulated.

Thrust bearing The bearing in the clutch assembly that is moved in to the release levers by clutch pedal action to disengage the clutch. Also referred to as a release bearing.

Timing belt A toothed belt which drives the camshaft. Serious engine damage may result if it breaks in service.

Timing chain A chain which drives the camshaft.

Toe-in The amount the front wheels are closer together at the front than at the rear. On rear wheel drive vehicles, a slight amount of toe-in is usually specified to keep the front wheels running parallel on the road by offsetting other forces that tend to spread the wheels apart.

Toe-out The amount the front wheels are closer together at the rear than at the front. On front wheel drive vehicles, a slight amount of toe-out is usually specified.

Tools For full information on choosing and using tools, refer to the *Haynes Automotive Tools Manual.*

Tracer A stripe of a second colour applied to a wire insulator to distinguish that wire from another one with the same colour insulator.

Tune-up A process of accurate and careful adjustments and parts replacement to obtain the best possible engine performance.

Turbocharger A centrifugal device, driven by exhaust gases, that pressurises the intake air. Normally used to increase the power output from a given engine displacement, but can also be used primarily to reduce exhaust emissions (as on VW's "Umwelt" Diesel engine).

U

Universal joint or U-joint A double-pivoted connection for transmitting power from a driving to a driven shaft through an angle. A U-joint consists of two Y-shaped yokes and a cross-shaped member called the spider.

V

Valve A device through which the flow of liquid, gas, vacuum, or loose material in bulk may be started, stopped, or regulated by a movable part that opens, shuts, or partially obstructs one or more ports or passageways. A valve is also the movable part of such a device.

Valve clearance The clearance between the valve tip (the end of the valve stem) and the rocker arm or tappet. The valve clearance is measured when the valve is closed.

Vernier caliper A precision measuring instrument that measures inside and outside dimensions. Not quite as accurate as a micrometer, but more convenient.

Viscosity The thickness of a liquid or its resistance to flow.

Volt A unit for expressing electrical "pressure" in a circuit. One volt that will produce a current of one ampere through a resistance of one ohm.

W

Welding Various processes used to join metal items by heating the areas to be joined to a molten state and fusing them together. For more information refer to the *Haynes Automotive Welding Manual.*

Wiring diagram A drawing portraying the components and wires in a vehicle's electrical system, using standardised symbols. For more information refer to the *Haynes Automotive Electrical and Electronic Systems Manual.*

Note: *References throughout this index are in the form - "**Chapter number**" • "**Page number**"*

R

S

T

U

V

W

Haynes Manuals – The Complete List

Title	Book No.
ALFA ROMEO	
Alfa Romeo Alfasud/Sprint (74 - 88) up to F	**0292**
Alfa Romeo Alfetta (73 - 87) up to E	**0531**
ALFA ROMEO	
Audi 80 (72 - Feb 79) up to T	**0207**
Audi 80, 90 (79 - Oct 86) up to D & Coupe (81 - Nov 88) up to F	**0605**
Audi 80, 90 (Oct 86 - 90) D to H & Coupe (Nov 88 - 90) F to H	**1491**
Audi 100 (Oct 82 - 90) up to H & 200 (Feb 84 - Oct 89) A to G	**0907**
Audi 100 & A6 Petrol & Diesel (May 91 - May 97) H to P	**3504**
Audi A4 (95 - Feb 00) M to V	**3575**
AUSTIN	
Austin/MG/Rover Maestro 1.3 & 1.6 (83 - 95) up to M	**0922**
Austin/MG Metro (80 - May 90) up to G	**0718**
Austin/Rover Montego 1.3 & 1.6 (84 - 94) A to L	**1066**
Austin/MG/Rover Montego 2.0 (84 - 95) A to M	**1067**
Mini (59 - 69) up to H	**0527**
Mini (69 - Oct 96) up to P	**0646**
Austin/Rover 2.0 litre Diesel Engine (86 - 93) C to L	**1857**
BEDFORD	
Bedford CF (69 - 87) up to E	**0163**
Bedford/Vauxhall Rascal & Suzuki Supercarry (86 - Oct 94) C to M	**3015**
BMW	
BMW 316, 320 & 320i (4-cyl) (75 - Feb 83) up to Y	**0276**
BMW 320, 320i, 323i & 325i (6-cyl) (Oct 77 - Sept 87) up to E	**0815**
BMW 3-Series (Apr 91 - 96) H to N	**3210**
BMW 3- & 5-Series (sohc) (81 - 91) up to J	**1948**
BMW 520i & 525e (Oct 81 - June 88) up to E	**1560**
BMW 525, 528 & 528i (73 - Sept 81) up to X	**0632**
CITROEN	
Citroën 2CV, Ami & Dyane (67 - 90) up to H	**0196**
Citroën AX Petrol & Diesel (87 - 97) D to P	**3014**
Citroën BX (83 - 94) A to L	**0908**
Citroën C15 Van Petrol & Diesel (89 - Oct 98) F to S	**3509**
Citroën CX (75 - 88) up to F	**0528**
Citroën Saxo Petrol & Diesel (96 - 98) N to S	**3506**
Citroën Visa (79 - 88) up to F	**0620**
Citroën Xantia Petrol & Diesel (93 - 98) K to S	**3082**
Citroën XM Petrol & Diesel (89 - 98) G to R	**3451**
Citroën ZX Diesel (91 - 93) J to L	**1922**
Citroën ZX Petrol (91 - 94) H to M	**1881**
Citroën 1.7 & 1.9 litre Diesel Engine (84 - 96) A to N	**1379**
COLT	
Colt/Mitsubishi 1200, 1250 & 1400 (79 - May 84) up to A	**0600**
FIAT	
Fiat 500 (57 - 73) up to M	**0090**
Fiat Cinquecento (93 - 98) K to R	**3501**
Fiat Panda (81 - 95) up to M	**0793**
Fiat Punto Petrol & Diesel (94 - Oct 99) L to V	**3251**
Fiat Regata (84 - 88) A to F	**1167**

Title	Book No.
Fiat Tipo (88 - 91) E to J	**1625**
Fiat Uno (83 - 95) up to M	**0923**
Fiat X1/9 (74 - 89) up to G	**0273**
FORD	
Ford Capri II (& III) 1.6 & 2.0 (74 - 87) up to E	**0283**
Ford Capri II (& III) 2.8 & 3.0 (74 - 87) up to E	**1309**
Ford Cortina Mk IV (& V) 1.6 & 2.0 (76 - 83) up to A	**0343**
Ford Escort (75 - Aug 80) up to V	**0280**
Ford Escort (Sept 80 - Sept 90) up to H	**0686**
Ford Escort & Orion (Sept 90 - 97) H to P	**1737**
Ford Escort Mk II Mexico, RS 1600 & RS 2000 (75 - 80) up to W	**0735**
Ford Fiesta (76 - Aug 83) up to Y	**0334**
Ford Fiesta (Aug 83 - Feb 89) A to F	**1030**
Ford Fiesta (Feb 89 - Oct 95) F to N	**1595**
Ford Fiesta Petrol & Diesel (Oct 95 - 97) N to R	**3397**
Ford Granada (Sept 77 - Feb 85) up to B	**0481**
Ford Granada & Scorpio (Mar 85 - 94) B to M	**1245**
Ford Ka (96 - 99) P to T	**3570**
Ford Mondeo Petrol (93 - 99) K to T	**1923**
Ford Mondeo Diesel (93 - 96) L to N	**3465**
Ford Orion (83 - Sept 90) up to H	**1009**
Ford Sierra 4 cyl. (82 - 93) up to K	**0903**
Ford Sierra V6 (82 - 91) up to J	**0904**
Ford Transit Petrol (Mk 2) (78 - Jan 86) up to C	**0719**
Ford Transit Petrol (Mk 3) (Feb 86 - 89) C to G	**1468**
Ford Transit Diesel (Feb 86 - 99) C to T	**3019**
Ford 1.6 & 1.8 litre Diesel Engine (84 - 96) A to N	**1172**
Ford 2.1, 2.3 & 2.5 litre Diesel Engine (77 - 90) up to H	**1606**
FREIGHT ROVER	
Freight Rover Sherpa (74 - 87) up to E	**0463**
HILLMAN	
Hillman Avenger (70 - 82) up to Y	**0037**
HONDA	
Honda Accord (76 - Feb 84) up to A	**0351**
Honda Civic (Feb 84 - Oct 87) A to E	**1226**
Honda Civic (Nov 91 - 96) J to N	**3199**
HYUNDAI	
Hyundai Pony (85 - 94) C to M	**3398**
JAGUAR	
Jaguar E Type (61 - 72) up to L	**0140**
Jaguar MkI & II, 240 & 340 (55 - 69) up to H	**0098**
Jaguar XJ6, XJ & Sovereign; Daimler Sovereign (68 - Oct 86) up to D	**0242**
Jaguar XJ6 & Sovereign (Oct 86 - Sept 94) D to M	**3261**
Jaguar XJ12, XJS & Sovereign; Daimler Double Six (72 - 88) up to F	**0478**
JEEP	
Jeep Cherokee Petrol (93 - 96) K to N	**1943**
LADA	
Lada 1200, 1300, 1500 & 1600 (74 - 91) up to J	**0413**
Lada Samara (87 - 91) D to J	**1610**
LAND ROVER	
Land Rover 90, 110 & Defender Diesel (83 - 95) up to N	**3017**
Land Rover Discovery Diesel (89 - 95) G to N	**3016**
Land Rover Series IIA & III Diesel (58 - 85) up to C	**0529**

Title	Book No.
Land Rover Series II, IIA & III Petrol (58 - 85) up to C	**0314**
MAZDA	
Mazda 323 (Mar 81 - Oct 89) up to G	**1608**
Mazda 323 (Oct 89 - 98) G to R	**3455**
Mazda 626 (May 83 - Sept 87) up to E	**0929**
Mazda B-1600, B-1800 & B-2000 Pick-up (72 - 88) up to F	**0267**
MERCEDES BENZ	
Mercedes-Benz 190, 190E & 190D Petrol & Diesel (83 - 93) A to L	**3450**
Mercedes-Benz 200, 240, 300 Diesel (Oct 76 - 85) up to C	**1114**
Mercedes-Benz 250 & 280 (68 - 72) up to L	**0346**
Mercedes-Benz 250 & 280 (123 Series) (Oct 76 - 84) up to B	**0677**
Mercedes-Benz 124 Series (85 - Aug 93) C to K	**3253**
MG	
MGB (62 - 80) up to W	**0111**
MG Midget & AH Sprite (58 - 80) up to W	**0265**
MITSUBISHI	
Mitsubishi Shogun & L200 Pick-Ups (83 - 94) up to M	**1944**
MORRIS	
Morris Ital 1.3 (80 - 84) up to B	**0705**
Morris Minor 1000 (56 - 71) up to K	**0024**
NISSAN	
Nissan Bluebird (May 84 - Mar 86) A to C	**1223**
Nissan Bluebird (Mar 86 - 90) C to H	**1473**
Nissan Cherry (Sept 82 - 86) up to D	**1031**
Nissan Micra (83 - Jan 93) up to K	**0931**
Nissan Micra (93 - 99) K to T	**3254**
Nissan Primera (90 - Aug 99) H to T	**1851**
Nissan Stanza (82 - 86) up to D	**0824**
Nissan Sunny (May 82 - Oct 86) up to D	**089**
Nissan Sunny (Oct 86 - Mar 91) D to H	**137**
Nissan Sunny (Apr 91 - 95) H to N	**321**
OPEL	
Opel Ascona & Manta (B Series) (Sept 75 - 88) up to F	**031**
Opel Ascona (81 - 88) *(Not available in UK see Vauxhall Cavalier 0812)*	**321**
Opel Astra (Oct 91 - Feb 98) *(Not available in UK see Vauxhall Astra 1832)*	**315**
Opel Calibra (90 - 98) *(See Vauxhall/Opel Calibra Book No. 3502)*	
Opel Corsa (83 - Mar 93) *(Not available in UK see Vauxhall Nova 0909)*	**316**
Opel Corsa (Mar 93 - 97) *(Not available in UK see Vauxhall Corsa 1985)*	**315**
Opel Frontera Petrol & Diesel (91 - 98) *(See Vauxhall/Opel Frontera Book No. 3454)*	
Opel Kadett (Nov 79 - Oct 84)	**063**
Opel Kadett (Oct 84 - Oct 91) *(Not available in UK see Vauxhall Astra & Belmont 1136)*	**319**
Opel Omega & Senator (86 - 94) *(Not available in UK see Vauxhall Carlton & Senator 1469)*	**315**
Opel Omega (94 - 99) *(See Vauxhall/Opel Omega Book No. 3510)*	
Opel Rekord (Feb 78 - Oct 86) up to D	**054**

itle	Book No
pel Vectra (Oct 88 - Oct 95)	
Not available in UK see Vauxhall Cavalier 1570)	3158
pel Vectra Petrol & Diesel (95 - 98)	
Not available in UK see Vauxhall Vectra 3396)	3523
PEUGEOT	
eugeot 106 Petrol & Diesel (91 - 98) J to S	1882
eugeot 205 (83 - 95) A to N	0932
eugeot 305 (78 - 89) up to G	0538
eugeot 306 Petrol & Diesel (93 - 99) K to T	3073
eugeot 309 (86 - 93) C to K	1266
eugeot 405 Petrol (88 - 96) E to N	1559
eugeot 405 Diesel (88 - 96) E to N	3198
eugeot 406 Petrol & Diesel (96 - 97) N to R	3394
eugeot 505 (79 - 89) up to G	0762
eugeot 1.7/1.8 & 1.9 litre Diesel Engine 2 - 96) up to N	0950
eugeot 2.0, 2.1, 2.3 & 2.5 litre Diesel Engines 4 - 90) up to H	1607
ORSCHE	
orsche 911 (65 - 85) up to C	0264
orsche 924 & 924 Turbo (76 - 85) up to C	0397
ROTON	
oton (89 - 97) F to P	3255
ANGE ROVER	
nge Rover V8 (70 - Oct 92) up to K	0606
ELIANT	
liant Robin & Kitten (73 - 83) up to A	0436
ENAULT	
nault 5 (Feb 85 - 96) B to N	1219
nault 9 & 11 (82 - 89) up to F	0822
nault 18 (79 - 86) up to D	0598
nault 19 Petrol (89 - 94) F to M	1646
nault 19 Diesel (89 - 95) F to N	1946
nault 21 (86 - 94) C to M	1397
nault 25 (84 - 92) B to K	1228
nault Clio Petrol (91 - May 98) H to R	1853
nault Clio Diesel (91 - June 96) H to N	3031
nault Espace Petrol & Diesel (85 - 96) C to N	3197
nault Fuego (80 - 86) up to C	0764
nault Laguna Petrol & Diesel 4 - 96) L to P	3252
nault Mégane & Scénic Petrol & Diesel - 98) N to R	3395
OVER	
ver 213 & 216 (84 - 89) A to G	1116
ver 214 & 414 (89 - 96) G to N	1689
ver 216 & 416 (89 - 96) G to N	1830
ver 211, 214, 216, 218 & 220 Petrol & Diesel c 95 - 98) N to R	3399
ver 414, 416 & 420 Petrol & Diesel ay 95 - 98) M to R	3453
ver 618, 620 & 623 (93 - 97) K to P	3257
ver 820, 825 & 827 (86 - 95) D to N	1380
ver 3500 (76 - 87) up to E	0365
ver Metro, 111 & 114 (May 90 - 96) G to N	1711
AB	
b 90, 99 & 900 (79 - Oct 93) up to L	0765
b 900 (Oct 93 - 98) L to R	3512
b 9000 (4-cyl) (85 - 95) C to N	1686

Title	Book No
SEAT	
Seat Ibiza & Cordoba Petrol & Diesel (Oct 93 - Oct 99) L to V	3571
Seat Ibiza & Malaga (85 - 92) B to K	1609
SKODA	
Skoda Estelle (77 - 89) up to G	0604
Skoda Favorit (89 - 96) F to N	1801
Skoda Felicia Petrol & Diesel (95 - 99) M to T	3505
SUBARU	
Subaru 1600 & 1800 (Nov 79 - 90) up to H	0995
SUZUKI	
Suzuki SJ Series, Samurai & Vitara (4-cyl) (82 - 97) up to P	1942
Suzuki Supercarry (86 - Oct 94) C to M	3015
TALBOT	
Talbot Alpine, Solara, Minx & Rapier (75 - 86) up to D	0337
Talbot Horizon (78 - 86) up to D	0473
Talbot Samba (82 - 86) up to D	0823
TOYOTA	
Toyota Carina E (May 92 - 97) J to P	3256
Toyota Corolla (Sept 83 - Sept 87) A to E	1024
Toyota Corolla (80 - 85) up to C	0683
Toyota Corolla (Sept 87 - Aug 92) E to K	1683
Toyota Corolla (Aug 92 - 97) K to P	3259
Toyota Hi-Ace & Hi-Lux (69 - Oct 83) up to A	0304
TRIUMPH	
Triumph Acclaim (81 - 84) up to B	0792
Triumph GT6 & Vitesse (62 - 74) up to N	0112
Triumph Spitfire (62 - 81) up to X	0113
Triumph Stag (70 - 78) up to T	0441
Triumph TR7 (75 - 82) up to Y	0322
VAUXHALL	
Vauxhall Astra (80 - Oct 84) up to B	0635
Vauxhall Astra & Belmont (Oct 84 - Oct 91) B to J	1136
Vauxhall Astra (Oct 91 - Feb 98) J to R	1832
Vauxhall/Opel Calibra (90 - 98) G to S	3502
Vauxhall Carlton (Oct 78 - Oct 86) up to D	0480
Vauxhall Carlton & Senator (Nov 86 - 94) D to L	1469
Vauxhall Cavalier 1600, 1900 & 2000 (75 - July 81) up to W	0315
Vauxhall Cavalier (81 - Oct 88) up to F	0812
Vauxhall Cavalier (Oct 88 - 95) F to N	1570
Vauxhall Chevette (75 - 84) up to B	0285
Vauxhall Corsa (Mar 93 - 97) K to R	1985
Vauxhall/Opel Frontera Petrol & Diesel (91 - Sept 98) J to S	3454
Vauxhall Nova (83 - 93) up to K	0909
Vauxhall/Opel Omega (94 - 99) L to T	3510
Vauxhall Vectra Petrol & Diesel (95 - 98) N to R	3396
Vauxhall/Opel 1.5, 1.6 & 1.7 litre Diesel Engine (82 - 96) up to N	1222
VOLKSWAGEN	
Volkswagen Beetle 1200 (54 - 77) up to S	0036
Volkswagen Beetle 1300 & 1500 (65 - 75) up to P	0039
Volkswagen Beetle 1302 & 1302S (70 - 72) up to L	0110
Volkswagen Beetle 1303, 1303S & GT (72 - 75) up to P	0159

Title	Book No.
Volkswagen Golf & Jetta Mk 1 1.1 & 1.3 (74 - 84) up to A	0716
Volkswagen Golf, Jetta & Scirocco Mk 1 1.5,1.6 & 1.8 (74 - 84) up to A	0726
Volkswagen Golf & Jetta Mk 1 Diesel (78 - 84) up to A	0451
Volkswagen Golf & Jetta Mk 2 (Mar 84 - Feb 92) A to J	1081
Volkswagen Golf & Vento Petrol & Diesel (Feb 92 - 96) J to N	3097
Volkswagen LT vans & light trucks (76 - 87) up to E	0637
Volkswagen Passat & Santana (Sept 81 - May 88) up to E	0814
Volkswagen Passat Petrol & Diesel (May 88 - 96) E to P	3498
Volkswagen Polo & Derby (76 - Jan 82) up to X	0335
Volkswagen Polo (82 - Oct 90) up to H	0813
Volkswagen Polo (Nov 90 - Aug 94) H to L	3245
Volkswagen Polo Hatchback Petrol & Diesel (94 - 99) M to S	3500
Volkswagen Scirocco (82 - 90) up to H	1224
Volkswagen Transporter 1600 (68 - 79) up to V	0082
Volkswagen Transporter 1700, 1800 & 2000 (72 - 79) up to V	0226
Volkswagen Transporter (air-cooled) (79 - 82) up to Y	0638
Volkswagen Transporter (water-cooled) (82 - 90) up to H	3452
VOLVO	
Volvo 142, 144 & 145 (66 - 74) up to N	0129
Volvo 240 Series (74 - 93) up to K	0270
Volvo 262, 264 & 260/265 (75 - 85) up to C	0400
Volvo 340, 343, 345 & 360 (76 - 91) up to J	0715
Volvo 440, 460 & 480 (87 - 97) D to P	1691
Volvo 740 & 760 (82 - 91) up to J	1258
Volvo 850 (92 - 96) J to P	3260
Volvo 940 (90 - 96) H to N	3249
Volvo S40 & V40 (96 - 99) N to V	3569
Volvo S70, V70 & C70 (96 - 99) P to V	3573
YUGO/ZASTAVA	
Yugo/Zastava (81 - 90) up to H	1453
AUTOMOTIVE TECHBOOKS	
Automotive Brake Manual	3050
Automotive Carburettor Manual	3288
Automotive Diagnostic Fault Codes Manual	3472
Automotive Diesel Engine Service Guide	3286
Automotive Disc Brake Manual	3542
Automotive Electrical and Electronic Systems Manual	3049
Automotive Engine Management and Fuel Injection Systems Manual	3344
Automotive Gearbox Overhaul Manual	3473
Automotive Service Summaries Manual	3475
Automotive Timing Belts Manual – Austin/Rover	3549
Automotive Timing Belts Manual - Ford	3474
Automotive Timing Belts Manual – Peugeot/Citroën	3568
Automotive Timing Belts Manual – Vauxhall/Opel	3577
Automotive Welding Manual	3053
In-Car Entertainment Manual (3rd Edition)	3363
OTHER TITLES	
Haynes Diesel Engine Systems & Data Book (91 -00)	3548
Haynes Petrol Models Data Book (94 - 00)	3718

CL09.04/00

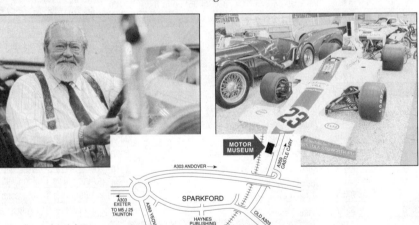